AF683822

# ENDANGERED and OTHER PROTECTED SPECIES:

## Federal Law and Regulation

# ENDANGERED and OTHER PROTECTED SPECIES:

## Federal Law and Regulation

RICHARD LITTELL

The Bureau of National Affairs, Inc., Washington, D.C.

Copyright © 1992
Richard Littell

**Library of Congress Cataloging-in-Publication Data**

Littell, Richard.
Endangered and other protected species / Richard Littell.
p. cm.
Includes bibliographical references and index.
ISBN 0-87179-747-X
1. Endangered species—Law and legislation—United States.
2. Wildlife conservation—Law and legislation—United States.
I. Title.
KF5640.L57 1992
346.7304'695—dc20 92-16020
[347.3064695] CIP

**Acknowledgments**

Association of Systematics Collections, for reprinting (with updating and revision) portions of Volume I of *Controlled Wildlife: Federal Permit Procedures,* 1984. The copyright for the revised and updated material, appearing in Appendix A of this book, is owned jointly by Richard Littell and Association of Systematics Collections.

*The New York Times,* for reprinting a portion of "The Last Chance Continent," by Stephen Jay Gould, Aug. 18, 1991. Copyright © 1991 by The New York Times Company. Reprinted by permission.

Viking Penguin, for reprinting a portion of *Wildlife in America* by Peter Matthiessen. Copyright © 1959, renewed 1987 by Peter Matthiessen. Used by permission of Viking Penguin, a division of Penguin Books USA Inc.

World Wide Fund For Nature, for reprinting a portion of *World Conservation Strategy* (1980).

Published by The Bureau of National Affairs, Inc.
International Standard Book Number: 0–87179–747–X
Printed in the United States of America

When man interferes with the Tao,
the sky become filthy,
the equilibrium crumbles,
creatures become extinct.

Lao-tzu
*Tao Te Ching*
About 500 B.C.

And of the species now living very few will transmit progeny of any kind to a far distant futurity; for . . . the greater number of species in each genus, and all the species in many genera, have left no descendants, but have become utterly extinct.

Charles Darwin
*On the Origin of Species by Means of Natural Selection*

The plain intent of Congress in enacting this statute was to halt and reverse the trend towards species extinction, whatever the cost.

Tennessee Valley Authority v. Hill,
437 U.S. 153, 184
U.S. Supreme Court, 1978

# Foreword

## Sustainable Conservation by and for the People

by
**Stephen R. Edwards**[1]

I am an optimist. My glass will always be half-full. At the same time I am a conservationist. I direct a global program for the "Sustainable Use of Wildlife" for IUCN—the World Conservation Union. My philosophy and professional responsibilities may appear to be a contradiction, if not a "fool's errand," in view of the plethora of laws enacted by the United States to protect the world from destruction. On the contrary, I have considerable hope and evidence that the future is not as bleak as some predict. As Richard Littell notes in this book,[2] the key lies in the statement by Stephen Jay Gould:

> [W]ildlife and habitats can only be preserved if long-term economic and social benefits will accrue to the . . . people for the effort. If no honorable argument can be made along these lines, the cause is lost. . . . Preservation must be defended "for reasons that go very much deeper than . . . 'conservation of a priceless heritage.'" . . . [A]ll the world needs a *humanistic* ecology of people protecting a bounteous nature for reasons of both soul and body—but especially the latter.[3]

In this foreword I will document the universality of the philosophy reflected in this statement and attempt to apply it to the basic conservation issues facing the United States—both in terms of its domestic legislation and its role as a leader in the international arena of global conservation and development.

We are all sensitive to the loss of species and the deterioration of the environment. We receive several solicitations per year from conservation organizations asking for money to protect one species or another. We read about elephants, rhinos, primates, parrots, and even butterflies being "exploited" to extinction. The electronic media commonly carry reports on one environmental disaster after another. And we respond. We give money. We express our concern. And, we may even support politicians who promote legislation like the U.S. Endangered Species Act. But does this protectionist approach really work or does it only serve to salve our consciences?

I have been struggling with this question for most of my professional career. What I have learned, above all, is that successful conservation depends on the commitment of the people living with the wild species—not us. Yes, we can give financial and technical support, but in the final analysis it will be

---

[1] Programme Director, Sustainable Use of Wildlife Programme. IUC–The World Conservation Union

[2] Chapter 9 at page 104.

[3] Stephen Jay Gould, *The Last Chance Continent,* N.Y. TIMES BOOK REVIEW, August 18, 1991.

those people who will make a difference. Not laws. Not government policies. And not our wishful thinking.

Over the years I have had many opportunities to visit rural communities all over the world. I have talked to the people, eaten their food, and listened to them describe their problems. I have seen how they are being exploited. I have walked with them in their country and seen the environmental problems that are affecting them. And, from a scientific perspective, I am probably more aware of the severity and complexity of these problems than they are.

On the other hand, I am equally aware that these people have survived under conditions that we cannot easily comprehend—poverty, drought, wars, authoritarian governments, deteriorating natural resources. And often their solutions to problems are ingenious and require efforts that we cannot conceive, such as the construction of a road 40 kilometers long out along the face of a cliff, built in just four years!

These people are also very sensitive to changes in their environment because they depend on it for food, fuel, fibers, construction materials, medicines, dies, religious purposes, and income. Furthermore, they are prepared to do something to protect their environment. To illustrate my point I recount two experiences from two distinctly different cultures. One in Panama and the other in Pakistan.

*Cocle, Panama*. This small Panamanian village is located in the center of the base of the country's "hammer-head" that extends into the Pacific Ocean. I was taken to this village in 1990 to see its green iguana management project. We left Panama City early in the morning. After several hours we left the highway following a dirt track, which often felt more like a river-bed than a road. As we drove the environment could only be described as "parched." There was little vegetation, extensive erosion, villages were dirt poor, and the children had distended bellies—typical of poor villages around the world. Frankly, I have become immune to these conditions and lost interest quickly. After what seemed like hours, I was jolted from my private thoughts by our guide thumping the roof, indicating he wanted to talk to us. We pulled over and piled out. The guide then told us that the village elders wanted to know why we wanted to visit their village. We answered correctly, but I had the distinct impression that if the answer was wrong, we would have been turned around. During this interrogation, I became aware that the scenery had changed. Trees were evident; agricultural plots were everywhere, some interspersed among plantations of trees. We were in an oasis. As we moved on, I began noticing children—animated, neatly dressed, and very healthy. I was very much aware that besides the obvious physical differences, this village was expressing considerable pride and determination.

We met the village elders in the shade of a thatched roof canopy, surrounded by hundreds of infant trees being tended by women. Coffee was served. We exchanged greetings and we were invited to sign their guest book. Amazing! What was different about this community? Why had they succeeded while others in the same area had not? As I grappled with these questions, the head of the village brought the meeting to order. He informed us that several years ago someone from CARE had visited their village. He had encouraged them to organize themselves and to undertake cooperative projects. Advice and technical assistance would be provided. They began by raising pigs and growing Caribbean pine (for the lumber) and added a project on agroforestry where vegetable crops are grown in combination with trees. Iguana management was added to their portfolio when they were visited by a woman working for the Smithsonian Institution who told them that it was important to save the species and they could possibly sell the animal. Finally, they had just begun an aquaculture project to raise talapia (a fish).

To coordinate the village activities a council was established. Each project activity had a representative on the council. Villagers (men and women) were required to work on one of the five projects for four days each week. On the other days they could develop and attend a personal (family) project chosen from the village portfolio. Work schedules and technical assistance were coordinated through the village council. Income from the village projects went to support the village activities. Income from personal projects went to the family.

I asked which one of the projects they liked most. "Pigs, because we can eat them and sell the meat," was the answer. They also thought the Caribbean Pine project held considerable promise "because they would be able to use the wood to build houses and sell the excess from the harvest." They expected to harvest their first trees the following year. When asked if they were making any money from the iguana management, the answer was no. They collected eggs, raised the hatchlings, and then released them. They wouldn't mind selling some—but they were doing it because they thought it was important to do.

The green iguana is native to the area. It reaches a length of over three feet. It is considered a delicacy and rural people throughout Central America have a tradition of eating them. The females lay over thirty eggs once a year. In the wild, mortality is very high in the first six months of their life, from predation on the eggs and hatchlings. Therefore, if the eggs are protected and the hatchlings are fed and protected from predators, the population can increase very quickly. Iguanas tend to stay in the area where they hatch (or are released) if the habitat meets their needs. They eat fruits, flowers, and leaves of trees. Consequently, to keep a resident population of green iguanas you have to be sure that there are adequate trees to produce the food and cover that they need.

Because of my interest in the iguana project, we were taken to several houses where families were raising them. In each case the house was surrounded by trees, and the trees were full of good-sized iguanas. It was obvious from the density of the animals and their size that the families had been doing this for several years. Also, I had no doubt that the species and its habitat were being conserved.

As we were leaving to return to Panama City, I said that if they wanted any help for their iguana management, they should prepare a brief proposal outlining what they needed. About two months later I received a letter from the council requesting $100 to buy cage materials so that more families could start managing iguanas. The money was provided and about six months later we received a full accounting of the expenditures. Since then we have provided another $300 in support. I have not been back, but my organization continues to support nominal requests for support. Besides being gratified for continuing conservation of the green iguana, I must admit that the lessons learned that day have had a profound effect on my approach to conservation. I had witnessed a rural community in the midst of abject poverty as reflected in the surrounding villages that was motivated to conserve a species because it thought it was the right thing to do.

*Northern Areas, Pakistan.* Northern Areas is administered by the federal government of Pakistan. In 1991, I was invited by a local nongovernment organization—the Aga Kahn Rural Support Programme (AKRSP)—to evaluate the feasibility of community-based wildlife management activities in the region. It took 18 hours to drive to Gilget, the administrative center of Northern Areas, from Islamabad, a distance of 600 kilometers. Because of the precipitous topography and relatively low rainfall (between 100 and 500 millimeters per year) ecologists have described the region as a "vertical desert." But the scenery is spectacular. At virtually any point, snow-capped mountains, some rising to over 20,000 feet, provide a backdrop for gray semi-arid valleys, each with a village at its entrance surrounded by patches of pink amid swatches of emerald green from flowering apricot and almond trees and emerging wheat. The life's blood for these communities is the cascading white-water rivers from melting glaciers that they have tapped by constructing irrigation channels out of solid rock, some several kilometers long.

The AKRSP has been working with villages in the region since 1982 to assist their economic development. The approach is unique. Through a series of dialogues with the villages, AKRSP offers to help the village undertake a major development project such as the construction of a link road, an irrigation channel, or a bridge. To receive the assistance the villages must form a village organization representing at least 50 percent of the households (normally consisting of eight people each), prepare a development plan that is approved by the village organization, and save a portion of any income they may receive. When the conditions are met AKRSP provides technical support, but the villages undertake the development project themselves. Funds are provided to pay the villagers and purchase supplies and needed material.

In the ten years since AKRSP began its program it has assisted over 1,400 villages in the region (out of approximately 1,500). While I do not know the total amount of money that has been saved by all of the villages, one village of 80 households has over 1,600,000 Rupees ($64,000) in savings! They have even borrowed against their savings to buy a tractor and thresher and an electric power generator.

To assess the status of the wildlife in the region I met with 19 villages over 15 days. Each village controlled a valley-watershed that it used for hunting and summer pasturage for its livestock. In most cases it required one or two days to reach the pasture area. Between two and ten people in each village were hunters. Game species commonly included: Himalayan ibex, Astor markhor, Marco Polo sheep, brown bear, Himalayan black bear, snow leopard, musk deer, marmot, ram chukker, chukker, snow cock, and several species of pheasant. Rainbow and brown trout have been introduced throughout the region; however, villagers showed little interest in them. Native tree species include juniper, birch, willow, and ash. While most historical forests have been eliminated, small pockets of comparatively natural habitat (with natural plant and animal communities) remain in a few unsettled valleys. Today, the favorite game is Himalayan ibex or Astor markhor. While government has many regulations to protect wild species, including a ban on hunting, enforcement is virtually impossible.

In all villages wildlife was not as plentiful as it had been five years ago—primarily because of outside hunters who were usually military personnel or government bureaucrats armed with sophisticated weapons and who coerced the villagers into providing guide service and took their firewood without paying for it.

This is a typical story of environmental degradation. But what was amazing was that all of the villages wanted to stop the illegal hunting and requested assistance in developing programs to manage their wildlife. In fact, a number of villages had taken the initiative to stop all hunting in their areas, including hunting by their own hunters.

In one case, a village sent a delegation to the local radio station, several kilometers away, to announce their hunting ban and the penalties if hunters were caught, including a fine of 5,000 Rupees ($200)—an astronomical sum in the context of the local economy where annual incomes are measured in hundreds of dollars—and confiscation of the rifle. The village also set aside areas in their valley where livestock grazing was not permitted and established a fine system for violators. Fifty volunteers patrol the valley. They have since apprehended two hunters and collected the fines. When asked what they did with the income, we were told that the villagers bought medicines for the village, books for the school, and 34,000 trees that they planted.

In another valley several kilometers away, villagers had prepared a proposal to organize ibex trophy-hunting for foreign hunters. Their valley covers approximately 440 square kilometers. Himalayan ibex, snow leopard, wolf, lynx, leopard cat, and ducks are found in the valley. Himalayan ibex had been hunted traditionally by villagers for the meat.

The villages banned all hunting and all villagers took an oath witnessed by the Administrator, who is the senior government official in Northern Areas, declaring that they would cease their hunting. World Wide Fund for Nature (WWF)–Pakistan advised the villagers on wildlife management techniques and agreed to lend the villagers funds to compensate for their loss of meat. The loan is to be repaid from revenues earned from the trophy hunting.

The village organization appointed six villagers, who had been hunters, to survey the Himalayan ibex population in the valley. Procedures were established to monitor changes in the population size and structure. And villagers patrol the valley and "arrest" anyone found hunting.

What conclusions can we draw from these examples? What are the conditions that these communities share? Are these conditions unique to these communities?

In each case the villagers are not dependent on the government to help them. They have established mechanisms to identify, discuss and address problems affecting their communities. It is also true that they have strong leaders that the villagers respect. It would also appear that an important factor is that they have some margin of economic security. They have the means to earn money and they have been successful at it.

They have not received much financial or technical assistance to conserve their wild resources. They are doing it because they have the economic freedom to respond to the concerns they have about the environment, and particular species that are important to them. In short, they conserve because they want to.

In most countries wild species are economically important. In the international conservation community, ensuring that uses of renewable natural resources are sustainable is a basic principle of conservation and sustainable development, as stated in the *World Conservation Strategy*[4] and its successor, *Caring for the Earth*.[5]

The same principle is articulated in the World Commission on Environment's treatise, *Our Common Future*.[6] More recently this principle was again endorsed in *Agenda 21,* which was adopted by the world community at the United Nations Conference on the Environment and Development (Earth Summit) in Rio de Janiero, Brazil in 1992.

Finally, IUCN–The World Conservation Union is in the process of developing a policy for the sustainable use of wild species. This policy provides criteria and requirements for assessing whether a use of a species is sustainable or not. It is based on two ethical statements from *Caring for the Earth:*[7]

- Within the limits of the Earth, people have "the right . . . to the resources needed for a decent standard of living, and hence a right to derive economic and other benefits from wild species.
- People have a responsibility to ensure "that their uses of renewable resources are sustainable."

In the examples I have given earlier, these conditions will be met through the local communities. It would be equally true if the managers of the resources were landowners. They will use their natural resources and they are policing themselves.

So how does this relate to U.S. law governing wildlife? This book summarizes no less than 19 different federal laws that relate to the protection of species, both domestically and internationally. Each is backed up by a labyrinth of regulations that are subject to varying interpretations. A number of these laws have been cloned at the state level.

In reading about each federal law, I was struck by the fact that they are a patch-quilt of reactions to specific conservation problems, rather then flowing from a comprehensive conservation policy. They do not embrace any of the principles outlined above. Where they address the status of species outside of

---

[4] International Union for Conservation of Nature and Natural Resources (World Conservation Union), *World Conservation Strategy* (IUCN-UNEP-WWF 1980).

[5] International Union for Conservation of Nature and Natural Resources (World Conservation Union), *Caring for the Earth: A Strategy for Sustainable Living* (Gland, Switzerland: IUCN-UNEP-WWF, 1991).

[6] World Commission on Environment and Development, *Our Common Future* (New York: Oxford University Press, 1987).

[7] *Supra* note 4.

the United States, they are restrictive and do not take into account the cultural systems in which the species exist. They clearly do not recognize the role that people can and should play in conservation of their natural resources. And, finally, they provide no basis for governments or people to acquire the capacity to care for their environment.

Why have we followed such a pattern of legislation when many of the concepts represented in these laws are alien to our own tradition of relying upon individual initiative? In part the answer derives from the history of wildlife protection. In an overview paper based on a series of case studies examining sport hunting as a sustainable use of wildlife,[8] Catherine Allen and I point out that there has been a progressive and systematic codification of laws over the past several hundred years. These laws have, for the most part, been directed at securing and maintaining land for wild game and controlling harvests of individual species. Historically, these controls were tied to property rights of the aristocracy in Europe and "common folk" were denied access. During the colonial era these concepts were transferred to Asia, Africa, and North America. In Asia and Africa, colonial laws controlled harvests by restricting access to particular species. Following independence of these countries, many of the laws remained in effect. As a result, most wild species remain controlled as "king's game" (*res nullius*) by government agencies with little or no authority granted to rural people to manage the resource directly. Nevertheless, basic principles of wildlife management began to emerge over the last century with the establishment of hunting reserves, harvest quotas, seasons, and the like under government authority.

In the United States, however, an entirely different approach to sport hunting has evolved. According to Burger and Teer,[9] the American Revolution effectively broke many traditions that impinged on individuals' rights—including controls over hunting of wild game. Following the Revolution wild game was considered the property of the state and all citizens ". . . had the right to harvest game without charge."

The consequence of this philosophy most likely contributed to the situation at the turn of the century, described by James Shaw,[10] where some individuals were predicting extinction for several large game mammals (e.g., elk, mountain sheep)—a situation not too different from what we see in many countries in the world today. Shaw points out that the extinctions did not occur because of a "combination of widespread public support, effective legal protection, and reintroduction of wild animals into areas from which they had been extirpated."

Shaw uses this vignette to highlight the status of wildlife in Latin America. While he does not elaborate on the relative contributions of these three factors

---

[8] Edwards, Stephen R., and Catherine M. Allen. *Sport Hunting as a Sustainable Use of Wildlife*. Policy paper submitted to WWF-International, 1992 (16 pages plus three Annexes.)

[9] J. Teer, G. Burger, and C. Deknatel, *State-Supported Habitat Management and Commercial Hunting on Private Lands in the United States: Transactions of Forty-Eighth North American Wildlife Conference* 445–456 (Kansas City, Missouri, 1983).

[10] J. Shaw, *The Outlook for Sustainable Harvests of Wildlife in Latin America,* printed in *Neotropical Wildlife Use and Conservation* (J. Robinson and K. Redford, eds) 25 (Chicago: University of Chicago Press, 1991).

to the success that we enjoy today, he does note that in Latin America government roles are not adequately defined—an obstacle in achieving sustainable use of renewable wild resources in most countries. Shaw apparently believes that the laws and science figured prominently in the successful conservation of these species. While I have no doubt that laws and science had considerable influence, I am more inclined to believe that the greatest contribution to the success rested with the understanding of the people. Because people were aware of the problem, they responded. They supported the laws and allowed the science to be developed and applied.

From an entirely different perspective, the history and development of commercial sport hunting in Texas by private landowners has been well documented.[11] In Texas, ranchers sell the rights to hunt native (and exotic) game on their land. The practice appears to be highly successful because many ranchers now actively promote maintenance of wild species on their property. Some have gone so far as to develop secondary markets for meat and other products. It is interesting to note that this approach is strongly objected to in many other states.

In Zimbabwe, the Parks and Wild Life Act of 1975 gives landholders the right to manage wildlife for their own benefit, thus providing an economic incentive to reinforce the scientific, aesthetic, and moral justifications for wildlife conservation. The government took this bold step because legislated protection of wildlife had failed in all but protected areas. Since 1975, rural communities have been encouraged to develop management plans for the sustainable use of wild species. Recent research in one district shows that 34 out of 37 ranches now keep wildlife. Four ranchers now raise only wildlife, while 31 have both cattle and wildlife. Aside from sport hunting and a growing wildlife-based tourist industry, game ranches also harvest wildlife to sell meat and hides to local and international markets.

In both of these examples, people have the incentive to manage the wild species for their benefit. Government has adopted a supportive role. It advises and assists the landowners (or communities) to obtain the highest value possible from their resources. This includes providing technical advice on managing the resource as well as marketing assistance.

In all of these examples, whether in other countries or the United States, I believe there are several underlying principles that should guide elaboration of our legal system if we are to assume a position of leadership in the world community:

- First, we must recognize that all humans, irrespective of their culture or financial status, care for their environment. In many cases those people are dependent on their environment for their survival, and past exploitation has left them with an environment that is severely impoverished.

---

[11] J. Teer, *Game Ranching in Texas,* printed in Volume 2, *The Behaviour of Ungulates and Its Relation to Management: The Papers of an International Symposium Held at the University of Calgary, Alberta, Canada 2–5 November* 1971 893–99 (IUCN publication new series, No 24, 1971).

- Second, wild resources are not inexhaustible if demand for them exceeds their capacity to reproduce.
- Third, use of wild species is a necessity for survival in poorer countries but is often driven by demands stemming from industrialized nations.
- Fourth, people living with the wild resources are far better equipped than agencies of governments to conserve those resources.
- Fifth, financial and technical assistance is needed to help rural people better manage their wild resources.

These principles are fundamental to a successful conservation policy. Their efficacy is demonstrated in the examples presented. The alternative—protectionist legislation—has not worked. Repeating past mistakes will not effectively change the rate at which we consume the resources of the planet. We must learn to adopt conservation policies that earn the support of the people.

In the final analysis, our success will not depend on how many laws are drafted, how many species are listed for total protection, how many government agencies have been formed, or how many people are arrested and convicted of misuse of the environment. Success can only be measured by the number of species that survive in sufficient numbers to reproduce naturally in the wild. Correlated with this yardstick would be the number of rural communities and landowners that value wildlife sufficiently to invest in its conservation and the number of government agencies capable of advising and assisting them to manage their wild resources.

—July 1992

# Preface

I finished writing this book at my mountain cabin. The cabin is perched on a slope of the Virginia Shenandoahs and overlooks a scene that is safe and serene. Nearby is a clear stream inhabited by wild brook trout, direct descendants of fish hunted by the original Native American Indians. Deer follow me as I fish in the midst of tall forests. Taking care to release the trout that mistake my barbless fly for a natural insect, I avoid any permanent intrusion on my environment.

Modern society's demands on our planet are not so benign. It is said that we do not own this Earth but only borrow it from our grandchildren. Today, wildlife species are disappearing at rates never before witnessed on this planet. We are depleting the inheritance of our grandchildren and of future generations.

Facing this threat, governments have enacted stringent laws that are designed, in the Supreme Court's words, "to halt and reverse the trend towards species extinction, whatever the cost."[1] These laws have sprouted an enormous outgrowth of court and agency rulings, creating a branch of law that is the subject of this book.

In many of the court decisions discussed, advocates of conservation clash with practitioners of development. Environmentalists often challenge government agencies that develop harbors, build roads, or dam rivers. Enterprises cannot dig mines, cut forests, or drill for oil and gas without intruding on the environment.

Private interests also find themselves hard pressed to accommodate conservation concerns. Shrimpers must try to find ways to harvest their catch without destroying turtles. Farmers are restricted as to where they may shoot grizzly bears and wolves that destroy their livestock. Importers misunderstand complex rules or are victimized by unscrupulous traders. Captive breeders, who mate fragile species in captivity and place animals back into the wild, can be prevented from financing that activity by trade. Scientists risk violating international law by acquiring primates for AIDS research.

We must strive to achieve better cooperation between advocates of conservation and practitioners of development. There is a need for accommodations. We "cannot fairly demand the perfect at the expense of the achievable."[2] If we do, "the best [becomes] an enemy of the good."[3] At present, conflicts between conservation and development are often damaging to conservation objectives. As the World Conservation Union emphasized in a 1980 report entitled "World Conservation Strategy,"[4] prepared in cooperation with the U.N. Envi-

---

[1] Tennessee Valley Auth. v. Hill, 437 U.S. 153, 184 (1978).

[2] American Pub. Gas Ass'n v. Federal Power Comm'n, 567 F.2d 1016, 1046 (D.C. Cir. 1977).

[3] Schwabacker v. United States, 334 U.S. 182, 193 (1948).

[4] International Union for Conservation of Nature and Natural Resources (World Conservation Union), *World Conservation Strategy* (IUCN-UNEP-WWF 1980).

ronmental Program and the World Wide Fund for Nature, "Too often [conservationists] have allowed themselves to be seen as resisting all development. . . . The result has been not to stop development, but to persuade many development practitioners, especially in developing countries, that conservation is not merely irrelevant, it is harmful and anti-social."[5]

The World Commission on Environment and Development, another U.N.-sponsored group, prescribed the best approach for harmonizing conservation and development.[6] That approach embodies the concept of "sustainable development"—that is, "development that meets the needs of the present without compromising the ability of future generations to meet their needs."[7]

On the eve of the 1992 Rio Conference, Vaclav Havel, the playwright and poet who recently resigned as Czechoslovakia's president, explained the importance of the concept of sustainable development:

> [T]he real theme of the conference is neither the environment alone nor development in itself. . . . The only solution lies in the combination of economic growth and respect for the environment. This has been the essence of the concept of sustainable development. . . . In other words, the key is to maintain economic development, yet to do it in a way that would be in keeping with the needs of both man and nature.[8]

This book reflects my belief in these words and in sustainable development. I hope that the book succeeds in illustrating why there are no easy answers. My goal is to help interested people understand the complexities of wildlife issues.

But this is a practical treatise, not an ideological tract. In addition to describing governmental statutes, treaties, and regulations, I cover the rulings that illustrate how the laws are applied to everyday transactions and projects. I write about court decisions, administrative agency rulings, and informal legal opinions. Instead of portraying the grand overview, I aim to provide useful advice to anyone whose affairs require passage through the maze of wildlife law.

For those seeking a broad, historical background, I recommend Michael Bean's masterful book[9] and Simon Lyster's excellent survey.[10] The first treatise is the definitive portrait of wildlife law's historical evolution; the second is a complete review of the text of international treaties on wildlife conservation. Although I follow a different route, I benefited from these pathbreaking achievements.

---

[5] *Id.* at Part 1(9).

[6] World Commission on Environment and Development, *Our Common Future* (New York: Oxford University Press, 1987).

[7] *Id.* at 43. The World Conservation Union defines sustainable development as a strategy for "[i]mproving the quality of human life while living within the carrying capacity of the supporting ecosystems." *Caring for the Earth: A Strategy for Sustainable Living* 211 (Gland, Switzerland: IUCN-UNEP-WWF, 1991).

[8] V. Havel, *Rio and the New Millennium,* N.Y. TIMES, June 3, 1992, at A-15.

[9] M. Bean, *The Evolution of National Wildlife Law* (New York: Praeger Scientific, 1983).

[10] S. Lyster, *International Wildlife Law* (Cambridge, Mass: Grotius, 1985).

* * *

As a matter of personal style, I depart from several conventions of the traditional law treatise. First, I rely heavily on sources that are not widely available to the general public. This does not mean that I neglect published court opinions, statute books, and congressional reports. On the contrary, I use published sources liberally.

Much of endangered species law, however, is hatched at more mundane levels. In cities like Albuquerque, Boston, and Atlanta, administrative law judges from the Departments of Interior and Commerce decide how the statutes are to be applied to ordinary people in the commonplace kinds of cases that rarely make their way to the courthouse. Those decisions are issued in mimeographed form, disseminated widely among agency personnel and practitioners, but not published in widely circulated books. I cite many of these administrative judges' opinions, particularly in Chapter 4. In the absence of *Bluebook* citation forms, I use the format shown on the decisions' title pages—for example, "U.S. Fish and Wildlife Service v. R.B. Woods, DOI Dkt. No. Boston 77-11 (ALJ ID dated September 14, 1978)." "DOI" stands for Department of Interior; "ALJ ID," for initial decision of an administrative law judge. A decision by a Department of Commerce law judge would have a "DOC" docket number.

In the same way, the Solicitor's Office of the Department of the Interior issues hundreds of legal interpretations that control the administration of many wildlife statutes. Some of these are published in a set called "Quinquennial Index Digest of the Department of Interior." More are kept in folders in a docket room opposite the Interior Department library. Most, however, are scattered around regional offices throughout the country. In 1991, the Solicitor's Office compiled more than 200 of these legal opinions in response to Freedom of Information Act requests, but has supplied me with only a handful so far. I refer to these documents by date, author, recipient, and subject matter.

For readers who are located outside Washington, D.C., those documents will not be easy to obtain. In this book, I try to describe the documents in a manner that can be cited or quoted. My own files contain copies of the documents that I cite. If readers need to obtain a complete copy of a document, I will try to respond to requests for access to my files.

In some instances, I indulge myself by departing from a dry, treatise-like statement of the facts and rulings. Writers of law treatises are like Scheherazade: they have a thousand and one stories to tell. Wildlife cases are often interesting. I do not hesitate to include details that give the full picture, even when they may not be crucial to the judge's decision. Such elaboration made this book more fun to write. If it also improves the reader's enjoyment, that is no offense either.

—RICHARD LITTELL
Washington, D.C.
July 1992

# CONTENTS

# Part I

## The Endangered Species Act

# Chapter 1
# Overview

Towering over the landscape of endangered species law is one monumental peak, the Supreme Court's 1978 opinion in *Tennessee Valley Authority v. Hill.*[1] That decision set the tone for all future interpretations of the law's purposes and policies.

## The *Hill* Decision

Today the Tellico Dam rises 129 feet above the Little Tennessee River, creating a 33-mile reservoir. Begun in 1967, the dam was 80 percent complete in August 1973 when a University of Tennessee ichthyologist discovered that the river was home to the snail darter, a previously unknown species. This discovery began prolonged contests that "pit the survival of an obscure fish against completion of a $100 million reservoir. . . ."[2]

The snail darter's fame was assured four months after its discovery, when Congress passed the Endangered Species Act of 1973.[3] That Act ordered the Secretary of the Interior to publish a list of endangered species. The snail darter was soon included on the endangered species list. Once that was done, the Tennessee Valley Authority (TVA), the dam's owner, was subject to the Act's command that federal agencies avoid action that jeopardizes the continued existence of endangered species.[4] As the Supreme Court later observed, "Congress . . . had chosen the snail darter over the dam."[5] So, in 1978, the Supreme Court affirmed an injunction against Tellico, "stopp[ing] the all-but-finished dam project dead in the water."[6]

For conservationists, the court victory proved to be only the first battle in a long war. Congressional critics argued that the Endangered Species Act put the interests of obscure species ahead of the interests of the people. After repeated attempts, Congress enacted legislation authorizing TVA to complete Tellico.[7]

---

[1] 437 U.S. 153.

[2] Hill v. Tennessee Valley Auth., 549 F.2d 1064, 1069 (6th Cir. 1977), *aff'd*, 437 U.S. 153 (1978).

[3] Pub. L. No. 93-205, 87 Stat. 884 (1973).

[4] *Id.* §7, 87 Stat. 884, 892.

[5] Weinberger v. Romero-Barcelo, 456 U.S. 305, 314 (1982).

[6] North Slope Borough v. Andrus, 642 F.2d 589, 607 (D.C. Cir. 1980).

[7] *See* Sequoyah v. Tennessee Valley Auth., 480 F. Supp. 608, 610 (E.D. Tenn. 1979),

In Tennessee, the *Hill* controversy left few permanent effects. The Tellico Dam was completed in 1979. And the snail darter survived. After the dam impounded the waters of the Little Tennessee River, the snail darter was found to exist in other rivers in Tennessee, Georgia, and Alabama, where it flourishes today. By 1984, as a result of these discoveries of additional snail darter populations, the government reclassified the snail darter as only "threatened" instead of "endangered."[8]

The Supreme Court ruling made an indelible imprint on the law.

## Facing the Threat of Species Extinction

In the *Hill* decision, the Court made clear that conservation is not to be sacrificed for other goals, no matter how worthy. The Court cited Congress' intention that "endangered species . . . be afforded the highest of priorities."[9] Congress had been warned repeatedly about wildlife extinction. At congressional hearings in 1973, the Assistant Secretary of the Interior observed that "half of the recorded extinctions of mammals over the past 2,000 years have occurred in the most recent 50-year period."[10]

The crisis that Congress envisioned has not abated. The World Commission on Environment and Development reported in 1987 that species are disappearing at rates never before witnessed on this planet.[11] The World Conservation Union detailed these losses in a 1980 study,[12] noting that 25,000 plant species and one thousand vertebrate species and subspecies are threatened with extinction. Many more small animal species—particularly invertebrates like mollusks, insects, and corals—disappear as their habitats are destroyed. Between 500,000 and one million species will become extinct by the end of this century, according to the study.

Equally important was the Court's recognition in the *Hill* decision that "Congress viewed the value of endangered species as 'incalculable.'"[13] One Senator observed, in an odd turn of phrase, that species "[e]xtinction is quite literally a fate worse than death."[14] Species, once extinct, are lost forever. Their loss reduces the genetic diversity of the world's ecosystem.

Preventing that loss would be justifiable on ethical, cultural, and scientific considerations alone. Economics provide another reason for preserving the

---

*cert. denied,* 449 U.S. 953 (1980). *See also* Chapter 2.

[8] 2 *Official World Wildlife Fund Guide to Endangered Species of North America* 922–23 (Washington: Beacham, 1990).

[9] *Supra* note 1, at 174.

[10] *Quoted in* National Wildlife Federation v. Nat'l. Park Serv., 669 F. Supp. 384, 386 (D. Wyo. 1987).

[11] World Comm'n on Environment and Development, *Our Common Future* 148 (New York: Oxford University Press, 1987) [hereinafter Our Common Future].

[12] International Union for the Conservation of Nature and Natural Resources (World Conservation Union), World Conservation Strategy §3.11 (IUCN-UNEP-WWF 1980).

[13] *Supra* note 1, at 187.

[14] 119 CONG. REC. 25,670 (1973).

genetic materials of diverse species. Agriculture is increasingly dependent upon genetic materials from wild relatives of crops like maize and wheat. In medicine, one-half of all prescriptions dispensed originate from organisms found in the wild. The commercial value of these medicines and drugs amounts to $14 billion yearly in the United States and $40 billion yearly world-wide. For industry, wildlife-derived materials contribute gums, oils, resins, dyes, tannins, vegetable fats and waxes, insecticides, and many other compounds. Many wild plants bear oil-rich seeds that can help in the manufacture of fibers, detergents, starch, and general edibles.[15] Conservation is truly everyone's business.

The *Hill* decision's most permanent legacy is the command "to halt and reverse the trend toward species extinction, whatever the cost."[16] In case after case, the federal courts invoke this precept to block actions that threaten species survival.[17]

## Role of United States Law

The United States cannot legislate a solution to a problem that is global in scope. The principal threat to species stems from the destruction of their habitats. While it is beyond our capacity to protect all habitats important to endangered species, Congress believed that this nation should still act to the extent of its ability to do so.[18]

Because of the United States' land area and population, our domestic legislation makes a major contribution by promoting conservation of animals and plants and their habitat within U.S. territory. Outside U.S. borders, the Endangered Species Act restricts prohibited conduct by persons subject to the jurisdiction of the United States.[19] To enforce this rule, the U.S. Government may conduct law enforcement investigations and research in foreign lands.[20]

The United States is also an important market for wildlife trade. Allowing unrestricted trade would increase the demand for endangered species and their products. It would give exploiters an incentive to violate the law.[21] By restricting that trade, Congress decided, this country can add a significant weapon to the arsenal of conservation.[22]

Although the federal government has the fundamental responsibility for species protection within the United States, Congress has encouraged state

---

[15] Our Common Future, *supra* note 11, at 155–56.

[16] *Supra* note 1, at 184.

[17] Roosevelt Campobello Int'l Park v. Environmental Protection Agency, 684 F.2d 1041, 1052–53 (1st Cir. 1982).

[18] H.R. REP. NO. 412, 93d Cong., 1st Sess. 5–6 (1973) [hereinafter 1973 House Report].

[19] 16 U.S.C. §1538(a) (1988). *Compare* United States v. Mitchell, 553 F.2d 996 (5th Cir. 1977) (Marine Mammal Protection Act).

[20] 16 U.S.C. §1537(d) (1988).

[21] People v. K. Sakai Co., 128 Cal. Rptr. 536, 539, 540, 56 Cal. App. 3d 531, 537 (1976).

[22] 1973 House Report, *supra* note 18, at 5.

conservation programs.[23] By limiting preemption Congress left room for strict but compatible laws at the local level.[24]

Finally, Congress also directed the U.S. government to be a catalyst for global reform. The Endangered Species Act of 1973 was expected to create an important precedent, exerting pressure on other countries to follow suit.[25] Moreover, in earlier legislation, Congress had directed the U.S. government to seek an international treaty on species conservation.[26] As a result, 80 nations met in Washington in March 1973 and agreed upon a treaty that now governs trade worldwide.[27]

The Endangered Species Act is the preeminent law protecting fragile species. The Act is complemented and supplemented by other federal statutes, which will be discussed further in later chapters.

---

[23] 16 U.S.C. §1535 (1988).

[24] *Id.* at §1535(f) (1988).

[25] 1973 House Report, *supra* note 18, at 6.

[26] Pub. L. No. 91-135, §5(b), 83 Stat. 275, 278 (1969).

[27] Convention on International Trade in Endangered Species of Wild Fauna and Flora, 1976, 27 U.S.T. 1087, T.I.A.S. No. 8249, *amended* June 22, 1979; T.I.A.S. No. 11,079.

# Chapter 2

# A Bird's-Eye View of the Legislation

In October 1966, President Johnson was in unusually high spirits as he signed seven new conservation bills, including the first endangered species statute. At a ceremony in the White House, the President accepted congratulations from conservationists and congressional leaders. President Johnson hailed the new package of legislation as "a milestone in the history of conservation."[1]

Actually, the 1966 Endangered Species Preservation Act[2] was too weak to have much impact. Within the next seven years the 1966 legislation was superseded by two endangered species statutes, the last of which was later amended many times. This chapter is a brief synopsis of those statutes and their antecedents.

## State Ownership Doctrine

Before 1966, the federal government had only "limited" involvement with endangered species.[3] The regulation of wildlife was considered a state function.[4]

This view was predicated upon the Supreme Court's 1896 decision in *Geer v. Connecticut*,[5] in which the Court upheld a Connecticut statute prohibiting the export of wild birds killed within the state. Geer had killed the birds legally, but was prosecuted for possessing the birds with the intent to ship them out of state. The Court rejected Geer's argument that the statute violated the Constitution's Commerce Clause. The Court reasoned that the states have a property interest in local wildlife and that this interest continues after the wildlife is killed and reduced to possession. By sanctifying the states' interest in wildlife, the Court relegated the federal government to a secondary role.

---

[1] *President Signs 7 Conservation Bills,* N.Y. TIMES, Oct. 16, 1966, at 40; *Johnson Signs Bill Creating Transportation Department,* WASHINGTON POST, Oct. 16, 1966, at A4.

[2] Pub. L. No. 89-669, 80 Stat. 926.

[3] *See* Tennessee Valley Auth. v. Hill, 437 U.S. 153, n.20 (1978).

[4] *See* R. Rosenberg, *Federal Protection of Unique Environmental Interests: Endangered and Threatened Species,* 58 N.C.L. REV. 491, 496–97 (1980).

[5] 161 U.S. 519 (1896).

The *Geer* doctrine reached its zenith in 1912. Then, in *The Abby Dodge*,[6] the Justices held that the state ownership doctrine precluded federal regulation of wildlife inside the boundary of Florida's territorial waters. In later years, as federal regulation expanded in other legal arenas, the *Geer* doctrine became outmoded. The Court limited *Geer* in a series of decisions[7] and finally overruled it in 1979.[8]

## Early Federal Statutes

The first federal statute protecting species was enacted in the shadow of the original *Geer* decision. The Lacey Act of 1900[9] provided federal sanctions only for the violation of other, non-federal laws. Together with the Bass Act of 1926,[10] the Lacey Act prohibited interstate transportation of fish or wildlife taken in violation of national, state, or foreign law.[11] "The effect of both these statutes was constrained . . . by the fact that prior to the passage of the Endangered Species Act of 1973, there were few laws regulating these creatures."[12]

The Migratory Bird Treaty Act, passed in 1918,[13] was more expansive, empowering the Secretary of the Interior to adopt regulations for the protection of migratory birds. Other measures concentrated on establishing refuges for wildlife.[14] During this period, the federal government followed policies that were "uncoordinated . . . protecting limited forms of wildlife for a wide range of purposes."[15]

## The 1966 Act

In 1966 Congress took its "first major"[16] action to preserve endangered species. The Endangered Species Preservation Act of 1966[17] declared a national policy to protect species that are threatened with extinction. The Secretary of

---

[6] 223 U.S. 166 (1912).

[7] Baldwin v. Fish & Game Comm'n, 436 U.S. 371 (1978); Douglas v. Seacoast Prod., 431 U.S. 265 (1977); Kleppe v. New Mexico, 426 U.S. 529 (1976); Takahashi v. Fish & Game Comm'n, 334 U.S. 410 (1948); Tommer v. Witsell, 334 U.S. 385 (1948); Foster-Fountain Packing Co. v. Haydel, 278 U.S. 1 (1928); Missouri v. Holland, 252 U.S. 416 (1920).

[8] Hughes v. Oklahoma, 441 U.S. 322 (1979).

[9] Ch. 553, §§1–5, 31 Stat. 187.

[10] Ch. 346, 44 Stat. 576.

[11] *See* Tennessee Valley Auth. v. Hill, *supra* note 3.

[12] *Id.*

[13] Ch. 128, §2, 40 Stat. 755.

[14] Tennessee Valley Auth. v. Hill, *supra* note 3, at n.20. (This is the Supreme Court's analysis of the early legislation.)

[15] *See* Rosenberg, *supra* note 4, at 498.

[16] *See* Tennessee Valley Auth. v. Hill, *supra* note 3, at 174.

[17] Pub. L. No. 89-669, 80 Stat. 926 (1966).

the Interior was authorized to acquire lands in order to protect threatened wildlife. But the Act's policy was hobbled by crippling limitations.

The Act protected only native fish and wildlife. Even for those species, the protections were qualified. Thus, the Secretary was directed to harmonize the Interior Department's programs with the Act's purposes, but only "to the extent practicable." In addition, the Secretary was to encourage other agencies to use their authority to further the Act's purposes "where practicable." Although these provisions were the lineal ancestor of the 1973 Act's section 7, they lacked the later statute's mandatory character. In addition, the 1966 Act directed federal agencies to protect threatened species only "insofar as is practicable and consistent with the agencies' primary purposes. . . ." This "practicability" and "consistency" language significantly weakened the 1966 Act's impact.

It is most important to note that the 1966 Act failed to prohibit the taking of endangered species, except on federal lands. Even on federal lands, the Secretary could allow the hunting and fishing of endangered species.[18]

This legislation gave the federal government another important responsibility—to determine which species were threatened and to publicize their identity. That function was to undergo major changes in later enactments. The 1966 Act, however, simply empowered the Secretary to publish the names of the species found to be threatened with extinction.

## The 1969 Act

The Endangered Species Conservation Act of 1969[19] continued the key provisions of the 1966 statute.[20] In addition, the 1969 Act broadened federal involvement in wildlife protection.[21]

The new legislation strengthened the 1966 Act's provisions for publication of the names of endangered species. If the Secretary found a species to be threatened, he was to include it in a list published in the *Federal Register*. The list was to include not only native wildlife, but also wildlife threatened with worldwide extinction. Astute commentators agree that the listing provision was the 1969 legislation's major innovation.[22]

The legislation's main impact was not domestic, but international. Congress directed the government to seek an international treaty on the conservation of endangered species. For the first time, Congress prohibited the importation of endangered species.[23] The Secretary, however, could permit imports to avoid undue economic hardship.

---

[18] *See* Tennessee Valley Auth. v. Hill, *supra* note 3, at 174–75.

[19] Pub. L. No. 91-135, 83 Stat. 275 (1969).

[20] *Id.* §12(d), at 283.

[21] *See* Tennessee Valley Auth. v. Hill, *supra* note 3, at 175–76.

[22] M. Bean, *The Evolution of National Wildlife Law* 321 (New York: Praeger Scientific, 1983); C. Goplerud, *The Endangered Species Act: Does It Jeopardize The Continued Existence of Species?* 1979 ARIZ. ST. L.J. 487, 489.

[23] *See* Delbay Pharmaceuticals v. Department of Commerce, 409 F. Supp. 637, 640 (D.D.C. 1976).

Congress tried an indirect approach to the problem of people taking endangered species. The legislation made it illegal to transport or sell wildlife taken in violation of federal, state, or foreign laws.

## The 1973 Act

Secluded at his San Clemente retreat during the throes of Watergate, Richard Nixon took time out to sign the Endangered Species Act of 1973.[24] Nixon congratulated Congress for "this important step," declaring that the legislation "provides the Federal Government with needed authority to protect an irreplaceable part of our national heritage—threatened wildlife."[25]

The presidential praise was on target. The Endangered Species Act of 1973 "represented the most comprehensive legislation for the preservation of endangered species ever enacted by any nation."[26]

More expansive than its predecessors,[27] the 1973 Act applied to all plants and animals that were either "endangered" or "threatened."[28]

The 1973 Act prohibited not only importation of endangered species, but also most takings, exports, and sales in interstate or foreign commerce. The legislation made it unlawful to deliver, receive, carry, transport, or ship an endangered species in interstate or foreign commerce in the course of commercial activities.

The Act's most far-reaching innovation was section 7, which directed federal agencies to consult with the Secretary of Interior and to insure that their actions "do not jeopardize" the continued existence of protected species or degrade those species' habitat.

## The 1978 Amendments

During the 1978 debates, Congress was preoccupied by the Supreme Court's interpretation of the 1973 Act in the *Hill* decision.[29] The Court's order had halted completion of the $100 million Tellico Dam. Soon after the Court decision was issued, the House of Representatives passed a bill that exempted the dam (and another project) from the Endangered Species Act.[30] The dam's supporters were determined to use the 1978 legislation to save Tellico.

---

[24] Pub. L. No. 93-205, 87 Stat. 884 (1973).

[25] Presidential Statement on Signing S. 1983 into Law, 10 Weekly Comp. Pres. Doc. 2 (Dec. 28, 1973).

[26] *See* Tennessee Valley Auth. v. Hill, 437 U.S. 153, 180 (1978).

[27] *Id.* at 176.

[28] *Id.* at 180.

[29] Tennessee Valley Auth. v. Hill, *supra* note 26.

[30] H.R. CONF. REP. NO. 1804, 95th Cong., 2d Sess. 24 (1978), *reprinted in* 1978 U.S. CODE CONG. & ADMIN. NEWS 9484, 9492.

In the end, the Endangered Species Act Amendments of 1978[31] were a compromise. The law did not authorize the Tellico Dam's completion. Instead, it established an Endangered Species Committee made up of six cabinet members empowered to grant exemptions from the Act. The committee was instructed to rule promptly on the Tellico Dam and another project.

The political battle for Tellico was not over. Signing the 1978 Amendments into law, President Carter attacked the exemption provision and warned the committee members to be "exceedingly cautious in considering exemptions."[32] Later, the committee denied an exemption for the Tellico Dam. Tellico remained in limbo until the next year. Then, in an unrelated money bill, the House forced the Senate to accept a rider requiring the dam's completion.[33]

The 1978 legislation's "most significant provision" was aimed at protecting critical habitat. Under the 1973 Act, the Secretary was not required to designate critical habitat. Changing this, the 1978 Amendments directed that, when adding a new species to the endangered species list, the Secretary must specify the species' critical habitat—"to the maximum extent prudent."[34] More importantly, in designating critical habitat, the Secretary was directed to consider economic impact. The result: the Secretary had to make economic assessments at the time of listing.

The Secretary was also instructed to follow new procedures for habitat designation, including notifying affected local governments, publishing notices in local newspapers, and holding public hearings.

In another part of the 1978 legislation, Congress modified the Act's penalty provisions.

## The 1979 Amendments

There was no controversy over the 1979 appropriations authorization for the Endangered Species Act.[35] Congress continued funding the Act for three more years.

This appropriations legislation also changed some of the Act's substantive provisions. The statute strengthened programs for protecting plants. It reorganized the government agencies that implemented the Convention on International Trade in Endangered Species. Finally, Congress tinkered with section 7's language requiring the federal government to insure that its actions are "not likely to" jeopardize any species' existence.

---

[31] Pub. L. No. 95-632, 92 Stat. 3751.

[32] Presidential Statement on Signing S. 2899 into Law, 14 Weekly Comp. Pres. Doc. 2002 (Nov. 10, 1978).

[33] Energy and Water Development Appropriations Act of 1980, Pub. L. No. 96-69, 93 Stat. 437, 449–50 (1979). *See* Sequoyah v. Tennessee Valley Auth., 480 F. Supp. 608 (E.D. Tenn. 1979), *cert. denied,* 449 U.S. 953 (1980).

[34] 124 CONG. REC. 38,666 (1978) (remarks of Rep. Murphy).

[35] Pub. L. No. 96-159, 93 Stat. 1225.

## The 1982 Amendments

The 1982 legislative program began in typical fashion, "with one side opposing any change in the act, the other side calling for drastic changes and hostility on both sides."[36] The congressional committees worked hard and "defused . . . a major legislative battle between conservation and development."[37]

What emerged was a "compromise bill which won [wide] support. . . ."[38] The Endangered Species Act Amendments of 1982[39] contained something for everyone.

In order to satisfy conservation groups, Congress nullified the 1978 legislation's most significant feature: the government requirement to make economic assessments about critical habitat at the time it listed any new species. Beginning in 1981, the Republican administration used economic considerations as a means to slow down new species listings, bringing the listing process "to a virtual standstill."[40]

To correct these "abuses,"[41] the 1982 Congress "eliminated all economic considerations from the species listing process."[42] Congress praised this change as the 1982 law's "principal purpose."[43]

Another change also pleased environmental groups. Congress established strict timetables for acting on proposals to list (or to delist) species. It shortened the time for final action from two years to one year.[44]

Congress met industry's concerns by paring down the timetable for the exemption process.[45] The Endangered Species Committee's timetable for granting exemption requests was reduced by nearly one-half.[46] To address the concerns of private landowners, Congress gave the Secretary power to permit "incidental" takings of endangered species.[47] Congress also deleted statutory language that "was perceived as an insult to sport hunters."[48]

Having achieved a consensus, Congress improved the protection for plants and refined other provisions of the Act.

---

[36] 128 CONG. REC. 26,189 (1982) (remarks of Rep. Jones).

[37] *Id.* at 12,957 (remarks of Rep. Jones).

[38] *Id.* at 12,960 (remarks of Rep. Lent).

[39] Pub. L. No. 97-304, 96 Stat. 1411.

[40] *See* S. REP. NO. 418, 97th Cong., 2d Sess. 4 (1982) [hereinafter 1982 Senate Report].

[41] 134 CONG. REC. S10,166 (daily ed. July 28, 1988) (remarks of Sen. Mitchell, a manager of the 1988 Amendments, who analyzed the 1978 and 1982 legislation).

[42] H.R. REP. NO. 567, 97th Cong., 2d Sess. 12 (1982), *reprinted in* 1982 U.S. CODE CONG. & ADMIN. NEWS 2807, 2812 [hereinafter 1982 House Report].

[43] H.R. CONF. REP. NO. 835, 97th Cong., 2d Sess. 19 (1982), *reprinted in* 1982 U.S. CODE CONG. & ADMIN. NEWS 2807, 2860 [hereinafter 1982 Conference Report].

[44] *Id.* at 23, 1982 U.S. CODE CONG. & ADMIN. NEWS at 2864.

[45] 1982 House Report, *supra* note 42, at 14, 1982 U.S. CODE CONG. & ADMIN. NEWS at 2814.

[46] *Id.;* 1982 Conference Report, *supra* note 43, at 28, 1982 U.S. CODE CONG. & ADMIN. NEWS at 2869.

[47] *Id.* at 29, 1982 U.S. CODE CONG. & ADMIN. NEWS at 2870.

[48] 1982 Senate Report, *supra* note 40, at 15.

## The 1988 Amendments

The Senate managers of the next legislation hoped to avoid any controversy. They proposed to reauthorize the Endangered Species Act with no changes in the Act's substantive provisions.[49] Other legislators, however, insisted upon enlivening the debates on the Endangered Species Act Amendments of 1988[50] with major new initiatives.

Gulf state senators obtained relief for the shrimp fishing industry. In order to protect sea turtles, the federal government had issued regulations requiring shrimp trawlers to equip their nets with turtle excluder devices. The new legislation postponed the regulations' effectiveness.

Culminating a ten-year effort, the House persuaded the Senate to accept legislation to protect the African elephant.

Changes in the Act proper were less noteworthy. Once again Congress increased protections for plants. It instituted a monitoring system so that species which were candidates for listing were less likely to become extinct before listing. Complaining that the Reagan administration had not funded some federal-state programs, Congress authorized funding.

Other amendments were fairly technical, with one exception concerning penalties. Since 1973, the cost of living had increased by 150 percent. Matching this, Congress increased both civil and criminal penalties for violating the Endangered Species Act. The worst offenders could now be fined up to $25,000 in a civil action and up to $50,000 in a criminal proceeding. Those penalties were needed, Congress said, "since the profits to be made from illegal activities often dwarf current penalties."[51]

## Future Prospects

Having nurtured endangered species legislation through so many amendments, some congressional leaders treat the Act with paternal solicitude. If the bureaucracy is thought to be working slowly, Congress imposes deadlines that "force action."[52] Court decisions that displease Congress are overruled,[53]

---

[49] 133 CONG. REC. 5029 (1987) (remarks of Sen. Mitchell introducing the legislation).

[50] Pub. L. No. 100-478, 102 Stat. 2306.

[51] S. REP. NO. 240, 100th Cong., 1st Sess. 13 (1987), *reprinted in* 1988 U.S. CODE CONG. & ADMIN. NEWS 2700, 2713 [hereinafter 1988 Senate Report].

[52] 1982 Conference Report, *supra* note 43, at 21, 1982 U.S. CODE CONG. & ADMIN. NEWS at 2862.

[53] Endangered Species Act Amendments of 1982, Pub. L. No. 97-304, §5, 96 Stat. 1411, 1421 (1982) (overruling Defenders of Wildlife v. Endangered Species Scientific Auth., 659 F.2d 168 (D.C. Cir.), *cert. denied sub nom.* International Ass'n of Fish and Wildlife Agencies v. Defenders of Wildlife, 454 U.S. 963 (1981)). *See* 1982 Conference Report, *supra* note 43, at 28–29, 1982 U.S. CODE CONG. & ADMIN. NEWS at 2869. *See also* Defenders of Wildlife v. Endangered Species Scientific Auth., 725 F.2d 726 (D.C. Cir. 1984).

criticized,[54] or circumvented.[55] So it is not surprising that, when the presidency and Congress are controlled by different political parties, Congress has no qualms about disagreeing with the Executive Department's policies.

The future promises no change. The 1988 Amendments provided appropriations for the Act's enforcement to continue only through Fiscal Year 1992. Congress will soon be faced with the need to enact additional legislation. Congress is likely to be the stage for new battles over the Act's policies. In a controversy over protecting the northern spotted owl,[56] the administration may support the timber industry's attempt to prevent a ban on logging in the Pacific Northwest's ancient forests. Repeating industry contentions that the ban will cost 30,000 jobs, *Time* magazine sees this as "an epic confrontation between ecology and economy."[57] The Secretary of the Interior promised to seek changes in the Endangered Species Act "that would make it easier to allow some species to diminish if preserving them would cause severe economic disruption."[58] Predictions are that the 1992 legislative session "promises to be a bloody political brawl between environmentalists who have used the act to restrain growth and business interests who think wildlife preservation is going too far."[59]

---

[54] *See* 1988 Senate Report, *supra* note 51, at 5–6, 17–19 (criticizing Sierra Club v. Clark, 755 F.2d 608 (8th Cir. 1985)); 1982 Senate Report, *supra* note 40, at 24–25 (attempting to resolve a conflict between United States v. Kepler, 531 F.2d 796 (6th Cir. 1976) and United States v. Molt, 624 F.2d 1092 (3d Cir. 1980)).

[55] *See* Sequoyah v. Tennessee Valley Auth., 480 F. Supp. 608 (E.D. Tenn. 1979), *cert. denied*, 449 U.S. 953 (1980).

[56] *See* Northern Spotted Owl v. Hodel, 716 F. Supp. 479 (W.D. Wash. 1988); Northern Spotted Owl v. Lujan; 758 F. Supp. 621 (E.D. Wash. 1991); 56 Fed. Reg. 40002 (1991) as corrected 56 Fed. Reg. 50701 (1991).

[57] *Owl vs. Man,* TIME, June 25, 1990, at 2, 56–63.

[58] *Softening Stand on Spotted Owl, Administration Delays Protection,* N.Y. TIMES, June 27, 1990, at A1.

[59] *Lobbyists' Smelt-and-Bird Campaign Is Assault Against Endangered Species Act Itself, Some Say,* WALL STREET JOURNAL, Aug. 29, 1991, at A14.

# Chapter 3

# The Listing Process Under Section 4

The Navajo and Hopi Indian tribes regard Arizona's San Francisco Peaks as sacred mountains. The tribes opposed a plan to develop a ski resort, believing that it threatened an alpine plant growing only on the Peaks. The court,[1] however, summarily rejected the tribes' arguments under the Endangered Species Act because the plant was not listed under the Act's section 4.[2] That court decision illustrates that "[t]he listing process under Section 4 is the keystone of the Endangered Species Act."[3]

## The Architects of Listing

The Act entrusts the listing process to "the Secretary."[4] Under the statutory definitions, "the Secretary" refers to the Secretary of the Interior or the Secretary of Commerce, depending upon the particular species that is threatened.[5] The two Secretaries exercise their powers under the Act through two departmental agencies—the U.S. Fish and Wildlife Service (for Interior) and the National Marine Fisheries Service (for Commerce).[6]

## Species Eligible for Listing

Congress has steadily expanded the list to embrace more and more life forms. The Endangered Species Preservation Act of 1966 directed the Secretary

---

[1] Wilson v. Block, 708 F.2d 735 (D.C. Cir.), *cert. denied,* 464 U.S. 956 (1983).

[2] 16 U.S.C. §1533 (1988).

[3] H.R. REP. NO. 567, 97th Cong., 2d Sess. 10 (1982), *reprinted in* 1982 U.S. CODE CONG. & ADMIN. NEWS 2807, 2810 [hereinafter 1982 House Report].

[4] 16 U.S.C. §1533(a) (1988).

[5] *Id.* §1532(15). *See also* Romero-Barcelo v. Brown, 643 F.2d 835, n.43 (1st Cir. 1981), *rev'd on other grounds sub nom.* Weinberger v. Romero-Barcelo, 456 U.S. 305 (1982); Reorg. Plan No. 4 of 1970, 84 Stat. 2090 (codified in 5 U.S.C. app. (1988)). In 1974 the Secretaries' Departments entered into a memorandum of understanding that detailed their jurisdictional responsibilities and procedures for listing under the Act. The Secretary of Agriculture also has responsibilities in connection with the export and import of plants.

[6] 50 C.F.R. §402.01(b) (1990). The National Marine Fisheries Service has jurisdiction over those marine species listed in 50 C.F.R. §§222.23(a), 227.4 (1990).

to publish the names of "*native* fish and wildlife found to be threatened with extinction . . ."[7] In 1969, as part of the Endangered Species Conservation Act,[8] Congress required the listing of all "fish and wildlife . . . threatened with worldwide extinction . . . ." Eligible creatures included wild mammals and birds, fish, amphibians, reptiles, mollusks, and crustaceans. As part of the Endangered Species Act of 1973,[9] Congress added invertebrates and plants. Any one of these life forms qualified for listing if it was "threatened" or "endangered."[10]

In the 18 years since the 1973 Act became law, Congress has made no substantive change in the definitions of "endangered species" and "threatened species." A species is "endangered" if it is in danger of extinction throughout all or a significant part of its range.[11] It is "threatened" if it is likely to become an endangered species within the foreseeable future.[12] By the term "species," the Act includes any species or subspecies of fish, wildlife, or plant.[13]

Some species are not imperiled throughout their entire geographic range, but only in a local geographic area. To protect wildlife in such cases, the Act allows the Secretary to protect any distinct population segment of any species of *vertebrate* fish or wildlife which interbreeds when mature.[14] As a consequence, the Secretary may limit a listing to a geographically isolated population of a species. Or he may list one population as endangered and another population as only threatened. For example, the green sea turtle is listed as endangered in Florida and on the Pacific coast of Mexico; it is listed as threatened elsewhere.[15] In the Endangered Species Act Amendments of 1978, Congress withdrew the Secretary's authority to divide invertebrates into distinct population segments.[16]

One life form is ineligible for listing as an endangered species. Congress defined the term "endangered species" to exclude a species of the class *Insecta* that constitutes a pest whose protection would present an overwhelming and overriding risk to humans.[17]

By May 1989, the Secretary had listed 1,046 species as endangered or threatened.[18] The Fish and Wildlife Service has identified more than 3,000 spe-

---

[7] Pub. L. No. 89-669, §1(c), 80 Stat. 926 (1966) (italics added).

[8] Pub. L. No. 91-135, §3(a), 83 Stat. 275 (1969).

[9] Pub. L. No. 93-205, §§3(5), (9), (11) and 4(c), 87 Stat. 884–87 (1973).

[10] *Id.* §§3(4), (15) and 4(c), 87 Stat. at 885–87.

[11] 16 U.S.C. §1532(6) (1988).

[12] *Id.* §1532(20).

[13] *Id.* §1532(16).

[14] *Id.*

[15] II *World Wildlife Fund Guide to Endangered Species* 724 (Beacham: Washington, D.C., 1990); 50 C.F.R. §17.11 (1990).

[16] Pub. L. No. 95-632, §2(5), 92 Stat. 3751, 3752 (1978). *See* H.R. CONF. REP. NO. 1804, 95th Cong., 2d Sess. 17 (1978), *reprinted in* 1978 U.S. CODE CONG. & ADMIN. NEWS 9453, 9485.

[17] 16 U.S.C. §1532(6) (1988). Although the statute excludes insect pests from the definition of "endangered species" only, the agency regulations exclude them from the definition of all "species." 50 C.F.R. §424.02(k) (1990).

[18] *See* Defenders of Wildlife v. Lujan, 911 F.2d 117, 123 (8th Cir. 1990), *rev'd on other grounds*, 60 U.S.L.W. 4495 (U.S. June 9, 1992). Of species that occur in the United States or its territories, the Secretary lists about 450 species as endangered and about 150 as threatened.

cies as candidates for eventual designation.[19] In fact, by 1987 the Fish and Wildlife Service acknowledged that it had sufficient information to propose the listing of another 950 candidate species, but it was unable to complete more than 50 new listings yearly.[20]

## Consequences of Listing Status

A species' right to protection can hinge on its status under section 4. The Act prescribes two types of protections for imperiled species. Under section 9,[21] private parties and governments are prohibited from harming or trafficking in endangered species. Under section 7,[22] the federal government is forbidden to take any action that is likely to jeopardize an imperiled species or to degrade its critical habitat. The two sections, however, are not coextensive in scope. The prohibitions listed in section 9 apply only to "endangered" species, while section 7's restrictions cover both "endangered" and "threatened" species.

### The Difference Between Endangered and Threatened

As a consequence of this difference in statutory language, the Act provides "two levels of protection . . ."[23] Thus, "although it expressly prohibited the killing of *endangered* species, Congress delegated to the Secretary the task of determining whether the killing of *threatened* species should also be prohibited."[24] Congress authorized, but did not require, the Secretary to extend section 9's protections to threatened species.[25] In the case of threatened species, the Secretary has considerable discretion to "issue such regulations as he deems necessary and advisable to provide for the conservation of such species."[26]

Generally, the Secretary exercises this discretion in favor of protection. After codifying the protections for endangered species, the Secretary issued a regulation that extends those same protections to most threatened species.[27]

---

M. Bean, S. Fitzgerald, and M. O'Connell, *Reconciling Conflicts Under the Endangered Species Act* 2 (Washington, D.C.: World Wildlife Fund, 1991). The Secretary of the Interior publishes the list in 50 C.F.R. §17.11 (for wildlife) and §17.12 (for plants).

[19] S. REP. NO. 418, 97th Cong., 2d Sess. 10 (1982) [hereinafter 1982 Senate Report].

[20] H.R. REP. NO. 467, 100th Cong., 1st Sess. 14 (1987); S. REP. NO. 240, 100th Cong., 1st Sess. 8 (1987), *reprinted in* 1988 U.S. CODE CONG. & ADMIN. NEWS 2700, 2707 [hereinafter 1988 House and Senate Reports].

[21] 16 U.S.C. §1538(a)(1)(A)–(G) and (a)(2)(A)–(E) (1988). *See* Chapter 4.

[22] *Id.* §1536(a). *See* Chapter 5.

[23] Sierra Club v. Clark, 755 F.2d 608, 614 (8th Cir. 1985).

[24] Christy v. Hodel, 857 F.2d 1324, 1333 (9th Cir. 1988), *cert. denied sub nom.* Christy v. Lujan, 490 U.S. 1114 (1989).

[25] *Id.*

[26] 16 U.S.C. §1533(d) (1988). For states that have entered into cooperative agreements with the Secretary, the regulations apply to species resident in those states, but only to the extent that those states adopt the regulations.

[27] 50 C.F.R. §§17.31(a) and 17.71(a) (1990).

There are significant exceptions, however, such as the grizzly bear. Although the Act's self-defense exception[28] does not extend to the protection of property,[29] the Secretary allows a government-supervised taking of grizzly bears that destroy livestock, crops, or beehives.[30] Similarly, the Secretary authorizes the importation of hides from Australian kangaroos, a threatened species, as a means to encourage conservation by the Australian government.[31]

The Secretary has authorized hunting and trapping of certain populations of threatened species. Two decisions illustrate both the scope and the limits of the Secretary's power to permit this activity. In one case,[32] the Secretary had authorized sport trapping of the Minnesota gray wolf, a threatened species. The court refused to uphold the Secretary. As part of the federal government's duty to conserve imperiled species, Congress authorized the Secretary to allow "regulated taking" only in "the extraordinary case where population pressures within a given ecosystem cannot be otherwise relieved . . . ."[33] In this case, the court found, the Secretary had no information satisfying this test, and so ruled that the sport trapping regulations violated the Act.

In the second case,[34] the Secretary's regulations prohibited the killing of grizzly bears in most parts of Montana, but permitted sport hunting of these bears in another part of the same state. The Secretary's regulations were challenged by a Montana sheep herder who was penalized for killing a grizzly bear outside the authorized hunting zone. The court accepted the view that sport hunting can be consistent with conservation goals where, as the Secretary found in this case, it is necessary to relieve population pressures in the region. The court held that permitting sport hunting in only parts of Montana was reasonable and, consequently, the sheep herder's penalty was not unconstitutional.

In other ways, the Act itself differentiates between endangered and threatened wildlife. The Act's most severe penalties are reserved for illegal acts involving endangered species.[35]

## The Importance of Being Listed

The Endangered Species Act protects only species that are listed. Take, for example, the case mentioned at the beginning of this chapter, in which Indian tribes objected to a ski resort that jeopardized a rare alpine plant. Before the lawsuit, the Secretary of the Interior proposed the plant for listing as an endangered species, but withdrew that proposal. Referring to section 7, one of

---

[28] 16 U.S.C. §1540(a)(3) and (b)(3) (1988).

[29] Christy v. Hodel, *supra* note 24.

[30] 50 C.F.R. §17.40(b)(1)(i)(c) (1990). The permission is subject to numerous safeguards.

[31] Defenders of Wildlife v. Watt, 12 Envtl. L. (Envtl. L. Inst.) 20,210 (D.D.C. 1981). *See* 50 C.F.R. §17.40(a)(1)(i)(B) (1990).

[32] Sierra Club v. Clark, *supra* note 23.

[33] 16 U.S.C. §1532(3) (1988). *See also id.* §1533(d).

[34] Christy v. Hodel, *supra* note 24.

[35] *See* Chapter 7.

the Act's major protections, the court ruled that the "structure of the Endangered Species Act confirms that §7(a)(2) applies only to listed species . . .[36] [T]o be protected under §7(a)(2) a species must be listed under §4."[37]

Other decisions reach the same result. One court allowed a Florida state-sponsored deer hunt to proceed because the target, the white-tailed deer, was not listed and did not interbreed with any protected deer species.[38] In another case, when a proposed highway threatened a newly discovered species of plant, the court held that the plant was not entitled to protection since it was neither listed nor proposed to be listed as an endangered species.[39]

The importance of being listed is illustrated by the recent saga of the spotted owl. In the 1980s, relying on the National Environmental Policy Act (NEPA),[40] environmentalists tried to halt harvesting of ancient forests in which the spotted owl nests. At first, the environmentalists "di[d] not [and could not] seek relief under the Endangered Species Act because the United States Fish and Wildlife Service ha[d] refused to declare the Northern Spotted Owl an endangered species."[41] The courts rejected the requests made under the National Environmental Policy Act.[42] In November 1988, a court ruled that the Fish and Wildlife Service's decision against listing the spotted owl was arbitrary and capricious.[43] Finally, in June 1989, the Service proposed to list the northern spotted owl as a threatened species, issuing its final rule one year later.[44] Soon a court set a timetable for the Service to designate a protected habitat for the owl.[45] If the spotted owl had remained unlisted, it would have remained unprotected as well.

The Secretary may list an unthreatened species as though it is endangered or threatened if it closely resembles a listed species. To do this, the Secretary must find that enforcement personnel would have substantial difficulty in differentiating between the listed species and the look-alike species, thus creating an additional threat for the listed species. In addition, the Secretary must find

---

[36] Wilson v. Block, 708 F.2d 735, 750 (D.C. Cir.), *cert. denied,* 464 U.S. 956 (1983).

[37] *Id.*, 708 F.2d at 751.

[38] Fund for Animals v. Florida Game & Fresh Water Fish Comm'n, 550 F. Supp. 1206 (S.D. Fla. 1982).

[39] Stop H-3 Ass'n v. Lewis, 538 F. Supp. 149 (D. Hawaii 1982), *remanded on other grounds sub nom.* Stop H-3 Ass'n v. Dole, 740 F.2d 1442 (9th Cir. 1984).

[40] 42 U.S.C. §4321 *et seq.* (1988).

[41] Portland Audubon Soc'y v. Hodel, 866 F.2d 302, 303 (9th Cir.), *cert. denied sub nom.* Northwest Forest Resource Council v. Portland Audubon Soc'y, 492 U.S. 911 (1989). For subsequent litigation, see Portland Audubon Soc'y v. Lujan, 712 F. Supp. 1456 (D. Ore. 1989), *aff'd in part and rev'd in part,* 884 F.2d 1233 (9th Cir. 1989), *cert. denied,* 494 U.S. 1026 (1990).

[42] *Id.*

[43] Northern Spotted Owl v. Hodel, 716 F. Supp. 479 (W.D. Wash. 1988).

[44] *See* Northern Spotted Owl v. Lujan, 758 F. Supp. 621 (E.D. Wash. 1991). *See also* Headwaters, Inc. v. BLM, Medford Dist., 914 F.2d 1174, 1184 (9th Cir. 1990) (dissenting opinion).

[45] Northern Spotted Owl v. Lujan, *supra* note 44. *See* 56 Fed. Reg. 40,002 (1991) as revised 56 Fed. Reg. 50,701 (1991). In January 1992, the Fish and Wildlife Service announced its designation of the owl's critical habitat. (U.S. Fish and Wildlife Service News Release 09-92 (Jan. 21, 1992)).

the Act's policies and enforcement will be aided by this treatment of the look-alike species.[46] In practice, the Secretary would add the look-alike species to the endangered species list with a "similarity of appearance" notation beside its name.[47]

Once the Secretary proposes to add a species to the endangered species list, its troubles are far from over. As the Act reads,[48] it requires only that government agencies "confer" informally with the Secretary about actions that are likely to jeopardize a proposed-to-be-listed species.[49] That is not much protection. Thus, after the Corps of Engineers went through the formality of conferring with the Fish and Wildlife Service, a court permitted the Corps to construct a harbor project that intruded upon a rare plant whose listing had not been made final.[50]

During the 1980s Congress became concerned with the lack of protection for proposed-to-be-listed species. In the Endangered Species Act Amendments of 1982,[51] Congress directed the Secretary to make a prompt finding if a proposed listing is warranted, even if it is precluded by the press of other pending proposals.[52] In the Endangered Species Act Amendments of 1988,[53] Congress required the Secretary to institute a system to monitor the status of these "warranted but precluded" species.[54] Additionally, the Secretary was granted power, under section 4(b)(7),[55] to issue emergency regulations "to prevent a significant risk to the well being of any such species."[56] In the case of a "warranted but precluded" species, Congress intended the Secretary to "use his emergency powers less cautiously—in a sense 'to shoot first and ask [all of the] questions later.'"[57]

The Fish and Wildlife Service publishes and periodically updates a notice that identifies species considered to be candidates for listing. When Congress enacted monitoring requirements, it expected the Service to apply the system to all candidate species.[58] Although the monitoring system is a step forward, the Act's substantive or procedural protections still do not apply to candidate species.[59]

---

[46] 16 U.S.C. §1533(e) (1988).

[47] *See* 50 C.F.R. §17.50–51 (1990).

[48] 16 U.S.C. §1536(a)(4) (1988).

[49] Wilson v. Block, *supra* note 36, at 751.

[50] Enos v. Marsh, 769 F.2d 1363 (9th Cir. 1985). *See also* County of Bergen v. Dole, 620 F. Supp. 1009, 1047–48, 1063 (D.N.J. 1985).

[51] Pub. L. No. 97-304, §2, 96 Stat. 1411, 1412 (1982).

[52] 16 U.S.C. §1533(b)(3)(B) (1988).

[53] Pub. L. No. 100-478, §1002(a), 102 Stat. 2306 (1988).

[54] 16 U.S.C. §1533(b)(3)(C)(iii) (1988).

[55] *Id.* §1533(b)(7).

[56] *Id.* §1533(b)(3)(C)(iii).

[57] City of Las Vegas v. Lujan, 891 F.2d 927, 932 (D.C. Cir. 1989).

[58] 1988 Senate Report, *supra* note 20, at 7–8, 1988 U.S. Code Cong. & Admin. News at 2706–07.

[59] 50 C.F.R. §424.15(b) (1990).

## Hybrid Populations

It is uncertain whether the Act protects hybrids—offspring of matings between an endangered species and another species or subspecies. In the Florida Everglades and nearby Big Cypress Swamp, for example, approximately 50 Florida panthers are the last of their line. Though these animals are listed as endangered, some of them have mated with animals from a captive stock having South American bloodlines. Between 1977 and 1984, Interior Department lawyers issued opinions suggesting that hybrids cannot be protected. Because of challenges to this semi-official "hybrid policy," the agency lawyers withdrew those rulings, but the Interior Department has not yet decided how to deal with these mixed animals.[60]

In an internal legal opinion, the Fish and Wildlife Service specified one limitation to the "hybrid policy." Planning to rebuild the Southern Selkirk Mountain caribou herd, the last remaining caribou herd in the contiguous 48 states, the Fish and Wildlife Service hoped to augment the Selkirk herd with nonendangered caribou from outside the Selkirks. The Service pondered whether the intermixed caribou would become "hybrids" and lose their protected status. The Service's lawyers found that offspring of parents of the same subspecies from two different geographic locations are not "hybrids," even though only one of the parent "populations" is listed as endangered.[61]

## Criteria for Listing

The Secretary is to determine whether a species is endangered or threatened according to five factors, listed as subparagraphs (A) through (E) of section 4(a)(1).[62] Those factors are:

- The present or threatened destruction, modification, or curtailment of the species' habitat or range
- Overutilization for commercial, recreational, scientific, or educational purposes[63]

---

[60] *See* S. O'Brien and E. Mayr, *Bureaucratic Mischief: Recognizing Endangered Species and Subspecies,* 251 Science Magazine 1187 (Mar. 8, 1991); *Entering the Hybrid Zone,* WASHINGTON POST, Mar. 18, 1991 at A9. *See* Letter from Assistant Solicitor, Fish and Wildlife, to Regional Solicitor, Northeast Region, Department of the Interior, entitled, "Status of the Offspring of Two Endangered Species" (Sept. 21, 1983); Memorandum from Assistant Solicitor, Fish and Wildlife, to Deputy Associate Director, Federal Assistance, Fish and Wildlife Service, entitled "Whether Hybrids Are Covered by the Endangered Species Act of 1973" (Aug. 2, 1977).

[61] Letter from Assistant Solicitor, Fish and Wildlife, to Associate Director, Federal Assistance, Fish and Wildlife Service, entitled, "Augmentation of the Southern Selkirk Mountain Caribou Herd" (Aug. 24, 1984).

[62] 16 U.S.C. §1533(a)(1) (1988).

[63] In the Endangered Species Act Amendments of 1982, Congress made a minor change in §4(a)(1)(B), which had allowed the Secretary to consider whether a species was imperiled because of "overutilization for commercial, sporting, scientific, or educational purposes." At the request

- Disease or predation
- The inadequacy of existing regulatory mechanisms
- Other factors affecting the species' continued existence

In addition to these five factors, the Secretary must also consider any efforts by state and foreign governments to protect the species.[64]

The American Fisheries Society stumbled over this two-pronged test when it asked the Secretary to list a population of California chinook salmon as endangered. The salmon's runs up the Sacramento River had declined, due primarily to a new dam and high water temperatures. Ruling that the salmon was not likely to become endangered, however, the Secretary relied entirely on the existence of a conservation plan by the California Department of Fish and Game and four federal agencies. The court upheld the Secretary.[65] In determining whether a species is endangered or threatened, the court said, the Secretary is entitled to consider subparagraph (A) through (E)'s factors "*and* the conservation activities of other federal and state agencies. . . ."[66]

The Secretary cannot make his listing decisions without being aware that species preservation is a global problem. The United States and other nations have entered into treaties and international agreements to protect species. One of these non-U.S. institutions, the Convention on International Trade in Endangered Species (CITES),[67] publishes its own lists of imperiled wildlife and plants. Recognizing this, the Secretary treats these designations by non-U.S. entities as evidence that the species are endangered or threatened.[68] Whenever one of the 50 states designates a species for protection, the Secretary also takes this into account in listing decisions.[69]

Congress forbids the Secretary from taking account of economic considerations, as explained later in this chapter. In addition, notwithstanding NEPA, the Secretary does not consider environmental matters that are extraneous to the Act, and therefore is not required to file an environmental impact statement.[70] The result is that the Secretary makes listing decisions "*solely* on the basis of the best available scientific and commercial information . . . , without reference to possible economic or other impacts of such determination."[71]

---

of sport hunters, Congress substituted the word "recreational" for the word "sporting." *See* Pub. L. No. 97-304, §2(a)(1)(C), 96 Stat. 1411 (1982). *See also* 1982 House Report, *supra* note 3, at 19, 1982 U.S. CODE CONG. & ADMIN. NEWS at 2819; 1982 Senate Report, *supra* note 19, at 15.

[64] 16 U.S.C. §1533(b)(1)(A) (1988).

[65] American Fisheries Soc'y v. Verity, Civ. No. 88-0174 RAR-JFM (E.D. Cal. Feb. 24, 1989).

[66] *Id.*, slip. op. at 11.

[67] 1976, 27 U.S.T. 1087, T.I.A.S. No. 8249, *amended* June 22, 1979, T.I.A.S. No. 11, 079.

[68] 50 C.F.R. §424.11(e) (1990). *See* 16 U.S.C. § 1533(b)(1)(B)(i) (1988).

[69] 50 C.F.R. §424.11(f) (1990). *See* 16 U.S.C. §1533(b)(1)(B)(ii) (1988).

[70] Pacific Legal Found. v. Andrus, 657 F.2d 829, 840 (6th Cir. 1981). *See* Glover River Org. v. Department of the Interior, 675 F. 2d 251 (10th Cir. 1982) (decided on standing issue).

[71] 50 C.F.R. §424.11(b) (1990).

In 1979, Congress directed the Secretary to establish a ranking system, thus identifying which species should receive priority reviews for listing.[72] During its 1982 review of the Act, Congress insisted that it wanted a scientifically based priority system, based on the degree of threat. The Secretary was told not to favor higher life forms over lower taxonomic orders.[73]

## The Procedure for Listing

Before 1982, the Act gave the Secretary a great deal of discretion about processing proposals to add new species to the list. If the Secretary proposed the listing, that official was required only to give notice and hold a public hearing. The Secretary could allow the proposal to languish for two years, after which it had to be withdrawn.[74] If the Secretary missed the deadline, "the proposal [was] simply dropped with no reviewable decision having been made."[75] When an outsider petitioned for a listing, the Secretary had to begin a review of the species' status within 90 days, but only if the Secretary found the petition presented substantial evidence that warranted a review.[76] In practice, the Secretary's status reviews often continued for many years.[77]

By 1982, the system had broken down. The 1978 Amendments on critical habitat had "burdened the listing process with nonbiological factors and, as a result, greatly decreased the number of listings."[78] The listing process came "to a virtual standstill."[79]

In the Endangered Species Act Amendments of 1982,[80] Congress reacted by streamlining the Act's procedures for listing. In order to "force action on listing,"[81] the 1982 Amendments laid down tight deadlines that "replace[d] the Secretary's discretion with mandatory, nondiscretionary duties."[82]

Under the 1982 Amendments, the Secretary must respond to a petition for listing, to the maximum extent practical,[83] within 90 days after the petition is received. Within that 90-day period, the Secretary must publish a finding

---

[72] Pub. L. No. 96-159, §3(6), 93 Stat. 1225, 1225–26 (1979).

[73] H.R. CONF. REP. NO. 835, 97th Cong., 2d Sess. 21, *reprinted in* 1982 U.S. CODE CONG. & ADMIN. NEWS 2807, 2862 [hereinafter 1982 Conference Report].

[74] 16 U.S.C. §1533(f)(5) (Supp. IV 1976).

[75] 1982 Senate Report, *supra* note 19, at 4.

[76] 16 U.S.C. §1533(c)(2) (Supp. IV 1976).

[77] 1982 Conference Report, *supra* note 73, at 20–21, 1982 U.S. CODE CONG. & ADMIN. NEWS at 2861–62.

[78] 1982 Senate Report, *supra* note 19, at 4.

[79] *Id.*

[80] Pub. L. No. 97-304, §2, 96 Stat. 1411–16.

[81] 1982 Conference Report, *supra* note 73, at 21, 1982 U.S. CODE CONG. & ADMIN. NEWS at 2862.

[82] *Id.* at 20, 1982 U.S. CODE CONG. & ADMIN. NEWS at 2861.

[83] The phrase "to the maximum extent practical" allows the Secretary and staff to delay the rulemaking process, but only if the existence of other proposals to list species of a greater degree of threat would make it unwise to allocate resources to the petition. 1982 Conference Report, *supra* note 73 at 21, 1982 U.S. CODE CONG. & ADMIN. NEWS at 2862.

on whether the petition presents substantial scientific or commercial information indicating that action may be warranted. The Secretary must begin a status review once the finding is published.[84]

For a substantiated petition, the Secretary has 12 months to complete the status review and publish one of three findings—that the requested action is *not* warranted, that it *is* warranted, or that it is warranted but a rulemaking is precluded by other pending listing proposals.[85] If the Secretary determines that the requested action is "warranted but precluded," it must also be shown that "expeditious progress" is being made to list qualified species (and to delist unqualified ones).[86]

The Secretary must keep close tabs on a "warranted but precluded" petition, treating it as having been resubmitted on the date the Secretary makes the "warranted but precluded" finding. It is also deemed to have been supported by substantial scientific and commercial information. Within 12 months, the Secretary must again publish a finding whether the requesting action is warranted.[87]

If the Secretary finds that the requested action is not warranted, or that it is "warranted but precluded," persons who disagree can appeal the Secretary's action to court.[88]

Once the Secretary finds that the requested action is warranted, a notice must be published in the *Federal Register,* accompanied by the text of a proposed regulation.[89] Also, the Secretary must notify local governments and affected foreign nations, give some form of notice to scientific organizations, and publish a summary of the regulation in a local newspaper. If requested, the Secretary must also hold one public hearing.[90]

Within one year after noticing a proposed regulation, the Secretary must adopt or withdraw the regulation, or extend its action date by up to six months.[91] In order to justify a six-month extension, the Secretary must find that there is substantial disagreement about the sufficiency or accuracy of the data.[92] The purpose of the six-month extension is to allow the Secretary to solicit additional data.[93] The regulation can be withdrawn if the Secretary finds that the evidence is insufficient to support it.[94]

If the regulation is withdrawn, the Secretary's action can be appealed to the courts.[95] The Secretary's decision to make a regulation final is also appealable. To appeal a listing, however, the complaining parties must show that they have standing. They must also show that the case is ripe for adjudication.

---

[84] 16 U.S.C. § 1533(b)(3)(A) (1988).
[85] *Id.* §1533(b)(3)(B)(i)–(iii).
[86] *Id.* §1533(b)(3)(B)(iii)(II).
[87] *Id.* §1533(b)(3)(C)(i).
[88] *Id.* §1533(b)(3)(C)(ii).
[89] *Id.* §1533(b)(3)(B)(ii).
[90] *Id.* §1533(b)(5)(E).
[91] *Id.* §1533(b)(6)(A).
[92] *Id.* §1533(b)(6)(B)(i).
[93] *Id.*
[94] *Id.* §1533(b)(6)(B)(ii).
[95] *Id.*

For example, Oklahoma landowners were not allowed to attack the Secretary's listing of the leopard darter, even though they said it could block the building of federal flood control projects. The landowners were unable to prove that, absent the listing, the government would build those projects. As a consequence, the court denied the landowners' appeal.[96]

### Emergency Listings

Normally, when proposing a listing, the Secretary must follow the Administrative Procedure Act's procedures for rulemaking,[97] as elaborated by the Endangered Species Act's special rules for notice, described above. These rules do not apply, however, if the Secretary issues a regulation "in regard to any emergency posing a significant risk to the [species'] well-being. . . ."[98] An emergency regulation becomes effective immediately upon publication. The Secretary has 240 days to complete the normal rulemaking procedures and to make the emergency regulation effective permanently.[99]

Recently the Secretary invoked these emergency procedures on behalf of the desert tortoise. In 1985 the Secretary found that the desert tortoise warranted endangered species protection. Nonetheless, the Secretary had not listed the species because he needed to devote his limited staff to listing other, more severely imperiled, species. In 1989, however, the Secretary changed his mind. He decided that new dangers created an emergency for the species. So he issued an emergency regulation that listed the desert tortoise as endangered. Because the emergency regulation was adopted without the normal notice and hearing, local governments and developers sought to enjoin its enforcement. The court upheld the regulation as a valid exercise of the Secretary's emergency powers.[100]

## Delisting

In 1982 the House committee stated its concern that the endangered species lists "harbor a number of improperly listed species."[101] In the Act's early years, the Secretary listed species without having the discipline of the Administrative Procedure Act's notice-and-comment procedure. The House committee was concerned about listings made "for emotional reasons or based on improper biological data. . . ."[102] So in 1982, Congress decided to speed up the process

---

[96] Glover River Org. v. Department of the Interior, 675 F.2d 251 (10th Cir. 1982).
[97] 5 U.S.C. §553 (1988).
[98] 16 U.S.C. §1533(b)(7) (1988).
[99] *Id.*
[100] City of Las Vegas v. Lujan, 891 F.2d 927 (D.C. Cir. 1989).
[101] 1982 House Report, *supra* note 3, at 22, 1982 U.S. CODE CONG. & ADMIN. NEWS at 2822.
[102] *Id.*

for removing species from the lists. Congress applied the new procedural deadlines to delisting as well as listing.

Four years earlier, in the Endangered Species Act Amendments of 1978,[103] Congress required the Secretary to make periodic reviews to determine whether to institute proceedings for delisting any species. A species will be delisted only if it is (1) extinct, (2) has recovered so it needs no protection, or (3) was listed on the basis of erroneous data.[104]

## Designation of Critical Habitat

Conservation of critical habitat has always been one of the Act's primary purposes. As the Supreme Court noted, Congress has been informed that the greatest threat to endangered species is the destruction of the species' natural habitat.[105] In the Act's Statement of Purposes,[106] Congress emphasized the need to conserve the ecosystems upon which endangered species and threatened species depend for survival.

Despite this, the statute has taken a zigzag course toward habitat protection. The 1973 Act did not require the Secretary to designate critical habitat; the legislation did not even define the term. By regulation, however, affected agencies defined "critical habitat" to include any "areas . . . the loss of which would appreciably decrease the likelihood of the survival and recovery of a listed species or a distinct segment of its population. . . ."[107] Critical habitat could include any portion of a listed species' present habitat, as well as additional areas for reasonable population expansion.[108]

The Endangered Species Act Amendments of 1978 made radical changes in the treatment of critical habitat. First, the 1978 statute "substantially limited"[109] the definition of critical habitat.[110] Under the new law, critical habitat was defined as the specific geographic areas which the species occupied at the time of listing. Even those areas could be protected only if they contain physical or biological features essential to the species' conservation, and if they may require special management consideration or protection. Critical habitat could not include areas outside those that the species occupied, unless the Secretary determined that they are essential to the species' conservation. The statute set out a bias against designating the entire geographical area that the species can occupy.[111]

---

[103] Pub. L. No. 95-632, §11(3), 92 Stat. 3751, 3764 (1978) (codified in 16 U.S.C. §1533(c)(2) (1988)).

[104] 50 C.F.R. §424.11(d) (1990).

[105] Tennessee Valley Auth. v. Hill, 437 U.S. 153, 179 (1978).

[106] 16 U.S.C. §1531(b) (1988).

[107] *See* H.R. REP. NO. 1625, 95th Cong., 2d Sess. 7–8 (1978), *reprinted in* 1978 U.S. CODE CONG. & ADMIN. NEWS 9453, 9457–58.

[108] *See* R. Rosenberg, *Federal Protection of Unique Environmental Interests: Endangered and Threatened Species,* 58 N.C.L. REV. 491, 507 n.66 (1980).

[109] *Id.* at 534.

[110] Pub. L. No. 95-632, §2(2), 92 Stat. 3751 (1978) (codified in 16 U.S.C. §1532(5) (1988)).

[111] 16 U.S.C. §1532(5)(C) (1988).

Secondly, the 1978 Amendments directed that, when the Secretary listed a new species, its critical habitat had to be specified "to the maximum extent prudent."[112] More importantly, in determining critical habitat, the Secretary had to consider economic impact, and was authorized to exclude an area from critical habitat for economic reasons.[113] "By virtue of these two related requirements, the listing process itself [became] heavily influenced by economic considerations and [was] no longer guided by strictly biological considerations."[114]

Not long after the 1978 Amendments became law, the Reagan Administration took office. As later testified in a Congressional subcommittee, the new Administration used economic reviews to hamstring the listing process, thus "effectively strangling the listing of new species."[115]

Congress responded by enacting the Endangered Species Act Amendments of 1982.[116] Declaring that "economic considerations have no relevance to determinations regarding the status of species . . . ,"[117] Congress put habitat designations and the listing process on separate tracks. The new system was designed "to prevent non-biological considerations from affecting" listing decisions.[118] The Secretary was instructed to base a listing decision solely on the best scientific and commercial data available.[119]

As a result of the 1982 legislation, the Secretary need not designate critical habitat at the same time a new species is listed. Thus, the Secretary still designates critical habitat concurrently with new listings, but only "to the maximum extent prudent and determinable."[120] The Secretary is expressly authorized to delay the critical habitat designation in two cases: when prompt listing of the species is essential to the species' conservation, and when the species' critical habitat is not then determinable.[121] The Secretary also will not specify a species' critical habitat when the designation will not benefit the species. An example is when identification of the habitat would disclose the species' location to unscrupulous collectors.[122]

Having uncoupled critical habitat from the listing of species, Congress left the Act's standards for the designation of critical habitat unchanged.[123] The Secretary was still directed to consider economic impact.[124] Any portion of an

---

[112] Pub. L. No. 95-632, §11(1), 92 Stat. 3751, 3764.

[113] *Id.* §11(7), 92 Stat. at 3766.

[114] *Endangered Species Act Reauthorization and Oversight: Hearings Before the Subcomm. on Fisheries and Wildlife Conservation and the Environment of the House Comm. on Merchant Marine and Fisheries,* 97th Cong., 2d Sess. 157 (1982) (statement of Michael Bean).

[115] *Id.* at 160.

[116] Pub. L. No. 97-304, §2, 96 Stat. 1411–16.

[117] 1982 Conference Report, *supra* note 73, at 20, 1982 U.S. CODE CONG. & ADMIN. NEWS at 2861.

[118] *Id.* at 19.

[119] *Id.* at 20.

[120] 16 U.S.C. §1533(a)(3) (1988).

[121] *Id.* §1533(b)(6)(C).

[122] 50 C.F.R. 424.12(a)(1) (1990).

[123] 1982 Conference Report, *supra* note 73, at 20, 1982 U.S. CODE CONG. & ADMIN. NEWS at 2861.

[124] 16 U.S.C. §1333(b)(2) (1988).

area will be excluded from critical habitat if the benefits of exclusion outweigh the benefits of inclusion. An area will not be excluded if that would result in a species' extinction.[125]

The Act did establish new deadlines for processing habitat designations.[126] Sometimes the Secretary cannot designate critical habitat at all. In a case decided under the 1978 statute, a court recognized that the Act "does not mandate a determination based on inadequate information. . . ."[127] That case concerned the Secretary's refusal to designate critical habitat for a plant that was listed as an endangered species. Since the plant had been found in a non-native habitat, the Secretary reasoned that the biological and physical features needed for the species' conservation could not be known. Upholding the Secretary, the court noted that the 1982 legislative changes "take account of the possibility that sufficient information may not be available to make a critical habitat designation."[128]

In practice, designations of critical habitat have not been numerous. Before the 1978 Amendments, the government designated critical habitats for only about 30 of the more than 185 species listed at the time by the U.S. as endangered or threatened. Of the more than 403 species added to the list since 1979, the government has designated critical habitats for only about 73.[129] In high profile cases, aggressive environmental groups complain that the Fish and Wildlife Service has been unreasonably slow in designating a protected habitat.[130]

## Recovery Plans

With the Endangered Species Act Amendments of 1978, Congress turned its attention to the need for developing and implementing recovery plans for listed species.[131] Congress elaborated this provision in the 1982 Amendments.[132] Then it told the Secretary to give priority to endangered and threatened species that would be most likely to benefit from recovery plans, especially those that are—or may be—in conflict with economic development. Congress was emphatic, however, that recovery plans should also be available for species that are endangered by causes other than human activity.[133]

---

[125] 50 C.F.R. §424.19 (1990).

[126] 16 U.S.C. §§1533(b)(3)(D), (b)(6)(A)(i)–(ii), (b)(6)(C) (1988).

[127] Enos v. Marsh, 769 F.2d 1363, 1371 (9th Cir. 1985).

[128] *Id.* at n.9.

[129] M. Bean, S. Fitzgerald, and M. O'Connell, *Reconciling Conflicts Under the Endangered Species Act* 3 (World Wildlife Fund: Washington, 1991).

[130] An example is the spotted owl case. *See* Revised Proposed Determination of Critical Habitat for the Northern Spotted Owl, 56 Fed. Reg. 40,002 (1991) as revised 56 Fed. Reg. 50,701 (1991). *See also* Northern Spotted Owl v. Hodel, 716 F. Supp. 479 (W.D. Wash. 1988); Northern Spotted Owl v. Lujan, 758 F. Supp. 621 (E.D. Wash. 1991).

[131] Pub. L. No. 95-632, §11(5), 92 Stat. 3751, 3765.

[132] Pub. L. No. 97-304, §2(a)(4)(D), 96 Stat. 1411, 1415.

[133] 1982 Conference Report, *supra* note 73, at 25, 1982 U.S. CODE CONG. & ADMIN. NEWS at 2866.

This statutory provision attained its present form[134] in the 1988 Amendments.[135] Congress had expressed displeasure at the Administration's allocation of funds primarily to help recovery of 12 species of birds, mammals, and sea turtles. Little or no money was being spent for the recovery of listed insects, mollusks, crustaceans, and plants. To correct this, Congress prohibited the Secretary, in developing recovery plans, from giving priority to species of the higher taxonomic classifications.[136]

Many recovery plans continue to benefit photogenic species like the Northern Rocky Mountain Wolf and the bald eagle.[137] The number of recovery plans, however, has increased. By 1991, 321 recovery plans had been formulated. Money remains a problem. According to a recent report from the Department of the Interior, $4.6 billion is needed in order to begin recovery efforts for all currently listed species. The current annual budget for recovery programs is $8 million.[138]

The Secretary's obligation to develop and implement recovery plans is not absolute. This task can be avoided if the Secretary finds that a recovery plan "will not promote the conservation of the species."[139] Illustrating this is a 1987 case in which the Secretary refused to close down a Wyoming campground that was the scene of incidents between tourists and grizzly bears. The environmentalists charged that the Secretary was shirking the obligation to implement a recovery plan. Noting that the Secretary is not obligated to initiate a plan that will not promote the species' conservation, the court held that the Secretary could delay implementing a plan pending additional study.[140]

The statute's call for recovery plans leans heavily on the concept of "conservation." As a basic policy objective, the Act directs the government to "conserve" protected species,[141] defining that term expansively.[142] Under that command, the Secretary "must do far more than merely avoid the elimination of protected species."[143] In addition, the Secretary "must bring these species back from the brink so that they may be removed from the protected class, and must use all methods necessary to do so."[144]

Even when a species recovers, the Secretary's duties are still not finished. For at least five additional years, the Secretary has to continue monitoring the species, in conjunction with the states. The Secretary is to use emergency powers to prevent a significant risk to the recovered species.[145]

---

[134] 16 U.S.C. §1533(f) (1988).

[135] Pub. L. No. 100-478, §1003, 102 Stat. 2306.

[136] 1988 Senate Report, *supra* note 20, at 8–9, 1988 U.S. CODE CONG. & ADMIN. NEWS at 2708.

[137] U.S. Fish and Wildlife Service, Northern Rocky Mountain Wolf Recovery Plan (1985); National Audubon Society, Audubon Wildlife Report 356 note (1986).

[138] WILDERNESS MAGAZINE, Summer 1991, at 8.

[139] 16 U.S.C. §1533(f)(1) (1988).

[140] National Wildlife Fed'n v. National Park Serv., 669 F. Supp. 384 (D. Wyo. 1987).

[141] 16 U.S.C. §1531(c)(1) (1988).

[142] *Id.* §1532(3)

[143] Defenders of Wildlife v. Andrus, 428 F. Supp. 167, 170 (D.D.C. 1977).

[144] *Id.*

[145] 16 U.S.C. §1533(g) (1988).

* * *

Joe DiMaggio, a baseball hero of the past, achieved a new sort of acclaim when his name was used in the hit song, "Mrs. Robinson," from the 1972 movie "The Graduate."[146] So too, as a federal judge observed, many an obscure species' "chief claim to fame is the fact that it succeeded in having its name inscribed on the endangered species list."[147] But this achievement "is a distinction without cause for celebration."[148] The government's listing of a species under section 4 is too often the species' obituary notice. Avoiding that end is the task of sections 9 and 7, which we will discuss in the next two chapters.

---

[146] P. Simon, *Simon and Garfunkel's Greatest Hits* (Columbia Records compact disk CK 31350).

[147] Sierra Club v. Lyng, 694 F. Supp. 1260, 1265 (E.D. Tex. 1988), *rev'd on other grounds sub nom*. Sierra Club v. Yeutter, 926 F.2d 429 (5th Cir. 1991).

[148] *Id*. at n.3.

# Chapter 4

# Acts Prohibited Under Section 9

Father Robert Walker, a Catholic Bishop, intended no mischief when he traveled to South America on church business. At missions in Columbia, the priest was given temporary use of artifacts, arrows, and skins for a New York exhibit on missionary work. He thought the skins came from a tiger or panther. In fact, the skins belonged to a jaguar, an endangered species. Imagine Father Walker's surprise when he was charged with violating Endangered Species Act Section 9[1] and, after a hearing, held liable to pay civil penalties.[2]

## Prohibitions of Section 9

Section 9 makes it unlawful "for any person subject to the jurisdiction of the United States"[3] to engage in a broad array of conduct "deemed threatening to . . . species."[4] Indeed, as the Supreme Court observed, "Virtually all dealings with endangered species, including taking, possession, transportation, and sale, were prohibited. . . ."[5]

The most important prohibitions are phrased in terms of "endangered" species only.[6] But the Secretary of the Interior has the power to apply the section 9 prohibitions to "threatened" species and, in general, has done so.[7]

## Unlawful Taking of Protected Species

Neither the Endangered Species Preservation Act of 1966 nor the Endangered Species Conservation Act of 1969 prohibited the taking of endangered

---

[1] 16 U.S.C. §1538 (1988).

[2] U.S. Fish and Wildlife Serv. v. Walker, DOI Dkt. No. Atlanta 78-3 (ALJ ID dated Sept. 6, 1978).

[3] 16 U.S.C. §1538(a)(1) (1988).

[4] Humane Society of the United States v. Hodel, 840 F.2d 45, 48 (D.C. Cir. 1988).

[5] Tennessee Valley Auth. v. Hill, 437 U.S. 153, 180 (1978).

[6] 16 U.S.C. §1538(a) (1988).

[7] *Id.* §1533(d). The Fish and Wildlife Service codified the statutory prohibitions regarding "endangered" wildlife and plants at 50 C.F.R. §§17.21, 17.61, and extended most of them to "threatened" wildlife and plants at 50 C.F.R. §§17.31(a), 17.71(a) (1990). In the case of states that have entered into cooperative agreements under 16 U.S.C. §1535(c), the Secretary's regulations protecting "threatened" wildlife apply to resident species of fish and wildlife only to the extent that the states adopt those regulations. 16 U.S.C. §1533(d) (1988).

species. This shortcoming was corrected in the 1973 Act, which proscribed the taking of an endangered species.[8]

The term "take" is "defined in . . . the broadest possible manner."[9] In the Act it means "to harass, harm, pursue, hunt, shoot, wound, kill, trap, capture, or collect, or to attempt to engage in any such conduct."[10] In its regulations, the Fish and Wildlife Service elaborates on the statutory definitions. The term "harass" is said to mean:

> [A]n intentional or negligent act or omission which creates the likelihood of injury to wildlife by annoying it to such an extent as to significantly disrupt normal behavior patterns which include, but are not limited to, breeding, feeding or sheltering.[11]

Similarly, "harm" is said to mean an act which actually kills or injures wildlife, including certain "significant" modifications or degradations of habitat.[12]

## Prohibitions Against Hunters

When it enacted the 1973 Act, Congress considered hunting regulations to be among the most important weapons in the fight to save vanishing species.[13] Hunting had been identified as one of the two major causes of species extinction.[14] The House managers had no tolerance for "those who would capture or kill [endangered animals] for pleasure or profit," and resolved to "make it less profitable for them to do so."[15]

Individuals who hunt endangered species within the United States do so at their peril. In one case, the Fish and Wildlife Service conducted an undercover operation to investigate the killing and sale of protected eagles. Posing as traders and collectors, the government agents purchased eagle carcasses and feathers from Dwight Dion and other tribal Indians. The Indians were charged with taking and selling protected species, and the Supreme Court upheld their conviction.[16] Other hunters have been prosecuted criminally for shooting a Florida panther[17] and a grizzly bear.[18] A person who shoots a protected animal can be made to pay civil penalties.[19]

---

[8] Codified in 16 U.S.C. §1538(a)(1)(B)–(C) (1988).

[9] Palila v. Hawaii Dep't of Land and Natural Resources, 852 F.2d 1106, 1108 (9th Cir. 1988) (quoting S. REP. NO. 307, 93d Cong., 1st Sess. 7 (1973), *reprinted in* 1973 U.S. CODE CONG. & ADMIN. NEWS 2989, 2995 [hereinafter 1973 Senate Report]).

[10] 16 U.S.C. §1532(19) (1988).

[11] 50 C.F.R. §17.3 (1990).

[12] *Id.*

[13] Defenders of Wildlife v. Andrus, 428 F. Supp. 167, 170 (D.D.C. 1977).

[14] Tennessee Valley Auth. v. Hill, *supra* note 5, at 179 (quoting the 1973 Senate Report, *supra* note 9, at 2, 1973 U.S. CODE CONG. & ADMIN. NEWS at 2990.

[15] 119 CONG REC. 30,162 (1973)(remarks of Rep. Sullivan).

[16] United States v. Dion, 762 F.2d 674 (8th Cir. 1985), *rev'd in part on other grounds,* 476 U.S. 734 (1986).

[17] United States v. Billie, 667 F. Supp. 1485 (S.D. Fla. 1987).

[18] United States v. St. Onge, 676 F. Supp. 1041 (D. Mont. 1987).

[19] Christy v. Hodel, 857 F.2d 1324 (9th Cir. 1988), *cert. denied sub nom.* Christy v. Lujan, 490 U.S. 1114 (1989).

The Endangered Species Act does not prohibit hunting worldwide. Most of the Act's provisions apply worldwide;[20] however, the prohibitions of Section 9 apply only to takings that occur within the United States, its territorial waters, or on the high seas.[21] Although Congress has the authority to regulate the conduct of United States citizens in other nations, the courts will not give statutes extraterritorial effect when the legislation does not require it.[22] As a result, hunters who "take" endangered species abroad will not be prosecuted under the Endangered Species Act for killing the wildlife, although they risk penalties and forfeiture if they bring their trophies back into this country.[23]

## Prohibitions Against Takings by the Government

Governmental agencies are among the persons instructed not to "take" endangered species.[24] This is extremely important, since governmental projects can degrade critical habitat. As Congress knew, the principal threat to species stems not from hunting, but from destruction of wildlife habitat.[25]

### *The Palila Cases*

Courts have not been reluctant to prohibit governmental intrusions upon critical habitat. The first of these rulings precipitated a head-on clash between a federal judge in Hawaii and the U.S. Fish and Wildlife Service. The dispute began when the State of Hawaii populated the exotic slopes of Mauna Kea with sheep and goats. These animals' grazing began to defoliate the area, which was home to the Palila, a six-inch-long finch-billed bird that exists nowhere else.

Finding that the defoliation endangered the Palila, the district court ruled that the state's maintenance of the sheep and goats constituted a "taking." The court rested its first order (*Palila I*)[26] upon the Fish and Wildlife Service's

---

[20] *But see* Lujan v. Defenders of Wildlife, 60 U.S.L.W. 4495, 4503–05 (U.S. June 9, 1992) (concurring opinion) (consultation provisions of Endangered Species Act do not extend to agency actions abroad).

[21] *Supra* note 6.

[22] *Compare* United States v. Mitchell, 553 F.2d 996 (5th Cir. 1977) (Marine Mammal Protection Act). On the extraterritorial effect of the 1973 Act generally, see H.R. CONF. REP. NO. 740, 93rd Cong., 1st Sess. 27 (1973), *reprinted in* 1973 U.S. CODE CONG. & ADMIN. NEWS 3001, 3005 [hereinafter 1973 Conference Report].

[23] *Compare* Carpenter v. Andrus, 485 F. Supp. 320 (D. Del. 1980) (no violation for accidental importation of leopard killed in Kenya) *with* U.S. Fish and Wildlife Serv. v. St. Clair, DOI Dkt. Nos. Albuquerque 78-1, 78-3 (ALJ ID dated April 18, 1978) *and* U.S. Fish and Wildlife Serv. v. Woods, DOI Dkt. No. Boston 77-11 (ALJ ID dated Sept. 14, 1978) (import violation only for red lechwe killed in Africa).

[24] Tennessee Valley Auth. v. Hill, *supra* note 5 at 184–85.

[25] *Id.* at 179. *See* 119 CONG. REC. 30,162 (1973) (remarks of Rep. Sullivan). *See also* World Comm'n on Environment and Development, *Our Common Future* 164 (New York: Oxford University Press, 1987).

[26] Palila v. Hawaii Dep't of Land and Natural Resources, 471 F. Supp. 985 (D. Hawaii 1979), *aff'd,* 639 F.2d 495 (9th Cir. 1981).

administrative elaboration of the statute, which defines "taking" so that it means to "harm" wildlife. "Harm" in turn was defined as an act or omission which "actually injures or kills wildlife"—including "significant environmental modification or degradation" which disrupts essential behavioral patterns.[27] In *Palila I,* the court had no doubt that the state's degradation of the Palila's habitat violated the Act.

After *Palila I,* the U.S. Secretary of the Interior proposed to amend the definition of "harm."[28] In the legal memorandum accompanying the proposed redefinition, the Fish and Wildlife Service acknowledged that the change was intended to prevent the result reached in *Palila I.*[29] But, after receiving 328 comments on the proposed redefinition, 262 of which were opposed, the Secretary abandoned the proposal, instead defining "harm" as:

> any action, including habitat modification, which actually kills or injures wildlife, rather than the present interpretation which might be read to include habitat modification or degradation alone without further proof of death or injury. Habitat modification as injury would only be covered by the new definition if it significantly impaired essential behavior patterns of a listed species.[30]

Just as importantly, the Secretary conceded that it is unnecessary to prove:

> direct physical injury to an individual member of the wildlife species. . . . The purpose of the redefinition was to preclude claims of a Section 9 taking for habitat modification alone without any attendant death or injury of the protected wildlife. Death or injury, however, may be caused by impairment of essential behavior patterns that can have significant and permanent effects on a listed species.[31]

Armed with this vindication, the district judge decided in *Palila II*[32] to continue the litigation for a trial of the facts.

The Palila was not safe yet. In *Palila III*[33] the state argued that the sheep no longer endangered the Palila because the bird's population had finally stopped declining. The district judge's patience was at an end. Ruling that injury can take place without "a decline in population numbers," the judge found that habitat modification is unacceptable if it "prevents the population from recovering. . . ."[34] The court of appeals affirmed the district court's finding that a "taking" had occurred. But the appeals court chose not to reach the issue of whether harm includes habitat degradation that prevents an endangered species' recovery.[35]

---

[27] *Quoted in* 46 Fed. Reg. 29,490 (1981).
[28] *Id.*
[29] *Id.* at 29,492.
[30] 46 Fed. Reg. 54,748 (1981). The Fish and Wildlife Service's current definition of "harm" is codified in 50 C.F.R. §17.3 (1990).
[31] 46 Fed. Reg. 54,748 (1981).
[32] Palila v. Hawaii Dep't of Land and Natural Resources, 631 F. Supp. 787 (D. Hawaii 1985).
[33] Palila v. Hawaii Dep't of Land and Natural Resources, 649 F. Supp. 1070 (D. Hawaii 1986), *aff'd,* 852 F.2d 1106 (9th Cir. 1988).
[34] *Id.,* 649 F. Supp. at 1077.
[35] Palila v. Hawaii Dep't of Land and Natural Resources, *supra* note 33, 852 F.2d at 1110.

*The Woodpecker Cases*

In two cases[36] after *Palila I,* the Sierra Club sought to enjoin the Park Service's policies for the cutting of old growth pine trees, located in national forests, that furnished the nests for the red-cockaded woodpecker.

The Sierra Club was successful in only one of the two cases. In the case concerning the Texas national forests, the Forest Service had endorsed clear-cutting in close proximity to woodpecker colonies, including the harvesting of older pine trees.[37] These practices caused and accelerated the species' decline.[38] Believing that the woodpeckers were on the verge of extinction,[39] the court ruled that "the Forest Service's actions constitute a taking under" the Act.[40] The court fashioned a remedy that was extraordinary, not contenting itself with enjoining the harmful practices. It also prescribed a substitute set of detailed management practices to be followed near the woodpecker colonies.[41]

The Sierra Club's second case concerned national forests in Mississippi, Arkansas, and Louisiana. There the Forest Service had a limited tree cutting program designed to control the southern pine beetle that was killing thousands of acres of pine trees in the southeastern United States. In addition to cutting down the infested trees, the Forest Service created buffer zones by cutting uninfested trees around the diseased ones. The Sierra Club was unable to demonstrate that the government's cutting of pine trees would harm the birds' habitat. Unlike the Texas case, the Forest Service had consulted with the Fish and Wildlife Service before fashioning its guidelines for cutting near woodpecker colonies. As a result, the Fish and Wildlife Service opined that the cutting program was not likely to jeopardize the woodpeckers. The court thought it was unlikely that a "taking" would occur.[42]

*Government Acquiescence*

Even passive government conduct can constitute a "taking."

One example is a case in which environmentalists battled against the Environmental Protection Agency (EPA), farmers, and ranchers.[43] For many years, the EPA had approved the registration of strychnine as an active ingredient in pesticides. Farmers and ranchers placed this poison in grain which was used as bait to kill prairie dogs that harmed their crops or land. The poison also killed black-footed ferrets, a protected species that lives near prairie dogs.

---

[36] Sierra Club v. Lyng, 694 F. Supp. 1260 (E.D. Tex. 1988), *rev'd on other grounds sub nom.* Sierra Club v. Yeutter, 926 F.2d 429 (5th Cir. 1991); Sierra Club v. Block, 614 F. Supp. 488 (D.D.C. 1985).

[37] Sierra Club v. Lyng, *supra* note 36, 694 F. Supp. at 1272.

[38] *Id.* at 1271.

[39] *Id.* at 1277.

[40] *Id.* at 1269.

[41] *Id.* at 1278. The Court of Appeals found this feature of the trial court's decision to be objectionable and, on this ground alone, vacated the judgment.

[42] Sierra Club v. Block, *supra* note 36.

[43] Defenders of Wildlife v. Administrator, Environmental Protection Agency, 882 F.2d 1294 (8th Cir. 1989).

When the Agency declined to cancel its registration of strychnine, the environmentalists filed suit. The court recognized that the issue was "whether the continued registration of a pesticide, as distinguished from the distribution or use of that pesticide, can constitute an illegal taking under the" Act.[44] The court answered that question affirmatively, saying that the Agency's "registrations constituted takings of endangered species."[45]

A similar case arose when the Fish and Wildlife Service allowed the use of lead shot ammunition. Bald eagles died from lead poisoning when they ate other birds that hunters had shot with lead pellets. The court held that the Service's authorization constituted a taking under the Act.[46]

### *The Puerto Rico Case*

The Navy was targeted in a controversy that reached the Supreme Court. The Navy used Vieques Island, a small island off the Puerto Rican coast, for bombing, artillery, and naval gunfire training. The governor of Puerto Rico and residents of the island sued to enjoin the Navy's operations. Among other things, Puerto Rico contended that the Navy's training activities constituted a taking under Endangered Species Act Section 9. Although the district court had rejected that contention, the court of appeals took a different view. It scolded the Navy for failing to obtain a timely biological opinion about the Vieques operation's impact on five protected species. The court of appeals remanded the section 9 claim to be considered in the light of a late-acquired biological opinion from the Fish and Wildlife Service.[47]

In the interim, the Navy's operations were enjoined because the Navy had failed to obtain a permit under the Federal Water Pollution Prevention and Control Act.[48] On review, the Supreme Court did not consider the Endangered Species Act issues.[49] It recognized, however, that the Act "contains a flat ban on the destruction of critical habitats."[50]

### *Unsuccessful Objections*

Sometimes, when environmentalists challenge government action under section 9, they fail because their lawsuits are premature. An example is the Park Service's refusal to close a Yellowstone National Park campground that intruded on the grizzly bear's habitat. The Park Service action was upheld because it was awaiting the results of an environmental impact study. The Fish and Wildlife Service had approved the interim operation of the campground. The court said that it "is hard pressed to understand how . . . the continued

---

[44] *Id.* at 1300.

[45] *Id.* at 1301.

[46] National Wildlife Fed'n v. Hodel, 23 ER Cases 1089, 1092–93 (E.D. Cal. 1985).

[47] Romero-Barcelo v. Brown, 643 F.2d at 835 (1st Cir. 1981), *rev'd on other grounds sub nom.* Weinberger v. Romero-Barcelo, 456 U.S. 305 (1982).

[48] 33 U.S.C. §1251 *et seq.* (1988).

[49] Weinberger v. Romero-Barcelo, *supra* note 47, at n.2.

[50] *Id.* at 314.

operation of [the campground] until the results of the EIS are received would constitute a taking."[51]

Other challenges fail because the government intrusion is not serious enough. Although a Florida State-sponsored deer hunt using airboats and all-terrain vehicles would be stressful to fish and small game, its temporary impact did not amount to a "taking."[52] Similarly, the government did not commit a "taking" when it granted a right-of-way permit for the laying of a pipeline across Puget Sound, since construction was contingent upon compliance with the Endangered Species Act.[53]

In another case, the Navy escaped a charge that it had engaged in a taking by leasing water rights to farmers. The lease program was alleged to imperil an endangered species of fish, the cui-ui (pronounced "kwee-wee"), by contributing to a significant decrease in the water level of Pyramid Lake, the fish's exclusive habitat. The Navy's saving grace was that it had consulted with the Fish and Wildlife Service before entering into the leases and had received the Service's opinion that the leases would not jeopardize the cui-ui. Since the evidence did not establish any harm to the cui-ui, the court ruled that "there is no 'taking' under section 9(a) (1)."[54]

Municipalities are among those governmental entities that can violate the Act by "taking" a protected species. A court dismissed a criminal suit against a California city charged with the unlawful taking of an endangered species of butterfly.[55] The Ninth Circuit ruled that the 1973 Act did not include a municipality within the definition of the term "person." Congress promptly amended the Act to override the court decision by specifying that municipalities are within the definition of "person."[56]

## Unlawful Harming of Plants

The Act's prohibitions against "taking" protect only "fish or wildlife,"[57] thus excluding "plants."[58] Indeed, before 1982, the Act did not prohibit the destruction of plants.[59] In the 1982 Amendments, Congress revised section 9(a) (2) (B)[60] by making it unlawful to remove and reduce to possession any endangered plant from federal land. The Act defines "plant" to mean "any member

---

[51] National Wildlife Fed'n v. National Park Serv., 669 F. Supp. 384, 389 (D. Wyo. 1987).

[52] Fund for Animals, Inc. v. Florida Game and Fresh Water Fish Comm'n, 550 F. Supp. 1206 (S.D. Fla. 1982).

[53] No Oilport! v. Carter, 520 F. Supp. 334, 365 (W.D. Wash. 1981).

[54] Pyramid Lake Paiute Tribe of Indians v. United States Dep't of the Navy, 898 F.2d 1410, 1420 (9th Cir. 1990).

[55] United States v. City of Rancho Palos Verdes, 841 F.2d 329 (9th Cir. 1988).

[56] Endangered Species Act Amendments of 1988, Pub. L. No. 100-478, §1001(a), 102 Stat. 2306 (codified in 16 U.S.C. §1532(13) (1988)). *See* 134 CONG. REC. S9759 (daily ed. July 25, 1988) (remarks of Sen. Mitchell).

[57] 16 U.S.C. §1538(a) (1988).

[58] *Compare id.* §1532(8) *and* §1532(14).

[59] S. REP. NO. 418, 97th Cong., 2d Sess. 26 (1982) [hereinafter 1982 Senate Report].

[60] Pub. L. No. 97-304, §9(b), 96 Stat. 1411, 1426 (1982).

of the plant kingdom, including seeds, roots and other parts thereof."[61] As a result of that definition, Congress prohibited the removal of parts and cuttings, as well as whole plants.[62] Congress did not, however, prohibit removals from areas other than federal lands.

The 1982 Amendments proved inadequate in two respects. First, they did not outlaw destruction of endangered plants, even on federal land, unless the plant was removed from federal jurisdiction. As a consequence, in 1986 and 1987, the Fish and Wildlife Service decided against identifying the critical habitat for 24 newly listed plant species. The Service feared that, if it identified the plants' location, it would make them vulnerable to illegal collection and vandalism.[63] So, in the 1988 Amendments, Congress expanded section 9 (a) (2) (B) by making it unlawful to "maliciously damage or destroy" an endangered plant on federal lands.[64]

The 1982 Amendment's other shortcoming was a failure to protect plants located on private and other non-federal land. As Congress recognized, private owners were not able to deter the theft or destruction of plants within their property. Congress thought that state trespass laws carried penalties that were too low to be effective. To create a "much stronger deterrent,"[65] Congress also expanded section 9(a) (2) (b) to cover actions on private land. The revised provision makes it unlawful to "remove, cut, dig up or damage or destroy" an endangered species in non-federal areas "in knowing violation of" any state law or regulation "or in the course of any violation of a State criminal trespass law."[66]

The Act does not ban all development activities that uproot and displace plants. In enacting the 1988 Amendments, the House committee noted that, for plants located on federal land, it was prohibiting "malicious" damage and destruction in order to protect against "willful acts of vandalism."[67] "It is not the Committee's intent that this prohibition interfere with otherwise lawfully permitted land use operations such as mining, logging, or grazing on federal lands which might incidently result in the taking of listed plants."[68] The Secretary has stated that he does not construe the statute as applying to development activities on federal land that physically displace endangered plants.[69] Additionally, the Senate committee stated that the 1988 Amendment "does not interfere with the rights traditionally accorded [private] landowners."[70]

---

[61] 16 U.S.C. §1532(14) (1988).

[62] 1982 Senate Report, *supra* note 59, at 26.

[63] S. REP. NO. 240, 100th Cong., 1st Sess. 12 (1987), *reprinted in* 1988 U.S. CODE CONG. & ADMIN. NEWS 2700, 2712 [hereinafter 1988 Senate Report].

[64] Pub. L. No. 100-478, §1006, 102 Stat. 2306, 2308 (codified in 16 U.S.C. §1538(a)(2)(B) (1988)).

[65] 1988 Senate Report, *supra* note 63, at 13, U.S. CODE CONG. & ADMIN. NEWS at 2712.

[66] 16 U.S.C. §1538(a)(2)(B) (1988).

[67] H.R. REP. NO. 467, 100th Cong., 1st Sess. 15 (1987) [hereinafter 1988 House Report].

[68] *Id.*

[69] 50 Fed. Reg. 39,681 at 39,686 (1985).

[70] 1988 Senate Report, *supra* note 63, at 12, 1988 U.S. CODE CONG. & ADMIN. NEWS at 2712.

## Protection of Trees

So far only a few tree species have been placed on the endangered species list. Even unlisted trees may be protected, however, where they make up forests that are the critical habitat for endangered wildlife or plants. Take the Pacific Northwest's old-growth forests as an example. Efforts to protect imperiled species have set off "a bitter dispute among environmentalists, loggers and the timber industry about management of the Pacific Northwest's oldest forests."[71] A court has set a timetable for the government to designate a protected habitat in those forests for the spotted owl.[72] In June 1991, the Fish and Wildlife Service proposed that another bird, the marbled murrelet, join the spotted owl on the list of endangered species in the forests.[73]

Another inhabitant of the Pacific Northwest's old-growth forests is the yew tree. According to the director of the National Cancer Institute, the bark of this tree yields a drug (taxol) that is "the most important new drug we have had in cancer for 15 years."[74] The U.S. Forest Service and the Bureau of Land Management own virtually all of the old-growth forests, but they offer little if any protection to the yew tree. Treating the tree as a weed, loggers typically rip out the yews and other noncommercial trees and burn them. In March 1991, at the request of environmental groups, the Forest Service instituted a moratorium on the burning of yews.[75] The lesson of the yew tree is that even plants that are considered to be weeds can be valuable.

## Other Trafficking in Protected Species

It is hard to envision anyone "taking" any member of the animal kingdom unless it is alive and in one piece. There are prohibitions, however, applying not only to live specimens, but also "to parts and products of 'fish or wildlife' (whether dead or alive) that are designated as 'endangered species.'"[76] Thus, the Act was invoked to prevent a drug manufacturer from selling a prescription drug containing *spermaceti,* a substance derived from the sperm whale.[77] Those who sell Indian crafts made from eagle feathers and parts have been convicted of violating the Act.[78]

---

[71] *Logging Called Threat to Murrelet,* WASHINGTON POST, June 18, 1991, at A3.

[72] Northern Spotted Owl v. Lujan, 758 F. Supp. 621 (E.D. Wash. 1991). *See* 56 Fed. Reg. 40,002 (1991) as revised 56 Fed. Reg. 50,701 (1991).

[73] *Bird Species in Northwest "Threatened,"* N.Y. TIMES, June 18, 1991, at C11.

[74] *Tree Yields a Cancer Treatment, But Ecological Cost May Be High,* N.Y. TIMES, May 13, 1991, at A1, A11.

[75] *Id.*

[76] Delbay Pharmaceuticals v. Department of Commerce, 409 F. Supp. 637, 640 (D.D.C. 1976) (interpreting the provision that is now 16 U.S.C. §1532(8) (1988)). The regulations define "animal" to include "any part, product, egg, or offspring thereof, or the dead body or parts thereof (excluding fossils), whether or not included in a manufactured or in a processed food product." 50 C.F.R. §10.12 (1990).

[77] Delbay Pharmaceuticals v. Department of Commerce, *supra* note 76.

[78] United States v. Dion, 762 F.2d 674 (8th Cir. 1985), *rev'd in part on other grounds,* 476

The ban on trafficking in parts of species is important because many species are prized more for their parts than for themselves. The world's consumption of ivory brought the African elephant near extinction in parts of Africa, prompting new U.S. domestic legislation[79] and increased restrictions on international trade.[80] Another endangered species that is sought for its parts is the hawksbill turtle. The Act is effective in banning imports of that species, whether the article is a whole turtle,[81] a turtle's shell,[82] or a portion of the shell contained in rings,[83] a lorgnette,[84] an inlaid clock,[85] hairpieces and earrings,[86] or other jewelry.[87]

## Prohibitions on Imports and Exports

In the Endangered Species Conservation Act of 1969, Congress for the first time prohibited the import of endangered species of fish and wildlife.[88] In the 1973 Act, Congress expanded the protected category to include plants.[89] And that Act prohibited exports as well as imports.[90]

### *What Is an Import?*

Taking its cue from the broadly worded statute,[91] the Fish and Wildlife Service classifies any shipment in transit through the United States as an import or export, whether or not it has entered the country for customs purposes.[92] Any contact with the United States puts a shipment at risk. One example was a consignment of crocodile hides which was being airlifted directly from Bolivia

---

U.S. 734 (1986).

[79] African Elephant Conservation Act, Pub. L. No. 100-478, §§2001 *et seq.*, 102 Stat. 2306, 2315–23 (1988).

[80] In 1987, an international organization of more than 100 nations—the Convention on International Trade in Endangered Species of Wild Fauna and Flora—imposed a ban on trade in African elephant ivory.

[81] U.S. Fish and Wildlife Serv. v. Feigler, DOI Dkt. No. Portland 77-1 (ALJ ID dated Aug. 30, 1977).

[82] *In re* John A. Sefcik, DOC Dkt. No. 235-037 (ALJ ID dated Nov. 26, 1982).

[83] U.S. Fish and Wildlife Serv. v. Cyntrex Export/Imports, DOI Dkt. No. Portland 77-2 (ALJ ID dated Nov. 2, 1977).

[84] U.S. Fish and Wildlife Serv. v. Fortunoff's Silver Sales, DOI Dkt. No. Boston 77-15 (ALJ ID dated Apr. 18, 1978).

[85] *Cf.* U.S. Fish and Wildlife Serv. v. Lewis, DOI Dkt. No. Portland 78-2 (ALJ ID dated June 6, 1978) (antique clock was exempt from Act's ban because purchased before Act's passage).

[86] U.S. Fish and Wildlife Serv. v. Damien Imports, DOI Dkt. No. Albuquerque 78-9 (ALJ ID issued Jan 26, 1979).

[87] U.S. Fish and Wildlife Serv. v. Nguyen Tu Thuy, DOI Dkt. No. Portland 78-1 (ALJ ID dated May 22, 1978).

[88] Pub. L. No. 91-135, 83 Stat. 275.

[89] Pub. L. No. 93-205, §311; 87 Stat. 884, 886.

[90] *Id.* at §9(a)(1)(A); 87 Stat. at 893–94.

[91] 16 U.S.C. §1532(10) (1988).

[92] 50 C.F.R. §§17.21(b), 17.61(b) (1990).

to Paris when the airplane was forced to make an unscheduled stop at Miami International Airport. The United States government seized the hides. Granting the government's request for forfeiture, the court construed these events as constituting an importation.[93]

Another trader met a similar misfortune when he shipped ivory jewelry from India to Mexico through a Texas post office. A customs broker picked up the items at the post office, took them to the Mexican border, and had Mexican customs officials process them. An administrative law judge found that there was an importation into the United States.[94]

In exceptional circumstances, however, courts will fashion their own solution to avoid unfair results under the Act's strict language. In one case, a hunter shot a leopard legally in Kenya and directed the shipping agent not to send the parts through the United States.[95] By mistake, however, the agent put the animal parts on board a Lufthansa Airlines flight that landed in New York en route from Kenya to Haiti. The Fish and Wildlife Service sought forfeiture of the goods. Although the court acknowledged that the Act "prohibits not only knowing importation but any importation of endangered species,"[96] it refused to sanction forfeiture. Its reasoning was that the hunter and owner had not violated the Act and, even if Lufthansa had done so, "forfeiture is [not] appropriate where . . . the owner had no involvement whatsoever in the violation of the Act."[97]

*The Naive Tourist*

The law's prohibition against importation usually ensnares what the Conference Report calls the "casual tourist who bought an item with no hint of its illegality or impropriety."[98]

Tourists cannot escape prosecution even when they make some effort to determine a wildlife product's suitability for import. It was no defense for tourists who made inquiries at a Customs Service office,[99] who obtained an invoice that misidentified the object as a nonendangered species,[100] or who obtained assurances from the foreign merchant that the law allowed importation.[101]

---

[93] United States v. 3,210 Crusted Sides of Caiman Crocodilus Yacare, 636 F. Supp. 1281 (S.D. Fla. 1986).

[94] U.S. Fish and Wildlife Serv. v. Marti's S.A., DOI Dkt. No. Albuquerque 78-4 (ALJ ID dated July 25, 1978).

[95] Carpenter v. Andrus, 485 F. Supp. 320 (D. Del. 1980). Under the 1982 Amendments, the transaction would probably have been regarded as a noncommercial transshipment, exempted under 16 U.S.C. §1539(i) (1988). *See* Chapter 6.

[96] *Id.* at 322.

[97] *Id.* at 323.

[98] 1973 Conference Report, *supra* note 22, at 28, 1973 U.S. CODE CONG. & ADMIN. NEWS at 3006.

[99] U.S. Fish and Wildlife Serv. v. Goel, DOI Dkt. No. Boston 79-7 (ALJ ID dated June 13, 1979).

[100] U.S. Fish and Wildlife Serv. v. Luhrs, DOI Dkt. No. Boston 78-14 (ALJ ID dated April 26, 1979).

[101] U.S. Fish and Wildlife Serv. v. Moss, DOI Dkt. No. Portland 77-3 (ALJ ID dated March 10, 1978).

Upon returning to the United States, unwary tourists are thus forced to surrender their foreign purchases of articles like fur coats and hats,[102] leather pocketbooks,[103] rugs,[104] ivory carvings,[105] or religious statues.[106] In most instances, tourists must also pay a civil penalty. The Fish and Wildlife Service's strict enforcement policy carries out the agency's belief that "[e]ven an inadvertent importation of a designated species violates the Act's purpose."[107]

### *The Naive Hunter*

Another casualty of the import prohibitions is the "casual hunter" who is an "ignorant violator."[108] A hunter may not import an endangered species even if it was acquired lawfully. In a decision under the Endangered Species Conservation Act of 1969, the court ordered forfeiture of a Kenya leopard that was shot before the leopard was placed on the endangered species list.[109] A hunter who shot a red lechwe in Africa before that species was listed violated the 1973 Act by shipping the headskin and skull to a Wyoming taxidermist after listing:

> [A] violation is complete when a product of an animal enumerated in 50 CFR 17.11 [the list of endangered and threatened wildlife] is imported into the United States.[110]

Indeed, someone who does not actually kill an endangered animal, but finds it after it is already dead, cannot lawfully bring it back to the United States.[111]

Hunters violate the import prohibitions even if they could not have known during the safari that their target was an endangered species. An administrative law judge fined a hunter whose Botswana safari misrepresented to him that his quarry was not on the endangered list.[112] If the animal is protected, the hunter cannot escape penalties for importation except, for example, where the government entrapped him into bringing the trophy into this country.[113]

---

[102] *Id.*; U.S. Fish and Wildlife Serv. v. Economou, DOI Dkt. No. Twin Cities 78-3 (ALJ ID dated March 22, 1978).

[103] U.S. Fish and Wildlife Serv. v. Unanue, DOI Dkt. No. Boston 77-13 (ALJ ID dated Feb. 21, 1978).

[104] *In re* Jack S. Gressen, DOI Dkt. No. Portland 74-1 (ALJ ID dated Nov. 12, 1973).

[105] U.S. Fish and Wildlife Serv. v. Luhrs, *supra* note 100.

[106] U.S. Fish and Wildlife Serv. v. Goel, *supra* note 99.

[107] *In re* John A. Sefcik, DOC Dkt. No. 235-037 (ALJ ID dated Nov. 26, 1982).

[108] 1973 Conference Report, *supra* note 22, at 28, 1973 U.S. CODE CONG. & ADMIN. NEWS at 3006.

[109] United States v. Species of Wildlife, Etc., 404 F. Supp. 1298 (E.D.N.Y. 1975).

[110] U.S. Fish and Wildlife Serv. v. Landis, DOI Dkt. No. Albuquerque 78-7 (ALJ ID dated July 26, 1978).

[111] *Cf.* U.S. Fish and Wildlife Serv. v. Hundley, DOI Dkt. No. Albuquerque 78-5 (ALJ ID dated Dec. 4, 1978) (Lacey Act prosecution for interstate transportation).

[112] U.S. Fish and Wildlife Serv. v. Woods, DOI Dkt. No. Boston 77-11 (ALJ ID dated Sept. 14, 1978).

[113] U.S. Fish and Wildlife Serv. v. Meredith, DOI Dkt. No. Boston 78-9 (ALJ ID dated Nov. 20, 1978).

## Trafficking in Illegally Taken Species

The Act makes it unlawful for any person subject to U.S. jurisdiction to "possess, sell, deliver, carry, transport, or ship" an endangered species of fish or wildlife that was "taken in violation of" the Act.[114] This prohibition does not come into play if the creature was not illegally taken. If there was an illegal taking, however, any trafficking is unlawful even if it is not part of a commercial activity.

Each of the enumerated acts is an independent violation. The regulations spell this out with an example:[115]

> A person captures a whooping crane in Texas and gives it to a second person, who puts it in a closed van and drives thirty miles, to another location in Texas. The second person then gives the whooping crane to a third person, who is apprehended with the bird in his possession. All three have violated the law—the first by illegally taking the whooping crane; the second by transporting an illegally taken whooping crane; and the third by illegally possessing an illegally taken whooping crane.

There is no comparable provision protecting plants.

## Trafficking in Endangered Species for Commercial Activities

The Act makes it illegal to "deliver, receive, carry, transport, or ship" an endangered species in interstate or foreign commerce "in the course of commercial activity." This prohibition is contained in parallel provisions that protect fish and wildlife[116] and plants.[117]

Under the statute, the term "commercial activity" means "all activities of industry and trade."[118] In its regulations and rulings, the Fish and Wildlife Service elaborates the statutory language. As used in the definition of "commercial activity," the term "industry or trade" means "the actual or intended transfer of wildlife or plants from one person to another person in the pursuit of gain or profit."[119] This includes transactions that result in a loss of money or a mere breaking even—as well as trades of same value species—if the dealer intended to make a profit.[120]

As a result of these definitions, the Service regards many transactions as not being "commercial activities." Excluded from that term, for example, are exhibitions of commodities by museums and similar cultural or historical

---

[114] 16 U.S.C. §1538(a)(1)(D) (1988).
[115] 50 C.F.R. §17.21(d) (1990).
[116] 16 U.S.C. §1538(a)(1)(E) (1988).
[117] *Id.* §1538(a)(2)(C).
[118] *Id.* §1532(2).
[119] 50 C.F.R. §17.3 (1990).
[120] Memorandum from Associate Solicitor, Conservation and Wildlife, to Regional Solicitor, Atlanta, Department of Interior, entitled, "Fish and Wildlife Service regulation defining 'industry and trade' for purposes of the Endangered Species Act" (June 2, 1978).

organizations.[121] In addition, the Senate committee explained that the term "commercial activity" does not encompass the lawful dealings of a hunter with his taxidermist. Nor, said the committee, does it encompass the hunter's dealings with his travel agent or an airline to arrange his hunting trip. When a professional guide offers his services to illegally obtain wildlife, that offer is a commercial activity within the meaning of the Act.[122]

### Sales and Offers for Sale

Under the Act, no person subject to U.S. jurisdiction may sell or offer to sell an endangered species in interstate or foreign commerce. The prohibition is contained in parallel provisions covering fish and wildlife[123] and plants.[124]

Selling wildlife or wildlife parts is risky business. The Supreme Court upheld criminal prosecutions in which tribal Indians were convicted of killing eagles and selling their carcasses, parts, and feathers.[125] In another case, a knifemaker who showed his wares at a guild craft show was assessed a civil penalty because he displayed a whale's tooth without a "not for sale" sign.[126]

### Violations of Regulations

Lastly, section 9(a) makes it unlawful for persons subject to U.S. jurisdiction to violate the Secretary's regulations pertaining to protected species. This prohibition covers endangered fish, wildlife, and plants. If the species are listed as threatened, they are also covered if the Secretary has issued a regulation extending the Act's protection to them.[127]

## Regulation of Importers and Exporters

Section 9(d)[128] of the Act makes it unlawful for importers or exporters of fish, wildlife, or plants to engage in business without obtaining a license. In 1988 Congress extended this prohibition to importers and exporters of African ivory. These traders must keep records, file reports, and conduct their business through designated ports.

The Act requires licenses from any business that imports or exports fish, wildlife, or plants—even if the species are not listed as threatened or endan-

---

[121] *Id.*
[122] 1982 Senate Report, *supra* note 59, at 27–28.
[123] 16 U.S.C. §1538(a)(1)(F) (1988).
[124] *Id.* §1538(a)(2)(D).
[125] United States v. Dion, 476 U.S. 734 (1986).
[126] *In re* Ronnie Wilson, DOC Dkt. No. 035-071 (ALJ ID dated Aug. 14, 1980).
[127] 16 U.S.C. §1538(a)(1)(G), (2)(E) (1988).
[128] As amended by the African Elephant Conservation Act, Pub. L. No. 100-478, §2301, 102 Stat. 2306, 2321 (1988) (codified in 16 U.S.C. §1538(d)(1) (1988)).

gered. There are only two exceptions. No license is required for persons who import unlisted shellfish and fishery products for food. Nor is a license required for persons who catch unlisted shellfish or fishery products by sport fishing in U.S. waters or on the high seas.

As a practical matter, the Fish and Wildlife Service does not require a license from everyone who is in the business of importing or exporting. The Service's regulations[129] have traditionally exempted common carriers, museums, circuses, and businesses whose yearly imports and exports are worth less than $25,000. In the 1988 Amendments, however, Congress required that all commercial importers and exporters of ivory obtain a license, regardless of the volume of their business.[130]

To obtain the needed licenses and permits, exporters and importers face a maze of regulations. The Fish and Wildlife Service and other federal agencies issue regulations under the Endangered Species Act and other statutes. The regulations governing licenses and permits are the subject of Chapter 15 and Appendix A of this book.

## International Conservation Convention

In the Endangered Species Conservation Act of 1969, Congress directed the United States government to seek an international convention on the conservation of endangered species.[131] The international agreement, called the Convention on International Trade in Endangered Species of Wild Flora and Fauna (CITES),[132] is discussed at length in Chapter 9. As explained there, the Endangered Species Act makes violation of the CITES Convention an unlawful act. No person subject to U.S. jurisdiction may trade in any specimens contrary to the CITES Convention or possess any specimens that were so traded.[133]

## Prohibition of Attempts and Instigations

The Act also makes it unlawful to attempt to commit any of the prohibited acts, to solicit another person to commit them, or to cause them to be committed. These prohibitions apply to any person subject to U.S. jurisdiction.[134]

---

[129] 50 C.F.R. §14.92 (1990).

[130] H. REP. NO. 827, 100th Cong., 2d Sess. 20 (1988), *reprinted in* 1988 U.S. CODE CONG. & ADMIN. NEWS 2719, 2733 (referring to the House version of Pub. L. No. 100-478, §2301, 102 Stat. 2306, 2321, codified in 16 U.S.C. §1538(d)(4) (1988)).

[131] Pub. L. No. 91-135, §5(b), 83 Stat. 275, 278.

[132] 1976, 27 U.S.T. 1087, T.I.A.S. No. 8249, *amended* June 22, 1979; T.I.A.S. No. 11079.

[133] 16 U.S.C. §1538(c)(1) (1988). *See* 50 C.F.R., Part 23 (1990).

[134] 16 U.S.C. §1538(g) (1988).

* * *

When he was young, Aldo Leopold was an avid hunter, "full of trigger-itch." One day, however, Leopold shot a wolf, contributing to that animal's extermination in the area. When he "reached the old wolf in time to watch a fierce green fire dying in her eyes," he "sensed that neither the wolf nor the mountain agreed" with his hunting philosophy.[135] Renouncing hunting, Leopold went on to found the Wilderness Society. In Endangered Species Act section 9, Congress enacted statutory prohibitions that protect wildlife from humans who lack Leopold's sensitivities.

---

[135] A. Leopold, *A Sand County Almanac and Other Essays from Round River* 138–39 (New York: Ballentine Books, 1991).

# Chapter 5

# Federal Agency Action Under Section 7

*Time* Magazine calls it "an epic confrontation between ecology and economy."[1] The *Time* article refers to the northern spotted owl, whose survival is threatened by logging. Once the owl became an endangered species, section 7 of the Act[2] required the government to protect the bird by barring the timber industry from many tracts in the Pacific Northwest's ancient forests. Recognizing this, the U.S. Fish and Wildlife Service delayed listing the owl as imperiled.[3] The courts, however, ruled that the Service's delay was arbitrary.[4] A reluctant administration was pushed towards a logging ban that may cost 38,000 jobs and more than $1.8 billion a year in lost personal income.[5] In reaction to this, the administration says that it will seek changes in section 7 "that would make it easier to allow some species to diminish if preserving them would cause severe economic disruption."[6]

With section 7 standing in the shadow of legislative change, let us examine it in detail.

## Introduction: The Structure of Section 7

Section 7 contains both substantive and procedural provisions. Under the substantive provisions, the Secretary must pursue conservation, and all federal agencies must avoid jeopardizing species and their habitat. The principal

---

[1] *Owl vs. Man,* TIME, June 25, 1990, at 2, 56–63.

[2] 16 U.S.C. §1536 (1988).

[3] Portland Audubon Soc'y v. Hodel, 866 F.2d 302, 303 (9th Cir.), *cert. denied sub nom.* Northwest Forest Resource Council v. Portland Audubon Soc'y, 492 U.S. 911 (1989). *See* Portland Audubon Soc'y v. Lujan, 712 F. Supp. 1456 (D. Ore.), *aff'd in part and rev'd in part*, 884 F.2d 1233 (9th Cir. 1989), *cert. denied*, 494 U.S. 1026 (1990).

[4] Northern Spotted Owl v. Hodel, 716 F. Supp. 479 (W.D. Wash. 1988); Northern Spotted Owl v. Lujan, 758 F. Supp. 621 (E.D. Wash. 1991). For the listing of critical habitat, see 56 Fed. Reg. 40,002 (1991) as revised by 56 Fed. Reg. 50,701 (1991), with the final decision announced by U.S. Fish and Wildlife Service News Release 09-92 (Jan. 21, 1992).

[5] *Owl vs. Man*, TIME, *supra* note 1, at 57; *Study: Logging Cut Needed to Save Northwest Forests*, WASHINGTON POST, July 25, 1991, at A3.

[6] *Softening Stand on Spotted Owl, Administration Delays Protection*, N.Y. TIMES, June 27, 1990, at A1.

procedural provision is section 7(b), which sets out a process of "consultation" whereby the Secretary issues a "biological opinion" determining the risk of jeopardy from an agency project. Under section 7(d), an agency is forbidden to make an "irreversible or irretrievable" commitment of resources during consultation.[7]

## The Substantive Obligation to Conserve

The Act imposes a special responsibility upon the Secretary, who is directed to "use programs administered by him to further the conservation purposes of" the Act.[8] Section 7(a)(1)[9] is the origin of this obligation, providing that the Secretary "shall" use programs "in furtherance of the purposes of this chapter," including a mandate that all federal agencies "seek to conserve" imperiled species.[10]

Three court decisions depict this requirement. In one case, municipal and industrial water users attacked the Secretary's refusal to sell them water from a dam project. The Secretary chose to use all the dam project's water to conserve two species of fish. And the Secretary intended to continue that practice until the fish ceased to be threatened or endangered. The court rejected the water users' contention that the Secretary was authorized only to take actions that avoid "jeopardizing" the species' continued existence. Since the Secretary is directed to "actively pursue a species conservation policy," the court ruled that the Act "supports the Secretary's decision to give priority to the fish until such time as they no longer need [the Act's] protection."[11]

The next decision overturned the Secretary's decision to allow bird hunters to continue using lead shot ammunition. Many bald eagles were poisoned when they fed upon other migratory birds that hunters had shot with lead pellets. Reading section 7(a) (1)'s duty to conserve together with the Act's definition of "conservation," the court said that the Act requires the Secretary:[12]

> '. . . to use . . . *all methods* which are necessary to bring any endangered . . . or threatened species to the point at which' the protections of the Act are no longer necessary.

Characterizing this language as "mandatory,"[13] the court found that the Secretary's action violated both sections 7(a) (1) and 9.

---

[7] 16 U.S.C. §1536(d) (1988).

[8] Carson-Truckee Water Conservancy Dist. v. Clark, 741 F.2d 257, 261 (9th Cir. 1984), *cert. denied sub nom.* Nevada v. Hodel, 470 U.S. 1083 (1985).

[9] 16 U.S.C. §1536(a)(1) (1988).

[10] *Id.* §1531(c)(1). Section 7(a)(2) also directs that all other federal agencies "shall" use their authorities to further the Act's purposes "by carrying out programs for the conservation of" imperiled species.

[11] Carson-Truckee Water Conservancy Dist. v. Clark, *supra* note 8, at 262.

[12] National Wildlife Fed'n v. Hodel, 23 ER Cases 1089, 1092 (E.D. Cal. 1985) (citing 16 U.S.C. §§1532(3), 1536(a)(2)).

[13] *Id.* at 1092.

In the third case, environmentalists objected to the Secretary's decision to allow sport hunting of migratory game birds from just before sunrise to sunset. At dawn and dusk, the environmentalists argued, visibility is so poor that hunters cannot distinguish between game birds and endangered species. The district judge was displeased that the Secretary had no information concerning the impact of the contested shooting hours on birds that should not be shot. Ruling against the Secretary, the court said that the Secretary's agency "must do far more than merely avoid the elimination of protected species. It must bring these species back from the brink so that they may be removed from the protected class, and it must use all methods necessary to do so."[14]

## The Substantive Obligation Not to Jeopardize

The Act's "principal substantive" provision is section 7(a) (2).[15] That provision requires each federal agency to "insure" that "agency action" is "not likely to jeopardize the continued existence" of any endangered species or threatened species.[16] The section also prohibits action that will destroy or adversely modify the species' habitat.

## The Definition of "Agency Action"

Courts will "interpret the term 'agency action' broadly."[17] The Act defines "agency action" as "*any* action authorized, funded, or carried out by" a federal agency.[18] The regulations[19] say that "action" means "all activities or programs of any kind authorized, funded, or carried out, in whole or in part, by Federal agencies." In those regulations, the Service tried to limit section 7 to agency action within the United States or on the high seas.[20] On review, the Supreme Court did not decide whether the consultation requirement of section 7 also applies to projects in foreign nations.[21]

The regulations contain a list of typical agency actions that are covered by section 7. They are:[22]

---

[14] Defenders of Wildlife v. Andrus, 428 F. Supp. 167, 170 (D.D.C. 1977). Two decisions discussing the Secretary's duty to "conserve," in a tangential manner, are: Enos v. Marsh, 616 F. Supp. 32, 59 (D. Haw. 1984), *aff'd,* 769 F.2d 1363 (9th Cir. 1985); National Wildlife Fed'n v. National Park Serv., 669 F. Supp. 384, 387–88 (D. Wyo. 1987).

[15] North Slope Borough v. Andrus, 642 F.2d 589, 607 (D.C. Cir. 1980) (referring to 16 U.S.C. §1536(a)(2) (1988)).

[16] 16 U.S.C. §1536(a)(2) (1988).

[17] Conner v. Burford, 848 F.2d 1441, 1453 (9th Cir. 1988), *cert. denied sub nom.* Sun Exploration & Production Co. v. Lujan, 489 U.S. 1012 (1989).

[18] 16 U.S.C. §1536(a)(2) (1988) (italics supplied).

[19] 50 C.F.R. §402.02 (1990).

[20] *Id.*

[21] Lujan v. Defenders of Wildlife, 60 U.S.L.W. 4495 (U.S. June 9, 1992) (but see concurring opinion).

[22] *Supra* note 19.

- Actions intended to conserve listed species or their habitat
- The promulgation of regulations
- The granting of licenses, contracts, leases, easements, rights-of-way, permits, or grants-in-aid
- Actions directly or indirectly causing modifications to the land, water, or air

Although the statute limits the term "agency action" to action by federal agencies, state agencies are covered when they build projects with federal funding.[23] Similarly, if the Federal Emergency Management Agency approves a community's eligibility for flood insurance under federal law, the community's flood plain development plan will become subject to section 7.[24]

One strained court decision on "agency action" deserves special notice. In 1980 the Court of Appeals for the D.C. Circuit was wrestling with a troublesome question: When the Interior Department prepares a biological opinion for sales of off-shore oil and gas leases, can it limit the opinion to the effects of the project's leasing phase—or must it also take account of the effects of possible exploration and drilling? The court chose the first (and more limited) option. Nonetheless, the court gave a nod in passing to the concept that "'agency action' . . . may signify the lease sale *and all subsequent activities.*"[25] Later in this chapter, I take up the leasing cases in the discussion of biological opinions and irreversible commitments.

## The Meaning of the "Not Likely to" Language

In 1979 Congress changed section 7 so that it requires agencies to insure only that their actions are "not likely to jeopardize" species.[26] Before that, section 7 was written more emphatically: Federal agencies had to insure that their actions "do not" jeopardize species.[27] In 1979 Congress recognized that the original wording might force the Secretary to oppose a project whenever he "cannot guarantee with certainty" that it will not jeopardize species.[28] By adopting the "not likely to jeopardize" language, Congress intended to permit the Secretary to frame his decision on the best available evidence.

---

[23] National Wildlife Fed'n v. Coleman, 529 F.2d 359, n.21 (5th Cir.), *cert. denied sub nom.* Boteler v. National Wildlife Fed'n, 429 U.S. 979 (1976).

[24] Letter from Associate Solicitor, Conservation and Wildlife, Department of Interior, to Regional Director, Region 4, Fish and Wildlife Service, entitled, "Application of Section 7 of the Endangered Species Act to Federal Flood Insurance" (Aug. 21, 1984).

[25] North Slope Borough v. Andrus, *supra* note 15, at 609 (italics added).

[26] Pub. L. No. 96-159, §4, 93 Stat. 1225, 1226 (1979).

[27] Pub. L. No. 93-205, §7, 87 Stat. 884, 892 (1973) *and* Pub. L. No. 95-632, §3, 92 Stat. 3751, 3752 (1978).

[28] H.R. REP. NO. 697, 96th Cong., 1st Sess. 12, *reprinted in* 1979 U.S. CODE CONG. & ADMIN. NEWS 2557, 2576 [hereinafter 1979 Conference Report].

Although the 1979 Amendments "softened" the obligation on an agency,[29] the legislative intent continues to give the benefit of the doubt to the species.[30]

## The Definition of "Jeopardize"

The regulations[31] state that the statutory term "jeopardize the continued existence of" means:

> . . . to engage in an action that reasonably would be expected, directly or indirectly, to reduce appreciably the likelihood of both the survival and recovery of a listed species in the wild by reducing the reproduction, numbers, or distribution of that species.

Among decisions holding that federal agency actions may "jeopardize" an endangered species, the most famous is the snail darter case, *Tennessee Valley Auth. v. Hill.*[32] There the Supreme Court halted the government agency's construction of a $100 million dam that threatened a paper-clip-sized fish. Since *Hill* was decided, however, most court decisions tend to turn on procedural questions. Did the agency follow section 7's procedures for "consultation"? If so, did it obtain a proper "biological opinion" that authorized its action? These questions will be discussed later in this chapter.

## The Definition of "Destruction" and "Adverse Modification"

When it enacted the Endangered Species Act of 1973, Congress was aware that the greatest threat to species survival was the destruction of natural habitat.[33] Consequently the statute forbids agency action that is likely to "result in the destruction or adverse modification of habitat." The regulations define the term "destruction or adverse modification" as meaning:

> . . . a direct or indirect alteration that appreciably diminishes the value of critical habitat for both the survival and recovery of a listed species. Such alterations include, but are not limited to, alterations adversely modifying any of those physical or biological features that were the basis for determining the habitat to be critical.[34]

In most instances, an agency action that destroys or adversely modifies habitat will also violate another one of the Act's prohibitions. Consider the State of Hawaii's action in placing sheep and goats on Mauna Kea's slopes,

---

[29] Roosevelt Campobello Int'l Park Comm'n v. Environmental Protection Agency, 684 F.2d 1041, 1048–49 (1st Cir. 1982).

[30] Village of False Pass v. Watt, 565 F. Supp. 1123, 1155 (D. Alaska 1983) (quoting 1979 House Conference Report, *supra* note 28), *aff'd sub nom.* Village of False Pass v. Clark, 733 F.2d 605 (9th Cir. 1984).

[31] *Supra* note 19.

[32] 437 U.S. 153 (1978).

[33] *Id.* at 179.

[34] *Supra* note 19.

causing defoliation of an exotic bird's only habitat. Certainly the State diminished that habitat's value within the meaning of section 7(a) (2). In addition, however, section 9 forbids anyone from "taking" a species—a concept that embraces harm caused by habitat degradation. In this circumstance, the courts held that the State of Hawaii had "taken" the endangered bird in violation of section 9.[35]

Similarly, in a case involving national forests, another court disapproved of Park Service policies that allowed clear-cutting in close proximity to woodpecker colonies. Again, the agency action harmed habitat. The court, however, referred to it as a "taking" under section 9 and an action that "jeopardized" wildlife under Section 7.[36]

The Service takes the position that section 9 cannot be violated by "habitat modification alone without any attendant death or injury of the protected wildlife."[37] In practice, however, courts are unlikely to be faced with cases of habitat degradation that do not injure species. As a consequence, the courts can usually avoid giving separate effect to section 7(a) (2)'s prohibition against habitat destruction.

## The Procedural Obligation to Consult

In order to insure proper agency action, section 7 instructs each federal agency to act "in consultation with" the Secretary. The Secretary administers these consultation provisions through "the Service"—the U.S. Fish and Wildlife Service (for the Secretary of the Interior) and the National Marine Fisheries Service (for the Secretary of Commerce).[38]

### Preliminary Consultation Procedures

An agency that ignores the consultation requirement can expect a lawsuit. The Forest Service learned this lesson when a diverse coalition—landowners, ranchers, outfitters, miners, hunters, fishermen, recreational users, and conservation organizations—attacked the agency's attempt to build a timber road in a national forest. The forest was home to an endangered species of wolf; it was also adjacent to the fabled Salmon River. Nonetheless, the Park Service did not follow the Act's procedures for consultation, believing that the road's effects were not harmful. The court of appeals was not satisfied.[39]

---

[35] Palila v. Hawaii Dep't of Land and Natural Resources, 852 F.2d 1106 (9th Cir. 1988); *id.*, 639 F.2d 495 (9th Cir. 1981). *See* Chapter 4.

[36] Sierra Club v. Lyng, 694 F. Supp. 1260, 1263 (E.D. Tex. 1988), *rev'd on other grounds sub nom.* Sierra Club v. Yeuttea, 926 F.2d 429 (5th Cir. 1991).

[37] *See* Palila v. Hawaii Dep't of Land and Natural Resources, 649 F. Supp. 1070, 1075–77 (D. Haw. 1986), *aff'd,* 852 F.2d 1106 (9th Cir. 1988) (quoting 46 Fed. Reg. 54,748 (1981)).

[38] 50 C.F.R. §402.02 (1990). *See* Village of False Pass v. Watt, *supra* note 30, at 1153.

[39] Thomas v. Peterson, 753 F.2d 754 (9th Cir. 1985).

As the court told the Forest Service, the statutory plan imposes a "three-step process" for consultation.[40] The first two steps serve a screening function to determine if formal consultation is required.

The first step requires that, when an agency proposes to take an action, it must inquire of the Service whether a protected species "may be present" in the action area.[41] If the answer to step one is affirmative, the agency must then prepare a "biological assessment" to determine whether the species or its habitat is likely to be affected by the action. The biological assessment may then be part of an environmental impact statement or environmental assessment.[42]

In failing to follow these procedures, the Forest Service had committed "a substantial procedural violation of" section 7—and "the remedy must be an injunction."[43] Similarly, the Navy was reprimanded for beginning training exercises in Puerto Rican waters without consulting with the Service.[44] "Once an agency has discovered that some action for which it is responsible crosses the low threshold of possible effect, it must consult" with the Service.[45]

In the case of these first and second steps, the agency must follow the procedures for species that are listed "or proposed to be listed."[46] Up to this point, "the obligations owed each group are co-extensive."[47]

## Formal Consultations

After the agency completes step two, its "biological assessment" may show a likely effect upon endangered or threatened wildlife or its habitat. If so, the agency must begin step three of the consultation process—formal consultations with the Service.[48] If the wildlife is not listed as an endangered or threatened species, but only proposed to be listed, the federal agency is not required to enter into formal consultations. The agency need only "confer" with the Service.[49]

"The [formal] consultation process is not precisely spelled out in the statute but has been implemented in detail in joint regulations promulgated by the . . . Fish and Wildlife Service and the National Marine Fisheries Service."[50]

---

[40] *Id.* at 763. *See* Enos v. Marsh, 769 F.2d 1363, 1368 (9th Cir. 1985).

[41] Thomas v. Peterson, *supra* note 39, at 763 (quoting 16 U.S.C. §1536(c)(1)).

[42] *Id.* In the regulations, the Secretary says that biological assessments are required only for "Federal actions that 'are major construction activities.'" 50 C.F.R. §402.12(b)(1) (1990). That limitation is hard to square with the broad definitions of "agency action" set forth in section 7(a)(2) ("any action authorized, funded, or carried out by such agency") and elsewhere in the Secretary's own regulations (50 C.F.R. §402.02 (1990)).

[43] Thomas v. Peterson, *supra* note 39, at 764.

[44] Romero-Barcelo v. Brown, 643 F.2d 835 (1st Cir. 1981), *rev'd on other grounds sub nom.* Weinberger v. Romero-Barcelo, 456 U.S. 305 (1982).

[45] *Id.*, 643 F.2d at 857.

[46] 16 U.S.C. §1536(c)(1) (1988).

[47] Enos v. Marsh, 769 F.2d 1363, 1368 (9th Cir. 1985).

[48] 50 C.F.R. §402.14 (1990).

[49] Enos v. Marsh, *supra* note 40 (interpreting 16 U.S.C. §1536(a)(4) (1985)).

[50] Village of False Pass v. Watt, *supra* note 30, at 1153.

Under those regulations,[51] the federal agency initiates consultation by submitting a written request. The requesting agency must provide the Service with a copy of the agency's biological assessment as well as detailed data.

The Service is to complete formal consultation within 90 days, although limited extensions are allowed. At the end of the consultation, the Service issues a "biological opinion," based upon the best scientific and commercial data available. Formal consultation is terminated with the issuance of the biological opinion.[52]

## The Biological Opinion

The biological opinion and its conclusions "are the pivots around which E[ndangered] S[pecies] A[ct] analysis must turn."[53]

### "Jeopardy" and "No-Jeopardy" Opinions

If the Service finds that the requesting agency's project is likely to jeopardize a listed species or to degrade its critical habitat, the Service issues a "jeopardy" biological opinion. When the Service issues a "jeopardy" opinion, it lists reasonable or prudent alternatives—or states that none are known. If the Service finds that the requesting agency's project is not likely to jeopardize or degrade, the Service issues a "no jeopardy" biological opinion.[54]

The Service may decide, in its biological opinion, to permit or recommend actions that result in incidental "takings" of listed species. As discussed in the next chapter, if the agency (or an allied applicant) "takes" a species in compliance with the Service's "incidental-take" authorization, the agency (or applicant) will not be deemed in violation of section 9. Incidental "takings" are permitted only if they are found not to violate section 7(a) (2)—that is, they do not jeopardize the species' survival or adversely modify critical habitat. If it allows incidental "takings," the Service specifies procedures for limiting and monitoring them.

### Effect of Biological Opinions

A favorable biological opinion puts the requesting agency in a strong position. It is true that the agency "may not rely solely upon a . . . biological opinion to establish conclusively its compliance with its *substantive* obligations under section 7(a) (2). . . . [I]ts decision to rely on a . . . biological opinion

---

[51] *Supra* note 48. *See* 16 U.S.C. §1536(b) (1988).
[52] 50 C.F.R. §402.14(*l*)(1) (1990).
[53] North Slope Borough v. Andrus, 642 F.2d 589, 609 (D.C. Cir. 1980).
[54] 50 C.F.R. §402.14(h) (1990).

must not have been arbitrary or capricious."[55] Still, "courts have accorded substantial weight to a sound biological opinion in determining an agency's compliance with [section] 7(a) (2)."[56] When the agency action is in conformity with a proper biological opinion, courts will generally uphold the agency.[57]

Can an agency continue with its project if the Service issues an unfavorable biological opinion? Several court decisions suggest that the Service does not have the last word. In one case, the Corps of Engineers refused the Service's request to postpone a dam project. Allowing the Corps of Engineers to proceed with the dam, the court said: "Consultation under Section 7 does not require acquiescence. Should a difference of opinion arise as to a given project, the responsibility for decision after consultation is not vested in the Secretary but in the agency involved."[58] Another court said in dictum that, "[Once] an agency has had meaningful consultation with the Secretary . . . the final decision of whether or not to proceed with the action lies with the agency itself."[59]

It is unclear how much weight these two decisions carry today. In its *Hill* decision, issued after these two court of appeals decisions, the Supreme Court emphasized that section 7's "no-jeopardize" language is an "affirmative command" that "admits of no exception."[60] The Ninth Circuit has since reiterated that the Service cannot "order other agencies to comply with its requests or . . . veto their decisions."[61] Nonetheless, the court held that the Corps of Engineers acted arbitrarily when it refused the Service's request to reinitiate consultations. The Service, said the court, "is primarily responsible for protecting endangered species," and "we defer to the agency with the more appropriate expertise."[62]

An agency need not follow the Service's recommendations: The agency may fashion alternatives to the Service's modifications. For example, in selling oil and gas leases off the Alaskan coast, an agency was allowed to adopt its own set of protections for whales, instead of another set that the Service had recommended.[63] Although it upheld the agency in that case, the court warned that, whenever an agency "deviates" from the Service's recommended alternatives, it "does so subject to the risk that [it] has not satisfied the standard of section 7(a) (2)."[64] In order to avoid that risk, the agency must show that it

---

[55] Pyramid Lake Paiute Tribe v. Dep't of Navy, 898 F.2d 1410, 1415 (9th Cir. 1990).

[56] Romero-Barcelo v. Brown, *supra* note 44, 643 F.2d at 857. *Accord,* Roosevelt Campobello Int'l Park Comm'n v. Environmental Protection Agency, 684 F.2d 1041, 1049 (1st Cir. 1982).

[57] *E.g.*, Environmental Coalition of Broward County, Inc. v. Myers, 831 F.2d 984 (11th Cir. 1987); Cabinet Mountain Wilderness v. Peterson, 685 F.2d 678 (D.C. Cir. 1982); Park County Resource Council, Inc. v. Department of Agriculture, 613 F. Supp. 1182 (D. Wyo. 1985), *aff'd,* 817 F.2d 609 (10th Cir. 1987).

[58] Sierra Club v. Froehlke, 534 F.2d 1289, 1303 (8th Cir. 1976).

[59] National Wildlife Fed'n v. Coleman, 529 F.2d 359, 371 (5th Cir.), *cert. denied sub nom.* Boteler v. National Wildlife Fed'n, 429 U.S. 979 (1976). Despite the court's language, it enjoined the road-building project pending environmental modifications.

[60] Tennessee Valley Auth. v. Hill, 437 U.S. 153, 173 (1978).

[61] Sierra Club v. Marsh, 816 F.2d 1376, 1386 (9th Cir. 1987).

[62] *Id.* at 1388.

[63] Tribal Village of Akutan v. Hodel, 869 F.2d 1185 (9th Cir. 1988).

[64] *Id.* at 1193 (quoting Village of False Pass v. Watt, 565 F. Supp. 1123, 1160–61 (D. Alaska 1983), *aff'd sub nom.* Village of False Pass v. Clark, 733 F.2d 605 (9th Cir. 1984)).

took "alternative, reasonably adequate steps to insure the continued existence of any endangered or threatened species."[65]

In the biological opinion, the Service may also offer so-called "discretionary conservation recommendations." These are advisory; they do not carry any binding legal force.[66]

## The Problem of Phase-by-Phase Agency Actions

In biological statements, how should the Service analyze agency action that is segmented into separate and successive phases? This problem is presented by the leasing of oil and gas rights on government territory. At the stage when the government sells the mineral lease, should it prepare a biological statement that examines the jeopardy posed by activities at the exploration stage? What about the later stages of development and production?

There is no obvious answer to these questions. It is true that the Act "insist[s] on foresight."[67] Yet, if the Service tries to assess the effect of all future steps, the information necessary for that determination may not be available. But by restricting its review to activities at the leasing phase, the Service may disregard the threats of subsequent activities. Not surprisingly, the courts have struggled with the choice.

It seems to turn on whether the matter is based on land or at sea. On land, the leading case[68] began when the Forest Service proposed to sell oil and gas leases on national forest land in Montana. The Fish and Wildlife Service divided the oil and gas activities into stages and, in its biological opinion, addressed the effects of only the leasing stage. The Ninth Circuit disagreed. It held that section 7 requires the Service "to consider all phases of the agency action, which includes post-leasing activities, in its biological opinion."[69] The court ordered a halt to all leasing until the Service "prepare[s] biological opinions assessing the potential impacts of all post-leasing activities."[70]

Faced later with oil and gas leases on other national forest lands, the Ninth Circuit reaffirmed its earlier ruling. Again it held that the biological opinion must "assess . . . the impact of the . . . leases and of all post-leasing activities on threatened and endangered species."[71]

The D.C. Circuit and other courts rejected this approach for oil and gas leases on lands submerged off the coast.[72] To justify its ruling, the D.C. Circuit

---

[65] Tribal Village of Akutan v. Hodel, *supra* note 63, at 1193.

[66] 50 C.F.R. §402.14(j) (1990).

[67] North Slope Borough v. Andrus, *supra* note 53, at 608.

[68] Conner v. Burford, 848 F.2d 1441 (9th Cir. 1988), *cert. denied sub nom.* Sun Exploration & Production Co. v. Lujan, 489 U.S. 1012 (1989).

[69] *Id.* at 1453.

[70] *Id.* at 1458.

[71] Bob Marshall Alliance v. Hodel, 852 F.2d 1223, 1228 (9th Cir. 1988), *cert. denied sub nom.* Kohlman v. Bob Marshall Alliance, 489 U.S. 1066 (1989).

[72] Village of False Pass v. Watt, *supra* note 64; North Slope Borough v. Andrus, *supra* note 53, at 607–09. *See also* California v. Watt, 520 F. Supp. 1359 (C.D. Cal. 1981), *aff'd in part and rev'd in part,* 683 F.2d 1253 (9th Cir. 1982), *rev'd sub nom.* Secretary of the Interior v.

relied upon the Outer Continental Shelf Lands Act (OCSLA),[73] which divides OCS projects into leasing, exploration, and production phases.[74] The D.C. Circuit was especially impressed that the Secretary can suspend activities on a lease if the activities harm marine life or the environment.[75] In the court's view, the OCSLA's mandatory stage-by-stage review "prevents the telescoping of any and every hazard . . . into one overwhelming statutory obstacle."[76] As a consequence, the court permitted the Service to limit its biological opinions to the leasing phase only.

## Indirect and Cumulative Effects of Agency Action

The biological opinion must detail how the agency action "affects" the species or its habitat.[77] "The case law . . . is clear that federal agencies are to consider many potential effects from a project on an endangered species."[78] These include direct and indirect effects, as well as cumulative effects.[79]

### Indirect Effects

The Fifth Circuit set the pattern in a 1976 decision[80] overturning a plan to build a federally funded highway transecting the habitat of the Mississippi sandhill crane, an endangered bird. Although the highway's direct effects were either unknown or manageable, its indirect effects—residential and commercial development—were "significant" and "feared."[81] Holding that it was questionable whether the crane could survive the loss of habitat caused "by the indirect effects of the highways" and other things,[82] the court ordered an injunction.

The Supreme Court followed a similar course in the snail darter case.[83] There the Court held that the Tennessee Valley Authority had to consider the effects caused by water that would back up from its dam, not just the direct physical impacts of the dam.

---

California, 464 U.S. 312 (1984); Conservation Law Foundation v. Andrus, 623 F.2d 712 (1st Cir. 1979).

[73] 43 U.S.C. §§1331 *et seq.* (1988).

[74] North Slope Borough v. Andrus, *supra* note 53, at 606.

[75] *Id.*

[76] *Id.* at 609.

[77] 15 U.S.C. §1536(b)(3)(A) (1985).

[78] Riverside Irrigation Dist. v. Andrews, 568 F. Supp. 583, 588 (D. Colo. 1983), *aff'd,* 758 F.2d 508 (10th Cir. 1985).

[79] 50 C.F.R. §402.02 (1990).

[80] National Wildlife Fed'n v. Coleman, 529 F.2d 359 (5th Cir.), *cert. denied sub nom.* Boteler v. National Wildlife Fed'n, 429 U.S. 979 (1976).

[81] *Id.*, 529 F.2d at 365, 372–73.

[82] *Id.* at 373.

[83] Tennessee Valley Auth. v. Hill, 437 U.S. 153 (1978), as construed in Riverside Irrigation Dist. v. Andrews, *supra* note 78, 568 F. Supp., at 588.

In the most recent case,[84] the Corps of Engineers blocked construction of a dam by refusing to give the dam developers permission to discharge sand and gravel into a navigable waterway. No one claimed that the sand and gravel itself would harm habitat. The dam developers, however, needed to deposit the sand and gravel in order to build their dam. In turn, the dam would allow greater consumption of the stream water, depleting stream flow, and thus impairing the crane's habitat. The court rejected the dam developers' argument that the Corps could not consider the depletion of water because it was an indirect effect. Upholding the Corps' decision, the court said:[85]

> To require [the Corps] to ignore the indirect effects that result from its actions would be to require it to wear blinders that Congress has not chosen to impose. . . . [T]he Corps was required to consider all effects, direct and indirect, of the discharge for which authorization was sought.

The Service takes the same view.[86] Its regulations state that the term "effects of the [agency] action" refers "to the direct and indirect effects. . . ."[87] The regulations define "indirect effects" as "those that are caused by the proposed action and are later [than the direct effects] in time, but still are reasonably certain to occur."[88]

## Cumulative Effects

Originally, the Interior Department took an expansive view of the impacts to be considered in evaluating a project. In two 1978 opinions, the Office of the Department's Solicitor said that federal agencies must consider the cumulative effects of all pending federal, state, and private projects.[89]

In 1981, however, the Solicitor's Office withdrew these opinions and substituted a more restrictive interpretation.[90] Under the 1981 interpretation, the department's consultation team is to consider:

- The *past* and *present* impacts of all projects
- The *anticipated* impacts of proposed federal projects that have received a favorable biological opinion
- The impacts of state or private projects that are contemporaneous with the federal project

---

[84] Riverside Irrigation Dist. v. Andrews, *supra* note 78, 758 F.2d 508.
[85] *Id.* at 512–13.
[86] *See* Cumulative Impacts Under Section 7 of the Endangered Species Act, 88 I.D. 903, 908 (1981).
[87] 50 C.F.R. §402.02 (1990).
[88] *Id.*
[89] *See* Cumulative Impacts Under Section 7 of the Endangered Species Act, *supra* note 86 (citing July 19, 1978 opinion, 85 I.D. 275, and July 24, 1978 opinion).
[90] *Id.*

- The cumulative impacts of *future* state or private projects that are reasonably certain to occur before the federal project is completed

The consultation team, however, is not to consider the "anticipated impacts of future federal projects which have *not* been previously reviewed under sec. 7."[91]

The current regulations are even more restrictive. They eliminate consideration of all federal projects, stating:

> Cumulative effects are those effects of future State or private activities, not involving Federal activities, that are reasonably certain to occur within the action area of the Federal action subject to consultation.[92]

As a justification for excluding federal projects from its analysis of cumulative effects, the Service reasoned that future federal projects would eventually be evaluated separately under section 7. As a result, these federal projects "could not occur unless they were able, in their own right, to avoid jeopardizing the continued existence of the affected species or destroying or adversely modifying critical habitat."[93]

## The Use of Scientific and Commercial Data

In fulfilling their "no-jeopardy" duties, federal agencies are told to use "the best scientific and commercial data available."[94] The Secretary is expected to use the same kind of information when deciding whether an imperiled species may be present in a project area.[95]

Sometimes, the available evidence is inadequate for a definitive opinion. In that event, the requesting agency has a continuing obligation to make a reasonable effort to develop better information. One court characterized the Secretary's duty to use the best scientific data as "ongoing."[96] Enjoining the Secretary from selling off-shore oil and gas leases, the court held that the Secretary's biological opinion was inadequate when it failed to incorporate incomplete studies. Once those studies were under way, they were within the concept of "the best scientific data."[97]

Another court overruled an agency that did not make a "first class effort" to acquire the best scientific data. In that case, in which the Environmental Protection Agency approved construction of an oil refinery and marine terminal, the First Circuit faulted the agency's failure to insist that certain oil-spill studies be done.[98] Invalidating another agency decision, the Ninth Circuit explained

---

[91] *Id.* at 906–08.
[92] 50 C.F.R. §402.02 (1990).
[93] 51 Fed. Reg. 19,926, 19,933 (1986).
[94] 16 U.S.C. §1536(a)(2) (1988).
[95] *Id.* §1536(c)(1).
[96] Conservation Law Foundation v. Watt, 560 F. Supp. 561, 572 (D. Mass.), *aff'd on other grounds sub nom.* Massachusetts v. Watt, 716 F.2d 946 (1st Cir. 1983).
[97] *Id.* at 272–73.
[98] Roosevelt Campobello Int'l Park Comm'n v. Environmental Protection Agency, 684 F.2d

that agencies cannot ignore available biological information.[99] An agency that proceeds with an action in the face of inadequate knowledge or information does so with the risk that it has not satisfied the standard of section 7(a) (2).[100]

The "best data" is not always the same as "perfect data." A biological opinion can rely on "admittedly weak" information in several situations. One is when a challenging party can claim no "new" information—that is, information the Service did not already take into account—which challenges the opinion's conclusions.[101] Another is when an opposing expert challenges the biological opinion's conclusions, but the expert's testimony contains no new information.[102]

If the Service uses complete data, it will usually be sustained even if its data is criticized. It is not considered an error for the Service to disregard alleged inconsistencies in its data if these criticisms are not brought to its attention until late in the litigation.[103] The agency will also be sustained if it presents scientifically respectable conclusions which its critics dispute with rival evidence of equal dignity.[104]

## The Prohibition Against Resource Commitments

Section 7(d) provides that, after formal consultation begins, the federal agency may not make any "irreversible or irretrievable commitment of resources" that "has the effect of foreclosing" alternatives to its project.[105] This prohibition remains in force throughout the consultation process and continues until the agency satisfies the requirements of section 7(a) (2).[106]

Section 7(d)'s "primary purpose . . . is to guarantee that no irreversible decisions are made until a definitive biological opinion can be prepared."[107] Congress intended to preclude investment of a massive amount of resources before the safety of an endangered species is assured.[108]

When is a commitment of resources "irreversible or irretrievable"? Neither the Act nor regulations define the term. One court said that a commitment is

---

1041, n.9 (1st Cir. 1982).

[99] Conner v. Burford, 848 F.2d 1441, 1454 (9th Cir. 1988), *cert. denied sub nom.* Sun Exploration & Production Co. v. Lujan, 489 U.S. 1012 (1989).

[100] Roosevelt Campobello Int'l Park Comm'n v. Environmental Protection Agency, *supra* note 98, at 1049 (citing 1979 Conference Report, *supra* note 28, at 12).

[101] Pyramid Lake Paiute Tribe v. United States Dep't of Navy, 898 F.2d 1410, 1416 (9th Cir. 1990).

[102] Stop H-3 Ass'n v. Dole, 740 F.2d 1442, 1460 (9th Cir. 1984), *cert. denied sub nom.* Yamasaki v. Stop H-3 Ass'n, 471 U.S. 1108 (1985).

[103] Friends of Endangered Species, Inc. v. Jantzen, 760 F.2d 976, 983 (9th Cir. 1985).

[104] Louisiana v. Verity, 853 F.2d 322, 329 (5th Cir. 1988).

[105] 16 U.S.C. §1536(d) (1988).

[106] 50 C.F.R. §402.09 (1990).

[107] Village of False Pass v. Watt, 565 F. Supp. 1123, 1155 (D. Alaska 1983), *aff'd sub nom.* Village of False Pass v. Clark, 733 F.2d 605 (9th Cir. 1984).

[108] North Slope Borough v. Andrus, 486 F. Supp. 326, 330 (D.D.C. 1979).

not irreversible or irretrievable when it is "salvageable."[109] By this, the court meant that the resources can be used in another project or in a different manner than that proposed in the original plan.[110]

Several courts examined whether the government's sale of off-shore oil and gas leases constitutes an irreversible or irretrievable commitment, as examined earlier in this chapter. The D.C. Circuit interpreted the Outer Continental Shelf Lands Act[111] as dividing off-shore oil and gas projects into separate phases—leasing, exploration, and development and production—with the Secretary having the right to suspend activities on a lease if they threatened harm to marine life or the environment. The court thus convinced itself that lease sales permitted only "preliminary activities" that "entail no 'irreversible or irretrievable commitment.'"[112] This is now "[t]he uniform conclusion of the reported cases."[113]

Section 7(d) does not protect all species. It applies only to formal consultations under section 7(a) (2). Those consultations concern projects affecting species that are already listed as endangered or threatened. Consequently, "federal agencies are not required to forego making resource commitments which could result in action adversely affecting" species that are only *proposed* for listing.[114]

## Belated Biological Assessments and Opinions

There have been instances where a federal agency takes action without a biological assessment or opinion, and then tries to justify its action by obtaining the document later. That tactic is not always successful, as demonstrated by the Navy's attempt to sustain training exercises that included naval and air bombardment of an island in Puerto Rican waters. When the Navy finally received a biological opinion, after the district court entered judgment, the court of appeals decided to disregard it. Noting that the biological opinion was not part of the record, the court said that the Navy's opponent should have the opportunity to challenge the adequacy of the opinion, both in terms of its factual basis and its recommendations.[115]

---

[109] North Slope Borough v. Andrus, 486 F. Supp. 332, 356 (D.D.C. 1980), *aff'd* 642 F.2d 589 (D.C. Cir. 1980).

[110] *Id.*, 486 F. Supp. at 356.

[111] 43 U.S.C. §§1331 *et seq.* (1988).

[112] North Slope Borough v. Andrus, *supra* note 109, 642 F.2d at 611.

[113] Village of False Pass v. Watt, *supra* note 107, at 1163. *See* California v. Watt, 520 F. Supp. 1359, 1387 (C.D. Cal. 1985), *aff'd in part and rev'd in part,* 683 F.2d 1253 (9th Cir. 1982), *rev'd sub nom.* Secretary of the Interior v. California, 464 U.S. 312 (1984); Conservation Law Foundation v. Andrus, 623 F.2d 712, 714–15 (1st Cir. 1979); *accord,* No Oilport! v. Carter, 520 F. Supp. 334, 365 (W.D. Wash. 1981).

[114] Enos v. Marsh, 769 F.2d 1363, 1369 (9th Cir. 1985).

[115] Romero-Barcelo v. Brown, 643 F. 2d 835, 858 (1st Cir. 1981), *rev'd on other grounds, sub nom.* Weinberger v. Romero-Barcelo, 456 U.S. 305 (1982).

Equally futile was the Forest Service's use of a tardy biological assessment for its timber road in a national forest. The assessment was completed after oral argument but before decision in the district court. On brief, the Forest Service characterized the assessment, but did not submit it to the court; the Service refused to show it to the conservation groups. The Ninth Circuit ruled against the Service. Although the court favored granting an injunction, it remanded the case so that the district court could examine the biological assessment.[116]

Federal agencies have been more successful when a biological assessment, though late, is completed in time for the district court to consider it. In a later decision, the Ninth Circuit emphasized that an environmental assessment was untimely although, for jurisdictional reasons, the court did not reach the merits of the Endangered Species Act issues.[117] In another case, the federal agency did not complete an environmental assessment until after it granted a right-of-way for a pipeline route. The court brushed this aside, noting that construction would not be permitted until the pipeline complied with the Act.[118]

## The Duty to Reinitiate Consultations

The regulations require federal agencies to reinitiate consultations "upon the receipt of new information that may affect endangered species."[119] For example, when the government sells leases for off-shore oil and gas projects, it is not able to predict all the impacts of drilling and exploration. Later, "[i]f new information develops which indicates that an endangered species might be threatened," the Act "would prohibit the further irreversible or irretrievable commitment of resources until consultation is reinitiated and a new biological opinion prepared."[120]

Citing the regulation, one court halted the Corps of Engineers' plan for a flood control project in Southern California. The Fish and Wildlife Service objected to the original plan because it would have destroyed 40 acres of California marshland, the habitat of endangered birds. To satisfy the Service's objections, the Corps agreed to have 188 acres of nearby wetlands transferred from private ownership to a publicly owned wildlife refuge for the birds. In 1981 the Service issued a "final opinion" approving the project.[121] But the Corps' woes were not over. To speed construction, the project's local sponsor, San Diego County, agreed to obtain the 188 acres and transfer it to the federal

---

[116] Thomas v. Peterson, 753 F.2d 754 (9th Cir. 1985).

[117] Save the Yaak Comm. v. Block, 840 F.2d 714 (9th Cir. 1988).

[118] No Oilport! v. Carter, *supra* note 113, at 364–65.

[119] *See* Sierra Club v. Lyng, 694 F. Supp. 1260, 1269 (E.D. Tex. 1988) (dictum), *rev'd on other grounds sub nom.* Sierra Club v. Yeutter, 926 F.2d 429 (5th Cir. 1991). *See also* 50 C.F.R. §402.16(b) (1990).

[120] *Cf.* Village of False Pass v. Watt, *supra* note 107, 565 F. Supp. at 1155 (citing Act §7(d), 16 U.S.C. §1536 (1988)).

[121] *See* Sierra Club v. Marsh, 816 F.2d 1376, 1379 (9th Cir. 1987).

government. By 1986, the County still had not performed. When the Service asked the Corps to reinitiate consultations, the Corps refused. The court ruled that the Corps had violated the law by refusing to reinitiate consultation.[122]

There are three other situations in which the regulations provide for consultations to be reinitiated: (1) when the agency's project is subsequently modified in a manner that causes an effect that was not considered in the agency opinion,[123] (2) when the project causes incidental "takings" that exceed expectations,[124] and (3) when the project affects newly listed species or newly designated habitat.[125]

* * *

Section 7 expresses the Act's policy of "institutionalized caution."[126] It makes the Secretary "an advocate within the bureaucratic system,"[127] whose role is to be our environmental nanny. Because the current Secretary believes the Act is overbalanced in favor of protection at the expense of development, he is calling for a reorientation of his statutory task.[128]

---

[122] *Id.* at 1388.
[123] 50 C.F.R. §402.16(c) (1990).
[124] *Id.* §412.16(a).
[125] *Id.* §402.16(d).
[126] Tennessee Valley Auth. v. Hill, 437 U.S. 153, 194 (1978).
[127] Rosenberg, *Federal Protection of Unique Environmental Interests: Endangered and Threatened Species,* 58 N.C. L. REV., 491, 495 (1980).
[128] *See* the first paragraph of this chapter.

# Chapter 6

# Exceptions and Exemptions Under Sections 7 and 9

In passing the Endangered Species Act of 1973, the Eighty-Ninth Congress "was . . . aware of certain instances in which exceptions to the statute's broad sweep would be necessary" and created "a number of limited 'hardship exemptions.'"[1] Since then, Congress has added other exceptions. All the exceptions to sections 7 and 9 of the Act, however, remain "extraordinarily narrow."[2]

## Hardship Cases

There is no general hardship exemption in the Act. The limited "hardship exemptions" specified in the statute are "the only 'hardship cases' Congress intended to exempt."[3] In the *Hill* case, for example, the Supreme Court held that the Act required halting completion of an almost-finished dam, notwithstanding "the loss of millions of unrecoverable dollars."[4] Similarly, another court upheld regulations requiring the shrimp boat industry to install turtle excluder devices on its fish nets, at a cost of $5.9 million. That court said:

> Congress has decided that these losses cannot compare to the 'incalculable' value of genetic heritage embodied in any protected living species. While we do not mean to imply that economic impact can never be considered in determining whether a particular regulation promulgated under [the Act] is arbitrary or capricious, the protections afforded by the regulations before us have not been shown to be achievable through less costly means. Thus, the costs shouldered by the industry are not arbitrary, but reasonably related to Congress' purpose.[5]

Nonetheless, Congress has not been entirely insensitive to the hardships of persons who have been "taking" or trading in a species that becomes protected. Congress recognized that those persons may need a period of adjustment after being notified by a Federal Register notice that a species is to be listed.

---

[1] Tennessee Valley Auth. v. Hill, 437 U.S. 153, 188 (1978).

[2] United States v. Billie, 667 F. Supp. 1485, 1488 (S.D. Fla. 1987).

[3] Tennessee Valley Auth. v. Hill, *supra* note 1.

[4] *Id.* at 187.

[5] Louisiana v. Verity, 853 F.2d 322, 331 (5th Cir. 1988) (quoting Tennessee Valley Auth. v. Hill, *supra* note 1, at 179) (footnotes omitted).

The Secretary is permitted, under section 10(b), to issue a limited exemption to persons showing undue economic hardship.[6]

An experienced commentator on the Act pointed out that the Secretary's authority is "of little practical significance" since the exemption cannot extend beyond one year from the date of the Federal Register notice,[7] and, except in emergency situations, "listings are seldom finalized within such one-year period."[8]

## Projects Designed for Scientific Purposes or Species' Survival

Under section 10(a), the Secretary can exempt transactions from section 9 if they are "for scientific purposes" or will "enhance the propagation or survival of affected species."[9]

The exemption is not automatic; the Secretary must issue a special permit. In the case of the Cayman Turtle Farm, a British West Indies facility that bred green sea turtles in captivity for scientific and commercial purposes, the farm was no longer able to export its turtle products for sale in the U.S. when the U.S. government classified the green sea turtle as a threatened species. The turtle farm fought the government regulation on the ground that, as applied to the farm, it was contrary to the exemption of section 10(a).[10] The farm lost in both the district court and on appeal. On appeal, however, the concurring judge observed that "if the existence of appellant's farm furthers 'scientific purposes' or 'enhance[s] the propagation or survival of the . . . species,' then the Secretaries of Interior and Commerce have discretion to permit the importation into and sale in the United States of products of the species."[11]

The Secretary's regulations[12] provide for requests under this exemption. They also give examples of conduct that enhances the propagation or survival of wildlife in captivity, including population management tactics such as culling, contraception, and euthanasia. The Secretary's examples also include educational exhibitions of live wildlife, as well as the holding and trading of wildlife that is not ready for scientific purposes or propagation.

The Secretary's discretion to grant an exemption is limited. The exemption must be applied for in good faith, and it must be demonstrated to the Secretary that an exemption will not lead to the species' disadvantage. In addition, the

---

[6] Pub. L. No. 93-205, §10(b), 87 Stat. 884, 896 (1973) (codified in 16 U.S.C. §1539(b) (1988)).

[7] Pub. L. No. 93-205 §10(b)(1)(A), 87 Stat. 884, 896 (1973), (codified in 16 U.S.C. §1539(b)(1)(A) (1988)).

[8] M. Bean, *The Evolution of National Wildlife Law* 349 (New York: Praeger Scientific, 1983).

[9] Pub. L. No. 93-205, §10(a), 87 Stat. 884, 896 (1973), (codified in 16 U.S.C. §1539(a)(1)(A))(1988).

[10] Cayman Turtle Farm v. Andrus, 478 F. Supp. 125, 129, 131–34 (D.D.C. 1979), *aff'd mem.*, D.C. Cir. No. 79-2031 (Dec. 12, 1980).

[11] *Id.*

[12] 50 C.F.R. §§17.3, 17.22 (1990).

Secretary must find that the exemption is consistent with the Act's purposes and policies, including the goal of conservation.[13]

## Alaskan Subsistence and Authentic Native Handicrafts

Alaska's Senator Stevens was one of the Senate managers of the 1973 Act and many of its amendments. Alaska's Senator Murkowski is still a member of the Senate committee that oversees endangered species legislation. It is therefore not surprising that the legislation is solicitous of Alaska's unique problems.

Section 10(e) is an exemption for Alaska's native residents and non-natives who permanently reside in Alaskan native villages.[14] Such persons may take endangered and threatened species if they do so primarily for subsistence purposes. The Alaskan natives and some of the nonresidents may also sell nonedible byproducts of species when made into authentic native articles of handcrafts and clothing.

The exemption is self-executing. It is effective without the Secretary issuing any order. The Secretary, however, may regulate the "taking" if it materially harms the species.

## Species Held in Captivity When They Attained Protected Status

In the 1973 Act, Congress exempted an entire class of wildlife from the prohibitions of Section 9—fish and animals held in captivity or in a controlled environment on December 28, 1973, the date when the Act became effective.[15] In later amendments, Congress extended this exemption to wildlife that is so held on the date when it is listed as endangered or threatened.[16]

This exemption, however, is not valid if the specimen is held, on those dates or thereafter, in the course of a commercial activity.[17] The Cayman Turtle Farm could not qualify its pre-1973 turtles because they were held for commercial as well as scientific purposes.[18] After Ray Kepler was convicted for transporting a cougar and a leopard across state lines, he could not overturn his conviction by claiming that the animals had been lawfully held in captivity since before the Act's passage. Kepler negated the exemption because he planned to sell the animals to a zoo.[19]

---

[13] Pub. L. No. 93-205, §10(d), 87 Stat. 884, 896–97 (1973), (codified in 16 U.S.C. §1539(d) (1988)).

[14] Pub. L. No. 93-205, §10(e), 87 Stat. 884, 897 (1973), (codified in 16 U.S.C. §1539(e) (1988)). The statutory language is defined partially in section 10(e)(3) and partially in 50 C.F.R. §17.3 (1990).

[15] Pub. L. No. 93-205, §9(b), 87 Stat. 884, 894 (1973).

[16] 16 U.S.C. §1538(b)(1) (1988).

[17] *Id.*

[18] Cayman Turtle Farm v. Andrus, *supra* note 10.

[19] United States v. Kepler, 531 F.2d 796 (6th Cir. 1976).

In its regulations,[20] the Fish and Wildlife Service offers two more examples of transactions which do not qualify for the pre-Act exemption. The first example is:

> On January 25, 1974, a tourist buys a stuffed hawksbill turtle (an endangered species listed since June 1970) in a foreign country. On December 28, 1973, the stuffed turtle had been on display for sale. The tourist imports the stuffed turtle into the United States on January 26, 1974. This is a violation of the Act since the stuffed turtle was held for commercial purposes on December 28, 1973.

The second example is:

> On January 15, 1974, a hunter kills a leopard legally in Africa. He has the leopard mounted and imports it into the United States in June 1974. This importation is a violation of the Act since the leopard was not in captivity or a controlled environment on December 28, 1973.

The distinction between commercial and noncommercial holdings is illustrated by two more cases, both concerning English antiques that contained tortoise shell from the hawksbill turtle. In one case, a woman purchased an antique clock in England in 1969 for her own use, so her husband was able to claim the pre-Act exemption to justify importing the clock in 1975.[21] In the second case, a London dealer owned an antique lorgnette when the Act was passed, and subsequently sold it to a buyer who later imported it into the United States. Since the dealer had held the antique in the course of commercial activity, the lorgnette was ruled to be ineligible for the exemption.[22]

The Secretary's regulations, however, provide an exemption for transactions in captive breeding of non-native wildlife that are designed to enhance the propagation or survival of the species.[23]

## The Pre-Act Species Parts Exemption

The 1976 Act was devoted primarily to providing a hardship exemption to scrimshaw artisans. The art of scrimshaw originated with New England whalers, who used whale bone to carve figures and etch designs. Under the 1973 Act, whales were an endangered species, and trade in whale scrimshaw was prohibited. Citing the late President Kennedy's affection for his own scrimshaw collection, Senator Ted Kennedy introduced legislation to enable scrimshanders to dispose of their stocks.[24]

---

[20] 50 C.F.R. §17.4 (1990).

[21] U.S. Fish and Wildlife Service v. Lewis, DOI Dkt. No. Portland 78-2 (ALJ ID dated June 6, 1978).

[22] U.S. Fish and Wildlife Service v. Fortunoff's Silver Sales, DOI Dkt. No. Boston 77-15 (ALJ ID dated Apr. 18, 1978).

[23] 50 C.F.R. §17.21(g) (1990).

[24] H.R. REP. NO. 823, 94th Cong., 2d Sess. 3–4 (1976), *reprinted in* 1976 U.S. CODE CONG. & ADMIN. NEWS 1685, 1686–87 [hereinafter 1976 House Report]; 122 CONG. REC. 20,162–63 (1976) (remarks of Sen. Kennedy).

The exemption[25] applies only if the scrimshaw product or its raw material was lawfully held in the United States in the course of a commercial activity on the date when the Act became effective. The Secretary is authorized to issue certificates of exemption, which were originally scheduled to last only three years. Under later legislation, the exemption was expanded and the Secretary is authorized to extend the certificates until October 1993.[26] Although the exemption originally extended to all qualifying scrimshaw, regardless of the owner, that is no longer true. Now, in order to benefit from the exemption, a person must have held the scrimshaw product or its raw material on October 13, 1982.[27]

The 1976 Act also included a second "pre-Act" exemption for sperm whale oil and its derivatives, if lawfully held in 1973 as part of a commercial activity. The exemption is designed to enable the U.S. General Services Administration to sell 14 million pounds of oil, stockpiled as a lubricant for emergencies.[28]

## Peregrine Falcons and Other Raptors

Since 1978 the Act has contained an exemption for captive bred raptors, or birds of prey.[29]

As noted earlier in this chapter, the 1973 Act exempted species—including raptors—that were held in captivity or a controlled environment on December 28, 1973. Congress was aware that biologists, conservationists, and falconers had been working to breed raptors in captivity. Congress wanted to exempt the captive-produced progeny of these pre-Act raptors, even if they were born after 1973. So it provided that section 9(a) (1) does not apply to raptors legally held in captivity or in a controlled environment on November 10, 1978, or to their progeny.[30]

The exemption expires when a raptor or its progeny is intentionally returned to the wild.[31] Congress wanted to encourage this replenishment of wild populations of raptors, particularly peregrine falcons. So it urged the Secretary to grant permits to breeders so that they can obtain additional brood stock from the wild. The breeders are to release the offspring of that breeding stock so that the overall wild population increases.[32]

---

[25] Pub. L. No. 94-359, §2, 90 Stat. 911 (1976).

[26] 16 U.S.C. §1539(f)(8)(A)(i) (1988).

[27] *Id.* at §1539(f)(8)(D).

[28] 1976 House Report, *supra* note 24, at 4–5, 1976 U.S. CODE CONG. & ADMIN. NEWS at 1687.

[29] Pub. L. No. 95-632, §4, 92 Stat. 3751, 3760 (1978), (codified in 16 U.S.C. §1538(b)(2) (1988)). "A raptor is a bird of prey, such as falcons, hawks, eagles, ospreys, and owls." United States v. Doyle, 786 F.2d 1440, n.5 (9th Cir.), *cert. denied,* 479 U.S. 984 (1986).

[30] H.R. CONF. REP. NO. 1804, 95th Cong., 2d Sess. 23 (1978), *reprinted in* 1978 U.S. CODE CONG. & ADMIN. NEWS 9453, 9490–91 [hereinafter 1978 Conference Report].

[31] 16 U.S.C. §1538(b)(2)(A) (1988).

[32] 1978 Conference Report, *supra* note 30, at 23, 1978 U.S. CODE CONG. & ADMIN. NEWS at 9491.

## Antique Articles

In the 1978 Amendments, Congress also created an exemption for imports of antique articles which meet rigid requirements. As the statute reads today,[33] the articles must be at least 100 years old. They cannot have been repaired or modified with part of a protected species since the Act was passed. If imported, they must be submitted for Custom Service inspection at a designated port of entry.

## Noncommercial Transshipments

In 1982 Congress sought to solve the problem created when an international carrier accidentally lands in the United States with an endangered species shipment on board. In many past cases, the government seized the shipment and sought forfeiture.[34] Congress believed that the Act should "avoid unnecessarily harsh forfeiture actions in certain noncommercial import violations."[35] It therefore enacted a "narrow" exemption for shipments that were truly "accidental."[36]

The exemption[37] applies only to shipments of fish or wildlife, not to plants. To qualify, the shipment must meet six tests: (1) the fish or wildlife must have been lawfully taken and exported from the country of origin; (2) the shipment must be en route to a country where the fish and wildlife can be lawfully imported; (3) the owner or exporter must have done everything reasonably possible to prevent entry into the United States; (4) the entry into the United States must have been caused by circumstances outside the owner's or exporter's control; (5) there must be no violation of the Convention on International Trade in Endangered Species of Wild Fauna and Flora;[38] and (6) the importation must not be part of a commercial activity.

## Incidental "Takings"

In 1982, while Congress was considering new endangered species legislation, it knew that its actions would determine the fate of land development plans for the San Bruno Mountain near San Francisco.[39] The mountain was

---

[33] 16 U.S.C. §1539(h) (1985) (revising Pub. L. No. 95-632, §5, 92 Stat. 3751, 3760 (1978)).

[34] *E.g.*, United States v. 3,210 Crusted Sides of Caiman Crocodilus Yacare, 636 F. Supp. 1281 (S.D. Fla. 1986); Carpenter v. Andrus, 485 F. Supp. 320 (D. Del. 1980).

[35] H.R. CONF. REP. NO. 835, 97th Cong., 2d Sess. 32 (1982), *reprinted in* 1982 U.S. CODE CONG. & ADMIN. NEWS 2807, 2873 [hereinafter 1982 Conference Report].

[36] *Id.* at 33.

[37] Pub. L. No. 97-304, §6, 96 Stat. 1411, 1424 (1982), (codified in 16 U.S.C. §1539(i) (1988)).

[38] 1976, 27 U.S.T. 1087, T.I.A.S. No. 8249, *amended* June 22, 1979; T.I.A.S. No. 11079.

[39] Friends of Endangered Species, Inc. v. Jantzen, 760 F.2d 976 (9th Cir. 1985).

inhabited by the mission blue butterfly, a species threatened with extinction because its grassland habitat would inevitably be lost to encroaching bush. The San Bruno development project offered to ensure the butterfly's survival by creating permanent open space as undisturbed habitat. Blessed by local governments and state conservation officials, the San Bruno development plan was viewed as a paradigm approach to reconciling conservation and development.

Nonetheless, the San Bruno plan risked violating section 9 because it would inevitably result in incidental "takings" of some butterflies. Congress wanted to correct this problem. In addition, it wanted to resolve an analogous problem for federal projects approved by the Secretary under section 7. The 1982 Amendments created two separate mechanisms to achieve these ends.

## Takings for Federal Projects

For federal agencies, section 9 posed an "apparent trap."[40] Before approving a federal project under section 7, the Secretary engages in a lengthy process to assure that the project is not likely to jeopardize the continued existence of any endangered or threatened species. What was the status of a no-jeopardy project, approved under section 7, that resulted in incidental "takings"? Federal agencies feared that—if they proceeded with such a no-jeopardy project—they might be criminally liable for violating section 9's prohibition against *any* "taking" of endangered wildlife.

To eliminate this apparent conflict between sections 7 and 9, Congress decided to provide federal agencies (and any nonfederal associate) with a statutory assurance that those unintentional takings will not subject them to penalties under section 9.[41]

As crafted in the 1982 Amendments, Congress' assurance had several parts. One new provision[42] authorizes the Secretary, after consultations under section 7, to provide a federal agency with a written statement of the incidental taking that is contemplated. For purposes of section 9, that taking "shall not be considered to be a prohibited taking of the species concerned."[43] In his written statement, the Secretary is required to specify the taking's impact on the species, the measures for minimizing that impact, and any other conditions imposed.

The courts will not allow federal agencies to immunize themselves by obtaining an incidental taking statement from the Secretary after the taking occurs. If an agency wants to rely upon the Secretary's statement, it "must have this written authorization before proceeding with action that results in an

---

[40] M. Bean, S. Fitzgerald, and M. O'Connell, *Reconciling Conflicts Under the Endangered Species Act* 5 (Washington, D.C.: World Wildlife Fund, 1991).

[41] H.R. REP. NO. 567, 97th Cong., 2d Sess. 26 (1982), 1982 U.S. CODE CONG. & ADMIN. NEWS 2807, 2826 [hereinafter 1982 House Report] and 1982 Conference Report, *supra* note 35, at 27, 1982 U.S. CODE CONG. & ADMIN. NEWS at 2807, 2868.

[42] Pub. L. No. 97-304, §4, 96 Stat. 1411, 1418, 1420 (1982), (codified in 16 U.S.C. §1536(b)(4), (o)(1988)).

[43] *Id.* at 16 U.S.C. §1536(o).

incidental taking."[44] Thus, the Eighth Circuit held that the Environmental Protection Agency's pesticide regulations, which led to the poisoning of protected species, constituted takings notwithstanding the Secretary's issuance of an incidental taking statement. The Secretary's statement, the court held, "does not retroactively excuse the takings that occurred before the Secretary issued the statement."[45]

Some federal actions concern the grant of a license or permit to a private party (or, perhaps, to a local government body). In those cases, the federal agency can consult with the Secretary under section 7 at the nonfederal party's request and with its cooperation.[46] The Secretary can then issue an incidental taking statement to the agency and the nonfederal applicant, immunizing the latter's incidental takings.[47]

## Takings for Nonfederal Projects

A different device was necessary for projects like San Bruno Mountain, undertaken by private developers who had no need for a federal clearance under section 7.

For these private land owners, Congress designed a solution through the permit provisions of section 10.[48] The Secretary is authorized to issue permits to individuals who demonstrate that the taking of an endangered species will be incidental to, but not the purpose of, their activities. Armed with the permit, the recipient is allowed to "take" endangered species without violating section 9.[49]

Congress intended that private developers are to get permits only if they make real environmental concessions. Applicants for a permit must submit "a conservation plan" showing that:[50]

- They will minimize and mitigate the impacts of the taking to the maximum extent practical
- They will ensure that adequate funds will be available to finance the conservation plan
- Their takings will not appreciably reduce the likelihood of the species' survival and recovery in the wild

---

[44] Defenders of Wildlife v. Administrator, Environmental Protection Agency, 882 F.2d 1294, 1300 (8th Cir. 1989).

[45] *Id.* at 1301. *Cf.* National Wildlife Fed'n v. Hodel, 23 ER Cases 1089, 1092–93 (E.D. Cal. 1985).

[46] 16 U.S.C. §1536(a)(3) (1988).

[47] Pub. L. No. 97-304, §4, 96 Stat. 1411, 1418, 1420 (1982), (codified in 16 U.S.C. §1536(b)(4), (o) (1988)).

[48] 16 U.S.C. §1539 (1988).

[49] Pub. L. No. 97-304, §6, 96 Stat. 1411, 1422 (1982), (codified at 16 U.S.C. §1539(a)(1)(B) (1988)). *See also* 1982 House Report, *supra* note 41, at 31, 1982 U.S. CODE CONG. & ADMIN. NEWS at 2831.

[50] *Id.*, 16 U.S.C. at §1539(a)(2).

Not surprisingly, the San Bruno Mountain project received the first permit issued under the new law. Notwithstanding protests from environmentalists, a court sustained the Secretary's decision to allow incidental takings connected with that project.[51]

So far, requests for incidental-take permits have concerned only land development, mostly in California. Including the San Bruno Mountain project, only seven incidental-take permits have been issued to private developers. Only 20 or so projects are under development.[52] Some observers believe that the procedure is appropriate for such activities as timber harvesting, grazing, pesticide spraying, and conversion of pasture to cropland.[53]

## Experimental Populations

In another part of the 1982 Amendments, Congress created a special status for "experimental populations." Black-footed ferrets—small weasel-like carnivores—are one example of an experimental population. The last known wild population of black-footed ferrets was discovered on a Wyoming ranch in 1981. After disease nearly wiped out the species in 1985–86, the government collected the last 18 ferrets to prevent the species' extinction. A captive breeding program increased the population to 300. Using a Wyoming wildlife management area, the government released 20 of these captive-raised ferrets in 1991, and more later, in an attempt to reestablish the species in the wild.[54]

Like the black-footed ferret, all experimental populations are composed of individual members of an imperiled species, usually bred in captivity, that are released into the wild. Before 1982, industry and landowners were reluctant to allow experimental populations on their land, fearing that the Act's prohibitions would then jeopardize development of their land. Wanting to calm these concerns, Congress added the experimental population provisions to the Endangered Species Act Amendments of 1982.[55]

Only the Secretary can create an experimental population and authorize its release into the wild.[56] The experimental population may be released outside the species' current range, but it must be kept geographically separate from the native populations of the same species.[57]

Experimental populations are not regarded as "endangered" species. Because of this, they are not entitled to section 9's protections unless the Secretary adopts a regulation conferring these protections. If the experimental

---

[51] Friends of Endangered Species, Inc. v. Jantzen, 760 F. 2d 976 (9th Cir. 1985).

[52] *See* Bean, *supra* note 40, at vii.

[53] *Id.* at xi.

[54] 56 Fed. Reg. 23,830 (1991) (to be codified in 50 C.F.R. §17.84).

[55] Pub. L. No. 97-304, §6, 96 Stat. 1411, 1422 (1982), (codified in 16 U.S.C. §1539(j)). *See* 1982 House Report, *supra* note 41, at 17, 31, 1982 U.S. CODE CONG. & ADMIN. NEWS at 2817, 2831; 1982 Conference Report, *supra* note 35, at 29, 33–34, U.S. CODE CONG. & ADMIN. NEWS at 2870, 2874–75.

[56] 16 U.S.C. §1539(j)(2) (1988).

[57] *Id.* §1539(j)(1)–(2)(A).

population inhabits a national park or wildlife refuge, or if the Secretary finds the population to be essential to the species' survival, it is treated as a threatened species. Otherwise, for purposes of section 7, it is treated as a candidate species, proposed-to-be-listed under section 4.[58] Congress intended that all experimental populations be treated as threatened,[59] thus giving the Secretary discretion about the degree of their protection.[60]

## The Endangered Species Committee

In 1978, Congress established an Endangered Species Committee empowered to grant exemptions from the Act.[61] This process "was intended to be a recourse of the last resort."[62] It is available only when the Secretary has found, after consultation, that a project will violate section 7's "no-jeopardy" mandate.[63]

The Endangered Species Committee is composed of six members of the President's cabinet and subcabinet, plus a representative from each affected state.[64] The Committee can grant an exemption if it finds, after hearing, that:[65]

- There are "no reasonable or prudent alternatives to the agency action"
- The project's benefits "clearly outweigh" the pro-conservation alternative
- The project is in the public interest
- The project is of regional or national significance
- No irreversible or irretrievable commitment of resources has been made on the project's behalf.

Among these criteria, the most important is the first. It requires the Committee to make a "positive finding" that there are *no* reasonable and prudent pro-conservation alternatives to the project.[66] The legislative history does not expressly state that a reasonable and prudent alternative is one which precludes jeopardy to the species or the destruction or adverse modification of its habitat.

---

[58] *Id.* §1539(j)(2)(C)(i). *See* 1982 Conference Report, *supra* note 35, at 33–35, 1982 U.S. CODE CONG. & ADMIN. NEWS at 2874–76.

[59] 1982 Conference Report, *supra* note 35, at 34, 1982 U.S. CODE CONG. & ADMIN. NEWS at 2875.

[60] *See* Chapters 3 and 4.

[61] Pub. L. No. 95-632, §3, 92 Stat. 3751, 3753–60 (1978), (codified as amended at 16 U.S.C. §1536(e)–(p) (1988).

[62] M. Bean, *The Evolution of National Wildlife Law* 371 (New York: Praeger Scientific, 1983).

[63] 16 U.S.C. §1536(g)(1) (1988).

[64] *Id.* §1536(e)(3), (g)(2)(B).

[65] *Id.* §1536(h)(1)(A).

[66] Memorandum from Associate Solicitor, Fish and Wildlife, to the Endangered Species Committee, regarding statutory standard and criteria for granting an exception for the Tellico or Graylocks Dam (Jan. 19, 1979).

"However, the intent of the legislative history forcefully implies this conclusion . . . as does the very structure of . . . section 7 and the purposes of the Act in section 2."[67]

The Committee's task is to use "a balancing approach taking into account all relevant environmental, economic, and cultural factors."[68] By telling the Committee to decide whether there are "reasonable" alternatives to the agency action, Congress meant to permit

> members of the Endangered Species Committee to consider a wide range of factors. It is the intent of the Environmental and Public Works Committee that the Cabinet-level panel . . . in evaluating alternatives examine not only engineering 'feasibility,' but also environmental and community impacts, economic feasibility and, other relevant factors.[69]

If a pro-conservation alternative is not "reasonable and prudent," the Committee would have to determine whether, even so, that alternative's benefits are "clearly outweigh[ed]" by those of the agency action. "Only then could [the Committee] grant an exemption. The legislative history indicates an especially broad definition of 'benefits' to allow the Committee to consider any ecological, economic or cultural fact deemed relevant."[70]

If the Committee grants an exemption from the Act, it must establish measures to minimize the project's adverse effects upon the species and its habitat.[71] The Committee's action, which must be based "on the record,"[72] is subject to judicial review.[73]

If the Committee favors the project, it can grant an exemption from both section 7's "no-jeopardize" prohibition and from section 9's "taking" prohibition.[74] The section 7 exemption is permanent with respect to all endangered or threatened species, with some exceptions.[75]

The Secretary of State can veto an exemption if the project would violate an international treaty or obligation.[76] The Secretary of Defense can compel the Committee to grant an exemption if it is necessary for national defense reasons.[77] And the President can dictate Committee decisions in the case of repairs to public facilities in presidentially declared disaster areas.[78]

The Committee procedure is so cumbersome that it does not invite use. Created in response to the *Hill* Court's halting of the Tellico Dam,[79] the

---

[67] *Id.* (citing 1978 Conference Report, *supra* note 30, at 20–21, 1978 U.S. CODE CONG. & ADMIN. NEWS at 9487–89).

[68] *Id.*

[69] 124 CONG. REC. 21,590 (1978) (remarks of Sen. Baker).

[70] Memorandum from Associate Solicitor, Fish and Wildlife, *supra* note 66.

[71] 16 U.S.C. §1536(h)(1)(B) (1988).

[72] *Id.* §1536(h)(1)(A).

[73] *Id.* §1536(n).

[74] *Id.* §1536(h)(1), (o).

[75] *Id.* §1536(h)(2).

[76] *Id.* §1536(i).

[77] *Id.* §1536(j).

[78] *Id.* §1536(p).

[79] Tennessee Valley Auth. v. Hill, 437 U.S. 153 (1978). *See* Chapters 1 and 2.

Committee procedure was rarely invoked.[80] Despite this bleak history, the Secretary of the Interior convened the Committee in 1991 with a request to permit logging in Oregon's old-growth forests, home of the spotted owl. In May 1992, the Committee voted 5 to 2 to allow logging in a portion of the acreage. Branded by some as "a largely symbolic attempt to please both logging and environmental interests," the Committee's decision "instead irritated both."[81]

The spotted owl is only one of several species whose protection threatens economic development. The delta smelt's survival may depend on curtailing California's water supplies from the Sacramento-San Joaquin River estuaries.[82] Hydroelectric dams along the Snake River may have to curb their practices in order to preserve the river's sockeye salmon.[83] To deal with these problems, an Endangered Species Committee-type mechanism could see a rebirth.

---

[80] Bean, *supra* note 62, at 370–71; *"God Squad" to Ponder Spotted Owl*, WASHINGTON POST, Oct. 21, 1991, at A17.

[81] *Panel Allows Logging in Site Vital to Owl*, WALL STREET JOURNAL, May 15, 1992, at A3.

[82] 56 Fed. Reg. 50,075 (1991); *Little Fish May Put California in Hot Water*, WALL STREET JOURNAL, July 10, 1991, at B1.

[83] *U.S. Designates Sockeye Salmon an Endangered Species*, WASHINGTON POST, Nov. 15, 1991, at A1.

# Chapter 7

# Enforcement and Penalties

Glacier National Park overlooks the Montana sheep farm where, on a July night in 1982, Richard Christy saw another grizzly bear about to attack his sheep. For over a week, bears from the park had hunted down Christy's herd every night, killing 20 sheep. Earlier, Christy's herder had failed in his attempts to frighten the bears away by building fires and shooting a gun in the air. This time Christy picked up his rifle and fired two shots, killing the bear. For violating the Act, Christy was assessed a $2,500 civil penalty, a penalty that the Supreme Court let stand.[1]

Christy was lucky that the bear was listed as only a threatened species. If the bear had been classified as endangered, Christy could have been assessed a criminal fine, jailed, or both. These and other options for enforcing the Act are this chapter's subject.

## Jurisdiction and Venue

The government chose to bring charges against Christy in an administrative forum. It could have brought an action in court: Federal district courts have jurisdiction over any actions arising under the Act.[2]

Having chosen administrative proceedings, the Secretary was required to accord Christy a full-fledged hearing, conducted in accordance with Administrative Procedure Act section 5.[3] If Christy refused to pay the penalty, the Attorney General could have sued to collect it.[4] The Attorney General may bring his lawsuit in a federal district court located in any district in which the person is found, resides, or does business. That district court has jurisdiction to hear and decide the case.[5]

---

[1] Christy v. Hodel, 857 F.2d 1324 (9th Cir. 1988), *cert. denied sub nom.* Christy v. Lujan, 490 U.S. 1114 (1989).

[2] 16 U.S.C. §1540(c) (1988).

[3] *Id.* §1540(a)(2) (referring to 5 U.S.C. §554 (1988)).

[4] *Id.* §1540(a).

[5] *Id.*

## Civil Money Penalties

The Secretary has considerable discretion about the civil penalties assessed. The stiffest penalties are reserved for persons who knowingly violate the Act. As Christy's case illustrates, the amount of penalties can also depend on whether the infraction concerns an endangered species or a threatened one. Thus, the Act establishes one level of civil penalties for knowing violations of section 9 provisions or regulations, concerning endangered species. For such infractions, violators may be assessed penalties up to $25,000 for each violation.[6]

Christy violated the "grizzly bear regulations."[7] The Secretary issued those regulations under section 4(d),[8] concerning threatened species, rather than under section 9. Because of this, Christy was not subject to the civil penalties cited in the last paragraph. Knowing violations of regulations like the grizzly bear regulations are punishable by a maximum civil penalty of $12,000 for each violation.[9] This is the penalty provision applied in Christy's case.

For inadvertent violations, the civil penalty cannot exceed $500 for each violation.[10]

## Violations As "Knowing"

Christy could not have escaped the large money penalty by pleading ignorance of the bear's protected status. "[I]gnorance of the law," the Supreme Court said,[11] "is no defense." The Endangered Species Act embodies this rule. It is true that the 1973 Act prescribed criminal penalties only for a person who "willfully" violated the Act.[12] In the Endangered Species Act Amendments of 1978, however, Congress made both civil and criminal penalties applicable if the person "knowingly" commits a violation.[13] The conference committee said that Congress did "not intend to make knowledge of the law an element of either civil penalty or criminal violations of the Act."[14]

Commercial importers and exporters can incur civil penalties for violating the Act even if the violation is not knowing. The 1978 Amendment[15] "subjects importers and exporters of fish and wildlife and plants to strict liability penalties

---

[6] *Id.*

[7] Christy v. Hodel, *supra* note 1, 857 F.2d at n.1.

[8] 16 U.S.C. §1533(d) (1988). *See* Chapter 3.

[9] *Id.* §1540(a).

[10] *Id.*

[11] United States v. International Minerals and Chemical Corp., 402 U.S. 558, 563 (1971).

[12] Pub. L. No. 93-205, §11 (b), 87 Stat. 884, 897–98 (1973).

[13] Pub. L. No. 95-632, §6, 92 Stat. 3751, 3761–62 (1978) (codified in 16 U.S.C. §1540(a)(1), (b)(1) (1988)).

[14] H.R. CONF. REP. NO. 1804, 95th Cong., 2d Sess. 26 (1978), *reprinted in* 1978 U.S. CODE CONG. & ADMIN. NEWS 9453, 9494 [hereinafter 1978 Conference Report].

[15] *Supra* note 13.

. . ." for noncriminal violations.[16] Even before the 1978 Amendments, the Act held commercial operators to a higher standard than others, but the 1978 Amendments made them "strictly liable."[17]

## Defense of Persons or Property

Christy tried to escape liability by pleading that he shot the bear in order to protect his property—an imaginative defense. Congress exempted persons from civil penalties if they could prove that they acted to protect themselves or others from bodily harm. This provision was added to the Act in 1978.[18]

But, as a court remarked in 1986:

> No similar statutory defense exculpates actions to protect property. Several state courts have held that, as a matter of state constitutional law, a person may kill wildlife contrary to the state's conservation laws where such action is necessary to protect his property. . . . No case has yet addressed whether a similar right exists under the United States Constitution, though the bodily injury defense contained in the Endangered Species Act suggests a congressional view that it does not.[19]

That was the state of the law when Christy raised his rifle. After Christy went to court to protest his $2,500 penalty, the district court and the court of appeals ruled against him. The appeals court declined Christy's "invitation to construe the fifth amendment as guaranteeing the right to kill federally protected wildlife in defense of property."[20]

In the Supreme Court, Justice White dissented from the denial of Christy's petition for review. He believed that Christy's claim of a constitutional right to defend his property "is not insubstantial."[21] "Even more substantial," said the Justice, is Christy's "claim that the Endangered Species Act operates as a governmental authorization of a 'taking' of his property. . . . [P]erhaps a government edict barring one from resisting the loss of his property is the constitutional equivalent of an edict taking such property in the first place."[22] Notwithstanding Justice White's views, Christy's case establishes that harming wildlife is not an acceptable way to protect property.

---

[16] 1978 Conference Report, *supra* note 14, at 26, 1978 U.S. CODE CONG. & ADMIN. NEWS at 9493.

[17] Newell v. Baldridge, 548 F. Supp. 39, 43 (W.D. Wash. 1982).

[18] Pub. L. No. 95-632, §§7, 8, 92 Stat. 3751, 3762 (1978) (codified in 16 U.S.C. §1540(a)(3), (b)(3) (1988)).

[19] Mountain States Legal Foundation v. Hodel, 799 F. 2d 1423, 1428 n.8 (10th Cir. 1986) (dictum), *cert. denied*, 480 U.S. 951 (1987).

[20] Christy v. Hodel, *supra* note 1, 857 F.2d at 1330.

[21] *Id.*, 490 U.S. at 1115.

[22] *Id.* at 1115–16.

## Forfeiture

In addition to money assessments, the government can impose other penalties. The Act specifies that wrongfully acquired fish, wildlife, or plants are subject to forfeiture.[23] Congress intended the Act's civil forfeiture provisions to be the preferred remedy for innocent violations by tourists and hunters.[24]

Before declaring a civil forfeiture, the government must show that grounds exist for assessment of a civil penalty.[25] That rule underlies the case where a hunter shot a leopard legally in Kenya and directed the shipping agent not to send it to the United States. The agent mistakenly violated his instructions, but the hunter was deemed innocent of any misdeed. The government sought to seize the articles as contraband. Rejecting this approach, the court ruled "that forfeiture is [not] appropriate where . . . the owner of the property has no involvement whatsoever in the violation of the Act."[26]

Criminal acts are treated more harshly. The government is not limited to seizing fish, wildlife, and plants. It can also force a forfeiture of all equipment and means of transportation used to aid the illegal act.[27]

The Endangered Species Act incorporates[28] the procedural provisions of the customs laws regarding forfeiture.[29] As a consequence, the government must show probable cause to believe that a violation occurred. Once that is done, the private party has the burden of persuasion about innocence.[30]

## Criminal Penalties

The most serious penalties are reserved for criminal violations. Those entail knowing violations of the Act, of a license, or of a regulation issued under section 9. For such infractions, a violator may be fined up to $50,000 or imprisoned for up to one year, or both. Knowing violations of other regulations may result in fines of up to $25,000 or imprisonment for up to six months, or both.[31] The government has no hesitation about prosecuting poachers who kill animals like Florida panthers[32] or grizzly bears.[33]

---

[23] 16 U.S.C. §1540(e)(4)(A) (1988).

[24] Carpenter v. Andrus, 485 F. Supp. 320, 322–23 (D. Del. 1980) (citing H.R. CONF. REP. NO. 740, 93d Cong., 1st Sess. 28 (1973), *reprinted in* 1973 U.S. CODE CONG. & ADMIN. NEWS 2989, 3006; H.R. CONF. REP. NO. 1804, 95th Cong., 2d Sess. 26 (1978), *reprinted in* 1978 U.S. CODE CONG. & ADMIN. NEWS 9453, 9493).

[25] *Cf.* United States v. Species of Wildlife Consisting of a Fully Mounted Leopard, 404 F. Supp. 1298, 1300 (E.D.N.Y. 1975).

[26] Carpenter v. Andrus, *supra*, note 24 at 323.

[27] 16 U.S.C. §1540(e)(4)(B) (1988).

[28] *Id.* at §1540(e)(5).

[29] 19 U.S.C. §1594 *et seq.* (1988).

[30] United States v. 2,507 Live Canary Winged Parakeets, 689 F. Supp. 1106, 1113 (S.D. Fla. 1988); United States v. 3,210 Crusted Sides of Caiman Crocodilus, 636 F. Supp. 1281, 1284 (S.D. Fla. 1986).

[31] 16 U.S.C. §1540(b) (1988).

[32] United States v. Billie, 667 F. Supp. 1485 (S.D. Fla. 1987).

[33] United States v. St. Onge, 676 F. Supp. 1041 (D. Mont. 1987).

Persons can avoid conviction if their actions were based upon a good faith belief that they were protecting themselves or other persons from bodily harm.[34]

It is not necessary that the violation be motivated by criminal intent. As noted in the civil penalties discussion, the Endangered Species Act Amendments of 1978 made criminal penalties applicable if the person "knowingly" commits a violation.[35] The purpose of this amendment was to "make criminal violations of the act a general rather than a specific intent crime."[36]

Illustrating this is the story of a Vietnamese fishing boat captain, Oanh Vu Nguyan. After boarding Nguyan's fishing vessel for a routine inspection, the Coast Guard discovered parts of an endangered sea turtle. Nguyan and his crew had caught the turtle by accident in their shrimp nets. In the subsequent prosecution for violating the Act, the trial judge instructed the jury that they could convict Nguyan even if he did not know that his conduct was illegal or that the turtle was a threatened species. The jury convicted Nguyan, and the Court of Appeals affirmed, saying:

> Congress intended to make violations of [the Act] a general intent crime. Thus, it is sufficient that Nguyan knew that he was in possession of a turtle. The government was not required to prove that Nguyan knew that this turtle is a threatened species or that it is illegal to transport or import it. . . . Congress deliberately dispensed with a *mens rea* requirement for violations of that statute.[37]

Another court ruled that a tribal Indian can be convicted of killing an endangered panther without proof that he knew what kind of panther he had hunted. According to the court, "the Government need prove only that the defendant acted with general intent when he shot the animal in question."[38]

Criminal convictions bring administrative consequences as well. Once a person is convicted, federal agencies may immediately modify, suspend, or revoke export and import licenses, land-use leases, and related permits.[39]

## Injunctions

Before 1982, the Act did not specifically authorize the Attorney General to seek injunctive relief. So the Department of Justice chose not to seek that relief, preferring to prosecute completed violations. Criticizing this practice, Congress noted that "[i]njunctions provide a greater opportunity to attempt resolution of conflicts before harm to a species occurs."[40] In the Endangered

---

[34] 16 U.S.C. §1540(b)(3) (1988).

[35] Pub. L. No. 95-632, §6, 92 Stat. 3751, 3761 (1978).

[36] H. R. REP. NO. 1625, 95th Cong., 2d Sess. 26, *reprinted in* 1978 U.S. CODE CONG. & ADMIN. NEWS 9453, 9776.

[37] United States v. Nguyan, 916 F.2d 1016, 1018, 1019–20 (5th Cir. 1990). The court recognized that it could have affirmed on the narrow ground that Nguyen knew it was illegal to keep the turtle, but the court chose to reach the broader issue.

[38] United States v. Billie, *supra* note 32, at 1493 (footnote omitted).

[39] 16 U.S.C. §1540(b)(2) (1988).

[40] S. REP. NO. 418, 97th Cong., 2d Sess. 24 (1982).

Species Act Amendments of 1982,[41] Congress empowered the Attorney General to ask for injunctions.

## Citizen Suits

Before 1986 the Secretary had interpreted the Act as requiring consultation when federal agencies authorized, funded, or carried out projects in foreign countries. In that year, however, the Secretary rescinded this ruling. Two environmental organizations challenged the Secretary's turnabout in a lawsuit, *Defenders of Wildlife* v. *Hodel,* resulting in a Supreme Court decision.[42]

The Act makes a specific provision for lawsuits like the *Defenders* case. Section 11(g),[43] entitled "Citizen Suits," allows interested persons to sue in federal courts "to force compliance with any provision of the Act."[44] More specifically, the citizen suit provision allows civil suits:

- To enjoin any person (including the government) from violating the Act or a regulation;
- To compel the Secretary to apply most prohibitions against "taking" protected species within the United States; and
- To order the Secretary to perform any non-discretionary duty under section 4.[45]

This citizen suit provision "establishes a private right of action."[46]

## Jurisdiction and Venue

The federal courts have jurisdiction of this type of lawsuit because of two separate statutory provisions. The first, section 11(c),[47] gives federal district courts jurisdiction over any actions arising under the Act. The second, section 11(g) (1),[48] gives district courts jurisdiction to act in citizen suits.

When they filed *Defenders,* the two environmental organizations had to select a court that has "venue." For citizen suits, section 11(g) (3) (A)[49] requires

---

[41] Pub. L. No. 97-304, §7, 96 Stat. 1411, 1425 (1982) (codified in 16 U.S.C. §1540(e)(6) (1988)).

[42] Defenders of Wildlife v. Hodel, 658 F. Supp. 43 (D. Minn. 1987), *rev'd,* 851 F.2d 1035 (8th Cir. 1988). The appeals court later reaffirmed its decision, upholding the environmentalists' standing, but the Supreme Court reversed. Lujan v. Defenders of Wildlife, 60 U.S.L.W. 4495 (U.S. June 9, 1992), *rev'g,* 911 F.2d 117 (8th Cir. 1990).

[43] 16 U.S.C. §1540(g) (1988).

[44] Tennessee Valley Auth. v. Hill, 437 U.S. 153, 180–81 (1978).

[45] 16 U.S.C. §1533 (1988).

[46] Defenders of Wildlife v. Administrator, Environmental Protection Agency, 882 F.2d 1294, 1298 (8th Cir. 1989).

[47] 16 U.S.C. §1540(c) (1988).

[48] *Id.* §1540(g)(1).

[49] *Id.* §1540(g)(3)(A).

the lawsuit to be brought in the judicial district in which the violation occurs. This "is a venue provision only"; it confers no jurisdiction.[50]

## Justiciability

Under Article III of the Constitution,[51] the role of federal courts is limited to the resolution of "cases" and "controversies." One purpose of this limitation is to insure that courts do not intrude into areas committed to other branches of government. In *Defenders,* six Justices ruled that the environmental organizations could not satisfy the Article III test because they lacked "standing."

### *Standing*

Although Endangered Species Act Section 11(g) (1) says that "any person" may commence a citizen's suit, that right is limited to persons who have "standing." When a litigant's standing is disputed, the question is whether the litigant is a proper party to request adjudication of a particular issue, not whether the issue itself is justiciable.

In order to have standing under Article III, litigants must satisfy three tests. One of these three constitutional tests is the so-called "injury-in-fact" test. Under it, litigants must show that they personally suffered some "actual or imminent" injury as a result of the challenged action.[52] Environmentalists cannot satisfy this injury-in-fact test by arguing their strong interest in the enforcement of the Act. The assertion of a right to have the government act in accordance with law is not sufficient, by itself, to confer standing.[53] Litigants may be able to establish injury-in-fact by showing damage to a habitat they personally visit or depletion of wildlife they go to view[54] —but only if they have "concrete plans" to visit the imperiled territory.[55]

In some instances, environmentalists can satisfy the injury-in-fact test in a second way. This was by showing that the agency violated the litigants' procedural rights.[56] In order to satisfy the constitutional tests for standing, litigants

---

[50] Colorado River Water Conservation Dist. v. Andrus, 476 F. Supp. 966, 968 (D. Col. 1979).

[51] U.S. CONST. art. III, §2.

[52] Lujan v. Defenders of Wildlife, *supra* note 42, 60 U.S.L.W. at 4498; Humane Soc'y of the United States v. Hodel, 840 F.2d 45, 51 (D.C. Cir. 1988); *compare* Lujan v. National Wildlife Fed'n, 110 S. Ct. 3177 (1990) (where environmentalists submitted affidavits indicating recreational use and aesthetic enjoyment of land "in the vicinity" of affected acreage, this held to be insufficient showing of actual injury).

[53] Humane Soc'y of the United States v. Hodel, *supra* note 52, at 51.

[54] Humane Soc'y of the United States v. Hodel, *supra* note 52, at 52. *But compare* Lujan v. Defenders of Wildlife, *supra* note 42, 60 U.S.L.W. at 4497 (environmentalists must be "'directly' affected").

[55] Lujan v. Defenders of Wildlife, *supra* note 42, 60 U.S.L.W. at 4498.

[56] *Id.,* 60 U.S.L.W. at 4500, n. 7 (in the case of "a person who has been accorded a procedural right to protect his concrete interests").

must also demonstrate that their injury is caused by the challenged conduct, and that their injury is likely to be redressed by a favorable decision.[57]

In addition to constitutional requirements, courts impose policy limitations on the right to bring a citizen suit. Called "prudential standing," this test requires that the litigants' interests be within the zone of interests that the statute seeks to protect.[58] All that is required is a plausible relationship between the litigants' interests and the statute's policies. Activities like observing and studying wildlife are within the zone of interests protected by the Act.[59] Indeed, the Eighth Circuit says that Congress has eliminated the prudential requirement for standing in citizen suits under the Act.[60]

In *Defenders,* the lawsuit was instituted by the two environmentalist organizations, rather than by their individual members. In the lower court opinion, the judges suggested that Congress intended to give environmental organizations procedural rights to bring citizen suits on their own behalf.[61] The prevailing view, however, is that:

> [A]n association has standing to bring suit on behalf of its members when: (a) its members would otherwise have standing to sue in their own right; (b) the interests it seeks to protect are germane to the organization's purpose; and (c) neither the claim asserted nor the relief requested requires the participation of individual members in the lawsuit.[62]

The Supreme Court's decision in the *Defenders* case makes it harder for environmentalists to establish standing under the Act.[63] Before *Defenders,* environmentalists had great success in establishing standing to contest numerous government actions, including challenges to agency decisions that expanded hunting in wildlife refuges[64] and that permitted the continued use of toxic pesticides.[65] *Defenders* casts a cloud over the future. Indeed, the dissenters[66] characterize the Court's decision as a "slash-and-burn expedition through the law of environmental standing."[67]

---

[57] *Id.*, 60 U.S.L.W. at 4497, 4499-4500. Applying this principle are: National Wildlife Fed'n v. Burford, 878 F.2d 429 (D.C. Cir. 1989), *rev'd on other grounds sub nom.* Lujan v. National Wildlife Fed'n, *supra* note 52; Humane Soc'y of the United States v. Hodel, *supra* note 52, at 51.

[58] Defenders of Wildlife v. Administrator, Environmental Protection Agency, 688 F. Supp. 1334, 1345 (D. Minn. 1988), *aff'd in part and rev'd in part,* 882 F.2d 1294 (8th Cir. 1989). *See* Allied-Signal, Inc. v. Lujan, 736 F. Supp. 1558, 1560 (N.D. Cal. 1990).

[59] Humane Soc'y of the United States v. Hodel, *supra* note 52, at 61; National Audubon Soc'y v. Hester, 801 F.2d 405, n.2 (D.C. Cir. 1986).

[60] Defenders of Wildlife v. Hodel, *supra* note 42, 851 F.2d at 1039; Region 8 Forest Serv. Timber Purchasers Council v. Alcock, 736 F. Supp. 267, 272 (N.D. Ga. 1990).

[61] Lujan v. Defenders of Wildlife, *supra* note 42, 911 F.2d at 121.

[62] Humane Soc'y of the United States v. Hodel, *supra* note 52, at 53 (quoting Hunt v. Washington State Apple Advertising Comm'n, 432 U.S. 333, 343 (1977)).

[63] *See* Lujan v. Defenders of Wildlife, *supra* note 42 (brief of *amici curiae* Washington Legal Foundation *et al.*, in No. 90-1424, Oct. term 1990).

[64] Humane Soc'y of the United States v Hodel, *supra* note 52.

[65] Defenders of Wildlife v. Administrator, Environmental Protection Agency, *supra* note 46.

[66] Justices Blackmun and O'Connor. Although Justice Stevens also disagreed with the majority decision on standing, he concurred in the result for other reasons.

[67] Lujan v. Defenders of Wildlife, *supra* note 42, 60 U.S.L.W. at 4509.

Other groups' attempts to bring citizen suits are not usually successful. One organization complained that the listing of an endangered fish jeopardized the likelihood of flood control projects; but the organization could not meet the constitutional tests for standing.[68] An industrial company, which was liable for hazardous waste cleanup costs at a naval station, did not have standing to object that the government's cleanup plan violated the Endangered Species Act.[69] And, if the court had applied the prudential standing test, it would have dismissed the timber companies' challenge of a Forest Service plan to protect woodpeckers by restricting timber cutting.[70]

*Mootness*

Another doctrine that stems from Article III of the Constitution is "mootness." Unlike standing, which focuses on the litigants' personal status, the "mootness" doctrine is concerned with the nature of the challenged order. A dispute is deemed to be "moot" if it has become academic because the relief cannot be granted. Under the "case" or "controversy" standard of Article III, federal courts may not judge abstract legal disputes without the existence of a present and live controversy.[71]

There is, however, an exception to the mootness doctrine for short-term orders that are "capable of repetition yet evading review."[72] This exception makes the controversy over legal points a real, non-moot issue for persons likely to be affected by the decision in the future.[73]

*Ripeness and Exhaustion*

Courts say that orders are "ripe" for judicial review when the litigants have "exhausted" their remedies before the agency. This standard enables courts to avoid reviewing interim orders that are only procedural in nature and do not have any meaningful impact or consequences.[74]

In the Endangered Species Act Amendments of 1982, Congress specified that judicial review is available when the Secretary decides against granting petitions to add a species to, or delete it from, the endangered species list.[75] Impatient with the Secretary's past performance,[76] the legislature wanted the

---

[68] Glover River Org. v. Department of Interior, 675 F.2d 251 (10th Cir. 1982).

[69] Allied-Signal, Inc. v. Lujan, *supra* note 58.

[70] Region 8 Forest Serv. Timber Purchasers Council v. Alcock, *supra* note 60.

[71] Greenpeace, U.S.A. v. Mosbacher, 719 F. Supp. 21, 22 (D.D.C. 1989).

[72] Defenders of Wildlife v. Endangered Species Scientific Auth., 659 F.2d 168, 175 (D.C. Cir.), *cert. denied sub nom.* International Ass'n of Fish and Wildlife Agencies v. Defenders of Wildlife, 454 U.S. 963 (1981) (quoting Southern Pacific Terminal Co. v. Interstate Commerce Comm'n, 219 U.S. 498, 515 (1911)).

[73] Greenpeace, U.S.A. v. Mosbacher, *supra* note 71, at 22.

[74] *Compare* Glover River Org., *supra* note 68, at 253 *with* Defenders of Wildlife v. Administrator, Environmental Protection Agency, *supra* note 58, 688 F. Supp. at 1343–44.

[75] Pub. L. No. 97-304, §2(a)(2), 96 Stat. 1411, 1413, 1414 (1982) (codified in 16 U.S.C. §§1533(b)(3)(C)(ii), 1533(b)(6)(B)(ii) (1988)).

[76] *See* chapter 3.

courts to test whether the Secretary's decision is justified in the light of available scientific evidence.[77] Congress did not explain why the Act needs a special judicial review provision for this purpose. The provision will, however, defeat any claim that the Secretary's action on listing proposals is not sufficiently final to qualify for judicial review.

## Prohibitions on Suits

Congress decided to limit the right to file citizens suits in certain situations.

### *Prior Notification*

Section 11(g)(2)[78] requires would-be litigants to give the Secretary written notice about their complaints and then wait 60 days before filing a citizens suit. Notice must also be given to government agencies or others whose actions the litigants will seek to enjoin. There is one exception to the 60-day waiting period. If the Secretary fails to list or delist a species, or to designate critical habitat, a lawsuit may be instituted immediately after written notice—but only if an emergency exists.

For many years, the courts were divided about how strictly to enforce the 60-day waiting period. Many courts decided to allow lawsuits even though they were filed with less than 60 days notice.[79] Other courts, however, recognized that the notice requirement is jurisdictional. Where litigants failed to wait the required 60 days after notice, those courts dismissed the lawsuits[80] and, in one instance, imposed a $250 fine against the litigant's attorney.[81]

A recent Supreme Court decision has probably settled the issue. In that case,[82] the Court construed the 60-day notice provision for citizen suits under the Resource Conservation and Recovery Act of 1976.[83] This notice provision, like the notice provision contained in the Endangered Species Act, was "patterned after" a section of the Clean Air Amendments of 1970.[84] The Court held that "the notice and 60-day delay requirements are mandatory conditions pre-

---

[77] H.R. CONF. REP. NO. 835, 97th Cong., 2d Sess. 21 (1982), *reprinted in* 1982 U.S. CODE CONG. & ADMIN. NEWS 2807, 2862.

[78] 16 U.S.C. §1540(g)(2) (1988).

[79] Sierra Club v. Froehlke, 534 F.2d 1289, 1302–03 (8th Cir. 1976); National Wildlife Federation v. Hodel, 23 ER Cases 1089, n.6 (E.D. Cal. 1985); Sierra Club v. Block, 614 F. Supp. 488, 492 (D.D.C. 1985); Jackson Hole Alliance for Responsible Planning v. Watt, 13 E.L.R. 20,994, 20,998 (D. Wyo. 1983); Libby Rod & Gun Club v. Poteat, 457 F. Supp. 1177, 1185 (D. Mont. 1978). *See* Village of Kaktovik v. Corps of Engineers, 12 ER Cases 1740, 1744 (D. Alaska 1978); Fund for Animals v. Andrus, 11 ER Cases 2189, 2199 (D. Minn. 1978).

[80] Save the Yaak Committee v. Block, 840 F.2d 714, 721 (9th Cir. 1988); Protect Our Eagles' Trees (POETs) v. City of Lawrence, 715 F. Supp. 996, 998 (D. Kan. 1989).

[81] Maine Audubon Soc'y v. Purslow, 907 F.2d 265 (1st Cir. 1990).

[82] Hallstrom v. Tillamook County, 493 U.S. 20 (1989).

[83] 42 U.S.C. §6972(b)(1)(1988).

[84] Hallstrom v. Tillamook County, *supra* note 82, at 23 and n.1 (citing 42 U.S.C. §7604 (1982)).

cedent to commencing suit under the [statute's] citizen suit provision; a District Court may not disregard these requirements at its discretion."[85] One court has already concluded that the Supreme Court's decision is controlling under the Endangered Species Act.[86]

*Pending Government Action*

By "[r]equiring citizens to comply with the notice and delay requirements," the statute "allows Government agencies to take responsibility for enforcing environmental regulations, thus obviating the need for citizen suits."[87] Consequently, the Act[88] does not allow a citizen suit to be commenced while the government is prosecuting an enforcement action. This rule accords with Congress' intent that "the citizen suit is meant to supplement rather than to supplant governmental action."[89]

## Intervention

Under section 11, a private party may sue a non-governmental violator without naming the federal government as a party.[90] The federal government has an interest in those lawsuits; it must be able to insure that the public interest is protected. So the Act[91] gives the Attorney General, at the Secretary's request, the right to intervene in such lawsuits. Under the Federal Rules of Civil Procedure, Rule 24(a),[92] the Attorney General's right to intervene is absolute. Persons can also intervene as a matter of right if the lawsuit impairs their ability to protect their property or transaction. Even then, courts may deny intervention if the persons' interests are adequately represented by existing parties.

Under Rule 24(b) of the Federal Rules,[93] courts have discretion to permit other persons to intervene when their claim or defense has questions of fact or law in common with the citizen suit. Intervention may also be granted when a federal statute confers a conditional right to intervene.

The courts can be very selective in deciding whether to allow intervention. Illustrating this is a citizens suit in which environmentalists challenged the Secretary's decision to open 28 wildlife refuges to hunting.[94] Two hunters'

---

[85] *Id.* at 31. If the government fails to object in the trial court to the suing party's failure to comply with the 60-day waiting period, the government waives the objection. The government may not avail itself of the objection for the first time on an appeal which seeks reversal of an unfavorable trial court judgment. Sierra Club v. Yeutter, 926 F.2d 429 (5th Cir. 1991).

[86] Humane Soc'y of the United States v. Lujan, 768 F. Supp. 360, 362 and n.3 (D.D.C. 1991).

[87] Hallstrom v. Tillamook County, *supra* note 82, at 29.

[88] 16 U.S.C. §§1540(g)(2)(A)(ii)–(iii), 1540(g)(2)(B)(ii) (1988).

[89] Hallstrom v. Tillamook County, *supra* note 82, at 29 (quoting Gwaltney of Smithfield v. Chesapeake Bay Found., 484 U.S. 49, 60 (1987)).

[90] *See* 16 U.S.C. §1540(g)(1)(A) (1988).

[91] *Id.* §1540(g)(3)(B).

[92] FED. R. CIV. P. 24(a).

[93] FED. R. CIV. P. 24(b).

[94] Humane Soc'y of the United States v. Clark, 109 F.R.D. 518 (D.D.C. 1985).

associations—the National Rifle Association and the Wildlife Legislative Fund—requested intervention. Those associations argued that they qualified for intervention as a matter of right under Rule 24(a). The judge disagreed, reasoning that the Secretary would represent the hunters' interests. The judge granted permissive intervention under Rule 24(b) to the Wildlife Legislative Fund. He denied any intervention to the National Rifle Association on the ground that its interests were represented by the Wildlife Legislative Fund.

## Injunctions

In citizen suits, the Act empowers litigants to ask for injunctions[95] without restricting their right to seek additional relief.[96]

There are two types of injunctions, "preliminary" and "permanent." A preliminary injunction is issued at the outset, before the court holds a full hearing on the merits. The purpose of a preliminary injunction is to preserve the *status quo* until the court has a chance to hold a full hearing. In determining whether to issue a preliminary injunction, a court normally considers four factors:[97]

- Whether the complaining party will suffer irreparable injury unless an injunction is granted
- Whether that injury outweighs any harm that an injunction would inflict on the other party
- Whether the complaining party has shown a likelihood of success on the merits
- Whether the public interest will be harmed by an injunction

The Ninth Circuit said, however, that "[t]his is not the test for injunctions under the Endangered Species Act."[98] In that case, the Corps of Engineers refused the Secretary's request to resume consultations after a major change in arrangements that justified a construction project. Viewing this as a procedural violation of the Act, the Ninth Circuit ruled that a preliminary injunction should be granted.[99]

After holding full hearings, courts can issue permanent injunctions if a statute has been violated. Under most statutes, courts have discretion whether or not to enjoin a violation; they can "balance the equities." In the *Hill* case, however, the Supreme Court decided that "Congress had foreclosed the exercise

---

[95] 16 U.S.C. §1540(g)(1)(A) (1988).

[96] *Id.* §1540(g)(5).

[97] Conservation Law Found. v. Watt, 560 F. Supp. 561, 568 (D. Mass.), *aff'd on other grounds sub nom.* Massachusetts v. Watt, 716 F.2d 946 (1st Cir. 1983); New England Naturalist Ass'n v. Larsen, 692 F. Supp. 75 (D.R.I. 1988).

[98] Sierra Club v. Marsh, 816 F.2d 1376, 1383 (9th Cir. 1987).

[99] *Id.* at 1388–89.

of the usual discretion possessed by a court of equity."[100] Consequently, once a substantial procedural violation of the Act is disclosed, "the remedy must be an injunction."[101] So the Ninth Circuit ruled that, absent "unusual circumstances," an injunction is the appropriate remedy for violation of the Act.[102]

## Attorneys Fees

Endangered Species Act section 11(g) (4)[103] allows courts to reimburse parties for their cost of litigation "whenever the court determines such award is appropriate."

When is an award of attorneys fees "appropriate"? Before 1983, some courts believed that, under the Endangered Species Act, parties were eligible for attorneys fees even though they lost on all issues.[104] That year, however, the Supreme Court reached a different conclusion. The Supreme Court was reviewing a request for attorneys fees under a statute similar to the Endangered Species Act.[105] The organizations requesting fees had achieved no success in their lawsuit. The Court denied fees, ruling that "some success on the merits [must] be obtained before a party becomes eligible for a fee award."[106]

The next question is: how much success is enough? In its 1983 decision, the Supreme Court said parties must "achiev[e] *some success,* even if not major success."[107] This means more than "trivial success on the merits, or purely procedural victories."[108] One court of appeals interpreted this as requiring "notable progress, short of full achievement, on any issue of substance."[109]

Winning on the merits is not a guarantee of a fec award. Litigants must also "make a substantial contribution to the goals of the statute."[110] For this reason, recovery was denied to an Indian tribe which argued only matters inconsistent with the Act's interpretation and implementation.[111] Opponents of offshore oil leases were refused attorneys fees because their contribution was neither substantial nor exceptional.[112] An individual who successfully opposed

---

[100] *See* Weinberger v. Romero-Barcelo, 456 U.S. 305, 313 (1982) (referring to Tennessee Valley Auth. v. Hill, 437 U.S. 153 (1978)). *Accord,* Amoco Production Co. v. Village of Gambell, 480 U.S. 531, n.9 (1987).

[101] Thomas v. Peterson, 753 F.2d 754, 764 (9th Cir. 1985).

[102] *Id.*; National Wildlife Fed'n v. Hodel, 23 ER Cases 1089, 1093, (E.D. Cal. 1985).

[103] 16 U.S.C. §1540(g)(4) (1988).

[104] *See* Village of Kaktovik v. Watt, 689 F.2d 222, 224 (D.C. Cir. 1982); North Slope Borough v. Andrus, 507 F. Supp. 106, 107 (D.D.C. 1981).

[105] Ruckelshaus v. Sierra Club, 463 U.S. 680 (1983) (interpreting 42 U.S.C. §7607(f) (1988)).

[106] *Id.,* 463 U.S. at 682.

[107] *Id.* at 688 (footnote omitted).

[108] *Id.* at n.9.

[109] Conservation Law Found. v. Secretary of the Interior, 790 F.2d 965, 967 (1st Cir. 1986) (fee approved under Outer Continental Shelf Lands Act, but not under Endangered Species Act).

[110] Carson-Truckee Water Conservancy Dist. v. Secretary of the Interior, 748 F.2d 523, 526 (9th Cir. 1984), *cert. denied sub nom.* Pyramid Lake Paiute Tribe v. Carson-Truckee Water Conservancy District, 471 U.S. 1065 (1985).

[111] *Id.*

[112] Village of Kaktovik v. Watt, *supra* note 104, at 225–28.

the Service's request for forfeiture of his property did not advance the Act's purposes "either in intent or in result" and, therefore, was not entitled to attorneys fees.[113]

If they qualify for fee awards, environmental organizations must also justify the amount of money requested. The starting point for calculating fees is called the "lodestar." The lodestar is the attorney's normal hourly billing rate, multiplied by the number of hours reasonably expended.[114] One appeals court approved increasing the lodestar rate to account for superior performance,[115] while another disapproved of a similar increase.[116] Enhancement of the lodestar is generally the exception rather than the rule.[117]

The Endangered Species Act is not the only source of attorneys fee awards. Environmental organizations have also won attorneys fees by filing claims under the Equal Access to Justice Act.[118]

## Standard of Review

The Endangered Species Act contains no comprehensive standard of review. As a consequence, judicial review is governed by the Administrative Procedure Act.[119] That statute provides several standards for court scrutiny of an agency's orders.

### De Novo Review

The most expansive type of review is *de novo* review, in which judges review the facts and make up their own minds about whether or not the facts justify the agency's decision. The Administrative Procedure Act[120] allows this form of review only in rare situations. The first is when the action is adjudicatory in nature and the agency's factfinding procedures are inadequate. The second situation is when, in a proceeding to enforce nonadjudicatory agency

---

[113] Carpenter v. Andrus, 499 F. Supp. 976, 979 (D. Del. 1980).

[114] Defenders of Wildlife v. Administrator, Environmental Protection Agency, 700 F. Supp. 1028, 1031 (D. Minn. 1988); Palila v. Hawaii Dep't of Land and Natural Resources, 512 F. Supp. 1006, n.1 (D. Haw. 1981); *Id.*, 118 F.R.D. 125, 127 (D. Haw. 1987).

[115] Sierra Club v. Clark, 755 F.2d 608, 619–20 (8th Cir. 1985).

[116] Conservation Law Found. v. Secretary of the Interior, *supra* note 109, at 970–71.

[117] Defenders of Wildlife v. Administrator, Environmental Protection Agency, *supra* note 114, at 1031–32.

[118] 28 U.S.C. §2412(d)(1)(A) (1988). *See* Thomas v. Peterson, 841 F.2d 332 (9th Cir. 1988); Washington Dep't of Wildlife v. Stubblefield, 739 F. Supp. 1428 (W.D. Wash. 1989).

[119] 5 U.S.C. §§701–706 (1988). *See* Tribal Village of Akutan v. Hodel, 869 F.2d 1185, 1193 (9th Cir. 1988); Friends of Endangered Species v. Jantzen, 760 F.2d 976, 981 (9th Cir. 1985); Village of False Pass v. Clark, 733 F.2d 605, 609 (9th Cir. 1984).

[120] 5 U.S.C. §706(2)(F) (1988).

action, the litigants raise issues that were not before the agency.[121] Courts uniformly refuse to engage in *de novo* review under the Endangered Species Act.[122]

## The Substantial Evidence Rule

Under the Administrative Procedure Act,[123] courts use the substantial evidence rule when they review agency adjudications and other cases required to be decided on the record after hearing. The courts take into account the *entire* record, considering evidence that cuts against—as well as in favor of—the agency's action.[124]

The Endangered Species Act provides for review under this standard in a few situations. Thus, when courts are reviewing attempts to collect civil penalties, the Act specifies that the courts should apply the substantial evidence standard.[125]

The government must sustain its charges against alleged violators by a preponderance of credible evidence.[126] If the evidence is evenly balanced, the government has failed to sustain its burden of proof.[127] Conversely, if accused violators seek to justify their actions by reason of any exception or permit, they have the burden of proving that defense.[128]

## The Arbitrary and Capricious Standard

Under the Endangered Species Act, court review of most agency decisions is governed by the arbitrary and capricious standard,[129] which allows an agency's action to be set aside only if it is arbitrary, capricious, or an abuse of discretion.

Under the arbitrary and capricious standard, the "scope of review . . . is very narrow."[130]

> The court is not to weigh the evidence in the record pro and con. . . . [I]f the agency considers the factors and articulates a rational relationship between the facts found and the choice made, its decision is not arbitrary or capricious.[131]

---

[121] Friends of Endangered Species v. Jantzen, *supra* note 119, at n.5; Cabinet Mountain Wilderness v. Peterson, 685 F.2d 678, 685–86 (D.C. Cir. 1982).

[122] *Id.;* Louisiana v. Verity, 853 F.2d 322, n.8 (5th Cir. 1988); Village of False Pass v. Clark, *supra* note 119, at 609–10.

[123] 5 U.S.C. §706(2)(E) (1988).

[124] Universal Camera Corp. v. National Labor Relations Bd., 340 U.S. 474, 488 (1951).

[125] 16 U.S.C. §1540(a)(1) (1988). *See* Newell v. Baldridge, 548 F. Supp. 39, 42 (W.D. Wash. 1982).

[126] U.S. Fish and Wildlife Serv. v. Luhrs, DOI Dkt. No. Boston 78-14 (ALJ ID dated April 26, 1979).

[127] *Id.*

[128] 16 U.S.C. §1539(g) (1988).

[129] 5 U.S.C. §706(2)(A) (1988).

[130] Louisiana v. Verity, *supra* note 122, at 327.

[131] *Id.*

Applying this standard, courts have upheld, for example, agency regulations,[132] approvals of permits,[133] and leases.[134] In other cases, under the same standard, courts have blocked agency regulations[135] and construction projects.[136]

When an agency changes prior policies, its actions will be carefully scrutinized. Courts will allow an agency to alter its policies, with or without a change in circumstances, so long as it explains its reasons.[137] If the agency does not provide a reasoned analysis for the change, its decision will be overturned as arbitrary and capricious.[138]

There is one class of cases in which courts give agencies unusual latitude. Under Endangered Species Act section 4(b) (7),[139] the Secretary is directed to short-cut ordinary procedures to protect species or their habitat in an emergency. "The statute . . . contemplates a somewhat less rigorous process of investigation and explanation for emergency regulations than for normal rulemaking. . . ."[140] As a result, one court concluded: "[W]hat might constitute arbitrary and capricious action or an unacceptable explanation for a regulation in the normal course of events might well pass muster under the emergency provisions."[141] Sustaining an emergency listing of the desert tortoise as endangered, the court said, "Congress . . . indicated that the Secretary was to use his emergency powers less cautiously—in a sense to 'shoot first and ask [all of the] questions later.'"[142]

In brief, agencies and courts share responsibility for enforcement of the Endangered Species Act. The agencies have the primary role in articulating policy. For this reason, judicial review is "at its most deferential where . . . the agency action is based *solely* upon environmental considerations."[143] Even when the issue is not purely a policy matter, the courts have only a limited supervising function. "The question for reviewing courts is not whether an agency decision is 'correct,' but rather whether the decision reflects sufficient attention to environmental concerns and is adequately reasoned and explained."[144]

---

[132] *Id.;* Cayman Turtle Farm v. Andrus, 478 F. Supp. 125, 131 (D.D.C. 1979), *aff'd mem.*, D.C. Cir. No. 79-2031 (Dec. 12, 1980).

[133] Friends of Endangered Species v. Jantzen, *supra* note 119.

[134] Cabinet Mountain Wilderness v. Peterson, *supra* note 121; Village of False Pass v. Clark, *supra* note 119.

[135] Connor v. Andrus, 453 F. Supp. 1037, 1041 (W.D. Tex. 1978); Defenders of Wildlife v. Andrus, 428 F. Supp. 167 (D.D.C. 1977).

[136] Sierra Club v. Marsh, 816 F.2d 1376, 1381–82 (9th Cir. 1987).

[137] National Audubon Soc'y v. Hester, 801 F.2d 405, 408 (D.C. Cir. 1986).

[138] Sierra Club v. Clark, 755 F.2d 608, 619 (8th Cir. 1985).

[139] 16 U.S.C. §1533(b)(7) (1988). *See* Chapter 3.

[140] City of Las Vegas v. Lujan, 891 F.2d 927, 932 (D.C. Cir. 1989).

[141] *Id.*

[142] *Id.* (brackets in original).

[143] National Audubon Soc'y v. Hester, *supra* note 137, at 407–08. *See* Louisiana v. Verity, *supra* note 122, at 329 ("[O]ur deference to the agency is greatest when reviewing technical matters within its area of expertise, particularly its choice of scientific data and statistical methodology") (footnote omitted).

[144] National Audubon Soc'y v. Hester, *supra* note 137, at 407.

* * *

The primary aim of the Act's penalty provisions is to discourage violations before they occur. Punishment is no substitute for prevention. "Extinct animals, like lost time, can never be brought back. They are gone forever."[145]

---

[145] Palladio, Inc. v. Diamond, 321 F. Supp. 630, 633 (S.D.N.Y. 1970), *aff'd,* 440 F.2d 1319 (2d Cir.), *cert. denied,* 404 U.S.983 (1971). The economists call this "irreversibility. . . . Once a species is lost it is gone forever." D. Pearce and R. Turner, *Economics of Natural Resources and the Environment* 50–51 (Baltimore: Johns Hopkins University Press, 1990).

# Chapter 8

# Federal Cooperation With The States

The states have regulated wildlife since colonial times. In the 1690s, Massachusetts enacted the first U.S. law protecting wildlife. It established a closed season on deer that every colony except Georgia emulated by the time of the Revolution.[1] New York State had less luck with an 1838 law forbidding hunters to use multiple guns against waterfowl. The Empire State had to repeal the statute after commercial hunters began wearing masks and vowing to execute informers.[2] Despite the infirmities of state enforcement, the states remained preeminent until Congress enacted the Endangered Species Preservation Act of 1966.[3]

Even then, although the federal government undertook the "fundamental responsibility"[4] for protecting endangered species, it did not obliterate the role of states.

## The Need for State Aid to Enforce the Law

Congress had a very practical reason for continuing state involvement. As the federal legislature noted, only state agencies "have the physical facilities and the personnel to see that state and federal endangered species policies are properly executed."[5] The federal government's main wildlife enforcement agency—the Fish and Wildlife Service—has only 200 special agents and 65 wildlife inspectors. Scattered throughout the United States, these agents try to enforce 11 federal laws and five international treaties. Agents from state wildlife agencies outnumber these federal agents 37 to 1.[6] Effective enforcement depends upon cooperation between state and federal agencies.

---

[1] P. Matthiessen, *Wildlife in America* 64–65, 303 (New York: Viking, 1987).

[2] *Id.* at 157.

[3] Pub. L. No. 89-669, 80 Stat. 926 (1966).

[4] H.R. Conf. Rep. No. 740, 93d Cong., 1st Sess. 25 (1973), *reprinted in* 1973 U.S. Code Cong. & Admin. News 2989, 3004 [hereinafter 1973 Conference Report].

[5] *Id.* at 26, 1973 U.S. Code Cong. & Admin. News at 3005.

[6] U.S. General Accounting Office, Report to Congress entitled, *Wildlife Protection: Enforcement of Federal Laws Could Be Strengthened* 2, 4 (Washington: GAO/RCED-91-44, 1991).

## The Plan of Section 6 for Federal–State Cooperation

The Endangered Species Act is infused with the concept of federal-state cooperation. The primary instrument is section 6.[7]

The 1966 Act laid down the basic precepts now embodied in section 6. In carrying out the Act's program, the Secretary was instructed to "cooperate to the maximum extent practicable with the" states.[8] To accomplish this, the Secretary is authorized to enter into agreements with states for the administration and management of conservation areas.[9] These provisions were incorporated into the Endangered Species Conservation Act of 1969.[10] And in 1973, with only minor language changes, the same provisions became section 6(a) and (b) of the Act as it exists today.[11]

The Endangered Species Act of 1973 embellished section 6 in several ways. First, the Secretary was empowered to enter into cooperative agreements with states whose conservation programs meet federal criteria.[12] Second, for states with cooperative agreements, the federal government agreed to pay the major share of program costs.[13] In later years, Congress expanded section 6. The 1977 Amendments made more state programs eligible for federal funding.[14] The 1978 Amendments authorized cooperative agreements for the conservation of plants.[15] Finally, the statute was amended in 1988 to provide assistance to states that aid in monitoring the status of candidate species and recovering species.[16]

From the beginning, the Secretary has also been instructed to consult with states before he acquires any land or water for conserving species.[17]

---

[7] 16 U.S.C. §1535 (1988).

[8] Pub. L. No. 89-669, §3(a), 80 Stat. 926, 927 (1966) (codified with minor change, at 16 U.S.C. §1535(a) (1988)).

[9] *Id.* §3(b), 80 Stat. 926, 927 (codified with minor changes, at 16 U.S.C. §1535(b) (1988)).

[10] Pub. L. No. 91-135, §12(d), 83 Stat. 275, 283.

[11] Pub. L. No. 93-205, §6(a), (b), 87 Stat. 884, 889–90 (codified in 16 U.S.C. §1535(a), (b) (1988)).

[12] Pub. L. No. 93-205, §6(c), 87 Stat. 884, 890 (codified in 16 U.S.C. §1535(c) (1988)).

[13] The original federal grant was up to 33⅓ percent of costs for single-state programs; up to 75 percent for multi-state programs. Pub. L. No. 93-205, §6(d), 87 Stat. 884, 890–91. In the Endangered Species Act Amendments of 1982, Pub. L. No. 97-304, §3, 96 Stat. 1411, 1416, the federal shares were increased to 75 percent and 90 percent respectively.

[14] Pub. L. No. 95-212, §1, 91 Stat. 1493 (codified in 16 U.S.C. §1535(c)(1)(E)(i), (ii) (1988)).

[15] Pub. L. No. 95-632, §10, 92 Stat. 3751, 3762–64.

[16] Pub. L. No. 100-478, §1005, 102 Stat. 2306, 2307–08 (codified in 16 U.S.C. §1535(d) (1988)). *See* H.R. CONF. REP. NO. 928, 100th Cong., 2d Sess. 21 (1988), *reprinted in* 1988 U.S. CODE CONG. & ADMIN. NEWS 2700, 2739.

[17] Pub. L. No. 89-669, §3(a), 80 Stat. 926, 927 (1966); Pub. L. No. 93-205, §6(a), 87 Stat. 884, 889 (1973) (codified in 16 U.S.C. §1535(a) (1988)). The Secretary has broad authority to establish and implement a conservation program by means of land acquisition, 16 U.S.C. §1534 (1988).

## Preemption of State Law

The Endangered Species Act "preempt[s] state wildlife conservation laws only to a very limited extent."[18] Indeed, the Act actually "invites state action."[19]

The Act is careful, for example, not to preempt all state and local laws prohibiting "taking" of wildlife. Instead, the Act provides:

> Any State law or regulation respecting the taking of an endangered species or threatened species may be more restrictive than the exemptions or permits provided for in this [Act] or in any regulation which implements this [Act] but not less restrictive than the prohibitions so defined.[20]

What this means is that state legislation "may not authorize any taking other than that authorized by the Act's permits and exceptions."[21] For this reason, the Interior Department ruled that a county ordinance was void insofar as it allowed "humane disposition," "confinement," or "impoundment" of federally protected species.[22] In contrast, a Florida court recognized that the state can enforce anti-taking prohibitions that are more restrictive than federal law.[23]

The Endangered Species Act preempts some—but not all—of the state and local laws relating to sale, to export, or to import. The Act specifies that:

> Any State law or regulation which applies with respect to the importation or exportation of, or interstate or foreign commerce in, endangered species or threatened species is void to the extent that it may effectively (1) permit what is prohibited by this [Act] or by any regulation which implements this [Act], or (2) prohibit what is authorized pursuant to an exemption or permit provided for in this [Act] or in any regulation which implements this [Act].[24]

Three cases from California illustrate this rule. In two of the cases, [25] importers attacked a California statute insofar as it prohibited them from trading in elephant products. In a third case,[26] a leather tannery complained that the local statute prohibited it from selling alligator products. Each of the three companies held federal licenses that permitted them to trade in products of the species. The courts invalidated the state prohibitions because they purported

---

[18] Cresenzi Bird Importers v. New York, 658 F. Supp. 1441, 1444 (S.D.N.Y. 1987), *aff'd*, 410 F. 2d 410 (2d Cir. 1987).

[19] Palladio, Inc. v. Diamond, 321 F. Supp. 630, 635 (S.D.N.Y. 1970), *aff'd*, 440 F.2d 1319 (2d Cir.), *cert. denied*, 404 U.S. 983 (1971).

[20] 16 U.S.C. §1635(f) (1988).

[21] Letter from Associate Solicitor, Fish and Wildlife, Dep't of Interior, to Assistant County Solicitor, Anne Arundel County, Maryland (Aug. 22, 1977).

[22] *Id.*

[23] State v. Billie, 497 So. 2d 889, 893–94 (Fla. App. 2 Dist. 1986), *review denied,* 506 So. 2d 1040 (1987).

[24] 16 U.S.C. §1535(f) (1988).

[25] Man Hing Ivory and Imports, Inc. v. Deukmejian, 702 F.2d 760 (9th Cir. 1983); H.J. Justin & Sons v. Deukmejian, 702 F.2d 758 (9th Cir. 1983).

[26] Fouke Company v. Brown, 463 F. Supp. 1142 (E.D. Cal. 1979).

"to prohibit what is authorized pursuant to an exemption or permit provided for by the . . . Act and regulations implementing it."[27]

Other than for this limited preemption, the Act "shall not . . . be construed to void any State law or regulation which is intended . . . to permit or prohibit sale of [migratory, resident, or introduced] fish or wildlife."[28] Thus, New York State could ban local sales of wild birds by importers who had no special permits or exemptions.[29] New York State[30] and California[31] could also prevent companies from trading in footwear made from skins of wildlife that the federal government had not listed.

## Other Special Treatment for States

Congress was solicitous of states in many other ways. When the Endangered Species Act of 1973 became law, Congress delayed the law's full application for a transition period. During that period, the Act's anti-taking prohibitions[32] did not normally apply to endangered or threatened species that resided within a state.[33] Instead, the Act gave the states the "fundamental roles with regard to resident species" during a period "during which it is expected that the states will adjust to the new federal program."[34] The transition period is now long past.

The Act still gives the states a special voice in many decisions. For example, the Secretary can decide by regulation to give a threatened species the full protection of the Act's anti-taking prohibitions. The Secretary's regulation, however, is not automatically effective in states that participate in federal-state cooperative agreements. In those states, the Secretary's anti-taking regulation applies to resident species only if the states adopt it.[35]

The states also have special status for listings under section 4.[36] At the outset of effective federal regulation in 1966, the Secretary was instructed not to list any species as imperiled except "after consultation with the affected States."[37] Even today, the Secretary makes sure that states have "actual notice" of federal proposals to list species or designate critical habitat,[38] and gives special consideration to listing species that a state has identified as in danger of extinction.[39] The Secretary may decline to list a species as imperiled after taking

---

[27] *Id.* at 1144.

[28] 16 U.S.C. §1535(f) (1988).

[29] Cresenzi Bird Importers v. New York, *supra* note 18.

[30] Palladio, Inc. v. Diamond, *supra* note 19.

[31] H.L. Justin & Sons v. Deukmejian, *supra* note 25.

[32] *See* Chapter 4.

[33] Pub. L. No. 93-205, §6(g), 87 Stat. 884, 891–92 (1973) (codified—though now obsolete—at 16 U.S.C. §1535(g) (1988)).

[34] 1973 Conference Report, *supra* note 4, at 26, 1973 U.S. CODE CONG. & ADMIN. NEWS at 3004.

[35] 16 U.S.C. §1533(d) (1988).

[36] *See* chapter 3.

[37] Pub. L. No. 89-669, §1(c), 80 Stat. 926.

[38] 16 U.S.C. §1533(b)(5)(A)(ii) (1988).

[39] *Id.* §1533(b)(1)(B)(ii).

into account state "efforts . . . to protect" it.[40] And, if the Secretary makes a listing decision to which a state objects, or if a state-requested regulation fails to be adopted, the Secretary must give the state a "written justification."[41]

* * *

The cooperation between federal and state wildlife regulators is inevitable. Until late in this century, the regulation of wildlife was considered a state function, with no room for federal interference.[42] Although the federal government's role has grown, most endangered species reside within state borders. The states continue to oversee sport fishing and hunting and numerous conservation activities. And, not least of all, the legislators who write the federal laws are elected by state citizens. The states are thus in a powerful position to insist, in the name of federalism, that they be given a significant voice in conservation programs.

---

[40] American Fisheries Soc'y v. Verity, Civ. No. 88-0174 RAR-JFM, slip op. at 14 (E.D. Cal. Feb. 24, 1989) (construing 16 U.S.C. §1533(b)(1)(A) (1988)).

[41] 16 U.S.C. §1533(i) (1988).

[42] *See* Chapter 2.

# Chapter 9
# International Aspects

In Japan, about 2,000 people earn their livelihood by making luxury items such as eyeglass frames from the shells of imported hawksbill turtles. The United States and the world community have banned trade in these endangered turtles for many years. At the beginning of 1991, however, Japan continued to reject international pleas to halt these imports. The United States got tough. In April 1991, President Bush informed Congress that he would impose trade sanctions against Japan for the turtle's sake. In Nagasaki, home of most hawksbill-trade workers, newspapers branded the U.S. pressure as "a second atomic bomb." But the pressure worked. Japan announced immediately that it would phase out the hawksbill trade within 18 months.[1]

This incident demonstrates an important truth: If species conservation is to succeed, the world community must be armed with weapons that can control international trade in endangered wildlife.

## The United States' Role in the Creation of CITES

The United States joins in numerous international treaties for the conservation of fish, wildlife, and plants facing extinction.[2] As part of the Endangered Species Conservation Act of 1969,[3] Congress instructed the U.S. government to convene a meeting of the world's nations. The meeting's purpose: to create an international convention on the conservation of endangered species.

The result was the Convention on International Trade in Endangered Species of Wild Fauna and Flora, known by its acronym, CITES.[4] Effective in 1975, CITES now has 113 member nations.[5] The purpose of CITES "is to protect 'certain species of wild fauna and flora against over-exploitation through international trade.'"[6] To accomplish this, CITES lists species in three Appen-

---

[1] 3 Marine Conservation News No. 3 (Washington: Center for Marine Conservation, 1991); *Sea Turtles Put New Friction in U.S.–Japan Trade Quarrels*, N.Y. TIMES, May 17, 1991, at A1.

[2] *See* Pub. L. No. 93-205, 87 Stat. 884 (codified in 16 U.S.C. §1531 (a)(4) (1988)).

[3] Pub. L. No. 91-135, §5(b), 83 Stat. 275, 278.

[4] 1976, 27 U.S.T. 1087, T.I.A.S. No. 8249, *amended* June 22, 1979; T.I.A.S. No. 11079.

[5] 56 Fed. Reg. 32,260 (1991), supplemented by the author's telephone conversation with the CITES Secretariat.

[6] Man Hing Ivory and Imports v. Deukmejian, 702 F.2d 760, 762 (9th Cir. 1983) (quoting

dices. Appendix I is for species threatened with extinction. Appendix II includes species that are not currently endangered but may become so if unrestricted commercial trade occurs.[7] Appendix III is for species that a country has identified as in need of protection.[8] Nations that are parties to CITES "agree that they 'shall not allow trade in specimens of species included in Appendices I, II and III except in accordance with the provisions of the . . . Convention.'"[9]

## The United States' Implementation of CITES

Having sponsored CITES, the United States promptly implemented it. CITES contemplates that member nations will establish their own Scientific and Management Authorities to carry out functions under the convention.[10] As part of the Endangered Species Act of 1973,[11] Congress directed the President to designate two agencies to act as the Scientific and Management Authorities.[12] Later, in the 1979 Amendments,[13] Congress designated the Secretary of the Interior as both the Scientific Authority and the Management Authority. Three years later the legislature polished these designations into their present form.[14]

The Scientific Authority spawned a major controversy in the late 1970s and early 1980s. Under CITES, a nation may export species listed on Appendix II only if its Scientific Authority determines that those exports will not be detrimental to the species' survival. The bobcat is one of the animals listed on Appendix II. In 1978 and 1979 the Scientific Authority approved the export of tens of thousands of bobcat pelts from approximately 30 states and the Navajo Nation. In 1981 the District of Columbia Circuit overturned the agency's decision because the Authority's no-detriment findings were based upon population trends, not actual population size.[15] Congress, however, amended the Act in 1982 to overrule the court's decision.[16] On a second appeal, the court accepted that the 1982 legislation invalidated its earlier decision.[17]

---

from CITES, *supra* note 4, 1976 27 U.S.T. at 1090).

[7] *See* Cayman Turtle Farm v. Andrus, 478 F. Supp. 125 (D.D.C. 1979), *aff'd mem.*, D.C. Cir. No. 79-2031 (1980).

[8] Man Hing Ivory and Imports v. Deukmejian, 702 F.2d 760, 762 (9th Cir. 1983).

[9] Defenders of Wildlife v. Endangered Species Scientific Auth., 659 F.2d 168, 171 (D.C. Cir.), *cert. denied sub nom.* International Ass'n of Fish and Wildlife Agencies v. Defenders of Wildlife, 454 U.S. 963 (1981).

[10] CITES, *supra* note 4, 1976 27 U.S.T. at 1103.

[11] *See* Defenders of Wildlife v. Endangered Species Scientific Auth., *supra* note 9, 659 F.2d at 174–75.

[12] *Id.* (referring to Pub. L. No. 93-205, §8(e), 87 Stat. 884, 893 (1973)).

[13] Pub. L. No. 96-159, §6, 93 Stat. 1225, 1228.

[14] Pub. L. No. 97-304, §5, 96 Stat. 1411, 1421 (1982) (codified in 16 U.S.C. §1537a(a)–(c) (1988)).

[15] Defenders of Wildlife v. Endangered Species Scientific Auth., *supra* note 9, 659 F.2d at 176–78.

[16] *See* Defenders of Wildlife v. Endangered Species Scientific Auth., 725 F.2d 726, 729–30 (D.C. Cir. 1984) (referring to Pub. L. No. 97-304, §5(1), 96 Stat. 1411, 1421 (1982), codified in 16 U.S.C. §1537a(c)(2) (1988)).

[17] *Id.*

## The United State's Leadership Role in CITES Controversies

The United States is one of the leading nations in CITES affairs. It is thus called upon to take an important role in deciding whether international trade in certain fragile species should be controlled—or totally banned.

That decision can be very controversial. For some species, a strong case can be made for a total ban. "A total ban is easier to enforce than a partial ban."[18] Even controlled trading in wildlife can increase consumer demand, creating an incentive for poaching.[19] Many believe that, if government prohibits all trade in wildlife, this "decreases the market therefore."[20] "A total ban may also encourage the search for other products, both natural and synthetic, to replace those derived from endangered species. This too will discourage the illegal taking of such species."[21]

Some total trade bans, however, can be counterproductive. Many species need protection but can thrive with controlled trade. Trade provides economic incentives that aid—and finance—wildlife conservation. Particularly in the regions where most wildlife lives—like South America, Asia, and Africa—governments cannot enforce conservation programs without local support. A total ban may deprive local populations of any lawful source of income from their wildlife.[22] In contrast, "well-regulated trade can provide sizable economic returns to local populations," thus encouraging conservation.[23]

The governments of industrialized nations and the less developed countries disagree about the choice between a total trade ban and controlled trade. In 1989, the world community wrestled with the question of whether to impose a total ban on trade in ivory from the African elephant. The elephant population in most of southern Africa was healthy and growing. In Zimbabwe, for example, the government had to cull 1,000 elephants yearly to prevent overpopulation. In other parts of Africa, however, elephant herds were near extinction. The southern African nations fought against a trade ban, believing that they were being punished for their northern neighbors' poor management practices and corruption. After much debate and anguish, the international trade agency approved a total ban, believing that a partial ban would prove ineffective.[24]

---

[18] Delbay Pharmaceuticals v. Department of Commerce, 409 F. Supp. 637, 642 (D.D.C. 1976).

[19] Cayman Turtle Farm v. Andrus, *supra* note 7, at 132; People v. K. Sakai Co., 128 Cal. Rptr. 536, 539–40 (Ct. App. 1976).

[20] People v. K. Sakai Co., *supra* note 19, 128 Cal. Rptr. at 540.

[21] Delbay Pharmaceuticals v. Department of Commerce, *supra* note 18.

[22] *See* B. Bull, *Incentives and the Rhino's Fate,* WALL STREET JOURNAL, Aug. 18, 1989, at A6; R. Simmons and U. Kreuter, *Save an Elephant—Buy Ivory,* WASHINGTON POST, Oct. 1, 1989, at D3; R. Littell, *"Culling" Ivory, Saving Elephants,* WASHINGTON POST, Feb. 23, 1992, at C5. *But see* M. Sutton, *Don't Let Them Buy Ivory,* WASHINGTON POST, Oct. 9, 1989, at A21; J. Wyerman, *Don't Help the Poachers*, WASHINGTON POST, Feb. 29, 1992, at A21.

[23] K. Fuller, foreword to S. Fitzgerald, *International Wildlife Trade: Whose Business Is It?* xiv (Washington: World Wildlife Fund, 1989).

[24] P. Matthiessen, *African Silences* 223 (New York: Random House, 1991).

The 1989 trade ban on elephants was debated on both scientific and non-scientific grounds. Many conservationists advocated the total trade ban for ethical reasons. The southern African nations opposed the ban, however, because it would deprive their impoverished tribespeople of a needed livelihood. The naturalist and scientist Stephan Jay Gould wrote:

> African wildlife and habitats can only be preserved if long-term economic and social benefits will accrue to the African people for the effort. If no honorable argument can be made along these lines, the cause is lost. . . . Preservation must be defended 'for reasons that go very much deeper than . . . conservation of a priceless heritage. . . .' Africa, and all the world, needs a *humanistic* ecology of people protecting a bounteous nature for reasons of both soul and body—but especially the latter.[25]

The United States and other CITES nations had an opportunity to revisit the African elephant issue in 1992. During the March 1992 CITES meeting, five southern African nations offered proposals to allow the resumption of trade in ivory and elephant parts. Those proposals were withdrawn, however, after meeting almost unanimous opposition.

## Sanctions Under the Endangered Species Act For Actions Against CITES

The United States Government treats certain violations of the CITES Convention as violations of United States domestic law. No person subject to United States jurisdiction may trade in any specimens contrary to the CITES Convention or possess any specimens that were so traded.[26] For example, a Sea World curator, who spent five years caring for sea turtles born of eggs that another person had unlawfully taken from Ascention Island, was reprimanded when he sought a permit to return the turtles to Ascention Island.[27] A hobbyist paid a fine for shipping two black-necked swans without a permit.[28] Because of improper documentation, one trader forfeited 3,210 crocodile hides,[29] while another forfeited 2,507 live parakeets.[30]

The Act contains a narrow exception for imports of certain fish and wildlife that are listed on CITES Appendix II. These imports are presumed "not in violation of" U.S. law if:[31]

- The species is not listed as "endangered" under U.S. law

---

[25] S. Gould, *The Last Chance Continent*, N.Y. TIMES BOOK REVIEW, August 18, 1991, at 3, 29. (underscoring and quotation marks in original).

[26] 16 U.S.C. §1538(c)(1) (1988). *See* 50 C.F.R., Part 23 (1990).

[27] *In re* Craig Smith, DOC Dkt. No. 635-241 (ALJ ID dated Oct. 31, 1989).

[28] U.S. Fish and Wildlife Serv. v. Davidson, DOI Dkt. No. Twin Cities 79-1 (Sept. 24, 1979).

[29] United States v. 3,210 Crusted Sides of Caiman Crocodilus Yacare, 636 F. Supp. 1281, 1285 (S.D. Fla. 1986).

[30] United States v. 2,507 Live Canary Winged Parakeets, 689 F. Supp. 1106 (S.D. Fla. 1988).

[31] 16 U.S.C. §1538(c)(2) (1988).

- The specimens were taken and exported in compliance with CITES
- All CITES requirements were complied with
- The importer has a U.S. license, keeps the required records, files the required reports, and uses an authorized port of entry
- The importation is not made in the course of a commercial activity[32]

The United States gives weight to other nations' views in formulating its own list of endangered and threatened species. In deciding whether to list or delist a species, the Secretary must take account of other nations' efforts to protect the species.[33] Before listing or delisting, the Secretary must try to notify each foreign nation concerned with the species.[34] And, in selecting species to be listed, the Secretary must consider species that foreign nations assert are in danger of extinction, are likely to become endangered, or are in need of protection from unrestricted trade.[35] The Secretary is not required to list a species for protection under the Act just because CITES has included it in Appendix I.[36]

## Sanctions Against Nations Whose Trade Policies Offend CITES

Although the Endangered Species Act contains sanctions for some violations of CITES, the sanctions are not aimed at other nations. To target governmental offenders, the United States can invoke other authority.

Under the Pelly Amendment to the Fisherman's Protection Act,[37] the President has the discretion to embargo wildlife products from a nation whose practices diminish the effectiveness of an international agreement like CITES. As mentioned at the beginning of this chapter, President Bush was successful in April 1991 in gaining Japan's cooperation to halt imports of hawksbill turtles. Japan is the seventh foreign nation that has been cited under the Pelly Amendment.[38]

As part of the Endangered Species Act Amendments of 1988, Congress made clear that the United States should apply sanctions under the Pelly Amendment to any country trading illegally in African elephant ivory.[39] Sanctions are

---

[32] For the meaning of the phrase "commercial activity," see Chapter 4 and 16 U.S.C. §1532(2) (1988).

[33] 16 U.S.C. §1533(b)(1)(A) (1988).

[34] *Id.* §1533(b)(5)(B).

[35] *Id.* §1533(b)(1)(B)(i).

[36] *See* 41 Fed. Reg. 24,062 (1976).

[37] 22 U.S.C. §1978 (1988).

[38] *Sea Turtles Put New Friction in U.S.–Japan Trade Quarrels,* N.Y. TIMES, *supra* note 1; U.S. Dep't of the Interior, Endangered Species Technical Bulletin 5 (Washington: July/Aug 1991).

[39] Pub. L. No. 100-478, §2303, 102 Stat. 2306, 2322 (1988). *See* H.R. CONF. REP. NO. 928, 100th Cong., 2d Sess. 31, *reprinted in* 1988 U.S. CODE CONG. & ADMIN. NEWS 2700, 2749 [hereinafter 1988 Conference Report].

not to be applied, however, in the case of occasional technical violations or minor violations.[40]

Conservationists have not been successful in forcing the Administration to impose sanctions under the Pelly Amendment. As part of a 1989 case,[41] Greenpeace challenged the Administration's decision not to certify Iceland, under the Pelly Amendment, as a nation that hurts the cause of international whaling conservation. Greenpeace argued that the Administration improperly took into account national security considerations, rather than just conservation ones. The court observed in passing that the Administration "must base its decision on conservation factors alone."[42] The court, however, dismissed the case as moot because Iceland had "abandoned" the whaling practices to which Greenpeace objected.[43]

The Pelly Amendment is not the only vehicle for retaliating against nations that disregard CITES. For example, although Thailand has been a party to CITES since 1983, it exercises very little control over imports or re-exports of non-native species. So Thailand has become the center of illegal trade in Indochina. To sanction Thailand, CITES recommended in 1991 that its member nations prohibit wildlife trade with that nation. The United States complied, prohibiting imports of listed species from Thailand. In its notice, the United States government warns importers who conduct prohibited trade with Thailand that they may be subject to criminal and civil prosecution, and their imports subject to forfeiture.[44]

## Direct U.S. Aid to Other Nations

The United States employs the carrot as well as the stick. As early as the Endangered Species Conservation Act of 1969,[45] Congress directed the government to provide technical assistance for wildlife protection programs. Four years later, as part of the Endangered Species Act of 1973, the legislature authorized grants of money and advisors to foreign countries in aid of conservation.[46] The statute reaffirmed "the commitment of the United States to the worldwide protection of endangered species and threatened species."[47]

---

[40] 1988 Conference Report, *supra* note 39.
[41] Greenpeace, U.S.A. v. Mosbacher, 719 F. Supp. 21 (D.D.C. 1989).
[42] *Id.* at 24.
[43] *Id.* at 23.
[44] 56 Fed. Reg. 32,260 (1991).
[45] *Supra* note 3, at §5, 83 Stat. at 278.
[46] *Supra* note 2, at §8, 87 Stat. at 892–93 (codified in 16 U.S.C. §1537 (1988)).
[47] *Supra* note 2, at §8(a), 87 Stat. at 892.

## United States Implementation of the Western Convention

In 1982, Congress also provided[48] for the United States to implement the Convention on Nature Protection and Wildlife Preservation in the Western Hemisphere, known as the "Western Convention."[49] This obscure convention, which has been in force since 1942, has been described as "a visionary instrument."[50] It was "the first agreement to have [the] objective" of "protect[ing] all native animals and plants from extinction through means within man's control."[51] The convention's second objective is to "protect and preserve scenery of extraordinary beauty . . . and natural objects of aesthetic, historic or scientific value."[52] Up to now, the Western Convention has been "'a sleeping treaty' of little or no practical value. . . . "[53] It remains to be seen whether United States activities will revitalize this international convention.

## Scope of Overseas Activities Under the Endangered Species Act

In addition to international agreements and treaties, the United States' law enforcement does not stop at the water's edge. The Act prohibits the taking of endangered fish or wildlife not only within the United States, but also in United States territorial waters and on the high seas.[54] The Act bans exports and imports of endangered species.[55] It bans sales of those species in both interstate and foreign commerce.[56] And it prohibits the delivery, receipt, carriage, transport, and shipment of those species in both interstate and foreign commerce in the course of a commercial activity.[57]

Not surprisingly, therefore, the Secretary is authorized to carry out law enforcement investigations abroad.[58]

There are, however, limits on the Endangered Species Act's application overseas. In the 1973 Act, Congress deliberately "did not make illegal [prohibited] actions if performed entirely with[in] one or more foreign countries."[59] The House committee expressed agreement with the government's 1976 view

---

[48] Pub. L. No. 97-304, §5, 96 Stat. 1411, 1421 (1982).

[49] 161 U.N.T.S. 193, T.S. No. 981, 56 Stat. 1354.

[50] S. Lyster, *International Wildlife Law* 97 (Cambridge, England: Grotius, 1985).

[51] *Id.* at 98.

[52] *Id.* at 99. The quotation is from the Preamble, *supra* note 49, 56 Stat. at 1356.

[53] Lyster, *supra* note 50, at 111.

[54] 16 U.S.C. §1538(a)(1)(B), (C) (1988).

[55] *Id.* §§1538(a)(1)(A), 1538(a)(2)(A).

[56] *Id.* §§1538(a)(1)(F), 1538(a)(2)(D).

[57] *Id.* §§1538(a)(1)(E), 1538(a)(2)(C). For the definition of the term "commercial activity," *see id.* at §1532(2) and Chapter 4.

[58] *Id.* §1537(d).

[59] H.R. CONF. REP. NO. 740, 93d Cong., 1st Sess. 27 (1973), *reprinted in* 1973 U.S. CODE CONG. & ADMIN. NEWS 2989, 3005. *Cf.* United States v. Mitchell, 553 F.2d 996 (5th Cir. 1977) (ruling that the criminal provisions of the Marine Mammal Protection Act do not have extraterritorial effect).

that the Act does not require the designation of critical habitat overseas.[60] Most recently, in a reversal of position, the Department of the Interior decided that federally funded projects overseas are not within the scope of the Act's consultative procedures. The court of appeals disagreed, and the Supreme Court reviewed the case. Only one Justice expressed a view on the merits of the case, however, with the majority ruling that the complaining parties lacked standing to litigate the issue.[61]

* * *

Encouraging conservation is easier at home than abroad. In the 1960s the industrialized nations were virtually alone in promoting environmentalism.[62] Even today, in developing countries, especially poor ones, people use up their natural resources in an effort to avoid starvation.[63] In the eyes of these developing countries, our preservationist values may seem to be unaffordable luxuries.

---

[60] H.R. REP. NO. 567, 97th Cong., 2d Sess. 20 (1982), *reprinted in* 1982 U.S. CODE CONG. & ADMIN. NEWS 2807, 2820.

[61] Lujan v. Defenders of Wildlife, 60 U.S.L.W. 4496 (U.S. June 9, 1992).

[62] *See* D. Pearce and R. Turner, *Economics of Natural Resources and the Environment* 23 (Baltimore: Johns Hopkins University Press, 1990).

[63] *Id.* at 342–43.

# Part II

# Other Federal Statutes Protecting or Regulating Wildlife

# Chapter 10

# The Lacey Act

The controversy over the Endangered Species Act[1] began with the Supreme Court's ruling in favor of the snail darter, a paper-clip-sized fish.[2] Recalling this, Justice Blackmun began a later case under the Lacey Act[3] with the words: "Once again, a little fish has caused a commotion."[4]

This time, the commotion centered around Bob Taylor, who operated a Maine bait business. When he bought 158,000 golden shiners from out of state, he violated a Maine statute prohibiting importation of live baitfish. The Lacey Act—a federal statute—makes it a federal crime to transport fish across state lines in violation of state law. Taylor's attempt to stop his prosecution under the federal law won him a full hearing before the U.S. Supreme Court. The only Justice to agree with Taylor was Justice Stevens, who declared: "There is something fishy about this case."[5]

## Historical Overview

The Lacey Act was one of the first federal wildlife laws.[6] Enacted in 1900,[7] the original Lacey Act was intended "to outlaw interstate traffic in birds and other animals illegally killed in their State of origin."[8] The original Lacey Act was amended many times.[9] In its early versions, it did not cover fish. Because

---

[1] 16 U.S.C. §§1531 *et seq.* (1988).

[2] Tennessee Valley Auth. v. Hill, 437 U.S. 153 (1978).

[3] 16 U.S.C. §§3371–78 (1988); 18 U.S.C. §42 (1988).

[4] Maine v. Taylor, 477 U.S. 131, 132 (1986).

[5] *Id.* at 151.

[6] *See* Chapter 2.

[7] Ch. 553, §§1–5, 31 Stat. 187.

[8] United States v. Carpenter, 933 F.2d 748, 751 (9th Cir. 1991) (quoting from S. REP. NO. 123, 97th Cong., 1st Sess. 2 (1981), *reprinted in* 1981 U.S. CODE CONG. & ADMIN. NEWS 1748, 1749 [hereinafter 1981 Senate Report]).

[9] Before the 1981 Lacey Act Amendments, the original Lacey Act, *supra* note 7, was amended in 1909 (ch. 321, §§241–43, 35 Stat. 1137), in 1935 (ch. 261, §201, 49 Stat. 380), in 1948 (Pub. L. No. 818, 62 Stat. 1096), in 1949 (ch. 139, §2, 63 Stat. 89), in 1960 (Pub. L. No. 86-702, 74 Stat. 753), and in 1969 (Pub. L. No. 91-135, §§7–8, 83 Stat. 275). The early history is discussed in M. Bean, *The Evolution of National Wildlife Law* 106–110 (New York: Praeger Scientific, 1983).

of this, Congress supplemented the Lacey Act with the Black Bass Act of 1926.[10]

In 1981, Congress overhauled the existing legislation, acting out of frustration at the inadequacy of the Lacey Act and the Black Bass Act, as written, to control the burgeoning trade in illegal fish and wildlife.[11] Designed to correct these deficiencies, the 1981 Amendments[12] combined the Lacey Act and the Black Bass Act into a single statute covering fish and wildlife and plants. Congress clarified the 1981 statute with amendments in 1988.[13]

## Offenses Under the Act

The modern version of the Lacey Act "federalizes the violation of most independent state, tribal [, foreign] and federal wildlife laws."[14]

### Trafficking in Violation of State Law

From the beginning the Lacey Act has been "a Federal tool to aid the States in enforcing their own laws concerning wildlife."[15] In its present form, section 3(a)(2)[16] provides that,

> It is unlawful for any person . . . to import, export, transport, sell, receive, acquire, or purchase in interstate or foreign commerce [any fish or wildlife or plant] taken, possessed, transported, or sold in violation of any law or regulation of any State.

Congress intended this provision to apply when someone violates state law by importing specimens into a state as well as by removing them from a state.[17] In the case discussed at the beginning of this chapter, Bob Taylor was violating a Maine law that forbids imports of baitfish into the state. Taylor convinced the federal court of appeals that the Maine law was an invalid restriction on interstate commerce. Disagreeing, the Supreme Court ruled[18] that Maine was legitimately concerned with protecting the state's fisheries from parasites that might be included in shipments. So Taylor's prosecution could proceed.

---

[10] Ch. 346, 44 Stat. 576 (1926).

[11] United States v. 594,464 Pounds of Salmon, 871 F.2d 824, 827 (9th Cir. 1989).

[12] Pub. L. No. 97-79, 95 Stat. 1073 (1981).

[13] Pub. L. No. 100-653, §§101–04, 102 Stat. 3825.

[14] United States v. Cameron, 888 F.2d 1279, 1280 (9th Cir. 1989).

[15] 1981 Senate Report, *supra* note 8, at 2, 1981 U.S. CODE CONG. & ADMIN. NEWS at 1749. *See* United States v. Bryant, 716 F.2d 1091, 1093 (6th Cir. 1983), *cert. denied,* 465 U.S. 1009 (1984).

[16] 16 U.S.C. §3372(a)(2) (1988).

[17] 1981 Senate Report, *supra* note 8, at 8, 1981 U.S. CODE CONG. & ADMIN. NEWS at 1755.

[18] Maine v. Taylor, *supra* note 4.

Taylor's case, however, illustrates an important principle. Lacey Act provisions like section 3(a)(2) do not "stand on their own."[19] In order to prosecute a case under section 3(a)(2), it is necessary to prove first that there has been a violation of state law,[20] which must, of course, be valid. If Taylor had succeeded in his attack on the Maine law, the federal prosecution would have failed too. Tribal Indians also use this type of defense when indicted under the Lacey Act for selling or transporting fish or wildlife taken contrary to state law. With varying success, the Indians assert that the state law is invalid because it infringes on their tribal rights and therefore does not support a Lacey Act prosecution.[21]

In most cases, however, persons indicted under the Lacey Act have no complaint against the state law they violate. Indeed, Lacey Act charges may be brought against persons who do not themselves commit the violation of state law. For example, a Connecticut fur dealer bought animal skins from a hunter who took the animals illegally in Vermont. The fur dealer was prosecuted under the Lacey Act for transporting the skins from Connecticut to New York.[22]

Under the Lacey Act, the government can often penalize the person who commits the underlying violation of state law. A Texan thought that he would escape penalties by testifying that he found a bighorn sheep, already dead, while on a hunting trip in Wyoming. By taking the horns and cape back to San Antonio, however, the hunter violated a Wyoming law that forbids removal of untagged sheep. So the hunter was held to have violated the Lacey Act by virtue of his "transport" of the sheep.[23] Another hunter, who shot wolverines out of season in Alaska, was penalized for arranging the "transport" of the hides to another state.[24] And a lecturer on wolves violated the Lacey Act when he "transported" three wolves from Illinois to New Jersey without getting a New Jersey permit for possession of the animals.[25]

## Trafficking in Violation of Federal Law

The current version of Lacey Act section 3(a) specifies[26] that:

> It is unlawful for any person . . . to import, export, transport, sell, receive, acquire, or purchase any fish or wildlife or plant taken, possessed, transported, or sold in violation of any law, treaty, or regulation of the United States or in violation of any Indian tribal law.

---

[19] 1981 Senate Report, *supra* note 8, at 4, 1981 U.S. CODE CONG. & ADMIN. NEWS at 1751.

[20] *Id.*

[21] *See* United States v. Alexander, 938 F.2d 942 (9th Cir. 1990); United States v. Skinna, 931 F.2d 530 (9th Cir. 1991); United States v. Williams, 898 F.2d 727 (9th Cir. 1990).

[22] U.S. Fish and Wildlife Serv. v. Picard, DOI Dkt. No. Boston 79-4 (ALJ ID dated April 19, 1979).

[23] U.S. Fish and Wildlife Serv. v. Hundley, DOI Dkt. No. Albuquerque 78-5 (ALJ ID dated Dec. 4, 1978).

[24] U.S. Fish and Wildlife Serv. v. Ramstad. DOI INV. 4-841, Alaska No. 78-1 (ALJ ID dated Aug. 24, 1978).

[25] U.S. Fish and Wildlife Serv. v. Harris, DOI Dkt. No. Boston 77-4 (ALJ ID dated Dec. 8, 1977).

[26] 16 U.S.C. §3372(a)(1) (1988).

Unlike the provision concerning wildlife taken in violation of state law, the federal law outlaws trafficking in intrastate commerce, as well as in interstate and foreign commerce. Before 1988 it was unlawful to traffick in specimens that had been illegally "taken or possess[ed]." The 1988 Amendments[27] expanded the prohibition so that it also covers transactions in articles "transported" or "sold" contrary to another federal law.[28]

Federal prosecutors and judges sometimes misunderstand one important limit to the Lacey Act. It punishes only trafficking in the illegally taken wildlife. It does not punish the violation of the underlying federal (or state) law. Forgetting this, the government mistakenly contended that a California goldfish farmer's "massacre" of birds was a violation of the Lacey Act.[29] Without doubt, the farmer violated the Migratory Bird Treaty Act[30] when his employees killed "thousands of birds . . . each year by shooting, poisoning or trapping."[31] But the Lacey Act does not itself prohibit unlawful takings:[32]

> In order to violate the Lacey Act a person must do something to wildlife that has already been "taken or possessed" in violation of [another] law. . . . The bird must be taken [in violation of another law] before acquiring it violates the Lacey Act. . . . The Lacey Act, as amended, did not intend to duplicate the Migratory Bird Treaty Act by making the very act of killing a bird a crime because the bird when shot fell on the property of the shooter.

The court reversed the farmer's conviction under the Lacey Act.

The Act also prohibits dealing in wildlife taken contrary to Indian tribal law. This applies to violations by both non-Indians and Indians.[33] Under the Lacey Act, Indians can also be prosecuted for violating federal regulations regarding tribal reservations.[34]

## Trafficking in Violation of Foreign Law

Lacey Act section 3(a)(2)[35] says that:

> It is unlawful for any person . . . to import, export, transport, sell, receive, acquire, or purchase in interstate or foreign commerce [any fish or wildlife (but not plants)] taken, possessed, transported, or sold . . . in violation of any foreign law.

---

[27] Pub. L. No. 100-653, 102 Stat. 3825.

[28] S. REP. NO. 563, 100th Cong., 2d Sess. 5 (1988), *reprinted in* 1988 U.S. CODE CONG. & ADMIN. NEWS, 5366, 5370 [hereinafter 1988 Senate Report].

[29] United States v. Carpenter, 933 F.2d 748, 750 (9th Cir. 1991).

[30] 16 U.S.C. §701 (1988). See Chapter 13.

[31] United States v. Carpenter, *supra* note 29, at 750.

[32] *Id.* at 750–51.

[33] United States v. Big Eagle, 881 F.2d 539 (8th Cir. 1989), *cert. denied*, 110 S. Ct. 1145 (1990); United States v. Sohappy, 770 F.2d 816 (9th Cir. 1985), *cert. denied*, 477 U.S. 906 (1986).

[34] United States v. Eberhardt 789 F.2d 1354 (9th Cir. 1986).

[35] 16 U.S.C. §3372(a) (1988).

Before the Lacey Act can be invoked, what kind of underlying law must be violated? In dealing with state and federal law violations, the Lacey Act specifically covers violations of any "regulation." In the Act's prohibition concerning foreign law, however, Congress did not mention regulations. Despite this, the courts ruled that foreign countries' regulations prohibiting fishing constitute "foreign law" under Lacey Act section 3(a)(2) and thereby support a Lacey Act prosecution.[36]

Violation of some foreign laws will not trigger a Lacey Act offense. In a controversial case, Pennsylvania wildlife importer Henry Molt was indicted under the Lacey Act for smuggling wildlife in violation of Fiji (and other) law. The Third Circuit ruled that the Lacey Act covered only foreign laws "designed and intended for the protection of wildlife in those countries."[37] Viewing the Fiji law as a revenue law, the court said that it did not trigger the applicability of the Lacey Act. Congress, however, disapproved of the Third Circuit's interpretation, labeling the quoted language as "too restrictive."[38]

Instead, Congress laid down this rule:[39]

> The Act's reference to 'any law, treaty or regulation' is not intended to include laws, treaties or regulations that are plainly *and solely* revenue laws with no specific reference to wildlife.

Congress meant the Lacey Act to cover laws that are revenue-producing or that concern safety if they also relate to wildlife protection.[40] Courts have not accepted the argument that the Lacey Act is unconstitutional because it takes into account the laws of foreign nations.[41]

## Trafficking Within U.S. Waters and Possessions

Lacey Act section 3(a)(3)[42] covers actions within the special maritime jurisdiction of the United States. Within that jurisdiction, it is unlawful to "possess" any fish or wildlife or plant taken, possessed, transported, or sold in violation of state law. The same section makes it unlawful to "possess" any fish or wildlife (but not plant) taken, possessed, transported, or sold in violation of foreign or tribal law.

Section 3(a)(3) incorporates the federal definition of special maritime and territorial jurisdiction. It includes the high seas and other waters within the United State's admiralty and maritime jurisdiction, but not within any state's

---

[36] United States v. Lee, 937 F.2d 1388, 1391 (9th Cir. 1991); United States v. 594,464 Pounds of Salmon, 871 F.2d 824, 825–28 (9th Cir. 1989).

[37] United States v. Molt, 599 F.2d 1217, 1218–19 (3rd Cir. 1979). *See id.*, 631 F.2d 258 (3d Cir. 1980).

[38] 1981 Senate Report, *supra* note 8, at 6, 1981 U.S. CODE CONG. & ADMIN. NEWS at 1753.

[39] *Id.* (italics added).

[40] *Id.*

[41] United States v. Rioseco, 845 F.2d 299 (11th Cir. 1988); United States v. Molt, *supra* note 37, 599 F.2d at n.1; United States v. 2,507 Live Canary Winged Parakeets, 689 F. Supp. 1106 (S.D. Fla. 1988).

[42] 16 U.S.C. §3372(a)(3) (1988).

jurisdiction. It also includes any U.S. ship or aircraft traveling on or over those waters. It also includes any U.S. flag vessel sailing on the Great Lakes, connecting waterways, or the St. Lawrence River.[43]

## Attempts to Commit Offenses

Lacey Act section (3)(a)(4)[44] makes it unlawful to attempt to commit any of the acts described so far. This provision also allows punishment of persons who cause a violation to be committed, even if they did not engage in the violative conduct themselves.[45]

## Sales of Guiding and Outfitting Services

The 1988 Amendments resolved a troublesome question. Many illegal expeditions are supported by outfitters who provide guiding services or false hunting licenses. Before 1988 the courts were splitting hairs about those outfitters' liability. If the outfitters did *more* than simply supply licenses or guiding services, they were culpable. For example, one guide was convicted under the Lacey Act when he conspired with the hunters to acquire elk taken contrary to Montana law.[46] An outfitter was convicted under the same statute when he aided others to transport bears killed contrary to Idaho law.[47]

But what if the outfitter only sold a hunting license or guiding services? In two cases,[48] courts ruled that the provision of guiding services or hunting permits did not constitute a "sale of wildlife" for purposes of the Lacey Act. The indictments against the outfitters were dismissed.

But that is not the end of the story. In the 1988 Amendments,[49] Congress decided that such outfitters and guides should not escape punishment. The legislature defined the term "sale," as it is used in the Lacey Act, to include the provision of guiding services and false licenses "for the illegal taking, acquiring, receiving, transporting, or possessing of fish or wildlife." "Thus, the apparent loophole in the law [was] closed."[50]

## Improper Marking of Packages

Since 1900[51] the Lacey Act has required that packages containing dead wildlife or wildlife parts be "plainly" marked so they can be readily inspected.

---

[43] 1981 Senate Report, *supra* note 8, at 8, 1981 U.S. CODE CONG. & ADMIN. NEWS at 1755.
[44] 16 U.S.C. §3372(a)(4) (1988).
[45] 1981 Senate Report, *supra* note 8, at 8, 1981 U.S. CODE CONG. & ADMIN. NEWS at 1755.
[46] United States v. Thomas, 887 F.2d 1341 (9th Cir. 1989).
[47] United States v. Powers, 923 F.2d 131 (9th Cir. 1990).
[48] United States v. DeMasters, 866 F.2d 327 (10th Cir. 1989); United States v. Stenberg, 803 F.2d 422, 435–37 (9th Cir. 1986).
[49] Pub. L. No. 100-653, §101, 102 Stat. 3825 (1988) (codified in 16 U.S.C. §3372(c)(1988)).
[50] United States v. DeMasters, *supra* note 48, at 330.
[51] Ch. 553, §4, 31 Stat. 187, 188.

In 1981 Congress decided that these statutory requirements were too "rigid," burdening the commercial seafood industry, among others.[52] So, in section 3(b) of the 1981 Amendments,[53] Congress gave the Secretary authority to craft standards. Section 3(b) now provides:

> It is unlawful for any person to import, export, or transport in interstate commerce [any container or package containing fish or wildlife unless it has been] plainly marked, labeled, or tagged in accordance with regulations issued pursuant to [the Act].

Under the Act,[54] "the Secretary" is either the Secretary of the Interior or the Secretary of Commerce, as program responsibilities are vested pursuant to Reorganization Plan 4 of 1970.[55] The Secretaries of the Interior and Commerce were told to issue joint regulations for the marking and labeling of packages. And they were instructed to craft regulations that are "in accordance with existing commercial practices."[56] The joint regulations are published in the Code of Federal Regulations.[57]

## False Records and Labels

In the prohibition against improper marking, Congress meant to cover mainly "simple, unintentional clerical violations."[58] In 1981 and 1988, Congress fashioned a second, more serious prohibition that covers deliberate false labeling—and also falsification of records and other documentation. This prohibition provides that:[59]

> It is unlawful for any person to make or submit any false record, account, or label for, or any false identification of, any fish, wildlife, or plant which has been, or is intended to be (1) imported, exported, transported, sold, purchased, or received from any foreign country, or (2) transported in interstate commerce.

False documentation is an offense "regardless of whether the wildlife was taken in violation of an underlying Federal or State law."[60] In other words, a person

---

[52] 1981 Senate Report, *supra* note 8, at 4, 8–9, 1981 U.S. CODE CONG. & ADMIN. NEWS at 1751, 1755–56.

[53] Pub. L. No. 97-79, §3(b), 95 Stat. 1073, 1074 (1981) (codified in 16 U.S.C. §3372(b)(1988)).

[54] 16 U.S.C. §3371(g) (1988).

[55] 84 Stat. 2090. The Secretary of Agriculture is the responsible official regarding the Act's provisions affecting the export and import of plants.

[56] Pub. L. No. 97-79, §7(a)(2), 95 Stat. 1073, 1078 (1981) (codified in 16 U.S.C. 3376(a)(2) (1988)).

[57] 50 C.F.R. §§14.81–82 (for the Fish and Wildlife Service) and §§246.1–246.2 (for the National Marine Fisheries Service) (1990).

[58] *See* 1981 Senate Report, *supra* note 8, at 9, 1981 U.S. CODE CONG. & ADMIN. NEWS at 1756.

[59] Pub. L. No. 100-653, §101, 102 Stat. 3825 (1988), amending a provision added by Pub. L. No. 97-79, §3(a)(4), 95 Stat. 1073, 1074 (1981). The current provision is codified in 16 U.S.C. §3372(d) (1988).

[60] 1988 Senate Report, *supra* note 28, at 5, 1988 U.S. CODE CONG. & ADMIN. NEWS at 5370.

violates the Lacey Act by dealing in wildlife with false documentation—even if the wildlife is legally taken under other laws.

## Exceptions

In section 8 of the Lacey Act,[61] Congress carved out several narrow exceptions to the Act's prohibitions.

Lacey Act section 8(a)[62] exempts certain activities that are regulated by a fishery management plan in effect under the Magnuson Fishery Conservation and Management Act of 1976.[63] In one case, a fishing boat captain was prosecuted under the Lacey Act for selling fish caught in a prohibited zone near Alaska. The fisherman pointed out that the prohibited zone was within a Magnuson Act management plan and, he argued, his activities were exempt from the Lacey Act. In fact, however, the management plan excluded the type of fish—halibut—that the fisherman had sold. So the Ninth Circuit upheld the fisherman's conviction.[64]

There is another limitation to the section 8(a) exemption. It exempts only activities concerning fish gained through violation of federal or tribal law. However, the Lacey Act continues to apply to violations of state law related to fish—even if the fish are caught within a zone under a federal fishery management plan.[65]

Lacey Act section 8 (b)(1)[66] exempts activities regulated by the Tuna Conventions Act of 1950[67] and the Atlantic Tunas Convention Act of 1975.[68] The purpose of this exemption is to avoid "duplicate enforcement."[69]

Lacey Act section 8 (b)(2)[70] exempts activities involving certain harvesting of highly migratory fish like tuna, which spawn and migrate over great distances. The United States takes the position that coastal nations do not have exclusive rights to manage tuna. Disagreeing, some of those nations assert management rights over tuna up to 200 miles off their coasts. If a fisherman catches tuna in violation of such a foreign law, and the United States refuses to recognize that law, the United States does not want to prosecute the fisherman under the Lacey act. This exemption insures that the fisherman will not be deemed in violation of the Lacey Act.[71]

---

[61] Pub. L. No. 97-79, §8, 95 Stat. 1073, 1078 (1981).

[62] 16 U.S.C. §3377(a) (1988).

[63] 18 U.S.C. §§1801–1882 (1988). Amended by the Fishery Conservation Amendments of 1990, Pub. L. No. 101-627, 104 Stat. 4436 (1990).

[64] United States v. Doubleday, 804 F.2d 1091 (9th Cir. 1986), *cert. denied*, 481 U.S. 1005 (1987).

[65] 1981 Senate Report, *supra* note 8, at 16, 1981 U.S. CODE CONG. & ADMIN. NEWS at 1763.

[66] 16 U.S.C. §3377(b)(1) (1988).

[67] 16 U.S.C. §§951–61 (1988).

[68] *Id.* §971–71(i).

[69] 1981 Senate Committee Report, *supra* note 8, at 17, 1981 U.S. CODE CONG. & ADMIN. NEWS at 1764.

[70] 16 U.S.C. §3377(b)(2) (1988).

[71] 1981 Senate Report, *supra* note 8, at 17, 1981 U.S. CODE CONG. & ADMIN. NEWS at 1764.

Finally, Lacey Act section 8(c)[72] exempts shipments if the fish, wildlife, or plants are legally taken and are en route to a state where they may be legally possessed. For example, a hunter legally shot bears in Maine and shipped them through New Jersey to a third state where bears were legally possessed. Under Lacey Act section 8(c), that is not a federal offense even if New Jersey's laws prohibit it.[73] "[T]he federal interest in prosecution is not great enough to warrant federal involvement."[74]

## Penalties and Sanctions

In an apparent attempt to try to make the punishment fit the crime, Congress constructed a bewildering variety of penalties.

## Civil Penalties

### *Major Violations*

The largest civil penalty is $10,000. This may apply where the violator should know, in the exercise of due care, that the articles were taken, possessed, transported, or sold contrary to an underlying law, treaty, or regulation. Normally, this penalty does not apply to violations of the prohibitions against improper marking or false labeling or documentation.[75] The 1988 Amendments made one change in that rule. If a person knowingly violates the prohibitions against false labeling or documentation, the 1988 Amendments allow the $10,000 penalty to be imposed.[76]

In 1981 Congress imposed the "due care" standard so that penalties can be tailored to the violators' "varying degrees of knowledge."[77] For example, the Senate committee observed, zoo curators are expected to know that a reptile is Australian and that Australia does not allow export of that reptile without special permits. So the curators would not be exercising due care unless they checked for those permits. On the other hand, the airline company which ships the reptile may be unaware that Australia does not allow the particular reptile to be imported. If the airline is notified of the problem and still tranships the reptile, then the airline would probably fail to pass the due care test.[78]

---

[72] 16 U.S.C. §3377(c) (1988).

[73] United States v. Martinell, 611 F. Supp. 399, 400 (M.D. Pa. 1985) (dictum).

[74] 1981 Senate Report, *supra* note 8, at 17, 1981 U.S. CODE CONG. & ADMIN. NEWS at 1764.

[75] 16 U.S.C. §3373(a) (1988).

[76] Pub. L. No. 100-653, §102(a), 102 Stat. 3825 (1988) (codified in 16 U.S.C. §3373(a)(1) (1988)).

[77] 1981 Senate Report, *supra* note 8 at 10, 1981 U.S. CODE CONG. & ADMIN. NEWS at 1757.

[78] *Id.*

### *Lesser Offenses*

Congress established a different punishment plan for "[r]elatively minor violations."[79] An offense is treated as relatively minor if it meets two criteria. The first is that it concerns fish, wildlife, or plants worth less than $350. The second is that the offense involves only the transportation, acquisition, or receipt of the articles. For such violations, Congress said that the penalty should not exceed the maximum provided for violation of the underlying state, federal, foreign, or tribal law.[80] Suppose, for example, that someone kills ducks worth less than $350 and thereby violates a state law having a maximum $450 civil penalty. Under the Lacey Act, the Secretary can impose a penalty for illegal interstate transportation, but that federal penalty may not exceed $450.[81]

Again,this penalty does not normally apply to violations of the prohibitions against improper marking or false labeling or documentation.[82]

### *Marking Violations*

The marking and labeling regulations are primarily intended as a regulatory tool to assist in identifying shipments of fish and wildlife. Because of this, Congress limited the penalty for "simple, unintentional clerical violations of the regulations" to a maximum $250 penalty.[83] Even before the 1988 Amendments, Congress and the courts recognized that this provision was not meant to immunize serious infractions. If a package is falsely marked in order to evade government scrutiny, Congress believed that "such mislabeling should not be treated as a mere marking offense."[84] A court applied this rule in a 1982 decision,[85] concerning a dealer in tropical fish who regularly sold sea turtles, shipping them in boxes mislabeled as containing pantherfish. Sales of sea turtles are prohibited under the Endangered Species Act and, by virtue of his shipments in interstate commerce, the dealer violated the Lacey Act. Assessed $1,000 for each of 11 Lacey Act violations, the dealer argued that he was subject, at most, to the maximum statutory penalty for mismarking of $250. The court ruled, however, that this limitation did not extend to "a continuous, multiviolation mislabeling scheme."[86] Under the current statute, as amended in 1988,[87] the trader would be subject to a penalty of up to $10,000 for a "knowing" violation of the marking prohibitions.

---

[79] *Id.* at 3, 1981 U.S. CODE CONG. & ADMIN. NEWS at 1750.

[80] 16 U.S.C. §3373(a) (1988).

[81] 1981 Senate Report, *supra* note 8, at 9–10, 1981 U.S. CODE CONG. & ADMIN. NEWS at 1756–57.

[82] *Id.*

[83] 1981 Senate Report, *supra* note 8, at 9, 1981 U.S. CODE CONG. & ADMIN. NEWS at 1756 (referring to the provision now codified at 16 U.S.C. §3373(a)(2) (1988)).

[84] *Id.*

[85] Newell v. Baldridge, 548 F. Supp. 39, 45–46 (W.D. Wash. 1982).

[86] *Id.* at 46.

[87] Pub. L. No. 100-653, §102(a), 102 Stat. 3825 (codified in 16 U.S.C. §3373(a) (1988)).

*Mitigation of Penalties*

The Secretary is given complete discretion to remit or mitigate any civil penalty.[88] In determining penalties, the Secretary is instructed to take into account the nature and gravity of the offense, as well as the violator's culpability and ability to pay.[89] Congress told the Secretary to administer the law so that innocent purchasers or consumers are not penalized. For example, Congress frowned on penalizing an individual when he voluntarily reports a technical violation such as receipt of several more species than appear on the export document.[90]

## Criminal Penalties

The Act punishes some violations as felonies and others as misdemeanors. Congress distinguishes between the two on the basis of both the nature of the activity and the perpetrator's culpability.[91]

*Felonies*

The most stringent penalties are a $20,000 fine, five years imprisonment, or both. These penalties are reserved for persons who violate the Act knowingly. Not all knowing violations are punished so severely, however. In the 1981 Amendments, Congress provided for felony punishment for any person who:

> (A) knowingly imports or exports any fish or wildlife or plants in violation of any provision of this [Act] (other than [the improper labeling or marking prohibitions]) or (B) violates any provision of this [Act] (other than [the improper labeling or marking prohibitions]) by knowingly engaging in conduct that involves the sale or purchase of, the offer of sale or purchase of, or the intent to sell or purchase, fish or wildlife or plants with a market value in excess of $350 [knowing that the articles are tainted by violation of an underlying law].[92]

Anyone who violates this provision "commits a felony."[93] Congress deliberately treated knowing importation and exportation as a felony, regardless of the article's value.[94]

In 1988, Congress also provided this most severe punishment for knowing violations of the false labeling prohibition if they involve:

---

[88] 16 U.S.C. §3373(a)(5) (1988).

[89] *Id.* §3373(a)(6).

[90] 1981 Senate Report, *supra* note 8, at 10, 1981 U.S. CODE CONG. & ADMIN. NEWS at 1757.

[91] *Id.* at 11, 1981 U.S. CODE CONG. & ADMIN. NEWS at 11.

[92] Pub. L. No. 97-79, §4(d), 95 Stat. 1073, 1076 (1981) (codified in 16 U.S.C. §1773(d)(1) (1988)).

[93] United States v. Thomas, 887 F.2d 1341, 1346 (9th Cir. 1989).

[94] 1981 Senate Committee Report, *supra* note 8, at 11, 1981 U.S. CODE CONG. & ADMIN. NEWS at 1758.

(i) the importation or exportation of fish or wildlife or plants, or (ii) the sale or purchase, offer of sale or purchase, or commission of an act with intent to sell or purchase fish or wildlife or plants with a market value greater than $350.[95]

The Senate committee defended the market value test as "useful to distinguish small scale commercial activity that may not warrant a felony penalty, such as the sale of one illegally taken duck, from commercial activity that does warrant such a penalty."[96]

The standard of culpability has changed over the years. Before the 1981 Amendments, the Lacey act imposed felony penalties for violations that were committed "knowingly and willfully."[97] A court interpreted this as requiring that felons have "guilty knowledge," knowing that their actions violate the law.[98] The 1981 Amendments deleted the requirement of "willfulness." One court said that the government must still show that the perpetrators acted with "scienter or knowledge."[99] Still, the government does not need to prove that the violators knew of the Lacey Act's existence.[100]

*Misdemeanors*

In 1981 Congress was concerned about the culpability of persons who do not actually know that certain fish, wildlife, or plants are tainted by violations of other laws. The Lacey Act is a general intent statute. Congress feared that individuals might be prosecuted even if they innocently obtained an illegal specimen and then transported it in interstate commerce. So Congress added a "due care" requirement. Thus, the statute requires proof that the individual should have known, in the exercise of due care, that the specimen was taken, possessed, transported, or sold in violation of another law.[101]

Violations of the "due care" provision are punishable with a $10,000 penalty, imprisonment for one year, or both. Anyone who violates this provision "commits a misdemeanor."[102]

The "due care" misdemeanor provision does not punish cases of improper marking or false labeling and documentation. In 1981, however, Congress provided that, if persons knowingly engage in false labeling or false documenta-

---

[95] Pub. L. No. 100-653, §102(b), 102 Stat. 3825, 3826 (1988) (codified in 16 U.S.C. §1773(d)(3)(A) (1988)).

[96] 1981 Senate Report, *supra* note 8, at 12, 1981 U.S. CODE CONG. & ADMIN. NEWS at 1759.

[97] Pub. L. No. 91-135, §7, 83 Stat. 275, 280 (1969).

[98] United States v. Jonas Brothers of Seattle, Inc., 368 F. Supp. 783, 784–85 (D. Alaska 1974).

[99] United States v. Cameron, 888 F.2d 1279, 1282 (9th Cir. 1989).

[100] United States v. Todd, 735 F.2d 146, 151 (5th Cir. 1984), *cert. denied*, 469 U.S. 1189 (1985) (citing 1981 Senate Committee Report, *supra* note 8, at 11, 1981 U.S. CODE CONG. & ADMIN. NEWS at 1758).

[101] 1981 Senate Report, *supra* note 8, at 12, 1981 U.S. CODE CONG. & ADMIN. NEWS at 1759 (referring to Pub. L. No. 97-79, §4(d)(2), 95 Stat. 1073, 1076 (codified in 16 U.S.C. §3373(d)(2)(1988)).

[102] United States v. Thomas, *supra* note 93.

tion, but do not qualify for the felony penalty, they may be fined under title 18 of the U.S. Code, imprisoned for one year, or both.[103]

## Permit Sanctions

Congress intended to rid the countryside and marketplace of persons who violate wildlife laws. The Secretary was given a free hand in suspending, revoking, or modifying export and import licenses held by persons convicted of criminally violating the Lacey Act. The Secretary was given the same power over permits to operate a quarantine station or rescue center for imported wildlife or plants. In the same way, hunters and fisherman can forfeit their permits and licenses. The Secretary can act without any obligation to pay compensation, reimbursement, or damages.[104]

## Forfeiture

### *Forfeiture of Wildlife*

Before 1981 the Lacey Act did not require violators to forfeit illegal shipments unless the government proved that the violators knowingly violated the Act or failed to exercise due care. The 1981 Amendments, however, changed this rule. Imposing "strict liability,"[105] Congress provided that:

> All fish or wildlife or plants imported, exported, transported, sold, received, acquired, or purchased contrary to the [Act or related regulations (except for marking violations)] shall be subject to forfeiture . . . notwithstanding any culpability requirements for civil penalty assessments or criminal prosecution.[106]

By imposing strict liability, Congress "placed the burden of assuring compliance with foreign law on the wildlife transporter."[107]

Congress took a tough attitude towards forfeiture because it wanted to treat illegal shipments as, in effect, contraband. Once the government makes a prima facie showing that a shipment is unlawful, the court must enter a decree of forfeiture. The owner's good faith or innocence is immaterial.[108]

---

[103] Pub. L. No. 100-653, §102(b), 102 Stat. 3825, 3825–26 (1988).

[104] 16 U.S.C. §3373(e) (1988).

[105] 1981 Senate Report, *supra* note 8, at 2, 13, 1981 U.S. CODE CONG. & ADMIN. NEWS at 1749, 1760.

[106] Pub. L. No. 97-79, §5(a), 95 Stat. 1073, 1076 (1981) (codified in 16 U.S.C. §3374 (a)(1) (1988)).

[107] United States v. 594,464 Pounds of Salmon, 871 F.2d 824, 828 (9th Cir. 1989).

[108] 1981 Senate Report, *supra* note 8, at 13, 1981 U.S. CODE CONG. & ADMIN. NEWS at 1760. *See* United States v. 2,507 Live Canary Winged Parakeets, 689 F. Supp. 1106, 1113, 1117–19 (S.D. Fla. 1988); United States v. 3,210 Crusted Sides of Caiman Crocodilus, 636 F. Supp. 1281, 1286–87 (S.D. Fla. 1986).

*Forfeiture of Equipment*

Violators can also be forced to forfeit their equipment and vehicles used in the offense. This type of forfeiture is limited to purchase-and-sale transactions. In addition, the owners must be privy to the infraction or should have known, in the exercise of due care, that their equipment or vehicles would be used in a criminal violation. Finally, the government must have obtained a felony conviction.[109]

It is not double jeopardy for the government to obtain a conviction and, subsequently, to seek forfeiture of the convicted person's vessel.[110]

*Forfeiture Administration*

Both the courts and the Secretary have authority to enforce the forfeiture sanctions.[111] Under the Interior Department's regulations, that Department can seek forfeiture through administrative proceedings if the property is not worth more than $100,000.[112]

Congress recognized that there will be cases where merchandise is seized because of a minor, technical violation. For example, as the result of an honest mistake, an individual may not have all the foreign documentation required. Later, even after a decree of forfeiture is entered, the individual may be able to supply exculpating proof from the foreign country. In such cases, Congress gave the government discretion to remit or mitigate the forfeiture.[113] Prompted by Congress, the Interior Department adopted regulations providing for return of property and restoration of proceeds.[114]

Congress also made violators liable for the costs incurred in storage, care, and maintenance of any fish, wildlife, or plants that the government seizes.[115] The regulations allow the agency to assess those costs.[116]

## Injurious Wildlife

The Lacey Act's most antique feature is its prohibition against importation of injurious wildlife. Enacted in 1900 as part of the original Lacey Act,[117] this provision was not incorporated into the Lacey Act Amendments of 1981. It remains part of Title 18.[118]

---

[109] 1981 Senate Report, *supra* note 8, at 13–14, 1981 U.S. CODE CONG. & ADMIN. NEWS at 1760–61 (referring to Pub. L. No. 97-79, §5(a)(2), 95 Stat. 1073, 1076–77 (1981) (codified in 16 U.S.C. §3374(a)(2) (1988)).

[110] United States v. U.S. Fishing Vessel Maylin, 725 F. Supp. 1222 (S.D. Fla. 1989).

[111] 16 U.S.C. §3375(a), (c) (1988).

[112] 50 C.F.R. §12.23 (1990).

[113] 1981 Senate Report, *supra* note 8, at 13, 1981 U.S. CODE CONG. & ADMIN. NEWS at 1760.

[114] 50 C.F.R. §§12.41, 12.51 (1990).

[115] 16 U.S.C. §3374(c) (1988).

[116] 50 C.F.R. §12.42 (1990).

[117] Ch. 553, §2, 31 Stat. 187, 188.

[118] 18 U.S.C. §42 (1988).

This provision's original purpose was to protect domestic agriculture and horticulture. It prohibited imports into the United States of the mongoose and the English sparrow, among other wild animals and birds. The Secretary of Agriculture was authorized to add other "injurious" animals and birds to the prohibited list.

Today the provision has been expanded in scope but not purpose. It still prohibits imports of various named species. The Secretary of the Interior can extend the "injurious" classification to other varieties—not only of wild mammals and birds—but also of fish (including mollusks and crustacea), amphibians, reptiles, and their eggs and offspring. In 1990 Congress amended this Lacey Act provision by specifying that the zebra mussel, which was infesting the Great Lakes, is an injurious species.[119]

As now written, this Lacey Act provision bans importation of injurious species into the United States or its territories or possessions. The provision also prohibits any shipment of those species between the continental United States, Hawaii, the District of Columbia, Puerto Rico, and U.S. possessions. The Secretary has issued comprehensive regulations implementing these prohibitions.[120] If persons import or ship injurious specimens, they commit a crime and may be fined up to $500, imprisoned for up to six months, or both.[121] The government has the right to export or destroy the prohibited articles at the importer's or consignee's expense.[122]

There are exceptions to the ban on injurious specimens. The prohibition does not restrict the importation of dead natural-history specimens for museums or for scientific collections. It does not restrict the importation of domesticated canaries, parrots, or other cage birds that the Secretary designates. And the Secretary can also permit imports of specimens for zoological, educational, medical, and scientific purposes.[123]

## Humane Transport of Wildlife

In 1949 Congress directed the Secretary of the Treasury to prescribe requirements for the transportation of "wild animals and birds" under humane and healthful conditions.[124] In the Lacey Act Amendments of 1981,[125] Congress transferred this function to the Secretary of the Interior.

Nothing much happened for years. Finally, in 1987 the Fish and Wildlife Service issued regulations that implemented this Lacey Act provision.[126] Zoos, airlines, and others protested that the regulations were faulty and would create

[119] Pub. L. No. 101-646, §1208, 104 Stat. 4761, 4772 (1990).
[120] 50 C.F.R. §§16.1–16.15 (1990).
[121] 18 U.S.C. §42(b) (1988).
[122] *Id.* §42(a)(1).
[123] *Id.* §42(a)(4). *See* 50 C.F.R. Part 16 (1990).
[124] Ch. 139, §2, 63 Stat. 89.
[125] Pub. L. No. 97-79, §9(d), 95 Stat. 1073, 1079 (codified in 18 U.S.C. §42(c) (1988)).
[126] 52 Fed. Reg. 53,274 (1987).

chaos in the trade. The Service tried to postpone the regulations' effective date. A court held, however, that the agency's attempted postponement was ineffective because of failure to comply with the Administrative Procedure Act.[127] The Service now has regulations in effect.[128]

Under the Lacey Act, it is unlawful for anyone to cause or permit wild animals or birds to be transported in inhumane or unhealthful conditions.[129] The statute attempts to lay down a standard of proof. It says that if the vessel or conveyance contains a substantial ratio of dead, crippled, diseased, or starving wildlife, that is *prima facie* evidence of a violation. Invoking this statute, the government indicted individuals who managed the "ill-fated shipment of eighty wild animals" from East Africa to New York.[130] Confined in cages on the ship's top deck, and subjected to heavy rain and cold weather, ten percent of the animals died during the voyage and another five percent died soon thereafter. The court, however, held that these facts did not establish a violation of the Lacey Act.

---

[127] Animal Welfare Inst. v. Hodel, No. 88-548 (D.D.C., filed March 1, 1988).
[128] 50 C.F.R. §§14.101–14.204 (1990).
[129] 18 U.S.C. §42(c) (1988).
[130] United States v. States Marine Lines, 334 F. Supp. 84, 85 (S.D.N.Y. 1971).

# Chapter 11

# The Marine Mammal Protection Act

The Ninety-Second Congress criticized the treatment of marine mammals as ranging from "malign neglect" to "virtual genocide."[1] Congress was especially outraged at the slaughter of dolphins by tuna fishermen in the eastern tropical Pacific Ocean.

In those waters, yellowfin tuna congregate with herds of dolphins, and the two groups move together. The dolphins swim near the top of the ocean, where they are visible as they break the surface to breathe and leap into the air. The tuna forage below the dolphins in deeper water. Fishing fleets hunt tuna by searching for dolphins. The fishermen surround groups of dolphins with cup-like purse-seine nets. The nets' open bottom is then drawn closed in the manner of a drawstring purse, trapping both the dolphins and the tuna below. Many of the dolphins are injured or drowned. Their carcasses are discarded into the sea.[2]

In 1970 and 1971, the U.S. tuna fleet's purse-seine fishing killed more than 600,000 dolphins.[3] Congress moved swiftly to enact the Marine Mammal Protection Act[4] the following year.

## Congress' Choice of Strategies

The 1972 Congress was asked to choose between opposing strategies for protecting marine mammals. The fishing industry wanted Congress to rely upon a scientific management program. Conservationists pressed for a total ban on the taking and importation of these mammals. Congress rejected the flat ban, not on principle, but because the ban was considered to be inflexible,

---

[1] H.R. REP. NO. 707, 92d Cong., 2d Sess. 11 (1971), *reprinted in* 1972 U.S. CODE CONG. & ADMIN. NEWS 4144 [hereinafter 1971 House Report].

[2] Earth Island Inst. v. Mosbacher, 929 F.2d 1449 (9th Cir. 1991), *aff'g* 746 F. Supp. 964 (N.D. Cal. 1990); American Tunaboat Ass'n v. Baldridge, 738 F.2d 1013 (9th Cir. 1984); Balelo v. Baldridge, 724 F.2d 753 (9th Cir.)(en banc), *cert. denied,* 467 U.S. 1252 (1984); Committee for Humane Legislation, Inc. v. Richardson, 540 F.2d 1141 (D.C. Cir. 1976), *aff'g in part* 414 F. Supp. 297 (D.D.C.).

[3] *Id.*

[4] Pub. L. No. 92-552, 86 Stat. 1027 (1972) (codified in 16 U.S.C. §§1361–1407 (1988)).

unrealistic, and unlikely to benefit the animals concerned. Instead the legislature adopted a compromise between the two approaches,[5] consisting of a two-track strategy: a management program combined with a partial moratorium.

## The Scientific Management Program

Administration of the Act is divided between government agencies. The Secretary of Commerce is responsible for whales, dolphins (porpoises), sea lions, and seals. The Secretary of the Interior has jurisdiction over polar bears, walruses, sea otters, and dugongs (sea cows or manatees).[6] The Act's references to "the Secretary" normally mean whichever of the two officials has responsibility for the species.[7]

Congress insisted that these officials manage the scientific program for the benefit of the animals and not for the benefit of commercial exploitation.[8] To this end, the Act establishes a "primary objective" for the management program: "to maintain the health and stability of the marine ecosystem."[9] Whenever consistent with that primary objective, the management program's "goal" is to maintain marine mammals at their "optimum sustainable population."[10]

These last three words—"optimum sustainable population"—have proven to be the Act's most important phrase. Nonetheless, the Act defines the phrase in the most opaque language:

> [W]ith respect to any population stock, the number of animals which will result in the maximum productivity of the population or the species, keeping in mind the carrying capacity of the habitat and the health of the ecosystem of which they form a constituent element.[11]

Maintaining marine mammals at their "optimum sustainable population" is the goal—not only of the management program—but of the entire Act.[12]

Driven by these goals, the government launched ambitious scientific initiatives. In 1972, when it enacted the new law, Congress found that existing federal programs for research and management were "quite small."[13] The 1972

---

[5] Committee for Humane Legislation v. Richardson, *supra* note 2, 414 F. Supp. at 300.

[6] H.R. REP. NO. 970, 100th Cong., 2d Sess. 14 (1988), *reprinted in* 1988 U.S. CODE CONG. & ADMIN. NEWS 6154, 6155 [hereinafter 1988 House Report]. *See* 50 C.F.R. §18.3 (1990).

[7] 16 U.S.C. §1362(11) (1988). In section 114, concerning interim exemptions for commercial fisheries, the term "Secretary" refers only to the Secretary of Commerce. 16 U.S.C. §1383a(o)(2).

[8] 1971 House Report, *supra* note 1, at 22, 1972 U.S. CODE CONG. & ADMIN. NEWS at 4154.

[9] 16 U.S.C. §1361(6) (1988).

[10] *Id.*

[11] 16 U.S.C. §1362(8)(1988). In 1981, Congress gave its approval to the Service's definition of "optimum sustainable population." It is any population level within a range of population levels. The upper bound of the range is the largest population that the ecosystem can support. The lower bound of the range is the population level that results in maximum net productivity. H.R. NO. 228. 97th Cong., 1st Sess. 16 (1981), *reprinted in* 1981 U.S. CODE CONG. & ADMIN. NEWS 1458, 1467 [hereinafter 1981 House Report.] *See* 50 C.F.R. §216.3 (1990).

[12] 16 U.S.C. §1361(2) (1988).

[13] 1971 House Report, *supra* note 1, at 13, 1972 U.S. CODE CONG. & ADMIN. NEWS at 4146.

Congress appropriated $15.3 million over a five-year period for an enhanced program.[14] In addition, Congress established a Marine Mammal Commission to review existing and proposed programs and to recommend improvements. Congress also established a Scientific Advisory Committee to aid the Commission and, if necessary, to carry out its own research.[15] In section 110 of the Act,[16] Congress established a fund from which the Secretary can make research grants. And, in section 111(a),[17] the Secretary was directed to undertake research and development to improve commercial fishing methods and gear.

In subsequent years, Congress augmented the research and management program. Often Congress created programs as companions to special exemptions for the commercial fishing industry. In 1981, for example, the legislature amended section 110 to subsidize research into methods to catch yellowfin tuna without killing dolphins.[18] Again in 1988, Congress told the Secretary to compile information, conduct studies, and make status reports and conservation plans concerning marine mammals.[19]

## The Moratorium

Congress put teeth in its two-track strategy by declaring a moratorium in sweeping language. Section 2 of the Act states, "There shall be a moratorium on the taking and importation of marine mammals and marine mammal products."[20] The term "moratorium" is defined as "a complete cessation" of taking and "a complete ban" on importation.[21] In fact, the moratorium is subject to exceptions in particular cases. Nonetheless, the moratorium's proscriptions are rigorous.

### Prohibitions on Taking

Subject to the Act's exemptions, both U.S. subjects and foreigners are forbidden to take marine mammals in U.S. territory. Persons subject to U.S. jurisdiction are also forbidden to take marine mammals on the high seas. If a ship, plane, or other conveyance is subject to U.S. jurisdiction, it may not be used to aid takings in U.S. territory or on the high seas.[22]

In addition to repeating these prohibitions, the National Marine Fisheries Service's regulations say that it is unlawful, during the moratorium, for any U.S. subject to take any marine mammal.[23] The prohibition purports to be

---

[14] *Id.*
[15] *Id. See* 16 U.S.C. §1401–03 (1988).
[16] Pub. L. No. 92-522, §110, 86 Stat. 1027, 1041 (1972).
[17] Pub. L. No. 92-522, §111(a), 86 Stat. 1027, 1041 (codified in 16 U.S.C. §1381(a) (1988)).
[18] Pub. L. No. 97-58, §5, 95 Stat. 979, 986–87 (codified in 16 U.S.C. §1380 (1988)).
[19] 16 U.S.C. §§1383a(g)–(h), 1383b (1988).
[20] *Id.* §1371(a).
[21] *Id.*§1362(7).
[22] *Id.* §1372(a).
[23] 50 C.F.R. §216.11(c) (1990).

effective without geographical restriction. Reading the regulation that way, the government prosecuted a U.S. citizen who captured 21 dolphins within the territorial waters of the Bahamas. The court of appeals set aside the conviction, ruling that the Act did not extend to actions occurring in the territory of another nation.[24]

The Act defines the term "taking" broadly. The term includes "actual or attempted harassing, hunting, capturing, and killing."[25] The agency regulations supplement this definition by prohibiting the collection of dead animals. They also ban the restraint or detention of an animal, or any negligent or intentional acts that disturb or molest an animal.[26] So, when a marine mammal entangles itself in a fishing net, the fisherman commits a "taking" even if the animal struggles free before it drowns.[27]

## Prohibitions on Importation

It is also unlawful to import marine mammals that were taken in violation of the Act. It is equally unlawful to import mammals that were taken illegally in another country. No one may import a product made from a marine mammal if the mammal was unlawfully taken, or if the product cannot be sold legally in the country of origin.[28]

Congress included a special prohibition aimed at foreign fishing fleets whose nets ensnare dolphins and other marine mammals. As just noted, the Act's anti-taking prohibitions apply to foreign fishermen only in U.S. territory. Congress needed to find another sanction that would affect the foreign fleets' catches on the high seas. So Congress directed the Secretary of the Treasury to "ban" imports of fish caught with commercial fishing techniques that do not meet U.S. standards.[29] To implement this, the Act makes it illegal to import fish caught by techniques which U.S. fishermen are forbidden to use.[30]

The Act[31] also makes it illegal to import marine mammals that were taken in an inhumane manner or are from populations that are depleted. Congress added a ban on the importation of mammals that, when taken, were pregnant, nursing, or underage. In enacting this last prohibition, Congress was responding to "emotional concerns."[32] Nonetheless, a court upheld the ban on imports of

---

[24] United States v. Mitchell, 553 F.2d 996 (5th Cir. 1977).

[25] Katelnikoff v. Department of the Interior, 657 F. Supp. 659, 662 (D. Alaska 1986)(referring to 16 U.S.C. §1362(12)).

[26] *Id. See* 50 C.F.R. §§18.3, 216.3 (1990).

[27] Federation of Japan Salmon Fisheries Coop. Ass'n v. Baldridge, 679 F. Supp. 37, 40 (D.D.C. 1987), *aff'd sub nom.* Kokechik Fisherman's Ass'n v. Secretary of Commerce, 839 F.2d 795 (D.C. Cir. 1988), *cert. denied sub nom.* Verity v. Center for Environmental Education, 488 U.S. 1004 (1989).

[28] 16 U.S.C. §1372(c) (1988).

[29] *Id.* §1371(a)(2).

[30] *Id.* §1372(c)(3).

[31] *Id.* §1372(b).

[32] Animal Welfare Inst. v. Kreps, 561 F.2d 1002, 1012 (D.C. Cir. 1977), *cert. denied sub nom.* Fouke Co. v. Animal Welfare Institute, 434 U.S. 1013 (1978).

nursing and underage mammals.[33] Some of these prohibitions are subject to exceptions discussed later.

## Other Prohibitions

The Act's prohibitions go beyond taking and importation. If a mammal was taken illegally, persons may not possess, transport, purchase, sell, or offer to purchase or sell the mammal (or any product made from the mammal). No one may use any U.S. port, harbor, or other place in connection with illegal taking or importation. And it is illegal for commercial fishermen to use any fishing method prohibited for their fishery.[34]

## The Secretary's Power to Grant Waivers

The Secretary is empowered to waive the moratorium and to allow both taking and importation in particular cases.[35] "Waiving the moratorium is a two-stage process. In the first stage, the [Secretary] must determine if there will be a waiver and promulgate regulations containing the terms of the waiver."[36]

## The Procedure for Issuing Regulations and Permits

Section 103 of the Act[37] specifies the regulations that allow the taking and importation. Before a regulation can be issued, the Secretary must follow prescribed procedures that track the Act's substantive policies. Thus, when the Secretary intends to grant a waiver, the intent must first be published in a Federal Register notice that contains:

1. A statement of the affected mammal's existing population
2. A statement of the waiver's impact on the mammal's optimum sustainable population
3. A statement describing the evidence on which the Secretary intends to rely

In addition, the Secretary must make public any government studies or recommendations relating to the proposed regulation.[38]

---

[33] Globe Fur Dyeing Corp. v. United States, 467 F. Supp. 177 (D.D.C. 1978), *aff'd*, 612 F.2d 586 (D.C. Cir. 1980).
[34] 16 U.S.C. §1372(a)(2)(B), (3)–(5) (1988).
[35] *Id.* §1371(a)(3)(A).
[36] Animal Welfare Inst. v. Kreps, *supra* note 32, at 1004.
[37] 16 U.S.C. §1373 (1988).
[38] *Id.* §1373(d).

Then the Secretary must make a decision "on the record," after granting an opportunity for a hearing.[39] The Secretary must insure that any taking "will not be to the disadvantage of" the species and population stock "and will be consistent with the [Act's] purposes and policies."[40]

The Secretary's regulation is not self-executing. In order to implement the regulation, the Secretary must issue a permit to a particular applicant. Here, too, the Act spells out detailed procedures to insure that the Secretary's action accords with the statutory policies for protecting marine mammals.[41]

The Secretary is authorized to hedge waivers with restrictions. These can limit the number of animals affected; their age, size, or sex; the season or place for the permitted action; or the fishing techniques to be used. The Secretary may also establish a quota for takings and importations.[42]

## Judicial Decisions That Invalidate Waivers

The Secretary has repeatedly tried to grant waivers to domestic and foreign fishing fleets. But in decision after decision, courts have found that the Secretary's actions failed to comply with statutory policies. The problem has frequently been obtaining the scientific evidence needed to show that a waiver will satisfy the Act's policies.

Two famous court decisions illustrate the Secretary's dilemma. The first is the *Richardson* case.[43] In this 1976 case, the Secretary granted permits that allowed U.S. fishermen to continue taking dolphins in the course of fishing for tuna. As noted earlier, the Act's key goal is maintaining marine mammals at their "optimum sustainable population." In the *Richardson* case, the Secretary lacked the scientific data needed to estimate the proposed taking's impact upon the dolphins' "optimum sustainable population." The court ruled that the missing data was "critical."[44] Without it, the court said, the Secretary cannot be assured "that the taking provided for will not be to the disadvantage of the marine mammals. . . . If he cannot make that finding, he cannot issue a permit."[45] So the court invalidated the permit.

The same problem emerged in the late 1980s, in the *Kokechik* case.[46] The Secretary chose to issue a waiver under which the Japanese fleet would be allowed to take some Dall's porpoises incidental to fishing for salmon with gillnets. Although the nets would also trap fur seals, the Secretary had no

---

[39] *Id.*

[40] *Id.* §1373(a).

[41] *Id.* §1374.

[42] *Id.* §§1373(c), 1374(b)(2)(D).

[43] Committee for Humane Legislation v. Richardson, 540 F.2d 1141 (D.C. Cir. 1976), *aff'g in part* 141 F. Supp. 297 (D.D.C.).

[44] *Id.*, 414 F. Supp. at 310.

[45] *Id.* at 309–10 (quoting 118 CONG. REC. 7686 (1972) (remarks of Rep. Dingell)).

[46] Federation of Japan Salmon Fisheries Coop. Ass'n v. Baldridge, 679 F. Supp. 37 (D.D.C. 1987), *aff'd sub nom.* Kokechik Fisherman's Ass'n v. Secretary of Commerce, 839 F.2d 795 (D.C. Cir. 1988), *cert. denied sub nom.* Verity v. Center for Environmental Education, 488 U.S. 1004 (1989).

evidence that the seals were at their "optimum sustainable population." As the court saw it, the Secretary was thus unable to make findings "which are an absolute requirement for the issuance of a permit and waiver."[47] Once again, the Secretary's waiver was invalidated.

Even when the Secretary can obtain the needed evidence, a waiver will be reversed unless the Secretary gives appropriate weight to the best scientific evidence available.[48] In 1980, when the government ruled on the U.S. tunaboat fleet's application for a waiver, the Secretary's delegatee disregarded scientific evidence that detracted from his conclusions. A court refused to endorse the regulation, holding it to be arbitrary.[49]

## Exemptions From the Moratorium

The Act and the Secretary's waivers have carved a number of exemptions from the moratorium.

### The Hardship Exception

The least important exception is for hardship cases. Enacted in 1972, it allowed the Secretary to exempt persons (other than commercial fishermen) for a period ending in 1973.[50] Although still on the statute books, this provision has no effect today.

### The Exemption for Alaskan Natives

When passing its version of the 1972 Act, the House of Representatives included an exemption allowing Alaskan natives to take marine mammals for subsistence purposes. The House bill, however, did not allow takings for handicraft purposes. Led by Alaska's Senator Stevens, the Senate succeeded in broadening the exemption to include takings for "purposes of creating and selling authentic native articles of handicrafts and clothing."[51]

What did Congress mean by "authentic native articles"? In a regulation, the Fish and Wildlife Service defined this term to mean that the items were commonly produced before the Act's 1972 effective date. An Aleut, Marina Rena Katelnikoff, tested this definition when she and her father shot 35 sea otters and she used the pelts to create craft items like stuffed bears and fur

---

[47] *Id.*, 839 F.2d at 801.

[48] 16 U.S.C. §1373(a) (1988).

[49] American Tunaboat Ass'n v. Baldridge, 738 F.2d 1013 (9th Cir. 1984).

[50] Pub. L. No. 92-522, §101(c), 86 Stat. 1027, 1031 (1972) (codified in 16 U.S.C. §1371(c) (1988)).

[51] 16 U.S.C. §1371(b) (1991). *See* United States v. Clark, 912 F.2d 1087, 1089 (9th Cir. 1990), *cert. denied,* 111 S. Ct. 705 (1991). Katelnikoff v. Department of the Interior, 657 F. Supp. 659, 663–65 (D. Alaska 1986).

flowers. The Service seized the articles because they were nontraditional. The court upheld the seizure and the regulation, ruling that Congress was concerned only "with the preservation of traditional aspects of native culture and life-style."[52]

Congress made any taking by Alaskan natives subject to another restriction: It must not be accomplished in a wasteful manner.[53] The Service's regulation defined "wasteful manner" as a process that results in the waste of a substantial portion of the animal. That definition led to a criminal prosecution against an Alaskan native who shot nine walrus but took only a small portion of the carcasses. Affirming the native's conviction, the Ninth Circuit viewed the statute as favoring a "careful husbanding of resources."[54]

## The Exemption for Scientific Research, Public Display, and Enhancement of Survival

Congress also authorized the Secretary to issue permits for taking and importing animals (or animal products) if they are to be used in scientific research or public display.[55] The taking or importation must be approved by the Marine Mammal Commission and the Committee of Scientific Advisors.[56]

To gain a permit under the exception for scientific research, applicants must justify the research. If the animal is to be killed, applicants must show that they cannot carry out the research by non-lethal methods. If the animal comes from a species or stock that is depleted, applicants must show that the research will benefit that species or is critically important.[57]

To gain a permit under the exemption for public displays, applicants must offer a program that includes education or conservation themes. The program also must satisfy professionally recognized standards, and the display facilities must be regularly open to the public.[58] Congress meant to favor zoos, aquariums, and similar institutions.[59]

Permits for public display are subject to additional restrictions. The Secretary cannot issue permits for animals that are depleted.[60] The Secretary cannot issue permits for the public display of animals that were taken when pregnant or nursing, or when less than eight months old.[61] Finally, the Secretary cannot issue permits for importing animals that were taken in an inhumane manner.[62]

---

[52] Katelnikoff v. Department of the Interior, *supra* note 51, at 666. *See* 50 C.F.R. §216.3 (1990).

[53] 16 U.S.C. §1371(b)(3) (1988).

[54] United States v. Clark, *supra* note 51, 912 F.2d at 1089.

[55] Pub. L. No. 92-522, §101(2)(1), 86 Stat. 1027, 1029 (1972) (codified in 16 U.S.C. §1371(a)(1) (1988)).

[56] 16 U.S.C. §§1401–03 (1988).

[57] *Id.* §1374(c)(3).

[58] *Id.* §1374(c)(2).

[59] *See* 1988 House Report, *supra* note 6, at 33–34, 1988 U.S. CODE CONG. & ADMIN. NEWS at 6174–75.

[60] 16 U.S.C. §§1371(a)(3)(B), 1372(b)(3) (1988).

[61] *Id.* §1372(b)(1), (2).

[62] *Id.* §1372(b)(4).

Congress waived these restrictions (for non-depleted animals) where importation is necessary for the animals' protection or welfare.[63]

Court decisions add another restriction on permits for scientific research or public display. In three cases,[64] courts sustained arguments that the Secretary could not issue certain permits without first preparing an environmental assessment or impact statement under the National Environmental Policy Act of 1969.[65]

In 1988 Congress authorized permits for a new exemption allowing the taking and importing of animals for purposes of enhancing the survival or recovery of a species or stock.[66] The Secretary must consult with the Marine Mammal Commission and allow public comment before issuing those permits. Applicants must show that the taking or importation is likely to contribute significantly to ensuring survival or recovery. The transaction must be consistent with the factors underlying any recovery plan.[67]

## The Exemption for the U.S. Tunaboat Industry

While Congress has been concerned about the U.S. tunaboat industry's kills of dolphins in the course of fishing for tuna, the legislature did not want to force tuna fishermen to cease operations.[68] Congress confronted the conflict between protecting marine mammals and protecting the fishing industry by establishing a "special,"[69] but "limited"[70] exemption for commercial fishermen. Under the exemption, the Secretary is empowered to award permits for the incidental taking of marine mammals in the course of commercial fishing.

### *The 1972 Legislation*

Congress inaugurated the Marine Mammal Protection Act by giving the fishing industry an exemption for two years. For the 1972–1974 period, fishermen were allowed to take marine mammals incidental to their fishing operations. Interim regulations required the use of fishing techniques producing the

---

[63] *Id.*

[64] Jones v. Gordon, 792 F.2d 821 (9th Cir. 1986); Progressive Animal Welfare Soc'y v. Department of the Navy, 725 F. Supp. 475 (W.D. Wash. 1989); Greenpeace U.S.A. v. Evans, 688 F. Supp. 579 (W.D. Wash. 1987).

[65] 42 U.S.C. §§4321 *et seq.* (1988).

[66] Pub. L. No. 100-711, §5(c), 102 Stat. 4755, 4769 (1988) (codified in 16 U.S.C. §1371(a)(1) (1988)).

[67] 16 U.S.C. §1374(c)(4) (1988).

[68] Committee for Humane Legislation v. Richardson, 540 F.2d 1141 (D.C. Cir. 1976), *aff'g in part* 414 F. Supp. 297 (D.D.C.).

[69] Committee for Humane Legislation v. Richardson, *supra* note 68, 414 F. Supp. at 301.

[70] Kokechik Fishermen's Ass'n v. Secretary of Commerce, 839 F.2d 795, 800 (D.C. Cir. 1988), *cert. denied sub nom.* Verity v. Center for Environmental Education, 488 U.S. 1004 (1989).

least practical hazard to marine mammals. Congress wanted to give the industry a two-year period in which to equip the fleet with new types of fishing gear.[71]

After 1974, the Secretary was given authority to issue permits for incidental takings. Before he can issue permits, however, the Secretary must satisfy two requirements. First, he must conduct formal rulemaking proceedings and issue regulations that authorize the taking. Second, he must determine that the taking does not disadvantage the affected species and is consistent with the Act's policies and purposes.[72] The law states:

> [I]t shall be the immediate goal that incidental kill or incidental serious injury of marine mammals permitted in the course of commercial fishing operations be reduced to insignificant levels approaching a zero mortality and serious injury rate.

These provisions remain part of the law today.[73]

In the 1970s the Secretary gave the U.S. tunaboat industry permits to continue incidental takings of dolphins. It was these waivers that led to the *Richardson* decision.[74] The district court invalidated the permit for the 1976 fishing season because of the Secretary's inability to make findings about the impact upon the dolphins' "optimum sustainable population." Although it affirmed the lower court on this point, the District of Columbia Circuit stayed its order, allowing the tuna fleet to continue operations.

For the next few years, the Secretary and the tuna fishermen sought to resolve the problem with half-measures and partial solutions.[75] Then, in 1980 the tunaboat industry applied for a new permit. The new permit incorporated an absolute ceiling on dolphin kills of 20,500. This ceiling was later drafted into the regulations and the Act itself.[76]

### *The 1981 Amendments*

By 1981 the tunaboat industry was "operating in fear of being shut down by lawsuits."[77] Congress rescued the industry. The 1981 Amendments reaffirmed the goal that incidental kills from commercial fishing should be reduced to levels approaching a zero mortality. But Congress specified that tuna fishermen should be deemed to satisfy this goal by continuing to use "the best marine mammal safety techniques and equipment that are economically and

---

[71] Committee for Humane Legislation v. Richardson, *supra* note 68, 414 F. Supp. at 301. The legislation is Pub. L. No. 92-522, §101(a)(2), 86 Stat. 1027, 1030 (1972).

[72] Kokechik Fisherman's Ass'n v. Secretary of Commerce, *supra* note 70, 839 F.2d at 800. *See* Pub. L. No. 92-522, §§101(a)(2), 103, 104, 86 Stat. 1027, 1029, 1030, 1033–36 (1972).

[73] 16 U.S.C. §§1371(a)(2), 1373, 1374 (1988).

[74] *See* text at notes 43–45.

[75] Described in M. Bean, *The Evolution of Wildlife Law* 309–10 (New York: Praeger Scientific, 1983).

[76] *See* Earth Island Inst. v. Mosbacher, 746 F. Supp. 964 (N.D. Cal. 1990), *aff'd*, 929 F.2d 1449 (9th Cir. 1991).

[77] 1981 House Report, *supra* note 11, at 13, 1981 U.S. CODE CONG. & ADMIN. NEWS at 1463.

technologically practicable."[78] Thus the fishing industry won a major exemption from the Act.

*The 1984 Amendments*

The 1984 hearings disclosed that the Secretary still lacked the data necessary to calculate the impact of incidental takings on many population stocks. Congress directed the Secretary to institute a five-year scientific research program to gather that data. In the interim, Congress extended the tunaboat industry's 1980 permit for an indefinite period, reaffirming the overall quota of 20,500 dolphins.[79] The U.S. tunaboat industry continues to operate under this permit today.

## The Exemption for the Rest of the U.S. Fishing Industry

Under the 1971 Act, the Secretary could and did grant permits to non-tuna fleets for incidental takings of marine mammals in the course of commercial fishing operations.

Congress recognized that some commercial fishermen are responsible for only a small number of incidental takings. In the 1981 Amendments, therefore, Congress created a special exemption for those small-take commercial fishermen. This exemption is contained in section 101(a)(4)(A).[80] It directs the Secretary to allow those incidental takings if he finds that the takings would have a negligible impact on the mammal. Congress intended this exemption to be available only to U.S. citizen fishermen whose takings are infrequent, unavoidable, and accidental.[81]

In 1988 another court decision threw the Secretary's permit process into "a state of paralysis."[82] This was the *Kokechik* decision.[83] Once again, the Secretary feared that the courts would not allow the issuance of a permit in the absence of a finding that the affected mammal was at its "optimum sustainable population."[84] The Secretary continued to lack adequate scientific information to make that determination. In the absence of that information, the *Kokechik* decision suggested that a permit could not be issued.[85]

This created a special problem for the U.S. non-tuna fishing fleets, whose permits were due to expire at the end of 1988. To aid those fishermen, Congress

---

[78] Pub. L. No. 97-58, §2, 95 Stat. 979, 980 (1981).

[79] Pub. L. No. 98-364, §102, 98 Stat. 440 (1984) (codified in 16 U.S.C. §1374(h) (1984)). *See* H.R. REP. NO. 758, 98th Cong., 2d Sess. 8–9 (1984), 1984 U.S. CODE CONG. & ADMIN. NEWS 635, 641–42.

[80] Pub. L. No. 97-58, §2, 95 Stat. 979, 980 (1981) (codified in 16 U.S.C. §1371(a)(4) (1988)). *See* 1981 House Report, *supra* note 11, at 14, 18–19, 1981 U.S. CODE CONG. & ADMIN. NEWS at 1464, 1468–69.

[81] 1988 House Report, *supra* note 6, at 17, 1988 U.S. CODE CONG. & ADMIN. NEWS at 6158.

[82] *Id.* at 18, 1988 U.S. CODE CONG. & ADMIN. NEWS at 6159.

[83] *See* text at notes 46–47.

[84] 1988 House Report, *supra* note 6, at 18, 1988 U.S. CODE CONG. & ADMIN. NEWS at 6159.

[85] *Id.*

enacted a new exemption authorizing permits for those U.S. fishing fleets, exempting them from the Act's other provisions through 1993.[86]

## The Exemption for Accidental Takings

The Secretary may also allow takings by U.S. citizens engaged in activities other than commercial fishing. This exemption is contained in section 101(a)(5)(A), enacted in 1981. Like section 101(a)(4)(A), just discussed, this exemption covers takings of only small numbers of mammals. Under this exemption, the takings must be accidental, and they must have only a negligible impact on the mammal.[87]

## The Exemption for Incidental Takings by Foreign Fleets

For almost two decades, Congress has been intensely concerned about the killing of marine mammals by foreign fishermen. Since 1972 the Act has directed the Secretary to "ban the importation" of commercial fish or fish products caught with "technology which results in the incidental kill or incidental serious injury of ocean mammals in excess of United States standards."[88] In 1984 and 1988 Congress toughened this embargo. It required foreign nations to submit proof about the effect of their fleets' technology on ocean mammals. In the case of tuna imports, Congress established acceptable rates of incidental taking.[89] When Mexico did not provide adequate proof of compliance, a court ruled in 1991 that the Secretary must embargo tuna imports from that country.[90] Mexico appealed that embargo to an international tribunal, which ruled that the embargo violates the General Agreement on Tariffs and Trade[91] because it impedes free trade. In 1992, however, Mexico, Venezuela, and the United States agreed to a five-year moratorium, beginning in 1994, on the use of purse-seine nets in Pacific tuna fishing.[92]

Embargos are not the only sanction facing foreign fishermen. When they operate in U.S. waters, foreign fishing fleets are subject to the Act's anti-taking prohibitions. In 1981 the Secretary granted the Japanese salmon fleet an exemption allowing it to make incidental takes of several species of marine mammals. After Congress extended the permit in 1972, the Japanese fleet applied in 1986 for a renewal. The Secretary renewed the permit in 1987, but the *Kokechik* decision[93] invalidated it. Congress deliberately left that decision's

---

[86] Pub. L. No. 100-711, §2, 102 Stat. 4755 (1988) (codified in 16 U.S.C. §1383a (1988)).

[87] Pub. L. No. 97-58, §2, 95 Stat. 979, 980–81 (1981) (codified in 16 U.S.C. §1371(a)(5)(A)). *See* 1981 House Report, *supra* note 11, at 18–19, 1981 U.S. CODE CONG. & ADMIN. NEWS at 1468–69.

[88] 16 U.S.C. §1371(a)(2) (1988).

[89] *Id.* §1371(a)(2)(A)–(C).

[90] Earth Island Inst. v. Mosbacher, *supra* note 76.

[91] 1947, 61 Stat. A1365, T.I.A.S. No. 1700; Geneva Protocol to the General Agreement on Tariffs and Trade, 1967, 19 U.S.T. 4, T.I.A.S. No. 6425.

[92] *See* MARINE CONSERVATION NEWS, Winter 1991, at 1 (Washington: Center for Marine Conservation, 1991); *U.S., Mexico, Venezuela Reach Accord to Protect Dolphins From Tuna Nets*, WALL STREET JOURNAL, March 20, 1992, at B10.

[93] *See* text at notes 46–47.

holding undisturbed with regard to the Japanese fleet.[94] Japanese commercial fishermen now have no permit authorizing them to make incidental takes of marine mammals in the course of their operations. As a consequence, the Japanese fishing fleets no longer practice net fishing in U.S. waters.

## The Exemption for Actions Permitted by International Treaties

The United States is not the only country concerned with the protection of marine mammals. In the Marine Mammal Protection Act[95] and elsewhere,[96] Congress has called for other nations to cooperate in protecting marine mammals. Recognizing this, the Marine Mammal Protection Act outlines[97] how the Act's provisions:

> shall be deemed to be in addition to and not in contravention of the provisions of any existing international treaty, convention, or agreement, or any statute implementing the same, which may otherwise apply to the taking of marine mammals.

The statute[98] and agency regulations[99] limit this exemption to international treaties, conventions, and agreements in force before December 21, 1972, and to which the United States was a party. The regulations mention only one convention: the Interim Convention for the Conservation of the North Pacific Fur Seal.[100]

This exemption was invoked during a controversy over the killing of fur seals under the Interim Convention. A Commission established under the Interim Convention awarded the United States government the right to kill 22,000 subadult North Pacific fur seals. Three animal welfare organizations sought to enjoin the United States government from conducting the planned killings. Under the Marine Mammal Protection Act, the moratorium would have prohibited these takings. So the court viewed the Act and the Interim Convention as in conflict. Nonetheless, citing the Act's exemption for conduct permitted by an international convention, the court denied any relief.[101]

## Exemption for Mammals Taken Before Protected Status

There is an exemption for importation of mammals that were taken before the Act's effective date, December 21, 1972. Also exempt are products made from mammals taken before that date. Although the Act does not normally

---

[94] 1988 House Report, *supra* note 6, at 21, 1988 U.S. CODE CONG. & ADMIN. NEWS at 6162.

[95] 16 U.S.C. §§1361(4), 1378(a) (1988).

[96] Pub. L. No. 95-426, §602, 92 Stat. 963, 985 (1978) (quoted at 16 U.S.C. §1361, note (1988)).

[97] 16 U.S.C. §1383 (1988).

[98] *Id.* §1372(a)(2).

[99] 50 C.F.R. §§18.21, 216.21 (1990).

[100] 1957, 8 U.S.T. 2283, T.I.A.S. No. 3948, 314 U.N.T.S. 105.

[101] International Fund for Animal Welfare v. Baldridge, 594 F. Supp. 129 (D.D.C. 1984).

allow importation of mammals that are classified as endangered or depleted, the Act exempts mammals (or mammal products) imported before the date when the mammals' classification was published in the Federal Register. A similar rule concerns mammals (and mammal products) that were imported before a foreign law made their taking or sale unlawful.[102]

## Penalties and Forfeiture

Congress specified a schedule of penalties. Any person who violates the Act, the regulations, or a permit is subject to a civil penalty of up to $10,000. The Secretary may assess the penalty administratively, after notice and opportunity for a hearing.[103] The Secretary usually relies on administrative proceedings in the case of individuals who take[104] or import[105] marine mammals or mammal products. In the administrative proceedings:[106]

> The Respondent's lack of awareness of the Act . . . is appropriate to consider as a mitigating factor; however, the provisions of the statute are binding and enforceable . . . even in the absence of actual knowledge. . . . Under the Marine Mammal [Protection] Act, only a showing that the acts involved were voluntary and intentional need be made. There is no specific requirement for a showing . . . of actual knowledge or wrongdoing.

The Secretary may remit or mitigate civil penalties. If the violator fails to pay a penalty assessment, the Secretary may also ask the Attorney General to bring a civil action.[107]

Penalties may also be assessed against vessels used in an unlawful taking. The penalty assessment may not exceed $25,000, and can be assessed only by a court having jurisdiction over the vessel.[108]

Congress took pity on individuals who unknowingly buy a marine mammal (or mammal product) while overseas and bring it into the United States without a permit. Although that action violates the Act, Congress believed that it is not appropriate to subject those individuals to a formal notice of violation procedure. So Congress amended the Act in 1981 to allow individuals to abandon the item at the port of entry. This procedure applies, however, only where the individuals imported the item for their own personal or family use.[109]

---

[102] 16 U.S.C. §1372(d) (1988). *See* 50 C.F.R. §§18.14, 216.14 (1990).
[103] 16 U.S.C. §1375(a)(1) (1988).
[104] *In re* Roger Ernest Jolma, DOC (NOAA) Dkt. No. 022-143 (ALJ ID dated Sept. 16, 1981).
[105] *In re* Mary K. Husby, DOC (NOAA) Dkt. No. 124-033 (ALJ ID dated August 14, 1981).
[106] *Id.*
[107] 16 U.S.C. §1375(a)(1) (1988).
[108] *Id.* §1376(b).
[109] Pub. L. No. 97-58, §3(b), 95 Stat. 979, 981–82 (1981) (codified in 16 U.S.C. §1375(a)(2) (1988)). *See* 1981 House Report, *supra* note 11, at 21, 1981 U.S. CODE CONG. & ADMIN. NEWS at 1471–72.

There are criminal penalties as well. Persons who knowingly violate the Act, the regulations, or a permit may be fined up to $20,000, imprisoned for up to one year, or both.[110]

The government may also seize the entire cargo of any U.S. vessel or other conveyance used in an unlawful taking.[111]

## Enforcement

In enforcing the Act, the Secretary may use personnel from other federal and state agencies. When those personnel observe a violation, they may make arrests without warrants. When they have reasonable cause to believe a violation took place, they may search vessels and other conveyances. They may seize the cargo of vessels and conveyances used to violate the Act. And, of course, they may seize marine mammals and mammal products taken or retained illegally.

Under the Act,[112] the U.S. fishing industry must allow the government to place observers on board vessels during fishing voyages. The Secretary's regulations[113] allow the observer to collect information for use in civil or criminal penalty proceedings. Captains of some tunaboats attacked the regulation as constituting an unconstitutional search, but they lost in the appeals court.[114] The tunaboat owners were equally unsuccessful in their opposition to the government's decision to include females among the observers.[115]

## The Problem of Treatment for "Depleted" Species

The Act has always recognized that "depleted" mammals need special treatment. In 1972 Congress began the Act with a finding that some mammals are in danger of "extinction or depletion."[116] In giving the Secretary power to waive the moratorium by means of permits, Congress erected special protections for "depleted" species. The Secretary was forbidden to issue permits for the taking of depleted species. No importation of depleted species was allowed.[117]

In 1986 Congress cleared the way for incidental takings of a few depleted species by persons other than commercial fishermen. This legislation was not intended as a change in policy, but only as correction of a technical problem created by a 1982 amendment of the Endangered Species Act. That Act lists many marine mammals as threatened or endangered. In the 1982 Amendments,

[110] 16 U.S.C. §1375(b) (1988).
[111] *Id.* §1376(a).
[112] *Id.* §§1381(d), 1383a(e).
[113] 50 C.F.R. §216.24(f)(1) (1990).
[114] Balelo v. Baldridge, 724 F.2d 753 (9th Cir.) (en banc), *cert. denied,* 467 U.S. 1252 (1984).
[115] Caribbean Marine Serv. Co. v. Baldridge, 844 F.2d 668 (9th Cir. 1988).
[116] 16 U.S.C. §1361(1) (1988).
[117] Pub. L. No. 92-522, §101(a)(3)(B), 86 Stat. 1027, 1031 (1972). As amended and codified in 16 U.S.C. §1371(a)(3)(B) (1988), the prohibition allows exceptions for scientific research, as well as for enhancing the survival or recovery of the stock.

Congress empowered the Secretary to authorize "incidental takings" of listed species.[118] But if any species is listed under the Endangered Species Act, the Marine Mammal Protection Act treats that species as "depleted."[119] Under its pre-1983 wording, therefore, the Marine Mammal Protection Act prohibited any taking of marine mammal species listed under the Endangered Species Act. Moreover, the more restrictive provision of the Marine Mammal Protection Act took precedence over the general provisions of the Endangered Species Act.[120] Congress recognized the result: the Endangered Species Act's 1982 Amendments "could not be used to authorize incidental taking of marine mammals, even if the take involved was non-lethal and resulted in no jeopardy."[121]

Congress decided to rectify this situation by harmonizing the Marine Mammal Act with the Endangered Species Act. The legislature accomplished this by changing Marine Mammal Protection Act section 101(a)(5)(A),[122] the provision under which the Secretary can authorize U.S. citizens to make incidental takings of "small numbers" of marine mammals. As enacted in 1981, section 101(a)(5)(A) applied only to takings of a species or population "that is not depleted."[123] The 1986 amendment deleted these quoted words.[124] It also made conforming amendments in other Marine Mammal Act provisions and in the Endangered Species Act.

Section 101(a)(5)(A) applies only to persons who are not commercial fishermen. So, in 1988, Congress was still able to declare: "There is no mechanism in the Act to allow the incidental take of depleted species by the fishing industry either through a general permit or a small take exemption."[125]

Ultimately, Congress decided to let even the fishing industry make takes of depleted species. Once again, the *Richardson* and *Kokechik* decisions[126] triggered the legislative change. As noted earlier, the Secretary was unable to make the "optimum sustainable population" findings for many species. Yet, under the Act, populations of marine mammals that are below optimum sustainable population are, by definition, "depleted."[127] What was the consequence for species that lacked an "optimum sustainable population" finding? Congress feared that, under the *Richardson* and *Kokechik* decisions, those species had become "de facto depleted."[128] In that event, Congress complained, many commercial fishermen "would be unable to fish."[129]

---

[118] 16 U.S.C. §§1536(b)(4), (o), and 1539(a)(1)(B) (1988).

[119] *Id.* §1362(1).

[120] *Id.* §1543.

[121] 132 CONG. REC. 31,294 (1986) (remarks of Sen. Danforth).

[122] 16 U.S.C. §1371(a)(5)(A) (1988).

[123] Pub. L. No. 97-58, §2, 95 Stat. 979, 980.

[124] Pub. L. No. 99-659, §411(a)(1), 100 Stat. 3706, 3741 (codified in 16 U.S.C. §1371(a)(5)(A) (1988)).

[125] 1988 House Report, *supra* note 6, at 17, 1988 U.S. CODE CONG. & ADMIN. NEWS at 6158.

[126] *See* text at notes 43–47.

[127] 1988 House Report, *supra* note 6, at 17, 1988 U.S. CODE CONG. & ADMIN. NEWS at 6158. *See* 16 U.S.C. §1362(1) (1988).

[128] 1988 House Report, *supra* note 6, at 18–19, 1988 U.S. CODE CONG. & ADMIN. NEWS at 6159.

[129] *Id.* at 17, 1988 U.S. CODE CONG. & ADMIN. NEWS at 6158.

Once again, Congress authored a special exemption to rescue commercial fishermen. The exemption allows non-tuna fishermen to make incidental takes of marine mammals, "including a population stock designated as depleted."[130] The exemption does not cover all marine mammals or all forms of taking. It does not authorize the taking of California sea otters. It does not authorize the "intentional lethal taking" of any Steller sea lion, cataceans, or marine mammals from a depleted population stock.[131] Nonetheless, the legislation significantly erodes the protection of depleted species.

## Federal Relations With the States

The Act creates a comprehensive federal system. "Congress intended to preempt the field so as to eliminate inconsistent State regulation while permitting regulation which complements the statute's design."[132] It achieved this result by means of section 109(a) of the Act,[133] "a broad and detailed preemption provision."[134] The Act generally prohibits states from enforcing any law or regulation "relating to the taking of any species . . . of marine mammals within the State."[135]

The Act's preemption is even more pervasive than the statute's literal reach. Soon after the Act became law, an importer of sealskins challenged a Maryland law that prohibited the *importation* of sealskins for commercial purposes. The importer argued that the Marine Mammal Protection Act (and other laws) preempted state regulation. The court recognized that section 109 covers only "taking within" a state. The section itself does not evidence a congressional intent to preempt state laws with respect to "importation." Nonetheless, the court ruled, "importation was, by the very nature of the enactment of the MMPA, necessarily preempted for federal control." The court declared the Maryland statute to be invalid.[136]

As part of the 1981 Amendments, Congress established a procedure under which the federal government can return marine mammal management to a state.[137] Before deciding to transfer this function to a state, the Secretary must make detailed findings that demonstrate the state's ability and commitment to

---

[130] Pub. L. No. 100-711, §2, 102 Stat. 4755, 4756 (1988) (codified in 16 U.S.C. §1383a(b)(2)(C) (1988)). Tuna fishermen did not need to be included in the exemption because their operations were already authorized under a permit of indefinite duration.

[131] *Id. See* 1988 House Report, *supra* note 6, at 22, 1988 U.S. CODE CONG. & ADMIN. NEWS at 6163.

[132] People of Togiak v. United States, 470 F. Supp. 423, 427 (D.D.C. 1979).

[133] Pub. L. No. 92-522, §109(a), 86 Stat. 1027, 1040 (1972).

[134] People of Togiak v. United States, *supra* note 132, at 425.

[135] 16 U.S.C. §1379(a) (1988).

[136] Fouke Co. v. Mandel, 386 F. Supp. 1341, 1360 (D. Md. 1974).

[137] Pub. L. No. 97-58, §4, 95 Stat. 979, 982–86 (1981) (codified in 16 U.S.C. §1379 (1988)). *See* 1981 House Report, *supra* note 11, at 9–10, 22–30, 1981 U.S. CODE CONG. & ADMIN. NEWS at 1460–61, 1472–80.

carry out federal standards.[138] The state must develop and implement a satisfactory management program, after complying with federal standards and procedures.[139] The Secretary is authorized to make grants to develop such management programs.[140]

Until the state actually implements its management program, the Secretary continues to regulate all takings within the state.[141] Even after the state program is implemented, the Secretary is still responsible for regulating any takings in the federal off-shore zone extending out to the 200-mile limit.[142] In addition, the Secretary continues to regulate takings for scientific research, public display, and the enhancement or recovery of a species.[143]

Many marine mammal populations inhabit both state and federal waters. For these populations, the Act contemplates that the Secretary and the state will enter into cooperative allocation agreements.[144] The Secretary can revoke a transfer of management authority. Before taking such action, however, the Secretary must give the state an opportunity to remedy deficiencies.[145]

## International Programs

Protecting marine mammals is an international task. Congress directed the U.S. government to begin negotiations "immediately to encourage the development of international arrangements for research on, and conservation of, all marine mammals."[146] In section 108,[147] the Secretary was given a detailed agenda to follow, acting in conjunction with the Secretary of State. In particular, the Secretaries were asked to negotiate with foreign governments having jurisdiction over commercial fishing fleets whose operations harm marine mammals. One important target is foreign governments with tuna fishing fleets. The Secretaries were directed to seek agreements with those governments to conserve marine mammals taken in the course of tuna fishing operations. The Secretaries were also told to encourage treaties for the protection of ocean or land regions important to the health and stability of marine mammal populations. The Secretaries were also to ask for amendment of existing treaties to bring them in line with the Act. Finally, they were to seek a multinational conference for the purpose of obtaining an international convention on mammal conservation and protection.

---

[138] 16 U.S.C. §1379(b)(1) (1988).
[139] *Id.* §1379(c).
[140] *Id.* §1379(j).
[141] *Id.* §1379(b)(2).
[142] *Id.* §1379(b)(3)(B)(i).
[143] *Id.* §1379(b)(3)(B)(ii).
[144] *Id.* §1379(d).
[145] *Id.* §1379(e).
[146] *Id.* §1361(4).
[147] *Id.* §1378.

* * *

Congress enacted the Marine Mammal Protection Act of 1972 in part as a response to the killing of 600,000 dolphins in 1970 and 1971. The Act's passage was undoubtedly effective in aiding that species. The U.S. tuna fleets' kills of dolphins decreased from 368,000 in 1972 to 18,573 in 1980 and to 13,992 in 1987. By 1987 the U.S. tuna fleet was responsible for less than 20 percent of the dolphins killed in the eastern tropical Pacific Ocean.[148]

The United States government continues to pressure foreign nations to abandon fishing practices that result in incidental kills of marine mammals. In 1991, in response to U.S. requests, Japan and South Korea agreed to ban drift-net fishing operations. Japan and the United States will sponsor a United Nations resolution outlawing the use of drift-nets by the end of 1992.[149] Because of U.S. government efforts, Mexico and Venezuela agreed in 1992 to cease purse-seine netting of dolphins by their Pacific tuna fleets.[150] Also in 1992, under the framework of the Inter-American Tropical Tuna Commission, ten nations that fish for tuna in the eastern Pacific Ocean agreed to cut the killing of dolphins by 80 percent during the 1990s.[151] Congress deserves a fair share of credit for these achievements.

---

[148] *See* 1988 House Report, *supra* note 6, at 15, 1988 U.S. CODE CONG. & ADMIN. NEWS at 6156.

[149] *South Koreans May End Use of Drift Nets,* WALL STREET JOURNAL, Nov. 27, 1991, at A6.

[150] *U.S., Mexico, Venezuela Reach Accord to Protect Dolphins From Tuna Nets,* WALL STREET JOURNAL, March 20, 1992, at B10.

[151] *10 Nations Reach Accord on Saving Dolphins,* N.Y. TIMES, May 12, 1992, at C4.

# Chapter 12

# The Bald Eagle and Golden Eagle Protection Act

In 1782 the Continental Congress adopted the bald eagle as a national symbol. Benjamin Franklin regretted that choice, complaining that "the Bald Eagle . . . is a Bird of bad moral Character; like those among Men who live by Sharping and Robbing, he is generally poor, and often very lousy."[1] As Franklin recognized, the bald eagle lives largely on carrion when it is not feasting on Alaskan salmon and other hapless prey. As national symbol and predator, the bald eagle was hunted down relentlessly by sportsmen, taxidermists, fishermen, and farmers. To protect the species from extinction, Congress enacted the Bald Eagle Protection Act in 1940.[2]

## Prohibited Conduct

Congress intended to ban all threats to the bald eagle's survival.[3] The Supreme Court described section 1[4] as a "sweepingly framed prohibition," encompassing "a full catalog of prohibited acts."[5] Section 1 makes it unlawful to "take, possess, sell, purchase, barter, offer to sell, purchase or barter, transport, export or import, at any time or in any manner, any" protected birds.

In 1962 Congress extended the Bald Eagle Protection Act to cover golden eagles. Congress' motive was partially to give more protection to bald eagles, which were often killed by persons who mistook them for golden eagles.[6]

---

[1] United States v. Hetzel, 385 F. Supp. 1311, 1315 n.1 (W.D. Mo.) (quoting letter to Sarah Bache, Jan. 26, 1784); *See also* P. Matthiessen, *Wildlife in America* 170 (New York: Viking, 1987).

[2] Ch. 278, 54 Stat. 250 (1940) (codified as amended at 16 U.S.C. §§668–668d (1988)).

[3] United States v. Fryberg, 622 F.2d 1010, 1015 (9th Cir. 1980), *cert. denied,* 449 U.S. 1004 (1980).

[4] 16 U.S.C. §668 (1988).

[5] Andrus v. Allard, 444 U.S. 51, 56–57 (1979).

[6] Pub. L. No. 87-884, 76 Stat. 1246 (1962). *See* United States v. Fryberg, *supra* note 3, at 1016.

It is illegal to commit the prohibited actions on these birds whether they are "alive or dead."[7] Moreover, the Act prohibits taking, removing, or destroying the birds' parts, nests, or eggs, as well as collecting their feathers.[8]

Congress defined the term "take" expansively. It includes "pursue, shoot, shoot at, poison, wound, kill, capture, trap, collect, or molest or disturb."[9] The original Act did not specify that poisoning was prohibited. Before the 1972 Amendments, the government's position was that the Act did not apply to poisoning unless the poison was deliberately put out to kill eagles. In 1972, Congress amended the definition of "take" to include the word "poison."[10]

## The Required Intent

When Congress enacted the 1940 legislation, it listed the prohibited acts ("pursue, shoot" and so forth) and added: "or otherwise *willfully* molest or disturb" eagles.[11] That language proved to be fortuitous for Richard Hetzel. In 1971, while at a wildlife refuge, Hetzel found a partially decomposed eagle that had been dead for several days. He removed the legs with the intent of taking the claws to Boy Scouts with whom he worked. A federal magistrate found Hetzel to be guilty of a criminal violation of the Act.

A U.S. district judge exculpated Hetzel, reading the Act as making "willfulness and specific criminal intent . . . essential elements of a . . . prosecution." The judge concluded that Hetzel "could not be convicted without proof beyond reasonable doubt that [he] had in fact *willfully* violated the Act."[12]

Hetzel's case immediately became a historical curiosity. Congress changed the law even before the judge acquitted Hetzel.

The new legislation was prompted by what Administration officials called a callous, deliberate defiance of the Act.[13] In 1971 sharpshooters in helicopters gunned down nearly 500 eagles over ranches in Wyoming and Colorado. Investigating this, Congress learned that the government had obtained only 32 convictions under the Act in the preceding five years, with fines and court costs totalling $2,235. Congress concluded that "the amount of knowledge required to be proved in order to obtain a conviction . . . should be reduced."[14]

As amended in 1972, the statute eliminates any requirement of criminal intent or willfulness. A prohibited act is unlawful if the perpetrator does it "knowingly, or with wanton disregard for the consequences of his act."[15] What

---

[7] 16 U.S.C. §668(a) (1988).

[8] *Id. See* Mountain States Legal Found. v. Hodel, 799 F.2d 1423, 1427 (10th Cir. 1986) (dictum), *cert. denied,* 480 U.S. 951 (1987).

[9] 16 U.S.C. §668c (1988). *See* 50 C.F.R. §22.3 (1990).

[10] Pub. L. No. 92-535, §4, 86 Stat. 1064, 1065 (1972). *See* United States v. Corbin Farm Serv., 444 F. Supp. 510, 532 (E.D. Cal.), *aff'd per curiam* 578 F.2d 259 (9th Cir. 1978).

[11] Ch. 278, §4, 54 Stat. 250, 251 (1940) (emphasis added).

[12] United States v. Hetzel, *supra* note 1, at 1315.

[13] S. REP. NO. 1159, 92d Cong., 2d Sess. 3 (1972), *reprinted in* 1972 U.S. CODE CONG. & ADMIN. NEWS 4285, 4287–88 [hereinafter 1972 Senate Report].

[14] *Id.*

[15] Pub. L. No. 92-535, §1, 86 Stat. 1064 (1972) (codified in 16 U.S.C. §668(a)).

does this language mean in the case, say, of persons tried for selling eagle feathers? It means that the government must prove that the persons knew that the feathers were from an eagle. They cannot be convicted of selling eagle feathers if they thought the feathers were turkey feathers.[16] By using the term, "wanton disregard," Congress meant to penalize conduct that is more than merely negligent. Although perpetrators need not intend to inflict injury, they must be conscious that their conduct will naturally and probably result in injury.[17]

## Exceptions and Exemptions

### Exemption for Pre-Act Products

Congress qualified the Act's general prohibitions with a list of exclusions. The Act exempts "possession or transportation" of bald eagles lawfully taken before the Act's 1940 effective date. It also exempts "possession or transportation" of golden eagles lawfully taken before those birds became protected under the Act's 1962 extension. The same exemption applies to "possession and transportation" of eagle parts, nests, and eggs.[18]

The Supreme Court refused to read this "narrow limitation" as authorizing "sale" or "purchase" of pre-Act bird products.[19] That lawsuit was filed by traders in Indian artifacts which were partly composed of eagle feathers. The artifacts had existed before the birds became protected by the Act. The traders argued that the Act did not forbid the sale of these artifacts insofar as their eagle parts were lawfully taken before the effective date of federal protection. Rejecting that contention, the Court said: "Congress specifically declined to except any activities other than *possession* and *transportation* from the general statutory ban."[20]

The Court also rejected claimed constitutional objections to the Act. The traders argued that the Act violated their Fifth Amendment property rights because it deprived them of the opportunity to earn a profit from their relics. But the court ruled: "[L]oss of future profits—unaccompanied by any physical property restriction—provides a slender reed upon which to rest a takings claim."[21] The Court recognized that the traders were forced to bear the costs of the Act's restriction. That, said the Court, "is a burden borne to secure 'the advantage of living and doing business in a civilized community.'"[22]

---

[16] United States v. Allard, 397 F. Supp. 429, 432 (D. Mont. 1975).
[17] 1972 Senate Report, *supra* note 13, at 5, 1972 U.S. CODE CONG. & ADMIN. NEWS at 4289.
[18] 16 U.S.C. §668(a) (1988).
[19] Andrus v. Allard, *supra* note 5, at 56–57.
[20] *Id.* at 56. *See* 50 C.F.R. §22.2 (1990).
[21] *Id.* at 66.
[22] *Id.* at 67 (quoting Pennsylvania Coal Co. v. Mahon, 260 U.S. 383, 422 (1922) (Justice Brandeis dissenting)).

## Exemption for Alaska

One exemption is of historical interest. Alaska was exempted from the 1940 Act.[23] The exemption lasted until 1959. Then, when Alaska was admitted as a state, Congress abolished the exemption.[24]

## Exemption for Activities Authorized by the Secretary

The Act enables the Secretary of the Interior to authorize the taking, possession, and transportation of specimens for several enumerated purposes. The Secretary can issue permits only if the activity is compatible with the species' preservation,[25] according to regulations governing requests for these permits.[26]

### *Scientific and Exhibition Purposes*

The Secretary may authorize the taking, possession, or transportation of eagles for scientific or exhibition purposes. Permits can be granted only to public museums, public scientific societies, or public zoological parks. The permits may cover whole birds, bird parts, nests, or eggs.[27]

### *Depredating Eagles*

The Secretary may also authorize the taking of bald and golden eagles in order to protect wildlife, agriculture, or other interests in a particular locality. If the Secretary issues a permit, the recipient may take the eagles with firearms, traps, or any other suitable means except by poison or from aircraft.

The Governor of a state can also ask the Secretary to authorize the taking of golden eagles in order to protect domesticated flocks or herds on a seasonal basis. If the Secretary issues an order granting the Governor's request, golden eagles may be taken without a permit. Bald eagles may not be taken under such an order, however. Persons can trap or shoot golden eagles, but they may not shoot them from airplanes or poison them.[28]

### *Falconry*

The Secretary may grant permits for the taking, possession, and transportation of golden eagles for the purpose of falconry. Golden eagles may be trapped only from an area in which they have been preying on livestock or wildlife.[29] When Congress enacted this exemption, in the 1972 Amendments,

---

[23] Ch. 278, §1, 54 Stat. 250 (1940).
[24] Pub. L. No. 86-70, §14, 73 Stat. 141, 143 (1959).
[25] 16 U.S.C. §668a (1988).
[26] 50 C.F.R. §§22.21–22.31 (1990).
[27] 16 U.S.C. §668a (1988); 50 C.F.R. §22.21 (1990).
[28] 16 U.S.C. §668a (1988); 50 C.F.R. §§22.23, 22.31 (1990).
[29] 16 U.S.C. §668a (1988); 50 C.F.R. §22.24 (1990).

conservation groups objected that too many golden eagles would be taken for purposes of falconry. Congress thought that the taking would be minimal. In any event, Congress concluded, "it is better to take an eagle and use it in falconry than to kill it."[30]

*Resource Development*

The Secretary may also permit the taking of golden eagle nests which interfere with resource development or recovery operations.[31] The regulations list many business activities that can qualify for permits. These include: mining, timbering, oil and gas drilling, geothermal energy development, and the construction of roads, dams, reservoirs, power plants, power transmission lines, and pipelines.[32]

The Secretary can require that business undertake mitigation measures that, if possible, encourage golden eagles to reoccupy the site. Only inactive nests may be taken.[33]

This exemption embodies Congress' view that golden eagles are entitled to less protection than bald eagles. The Act was extended to cover golden eagles, after all, because their fledglings look like bald eagles. Golden eagle populations were thriving and in no danger. Congress decided that the Secretary should have discretion to resolve conflicts between the Act and resource development projects.[34]

*Indian Religious Purposes*

Another exemption concerns Indian tribal rights. In 1962, Congress empowered the Secretary to grant permits that authorize takings for "the religious purposes of Indian tribes."[35] Eagles have an exalted place in Indian religions. Experts have likened the status of the eagle feather in tribal rites to that of the cross in Christianity.[36]

This is the most litigated of the Act's exemptions. The controversy began when Jackie White, a member of the Red Lake Band of Chippewa Indians, shot at a bald eagle within the confines of the Red Lake Reservation. The government charged White with a criminal violation of the Act, but the trial court dismissed the case. The Eighth Circuit affirmed, holding that White's tribe had a treaty right to hunt on the reservation. The court did not doubt that Congress has authority to abrogate that treaty right. The court, however, concluded that Congress had not done so in the Act. Although the Act's exemption for Indian religious purposes requires that the Secretary issue a permit, the

---

[30] 1972 Senate Report, *supra* note 13, at 5, 1972 U.S. CODE CONG. & ADMIN. NEWS at 4289.

[31] 16 U.S.C. §668a (1988).

[32] 50 C.F.R. §22.3 (1990).

[33] *Id.* §22.25

[34] S. REP. NO. 1175, 95th Cong., 2d Sess. 6–7 (1978), *reprinted in* 1978 U.S. CODE CONG. & ADMIN. NEWS 7641, 7645–46.

[35] Pub. L. No. 87-884, 76 Stat. 1246 (1962) (codified in 16 U.S.C. §668a (1988)).

[36] United States v. Thirty Eight (38) Golden Eagles or Eagle Parts, 649 F. Supp. 269, 276 (D. Nev. 1986), *aff'd*, 829 F.2d 41 (9th Cir. 1987).

Eighth Court was unimpressed. It refused to read the exemption as a "back-handed way" to abrogate Indian hunting rights.[37]

Another Indian, Jose Abeyta, invoked the White decision after he killed an eagle to obtain feathers for ceremonial purposes. The court refused to hold that Abeyta had to apply for a permit in order to qualify for the exemption. Instead, the court disparaged the permit regulations as establishing a "labyrinthine application procedure."[38] Moreover, said the court, Abeyta could ignore the regulations because they cannot "fulfill the pueblos' need for eagle feathers for ceremonial use."[39]

Those two decisions are of questionable value today. Other federal courts have criticized the two decisions.[40] Moreover, two months after the Abeyta decision was issued, the Supreme Court decided that the Bald and Golden Eagle Protection Act did, in fact, abrogate Indians' treaty rights to hunt eagles.[41]

Under the regulations, the Secretary can authorize tribal members to possess and transport (as well as take) eagles, parts of eagles, nests or eggs.[42]

## Enforcement and Penalties

Only the government can enforce the Act's provisions. Unlike the Endangered Species Act,[43] the Bald and Golden Eagle Protection Act does not establish a private right of action. Three decisions illustrate this. In one, an animal protection group challenged the Environmental Protection Agency's decision to continue registration of a pesticide. In the second decision, another group sought to stop the hunting of migratory birds with lead shot. Although eagles were not the target of the pesticide or the lead shot, the birds were poisoned when they consumed the pesticide or the shot or animals that had been killed by either. In the third case, an animal protection society and homeowners wanted to block a deer hunt in an eagle refuge. In all three cases, the litigants sued under the Endangered Species Act, the Bald and Golden Eagle Protection Act, and the Migratory Bird Treaty Act.[44] Two of the courts ruled that neither the Bald and Golden Eagle Protection Act nor the Migratory Bird Treaty Act

---

[37] United States v. White, 508 F.2d 453, 458 (8th Cir. 1975).

[38] United States v. Abeyta, 632 F. Supp. 1301, 1303 (D.N.M. 1986).

[39] *Id.*

[40] United States v. Fryberg, 622 F.2d 1010 (9th Cir. 1980), *cert. denied,* 449 U.S. 1004 (1980); United States v. Thirty Eight (38) Golden Eagles or Eagle Parts, *supra* note 36; United States v. Allard, 397 F. Supp. 429 (D. Mont. 1975). *See* United States v. Top Sky, 547 F.2d 486 (9th Cir. 1976).

[41] United States v. Dion, 476 U.S. 734 (1986).

[42] 50 C.F.R. §22.22 (1990).

[43] *See* 16 U.S.C. §1540(g) (1988). *See also* Chapter 7.

[44] 16 U.S.C. §§703–712 (1988).

provides a private right of action.[45] The third court declined to reach the claims under those two statutes.[46]

The Act gives government officials the customary powers of enforcement.[47] In the 1972 Amendments, Congress "reinforced"[48] the penalties for violating the Act. It increased the criminal penalty, for a first offense, from a possible $500 fine to a $5,000 fine. It increased the possible prison sentence, for a first offense, from six months to one year. For second and subsequent offenses, Congress decreed possible punishments of a $10,000 fine, two years in jail, or both. The government was authorized to pay one-half of the fine, up to $2,500, to informers.[49]

Violators may also be assessed civil penalties of up to $5,000 for each violation. The Secretary must give the violator the opportunity to have an administrative hearing. In determining the amount of a penalty, the Secretary should consider the violation's gravity and the perpetrator's good faith. The Secretary may remit or mitigate a penalty. If the violator refuses to pay a penalty, the Department of Justice may institute a court action to collect. The court is instructed to sustain the Secretary's action if it is supported by substantial evidence.[50]

After the government obtains a criminal conviction, it may cancel any authority that the perpetrator has for grazing domestic livestock on federal lands.[51]

The Act also provides for forfeiture of all illegally acquired eagles, eagle parts, nests, or eggs.[52] The provision, in effect, "prohibits the private possession of these animals or any part of them without permission."[53] In addition, the Act allows forfeiture of vessels, vehicles, aircraft, traps, nets, guns, and other instruments used in violations. Forfeiture is not mandatory: these articles are only "subject to forfeiture." Congress gave U.S. Attorneys discretion to decline to seek forfeiture when that penalty is disproportionate to the crime.[54]

Forfeiture proceedings are governed by the customs laws.[55] The effect is to give the Secretary authority over forfeitures except where the value of the birds or equipment exceeds $2,500 (or someone files a claim and bond). A U.S. Attorney prosecutes these excepted forfeitures in court proceedings. The

---

[45] Defenders of Wildlife v. Administrator, Environmental Protection Agency, 882 F.2d 1294, 1301–02 (8th Cir. 1989); Humane Soc'y of the United States v. Lujan, 768 F. Supp. 360, 362 n.4 (D.D.C. 1991).

[46] National Wildlife Fed'n v. Hodel, 23 ER Cases 1089, 1093 n.7 (E.D. Cal. 1985).

[47] 16 U.S. C. §668b (1988).

[48] Andrus v. Allard, 441 U.S. 51, n.8 (1979). *See* United States v. Fryberg, *supra* note 40, at 1016; United States v. Allard, *supra* note 37, at 432.

[49] 16 U.S.C. §668(a) (1988).

[50] *Id.* §668(b).

[51] *Id.* §668(c).

[52] *Id.* §668b(b).

[53] United States v. Thirty Eight (38) Golden Eagles or Eagle Parts, *supra* note 36, at 272.

[54] 16 U.S.C. §668b(b) (1988). *See* 1972 Senate Report, *supra* note 13, at 7, 1972 U.S. CODE CONG. & ADMIN. NEWS at 4290–91.

[55] 16 U.S.C. §668b(c).

customs laws also protect persons who have a proprietary right in equipment used in a violation if they were not significantly involved in the crime.[56]

## Relationship to Other Statutes

Eagles are protected under several statutes. In 1972, eagles were brought within the Migratory Bird Treaty Act[57] by a presidential agreement. The consequence is that eagles are protected under the Migratory Bird Treaty Act as well as under the Bald and Golden Eagle Protection Act.[58] This was of little solace to two persons who sold whole eagles and eagle parts to undercover agents. Trying to overturn their convictions under the Bird Treaty Act, they argued that they should have been prosecuted under the more specific Eagle Act. The court disagreed. The rule is that the government may elect to prosecute under either statute.[59]

Bald eagles are also protected under the Endangered Species Act. The bald eagle is an endangered species, and the Endangered Species Act makes it unlawful to take a specimen of an endangered species.[60]

* * *

When it adopted the Act in 1940, Congress declared that the bald eagle was threatened with extinction. Notwithstanding Benjamin Franklin's reservations, Peter Matthiessen captured this Nation's belief when he wrote of the bald eagle:[61]

> [I]t is a species of much more than mere biological interest. White-headed and austere on a solitary tree, or flapping and sailing, stiff-winged and spread-fingered, over southern waterways or northern river deltas, inland river swamps or outer beaches, coursing the nation in summer and winter from the Columbia to the Merrimack, from the Everglades to the Yukon, the bald eagle is magnificent.

Under our environmental laws, the bald eagle is making an encouraging comeback all over the country.[62]

---

[56] 1972 Senate Report, *supra* note 13, at 7, 1972 U.S. CODE CONG. & ADMIN. NEWS at 4290–91.

[57] *Supra* note 44.

[58] United States v. Mackie, 681 F.2d 1121, 1123 (9th Cir. 1982).

[59] *Id.* at 1122–23.

[60] Humane Soc'y of the United States v. Lujan, *supra* note 45, at 361 (citing 16 U.S.C. §1538(a)(1)(B)). *See* Chapter 4.

[61] P. Matthiessen, *Wildlife in America,* 170–71 (New York: Viking, 1987).

[62] M. Bean, "Looking Back Over the First Fifteen Years," in K. Kohm, ed., *Balancing on the Brink of Extinction* 38 (Washington, D.C.: Island Press, 1991).

# Chapter 13

# The Migratory Bird Treaty Act

The skies were once darkened by vast flocks of passenger pigeons migrating over the North American continent. In 1813 Audubon observed a flock so numerous that "[t]he light of the noonday sun was obscured, as if by an eclipse." Following the birds to their roosting place, Audubon watched them shot and clubbed to death by an army of human foes.[1] Although the passenger pigeon had been the most numerous of all bird species, hunting soon made it rare. No large breeding colonies were found after 1860; the last nest was observed in 1894.[2] The passenger pigeon became extinct when Martha, a 29-year-old female residing in the Cincinnati Zoological Gardens, died in September 1914.[3]

Although he was too late to help the passenger pigeon, President Wilson signed a 1916 treaty with Great Britain (on behalf of Canada) for the protection of the "[m]any species of birds [which] in their annual migration traverse certain parts of the United States and . . . Canada."[4] In later years, the United States signed similar treaties with Mexico, Japan, and the Soviet Union.[5]

Congress implemented the treaty with Great Britain by enacting the Migratory Bird Treaty Act.[6] By amendments Congress incorporated the treaties of Mexico, of Japan, and of the USSR into the statute.[7]

---

[1] Quoted in M. Reisner, *Game Wars* 259–61 (New York: Viking 1991). *See* V. Ziswiler, *Extinct and Vanishing Animals* 2–3 (New York: Springer-Verlag, 1967).

[2] Ziswiler, *supra* note 1, at 3–4.

[3] *Id.*; W. Reffalt, "The Endangered Species Lists: Chronicles of Extinction?," in K. Kohm, ed., *Balancing on the Brink of Extinction* 77 (Washington, D.C.: Island Press, 1991); P. Matthiessen, *Wildlife in North America* 181 (New York: Viking, 1987).

[4] Convention for the Protection of Migratory Birds, 1916, 39 Stat. 1702.

[5] Convention for the Protection of Migratory Birds and Game Mammals, United States-Mexico, 1936, 50 Stat. 1311; Convention for the Protection of Migratory Birds, United States- Japan, 1972, 25 U.S.T. 3329, T.I.A.S. No. 7990; and Convention Concerning the Conservation of Migratory Birds and Their Environment, United States-Soviet Union, 1976, 29 U.S.T. 4647, T.I.A.S. No. 9073.

[6] Ch. 128, 40 Stat. 755 (1918) (codified in 16 U.S.C. §§703–711 (1988)).

[7] Ch. 634, §1, 49 Stat. 1555–56 (1936) (Mexico); Pub. L. No. 93-300, 88 Stat. 190 (1974) (Japan); Pub. L. No. 101-233, §15, 103 Stat. 1968, 1977 (1989) (USSR).

## Scope of the Act's Protection for Migratory Birds

The Act absolutely forbids killing, possessing, or trading in migratory birds except in accordance with regulations prescribed by the Secretary of the Interior. Section 2's prohibition can be violated by persons who:

> at any time, by any means or in any manner, . . . pursue, hunt, take, capture, kill, attempt to take, capture, or kill, possess, offer for sale, sell, offer to barter, barter, offer to purchase, purchase, deliver for shipment, ship, export, import, cause to be shipped, exported, or imported, deliver for transportation, transport or cause to be transported, carry or cause to be carried, or receive for shipment, transportation, carriage or export [migratory birds].[8]

The term "migratory bird" encompasses not only whole birds, but also parts of birds.[9] From its beginning, the statute has also protected bird nests and eggs.[10] In 1974 Congress extended the statute's protection to "any product, whether or not manufactured, which consists, or is composed in whole or part, of any such bird or any part, nest or egg thereof."[11]

The Act protects species of migratory birds that are included within the terms of the treaties with Great Britain, Mexico, Japan,[12] and the Soviet Union.[13] This includes species that the Presidents of the United States and Mexico added by executive agreement after the signing of the treaty between the two countries.[14] The U.S. regulations extend the Act's protections to mutations and hybrids of those species.[15] The regulations contain a list of migratory birds protected by the treaties and the Act.[16]

Unquestionably, the Act protects migratory birds that are wild. Does it also cover migratory birds that are raised in captivity? That question was raised by a college professor who began to breed sparrow hawks before they became subject to federal protection. In order to test the new federal regulation, the professor sold three captive-bred hawks. When the professor was convicted and sentenced to 18 months in jail, the Tenth Circuit confessed in 1978 that "[t]he severity of the sentence appalls us."[17] Nonetheless, the majority of the judges upheld the conviction under an administrative regulation that defines "migratory bird" to include any bird "whether or not raised in captivity."[18] The dissenting judge would have invalidated the regulation.

The next year, the Tenth Circuit revisited the same question in a different guise. This time members of a club were training dogs to retrieve birds; the

---

[8] 16 U.S.C. §703 (Supp. I 1989).
[9] United States v. St. Pierre, 578 F. Supp. 1424, 1426 (D.S.D. 1983).
[10] Ch. 128, §3, 40 Stat. 755 (1918).
[11] Pub. L. No. 93-300, §1(1), 88 Stat. 190 (codified in 16 U.S.C. §703 (1988)).
[12] 16 U.S.C. §703 (1988).
[13] Pub. L. No. 101-233, §15, 103 Stat. 1968, 1977 (1989).
[14] United States v. Blanket, 391 F. Supp. 15, 18 (W.D. Okla. 1975).
[15] 50 C.F.R. §10.12 (1990). *See id.* §20.11(a).
[16] *Id.* §10.13.
[17] United States v. Richards, 583 F.2d 491, 497 (10th Cir. 1978).
[18] *Id.* at 493–96 (citing 50 C.F.R. §10.12).

club members threw mallard ducks into a pond and released their dogs to fetch the birds. The club members insisted that they had used captive-reared ducks, purchased from legitimate suppliers. The trial court, however, convicted a club member of violating the Act. This time the Tenth Circuit ruled that, if the birds were reared in captivity, the charges should be dismissed. In the appeals court's opinion, the crucial factor was that the treaties with Great Britain and Mexico mentioned only "wild" ducks. The U.S. regulation referred specifically to "wild ducks." So the court majority ruled that the Act does not apply to the killing of captive-reared ducks.[19]

## Misdemeanors, Felonies, and the Required Intent

Unlike most wildlife statutes, the Act does not provide civil penalties for violations. Instead, violations are punishable only by criminal sanctions (and forfeiture).

### The Law Before 1960

For the first 42 years of the statute's life, all violations were treated alike. Under the original legislation,[20] anyone violating the Act or regulations was guilty of a misdemeanor. The maximum penalty was $500 or six months imprisonment, or both. Scienter was not mentioned as an element of the offense. The Act was regarded as containing a strict liability standard.[21]

### The 1960 Amendment

The Eighty-Sixth Congress made a radical change in the law's penalties. It retained the preexisting misdemeanor provision as subsection 6(a). It added an entirely new subsection 6(b) which makes the sale of a protected species a felony. Section 6(b) also makes it a felony to take a protected species with intent to sell it. The fine for felonies was set at $2,000; the maximum jail term at two years. Despite this increase in penalties, the 1960 Congress did not require that the felony be committed "knowingly."[22]

By this Amendment, Congress intended to provide more severe penalties for a so-called "commercial" or "market" hunter who "slaughters" migratory

---

[19] United States v. Connors, 606 F.2d 269 (10th Cir. 1979) (citing 50 C.F.R. §20.11 (1977)). The regulation cited by the court has since been changed to refer to "ducks" instead of "wild ducks." Another regulation allows the killing of properly marked, captive-reared mallard ducks, but normally not by shooting. 50 C.F.R. §21.13(d) (1990).

[20] Ch. 128, §5, 40 Stat. 755, 756 (1918).

[21] United States v. Engler, 806 F.2d 425, 431 (3rd Cir. 1986), *cert. denied,* 481 U.S. 1019 (1987). *See* United States v. Schultze, 28 F. Supp. 234 (W.D. Ky. 1939); United States v. Reese, 27 F. Supp. 833 (W.D. Tenn. 1939).

[22] Pub. L. No. 86-732, §6(a), (b), 74 Stat. 866 (1960).

birds in order to sell them. The misdemeanor provisions were retained for an individual "who hunts migratory birds for pleasure."[23]

## Misdemeanors: Required Intent

For misdemeanor prosecutions, most courts continue to treat the Act as imposing strict liability. According to the majority rule, "it is not necessary to prove that a defendant violated the . . . Act with specific intent or guilty knowledge."[24]

Believing that strict liability "is a harsh rule," several courts express "a reluctance to charge anyone with a crime which he does not know he is committing."[25] Those courts, however, adhere to the strict liability standard, contenting themselves with expressing the hope that the government will avoid prosecuting innocent technical violations or, at least, seek only nominal fines.

A minority of courts refuse to apply the strict liability rule, even for misdemeanors. For example, a district judge in Idaho refused to convict a farmer who sprayed his alfalfa field with pesticide, thus killing a flock of geese who ate the alfalfa. The farmer and his neighbors had used the pesticides in the past without ever killing geese. Labeling the farmer's application of the pesticides as an "innocent act," the judge confessed to being "queasy about the reach of strict liability criminal statutes." So he ruled that the Act was unconstitutionally vague as applied to the farmer.[26]

Another minority court is the Fifth Circuit. "Unique among the Circuits,"[27] that court has issued two opinions saying that hunters cannot be held strictly liable for violating the Act. Both cases concerned hunters who baited their fields with grain in violation of the regulations. In both decisions, the court recognized that—if it required actual guilty knowledge—the regulations would be very hard to enforce. So the court settled for "a minimum form of scienter—the 'should have known' form—[a]s a necessary element of the offense."[28] Applying that standard, the court found that the hunters had violated the Act in both cases.

---

[23] S. Rep. No. 1779, 86th Cong., 2d Sess. 1 (1960), *reprinted in* 1960 U.S. Code Cong. & Admin. News 3459 [hereinafter 1960 Senate Report]. *See* United States v. Engler, *supra* note 21, at 431.

[24] United States v. Manning, 787 F.2d 431, 435 n.4 (8th Cir. 1986). *Accord* United States v. Catlett, 747 F.2d 1102, 1104 (6th Cir. 1984), *cert. denied,* 471 U.S. 1074 (1985); United States v. Chandler, 753 F.2d 360, 363 (4th Cir. 1985); United States v. Green, 571 F.2d 1, 2 (6th Cir. 1977); United States v. FMC Corp., 572 F.2d 902, 905–08 (2d Cir. 1978).

[25] United States v. Catlett, *supra* note 24, at 1105. *See* United States v. FMC Corp., *supra* note 24, at 905.

[26] United States v. Rollins, 706 F. Supp. 742, 744–45 (D. Idaho 1989).

[27] United States v. Sylvester, 848 F.2d 520, 522 (5th Cir. 1988), citing United States v. Delahoussaye, 573 F.2d 910, 913 (5th Cir. 1978). Also citing United States v. Delahoussaye, Justice White voted to grant certiorari in United States v. Catlett, *supra* note 24, 471 U.S. at 1074–75, "to resolve the split among the Courts of Appeals."

[28] United States v. Delahoussaye, *supra* note 27, at 912.

This minority view is at odds with Congress' latest expression of intent. In 1986, when Congress amended the Act's penalty provisions, it reenacted the misdemeanor provision without significant change. Congress stated then that it had decided not to "alter the 'strict liability' standard for misdemeanor prosecutions."[29]

## Felonies: Required Intent

Several courts refused to go along with Congress' decision, in the 1960 amendment, to punish sales as a felony without proof of improper intent. Relying upon a 1952 Supreme Court ruling[30] in a non-wildlife case, those courts reasoned that strict liability statutes are constitutional only where the penalties are relatively small, and conviction does not damage an offender's reputation. Thus, a South Dakota district court concluded in 1983 that the Migratory Bird Treaty Act's strict-liability felony provision violates due process.[31] Two years later, the Sixth Circuit reached the same result in the *Wulff* case.[32] Affirming the dismissal of an indictment, the *Wulff* court said that "in order for one to be convicted of a felony under the [Act] . . . Congress must require the prosecution to prove the defendant acted with some degree of scienter."[33]

Congress acquiesced, acknowledging that the *Wulff* decision had made the Act's felony provision meaningless within the Sixth Circuit and of uncertain validity elsewhere.[34] To "cure the unintended infirmity,"[35] Congress amended the felony provision in 1986 by requiring that violations must be committed "knowingly."[36] Congress explained:[37]

> [T]he amendment will require proof that the defendant knew (1) that his actions constituted a taking, sale, barter, or offer to sell or barter, as the case may be and (2) that the item so taken, sold, or bartered was a bird or portion thereof.

But Congress did not insist that the offender act with evil intent:[38]

> It is not intended that proof be required that the defendant knew the taking, sale, barter or offer was a violation of the [Act], nor that he know the particular bird was listed in the various international treaties implemented by this Act.

Interestingly, a few weeks after Congress changed the law, the Third Circuit issued an opinion disagreeing with *Wulff;* the court upheld strict liability

---

[29] S. REP. NO. 445, 99th Cong., 2d Sess. 16 (1986), *reprinted in* 1986 U.S. CODE CONG. & ADMIN. NEWS 6113, 6128 [hereinafter 1986 Senate Report].

[30] Morissette v. United States, 342 U.S. 246 (1952).

[31] United States v. St. Pierre, 578 F. Supp. 1424, 1427–29 (D.S.D. 1983).

[32] United States v. Wulff, 758 F.2d 1121 (6th Cir. 1985).

[33] *Id.* at 1125.

[34] 1986 Senate Report, *supra* note 29.

[35] *Id.*

[36] *Id.*

[37] *Id.*

[38] *Id.*

under the Act's felony provision without proof of scienter. The Third Circuit made no mention of Congress' recent action,[39] which effectively nullifies the Third Circuit decision's future effect.

## Actions Permitted or Prohibited by the Regulations

The Act allows the Secretary of the Interior[40] to prescribe exceptions to the Act's general prohibitions. The Secretary is empowered to specify "when, to what extent, if at all, and by what means," migratory birds may be taken or used.[41] Those regulations must, of course, be compatible with the terms and purposes of the conventions.[42] Subject to that guideline, the Secretary has broad discretion in determining the regulations' content.[43] The courts have generally rejected challenges to the regulations' constitutionality.[44]

### Forbidden Hunting Methods

In the 1916 treaty between the United States and Great Britain, the "essential articles" establish closed seasons during which bird hunting is forbidden.[45] "If Congress may prohibit duck and geese shooting entirely," the Seventh Circuit ruled:[46]

> [I]t follows that the same authority may provide for a short open season, but limit the number of game birds a hunter may kill in a day, as well as prohibit the use of lures to attract birds to hunters' blinds and also may prescribe the guns or other instruments which the hunter may use to kill the birds.

The regulations contain all these restrictions and more.

#### *Traps, Guns, and Poison*

One regulation forbids hunting with traps, snares, nets, various kinds of guns, fish hooks, explosives, drugs, and poisons.[47]

The statute does not mention poisoning by name. That omission became an issue when a farmer had his alfalfa field sprayed with a pesticide, leading to the death of waterfowl. The pilot who sprayed the field argued that the Act

---

[39] United States v. Engler, *supra* note 21.

[40] Although the original Act granted regulatory authority to the Secretary of Agriculture (ch. 128, §3, 40 Stat. 755 (1918)), that function was later transferred to the Secretary of the Interior. *See* Reorganization Plan No. II of 1939, §3(f), 53 Stat. 1431, 1433 (1939).

[41] 16 U.S.C. §704 (1988). *See* United States v. Manning, *supra* note 24, at 434.

[42] *Id.*, §704.

[43] Alaska Fish and Wildlife Fed'n v. Dunkle, 829 F.2d 933, 940 (9th Cir. 1987), *cert. denied,* 485 U.S. 988 (1988).

[44] United States v. Manning, *supra* note 24, at 437, and cases cited therein.

[45] Cochrane v. United States, 92 F.2d 623, 625 (7th Cir. 1937), *cert. denied,* 303 U.S. 636 (1938) (quoting 39 Stat. 1702 (1916)).

[46] *Id.*, 92 F.2d at 626–27.

[47] 50 C.F.R. §20.21(a) (1990).

does not encompass "poisoning." Disagreeing, the court interpreted the statute to include poisoning as a prohibited act within the meaning of the Act's ban on killing "by any means or in any manner."[48]

The majority of courts will punish poisoning even when it is not intentional. The aerial spraying case, just discussed, is one example.[49] Another case concerned a chemical company that inadvertently discharged a pesticide into a pond where it poisoned birds. The court upheld the company's conviction under strict liability rules.[50] In a third case, a city government told a homeowner to get rid of pigeons that infested a vacant lot near his property. He did so, first by shooting them, then by spreading poisoned corn and wheat. Four migratory birds joined the feast and died. The court held that, under the strict liability standard, the homeowner could be convicted without establishing that his tactics could be expected to kill migratory birds.[51] And in the minority jurisdiction mentioned earlier, an Idaho district court refused to convict a farmer who accidentally killed birds by spraying his field with pesticides.[52]

### *Shotguns*

Hunters are forbidden to use shotguns capable of holding more than three shells, unless the extra capacity is plugged.[53]

### *Motorized Conveyance*

Hunters may not shoot birds from motorboats, sailboats, motor vehicles, or aircraft. They may, however, operate a craft under power to retrieve dead or crippled birds.[54] When does a powerboat cease to be a powerboat? One hunter asked that question when he shot a bird after shutting off his outboard motor and lifting the propeller clear of the water. In that 1941 decision, the judge concluded that the craft remained a powerboat until the engine had been detached from the stern and placed in the boat.[55] The current regulations allow shooting from a powerboat once its motor has been completely shut off and its motorized progress has ceased.[56]

### *Decoys, Bird Calls, and Herding*

The regulations forbid a variety of tactics that are unsporting. One of these is the use of live birds as decoys. Among other things, it is unlawful to take

---

[48] United States v. Corbin Farm Serv., 444 F. Supp. 510, 531–32 (E.D. Cal.) (citing 16 U.S.C. §703), *aff'd on other grounds per curiam,* 578 F.2d 259 (9th Cir. 1978).
[49] *Id.*, 444 F. Supp. at 532–36.
[50] United States v. FMC, 572 F.2d 902 (2d Cir. 1978).
[51] United States v. Van Fossan, 899 F.2d 636 (7th Cir. 1990).
[52] United States v. Rollins, 706 F. Supp. 742 (D. Idaho 1989).
[53] 50 C.F.R. §20.21(b) (1990).
[54] *Id.* §20.21(d), (e).
[55] United States v. Olson, 41 F. Supp. 433 (W.D. Ky. 1941).
[56] 50 C.F.R. §20.21(e) (1990).

waterfowl in an area where tame or captive live ducks or geese are present unless they have been there for 10 days before the shoot. In addition, the tame or captive birds have to be confined in an enclosure so that the wild birds cannot see or hear them.[57] The owner of Mebane Farms, where 4,500 ducks had been raised over two years, violated the regulations when he conducted a hunt on the farm.[58]

The use of recorded or electronic bird calls is banned as well.[59] Hunters also may not use motorized conveyances or sailboats to flush or drive birds.[60]

### *Bait*

The regulations also "prohibit the taking of waterfowl that are lured to an area by bait."[61] Baiting consists of scattering feed where it can lure birds within shotgun range.

The regulation's prohibition is stated in the disjunctive: Migratory birds may not be taken either "[b]y the aid of baiting, or on or over any baited area."[62] Several courts held that, to be convicted for taking birds "by the aid of baiting," the hunters must have taken some part in the baiting or, at least, it must have been done for their benefit.[63] To be convicted for shooting "on or over any baited area," hunters need not be connected in any way with placing the bait.[64]

It is not necessary that the baiting take place during the hunting season. The regulation is violated by baiting before the season in order to keep the birds there to be shot after the season begins.[65]

Baiting exists even if the bait is gone by the time of the shoot. In one case,[66] for example, a court convicted two hunters who quit baiting two to five days before the 1962 hunting season began. A decade later, the regulation was amended to declare that an area remains a baited area for ten days following "complete removal" of all feed. So, where a field had been baited three days before the hunt, a court[67] upheld a conviction even though the bait was removed by the time of the shooting.

This 10-day rule appears to allow conviction of hunters who enter the area after the bait has been removed, even if they have no reason to know that the area was ever baited. When defendants complained that this possibility renders the rule unconstitutional, a Wisconsin district court dismissed their objection.[68]

---

[57] *Id.* §20.21(f).
[58] United States v. Mebane, 839 F.2d 230 (4th Cir. 1988).
[59] 50 C.F.R. §20.21(g).
[60] *Id.* §20.21(h).
[61] United States v. Chandler, 753 F.2d 360, 362 (4th Cir. 1985).
[62] *Id.*; 50 C.F.R. §20.21(i) (1990).
[63] Allen v. Merovka, 382 F.2d 589, 591 (10th Cir. 1967); United States v. Bryson, 414 F. Supp. 1068 (D. Del. 1976).
[64] United States v. Chandler, *supra* note 61, at 363.
[65] Koop v. United States, 296 F.2d 53, 58 (8th Cir. 1961); Cerritos Gun Club v. Hall, 96 F.2d 620, 624 (9th Cir. 1938).
[66] United States v. Tarmon, 227 F. Supp. 480 (D. Md. 1964).
[67] United States v. Jarman, 491 F.2d 764 (4th Cir. 1974).
[68] United States v. Atkinson, 468 F. Supp. 834, 836–37 (E.D. Wis. 1979).

Under its "unique" requirement of scienter, the Fifth Circuit insists that "the bait . . . must have been so situated that [its] presence could reasonably have been ascertained by a hunter properly wishing to check the area of his activity for illegal devices."[69] So the Fifth Circuit would probably not enforce the 10-day rule against hunters who had no reason to suspect previous baiting.

If hunters position themselves at a distance from the feed, are their bird kills made (in the regulation's words) "on or over any baited area"? In 1976 a Delaware district judge answered this question in the negative. Giving the quoted words "their literal meaning," the judge ruled that the regulation's prohibition did not apply to hunters who shot geese from a blind located approximately 100 yards from the deposit of feed.[70] Other courts reach a different result. In the majority view, "[t]he term 'baited area' plainly means the area within which and over which scattered bait exercises an attraction."[71] The area's geographical limits are "defined only by the capacity of bait placed anywhere within it to act as an effective lure for the particular hunter charged."[72]

There are two exceptions to the prohibition against baiting. One exception allows hunting over standing crops or grain scattered as the result of normal farm planting or harvesting.[73] But the farmer must undertake those activities with the primary goal of producing a crop—not enticing migratory birds[74] or feeding livestock.[75] A second exception allows hunting (except for waterfowl[76]) over lands where grain has been scattered "as a result of *bona fide* agricultural operations or procedures."[77] For this exception, too, the farming operation or procedure must be done for a purpose related to the growing of crops, such as erosion control.[78]

### *Lead Shot*

Lead poisoning has long plagued migratory waterfowl, which are poisoned when they ingest spent lead ammunition. After much research, the government banned hunting except with steel shot or other nontoxic shot.[79] When the National Rifle Association challenged the early version of this regulatory scheme, the court upheld the regulation.[80]

---

[69] United States v. Delahoussaye, 573 F.2d 910, 912 (5th Cir. 1978).

[70] United States v. Bryson, 414 F. Supp. 1068, 1071, 1073–74 (D. Del. 1976).

[71] United States v. Manning, 787 F.2d 431, 437 (8th Cir. 1986); United States v. Delahoussaye, *supra* note 69, at 912.

[72] United States v. Chandler, *supra* note 61, at 363. *See also* United States v. Angueira, 744 F. Supp. 36, 39 (D.P.R. 1990); Yandell v. United States, 550 F. Supp. 572, 575 (N.D. Miss. 1982), *aff'd,* 712 F.2d 218 (5th Cir. 1983).

[73] 50 C.F.R. §20.21(i)(1) (1990).

[74] United States v. Brandt, 717 F.2d 955, 958 (6th Cir. 1983).

[75] United States v. Manning, *supra* note 71, at 436.

[76] *Id.*

[77] 50 C.F.R. §20.21(i)(2) (1990).

[78] United States v. Brandt, *supra* note 74, at 958.

[79] 50 C.F.R. §§20.21(j), 20.134 (1990).

[80] National Rifle Ass'n v. Kleppe, 425 F. Supp. 1101 (D.D.C. 1976), *aff'd sub nom.* National Rifle Ass'n v. Andrus, 571 F.2d 674 (D.C. Cir. 1978).

*Takings During Closed Seasons*

The taking of migratory game birds is forbidden except during open seasons.[81] In one case, environmentalists challenged the government's declaration of an open season for duck hunting. They noted that, when the Secretary decides to allow hunting, he is required by law to give regard to such factors as "distribution, abundance, economic value, [and] breeding habits" of the birds.[82] The duck population had been declining, although the species was not endangered. The government promised to reexamine hunting limits for the following year. "[N]ot convinced that the species would be unable to repair itself in subsequent years,"[83] the court upheld the open-season regulation.[84]

*Hunting Outside Shooting Hours*

The regulations allow hunting only during prescribed shooting hours.[85]

*Kills Exceeding the Daily Limit*

On any day, hunters may not exceed a prescribed bag limit of birds.[86] One case suggests, though it does not decide, that a hunter violates the regulation when he shoots more than the bag limit even if he does not retrieve all his birds.[87]

*Wanton Waste*

Hunters are required to retrieve any bird that they kill or cripple.[88] The rule's purpose is to prevent hunters from killing more ducks than they are allowed to keep, leaving the excess uncollected. Hunters who do that are guilty of wanton waste.[89]

## Other Forbidden Conduct

The statute[90] proscribes not only taking, but also other uses of migratory birds. The regulations implement those prohibitions.

---

[81] 50 C.F.R.§§20.22, 20.100 (1990).
[82] 16 U.S.C. §703 (1988).
[83] Humane Soc'y of the United States v. Watt, 550 F. Supp. 47, 49 (D.D.C. 1982).
[84] Humane Soc'y of the United States v. Watt, 551 F. Supp. 1310 (D.D.C. 1982), *aff'd*, 713 F.2d 865 (1983).
[85] 50 C.F.R. §§20.23, 20.100 (1990).
[86] *Id.* §§20.24, 20.100 (1990).
[87] United States v. Chew, 540 F.2d 759, 761–62 (4th Cir. 1976), *cert. denied*, 429 U.S. 1043 (1977).
[88] 50 C.F.R. §20.25 (1990).
[89] United States v. Lyon, 949 F.2d 240; 243 (8th Cir. 1991).
[90] 16 U.S.C. §703 (1988).

*Failure to Tag*

Hunters may not leave birds anyplace (except at home) unless they are tagged with information identifying the hunters and the date and number of their kill.[91] Illustrating this rule is the case of three hunters who killed 37 ducks, cleaning 10 and leaving the remaining 27 ducks untagged at the campsite. Their conduct earned each a $300 fine.[92]

*Forbidden Possession*

The prohibitions against illegal possession of migratory birds are numerous. No one may possess a bird that was taken in violation of the hunting rules just discussed. No one may possess a freshly killed bird during the closed season, or possess more than the bagged limits. Nor may anyone possess live or untagged birds.[93]

*Forbidden Transportation and Trade*

No one may transport or export any migratory bird taken in violation of the hunting regulations. No one may import a bird belonging to another or transport it if untagged. Nor may anyone export or import or transport a bird unless it is complete enough so that its species can be identified. Shipping packages must be marked appropriately. Imports from Mexico and Canada are limited for some species.[94]

*Use of Feathers and Skins*

Generally, persons are allowed to use the feathers of legally killed migratory waterfowl for commercial purposes. There are exceptions, however. No one may trade in those feathers for millinery or ornamental use. And no one may trade in mounted specimens of migratory game birds. For their own use, however, people may possess, transport, ship, import, and export feathers and skins of lawfully taken birds.[95]

## Violations of Other Federal Laws

In its regulations, the government also forbids the taking, possession, transportation, or export of any migratory bird (or part, nest, or egg) in violation of any congressional statute or related regulation.[96]

---

[91] 50 C.F.R. §20.36 (1990).

[92] United States v. Mielke, 367 F. Supp. 518 (W.D. Okla.), *aff'd sub nom.* United States v. Ray, 488 F.2d 15 (10th Cir. 1973).

[93] 50 C.F.R. §§20.31–20.35, 20.37–20.40, 20.100 (1990).

[94] *Id.* §§20.41–20.66.

[95] *Id.* §§20.91–20.92.

[96] *Id.* §20.71.

## Violations of State or Foreign Law

Section 2, which protects migratory birds, is not the Act's only prohibition. An obscure provision, Section 4,[97] makes it unlawful to ship, transport, or carry, in an interstate or foreign journey, any bird that is tainted by a violation of state or local law. It is also unlawful to import any bird that is tainted by a violation of Canadian law. These restrictions apply not only to whole birds, but also to bird parts, nests, and eggs.

In 1936 Congress added a provision making it unlawful to import game mammals from Mexico, without a permit,[98] but repealed this in 1969.[99]

Unlike Section 2, Section 4 speaks in terms of "any bird," not "any migratory bird." Because of that difference in language, one court said 60 years ago that Section 2 "may not be read as limited to migratory birds."[100] Nonetheless, the regulations apply only to "any migratory bird" (or part, nest, or egg) acquired in violation of state or foreign law.[101]

## Exemptions

Although the Act itself contains only a few exemptions, the agency rules except numerous transactions from regulation or, at least, from the need to obtain permits.

### *Alaskan Natives*

In 1978, Congress amended the Act to implement the convention with the Soviet Union. That amendment authorizes the Secretary to adopt regulations permitting subsistence hunting by Alaskan natives.[102] Those regulations must not, however, contravene the treaties with Canada, Japan, Mexico, or the Soviet Union. For that reason, a court invalidated several federal agreements that violated the treaties.[103]

### *Captive-Bred Birds*

Congress took pains to legalize the breeding of migratory birds on farms and preserves, as well as the sale of those birds for the purpose of increasing the food supply. The government may regulate the manner of those sales.[104]

---

[97] 16 U.S.C. §705 (1988).

[98] Ch. 634, §4, 49 Stat. 1555, 1556 (1936).

[99] Pub. L. No. 91-135, §10, 83 Stat. 275, 282 (1969). *See* S. Rep. No. 526, 91st Cong., 1st Sess. 17 (1969), *reprinted in* U.S. Code Cong. & Admin. News 1413, 1430.

[100] Bogle v. White, 61 F.2d 930, 931 (5th Cir. 1932).

[101] 50 C.F.R. §§20.72–20.73 (1990).

[102] Convention Concerning the Conservation of Migratory Birds and Their Environment, 1976, 29 U.S.T. 4647, T.I.A.S. No. 9073. *See* 50 C.F.R. §20.132 (1990).

[103] Alaska Fish & Wildlife Fed'n v. Dunkle, 829 F.2d 933 (9th Cir. 1987), *cert. denied,* 485 U.S. 988 (1988).

[104] 16 U.S.C. §711 (1988).

The regulations also allow the use of certain captive-bred birds, under strict controls, for food sales, dog training, and other purposes.[105]

### *Pre-Act Articles*

The regulations allow possession and transportation of migratory birds (or parts, nests, and eggs) lawfully acquired before the advent of protection under the Act. No permit is required. The exemption does not apply to the offspring of these birds. The regulation forbids the importation, exportation, purchase, sale, or barter of these birds.[106]

The Supreme Court upheld the regulation's prohibition on sales of pre-Act birds and their parts.[107]

### *Zoos and Institutions*

Public parks, zoos, and scientific and educational institutions are allowed to have lawfully acquired migratory birds. Those facilities may acquire, possess, transport, and dispose of birds, subject to record keeping and other safeguards.[108]

### *Indian Treaty Rights*

Two lower courts ruled that Native Americans whose tribes have treaty rights to hunt may not be prosecuted under the Act for killing migratory birds[109] or for selling their feathers.[110] The latter decision attempted to distinguish a Supreme Court ruling[111] that the Bald and Golden Eagle Act abrogated hunting rights granted by tribal treaties. The status of Indian hunting rights under the Migratory Bird Treaty Act should still be regarded as unsettled.

### *Protection of Property*

A familiar question is whether a landowner has a right to kill protected wildlife in defense of property.[112] When Billy Joe Darst's chickens were being killed by great horned owls, Darst set traps to protect his fowl. He caught and killed two owls. The court rejected Darst's assertion of a constitutional right to protect property.[113]

---

[105] 50 C.F.R. §§21.13–21.14 (1990).
[106] *Id.* §21.2(a).
[107] Andrus v. Allard, 444 U.S. 51, 59–62 (1979).
[108] 50 C.F.R. §21.12(b) (1990).
[109] United States v. Cutler, 37 F. Supp. 724 (E.D. Idaho 1941).
[110] United States v. Bresette, 761 F. Supp. 658 (D. Minn. 1991).
[111] United States v. Dion, 476 U.S. 734 (1986), discussed in Chapter 12.
[112] *See* Chapter 7.
[113] United States v. Darst, 726 F. Supp. 286 (D. Kan. 1989).

## Enforcement

Unlike many environmental statutes, the Migratory Bird Treaty Act contains no provision for private rights of action.[114] Nor does the Act impose civil penalties. The federal government can seek to impose sanctions only by means of the provisions for criminal penalties and forfeiture.

### *Right to Jury Trial*

The Act's misdemeanor provision constitutes a petty offense that was not triable by a jury at common law. So, generally, persons charged with a misdemeanor under the Act do not have the right to trial by jury.[115] An exception is where the government combines a number of misdemeanor counts in a single prosecution, creating the potential for substantial penalties. In that instance, the accused is entitled to a jury trial.[116]

### *Multiple Counts*

A single action can lead to the death of many birds. By one application of pesticide to his field, for example, a farmer killed 10 migratory birds. The government argued that each killing was a separate violation of the statute, justifying separate counts in the indictment. The court disagreed. Concluding that only one offense had occurred, the court dismissed nine of ten counts.[117]

### *Arrests and Searches*

The Act authorizes the Secretary's employees to make arrests, without a warrant, for violations committed in their presence. They also have authority, with a search warrant, to search "any place."[118] In one instance, federal agents searched a hunter's automobile. The search was not made as an incident to a lawful arrest or under authority of a search warrant. Ruling that the evidence should have been suppressed, the court reversed the conviction.[119] Not all areas are protected against warrantless searches, however. For example, federal agents do not need a warrant to search open fields.[120]

---

[114] Defenders of Wildlife v. Administrator, Environmental Protection Agency, 882 F.2d 1294, 1301 (8th Cir. 1989).

[115] United States v. Bullock, 579 F.2d 1116, 1118 (8th Cir.) *cert. denied,* 439 U.S. 967 (1978); United States v. Coates, 573 F.2d 257, 258 (5th Cir. 1978); United States v. Jarman, 491 F.2d 764, 767 (4th Cir. 1974); United States v. Ireland, 493 F.2d 1208, 1209 (4th Cir. 1973); United States v. Cain, 454 F.2d 1285, 1287–88 (7th Cir. 1972). *But compare* Smith v. United States, 128 F.2d 990 (5th Cir. 1942).

[116] United States v. FMC Corp., 428 F. Supp. 615, 619–20 (W.D.N.Y. 1977), *aff'd on other grounds,* 572 F.2d 902 (2d Cir. 1978).

[117] United States v. Corbin Farm Serv., 444 F. Supp. 510, 527–31 (E.D. Cal.), *aff'd per curiam,* 578 F.2d 259 (9th Cir. 1978).

[118] 16 U.S.C. §706 (1988).

[119] Aiuppa v. United States, 338 F.2d 146 (10th Cir. 1964).

[120] United States v. Swann, 377 F. Supp. 1305 (D. Md. 1974).

Some state laws allow searches, upon probable cause, without a warrant. In such a state, if a state game warden acts independently to conduct a warrantless search, and discovers incriminating evidence, it may be used in a federal prosecution.[121]

*Crime Against Eagles*

Bald and golden eagles are migratory birds.[122] They are protected under both the Migratory Bird Treaty Act and the Bald and Golden Eagle Protection Act.[123] The government may elect to prosecute illegal sales of eagles and eagle parts under either statute.[124]

*Forfeiture*

The Act has always allowed the government to seize illegally acquired birds, parts, nests, and eggs.[125] In 1960 Congress complained that this provision did not permit the forfeiture of the culprits' guns and equipment. To increase the statutory deterrent, the legislature enacted a separate forfeiture section that provides for the "loss of boats, automobiles, motors and equipment."[126]

In order to keep seized wildlife, the government does not have to win conviction of the offender. A 1981 case illustrates this. Believing that the government was guilty of misconduct, a district judge dismissed an indictment against Warren Dean Drake, who had illegally sold two American flamingos. The judge also ordered the government to return the flamingos to Drake. The court of appeals found, however, that the government had not misbehaved. Allowing the trial to proceed, the appeals court also let the government keep the birds. "Even if Drake is not convicted . . . , if the birds are found to be 'possessed contrary to [the Act],' they are to be forfeited to the United States."[127]

## Relationship to State Law

The Act leaves states and territories free to play a major role in wildlife protection. These local governments are allowed to make and enforce laws and regulations that are consistent with the Act and related treaties. They may even

---

[121] United States v. Verret, 302 F. Supp. 492 (E.D. La. 1969).

[122] 50 C.F.R. §10.13 (1990).

[123] *See* Chapter 12.

[124] United States v. Mackie, 681 F.2d 1121 (9th Cir. 1982).

[125] Ch. 128, §5, 40 Stat. 755, 756 (1918) (codified at 16 U.S.C. §706 (1988)), as amended by the Fish and Wildlife Improvement Act of 1978, Pub. L. No. 95-616, §3(h), 92 Stat. 3110, 3111–12 (1978)).

[126] 1960 Senate Report, *supra* note 23. *See* Pub. L. No. 86-732, 74 Stat. 866 (1960) (codified in 16 U.S.C. §707(c) (1988)).

[127] United States v. Drake, 655 F.2d 1025, 1028 (10th Cir. 1981) (referring to 16 U.S.C. §706).

give additional protection to migratory birds, their nests, and eggs. They may not, however, extend the open seasons for hunting.[128]

The states have taken advantage of these powers. The Minnesota Supreme Court ruled that the state could prohibit hunters from taking three ducks daily, although the federal limit was four ducks.[129] The South Dakota Supreme Court approved the state's refusal to issue bird hunting licenses to nonresidents.[130]

* * *

The Migratory Bird Treaty Act, together with complementary legislation,[131] obligates the United States to preserve and protect migratory birds through the regulation of hunting, the establishment of refuges, and the protection of bird habitats.[132] Upholding the constitutionality of both the 1916 treaty with Great Britain and the Migratory Bird Treaty Act, Justice Holmes wrote:[133]

> Here a national interest of very nearly the first magnitude is involved. It can be protected only by national action in concert with that of another power. . . . But for the treaty and the statute, there soon might be no birds for any powers to deal with.

---

[128] 16 U.S.C. §708 (1988). *See* 50 C.F.R. §20.2(b) (1990). *See also* Carey v. South Dakota, 250 U.S. 118 (1919).

[129] State *ex rel.* Duck Hunters Ass'n v. Olson, 266 Minn. 571, 123 N.W.2d 679 (1963).

[130] State v. Kemp, 73 S.D. 458, 44 N.W.2d 214 (1950).

[131] Migratory Bird Conservation Act, Ch. 257, 45 Stat. 1222 (1929); Migratory Bird Hunting and Conservation Stamp Act., Ch. 71, 48 Stat. 451 (1934); Wetlands Loan Act, Pub. L. No. 87-383, 75 Stat. 813 (1961) (all codified in 16 U.S.C. §715 *et seq.* (1988)).

[132] *See* United States v. Brandt, 717 F.2d 955, 956 n.1 (6th Cir. 1983); United States v. North Dakota, 650 F.2d 911, 913–14 (8th Cir. 1981), *aff'd,* 460 U.S. 300 (1983).

[133] Missouri v. Holland, 252 U.S. 416, 435 (1920).

# Chapter 14

# Other Federal Statutes

Chapters 1 through 13 discuss five laws that are prominent in the protection and control of fish, wildlife, and plants. This chapter will summarize the provisions of 14 other federal statutes that play an important role in environmental protection.

## The Airborne Hunting Act

In 1971, Congress amended the Fish and Wildlife Act of 1956 by adding legislation commonly referred to as the Airborne Hunting Act. Instigated by media reports of the shooting of wolves and eagles from aircraft,[1] the statute makes it unlawful for anyone while airborne in an aircraft to shoot or attempt to shoot for the purpose of capturing or killing any bird, fish, or animal. It is also unlawful for anyone to use an aircraft to harass any bird, fish, or animal. In addition, it is unlawful for anyone to knowingly participate in using an aircraft for those purposes.[2]

Violators are subject to a $5,000 fine, one year in prison, or both. In addition, the hunters may forfeit their guns and aircraft, as well as the birds, fish, or animals shot.[3]

The statute contains significant exceptions, however. It does not apply to government agents working to protect land, water, livestock, domesticated animals, human life, or crops. Nor does the statute apply to persons operating under a license or permit issued for those purposes.[4] Congress did not intend to prohibit ranchers from using aircraft to work or move cattle or other kinds of domesticated livestock or even privately owned and managed wildlife.[5]

---

[1] S. Rep. No. 421, 92d Cong., 1st Sess. 3 (1971), *reprinted in* 1971 U.S. Code Cong. & Admin. News 1735 [hereinafter Senate Report 92-421].

[2] 16 U.S.C. §742j–1(a) (1988). The Act was upheld in United States v. Helsley, 615 F.2d 784 (9th Cir. 1979).

[3] *Id.* §742j–(1)(a), (e).

[4] *Id.* §742j–(1)(b)(1).

[5] Senate Report 92-421, *supra* note 1, at 4, 1971 U.S. Code Cong. & Admin. News at 1737–38.

## The Wild Free-Roaming Horses and Burros Act

In the 1950s President Eisenhower signed the first federal law designed to protect wild horses and burros.[6] The legislature was motivated by widespread public objection to the use of motorized vehicles or aircraft to hunt those animals on land belonging to the United States. The legislation prohibited this hunting tactic. During the 1960s Congress considered other legislation to increase protection for wild horses and burros. Those proposals were not enacted, however.[7]

Finally, in 1971 Congress passed a statute known as the Wild Free-Roaming Horses and Burros Act.[8] Declaring these animals to be living symbols of our pioneer heritage, Congress directed that the animals be considered an integral part of our system of public lands.[9]

The statute incorporates two strategies for protection. The first makes it unlawful[10] to:

- Willfully remove a free-roaming horse or burro from public lands, without the Secretary's permission
- Convert any of these animals to private use, without the Secretary's permission
- Maliciously cause the death or harassment of any of these animals
- Process the remains of any of these animals into commercial products
- Sell any of these animals (or their remains) if the animal was maintained on private or leased land
- Violate a regulation issued under the Act

Violators are subject to fines of up to $2,000, up to one year's imprisonment, or both.

The Act's second strategy is to place all wild free-roaming horses and burros "under the jurisdiction of the Secretary for the purpose of management and protection." The Secretary is directed to protect and manage these animals "as components of the public lands."[11] Under this regulatory scheme, federal agencies are called upon to manage public lands by taking into account multiple uses, including the needs of wild free-roaming horses and burros, of "other wildlife species,"[12] and other purposes.[13]

---

[6] Pub. L. No. 86-234, 73 Stat. 470 (1959) (codified in 18 U.S.C. §47 (1988)).

[7] S. REP. NO. 242, 92d Cong., 1st Sess. 2 (1971), *reprinted in* 1971 U.S. CODE CONG. & ADMIN. NEWS 2149 [hereinafter Senate Report 92-242].

[8] 16 U.S.C. §§1331–1340 (1988). The Supreme Court upheld the Act's constitutionality in Kleppe v. New Mexico, 426 U.S. 529 (1976).

[9] *Id.* §1331.

[10] *Id.* §1338.

[11] *Id.* §1333(a).

[12] *Id.*

[13] The duties imposed on federal land managers are discussed in M. Bean, *The Evolution of National Wildlife Law* 160–66 (New York: Praeger Scientific, 1983).

The 1971 Act contained a brief section allowing the Secretary to have infirm animals destroyed in overpopulated areas. The Secretary was also allowed to have excess animals captured and removed from such areas for private maintenance.[14] In 1978, Congress amended this provision to allow qualified private individuals to adopt the excess animals. No one is allowed to adopt more than four animals in a year without special permission from the Secretary.[15]

The Act also specifies the treatment of wild free-roaming horses and burros that stray onto private lands. Private landowners must notify federal officials, who "shall arrange to have the animals removed."[16] In one case, when the Secretary failed to remove wild horses from grazing lands, the landowners alleged that the Secretary's nonaction constituted a "taking" of their property under the Fifth Amendment. The court disagreed, relying upon "an unbroken line" of Supreme Court decisions upholding land-use regulations related to the public interest.[17] Also, private landowners may choose to maintain the animals on private lands if the animals are protected from harassment.[18]

## The Animal Welfare Act

The Animal Welfare Act[19] has only an incidental effect on wildlife. As first enacted in 1966, the Animal Welfare Act was aimed at preventing theft and sale for use in research of pet cats and dogs. It was also designed to foster humane treatment by dealers and research facilities of cats, dogs, and certain other laboratory animals.[20] In 1970 the Act's coverage was extended to most live or dead warm-blooded animals. Exhibitors and auction sales were subjected to regulation. The Secretary's powers were increased and extended to cover activities which substantially affect interstate commerce.[21]

The 1976 amendments addressed two additional problems. One was the mistreatment of animals during their transportation. Airlines, railroads, truckers and other carriers of animals, and animal handlers, were required to adhere to humane standards. The second problem was animal fighting ventures. The legislation made it a crime to promote, sponsor, or abet animal fighting ventures.[22] In the case of this fighting-ventures provision, the term "animal" is defined to mean "any live bird, or any live dog or other mammal, except man."[23]

---

[14] Pub. L. No. 92-195, §3(b), 85 Stat. 649, 650.

[15] Public Rangelands Improvement Act of 1978, Pub. L. No. 95-514, §14, 92 Stat. 1803, 1808–10 (codified in 16 U.S.C. §1333(b)–(d) (1988)).

[16] 16 U.S.C. §1334 (1988). *See* 43 C.F.R. §4720.2–1 (1991).

[17] Mountain States Legal Found. v. Hodel, 799 F.2d 1423 (10th Cir. 1986), *cert. denied,* 480 U.S. 951 (1987), and cases cited therein.

[18] 16 U.S.C. §1334 (1988).

[19] 7 U.S.C. §§2131–2157 (1988).

[20] Pub. L. No. 89-544, 80 Stat. 350 (1966).

[21] Pub. L. No. 91-579, 84 Stat. 1560 (1970).

[22] Pub. L. No. 94-279, 90 Stat. 417 (1976).

[23] Pub. L. No. 94-279, §17, 90 Stat. 417, 423 (codified in 7 U.S.C. §2156 (1988)).

In 1978 Congress strengthened the Secretary's powers and obligations to ensure humane treatment of animals, particularly in research facilities.[24]

The Secretary may assess civil penalties for violations. Those who violate the Act, regulations, or the Secretary's standards may be penalized up to $2,500 for each violation. The Secretary may also enter a cease and desist order. If persons knowingly fail to obey a cease and desist order, they may be subject to a civil penalty of up to $1,500 for each day of noncompliance. Knowing violations may also be punished by criminal fines of up to $2,500, imprisonment for up to one year, or both.[25]

## The Federal Power Act

Under the Federal Power Act,[26] the Federal Energy Regulatory Commission issues licenses to build and operate dams, reservoirs, transmission lines, and other power projects. The Endangered Species Act requires federal agencies like the Commission to insure that their actions are not likely to jeopardize the continued existence of endangered or threatened species.[27] Moreover, in 1986, Congress amended[28] the Federal Power Act by requiring the Commission to give consideration to "environmental values, including fish and wildlife. . . , in deciding whether to issue" a license.[29]

The Commission now follows elaborate procedures in determining whether to issue hydroelectric and other licenses. The Commission issues licenses that include conditions to protect, enhance, and mitigate damages to fish and wildlife (including related spawning grounds and habitat).[30] In one recent case involving a dam, the owner was required to increase water flows in order to protect downstream fish and other aquatic animals, including an endangered species of snail.[31]

In the future the Commission is likely to be busy with requests to protect fish and wildlife. Federal licenses for 231 hydroelectric power dams in 24 states will expire by the end of 1993. Power companies will be seeking renewal of their 50-year licenses. Environmental agencies and groups are planning to ask

---

[24] Food Security Act of 1985, Pub. L. No. 99-198, §§1751–1753, 99 Stat. 1354, 1645–49 (codified in 7 U.S.C. §§2143, 2146(a) (1988)).

[25] 7 U.S.C. §2149(b) (1988).

[26] 16 U.S.C. §§791(a)–828c (1988).

[27] *Id.* §1536(a)(2).

[28] Electric Consumers Protection Act, Pub. L. No. 99-495, §3, 100 Stat. 1243–44 (1986) (codified in 16 U.S.C. §§797(e), 803(a) and (j) (1988)).

[29] Platte River Whooping Crane Critical Habitat Maintenance Trust v. Federal Energy Regulatory Comm'n, 876 F.2d 109, 118 (D.C. Cir. 1989) (quoting H. CONF. REP. NO. 934, 99th Cong., 2d Sess. 21–22 (1986), *reprinted in* 1986 U.S. CODE CONG. & ADMIN. NEWS 2496, 2538)).

[30] Allegheny Electric, 48 F.E.R.C. ¶61,363 (1989), *aff'd on other grounds sub nom.* U.S. Dep't of Interior v. Federal Energy Regulatory Comm'n, 952 F.2d 538 (D.C. Cir. 1992).

[31] Alabama Power Co., 56 F.E.R.C. ¶61,173 (1991), *appeal filed,* No. 91-1466 (D.C. Cir. 1991).

the Commission to condition any new licenses by requiring equipment to protect fish and assist their migration. The dam operators will be asked to accept modifications that improve water quality and protect fish.[32] The relicensing arena will test the Commission's commitment to its new powers to protect the environment and wildlife.

## The Whaling Convention Act

The Whaling Convention Act[33] implements the 1946 International Convention for the Regulation of Whaling.[34] The Convention prohibits wasteful whaling practices and establishes an International Whaling Commission empowered to protect certain types of whales, establish whaling seasons, set size and catch limits, and prescribe whaling methods. Under the Whaling Convention Act, the Secretary of Commerce publishes the Whaling Commission's regulations, thus making them binding on persons subject to U.S. jurisdiction.[35]

The Whaling Convention Act makes it unlawful for persons subject to U.S. jurisdiction to engage in whaling operations in violation of the Convention. They may not engage in whaling operations contrary to the Whaling Commission or the Secretary's regulations. They may not ship, transport, purchase, sell, export, import, or possess any illegal whale or whale products. They may not fail to provide any required report. It is also unlawful for any person or vessel subject to U.S. jurisdiction to do any act prohibited by the Convention or regulations, or to fail to do any act so required.[36]

The Secretary is authorized to issue licenses that allow the taking of whales and the conducting of biological experiments for scientific purposes.[37]

Violations are punishable by sanctions. Except for infractions of the reporting requirements, violators may be fined up to $10,000 or imprisoned for up to one year, or both.[38]

## Public Health Service Act

Under the Public Health Service Act the Public Health Service has been given broad powers to prevent the spread of communicable diseases from foreign countries into the United States. In order to carry out these duties, the Health Service is empowered to provide for the inspection, fumigation, disin-

---

[32] *A Watershed in Debate on Hydropower,* WASHINGTON POST, January 26, 1992, A3.

[33] 16 U.S.C. §916–916(*l*) (1988).

[34] 1946, 62 Stat. 1716, T.I.A.S. No. 1849. The 1946 Convention supplemented the Convention for the Regulation of Whaling, 1931, 49 Stat. 3079, T.S. No. 880.

[35] 16 U.S.C. §916k (1988). Administration of the Act was transferred from the Secretary of the Interior to the Secretary of Commerce by Reorganization Plan No. 4 of 1970, 84 Stat. 2090.

[36] *Id.,* 16 U.S.C. at §916c.

[37] *Id.* §916i.

[38] *Id.* §916f.

fection, sanitation, pest extermination and destruction of animals and articles thought to be dangerous.[39] The Health Service's regulations[40] expand the Service's right to quarantine animal imports. Persons who violate quarantine laws may be punished by fines of up to $1,000 or by imprisonment of up to one year, or both. Vessels that violate those laws may be assessed a fine of up to $5,000.[41]

## Nonindigenous Aquatic Nuisance Prevention and Control Act of 1990

In the late 1980s, zebra mussels were first discovered in the Great Lakes, to which they had been transported in the ballast water of transocean ships. The tiny mollusk soon spread through U.S. waterways and was feared to threaten the supply of plantlife and tiny animals that constitute the food chains for fish. In response to this threat, Congress enacted the Nonindigenous Aquatic Nuisance Prevention and Control Act of 1990.[42]

The Act specifies a program of studies and actions designed to control the zebra mussel. In addition, the Act adds the zebra mussel to the list of non-indigenous species which are banned under the Lacey Act.[43]

## The African Elephant Conservation Act

As part of the 1988 Amendments to the Endangered Species Act, Congress passed the African Elephant Conservation Act.[44] This Act directs the Secretary to establish a moratorium on imports of ivory from the African elephant from certain countries.[45] Under the Act, it is unlawful:[46]

- To import ivory tusks from any country other than an "ivory producing country" (which is an African country that has an elephant population)
- To import ivory that was exported from an ivory producing country in violation of its laws or of quotas established by the Convention on International Trade in Endangered Species of Wild Flora and Fauna (CITES)[47]
- To export ivory tusks from the United States

---

[39] 42 U.S.C. §264(a) (1988).
[40] 42 C.F.R. Part 71 (1990).
[41] 42 U.S.C. §271 (1988).
[42] Pub. L. No. 101-646, 104 Stat. 4761–88.
[43] Pub. L. No. 101-646, §1208, 104 Stat. 4761, 4772.
[44] Pub. L. No. 100-478, Title II, 102 Stat. 2306, 2315–23 (codified in 16 U.S.C. §§4201–45 (1988)).
[45] *Id.*, 16 U.S.C. at §4222.
[46] *Id.* §4223.
[47] *See* Chapter 9.

- To import ivory products, other than personal effects, unless the exporting country certifies that the ivory was derived from a legal source
- To import ivory from a country for which the Secretary has declared a moratorium

The Act contains an exemption for sport-hunted trophies.[48] Individuals are allowed to import sport-hunted elephant trophies that they have legally taken in an ivory producing country that has submitted a quota to CITES. In enacting this exemption, Congress declared that sport hunting is not part of the poaching that contributes to illegal trade. To the contrary, Congress asserted, the proper use of well-managed elephant populations helps provide funds for African elephant conservation programs.[49]

Although the government has not issued regulations under the Act, it published some explanatory guides.[50]

For civil violations, the Secretary may assess penalties of up to $5,000 for each violation.[51] For criminal violations, the Act imposes fines under title 18, imprisonment for up to one year, or both. The fines imposed by title 18 are a maximum of $100,000 for an individual and $200,000 for an organization.

The Fish and Wildlife Service enforces this law with vigor. In 1991, a New York wholesaler was prosecuted for illegally importing $50,000 of African ivory. Originating in the Sudan, the ivory was shipped to China, where it was carved into 13 figurines, and then shipped to the United States for sale to private collectors. Not only did the wholesaler forfeit the carved ivory figures, but it also paid a $100,000 fine.[52]

## Fur Seal Act

In 1911 the United States, Japan, Russia, and Great Britain concluded a treaty to protect North Pacific fur seals.[53] That treaty was superceded by later treaties.[54] Under the treaties, Canada and Japan abstained from taking seals on the high seas; Russia and the United States harvested the seals and gave the other two nations a share of their seal revenues.[55]

---

[48] *Id.* §4222(e).

[49] *Id.* §4202(9).

[50] *See e.g.*, Fish and Wildlife Service News Release entitled *Fish and Wildlife Service Imposes Moratorium on African Elephant Ivory From Certain Countries* (Newton Corner, Mass.: Dec. 30, 1988); Fish and Wildlife Service News Release entitled *Fish and Wildlife Facts: Imports and Exports of African Elephants and Their Products* (Arlington, Va.: revised June 1990).

[51] 16 U.S.C. §4224(a), (b) (1988).

[52] U.S. Fish and Wildlife Service News Release 91-14 (Boston: March 18, 1991).

[53] Treaty for the Preservation and Protection of Fur Seals, 1911, 37 Stat. 1542, T.S. No. 564.

[54] *See* S. Lyster, *International Wildlife Law* 40–48 (Cambridge: Grotius, 1985).

[55] H. Rep. No. 2154, 89th Cong., 2d Sess. 4 (1966), *reprinted in* 1966 U.S. Code Cong. & Admin. News 3628, 3630.

Congress implemented these international agreements by means of the Fur Seal Act,[56] which prohibits unauthorized U.S. subjects or vessels from taking fur seals in U.S. waters or in the North Pacific Ocean. In addition, the statute prohibits any persons from transporting, importing, possessing, or selling illegally taken seals (or seal parts) in the United States or on U.S. vessels. On the high seas, U.S. sealing ships must allow Canadian, Japanese, and Russian officials to board in order to inspect whether the ships are being used to violate the treaty.

Aleuts, Eskimos, and Indians who live on the coasts can take seals for subsistence purposes, but only in small, non-motorized canoes. They may also dispose of the skins after marking and certification. The exemptions do not apply if the coast-dwellers are employed to take skins for, or to deliver them to, others.

The Secretary is empowered to allow the taking, import, export, or possession of fur seals (or parts) for educational, scientific, or exhibition purposes. The statute contains special provisions concerning the taking of seals on the Pribilof Islands.

The Act imposes both criminal and civil penalties. For knowing violations, the government may impose criminal fines of up to $20,000 for each violation, imprisonment of up to one year, or both. The Secretary may assess civil penalties of up to $10,000. Violators may be forced to forfeit not only their seals, but also their vessels and equipment.

The National Marine Fisheries Service, which administers the Act, issues regulations detailing allowable subsistence uses and exhibitions.[57]

## Tariff Act

The Tariff Act is the source of a quota for certain bird feathers.[58] The Act generally prohibits importation of the feathers or skins of birds (or artifacts containing skins or feathers) except under quota. One set of quotas is for listed birds whose feathers are used in the manufacture of artificial flies used for fishing. Another quota is for other listed birds whose feathers are used for millinery purposes or for the manufacture of artificial flies used for fishing. Importers need a permit in order to bring in skins and feathers under the quotas.

There are exceptions to the Act's prohibitions. There is no prohibition on the import of live birds. For many birds, such as domesticated chickens, turkeys, and ducks, there is no prohibition on importation, dead or alive. Also exempt are imports for scientific or educational purposes. And there is no prohibition on the import of fully manufactured artificial flies used for fishing.

The government issues regulations that specify the procedures for obtaining permits to import under the quotas.[59]

---

[56] 16 U.S.C. §§1151–1175 (1988).

[57] 50 C.F.R. Part 215 (1990).

[58] *See* 19 U.S.C.A. §1202, Sch. 1, Part 15D, Headnote 2 (1978). *See also* Pub. L. No. 100-418, §§1201–1214, 102 Stat. 1107, 1147–56 (annotated in 19 U.S.C. Ch. 4, Subtitle I (1988)).

[59] 50 C.F.R. Part 15 (1990).

## Plant Pest Act

Like the Nonindigenous Aquatic Nuisance Prevention and Control Act, the Plant Pest Act[60] is intended to prevent the importation of injurious wildlife. In this statute, however, the subject matter is plant pests. In cooperation with Canada and Mexico and other foreign nations, the Secretary of Agriculture is directed to carry out programs to control and prevent the spread of plant pests. Except as the Secretary authorizes, persons are not permitted to move any plant pest from a foreign country into or through the United States. Nor may anyone accept delivery of such a plant pest.

If persons knowingly violate those prohibitions or the regulations, or knowingly forge or change a permit, they may be fined up to $5,000, imprisoned for up to one year, or both. In the case of violations that are not "knowing," the Secretary may assess a civil penalty of up to $1,000.

## Plant Quarantine Act

The Plant Quarantine Act[61] regulates the importation of nursery stock and other plants and plant products. It authorizes the Secretary of Agriculture to establish and maintain quarantine districts for plant diseases and plant pests. The Secretary is also authorized to control the movement of fruits, plants, and vegetables from the quarantine districts.

Under the Act, it is unlawful to import any nursery stock, or to offer it for entry, without a permit. It is unlawful to ship, carry, or transport fruits, plants, or vegetables that the Secretary has placed under quarantine.

Persons who knowingly violate those prohibitions or the regulations, or who knowingly forge or change a permit, are subject to fines up to $5,000, imprisonment for up to one year, or both. For violations that are not "knowing," the Secretary may impose a civil penalty of up to $1,000.

## Federal Noxious Weed Act

In the Federal Noxious Weed Act of 1974,[62] Congress acted to prevent the spread of noxious weeds that interfere with the growth of other plants, clog waterways and interfere with navigation, cause disease, or impair agriculture. The Secretary of Agriculture is directed to identify weeds that are noxious, quarantine them, and act to prevent their dissemination.

Under the Act, persons are prohibited from knowingly moving any noxious weed into or through the United States. There are exceptions, however, for

---

[60] 7 U.S.C. §§149, 150aa–150jj (1988).
[61] 7 U.S.C. §§151–167 (1988).
[62] 7 U.S.C.A. §§2801–2813 (1988 and Supp. 1992).

movements that are from Canada, or authorized by a permit from the Secretary and made in accordance with the Secretary's conditions. Persons are also prohibited from knowingly selling, purchasing, exchanging, giving, or receiving noxious weeds that have been illegally moved. And the Act restricts the transport of advertisements for noxious weeds.

Persons who knowingly violate those prohibitions, or who violate quarantine orders or the Secretary's regulations, are guilty of a misdemeanor. The penalty may be a fine up to $5,000, one year's imprisonment, or both.

## National Environmental Policy Act

No discussion of environmental protection statutes would be complete without mention of the National Environmental Policy Act.[63] It requires federal agencies to prepare an environmental impact statement before approving any "major federal actions significantly affecting the quality of the human environment."[64] Under the Fish and Wildlife Service's internal regulations, the Act's requirements apply to issuing permits that "involve the killing, the removal from natural habitat or the permanent impairment of reproductive capability of endangered species, threatened species, eagles or marine mammals."[65]

But the Act does not require a full-fledged impact statement for every major project that could affect the environment. Preparing an environmental impact statement is both expensive and time-consuming. To decide whether an impact statement is necessary, an agency begins with an intermediate document: the so-called environmental assessment. Thus, the Fish and Wildlife Service requires an agency to prepare an environmental assessment to determine whether a project will:[66]

> Have adverse effects on species listed or proposed to be listed on the List of Endangered or Threatened Species, or have adverse effects on designated Critical Habitat for these species.

After compiling an environmental assessment, the agency may conclude that a project will have no significant effect on the environment. In that event, the agency will consider itself free to approve a project without preparing an environmental impact statement.

The agency's decision, however, may not be decisive. Whether a court will uphold that decision depends upon the quality of the environmental assessment's conclusions and analysis. In one case,[67] environmentalists appealed the Forest Service's approval of a mineral drilling project in grizzly bear territory. Before approving the project, the Forest Service consulted with the

---

[63] 42 U.S.C. §§4321–4370 (1988).

[64] *Id.* §4332.

[65] Department of the Interior, Departmental Administrative Manual Environmental NEPA Handbook, at 516 DM 6, App. 1 (1984).

[66] *Id.* at 516 IM 2, App. 2.

[67] Cabinet Mountains Wilderness v. Peterson, 685 F.2d 678 (D.C. Cir. 1982).

Fish and Wildlife Service, which recommended modifications in the project in order to protect the grizzly bears. In its environmental assessment, the Forest Service insisted that those modifications be made. In view of this, the appeals court upheld the Forest Service's environmental assessment. This allowed the drilling project to proceed without an environmental impact statement.

A second case reached a similar result. The Fish and Wildlife Service decided not to prepare an environmental impact statement before granting a permit that allowed a real estate developer to build office and residential buildings. The project would result in incidental takings of the Mission Blue butterfly. In its permit, the Fish and Wildlife Service imposed conditions that improved the butterfly species' chances of survival. As a result, local, state, and federal authorities—and most environmental groups—supported the developer's project. When a dissident environmental group attacked the Service's environmental assessment, the court upheld the Service.[68]

If the agency fails to take a "'hard look' at the environmental consequences of its action,"[69] however, the courts will not uphold an environmental assessment. Illustrating this rule is another case in which the Forest Service prepared an environmental assessment, but not an impact statement. This time, the issue was whether to grant a permit for the reconstruction of a road through a national forest. Noting that the road intruded upon the habitat of Bighorn sheep, the court found that the agency had shunted the problem aside with mere conclusory statements. Overturning the agency's decision, the court ruled that the agency had been unreasonable in determining that it could dispense with an environmental impact statement.[70]

* * *

In the 19 statutes discussed so far, the federal government has laid down a variety of rules concerning fish, animals, and plants. Many of these regulatory schemes, like the Endangered Species Act, are designed primarily to protect species from harm. Other statutes, like the Noxious Weed Act and part of the Lacey Act, prohibit the dissemination of injurious animals or plants. Most statutes, however, allow trade in fish, animals, and plants—subject to controls. The government exercises those controls primarily by means of issuing licenses and permits. It is to this system of licenses and permits that we turn next.

---

[68] Friends of Endangered Species, Inc. v. Jantzen, 760 F.2d 976 (9th Cir. 1985). The court decision is discussed in Chapter 6.

[69] Foundation for N. Am. Wild Sheep v. Department of Agriculture, 681 F.2d 1172, 1178 (9th Cir. 1982) (quoting Kleppe v. Sierra Club, 427 U.S. 390, 410, n.21 (1976)).

[70] *Id.*

# Chapter 15

# Permits and Licenses for Trading In Protected Species

With guns on their hips, wildlife enforcement officers strode into Lord & Taylors' fashionable New York store and threatened to kick in the showcases if the imported leather handbags, wallets, and belts were not delivered to them. Despite management's protests, the state officers, accompanied by a federal law enforcement agent, seized the merchandise. Across the continent, on Rodeo Drive in Beverly Hills, armed officers confiscated $50,000 of leather merchandise from Neiman-Marcus.[1]

Although it is unusual for government agents to act with such force, seizures of protected wildlife and its products are common. About 2000 shipments of wildlife and plants are seized each year because people fail to comply with legal requirements for trade in protected species.[2] For example, traders had to forfeit a shipment of 3,210 crocodile hides when the accompanying permits were defective.[3] A bird breeder forfeited a shipment of parrots that he imported without obtaining appropriate documentation.[4] And a shipment of 2507 parakeets was subject to seizure, even though the importer was unaware that the government official who signed the permits lacked proper authority.[5]

## Licenses for Exporters and Importers

Most persons who operate commercial export or import businesses must obtain a license.[6] The many types of businesses that require a license include animal dealers, pet dealers and suppliers, laboratory research suppliers, fur dealers, and fur manufacturers. Businesses also need a license if they import

---

[1] *Endangererd Species Act Reauthorization and Oversight: Hearings Before the Subcomm. on Fisheries and Wildlife Conservation and the Environment of the House Comm. on Merchant Marine and Fisheries*, 97th Cong., 2d Sess. 115–16 (1982).

[2] C. Estes and K. Sessions, Introduction to 1 *Controlled Wildlife: Federal Permit Procedures* (Lawrence, Kan.: Ass'n of Systematics Collections, 1984).

[3] United States v. 3,210 Crusted Sides of Caiman Crocodilus, 636 F. Supp. 1281 (S.D. Fla. 1986).

[4] United States v. Fifty-Three (53) Eclectus Parrots, 685 F.2d 1131 (9th Cir. 1982).

[5] United States v. 2,507 Live Canary Winged Parakeets, 689 F. Supp. 1106 (S.D. Fla. 1988).

[6] 16 U.S.C. §1538(d) (1988).

or export wildlife in the form of hides or skin for tanning, manufacture, or sale. So do wholesalers and retailers who deal in wildlife products such as garments, bags, shoes, jewelry, rugs or curios. Taxidermists need a license as well.[7]

There is controversy about the licensing requirement for exporters and importers. Congress imposed the requirement upon "any person" who engages in these activities.[8] As noted earlier,[9] however, the Fish and Wildlife Service's regulations[10] exempt businesses that export and import wildlife worth less than $25,000 yearly. Reviewing this exemption in 1988, the House committee expressed concern that the Service will not be able to monitor commercial trade in wildlife unless it licenses the smaller exporters and importers. The committee stated its expectation that the Service will expand its licensing program to cover all exporters and importers.[11]

The Service's regulations[12] exempt other groups as well. Thus, museums, schools, and scientific institutions are exempt when they acquire wildlife for research or educational purposes, but not for resale. Circuses do not ordinarily need a license if they exhibit their wildlife and do not sell or transfer it. Neither do public museums and other scientific or educational institutions if their imports and exports are for research or scientific purposes and not resale. Also exempt are common carriers, custom house brokers, and government agencies.

## The Federal Permit Process

Commercial importers and exporters are not the only persons who must concern themselves with obtaining permits. Although other persons do not need licenses, they are often required to obtain permits in order to obtain, import, export, ship, transport, possess, trade in, or use protected species or products of those species. Unless exempted by law, most transactions in protected wildlife and plants require a federal permit. A number of federal agencies issue permits. These include the Fish and Wildlife Service, the National Marine Fisheries Service, the Department of Agriculture, the U.S. Health Service, and others. These agencies issue detailed regulations that prescribe procedures for obtaining permits. In the statutes explaining these procedures, Congress usually mandates penalties for those who fail to comply with the agency regulations.

It would be fair to say that the agencies' permit rules, like the Internal Revenue Service's regulations, are complex and difficult to follow. In 1984, the Association of Systematics Collections published a guide to the permit rules that clarified them by the use of schematic diagrams.[13] With the Association's

---

[7] 50 C.F.R. §14.91 (1990).
[8] 16 U.S.C. §1538(d) (1988).
[9] *See* Chapter 4.
[10] 50 C.F.R. §14.92(b)(6) (1990).
[11] H. Rep. No. 467, 100th Cong., 1st Sess. 9 (1987).
[12] 50 C.F.R. §14.92(b)(1)–(5) (1990).
[13] C. Estes and K. Sessions, 1 *Controlled Wildlife: Federal Permit Procedures, supra* note 2.

permission, this guide is updated and revised and included in this volume as Appendix A. Appendix B contains updated permit application forms. I hope that these documents will aid readers to negotiate the maze of federal permit regulations.

# APPENDIX A
# FEDERAL PERMIT PROCEDURES

The material in this appendix has been adapted and updated from Volume I of *Controlled Wildlife: Federal Permit Procedures*, published in 1984 by Association of Systematics Collections. The copyright for the material in this appendix is owned jointly by Richard Littell and Association of Systematics Collections.

## TABLE OF CONTENTS

## A-IV *Endangered and Other Protected Species*

# INTRODUCTION

This guide has been designed to provide the user with a streamlined method for identifying the requirements of a particular transaction without wading through volumes of statutes and regulations. The guide assembles and reorganizes the requirements of various wildlife protection laws into a digestible format. It is a handy reference that will direct the user to the applicable laws, regulations, and their requirements. The guide is not a substitute for reading those laws and regulations. Moreover, Congress periodically amends its wildlife laws, and the government agencies review their regulations too. The careful reader will refer to the laws and regulations to insure compliance with current rules. It is also wise to consult with the responsible government agencies to determine how they are interpreting the law.

One final note: this guide is directed at federal law, including U.S. laws relating to compliance with the Convention on International Trade in Endangered Species of Wild Fauna and Flora. States and localities, as well as foreign countries, also have laws affecting trafficking in fish, wildlife, and plants. The reader must take care to meet the requirements of these non-federal laws protecting or controlling transactions.

## Protected and Endangered Species

HOW TO USE THIS GUIDE

This guide contains a section on each wildlife law. Once you have determined which laws protect or control your species, follow the steps outlined below to determine the requirements for a particular activity involving that species.

STEP 1: TURN TO THE "STARTING POINT" SECTION ON PAGE A-3

The introductory material on this page will provide you with essential background information before you begin the question and answer process that will lead you to information on your proposed activity.

STEP 2: ANSWER THE QUESTIONS AND FOLLOW THE INSTRUCTIONS IN THE GUIDE.

Through the questions and instructions in the decision trees, you will be led through a number of cases which may apply to your activities, including:

1. exemptions to the normal permit requirements,
2. special cases that apply to certain species,
3. multiple law combinations and the proper permit applications to file,
4. available permits, and
5. general requirements.

Again, the decision trees have been designed to help you select the pieces of information that apply to your transaction from among the myriad statutes, regulations and exceptions that deal with the use of wildlife. In essence, the decision tree system provides a shortcut as well as a roadmap to the permit process as it applies to your case. Follow the signposts.

STEP 3: MAKE SURE YOU HAVE CONSULTED EACH SECTION THAT APPLIES TO YOUR SPECIES, INCLUDING THE "GENERAL REQUIREMENTS" SECTION.

At the end of each chapter, in the "OTHER CONSIDERATIONS" section you will be directed to sections dealing with other laws. Unless you have been advised in the "MULTIPLE LAWS" section that you have met the requirements of two or more laws simultaneously, you must meet the requirements of each law that affects your species separately.

STEP 4: CONFIRM THE INFORMATION WITH THE APPROPRIATE AGENCY OR AGENCIES.

In order to avoid the consequences of an unintentional violation of the law, which may include delays, seizure and confiscation of your shipment, fines or imprisonment, check with the appropriate agency or agencies before you undertake your transaction.

## STARTING POINT

The first step in using the guide is to determine which laws regulate activities with the species. The species protected under federal law are listed in Volume 50 of the Code of Federal Regulations (hereinafter referred to as "CFR"). For example, migratory birds are listed in 50 CFR Part 10; injurious wildlife, in 50 CFR Part 16; endangered and threatened wildlife, in 50 CFR Part 17; and marine mammals, in 50 CFR Part 18.

CAUTION: If your species is not listed in 50 CFR, you cannot assume that no laws apply. Many listings are by scientific or common names. Moreover, many protected species are not listed specifically in the law by species name, but are included in group listings. Generally speaking, a "species" is the smallest scientific classification (taxon) for a type of animal or plant, although species are sometimes divided into smaller groups called "subspecies." To form the taxonomic hierarchy, species are lumped into larger and larger groups, based on biological relationships. Although biologists recognize a number of additional categories, the hierarchy that appears in the law is:

Order
Family
Subfamily
Genus
Species
Subspecies

Thus protected wildlife may be included in a group listing higher up on the taxonomic ladder. This means that the species name of the wildlife with which the reader is concerned may not be listed separately.

YOU MUST COMPLY WITH ALL LAWS THAT APPLY TO YOUR SPECIES OR YOUR PROPOSED ACTIVITY. In addition to the law(s) discussed for your species, there are regulations that deal in general with transactions involving wildlife and plants, regardless of species. You will be directed to the General Requirements section of this Appendix if these regulations affect your specific activity. States also regulate certain activities with wildlife and wild plants. Finally, there may be local ordinances and regulations with which you must comply. **To make certain that your information is current and complete, and to avoid mistakes that may result in delays, seizure and confiscation of your shipment, fines or imprisonment, contact the agencies involved before undertaking any activity involving wildlife or plants.**

Once you have identified the laws that apply to your species, you are ready to begin the question and answer process below—a process designed to guide you to the specific information on your proposed activity by the most efficient route. Depending on the laws and type of activity involved, you will be referred to various locations throughout this appendix. Be sure to answer the questions and follow the instructions in the boxes on each page. If your species is covered by more than one law, refer to the applicable sections in the order they are presented. By turning to the first section listed below that applies to your species, you will avoid wasted effort in satisfying requirements unnecessarily.

TURN TO PAGE A-4 ANSWER THE QUESTIONS AND FOLLOW THE INSTRUCTIONS IN THE BOXES

CAUTION: THE FOLLOWING PROHIBITION AFFECTS MOST TRANSACTIONS INVOLVING WILDLIFE, AND SHOULD BE KEPT IN MIND AT ALL TIMES: **Under the Lacey Act Amendments of 1981, it is unlawful to receive or sell wildlife taken or transported in violation of national, state, foreign or Indian tribal law, and plants taken or transported in violation of national, state or Indian tribal law.** Violation of this provision of the Lacey Act may result in a civil penalty if evidence establishes that a person exercising "due care" should have known that the wildlife or plants had been taken, possessed, transported or sold in violation of an underlying law. However, a "knowing violation" of this provision of the Lacey Act is a felony, punishable with a fine and/or prison sentence.

Is your species protected or regulated by law?

— NO — Contact the U.S. Fish and Wildlife Service, Wildlife Permit Office, 4401 N. Fairfax Drive, Room 432, Arlington, Virginia, 22203, to make sure that the status of your species has not changed. (For plants, contact Animal and Plant Health Inspection Service, U.S. Department of Agriculture, Hyattsville, Maryland.) If WPO or APHIS confirms that your species is not specifically controlled, TURN TO PAGE A-149, "GENERAL REQUIREMENTS"

YES

Do you wish to obtain, amend, or renew an existing permit?

—YES— TURN TO PAGE A-149, "GENERAL REQUIREMENTS"

NO

TURN TO THE FIRST SECTION THAT APPLIES TO YOUR SPECIES:



NOTE: The requirements of the Plant Quarantine Act (PQA) and Plant Pest Act (PPA) are included in the "General Requirements" section.

## MULTIPLE LAWS

IMPORTANT: Many listed species are protected under more than one law. While the requirements of all laws must be met, it is possible in some cases to file a single permit application that fulfills the requirements of the multiple laws affecting a species. The table presented below summarizes the different combinations of laws (that expressly list species), identifies the permit requirements that take precedence for particular activities and directs the reader to the appropriate sections in this book. HOWEVER, IRRESPECTIVE OF THE "PRIORITIES" REFERENCED IN THIS TABLE, QUARANTINE LAWS AND CERTAIN PROVISIONS OF THE LACEY ACT (I.E., ACQUISITION OF PLANTS FROM FEDERAL LANDS, AND REQUIREMENTS TO DOCUMENT THAT SPECIMENS OBTAINED IN A FOREIGN COUNTRY WERE ACQUIRED LEGALLY UNDER THE LAWS OF THAT NATION), TAKE PRECEDENCE OVER ALL OTHER PERMIT REQUIREMENTS, AND FAILURE TO SATISFY THOSE REQUIREMENTS COULD RESULT IN THE LOSS OR DESTRUCTION OF THE SPECIMENS. Further, state and local laws may affect the activity you wish to undertake.

| LAW COMBINATIONS | PROPOSED ACTIVITY | ACTION REQUIRED |
|---|---|---|
| **Endangered Species Act (ESA)** plus **Convention on International Trade in Endangered Species (CITES)** | Import, Export, Reexport | A permit application filed under the ESA will meet the CITES requirements. However, you must also provide foreign documentation that meets CITES requirements, see page A-51, and TURN TO PAGE A-20, "ENDANGERED ANIMALS: ACTIVITIES REQUIRING A PERMIT" or PAGE A-21, "ENDANGERED PLANTS: ACTIVITIES REQUIRING A PERMIT" |
| | All other | A permit application which meets the requirements of the ESA may also satisfy CITES requirements. TURN TO PAGE A-20, "ENDANGERED ANIMALS: ACTIVITIES REQUIRING A PERMIT" or PAGE A-21, "ENDANGERED PLANTS: ACTIVITIES REQUIRING A PERMIT" |
| **Endangered Species Act (ESA)** plus **Marine Mammal Protection Act (MMPA)** | Take | An application filed under the MMPA may also satisfy the requirements of ESA. TURN TO PAGE A-77, "MARINE MAMMAL PROTECTION ACT: INTRODUCTION" |
| | Import | An application filed under the MMPA may also satisfy the requirements. TURN TO PAGE A-77, "MARINE MAMMAL PROTECTION ACT: INTRODUCTION" |
| | Export, Interstate and Foreign Commerce | An application filed under the ESA may also satisfy the requirements. TURN TO PAGE A-20, "ENDANGERED ANIMALS: ACTIVITIES REQUIRING A PERMIT" |

| LAW COMBINATIONS | PROPOSED ACTIVITY | ACTION REQUIRED |
|---|---|---|
| **Endangered Species Act (ESA)** plus **Migratory Bird Treaty Act (MBTA)** | Possession | Since the ESA does not prohibit possession of legally acquired specimens, you must file a permit application under the MBTA. TURN TO PAGE A-87, "MIGRATORY BIRD TREATY ACT" |
| | All other | An application filed under the ESA may also satisfy the requirements of MBTA. TURN TO PAGE A-20, "ENDANGERED ANIMALS: ACTIVITIES REQUIRING A PERMIT" |
| **Endangered Species Act (ESA)** plus **Convention on International Trade in Endangered Species (CITES)** plus **Migratory Bird Treaty Act (MBTA)** plus **Bald Eagle Protection Act (BEPA)** | Import, Export, Commerce | Not allowed because of BEPA. |
| | All other | The BEPA takes precedence over other laws and severely restricts the types of activities that are allowed with these species. TURN TO PAGE A-105, "BALD EAGLE PROTECTION ACT" |
| **Endangered Species Act (ESA)** plus **Convention on International Trade in Endangered Species (CITES)** plus **Marine Mammal Protection Act (MMPA)** | Take, Import | An application filed under the MMPA may also satisfy the requirements of ESA and CITES. However, you must also provide documentation that meets CITES requirements, see page A-70, and TURN TO PAGE A-77, "MARINE MAMMAL PROTECTION ACT: INTRODUCTION" |
| | All other | An application filed under the ESA may also satisfy the requirements of MMPA and CITES, TURN TO PAGE A-20, "ENDANGERED ANIMALS: ACTIVITIES REQUIRING A PERMIT" |

| LAW COMBINATIONS | PROPOSED ACTIVITY | ACTION REQUIRED |
|---|---|---|
| **Endangered Species Act (ESA)** plus **Convention on International Trade in Endangered Species (CITES)** plus **Migratory Bird Treaty Act** | Commerce | Generally not allowed under MBTA; allowed for captive reared waterfowl, cranes, and certain properly marked raptors |
| | Possession | Since the ESA does not prohibit possession of legally acquired specimens, you must file a permit application under the MBTA. CITES applies only to import, export and reexport. TURN TO PAGE A-87, "MIGRATORY BIRD TREATY ACT" |
| | Import, Export, Reexport | An application filed under the ESA satisfies the requirements of CITES. However, you must provide foreign documentation that meets CITES requirements. CONSULT the CITES section, page A-70, and TURN TO PAGE A-20, "ENDANGERED ANIMALS: ACTIVITIES REQUIRING A PERMIT," MBTA does not restrict import, export or reexport of legally possessed migratory birds. |
| | All other | An application filed under the ESA may also satisfy the requirements of CITES and MBTA. TURN TO PAGE A-20, "ENDANGERED ANIMALS: ACTIVITIES REQUIRING A PERMIT" |

| LAW COMBINATIONS | PROPOSED ACTIVITY | ACTION REQUIRED |
|---|---|---|
| **Convention on International Trade in Endangered Species (CITES)** plus **Marine Mammal Protection Act (MMPA)** | Take, Import | An application filed under the MMPA may also satisfy the requirements of CITES. TURN TO PAGE A-77, "MARINE MAMMAL PROTECTION ACT: INTRODUCTION" |
| | Export, Reexport, Foreign Commerce | An application filed under the MMPA may also satisfy the requirements of CITES. However, you must also provide foreign documentation that meets CITES requirements. CONSULT the CITES section, page A-70, and TURN TO PAGE A-77. |
| | All other | An application filed under the MMPA may also satisfy the requirements of CITES. TURN TO PAGE A-77, "MARINE MAMMAL PROTECTION ACT: INTRODUCTION" |
| **Convention on International Trade in Endangered Species (CITES)** plus **Migratory Bird Treaty Act (MBTA)** | Commerce | Not allowed except captive-reared mallards, etc. TURN TO PAGE A-87, "MIGRATORY BIRD TREATY ACT: INTRODUCTION" |
| | Possession | Since the CITES does not prohibit possession of legally acquired specimens, you must file a permit application under the MBTA. CITES applies only to import, export and reexport. TURN TO PAGE A-87, "MIGRATORY BIRD TREATY ACT" |
| | Import, Export, Reexport | An application filed under the CITES may also satisfy the requirements of MBTA. TURN TO PAGE A-51, "CONVENTION ON INTERNATIONAL TRADE IN ENDANGERED SPECIES" |
| | All other | An application filed under the MBTA may also satisfy the requirements of CITES. TURN TO PAGE A-87, "MIGRATORY BIRD TREATY ACT" |

# ENDANGERED SPECIES ACT
## U.S. Fish and Wildlife Service
## National Marine Fisheries Service

## INTRODUCTION

The U.S. Endangered Species Act (ESA) was enacted by Congress in December 1973, to halt the serious decline in numbers of many species of wild animals and plants. The ESA provides two levels of protection for listed species. Species considered to be in danger of extinction are listed as "Endangered," and are provided the most stringent protection. Species likely to **become** Endangered are listed as "Threatened," and protected by less restrictive regulations.

The ESA places restrictions on a wide range of activities involving protected animals and plants to help ensure their continued survival. With limited exceptions, the ESA prohibits the use, taking, possession, sale, or advertising for sale in interstate and foreign commerce of listed species unless authorized by permit. Administration of the ESA is shared by the U.S. Fish & Wildlife Service (FWS) and the National Marine Fisheries Service (NMFS).

Commercial activities involving **legally acquired** Endangered or Threatened species that take place entirely within one's state of residence are not prohibited by the Act. However, advertisements in publications that have interstate circulation must include a warning that an Endangered/Threatened Species Permit is required to purchase the ESA listed plant or animal in interstate or foreign commerce. Many states also regulate activities involving protected species.

Does your proposed activity involve an ESA listed animal or plant?

YES

TURN TO PAGE A-10, "ENDANGERED AND THREATENED ANIMALS: PROHIBITED ACTIVITIES" **OR,** "ENDANGERED AND THREATENED PLANTS: PROHIBITED ACTIVITIES"

In exceptional cases, applicants can also receive permits granting very limited authority for incidental takings, 50 C.F.R. 17.22(b), and work with experimental populations. (See Appendix B, "Sample Application: Incidental Take of Species.")

## ENDANGERED AND THREATENED ANIMALS: PROHIBITED ACTIVITIES

**Without a permit, it is unlawful** to commit, attempt to commit, solicit another to commit, or cause to be committed any of the following activities involving a listed species:

1. Import or export.
2. Deliver, receive, carry, transport, or ship in interstate or foreign commerce in the course of a commercial activity.
3. Sell or offer for sale in interstate or foreign commerce.
4. "Take," which means to harm, harass, pursue, hunt, shoot, wound, trap, kill, capture, or collect, or attempt to engage in any such conduct.
5. Possess, ship, deliver, carry, transport, sell, or receive unlawfully taken Endangered or Threatened wildlife.
6. Violate any federal regulation pertaining to listed species.
7. Engage in business as an importer or exporter without a license.
8. Import or export ivory in violation of the African Elephant Conservation Act.

**These prohibitions apply equally to live or dead animals, their progeny, and any parts or products derived from them.**

## ENDANGERED AND THREATENED PLANTS: PROHIBITED ACTIVITIES

**Without a permit, it is unlawful** to commit, attempt to commit, solicit another to commit, or cause to be committed any of the following activities involving a listed species:

1. Remove and reduce to possession from areas under federal jurisdiction.
2. Maliciously damage or destroy on areas under federal jurisdiction.
3. Remove, cut, dig up, or damage or destroy on non-federal areas in knowing violation of state laws or in violation of state criminal trespass laws.
4. Import or export.
5. Deliver, receive, carry, transport, or ship in interstate or foreign commerce in the course of a commercial activity.
6. Sell or offer for sale in interstate or foreign commerce.
7. Violate any federal regulation pertaining to listed species.
8. Engage in business as an importer or exporter without a license.

**These prohibitions apply equally to live, dead, wild or artificially propagated plants, their seeds, and any parts or products derived from them. The only exception is seeds of artificially propagated Threatened species.**

TURN TO PAGE A-11, "SPECIAL SITUATIONS AND EXEMPTIONS"

## SPECIAL SITUATIONS AND EXEMPTIONS

In certain cases, exemptions may be claimed from the standard ESA permit requirements if specific criteria are met. These exemptions include the activities listed in the box below. Turn to the first section which seems to apply to your situation. The information provided there will help you determine if you qualify for that exemption, and what documentation is required, if any.

CAUTION: Some form of documentation is nearly always required for any transaction involving a listed species, whether or not an exemption or special situation applies. If you attempt to conduct an otherwise illegal activity but cannot document the fact that your activity is exempt, AND you have not obtained a permit, you are in violation of the law. Therefore, even though you may not need an ESA permit, you must be able to prove that you don't.

To determine if any exemptions or special situations apply to your proposed activity, refer to the sections listed below:



THEN

IF NO EXEMPTIONS OR SPECIAL SITUATIONS APPLY **AND** YOUR SPECIES IS LISTED AS ENDANGERED TURN TO PAGE A-20 "ENDANGERED ANIMALS: ACTIVITIES REQUIRING A PERMIT" **OR** PAGE A-21 "ENDANGERED PLANTS: ACTIVITIES REQUIRING A PERMIT"
**AND**
TURN TO PAGE A-5 "MULTIPLE LAWS"

THEN

IF YOUR SPECIES IS LISTED AS THREATENED TURN TO PAGE A-24 "THREATENED ANIMALS: SPECIAL RULES" **OR** PAGE A-45 "THREATENED PLANTS: ACTIVITIES REQUIRING A PERMIT"

## EXEMPTION: PRE-ACT SPECIMENS

An exemption may be claimed for specimens of listed species which were held for purposes not contrary to the Act on December 28, 1973, or before the date the species was listed on the ESA. THIS EXEMPTION ESSENTIALLY ALLOWS ONLY NONCOMMERCIAL IMPORT AND EXPORT of personal items. If the specimens are intended for sale in interstate or foreign commerce, or were held for commercial purposes on or before their Pre-Act date, the exempt status does not apply. **Any Endangered or Threatened animals born in captivity from Pre-Act parents are fully protected and not afforded any "exempt" status.** Persons requesting an exemption for Pre-Act specimens must be able to document the exempt status of the specimens. The date a species was listed under the ESA can be found by referring to the listing in 50 CFR Part 17. Contact the U.S. Fish and Wildlife Service, Wildlife Permit Office, for any listing subsequent to the issue date of the CFR volume.

Does your proposed activity meet the criteria described above?

—YES— If you can document the exempt status of your specimen, you are exempt from ESA permit requirements. HOWEVER, the exempt status is "lost" if the specimen enters into a commercial activity. Further, you must either qualify for an exemption or meet the requirements under **each** of the laws that protects your species. TURN TO PAGE A-49, "OTHER CONSIDERATIONS"

NO

To find out if any **other** exemptions or special situations apply, TURN TO PAGE A-11, "SPECIAL SITUATIONS AND EXEMPTIONS"

## EXEMPTION: ANTIQUES

An exemption from all ESA prohibitions may be claimed for certain antiques that incorporate Endangered or Threatened species or their parts. However, the antique may not be less than 100 years old, and may not have been repaired or modified since December 28, 1973, or the date of the species listing on the ESA, with any part of a listed species. Such antiques must enter through a port designated by the U.S. Customs Service, and must be accompanied by documentation authenticating this exempt status. Documentation should be in the form of a bill of sale, antiquities export statement, etc.

Does your proposed activity meet the criteria described above?

—YES— If you can document the exempt status of your specimen, you are exempt from ESA permit requirements. HOWEVER, you must either qualify for an exemption or meet the requirements under **each** of the laws that protects your species. TURN TO PAGE A-49, "OTHER CONSIDERATIONS"

NO

To find out if any **other** exemptions or special situations apply, TURN TO PAGE A-11, "SPECIAL SITUATIONS AND EXEMPTIONS"

## SPECIAL SITUATION: LOANS AND GIFTS

Legally acquired Endangered or Threatened species may be shipped **interstate** as a *bona fide* gift or loan if there is no barter, credit, or other form of compensation involved, provided you are not prohibited from doing so by permit or other legal restrictions.

Does your proposed activity meet the criteria described above?

—YES— No documentation is required under the ESA. HOWEVER, you must either qualify for an exemption or meet the requirements under **each** of the laws that protects your species. TURN TO PAGE A-49, "OTHER CONSIDERATIONS"

NO

To find out if any **other** exemptions or special situations apply, TURN TO PAGE A-11, "SPECIAL SITUATIONS AND EXEMPTIONS"

## EXEMPTION: IMPORT (FROM THE SEA) OR TAKE BY ALASKAN NATIVES

"Alaskan native" is defined as:

> ". . . a person defined in the Alaska Native Claims Settlement Act . . . as a citizen of the United States who is of one-fourth degree or more Alaska Indian (including Tsimshian Indians enrolled or not enrolled in the Metlaktla Indian Community), Eskimo, or Aleut blood, or combination thereof. The term includes any Native, as so defined, either or both of whose adoptive parents are not Natives. It also includes, in the absence of proof of a minimum blood quantum, any citizen of the United States who is regarded as an Alaska Native by the Native village or town of which he claims to be a member and whose father or mother is (or, if deceased, was) regarded as Native by any Native village or Native town. Any citizen enrolled by the Secretary pursuant to Section 5 of the Alaska Native Claims Settlement Act shall be conclusively presumed to be an Alaskan Native for purposes of this part . . ." (50 CFR 17.3).

Alaskan natives may (1) import only species taken pursuant to this section, or (2) take Endangered or Threatened wildlife primarily for subsistence. The byproducts of these taken animals may be used as raw materials for the production of authentic native handicrafts and clothing, which may be sold in interstate commerce without federal permits. It would be advisable to have some way to document the origin of the specimen.

Does your proposed activity meet the criteria described above?

—YES— If you can document the exempt status of your specimen, you are exempt from ESA permit requirements. HOWEVER you must either qualify for an exemption or meet the requirements under **each** of the laws that protects your species. TURN TO PAGE A-49, "OTHER CONSIDERATIONS"

NO

To find out if any other exemptions or special situations apply, TURN TO PAGE A-11,"SPECIAL SITUATIONS AND EXEMPTIONS"

## EXEMPTION: RAPTORS HELD IN CAPTIVITY ON NOVEMBER 10, 1978

Prohibitions under the ESA do not apply to any Endangered or Threatened raptors LEGALLY HELD IN CAPTIVITY IN THE U.S. ON NOVEMBER 10, 1978, or to their U.S. born progeny, provided that documents or records outlined below are available to substantiate the exempt status (50 CFR 17.7).

1. The prohibitions which normally apply to Endangered and Threatened species do not apply to any raptor (a live migratory bird of the Order Falconiformes or the Order Strigiformes, other than a bald eagle *(Haliaeetus leucocephalus)* or a golden eagle *(Aquila chrysaetos))* legally held in captivity or in a controlled environment on November 10, 1978, or to any of its progeny, which is:

   a. Possessed and banded in compliance with the terms of a valid FWS permit; or

   b. Identified in the earliest applicable annual report required under a FWS permit as in a permittee's possession on November 10, 1978, or as the progeny of such a raptor.

2. This exemption does not apply to any raptor intentionally returned to the wild.

Does your proposed activity meet the criteria described above?

—YES—

You have met the requirements for an exemption to ESA permit requirements. No **further** documentation is required under the ESA. HOWEVER, you must either qualify for an exemption or meet the requirements under **each** of the laws that protect your species. TURN TO PAGE A-49, "OTHER CONSIDERATIONS"

NO

To find out if any **other** exemptions or special situations apply, TURN TO PAGE A-11, "SPECIAL SITUATIONS AND EXEMPTIONS"

## CAPTIVE-BRED ENDANGERED AND THREATENED WILDLIFE

The captive-bred wildlife registration regulation became effective on September 17, 1979, and is now codified at 50 CFR 17.21(g). The registration system was implemented by the Fish and Wildlife Service in an effort to decrease the federal permit requirements for captive-born, exotic, endangered and threatened wildlife, when the prohibited activities being carried out with such wildlife could be shown to enhance the propagation or survival of the affected species.

Types of Wildlife Covered

Living wildlife listed as Endangered or Threatened under the Endangered Species Act, having a natural geographic distribution (including historical range) not including any part of the United States, and bred in captivity in the United States may be covered by the registration. On a species-by-species basis, the Director of the Service may determine that particular species native to the United States are eligible for the registration. At the present time, the only native species that has been granted eligibility under the registration is the Laysan duck *(Anas laysanensis)*.

Activities Authorized by Registration

The registration authorizes take for normal husbandry purposes and interstate commerce, PROVIDED the purpose of the take or commerce is to enhance the propagation or survival of the affected species. Take for normal husbandry covers activities including, but not limited to, drawing blood, collecting semen, culling and euthanasia, provided such activities are necessary to maintain a genetically viable, self-sustaining captive population of the affected species. Interstate commerce pertains to the purchase and sale of the affected species among captive-bred wildlife registrants who are not residents of the same state and who are registered for the species involved. Registrants must comply with any applicable state laws.

Limitations

1. Activities involving non-living wildlife and their parts and products are not authorized under the registration. Authorized activities may be conducted only with living wildlife born and held in captivity in the United States.
2. The registrations may be issued only when the applicant documents that his activities will serve to enhance the propagation or survival of the endangered or threatened species, as defined in 50 CFR 17.3.
3. Authorized activities may be conducted only with other captive-bred wildlife registrants who are registered for the same species.

Does your proposed activity involve the Laysan duck (*Anas laysanensis*) or **non-native** Endangered or Threatened species **born in captivity in the U.S.?**

— NO —

Your activity is not allowed under the CBW program. However, it may be allowed under an Endangered/Threatened Species Permit. Is your species listed as Endangered?

YES

TURN TO PAGE A-20, "ENDANGERED ANIMALS: ACTIVITIES REQUIRING A PERMIT" **AND** PAGE A-5 "MULTIPLE LAWS"

NO

TURN TO PAGE A-24, "THREATENED ANIMALS: SPECIAL RULES"

YES

Does your activity involve first-time import or take within the U.S.?

—YES—

Your activity is not allowed under the CBW program. However, it may be allowed under an Endangered/Threatened Species Permit. Is your species listed as Endangered?

YES

TURN TO PAGE A-20, "ENDANGERED ANIMALS: ACTIVITIES REQUIRING A PERMIT" **AND** PAGE A-5 "MULTIPLE LAWS"

NO

TURN TO PAGE A-24, "THREATENED ANIMALS: SPECIAL RULES"

NO

Is the purpose of your activity listed below?

1. Enhancement of propagation or survival.
2. Zoological exhibition.
3. Educational purposes.

— NO —

Your activity may not be allowed under the CBW program. Contact the Wildlife Permit Office for further information.

YES

TO PAGE A-17

FROM PAGE A-16

**Does your proposed activity involve interstate commerce in live animals?**

- **YES** → Is the person with whom you wish to conduct interstate commerce registered under the CBW program for the family of animals you are dealing with?
  - **YES** → TURN TO PAGE A-18, "APPLICATION INFORMATION: CAPTIVE BRED WILDLIFE REGISTRATION
  - **NO** → Your activity is not allowed. Contact the appropriate office for further information: FWS Wildlife Permit Office
- **NO** → Does your proposed activity involve one of the following:
  1. Export of live animals in foreign commerce, or
  2. Export and reimport of the same live animals

  - **YES** → TURN TO PAGE A-18, "APPLICATION INFORMATION: CAPTIVE BRED WILDLIFE REGISTRATION"
  - **NO** → Your activity is not allowed under the CBW program. However, your activity may be allowed under an Endangered/Threatened Species Permit. Is your species listed as Endangered?
    - **NO** → TURN TO PAGE A-24, "THREATENED ANIMALS: SPECIAL RULES"
    - **YES** → TURN TO PAGE A-20, "ENDANGERED ANIMALS: ACTIVITIES REQUIRING A PERMIT" **AND** PAGE A-5 "MULTIPLE LAWS"

## APPLICATION INFORMATION: CAPTIVE BRED WILDLIFE REGISTRATION

A CBW registration permit application consists of three parts:

1. FORM 3-200
   Form 3-200 requests general information about you and your proposed activity. (A detailed explanation of each question may be found in Appendix B.)
2. SUPPLEMENTARY INFORMATION
   A series of questions (usually found on the back of Form 3-200) which request specific information about your proposed activity.
3. APPLICATION FEE
   The application fee must be paid by certified check or money order, made payable to the U.S. Fish and Wildlife Service. The fee for CBW registration is $25.

**Be sure to answer all questions, supply all of the information required, and include a check or money order for the application fee.** An incomplete application will be returned to you for completion, resulting in considerable delay.

### WHERE TO OBTAIN APPLICATION FORMS

Federal Wildlife Permit Office
U.S. Fish and Wildlife Service
4401 N. Fairfax Drive, Room 432
Arlington, Virginia 22203

### WHEN TO APPLY

Submit your completed application, accompanying documents, and a check or money order for $25 to the address listed below AT LEAST 60 days before you need the permit.

### WHERE TO SUBMIT THE COMPLETED APPLICATION

Federal Wildlife Permit Office
U.S. Fish and Wildlife Service
4401 N. Fairfax Drive, Room 432
Arlington, Virginia 22203

TURN TO APPENDIX B
"SAMPLE APPLICATION: CBW REGISTRATION"
**AND**
TURN TO PAGE A-49, "OTHER CONSIDERATIONS"

## EXEMPTION: SEEDS OF ARTIFICIALLY PROPAGATED THREATENED PLANTS

No ESA permits are required for interstate or foreign commerce, import, and export involving seeds of artificially propagated specimens of Threatened plants. However, seeds must be accompanied by a label which includes the name of the species and a statement that the seeds are of cultivated origin.

Does your proposed activity meet the criteria described above?

—YES— No documentation is required under the ESA. HOWEVER, you must either qualify for an exemption or meet the requirements under each of the laws that protects your species. TURN TO PAGE A-49, "OTHER CONSIDERATIONS"

NO

To find out if any **other** exemptions or special situations apply, TURN TO PAGE A-11, "SPECIAL SITUATIONS AND EXEMPTIONS"

## ENDANGERED ANIMALS: ACTIVITIES REQUIRING A PERMIT

Permits authorizing prohibited activities affecting ENDANGERED animals may be issued ONLY for scientific research, or to enhance the propagation or survival of the species. You may apply for a permit to conduct prohibited activities to alleviate undue economic hardship caused by the listing of that species, if you had entered into a contract that involves the species prior to the notice of listing or actual listing of the species (whichever occurs first). However, any hardship exemption will terminate not more than one year after the date when the government publishes a Federal Register notice that it is considering the classification of the species as protected. In exceptional cases, applicants can also receive permits granting *very limited* authority for incidental takings, 50 CFR 17.22(b), and work with experimental populations.

Is your proposed activity listed below?

1. Import or export.
2. Deliver, receive, carry, transport or ship Endangered species in interstate or foreign commerce in the course of a commercial activity.
3. Sale or offer for sale in interstate or foreign commerce of species listed as Endangered.
4. Possession, shipment, delivery, carrying, transport, sale or receipt of **unlawfully taken** Endangered wildlife.
5. Take (harm, harass, pursue, hunt, shoot, wound, trap, kill, capture or collect) Endangered wildlife, or attempt to engage in any such activity.
6. Import or export ivory.

— NO — Your activity is not specifically regulated by the ESA. If you are dealing with a terrestrial species, contact:

FWS, Wildlife Permit Office

If you are dealing with a marine species, contact:

NMFS, Office of Protected Species and Habitat Conservation.

YES

Do you plan to justify your permit request on the basis of economic hardship?

—YES— TURN TO PAGE A-22, "PERMIT INFORMATION: ECONOMIC HARDSHIP"

NO

Is the purpose of your activity listed below?

1. Scientific research.
2. Enhancement or propagation or survival of the species.
3. Import or Export ivory.

— NO — Your activity is not allowed, and no permit will be issued. If you are dealing with a terrestrial species, contact:

FWS, Wildlife Permit Office

If you are dealing with a marine species, contact:

NMFS, Office or Protected Species and Habitat Conservation.

YES

TURN TO PAGE A-46, "APPLICATION INFORMATION: ENDANGERED/THREATENED SPECIES (FWS)" **OR** for marine species (animals only) TURN TO PAGE A-47, "APPLICATION INFORMATION: ENDANGERED/THREATENED SPECIES (NMFS)" **OR** for raw or worked ivory TURN TO PAGE A-28, "SPECIAL RULE—AFRICAN ELEPHANT"

## ENDANGERED PLANTS: ACTIVITIES REQUIRING A PERMIT

Permits authorizing activities affecting Endangered species are issued *only* for purposes of scientific research, enhancement of propagation or survival of the species. However, within one year of the listing of the species you may also apply for a permit to conduct prohibited activities to alleviate undue economic hardship caused by the listing of a species, if you had entered into a contract that involves the species prior to the notice of listing or actual listing of the species (whichever comes first). In exceptional cases, applicants can also receive permits granting very limited authority for incidental takings, 50 CFR 17.22(b).

Is your proposed activity listed below?

1. Remove and reduce to possession from lands under federal jurisdiction.
2. Import or export.
3. Deliver, receive, carry, transport, or ship species listed as Endangered in interstate or foreign commerce in the course of a commercial activity.
4. Sell or offer for sale in interstate or foreign commerce species listed as Endangered.
5. Maliciously damage or destroy on areas under federal jurisdiction.
6. Remove, cut, dig up, or damage or destroy on non-federal areas in knowing violation of state laws or in violation of state criminal trespass laws.
7. To engage in business as an importer or exporter without a license.

— NO — Your activities are not specifically regulated by ESA. Contact the Wildlife Permit Office and the Plant Protection and Quarantine Office of USDA for further information.

YES

Do you plan to justify your permit request on the basis of economic hardship?

—YES— TURN TO PAGE A-22, "PERMIT INFORMATION: ECONOMIC HARDSHIP"

NO

Is the purpose of your activity listed below?

1. Scientific research.
2. Enhancement of propagation or survival of the species.

— NO — Your activity is not allowed, and no permit will be issued. Contact the Wildlife Permit Office, and the Plant Protection and Quarantine Office of USDA, for further information.

YES

Does your proposed activity involve interstate commerce or export of artificially propagated specimens?

—YES— TURN TO PAGE A-48, "APPLICATION INFORMATION: ARTIFICIALLY PROPAGATED ENDANGERED OR THREATENED SPECIES"

NO

TURN TO PAGE A-46, "APPLICATION INFORMATION: ENDANGERED/THREATENED SPECIES"

## Protected and Endangered Species

## PERMIT INFORMATION: ECONOMIC HARDSHIP

Economic Hardship permit applications are available to persons allegedly suffering undue economic hardship because their desired activity was contracted for, but has since been prohibited under the ESA. However, any hardship exemption will terminate not more than one year after the date when the government publishes a Federal Register notice that it is considering the classification of the species as protected.

Does your proposed activity meet the criteria described above?

— NO — Your activity is not allowed. If you are dealing with a terrestrial species, contact: FWS, Wildlife Permit Office
If you are dealing with a marine species (animals only), contact:
NMFS, Office of Protected Species and Habitat Conservation.

YES

TURN TO PAGE A-23, "APPLICATION INFORMATION: ECONOMIC HARDSHIP" **AND** CONTACT: FWS, Wildlife Permit Office.

## APPLICATION INFORMATION: ECONOMIC HARDSHIP

A permit application for Economic Hardship consists of three parts:

1. FORM 3-200
   Form 3-200 requests general information about you and your proposed activity. (A detailed explanation of each question may be found in Appendix B.)
2. SUPPLEMENTARY INFORMATION
   A series of questions (usually found on the back of Form 3-200) which requests specific information on your proposed activity (see 50 CFR 17.23).
3. APPLICATION FEE
   The application fee must be paid by certified check or money order, made payable to the U.S. Fish and Wildlife Service. The fee for this permit is $25.

**Be sure to answer all questions, provide all of the information required, and include a check or money order for the application fee.** An incomplete application will be returned to you for completion, resulting in considerable delay.

### WHERE TO OBTAIN APPLICATION FORMS

Federal Wildlife Permit Office
U.S. Fish and Wildlife Service
4401 N. Fairfax Drive, Room 432
Arlington, Virginia 22203

**OR** for marine species (animals only):

Office of Protected Species and Habitat Conservation
National Marine Fisheries Service
U.S. Department of Commerce
Washington, DC 20235

### WHEN TO APPLY

Submit your completed application, accompanying documents, and a check or money order for $25 (FWS only) to the address listed below AT LEAST 30 days before you need the permit.

### WHERE TO MAIL THE COMPLETED APPLICATION

Federal Wildlife Permit Office
U.S. Fish and Wildlife Service
4401 N. Fairfax Drive, Room 432
Arlington, Virginia 22203

**OR** for marine species (animals only):

Office of Protected Species and Habitat Conservation
National Marine Fisheries Service
U.S. Department of Commerce
Washington, DC 20235

Contact FWS OR NMFS, Office of Protected Species and Habitat Conservation for further information on application procedures for this permit AND TURN TO PAGE A-49, "OTHER CONSIDERATIONS"

## THREATENED ANIMALS: SPECIAL RULES

A few species listed as Threatened are covered by Special Rules under the ESA. These rules may allow limited commercial activity, or may specify other requirements which are less restrictive than those which would normally apply to Threatened species. Refer to the chart below to determine whether or not a Special Rule applies to your species.

IS YOUR SPECIES LISTED BELOW? — NO — TURN TO PAGE A-5, "MULTIPLE LAWS"

YES

TURN TO THE PAGE INDICATED

**Mammals**

| | | |
|---|---|---|
| Bears: | GRIZZLY BEAR, *Ursus arctos horribilis* | A-26 |
| Elephants: | AFRICAN ELEPHANT, *Loxodonta africana* | A-28 |
| Kangaroos: | | A-31 |
| | Species covered:<br>EASTERN GRAY KANGAROO, *Macropus giganteus*, all subspecies except *tasmaniensis*<br>RED KANGAROO, *Macropus (=Megaleia) rufus*<br>WESTERN GRAY KANGAROO, *Macropus fuliginosus* | |
| Leopards: | LEOPARD, *Panthera pardus* | A-32 |
| Primates: | | A-33 |
| | Species covered:<br>BLACK HOWLER MONKEY, *Alouatta pigra*<br>CHIMPANZEE, *Pan troglodytes*<br>FORMOSAN ROCK MACAQUE, *Macaca cyclopis*<br>GELADA (BABOON), *Theropithecus gelada*<br>JAPANESE MACAQUE, *Macaca fuscata*<br>LESSER SLOW LORIS, *Nycticebus pygmaeus*<br>LONG-TAILED LANGUR, *Presbytis potenzani*<br>PHILIPPINE TARSIER, *Tarsius syrichta*<br>PIGMY CHIMPANZEE, *Pan paniscus*<br>PURPLE-FACED LANGUR, *Presbytis senex*<br>STUMP-TAILED MACAQUE, *Macaca arctoides*<br>TONKIN SNUB-NOSED MONKEY, *Pygathrix (=Rhinopithecus) avunculus*<br>TOQUE MACAQUE, Macaca sinica<br>WHITE-FOOTED TAMARIN, *Saguinus leucopus* | |

## SPECIAL RULE—GRIZZLY BEAR

The grizzly bear *(Ursus arctos horribilis)* is listed as Threatened only in the 48 coterminous United States. The Special Rule under the ESA authorizes limited take, import, export and interstate and foreign commerce involving this population of the grizzly bear and its parts and products without an ESA permit when certain conditions are met (50 CFR 17.40(b)). However, all brown bears *(Ursus arctos),* including the grizzly *(Ursus arctos horribilis),* are protected on Appendix II of CITES and require CITES documents for import, export and reexport.

Do you plan to take a grizzly bear?

— YES— Take may be allowed under limited conditions. Check with WPO.

NO

Do you plan to import a grizzly bear?

— YES— Are you a public zoological institution?

NO

Are you a federal or state employee importing a bear for scientific or research purposes?

YES

No ESA permit required. However, CITES requirements must be met. TURN TO PAGE A-64, "CITES APPENDIX II: ACTIVITIES REQUIRING A PERMIT"

NO

Your activity is not allowed under this Rule, and no permit is otherwise available to authorize imports.

YES

No ESA permit required. However, CITES requirements must be met. TURN TO PAGE A-64, "CITES APPENDIX II: ACTIVITIES REQUIRING A PERMIT."

NO

TO PAGE A-27

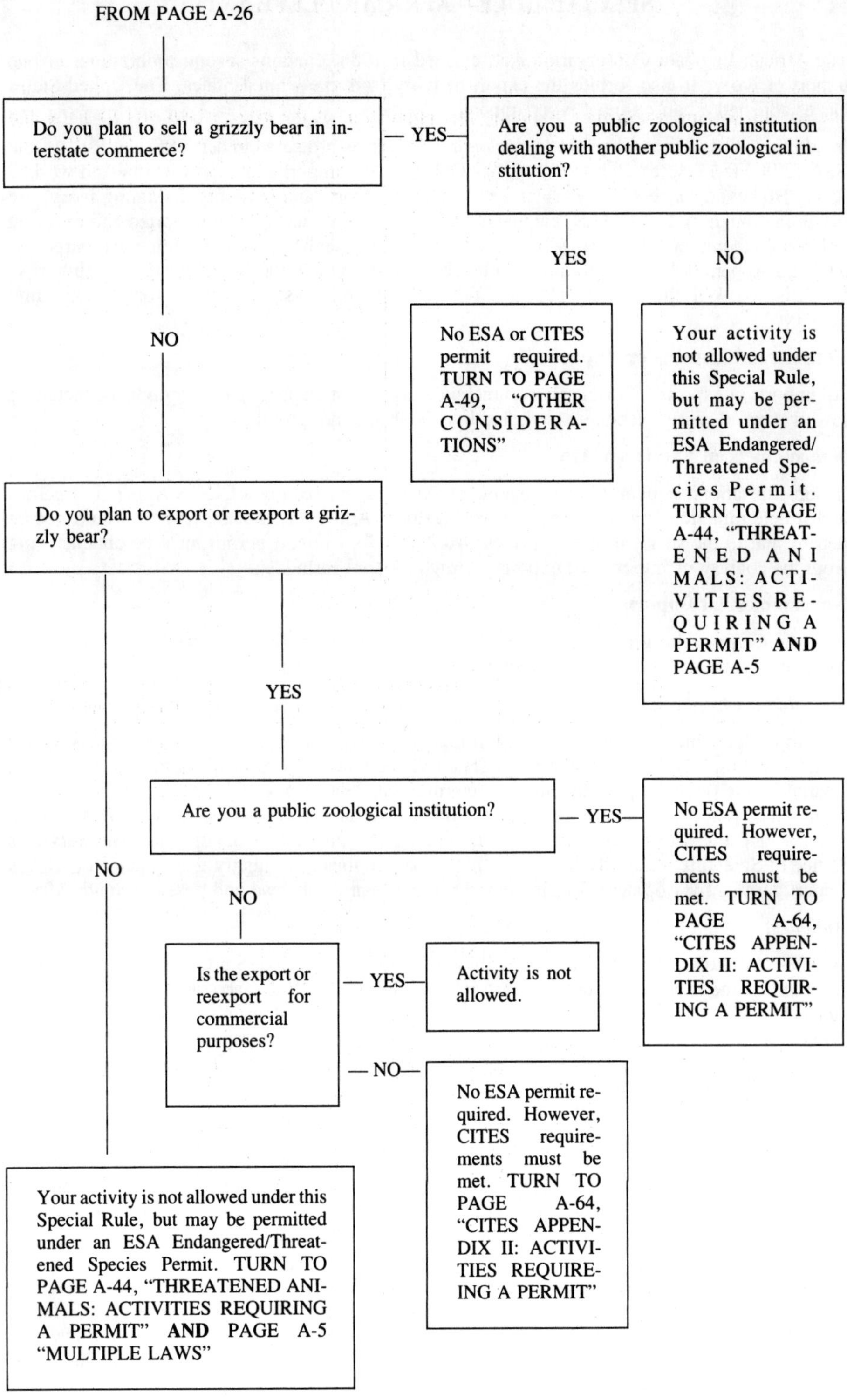
FROM PAGE A-26
Do you plan to sell a grizzly bear in interstate commerce?
YES
Are you a public zoological institution dealing with another public zoological institution?
YES
No ESA or CITES permit required. TURN TO PAGE A-49, "OTHER CONSIDERATIONS"
NO
Your activity is not allowed under this Special Rule, but may be permitted under an ESA Endangered/Threatened Species Permit. TURN TO PAGE A-44, "THREATENED ANIMALS: ACTIVITIES REQUIRING A PERMIT" AND PAGE A-5
NO
Do you plan to export or reexport a grizzly bear?
YES
Are you a public zoological institution?
YES
No ESA permit required. However, CITES requirements must be met. TURN TO PAGE A-64, "CITES APPENDIX II: ACTIVITIES REQUIRING A PERMIT"
NO
Is the export or reexport for commercial purposes?
YES
Activity is not allowed.
NO
No ESA permit required. However, CITES requirements must be met. TURN TO PAGE A-64, "CITES APPENDIX II: ACTIVITIES REQUIRE-ING A PERMIT"
NO
Your activity is not allowed under this Special Rule, but may be permitted under an ESA Endangered/Threatened Species Permit. TURN TO PAGE A-44, "THREATENED ANIMALS: ACTIVITIES REQUIRING A PERMIT" AND PAGE A-5 "MULTIPLE LAWS"

## SPECIAL RULE—AFRICAN ELEPHANT

The African Elephant Conservation Act, enacted in 1988, contains several prohibitions on the import of ivory. It also forbids the export of ivory from the United States. The United States has established a ban on most ivory imports.

In addition, the African elephant *(Loxodonta africana)* is protected under a Special Rule of the ESA (50 CFR 17.40(e)). This rule applies ONLY to the import and export of raw and worked ivory. However, since LIVE African elephants (their parts and products, including ivory) are listed on Appendix I of CITES, elephants and elephant products can be imported and exported only for noncommercial purposes. In order to import live elephants for noncommercial purposes, a CITES Appendix I import permit must be obtained from the Office of Management Authority, U.S. Fish and Wildlife Service. Then a CITES export permit must be obtained from the exporting country.

### Commercial Imports or Export

All imports or exports for primarily commercial purposes of elephant parts or products, including raw or worked ivory, elephant skins, and live elephants, are prohibited.

### Noncommercial Exports of Ivory

In some instances, noncommercial exports of *worked* ivory require a CITES Appendix I permit and a determination, by the Office of Management Authority, that the export would not be detrimental to the survival of the species. An Appendix I import permit must be obtained first from the country of import. All exports of *raw* ivory are forbidden.

### Noncommercial Imports of Ivory

Most noncommercial ivory *imports* are prohibited, including tourist souvenirs. However, the following types of imports are allowed under certain circumstances:

*Sport-hunted trophies:*

An Appendix I import permit for a sport-hunted trophy must first be obtained. Such import permits will only be issued if: the range state has submitted an export quota to the CITES Secretariat for the year of export; the Service determines that the trophy will not be used for primarily commercial purposes, that the import of the trophy will not be detrimental to the survival of the species, and the take of the elephant will enhance the survival of the species. The Service's Office of Scientific Authority has noted that it may be unable to justify the issuance of CITES import permits for trophies taken in countries other than Zimbabwe and possibly South Africa.

*Antiques:*

Articles of antique worked ivory can be imported, provided: a CITES pre-convention certificate is issued by the exporting country, certifying that the specimen was acquired on or before February 4, 1977; it is a bona fide antique object of worked ivory; the importer has proof that the article is not less than 100 years old on the date of export; it is composed in whole or in part of African elephant ivory; and it has not been repaired or modified with any ivory on or after February 4, 1977.

*Personal effects:*

A limited exemption exists for some personal effects. These are defined as articles that are not intended for sale and are part of a shipment of the household effects of a person who is moving her or his residence to or from the United States, or are included in personal accompanying baggage. This exemption is *not* available for elephant parts or products acquired outside of the United States and being imported into the United States for the first time. Worked ivory that is included as personal effects may only be imported if: it was acquired in the United States; it was properly registered with a Customs officer on export; a Certificate of Registration for Personal Effects Taken Abroad was obtained prior to export and presented upon importation; and it is part of an article having a serial number, or other distinctive, permanently affixed unique markings that can be registered with the U.S. Customs Service.

Do you plan to import live African elephants or their parts or products? — YES — African Elephant Conservation Act and CITES requirements must be met. TURN TO PAGE A-61, "CITES APPENDIX I: ACTIVITIES REQUIRING A PERMIT"

NO

Do you plan to export a live African elephant? — YES — (see above)

NO

Do you plan to reexport a live African elephant (elephant previously imported)? — YES — A CITES Reexport Certificate is required. TURN TO PAGE A-63, "APPLICATION PROCEDURES: REEXPORT FROM THE U.S."

NO

Do you plan to reexport African elephant ivory parts and products? — YES — (see above)

NO

Do you plan to conduct interstate commerce in legally imported African elephant products other than ivory? — YES — No permit is required.

TO PAGE A-30

FROM PAGE A-29

Do you plan to conduct interstate commerce in African ivory or ivory products?

— YES —

No permit is required for interstate commerce of legally imported African elephant ivory.

## SPECIAL RULE—KANGAROOS

A Special Rule provides for import of three species of kangaroos from Australia: EASTERN GRAY KANGAROO, *Macropus giganteus* (all subspecies except *tasmaniensis),* RED KANGAROO, *Macropus (=Megaleia) rufus,* and WESTERN GRAY KANGAROO, *Macropus fuliginosus*. The above-listed kangaroos, including their parts and products, which have been identified as harvested in accordance with the management plans of Australian States, may be imported into the U.S. without an ESA permit. Shipments imported directly from Australia require a copy of the Australian export license. Note that the original Australian license is collected by Australian Customs. However, other laws may apply. Check with the U.S. Department of Agriculture on the importation of meat and meat products. If a shipment is reexported from another country to the United States, a document must be provided that proves the shipment was originally exported from Australia in accordance with the U.S. Endangered Species Act.

Do you plan to import from Australia any of the above listed species of kangaroos, or their parts and products?

— NO — Your activity is not covered by this Special Rule, but may be allowed under an ESA Endangered/Threatened Species Permit. TURN TO PAGE A-44, "THREATENED ANIMALS: ACTIVITIES REQUIRING A PERMIT" AND PAGE A-5, "MULTIPLE LAWS"

YES

TURN TO PAGE A-49, "OTHER CONSIDERATIONS"

## SPECIAL RULE—LEOPARD

On March 1, 1982, leopard *(Panthera pardus)* populations occurring in Africa to the south of a line running along the borders of the following countries were down-listed from Endangered to Threatened: Gabon/Rio Muni; Gabon/Cameroon; Congo/Cameroon; Congo/Central African Republic; Zaire/Central African Republic; Zaire/Sudan; Uganda/Sudan; Kenya/Sudan; Kenya/Ethiopia; Kenya/Somalia. However, all leopards still are listed on Appendix I of CITES. A sport-hunted leopard trophy legally taken AFTER March 1, 1982, from an area south of the line delineated above may be imported into the U.S. without a Threatened Species permit, provided that the appropriate CITES documents have been obtained. However, CITES has approved only certain countries for import into the U.S., under a quota, of sport-hunted leopard trophies. A sport-hunted leopard trophy legally taken BEFORE March 1, 1982, from an approved area south of the line delineated above, may be imported into the U.S. provided CITES permits have been obtained. These steps must be followed to import a trophy of a legally taken sport-hunted leopard into the United States:

1. First, obtain a CITES import permit from the Federal Wildlife Permit Office.
   a. Permits are available for sport-hunted trophies only. This means the trophy must be imported by the person who shot it and must be for personal use or display only. It does not include leopards shot by other people, nor does it include purchased skins.
   b. Sport hunters should allow approximately 60 days for processing of these permits.
2. Take the leopard according to the foreign country's laws.
3. Obtain a CITES export permit from the CITES Management Authority of a Party country or equivalent CITES documentation from a competent authority in a non-Party country. "In lieu of" documents from Party countries are not acceptable.
4. Import your specimen through a port designated for wildlife pursuant to 50 CFR Part 14.
5. Present the ORIGINAL of CITES import and export permits and a completed Wildlife Declaration (Form 3-177) to a U.S. Fish and Wildlife Service inspector at a designated port upon import.

Does your activity involve the import of a personal, legally taken, sport-hunted trophy from an approved area?

— NO — Your activity is not allowed under this Special Rule, but may be permitted under an ESA Endangered/Threatened Species Permit. TURN TO PAGE A-44, "THREATENED ANIMALS: ACTIVITIES REQUIRING A PERMIT" **AND** PAGE A-5, "MULTIPLE LAWS"

YES

You must obtain a CITES leopard import permit. TURN TO APPENDIX B "SAMPLE APPLICATION: IMPORT OF SPORT-HUNTED TROPHY"

## SPECIAL RULE—PRIMATES

If certain conditions are met, no federal permit is required to buy or sell the species listed below in interstate commerce, and no ESA permit is required for export or reimport, although appropriate CITES documents must be obtained. The conditions are: the specimens involved must have been held in captivity on or before November 18, 1976, or born in captivity to parents that were held in captivity on or before that date, or born in captivity to parents legally imported after that date.

BLACK HOWLER MONKEY, *Alouatta pigra*
CHIMPANZEE, *Pan troglodytes*
FORMOSAN ROCK MACAQUE, *Macaca cyclopis*
GELADA (BABOON), *Theropithecus gelada*
JAPANESE MACAQUE, *Macaca fuscata*
LESSER SLOW LORIS, *Nycticebus pygmaeus*
LONG-TAILED LANGUR, *Presbytis potenziani*
PHILIPPINE TARSIER, *Tarius syrichta*
PURPLE-FACED LANGUR, *Presbytis senex*
STUMP-TAILED MACAQUE, *Macaca arctoides*
TONKIN SNUB-NOSED MONKEY, *Pygathrix (=Rhinopithecus) avunculus*
TOQUE MACAQUE, *Macaca sinica*
WHITE-FOOTED TAMARIN, *Saguinus leucopus*

To engage in any activity involving the species listed above that is normally prohibited, you must be able to provide sufficient documentary evidence of the U.S. captive status of your specimen on November 18, 1976, or that it was born in captivity in the U.S. Records in the form of studbooks or inventories kept in the normal course of business will be acceptable as evidence, provided that a notarized statement accompanies the records (see 50 CFR 17.40(c)).

Was your Special Rule primate held in captivity in the U.S. on or before November 18, 1976 or born in captivity in the U.S. to parents legally held in captivity on November 18, 1976, or to parents legally imported after that date?

— NO — Your activity is not covered by this Special Rule, but may be allowed under an ESA Endangered/Threatened Species Permit. TURN TO PAGE A-44, "THREATENED ANIMALS: ACTIVITIES REQUIRING A PERMIT" **AND** PAGE A-5, "MULTIPLE LAWS"

YES

Do you wish to buy or sell such a specimen in interstate commerce?

—YES — No ESA or CITES permit is required. TURN TO PAGE A-49, "OTHER CONSIDERATIONS"

NO

Do you wish to export or reimport such a specimen?

—YES — No ESA permit required; however, CITES requirements must be met. TURN TO PAGE A-51, "CITES: INTRODUCTION"

NO

Your activity is not covered by this Special Rule, but may be allowed under an ESA Endangered/Threatened Species Permit. TURN TO PAGE A-44, "THREATENED ANIMALS: ACTIVITIES REQUIRING A PERMIT" **AND** PAGE A-5, "MULTIPLE LAWS"

## SPECIAL RULE—GRAY WOLF

A Special Rule authorizes limited taking of the gray wolf *(Canis lupus)* in Minnesota under the conditions listed below. Other activities normally prohibited by the ESA are also prohibited in the case of the gray wolf; however, Threatened species permits are available in these cases.

1. Any person may take a gray wolf in defense of his own life or the lives of others.
2. Any employee or agent of the FWS or federal land management agency may, when acting in the course of his official duties, take a gray wolf in Minnesota without a permit if such action is necessary to:
   a. Aid a sick, injured, or orphaned specimen;
   b. Dispose of a dead specimen;
   c. Salvage a dead specimen which may be useful for scientific study; or
   d. Remove an animal committing significant depredations on livestock from certain zones in the state (see 50 CFR 17.40(d)).
3. Any employee or agent of the FWS or the Minnesota Department of Natural Resources, when operating under a Cooperative Agreement with the FWS, who is designated by his agency for such purposes, may take a gray wolf in Minnesota to carry out scientific research or conservation programs.

Does your proposed activity meet the guidelines listed in 1, 2, or 3 above?

—YES — No special documentation is required under the ESA. HOWEVER, you must meet the requirements of all laws that protect your species. TURN TO PAGE A-49, "OTHER CONSIDERATIONS"

NO

Your activity is not covered under this Special Rule, but may be permitted under an ESA Endangered/Threatened Species Permit. TURN TO PAGE A-44, "THREATENED ANIMALS: ACTIVITIES REQUIRING A PERMIT" **AND** PAGE A-5, "MULTIPLE LAWS"

## SPECIAL RULE—SEA TURTLES

A Special Rule permits incidental catch and subsistence taking of the following species (these do not include populations listed as Endangered):

Green sea turtle, *Chelonia mydas*
Loggerhead sea turtle, *Caretta caretta*
Olive ridley sea turtle, *Lepidochelys olivacea*

Does this special situation apply to your activities?

—YES — No ESA documentation is required. Contact NMFS Office of Protected Resources for further information.

NO

Your activity is not allowed under this Special Rule, but may be allowed under an ESA Endangered/Threatened Species Permit. TURN TO PAGE A-44, "THREATENED ANIMALS: ACTIVITIES REQUIRING A PERMIT" AND PAGE A-5, "MULTIPLE LAWS"

## SPECIAL RULE—AMERICAN ALLIGATOR

At one time the American alligator, *Alligator mississippiensis,* underwent severe population declines, but in recent years this species has made a remarkable comeback. Thus, it is listed as Threatened and Threatened by Similarity of Appearance (T/SA) in areas where a limited harvest and commercial trade is allowed under strict state and federal controls. This species is also listed on Appendix II of the Convention on International Trade in Endangered Species (CITES), allowing regulated international trade. It is prohibited to possess, sell, deliver, carry, transport, or ship **unlawfully taken** American alligators.

Persons may take alligators in the wild or those born in captivity when that taking is in accordance with state law. Persons may also deliver, receive, carry, transport, ship, sell, offer to sell, purchase, or offer to purchase alligators when that is in accordance with state law. But all these activities are subject to the following conditions. State officials must tag the hides with an FWS-approved tag. Hide, meat, or parts may be sold or otherwise transferred only in accordance with state law. Imports and exports must comply with CITES. Record keeping requirements must be met.

This page intentionally left blank.

This page intentionally left blank

## SPECIAL RULE—SAN MARCOS SALAMANDER

A Special Rule permits the taking of the San Marcos salamander *(Eurycea nana)* in accordance with state law (Texas). However, any violation of state law is also a violation of the Endangered Species Act.

Does this Special Rule apply to your activities.

—YES — Refer to Texas law for information pertaining to this species. TURN TO PAGE A-49, "OTHER CONSIDERATIONS"

NO

Your activity is not covered by this Special Rule.

## SPECIAL RULE—FISHES

A Special Rule permits the taking of the fishes listed below in accordance with state law. Any violation of state law also is a violation of the Endangered Species Act.

Arizona trout, *Salmo apache*
Bayou darter, *Etheostoma rubrum*
Greenback cutthroat trout, *Salmo clarki stomias*
Lahontan cutthroat trout, *Salmo clarki henshawi*
Leopard darter, *Percina pantherina*
Little Kern golden trout, *Salmo aguabonita whitei*
Paiute cutthroat trout, *Salmo clarki seleniris*
Slackwater darter, *Etheostoma boschungi*
Slender chub, *Hybopsis cahni*
Spotfin chub, *Hybopsis monacha*
Yellowfin madtom, *Noturus flavipinnis*

Does this Special Rule apply to your activities?

—YES — Consult state wildlife laws. TURN TO PAGE A-49, "OTHER CONSIDERATIONS"

NO

Your activity is not covered by this Special Rule.

## SPECIAL RULE—CRUSTACEANS

A Special Rule provides that specimens of the Madison Cave isopod *(Antrolana litra)* may be taken for scientific purposes without federal permit, *provided,* that all other federal, state, and local laws, regulations, ordinances, or other restrictions or limitations have been complied with.

| Does this Special Rule apply to your activity? | —YES — | No ESA permit is required. TURN TO PAGE A-49, "OTHER CONSIDERATIONS" |
|---|---|---|
| NO | | |
| Your activity is not covered by this Special Rule, but may be allowed under an ESA Endangered/Threatened Species Permit. TURN TO PAGE A-44, "THREATENED ANIMALS: ACTIVITIES REQUIRING A PERMIT" AND PAGE A-5, "MULTIPLE LAWS" | | |

## THREATENED ANIMALS: ACTIVITIES REQUIRING A PERMIT

Permits authorizing prohibited activities affecting THREATENED animals may be issued **only** for purposes of scientific research, enhancement of propagation or survival of the species, zoological exhibition, educational purposes, and special purposes consistent with the Act. In exceptional cases, applicants can also receive permits granting very limited authority for incidental takings, 50 CFR 17.22(b), and work with experimental populations.

Is your activity listed below?
1. Import or Export.
2. Deliver, receive, carry, transport, or ship species listed as Threatened in interstate or foreign commerce in the course of a commercial activity.
3. Sell or offer for sale in interstate or foreign commerce species listed as Threatened.
4. Possess, ship, deliver, carry, transport, sell or receive unlawfully acquired Threatened wildlife.
5. Taking of a Threatened Species that is not subject to a special rule that allows taking.

— NO —

Your activity is not specifically regulated by the ESA. If you are dealing with a terrestrial species, contact:
FWS, Federal Wildlife Permit Office
If you are dealing with a marine species, contact:
NMFS, Office of Protected Resources

YES

Is the purpose of your activity listed below?
1. Scientific research.
2. Enhancement of propagation or survival of the species.
3. Zoological exhibition.
4. Educational purposes.
5. Special purposes consistent with the Act.
6. Import or export of African elephant ivory.

— NO —

Your activity is not allowed, and no permit will be issued. If you are dealing with a terrestrial species, contact:
FWS, Federal Wildlife Permit Office
If you are dealing with a marine species, contact:
NMFS, Office of Protected Resources

YES

TURN TO PAGE A-46, "APPLICATION INFORMATION: ENDANGERED/THREATENED SPECIES (FWS)"
**OR** for marine species (animals only)
TURN TO PAGE A-47, "APPLICATION INFORMATION: ENDANGERED/THREATENED SPECIES (NMFS)"
**OR** for ivory
TURN TO PAGE A-28, "SPECIAL RULE: AFRICAN ELEPHANT"

## THREATENED PLANTS: ACTIVITIES REQUIRING A PERMIT

Permits authorizing prohibited activities involving Threatened species are issued for purposes of scientific research, enhancement of propagation or survival, zoological, horticultural or botanical exhibition, education, or special purposes which are consistent with the goals of the ESA. Seeds of cultivated specimens of Threatened species are exempt if accompanied by a statement that the seeds are of "cultivated origin." 50 CFR 17.71(a). In exceptional cases, applicants can also receive permits granting very limited authority for incidental takings, 50 CFR 17.22(b).

Is your proposed activity listed below?

1. Remove and reduce to possession from areas under federal jurisdiction.
2. Maliciously damage or destroy on areas under federal jurisdiction.
3. Remove, cut, dig up, or damage or destroy on non-federal areas in knowing violation of state laws or in violation of state criminal trespass laws.
4. Import or export.
5. Deliver, receive, carry, transport, or ship species listed as Threatened in interstate or foreign commerce in the course of a commercial activity.
6. Sell or offer for sale in interstate or foreign commerce species listed as Threatened.

— NO — Your activity is not specifically regulated by ESA. However, other laws may affect your species; contact the Wildlife Permit Office and the Plant Protection and Quarantine Office of USDA.

YES

Is the purpose of your activity listed below?

1. Scientific research.
2. Enhancement of propagation or survival of the species.
3. Horticultural or botanical exhibition.
4. Educational purposes.
5. Special purposes consistent with the Act.

— NO — Your activity is not allowed, and no permit will be issued. Contact the Wildlife Permit Office and the Plant Protection and Quarantine Office of USDA for further information.

YES

Does your proposed activity involve interstate commerce or export of artificially propagated specimens?

—YES — TURN TO PAGE A-48, "APPLICATION INFORMATION: ARTIFICIALLY PROPAGATED ENDANGERED/THREATENED PLANTS"

NO

TURN TO PAGE A-46, "APPLICATION INFORMATION: ENDANGERED/THREATENED SPECIES"

## APPLICATION INFORMATION: ENDANGERED/THREATENED SPECIES (FWS)

A permit application for Endangered/Threatened Species consists of three parts:

1. FORM 3-200
   Form 3-200 requests general information about you and your proposed activity. (A detailed explanation of each question may be found in Appendix B.)
2. SUPPLEMENTARY INFORMATION
   A series of questions (usually found on the back of Form 3-200) which requests specific information on your proposed activity.
3. APPLICATION FEE
   The application fee must be paid by certified check or money order, made payable to the U.S. Fish and Wildlife Service. The fee for this permit is $25.

**Be sure to answer all questions, provide all of the information required, and include a check or money order for the application fee.** An incomplete application will be returned to you for completion, resulting in considerable delay.

### WHERE TO OBTAIN APPLICATION FORMS

Federal Wildlife Permit Office
U.S. Fish and Wildlife Service
4401 N. Fairfax Drive, Room 432
Arlington, Virginia 22203

Plant Protection and Quarantine Office
Animal and Plant Health and Inspection Service
U.S. Department of Agriculture
Federal Building
Hyattsville, Maryland 20782

### WHEN TO APPLY

Submit your completed application, accompanying documents, and a check or money order for $25 to the address listed below AT LEAST 90 days before you need an Endangered Species permit and 60 days before a Threatened Species Permit.

### WHERE TO MAIL THE COMPLETED APPLICATION

Federal Wildlife Permit Office
U.S. Fish and Wildlife Service
4401 N. Fairfax Drive, Room 432
Arlington, Virginia 22203

TURN TO APPENDIX B, "SAMPLE APPLICATION: ENDANGERED/THREATENED SPECIES (FWS)" AND "SAMPLE APPLICATION: INCIDENTAL TAKE OF SPECIES"
**AND**
TURN TO PAGE A-49, "OTHER CONSIDERATIONS"

## APPLICATION INFORMATION: ENDANGERED/THREATENED SPECIES (NMFS)

A permit application to the NMFS requires completing a questionnaire that is too long to be included in this appendix. You should obtain the application form from:

NMFS Office of Protected Resources
1335 East-West Highway
Silver Spring, Maryland 20910

### Where to Send Applications

Submit an original and two signed copies of the completed application to the Office of Protected Resources at the address listed above.

### Give Complete Information

NMFS endeavors to process all applications as quickly as possible. An application must be complete before it is forwarded to reviewers and before a Notice of Receipt is published in the *Federal Register*. Incomplete applications will not be processed; additional information will be requested or the application returned. Therefore, it is in your interest to furnish complete and specific information. Review time is shorter when the proposed methods, objectives, and potential adverse impacts are clearly addressed.

The sufficiency of a permit application will be determined by NMFS based on the requirements of the appropriate regulations. The information provided will be used to determine whether the application is complete and whether a permit should be issued. Reports required under previous permits must be up-to-date for a new application to be considered.

TURN TO PAGE A-49, "OTHER CONSIDERATIONS"

## APPLICATION INFORMATION: ARTIFICIALLY PROPAGATED ENDANGERED/THREATENED PLANTS

A permit application for Artificially Propagated Endangered and Threatened Species consists of three parts:

1. FORM 3-200
   Form 3-200 requests general information about you and your proposed activity. (A detailed explanation of each question may be found in Appendix B.)
2. SUPPLEMENTARY INFORMATION
   A series of questions (usually found on the back of Form 3-200) which requests specific information about your proposed activity.
3. APPLICATION FEE
   The application fee must be paid by certified check or money order, made payable to the U.S. Fish and Wildlife Service. The fee for this permit is $25.

**Be sure to answer all questions, provide all of the information required, and include a check or money order for the application fee.** An incomplete application will be returned to you for completion, resulting in considerable delay.

### WHERE TO OBTAIN APPLICATION FORMS

Federal Wildlife Permit Office
U.S. Fish and Wildlife Service
4401 N. Fairfax Drive, Room 432
Arlington, Virginia 22203

### WHEN TO APPLY

Submit your completed application, accompanying documents, and a check or money order for $25 to the address listed below AT LEAST 90 days before you need an Endangered Species permit and 60 days before a Threatened Species Permit.

### WHERE TO MAIL THE COMPLETED APPLICATION

Federal Wildlife Permit Office
U.S. Fish and Wildlife Service
4401 N. Fairfax Drive, Room 432
Arlington, Virginia 22203

TURN TO APPENDIX B, "SAMPLE APPLICATION: ARTIFICIALLY PROPAGATED ENDANGERED AND THREATEND PLANTS"
**AND**
TURN TO PAGE A-49, "OTHER CONSIDERATIONS"

## OTHER CONSIDERATIONS

If you have followed the steps outlined in this chapter, you have completed the permit process under the ESA. However, you must fulfill the requirements of **each** law that applies to your species. Be sure to check each applicable section of this Appendix. For best results, consult the sections that pertain to your species **in the order listed.**



IF YOU HAVE CONSULTED ALL OF THE SECTIONS THAT PERTAIN TO YOUR SPECIES, TURN TO PAGE A-149, "GENERAL REQUIREMENTS: ANIMAL"
**OR**
PAGE A-167, "GENERAL REQUIREMENTS: PLANTS"

This page intentionally left blank.

# CONVENTION ON INTERNATIONAL TRADE IN ENDANGERED SPECIES OF WILD FAUNA AND FLORA

## U.S. Fish and Wildlife Service

## GENERAL INTRODUCTION

The United States and over 100 other nations are Parties to an international agreement known as the Convention on International Trade in Endangered Species of Wild Fauna and Flora (CITES). The purpose of the Convention is to regulate trade in certain imperiled species of wildlife and plants. A species considered to be imperiled or subject to heavy trade may be listed in Appendix I, II or III of the Convention, depending on the degree to which it is threatened by trade.

Each country that is Party to the Convention is required to designate two administrative bodies, a Management Authority and a Scientific Authority. The Management Authority of each Party country issues permits and certificates; the Scientific Authority determines whether or not a particular activity will pose a threat to the survival of listed species in the wild. Therefore, the approval of the Scientific Authority is required before a permit can be issued by the Management Authority. In the U.S., the Management Authority and the Scientific Authority are within the U.S. Fish and Wildlife Service.

U.S. regulations require that imports (including the introduction of listed species from the sea), exports or reexports* of wildlife and plants listed on any of the three Appendices of the Convention be accompanied by proper permits or certificates of exception. CITES export documentation is almost always required; import permits are necessary only for species listed in Appendix I, or for Appendix II species introduced from the sea.

NOTE: Any Party may enact stricter legislation, or may enter a specific reservation with regard to any species included in Appendix I, II or III, or any parts or derivatives specified in an Appendix III listing. If a Party country enters a reservation to a particular species, part or derivative, that country will be treated as a Non-Party country with respect to that particular species. Information on reservations is available from the Fish and Wildlife Service.

Appendix I includes species presently threatened with extinction. The Convention's most stringent controls are directed at commercial activities involving these animals and plants.

Appendix II species are those species which are not presently threatened with extinction but may become so unless trade is strictly regulated. CITES controls are less restrictive for Appendix II species than for those listed in Appendix I.

Appendix III includes species that are regulated for conservation purposes by a Party country and need Treaty protection to enforce the Party's domestic controls on a listed species.

NOTE: During the eight CITES conferences, the Parties have adopted resolutions regarding implementation of the Convention. The U.S. Fish and Wildlife Service uses many of these resolutions in interpreting and implementing CITES even if the resolutions have not been incorporated into the U.S. regulations. In addition, some resolutions allow trade in Appendix I species as a result of establishing a quota or ranching system. For example, people are allowed to keep leopard skins (including hunting trophies) that they acquire in certain African countries and take back to their homeland. CITES Resolution Conf. 7.7.

TURN TO PAGE A-52 "SPECIAL SITUATIONS AND EXEMPTIONS"

*"Reexport" is defined as the export of materials previously legally imported.

## SPECIAL SITUATIONS AND EXEMPTIONS

In some cases, exemptions may be claimed from the standard CITES permit requirements if specific criteria are met. These exemptions include the activities listed in the box below. Turn to the first section which seems to apply to your situation. The information provided there will help you determine whether or not you qualify for that exemption, and what documentation is required, if any.

CAUTION: Although CITES provides exceptions relating to some wildlife or plants listed in CITES Appendices, those species may also be subject to regulation under the U.S. Endangered Species Act or Marine Mammal Protection Act. An exception provided under CITES does not necessarily allow activities that are prohibited under the U.S. laws. 50 CFR 23.13(a).

To determine if any exemptions or special situations apply to your proposed activity, refer to the sections listed below:



THEN

IF NO EXEMPTIONS OR SPECIAL SITUATIONS APPLY, TURN TO THE SECTION ON THE CITES APPENDIX WHICH LISTS YOUR SPECIES:

## EXEMPTION: PRE-CONVENTION SPECIMENS

This exemption applies to specimens of species listed under CITES that were acquired before the species was listed by CITES. To qualify for this exemption, you must obtain a CITES Certificate of Exemption from the Management Authority of the country of origin, stating that the specimen (including parts or products) was acquired before the time the species was listed in a CITES appendix. The date a species was listed under CITES can be found by referring to 50 CFR 23.23. If more than one date is listed, contact the Wildlife Permit Office for information on which date determines Pre-Convention status.

Does your proposed activity meet the criteria described above?

—YES — TURN TO PAGE A-75, "APPLICATION INFORMATION: PRE-CONVENTION CERTIFICATE"

NO

To find out if any **other** exemptions or special situations apply, TURN TO PAGE A-52, "SPECIAL SITUATIONS AND EXEMPTIONS"

## EXEMPTION: APPENDIX I WILDLIFE BRED IN CAPTIVITY

A CITES Certificate of Exemption for captive-bred wildlife, or parts and products of captive-bred wildlife, must be obtained from the Management Authority of the country of origin. The document must state that the wildlife was bred in captivity. The wildlife or parts or products must qualify under the definition of "captive-bred" in accordance with CITES Resolution (Conf. 2.12) outlined below, passed at the second meeting of the Conference of the Parties to CITES, San Jose (Costa Rica), 19-30 March 1979:

"THE CONFERENCE OF THE PARTIES TO THE CONVENTION RECOMMENDS:

a) . . . Specimens of animal species in Appendix I bred in captivity for commercial purposes . . . shall be treated as if they were in Appendix II. . . .

b) . . . that the term 'bred in captivity' be interpreted to refer only to offspring, including eggs, born or otherwise produced in a controlled environment, either of parents that mated or otherwise transferred gametes in a controlled environment, if reproduction is sexual, or of parents that were in a controlled environment when development of the offspring began, if reproduction is asexual. The parental breeding stock must be to the satisfaction of the competent government authorities of the relevant country:

i. established in a manner not detrimental to the survival of the species in the wild;

ii. maintained without augmentation from the wild, except for the occasional addition of animals, eggs or gametes from wild populations to prevent deleterious inbreeding, with the magnitude of such addition determined by the need for new genetic material and not by other factors; and

iii. managed in a manner designed to maintain the breeding stock indefinitely.

"A controlled environment for animals is an environment that is intensively manipulated by man for the purpose of producing the species in question, and that has boundaries designed to prevent animals, eggs or gametes of the selected species from entering or leaving the controlled environment. General characteristics of a controlled environment may include but are not limited to artificial housing, waste removal, health care, protection from predators, and artificially supplied food. A parental breeding stock shall be considered to be 'managed in a manner designed to maintain the breeding stock indefinitely' only if it is managed in a manner which has been demonstrated to be capable of reliably producing second-generation offspring in a controlled environment. . . ."

Is your species listed in Appendix II or III?

—YES—

Your activity will require the permits normally required for activities involving **Appendix II or III** species. TURN TO PAGE A-64, "CITIES APPENDIX II" OR PAGE A-69, "CITIES APPENDIX III"

NO

Is your species listed in Appendix I, and were your specimens bred in captivity **for commercial purposes?**

—YES—

TURN TO PAGE A-75, "APPLICATION INFORMATION: CAPTIVE-BRED CERTIFICATE" AND PAGE A-76 "OTHER CONSIDERATIONS"

NO

To find our it any **other** exemptions or special situations apply, TURN TO PAGE A-52, "SPECIAL SITUATIONS AND EXEMPTIONS"

## EXEMPTION: ARTIFICIALLY PROPAGATED PLANTS

A CITES Certificate of Exemption for artificially propagated plants or parts and products of artificially propagated plants, must be obtained from the Management Authority of the country of origin. The document must state that the plants were artificially propagated. The plant, plant part or product must qualify under the definition of "artificially propagated" in accordance with CITES Resolution, Conf. 2.12 outlined below, passed at the second meeting of the Conference of the Parties to CITES, San Jose (Costa Rica), 19–30 March 1979.

"THE CONFERENCE OF THE PARTIES TO THE CONVENTION RECOMMENDS:

a) . . . plant species in Appendix I artificially propagated for commercial purposes shall be treated as if they were in Appendix II. . . .

c) that the term 'artificially propagated' be interpreted to refer only to plants grown by man from seeds, cuttings, callus tissue, spores or other propagules under controlled conditions. The artificially propagated stock must be:

i. established and maintained in a manner not detrimental to the survival of the species in the wild, and

ii. managed in a manner designed to maintain the artificially propagated stock indefinitely.

"Controlled conditions for plants [means plants maintained] under an environment that is intensively manipulated by man for the purpose of producing selected species. General characteristics of controlled conditions may include but are not limited to tillage, fertilization, weed control, irrigation, or nursery operations such as potting, bedding, or protection from weather. . . ."

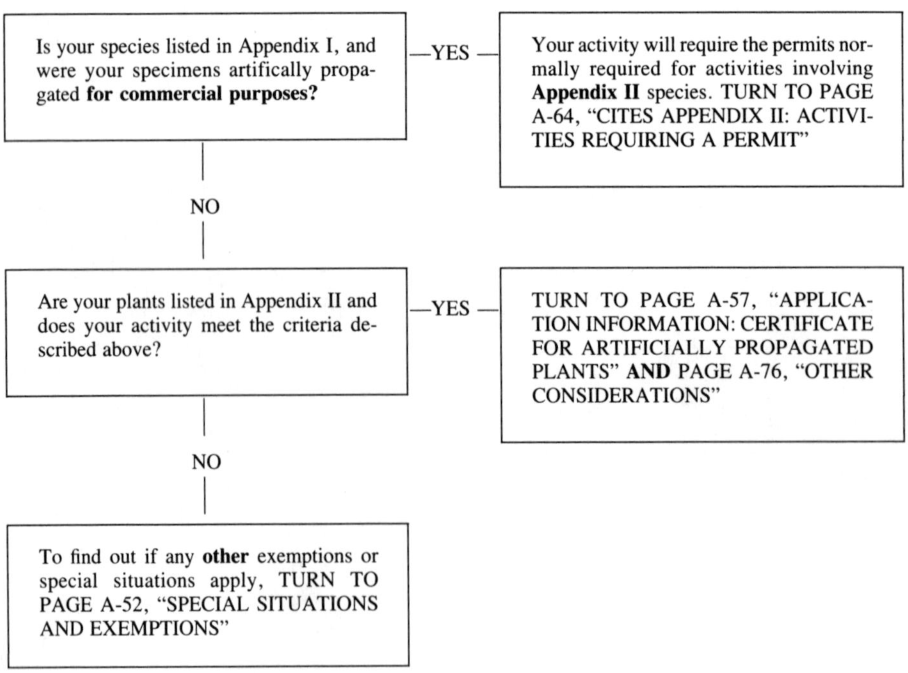

## APPLICATION INFORMATION: CERTIFICATE FOR ARTIFICIALLY PROPAGATED PLANTS

An application for a Certificate for Artificially Propagated Plants consists of three parts:

1. FORM 3-200
   Form 3-200 requests general information about you and your proposed activity. (A detailed explanation of each question may be found in Appendix B.)
2. SUPPLEMENTARY INFORMATION
   A series of questions (usually found on the back of Form 3-200) which requests specific information on your proposed activity.
3. APPLICATION FEE
   The application fee must be paid by certified check or money order, made payable to the U.S. Fish and Wildlife Service. The fee for this permit is $25.

**Be sure to answer all questions, provide all of the information required, and include a check or money order for the application fee.** An incomplete application will be returned to you for completion, resulting in considerable delay.

### WHERE TO OBTAIN APPLICATION FORMS

Federal Wildlife Permit Office
U.S. Fish and Wildlife Service
4401 N. Fairfax Drive, Room 432
Arlington, Virginia 22203

### WHEN TO APPLY

Submit your completed application, accompanying documents, and a check or money order for $25 to the address listed below AT LEAST 30 days before you need the permit.

### WHERE TO MAIL THE COMPLETED APPLICATION

Federal Wildlife Permit Office
U.S. Fish and Wildlife Service
4401 N. Fairfax Drive, Room 432
Arlington, Virginia 22203

TURN TO APPENDIX B, "SAMPLE APPLICATION: CERTIFICATE FOR ARTIFICIALLY PROPAGATED PLANTS"
**AND**
TURN TO PAGE A-76, "OTHER CONSIDERATIONS"

## EXEMPTION: SCIENTIFIC EXCHANGE OF HERBARIUM OR MUSEUM SPECIMENS

Scientific exchange is allowed for preserved, dried or embedded museum or herbarium specimens, or live plant material under the following conditions:

1. The activity must be a non-commercial loan, donation, or exchange;
2. It must involve only legally accessioned specimens;
3. The exchange must be between scientists and scientific institutions that have been registered with the CITES Secretariat by the Management Authority of their country. Additional documentation is needed for ESA listed species; for further information contact WPO.
4. An appropriate label must be affixed to the package or container.

A CITES Certificate of Exemption for scientific exchange and the accompanying assigned code must be obtained from the Management Authority of the country of origin. CITES Resolution Conf. 2.14.

Does your proposed activity meet the criteria described above?

—YES —

TURN TO PAGE A-59, "APPLICATION INFORMATION: REGISTRATION OF SCIENTIFIC INSTITUTIONS" AND PAGE A-76, "OTHER CONSIDERATIONS"

NO

To find out if any **other** exemptions or special situations apply, TURN TO PAGE A-52, "SPECIAL SITUATIONS AND EXEMPTIONS"

## APPLICATION INFORMATION: REGISTRATION OF SCIENTIFIC INSTITUTIONS

A permit application for Registration of Scientific Institutions under CITES consists of three parts:

1. FORM 3-200
   Form 3-200 requests general information about you and your proposed activity. (A detailed explanation of each question may be found in Appendix B.)
2. SUPPLEMENTARY INFORMATION
   A series of questions (usually found on the back of Form 3-200) which requests specific information on your proposed activity.
3. APPLICATION FEE
   The application fee must be paid by certified check or money order, made payable to the U.S. Fish and Wildlife Service. The fee for this permit is $25.

**Be sure to answer all questions, provide all of the information required, and include a check or money order for the application fee.** An incomplete application will be returned to you for completion, resulting in considerable delay.

### WHERE TO OBTAIN APPLICATION FORMS

Federal Wildlife Permit Office
U.S. Fish and Wildlife Service
4401 N. Fairfax Drive, Room 432
Arlington, Virginia 22203

### WHEN TO APPLY

Submit your completed application, accompanying documents, and a check or money order for $25 to the address listed below AT LEAST 30 days before you need the permit.

### WHERE TO MAIL THE COMPLETED APPLICATION

Federal Wildlife Permit Office
U.S. Fish and Wildlife Service
4401 N. Fairfax Drive, Room 432
Arlington, Virginia 22203

TURN TO APPENDIX B, "SAMPLE APPLICATION: REGISTRATION OF SCIENTIFIC INSTITUTIONS"
**AND**
TURN TO PAGE A-76, "OTHER CONSIDERATIONS"

## EXEMPTION: TRANSSHIPMENT THROUGH THE U.S.

No CITES permits or certificates are needed to import, export or reexport CITES listed species that are being transshipped through the U.S., provided that the shipment remains in Customs custody. Species also listed under the Endangered Species Act or the Marine Mammal Protection Act may **not** be transshipped through the U.S. If you are uncertain that your shipment qualifies, contact the U.S. Fish & Wildlife Service's Division of Law Enforcement.

Does your proposed activity meet the criteria described above?

—YES — No special documentation is required under CITES. However, you must either qualify for an exemption or meet the requirements of each of the laws that protect your species. TURN TO PAGE A-76, "OTHER CONSIDERATIONS"

NO

To find out if any **other** exemptions or special situations apply, TURN TO PAGE A-52, "SPECIAL SITUATIONS AND EXEMPTIONS"

## EXEMPTION: PERSONAL BAGGAGE OR HOUSEHOLD EFFECTS

No CITES permits or certificates are needed to import, export or reexport listed animals or plants that are accompanying the personal baggage or household effects of persons moving to or from the U.S. This exemption does **not** apply to the following:

1. Importation by U.S. residents of Appendix I listed species acquired outside of the United States;
2. Importation by U.S. residents of Appendix II listed species (particularly live animals) that were taken from the wild in a foreign country, if that country requires an export permit;
3. Species also listed under the Endangered Species Act, the Bald Eagle Protection Act or the Marine Mammal Protection Act.

The U.S. Department of Agriculture's Animal and Plant Health Inspection Service (APHIS) also has rules for importing plants and pet birds into the U.S. You will be directed to information on these rules as you follow the process outlined in this Appendix.

**CAUTION:** Many countries do not recognize the personal baggage/household effects exception, including Canada, most European countries and the United Kingdom. Therefore, you may not import, export or reexport animals or plants, or their parts or products, to or from these countries without a CITES permit. Check with the Management Authority of the foreign country involved before you leave the U.S.

Does your proposed activity meet the criteria described above?

—YES — No special documentation is required under CITES. HOWEVER, you must either qualify for an exemption or meet the requirements of **each** of the laws that protect your species. TURN TO PAGE A-76, "OTHER CONSIDERATIONS"

NO

To find out if any **other** exemptions or special situations apply, TURN TO PAGE A-52, "SPECIAL SITUATIONS AND EXEMPTIONS"

## CITES APPENDIX I

### CITES APPENDIX I: ACTIVITIES REQUIRING A PERMIT

Appendix I includes species presently threatened with extinction. The Convention's most stringent controls are directed at activities involving these animals and plants. All shipments of these species, or their parts and derivatives, require two permits—one from the importing country (obtained first) and another from the exporting country. Such permits will be issued only when the purpose for import is **not** primarily commercial and will not be detrimental to the survival of the species. In the instance of African elephant parts and products, the African Elephant Conservation Act allows only limited trade for noncommercial purposes.

Is your proposed activity IMPORT or INTRODUCTION FROM THE SEA, which is defined as the importation of specimens of any listed species which were taken in the marine environment not under the jurisdiction of any country?

—YES — TURN TO PAGE A-62, "APPLICATION PROCEDURES: IMPORT"

NO

Is your activity REEXPORT from the U.S. of previously legally imported materials?

—YES — TURN TO PAGE A-63, "APPLICATION PROCEDURES: REEXPORT FROM THE U.S."

NO

Is your activity EXPORT from the U.S.?

—YES — TURN TO PAGE A-62, "APPLICATION PROCEDURES: EXPORT FROM THE U.S."

NO

If your activity is something **other** than introduction from the sea, import from a foreign nation, reexport from the U.S., it is not regulated by CITES. TURN TO PAGE A-76, "OTHER CONSIDERATIONS"

## APPLICATION PROCEDURES: IMPORT

To import Appendix I wildlife or plants, or their parts and products into the U.S., two permits are required:

1. FIRST, obtain a CITES Import Permit from the U.S. Management Authority for CITES.
2. THEN, obtain an export permit from the country of export.

NOTE: No CITES Export Permit will be issued until you have obtained a CITES Import Permit.

CONSULT **BOTH** OF THESE SECTIONS FOR INFORMATION ON THE TWO CITES PERMITS REQUIRED:

| | Page |
|---|---|
| 1. "CITIES FOREIGN DOCUMENTATION REQUIREMENTS" . . . . . . . . . . . . . . . | A-70 |
| 2. "APPLICATION INFORMATION" . . . . . . . . . . . . . . . . . . . . . . . . . . . . . . . . | A-74 |

THEN

TURN TO APPENDIX B, "CITES HARMONIZED PERMIT" **AND** TURN TO PAGE A-76, "OTHER CONSIDERATIONS"

## APPLICATION PROCEDURES: EXPORT FROM THE U.S.

To export Appendix I wildlife or plants, or their parts and products, you must obtain two permits:

1. FIRST, obtain an import permit from the country of import.
2. THEN, obtain a CITES Export Permit from the U.S. Management Authority.

NOTE: No CITES Export Permit will be issued until you have obtained a CITES Import Permit from the importing country.

CONSULT **BOTH** OF THESE SECTIONS FOR INFORMATION ON THE TWO CITES PERMITS REQUIRED:

| | Page |
|---|---|
| 1. "CITIES FOREIGN DOCUMENTATION REQUIREMENTS" . . . . . . . . . . . . . . . | A-70 |
| 2. "APPLICATION INFORMATION: CITES EXPORT PERMIT" . . . . . . . . . . . . . . | A-75 |

THEN

TURN TO APPENDIX B, "CITES HARMONIZED PERMIT" **AND** TURN TO PAGE A-76, "OTHER CONSIDERATIONS"

## APPLICATION PROCEDURES: REEXPORT FROM THE U.S.

"Reexport" is defined as the export of wildlife or plants, or their parts or products, that were previously legally imported. To reexport Appendix I species, two permits are required:

1. FIRST, obtain an import permit from the country of import.
2. THEN, obtain a CITES Reexport Certificate from the U.S. Management Authority.

NOTE: No CITES Reexport Certificate will be issued until you have obtained a CITES Import Permit from the importing country.

CONSULT **BOTH** OF THESE SECTIONS FOR INFORMATION ON THE TWO CITES PERMITS REQUIRED:

| | Page |
|---|---|
| 1. "CITES FOREIGN DOCUMENTATION REQUIREMENTS" . . . . . . . . . . . . . . . . | A-70 |
| 2. "APPLICATION INFORMATION: CITES REEXPORT PERMIT" . . . . . . . . . . . . . . | A-75 |

THEN

TURN TO APPENDIX B, "CITES HARMONIZED PERMIT" **AND** TURN TO PAGE A-76, "OTHER CONSIDERATIONS"

## CITES APPENDIX II: ACTIVITIES REQUIRING A PERMIT

Appendix II species are those species which are not presently threatened with extinction but may become so unless trade is regulated. CITES controls are less stringent for Appendix II species than for those listed in Appendix I.

U.S. import permits are not needed for Appendix II species unless they are introduced from the sea, but foreign export permits or certificates of exemption must accompany each import shipment. A U.S. export permit or reexport certificate must accompany each export shipment. Export permits for Appendix II species can be issued for almost any purpose, as long as the export is not detrimental to the survival of the species. Reexport certificates are required for items previously legally imported, including items subsequently converted to manufactured goods.

Does your proposed activity involve the **export** or **reexport** of wild or cultivated American ginseng?

—YES — TURN TO PAGE A-66, "APPLICATION PROCEDURES: AMERICAN GINSENG"

NO

Is your proposed activity INTRODUCTION FROM THE SEA, which is defined as the importation of a specimen of any listed species which was taken in the marine environment not under the jurisdiction of any country?

—YES — A CITES Import Permit is required. TURN TO PAGE A-74, "APPLICATION INFORMATION"

NO

Is your proposed activity IMPORT from a foreign country?

—YES — No CITES import permit is required. HOWEVER, you must obtain an export permit or certificate of exemption from the country of export. TURN TO PAGE A-70, "CITES FOREIGN DOCUMENTATION REQUIREMENTS"

NO

Is your proposed activity REEXPORT from the U.S. of previously legally imported specimens or their parts or products, including manufactured products.

—YES — Do you plan **multiple** reexports of CITES II Specimens, either live or their parts and products?

YES — TURN TO PAGE A-72, "PERMIT INFORMATION: LETTER OF AUTHORIZATION

NO — TURN TO PAGE A-75, "APPLICATION INFORMATION: CITES REEXPORT CERTIFICATEŒ

NO

TO PAGE A-65

# CITES APPENDIX II

FROM PAGE A-64

Is your proposed activity EXPORT from the U.S.?

— NO — If your proposed activity is something other than introduction from the sea, import from a foreign country, export or re-export, it is not regulated by CITES. TURN TO PAGE A-76, "OTHER CONSIDERATIONS"

YES

Do you plan to export pelts, hides or products of any of the following species?
Alaskan brown bear *(Ursus arctos)*
Alaskan gray wolf *(Canis lupus)*
American alligator *(Alligator mississippiensis)*
Bobcat *(Lynx rufus)*
Lynx *(Lynx canadensis)*
River otter *(Lutra canadensis)*

—YES — For multiple shipments, TURN TO PAGE A-72, "PERMIT INFORMATION: LETTER OF AUTHORIZATION"
For single shipments, TURN TO PAGE A-75, "APPLICATION INFORMATION: CITES EXPORT PERMIT"

NO

TURN TO PAGE A-75, "APPLICATION INFORMATION: CITES EXPORT PERMIT"

## APPLICATION INFORMATION: AMERICAN GINSENG *(Panax quinquefolius)*

American ginseng *(Panax quinquefolius)* root is listed in CITES Appendix II, which regulates the import, export and reexport of this species. Special procedures have been developed for export and reexport of this species; they are outlined below. However, CITES does not regulate the harvest of American ginseng or its shipment in interstate commerce, although other federal and state laws may apply.

**Wild Ginseng**

The U.S. Management Authority may issue CITES export permits for wild American ginseng root only after it has been determined that the export will not be detrimental to the survival of the species in the wild in the specific state in which it was harvested. Upon purchase of wild ginseng root intended for export, the buyer must obtain a State Certificate of Legal Take, which verifies that the roots were legally harvested in a state approved for that harvest season. (For a list of state contacts, contact the U.S. Management Authority.) Exporters must collect these state certificates for each shipment and present them to a port inspector of the USDA Animal and Plant Health Inspection Service (APHIS), Division of Plant Protection and Quarantine (PPQ), upon export, together with the federal export permit and export report (an export report form will be attached to the original export permit sent by the U.S. Management Authority).

The PPQ inspector will sign and stamp the federal export permit and export report for validation ONLY when proper state documents are presented. Because the list of approved states and conditions for export may vary from year to year, exporters will need separate CITES export permits for wild ginseng collected during different harvest seasons. For example, if an exporter wishes to export wild root collected between October 1981 and October 1982, two export permits specific to the harvest season will be necessary, as well as the applicable state certificates.

**Cultivated Ginseng**

Valid CITES export documents are necessary for exporting artificially propagated or cultivated ginseng root. A Certificate of Artificially Propagated Plants is issued for cultivated ginseng. In addition, the exporter must maintain valid state documents certifying that the ginseng was artificially propagated. Copies of state documents, the export report, and the federal export certificate must be presented to a USDA/APHIS/PPQ inspector for validation upon export.

**Foreign Ginseng (Reexports)**

Reexport from the U.S. of foreign-grown American ginseng root requires a valid U.S. CITES Reexport Certificate. The U.S. exporter should obtain a CITES Reexport Certificate from the U.S. Management Authority. Reexporters must retain a copy of the foreign CITES export document showing legal import into the U.S. for presentation to a PPQ port inspector upon reexport. The PPQ inspector will validate the reexport documents only when assured that the ginseng was legally imported into the U.S. The procedure for reexport is similar to the procedure for cultivated or wild ginseng, except that a copy of valid foreign CITES export documents must be presented upon shipment.

**Permit Endorsement at the Port**

Export may be made only through ports designated by the USDA. For each shipment, exporters must present one copy of each State Certificate of Legal Take for the ginseng being shipped (or foreign export document for reexports) and two copies of the completed CITES export document for ginseng to a PPQ port inspector. Both copies of the permit and the export report must be completely filled out by the exporter in accordance with the instructions on the permit. The permits and export report must then be signed and stamped by the PPQ port inspector for validation. The completed export report (including the State Certificates of Legal Take) and one copy of the CITES export document are collected by the APHIS agent; the other CITES export document must accompany the shipment.

Does your activity involve export of wild or cultivated American ginseng?

—YES — TURN TO PAGE A-68, "APPLICATION INFORMATION: EXPORT OF WILD AND CULTIVATED AMERICAN GINSENG"

NO

TURN TO PAGE A-75, "APPLICATION INFORMATION: CITES REEXPORT CERTIFICATE"

## APPLICATION INFORMATION: EXPORT OF WILD AND CULTIVATED AMERICAN GINSENG

Although the same application form is used for both wild and cultivated ginseng, a separate application must be filed if the exporter is seeking both an export permit for wild roots and a Certificate for Artificially Propagated Plants for cultivated roots. The U.S. Management Authority coordinates the review of applications and makes the final determination whether a permit or certificate can be issued. The documents should be obtained by the person who will actually export the roots out of the U.S. A permit application for Export of American Ginseng or a Certificate for Artificially Propagated Plants consist of three parts:

1. FORM 3-200
   Form 3-200 requests general information about the applicant and his proposed activity. (A detailed explanation of each question may be found in Appendix B.)
2. SUPPLEMENTARY INFORMATION
   A series of questions (usually found on the back of Form 3-200) which requests specific information on your proposed activity.
3. APPLICATION FEE
   The application fee must be paid by certified check or money order, made payable to the U.S. Fish and Wildlife Service. The fee for this permit is $25.

**Be sure to answer all questions, provide all of the information required, and include a check or money order for the application fee.** An incomplete application will be returned to you for completion, resulting in considerable delay.

### WHERE TO OBTAIN APPLICATION FORMS

Office of Management Authority
U.S. Fish and Wildlife Service
4401 N. Fairfax Drive, Room 432
Arlington, Virginia 22203

### WHEN TO APPLY

Submit your completed application, accompanying documents, and a check or money order for $25 to the address listed below AT LEAST 45 days before you need the permit.

### WHERE TO MAIL THE COMPLETED APPLICATION

Office of Management Authority
U.S. Fish and Wildlife Service
4401 N. Fairfax Drive, Room 432
Arlington, Virginia 22203

TURN TO APPENDIX B, "SAMPLE APPLICATION: EXPORT OF WILD AND CULTIVATED AMERICAN GINSENG"
**AND**
TURN TO PAGE A-76, "OTHER CONSIDERATIONS"

## CITES APPENDIX III

### CITES APPENDIX III: ACTIVITIES REQUIRING A PERMIT

Appendix III includes species which do not fall in the Appendix I or II categories, but are regulated for conservation purposes by a Party country. The U.S. has not listed any species on Appendix III. International shipment of Appendix III species requires either an export permit from the country that listed the species or a reexport certificate or certificate of origin from any other country. No CITES import permit is necessary.

Is your proposed activity IMPORT from a foreign country?

YES

No U.S. import permit is necessary. Are you importing the specimen from the country that listed the species?

—YES —

You must obtain an export permit from the country of export. TURN TO PAGE A-70, "CITES FOREIGN DOCUMENTATION REQUIREMENTS: PARTY COUNTRIES"

NO

Was your specimen previously imported into the foreign country from which you will receive it?

—YES —

You must obtain a reexport certificate from the country of reexport. TURN TO PAGE A-70, "CITES FOREIGN DOCUMENTATION REQUIREMENTS: PARTY COUNTRIES"

— NO —

You must obtain a certificate of origin from the country of export. TURN TO PAGE A-71, "CITES FOREIGN DOCUMENTATION REQUIREMENTS: NON-PARTY COUNTRIES"

NO

Is your proposed activity REEXPORT from the U.S. of previously imported materials?

—YES —

For single shipments:
TURN TO PAGE A-72, "PERMIT INFORMATION: LETTER OF AUTHORIZATION"
For multiple shipments:
TURN TO PAGE A-75, "APPLICATION INFORMATION: CITES REEXPORT CERTIFICATE"

NO

Is your proposed activity EXPORT from the U.S.?

YES

To apply for a Certificate of Origin, complete the application for a CITES export permit. TURN TO PAGE A-75, "APPLICATION INFORMATION: CITES EXPORT PERMIT"

NO

For Appendix III species, if your proposed activity is something OTHER than import from a foreign country, reexport or export from the U.S., your activity is not regulated by CITES. TURN TO PAGE A-76, "OTHER CONSIDERATIONS"

## CITES FOREIGN DOCUMENTATION REQUIREMENTS

Does your activity involve a country that is a party to CITES?

— NO — TURN TO PAGE A-71, "CITES FOREIGN DOCUMENTATION REQUIREMENTS: NON-PARTY COUNTRIES"

YES

SEE BELOW: "CITES FOREIGN DOCUMENTATION REQUIREMENTS: PARTY COUNTRIES"

## CITES FOREIGN DOCUMENTATION REQUIREMENTS: PARTY COUNTRIES

CITES documents must be issued by the Party country's Management Authority as recognized by the Secretariat. The Parties have agreed to adopt a standardized format for CITES documents, often referred to as the Harmonized Permit (see Appendix B). This form, or a similar one, should be in use by all Party countries.

Shipments of listed species must be accompanied by an original CITES document. A copy may be used **only** if it has an original endorsement by a government official of or designated by, the Management Authority, which validates the document for use in place of the original.

The CITES document must contain the following information:

1. The title of the Convention, the name, address and country of the issuing Management Authority, the signature of the issuing official and the identifying stamp of the Management Authority.
2. A document control number and, in the case of an export permit, an effective date and expiration date showing the period which the permit may be used for export. Such a time period may not exceed six months from the date the permit was granted.
3. The name, address and country of the person to whom such document was issued, and the name, address and country of the receiving person.
4. The number of specimens being imported, the appendix in which the wildlife or plant is listed, a description of any mark affixed thereto, and the scientific and common names.
5. The sex of living wildlife, if practicable.
6. The country of origin of the wildlife or plant being imported and the permit number of the export permit issued by such country, or contain justification for omitting such information.

# CITES FOREIGN DOCUMENTATION

## CITES FOREIGN DOCUMENTATION: NON-PARTY COUNTRIES

Documents comparable to the CITES documents issued by Party countries are required from countries that are not party to CITES for shipments of listed wildlife, or their parts or products. The documents may be in the form of a permit, letter, or any other form, but must be issued by a competent issuing authority. A nature conservation authority is considered competent unless the country concerned has designated another governmental authority for that purpose and has informed the CITES Secretariat. To be acceptable as a "comparable document," a document must be an **original,** unless it has an original endorsement by a government official of, or designated by, the competent issuing authority, validating the document for use in place of the original. These documents must contain the same information required in a CITES document issued by a Party country (items 1–6 below) and certify the information requested for your activity in item 7, 8 or 9 below.

1. The title of the Convention, the name, address and country of the issuing Management Authority, the signature of the issuing official and the identifying stamp of the Management Authority.
2. A document control number and, in the case of an export permit, an effective date and expiration date until which the permit may be used for export. Such dates of use may not exceed six months from the date the permit was granted.
3. The name, address and country of the person to whom such document was issued, and the name, address and country of the receiving person.
4. The number of wildlife or plants being imported, the appendix in which the wildlife or plant is listed, a description of any mark affixed thereto, and the scientific and common names.
5. The sex of living wildlife, if practicable.
6. The country of origin of the wildlife or plant being imported and the permit number of the export permit issued by such country, or contain justification for such information.
7. FOR IMPORT ONLY:
   a. that the import will be for purposes which are not detrimental to the survival of the species involved;
   b. that the wildlife or plants are not to be used for primarily commercial purposes;
   c. that, in the case of live wildlife and plants, the proposed recipient is suitably equipped to house and care for them.
8. FOR EXPORT ONLY:
   a. that export will not be detrimental to the survival of the species;
   b. that the wildlife or plant was not obtained in contravention of the laws of the exporting country;
   c. that, in the case of live wildlife and plants, transport will be in a manner which will minimize the risk of injury, damage to health, or cruel treatment.
9. FOR REEXPORT ONLY:
   a. that the competent authority of the country of origin has issued an export document which substantially meets the requirements of the Convention; and
   b. that, in the case of live wildlife and plants, transport will be in a manner which will minimize the risk of injury, damage to health, or cruel treatment.

CAUTION: U.S. regulations also specify a format for the statement certifying that the activity will not be detrimental and is in compliance with the laws of the country, and that the transportation will meet CITES requirements. 50 CFR 23.14(b).

## PERMIT INFORMATION: LETTER OF AUTHORIZATION (LOA) EXPORT/REEXPORT

In an attempt to expedite the permit process for exporters who deal with multiple shipments of the same wildlife, the U.S. Management Authority has established the Letter of Authorization (LOA). The LOA is **not** a permit, but simply a procedure designed to provide export permits or reexport certificates for multiple shipments of eligible species quickly. With a valid LOA, the exporter can obtain the necessary original CITES documents at the FWS port office or district office, provided that the exporter satisfies other export criteria. Although use of the LOA is optional, it does eliminate the inconvenience of filing a separate application form for each shipment. An LOA is valid for two years. You may apply for an LOA to:

1. Export pelts, hides or products of the following species:
   a. Alaskan brown bear *(Ursus arctos)*
   b. Alaskan gray wolf *(Canis lupus)*
   c. American alligator *(Alligator mississippiensis)*
   d. Bobcat *(Lynx rufus)*
   e. Lynx *(Lynx canadensis)*
   f. River otter *(Lutra canadensis)*
2. Reexport live specimens, or products of other CITES Appendix II wildlife. This system does not include any species listed under the U.S. Endangered Species Act except: American alligator hides or hide products.*

Does your proposed activity meet the criteria described above?

—YES — TURN TO PAGE A-73, "APPLICATION INFORMATION: LETTER OF AUTHORIZATION"

NO

TURN TO PAGE A-75, "APPLICATION INFORMATION: CITES EXPORT PERMIT, CITES REEXPORT CERTIFICATE"

*If you have not already read the sections in the ESA Special Rules which deal with these species, be sure to do so before applying for a permit.

"SPECIAL RULE—AMERICAN ALLIGATOR," PAGE A-36

## CITES APPENDIX II AND III

## APPLICATION INFORMATION: LETTER OF AUTHORIZATION

An application for a Letter of Authorization consists of three parts:

1. FORM 3-200
   Form 3-200 requests general information about you and your proposed activity. (A detailed explanation of each question may be found in Appendix B.)
2. SUPPLEMENTARY INFORMATION
   A series of questions (usually found on the back of Form 3-200) which requests specific information on your proposed activity.
3. APPLICATION FEE
   There is no fee for a Letter of Authorization. However, there is a fee of $25 for each permit or certificate issued under the LOA. The fee must be paid by certified check or money order, made payable to the U.S. Fish and Wildlife Service.

**Be sure to answer all questions, provide all of the information required, and include a check or money order for the application fee.** An incomplete application will be returned to you for completion, resulting in considerable delay.

### WHERE TO OBTAIN APPLICATION FORMS

Office of Management Authority
U.S. Fish and Wildlife Service
4401 N. Fairfax Drive, Room 432
Arlington, Virginia 22203

### WHEN TO APPLY

Submit your completed application, accompanying documents and a check or money order for $25 to the address listed below AT LEAST 30 days before you need the permit.

### WHERE TO MAIL THE COMPLETED APPLICATION

Office of Management Authority
U.S. Fish and Wildlife Service
4401 N. Fairfax Drive, Room 432
Arlington, Virginia 22203

TURN TO APPENDIX B, "SAMPLE APPLICATION: LETTER OF AUTHORIZATION"
**AND**
TURN TO PAGE A-76, "OTHER CONSIDERATIONS"

## APPLICATION INFORMATION

A permit application consists of three parts:

1. FORM 3-200
   Form 3-200 requests general information about you and your proposed activity. (A detailed explanation of each question may be found in Appendix B.)
2. SUPPLEMENTARY INFORMATION
   A series of questions (usually found on the back of Form 3-200) which requests specific information on your proposed activity.
3. APPLICATION FEE
   The application fee must be paid by certified check or money order, made payable to the U.S. Fish and Wildlife Service. The fee for this permit is $25.

**Be sure to answer all questions, provide all of the information required, and include a check or money order for the application fee.** An incomplete application will be returned to you for completion, resulting in considerable delay.

### WHERE TO OBTAIN APPLICATION FORMS

Office of Management Authority
U.S. Fish and Wildlife Service
4401 N. Fairfax Drive, Room 432
Arlington, Virginia 22203

### WHEN TO APPLY

Submit your completed application, accompanying documents, and a check or money order for $25 to the address listed below AT LEAST 30 days before you need the permit.

### WHERE TO MAIL THE COMPLETED APPLICATION

Office of Management Authority
U.S. Fish and Wildlife Service
4401 N. Fairfax Drive, Room 432
Arlington, Virginia 22203

TURN TO APPENDIX B, "SAMPLE APPLICATION: ENDANGERED/THREATENED SPECIES PERMIT"
**AND**
TURN TO PAGE A-76, "OTHER CONSIDERATIONS"

# CITES APPENDIX I, II, AND III

APPLICATION INFORMATION: CITES EXPORT PERMIT
CITES REEXPORT CERTIFICATE
PRE-CONVENTION CERTIFICATE
CAPTIVE-BRED CERTIFICATE

An application for the CITES permits and certificates listed above consists of three parts:

1. FORM 3-200
   Form 3-200 requests general information about you and your proposed activity. (A detailed explanation of each question may be found in Appendix B.)
2. SUPPLEMENTARY INFORMATION
   A series of questions (usually found on the back of Form 3-200) which request specific information on your proposed activity.
3. APPLICATION FEE
   The application fee must be paid by certified check or money order, made payable to the U.S. Fish and Wildlife Service. The fee for these permits is $25.

**Be sure to answer all questions, provide all of the information required, and include a check or money order for the application fee.** An incomplete application will be returned to you for completion, resulting in considerable delay.

## WHERE TO OBTAIN APPLICATION FORMS

Office of Management Authority
U.S. Fish and Wildlife Service
4401 N. Fairfax Drive, Room 432
Arlington, Virginia 22203

## WHEN TO APPLY

Submit your completed application, accompanying documents, and a check or money order for $25 to the address listed below AT LEAST 30 days before you need the permit.

## WHERE TO MAIL THE COMPLETED APPLICATION

Office of Management Authority
U.S. Fish and Wildlife Service
4401 N. Fairfax Drive, Room 432
Arlington, Virginia 22203

TURN TO APPENDIX B, "SAMPLE APPLICATION: CITES EXPORT PERMIT" OR "CITES HARMONIZED PERMIT"
**AND**
TURN TO PAGE A-76, "OTHER CONSIDERATIONS"

## OTHER CONSIDERATIONS

If you have followed the steps outlined in this chapter, you have completed the permit process under CITES. However, you must also fulfill the requirements of **each** law that applies to your species. Be sure to check each applicable section of this volume.



IF YOU HAVE CONSULTED ALL OF THE SECTIONS THAT PERTAIN TO YOUR SPECIES, TURN TO PAGE A-149, "GENERAL REQUIREMENTS: ANIMALS" **OR** PAGE A-167, "GENERAL REQUIREMENTS: PLANTS"

# MARINE MAMMAL PROTECTION ACT
## National Marine Fisheries Service
## U.S. Fish and Wildlife Service

## INTRODUCTION

The Marine Mammal Protection Act (MMPA) was enacted on December 21, 1972, to protect all species of whales, dolphins, seals, polar bears, walrus, manatees or sea cows, and sea otters. It is jointly administered by the National Marine Fisheries Service (NMFS) and the U.S. Fish and Wildlife Service (FWS). Eight marine mammal species are managed by the FWS (those species that are associated with land), and the NMFS has jurisdiction over all other marine mammals.

Species Managed by the U.S. Fish and Wildlife Service:

Amazonian manatee *(Trichechus inunguis)*
Dugong *(Dugong dugon)*
Marine otter *(Lutra felina)*
Polar bear *(Ursus maritimus)*
Sea otter *(Enhydra lutris)*
Walrus *(Odobenus rosmarus)*
West African manatee *(Trichechus senegalensis)*
West Indian manatee *(Trichechus manatus)*

The MMPA prohibits the taking of marine mammals and the importation of marine mammals into the United States, EXCEPT that:

1. Permits may be issued for the taking of marine mammals for purposes of scientific research, public display, or enhancing the mammals' survival or recovery. If the animal is to be killed for scientific research, the applicant must show that the research could not be carried out by non-lethal means. Only rarely will permits be issued for public display of animals that were taken when pregnant or immature, or taken in an inhumane manner. If the population of mammals is depleted, more stringent limitations apply.

2. Marine mammals may be taken incidentally in the course of commercial fishing operations. However, permits authorizing incidental take are required. There is no standard application form for incidental take permits. Contact the NMFS Office of Protected Species and Habitat Conservation for further information.

TURN TO PAGE A-78, "SPECIAL SITUATIONS AND EXEMPTIONS"

## SPECIAL SITUATIONS AND EXEMPTIONS

In some cases, exemptions may be claimed from the standard MMPA permit requirements if specific criteria are met. These exemptions include the activities listed in the box below. Turn to the first section which seems to apply to your situation. The information provided there will help you determine whether or not you qualify for that exemption, and what documentation is required, if any.

CAUTION: Some form of documentation is nearly always required for transactions involving a protected species, whether or not an exemption or special situation applies. If you cannot document the fact that your activity is exempt, and you have not obtained a permit, you cannot conduct an otherwise prohibited activity. In other words, you may not need an MMPA permit, but you must be able to prove that you don't.

To find out if any of the following exemptions or special situations apply to your proposed activity, TURN TO THE SECTIONS WHICH APPLY TO YOUR ACTIVITY:



THEN

IF NO EXEMPTIONS OR SPECIAL SITUATIONS APPLY, is your species also covered by other laws?

NO

TURN TO PAGE A-82, "ACTIVITIES REQUIRING A PERMIT"

YES

TURN TO PAGE A-5, "MULTIPLE LAWS"

## EXEMPTION: TAKING OF MARINE MAMMALS BY INDIAN, ALEUT OR ESKIMO

To qualify for this exemption to standard MMPA permit requirements, the following requirements must be met:

1. The taking of the marine mammal must be done for subsistence purposes, or for purposes of creating and selling authentic native articles of handicrafts and clothing; and
2. The taking must not be done in a wasteful manner.

Under this exemption, anyone taking a marine mammal or its parts must comply with the following restrictions. Specifically, no marine mammal may be sold or transferred to anyone other than an Alaskan native [as defined in the Alaska Native Claims Settlement Act (see page A-13)], or delivered, carried, transported, or shipped in interstate or foreign commerce, unless it is either:

1. sent by an Alaskan native, either directly or through a registered agent, to a registered tannery for the purpose of processing, and returned directly or through a registered agent to the Alaskan native; or,
2. sold or transferred to a registered agent in Alaska for resale or transfer to an Alaskan native; or,
3. an edible portion and is sold in an Alaskan native village or town; or
4. an authentic native handicraft (with no mass production involved) made by an Alaskan native.

Does your proposed activity meet the criteria described above?

—YES —

If you can document the exempt status of your specimen, you are exempt from MMPA requirements. HOWEVER, you must either qualify for an exemption under or meet the requirements of **each** of the other laws that protects your species. TURN TO PAGE A-5, "MULTIPLE LAWS" **AND** PAGE A-86 "OTHER CONSIDERATIONS"

NO

To find out if any **other** exemptions or special situations apply, TURN TO PAGE A-78, "SPECIAL SITUATIONS AND EXEMPTIONS"

## EXEMPTION: PRE-ACT MARINE MAMMALS OR PARTS

Specimens taken on or before December 21, 1972, are exempt from MMPA restrictions and requirements. To establish Pre-Act status, it is necessary to file an affidavit with the agency responsible for the management of the species in question (either the FWS or the NMFS). However, marine mammals listed under the ESA cannot qualify as Pre-Act items (see page A-12), if they are to enter interstate or foreign commerce.

Does your specimen meet the criteria described above?

—YES — Is your species managed by the FWS?

YES — TURN TO APPENDIX B "SAMPLE APPLICATION: PRE-ACT AFFIDAVIT, REQUIREMENTS, FWS"

NO — TURN TO APPENDIX B "SAMPLE APPLICATION: PRE-ACT AFFIDAVIT, REQUIREMENTS, NMFS"

NO — To find out if any **other** exemptions or special situations apply, TURN TO PAGE A-78, "SPECIAL SITUATIONS AND EXEMPTIONS"

## EXEMPTION: INTERSTATE COMMERCE IN AUTHENTIC NATIVE HANDICRAFTS—REGISTERED AGENTS AND TANNERIES

Registered agents and tanneries are exempt from MMPÁ prohibitions against the buying and selling of marine mammals or their parts or products if 50 CFR 18.23 is complied with. Registration must be made with the agency with jurisdiction over the species in question. This exemption applies only to marine mammals and parts taken by Alaskan natives (as defined in the Alaska Native Claims Act, see page A-13).

Do you wish to buy and sell marine mammals as a registered agent or tanner?

—YES — Is your species managed by the FWS?

NO — TURN TO PAGE A-83, "APPLICATION INFORMATION: NMFS"

YES — TURN TO PAGE A-81, "APPLICATION INFORMATION: REGISTERED AGENT OR TANNERY, FWS"

NO — To find out if any **other** exemptions or special situations apply, TURN TO PAGE A-78, "SPECIAL SITUATIONS AND EXEMPTIONS"

## APPLICATION INFORMATION: REGISTERED AGENT OR TANNERY (FWS)

An application for registration as an agent or tanner consists of three parts:

1. FORM 3-200
   Form 3-200 requests general information about you and your proposed activity. (A detailed explanation of each question may be found in Appendix B.)
2. SUPPLEMENTARY INFORMATION
   A series of questions (usually found on the back of Form 3-200) which requests specific information on your proposed activity.
3. APPLICATION FEE
   The application fee must be paid by certified check or money order, made payable to the U.S. Fish and Wildlife Service. The fee for this permit is $25.

**Be sure to answer all questions, provide all of the information required, and include a check or money order for the application fee.** An incomplete application will be returned to you for completion, resulting in considerable delay.

### WHERE TO OBTAIN APPLICATION FORMS

Office of Management Authority
U.S. Fish and Wildlife Service
4401 N. Fairfax Drive, Room 432
Arlington, Virginia 22203

### WHEN TO APPLY

Submit your completed application, accompanying documents and a check or money order for $25 to the address listed below AT LEAST 30 days before you need the permit.

### WHERE TO MAIL THE COMPLETED APPLICATION

Office of Management Authority
U.S. Fish and Wildlife Service
4401 N. Fairfax Drive, Room 432
Arlington, Virginia 22203

TURN TO APPENDIX B, "APPLICATION INFORMATION: REGISTERED AGENT/TANNERY, FWS"
**AND**
TURN TO PAGE A-86, "OTHER CONSIDERATIONS"

## ACTIVITIES REQUIRING A PERMIT

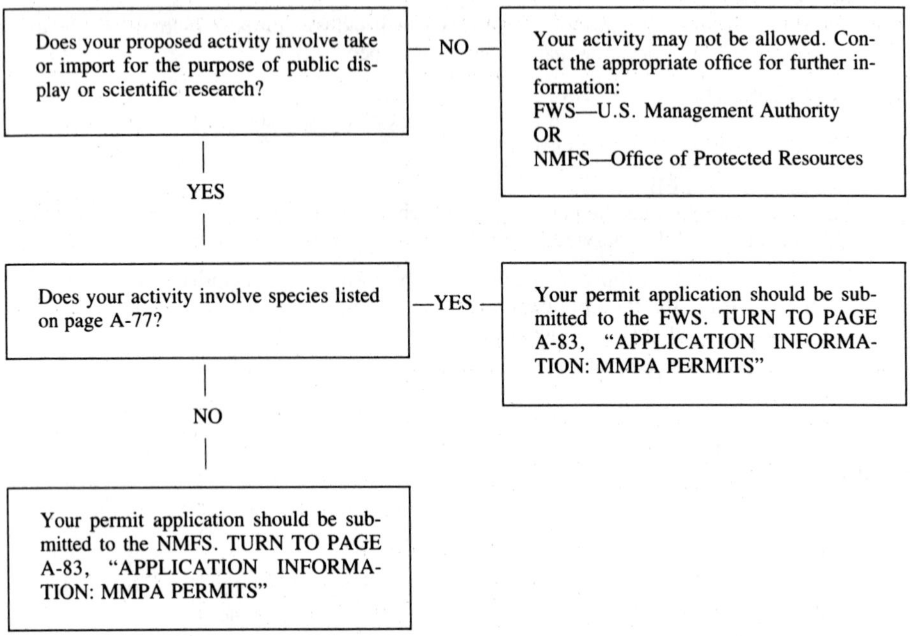

## APPLICATION INFORMATION: MMPA PERMITS

Permits are issued under the MMPA for purposes of public display, scientific research, incidental take in commercial fisheries and other purposes, including take and import. Permit application forms for public display and scientific research under the MMPA are available from the U.S. Management Authority for the eight species under its jurisdiction, and from the National Marine Fisheries Service for all other marine mammal species. The application should be submitted to the appropriate agency.

Both the FWS and the NMFS cooperate with APHIS in the issuance of public display permits, which can be issued only to APHIS licensees. In other words, FWS and NMFS issue permits to take from the wild, but standards for maintenance of the animals in captivity are established and enforced by the Department of Agriculture. Failure to comply with APHIS standards may be cause for revocation of a permit issued by the FWS and NMFS (see Animal Welfare Act, page A-125).

The law requires that notice of the receipt of an application be published in the *Federal Register* to provide the public with a 30 day comment period on each application. This informs the public that the Director of the appropriate agency will entertain considerations for a public hearing on each application. The Marine Mammal Commission and its Committee of Scientific Advisors reviews all applications for scientific research and public display permits within a 30 day period from application date. However, allow at least 90 days for the total processing time for these applications.

TURN TO PAGE A-84, "APPLICATION INFORMATION (FWS)"
**OR**
TURN TO PAGE A-85, "APPLICATION INFORMATION (NMFS)"

## APPLICATION INFORMATION: MARINE MAMMAL PROTECTION ACT (FWS)

An FWS application for a permit under the MMPA consists of three parts:

1. FORM 3-200
   Form 3-200 requests general information about you and your proposed activity. (A detailed explanation of each question may be found in Appendix B.)
2. SUPPLEMENTARY INFORMATION
   A series of questions (usually found on the back of Form 3-200) which requests specific information on your proposed activity.
3. APPLICATION FEE
   The application fee must be paid by certified check or money order, made payable to the U.S. Fish and Wildlife Service. The fee for this permit is $100.

**Be sure to answer all questions, provide all of the information required, and include a check or money order for the application fee.** An incomplete application will be returned to you for completion, resulting in considerable delay.

### WHERE TO OBTAIN APPLICATION FORMS

Office of Management Authority
U.S. Fish and Wildlife Service
4401 N. Fairfax Drive, Room 432
Arlington, Virginia 22203

### WHEN TO APPLY

Submit your completed application, accompanying documents and a check or money order for $100 to the address listed below AT LEAST 90 days before you need the permit.

### WHERE TO MAIL THE COMPLETED APPLICATION

Office of Management Authority
U.S. Fish and Wildlife Service
4401 N. Fairfax Drive, Room 432
Arlington, Virginia 22203

TURN TO APPENDIX B, "SAMPLE APPLICATION: MARINE MAMMAL PROTECTION ACT (FWS)"
**AND**
TURN TO PAGE A-86, "OTHER CONSIDERATIONS"

# APPLICATION INFORMATION: MARINE MAMMAL PROTECTION ACT (NMFS)

A permit application to the NMFS requires completing a questionnaire that is too long to be included in this volume. You should obtain the application form from:

NMFS Office of Protected Resources
1335 East-West Highway
Silver Spring, Maryland 20910

**Where to Send Applications**

Submit an original and two signed copies of the completed application to the National Marine Fisheries Service, Office of Protected Resources. If you have questions or need assistance, please contact the Office of Protected Resources.

**Give Complete Information**

NMFS endeavors to process all applications as quickly as possible. An application must be complete before it is forwarded to reviewers and before a Notice of Receipt is published in the *Federal Register*. Incomplete applications will not be processed; additional information will be requested or the application returned. Therefore, it is in your interest to furnish complete and specific information. Review time is shorter when the proposed methods, objectives, and potential adverse impacts are clearly addressed.

The sufficiency of a permit application will be determined by NMFS based on the requirements of the appropriate regulations. The information provided will be used to determine whether the application is complete and whether a permit should be issued. Reports required under previous permits must be up-to-date for a new application to be considered.

TURN TO PAGE A-86, "OTHER CONSIDERATIONS"

## OTHER CONSIDERATIONS

If you have followed the steps outlined in this chapter, you have completed the permit process under the MMPA. However, you must also fulfill the requirements of **each** law that applies to your species. Be sure to check each applicable section of this volume.



IF YOU HAVE CONSULTED ALL OF THE SECTIONS THAT PERTAIN TO YOUR SPECIES, TURN TO PAGE A-149, "GENERAL REQUIREMENTS: ANIMALS"

# MIGRATORY BIRD TREATY ACT
## U.S. Fish and Wildlife Service

## INTRODUCTION

The Migratory Bird Treaty Act (MBTA) implemented treaties between Great Britain (for Canada), Mexico, Japan, the USSR and the United States for the protection of migratory birds, birds in danger of extinction, game mammals, and their environment. 50 CFR 10.13 lists the protected bird species under the MBTA. 50 CFR 20.11(a) lists the families of migratory game birds that are protected. Current regulations make it unlawful to take, possess, buy or sell a listed migratory bird. Possession or transportation of specimens acquired before the effective date of protection (Pre-Act Specimens) is allowed; purchase or sale is prohibited. The Fish and Wildlife Service issues permits for banding and marking migratory birds, scientific collecting, depredation control, taxidermy, waterfowl sale and disposal, falconry, and special purposes. Import and export are allowed if the controlled birds are possessed under MBTA permits or are possessed by a public scientific institution, public education institution, museum, or zoological park.

TURN TO PAGE A-88, "SPECIAL SITUATIONS AND EXEMPTIONS"

## SPECIAL SITUATIONS AND EXEMPTIONS

In certain cases, exemptions may be claimed from the standard MBTA permit requirements if specific criteria are met. These exemptions include the activities listed in the box below. Turn to the first section which seems to apply to your situation. The information provided there will help you determine whether or not you qualify for that exemption, and what documentation is required, if any.

To determine if any exemptions or special situations apply to your proposed activity, refer to the sections listed below:



IF NO EXEMPTIONS OR SPECIAL SITUATIONS APPLY, is your species also covered by other laws?

NO

TURN TO PAGE A-92, "ACTIVITIES REQUIRING A PERMIT"

YES

TURN TO PAGE A-104, "OTHER CONSIDERATIONS" **AND** PAGE A-5, "MULTIPLE LAWS"

## EXEMPTION: PUBLIC SCIENTIFIC OR EDUCATIONAL INSTITUTIONS

This exemption is available to state game departments, municipal game farms or parks and public museums, public zoological parks, accredited institutional members of the American Association of Zoological Parks and Aquariums, and public scientific or educational institutions. Under this exemption, these institutions may acquire by gift or purchase, possess, transport, and by gift or sale dispose of lawfully acquired migratory birds or their progeny, parts, nests, or eggs without a permit. However, the specimen must be acquired from similar institutions, or the holder of a valid Possession Permit which also authorizes disposal, or from federal or state game authorities. Any person exercising a privilege granted under this exemption is required to keep accurate records of its operations showing the species and numbers of birds acquired, possessed, and disposed of; the names and addresses of the persons to whom the birds were donated or sold; and the dates of those transactions. The records must be retained for five years following the end of the calendar year covered by the records.

Does your proposed activity meet the criteria described above?

—YES — There are no further requirements under the MBTA. HOWEVER, you must either qualify for an exemption or meet the requirements under **each** of the laws that protects your species. TURN TO PAGE A-104, "OTHER CONSIDERATIONS"

NO

To find out if any **other** exemptions or special situations apply, TURN TO PAGE A-88, "SPECIAL SITUATIONS AND EXEMPTIONS"

## EXEMPTION: ACQUISITION OF CAPTIVE-REARED MIGRATORY WATERFOWL

This exemption allows the acquisition, possession, and transportation of properly marked and captive-reared migratory waterfowl of all species other than mallard ducks, alive or dead, or their eggs, **solely for private use,** and subject to the following conditions and restrictions: Birds may be lawfully acquired without permit only from the holder of a valid Waterfowl Sale and Disposal Permit, and provided:

1. Birds may be lawfully disposed of only after a Waterfowl Sale and Disposal Permit has been obtained. However, the permit is not required of food establishments or dealers in meat and game when selling to customers.
2. When disposing of captive-bred migratory waterfowl, the seller must furnish the buyer with a copy of Form 3-186, Notice of Waterfowl Sale or Transfer, and the buyer must keep the document on file for as long as he possesses the birds.
3. The offspring of birds hatched, reared and retained in captivity must be marked according to one of the approved methods listed below. The marking must remain in place at all times during possession, transportation, and storage until the raw carcasses of the birds are processed immediately before cooking, smoking, or canning.
   a. Removal of the hind toe from the right foot.
   b. Pinioning of a wing; specifically, the removal of the metacarpal bones of one wing, or a portion of the metacarpal bones, which renders the bird permanently incapable of flight.
   c. Banding of one metatarsus with a seamless metal band.
   d. Tattooing of a readily discernible number, letter, or combination on the web of one foot.

Do you plan to acquire captive-reared migratory waterfowl from a holder of a Waterfowl Sale and Disposal Permit?

—YES — No permit is required. TURN TO PAGE A-104, "OTHER CONSIDERATIONS"

NO

Do you plan to obtain captive-reared migratory waterfowl from another source?

—YES — Waterfowl Sale and Disposal Permit is required. TURN TO PAGE A-101, "APPLICATION INFORMATION: WATERFOWL SALE AND DISPOSAL"

NO

To find out if any **other** exemptions or special situations apply, TURN TO PAGE A-88, "SPECIAL SITUATIONS AND EXEMPTIONS"

## EXEMPTION: CAPTIVE-REARED MALLARD DUCKS

This exemption to the MBTA allows the acquisition, possession, sale, and exportation of captive-reared and properly marked mallard ducks, subject to the following conditions and restrictions:

1. Taking birds or eggs from the wild is prohibited.
2. Birds and their progeny must have been marked before reaching six weeks of age by one of the approved methods listed below:
   a. Removal of the hind toe from the right foot.
   b. Pinioning of a wing; specifically, the removal of the metacarpal bones of one wing, or a portion of the metacarpal bones, which renders the bird permanently incapable of flight.
   c. Banding of one metatarsus with a seamless metal band.
   d. Tattooing of a readily discernible number, letter, or combination on the web of one foot.

The marking must remain in place at all times during possession, transportation, and storage, until final processing before cooking, smoking, or canning. (Operators of game farms or shooting preserves under a state license, permit, or other authorization, may remove the marked foot or wing when either (a) the number of his state license, permit or authorization has first been legibly stamped in ink on the back of each carcass and on the container in which each carcass is maintained, or (b) each carcass is identified by a state band on a leg or wing according to the requirements of his state license, permit, or authorization.)

Do you plan to acquire, possess, sell, or export captive-reared mallard ducks according to the criteria described above?

—YES — No permit is required. TURN TO PAGE A-104, "OTHER CONSIDERATIONS"

NO

To find out if any **other** exemptions or special situations apply, TURN TO PAGE A-88, "SPECIAL SITUATIONS AND EXEMPTIONS"

## ACTIVITIES REQUIRING A PERMIT

Do you plan to engage in falconry?
—YES — TURN TO PAGE A-93, "PERMIT INFORMATION: FALCONRY." Also, consult state falconry requirements.

NO

Do you plan to perform taxidermy services involving species protected by the MBTA?
—YES — TURN TO PAGE A-98, "APPLICATION INFORMATION: TAXIDERMY"

NO

Do you plan to band or mark species protected by the MBTA?
—YES — TURN TO PAGE A-99, "APPLICATION INFORMATION: BANDING OR MARKING"

NO

Do you plan to collect, for scientific purposes, species protected by the MBTA?
—YES — TURN TO PAGE A-100, "APPLICATION INFORMATION: SCIENTIFIC COLLECTING"

NO

Do you plan to sell or dispose of captive bred waterfowl protected by the MBTA?
—YES — TURN TO PAGE A-101, "APPLICATION INFORMATION: WATERFOWL SALE AND DISPOSAL"

NO

Do you plan to capture, kill or harrass, for depredation control, species protected by the MBTA?
—YES — TURN TO PAGE A-102, "APPLICATION INFORMATION: DEPREDATION CONTROL"

NO

TURN TO PAGE A-103, "APPLICATION INFORMATION: SPECIAL PURPOSES"

## PERMIT INFORMATION: FALCONRY

A falconry permit is required before anyone may take, transport, sell, purchase, or possess raptors for falconry purposes. Falconry is defined as the sport of taking quarry by means of a trained raptor. A falconry permit will not be issued by the FWS unless there is a joint concurrence in that decision by the FWS and an appropriate official of one of the states listed below.

States Meeting Federal Falconry Standards

The following states meet or exceed the minimum federal standards for regulating the taking, possession, and transportation of raptors for the purpose of falconry. They are also participants in a joint federal/state permit system.

| | | | |
|---|---|---|---|
| Alabama | Iowa | Nebraska | South Carolina |
| Alaska | Kentucky | Nevada | South Dakota |
| Arizona | Louisiana | New Jersey | Tennessee |
| Arkansas | Maine | New Mexico | Texas |
| California | Massachusetts | New York | Utah |
| Colorado | Maryland | North Dakota | Virginia |
| Florida | Michigan | North Carolina | Washington |
| Georgia | Minnesota | Ohio | Wisconsin |
| Idaho | Mississippi | Oklahoma | Wyoming |
| Illinois | Missouri | Oregon | |
| Indiana | Montana | Pennsylvania | |

A person who has obtained a valid falconry permit issued by the FWS may take, possess and transport raptors for falconry in a state only in accordance with laws and regulations of that state. He may not violate any of the minimum federal standards, restrictions, conditions, or requirements, even if they have not been adopted by the state. However, states may adopt laws which are more restrictive than federal laws. States may have any number of classes of falconry permits, provided the standards are not less restrictive than the following federal standards:

Apprentice Class

1. The permitee must be at least 14 years old.
2. A sponsor, who is a holder of a General or Master Falconry Permit or equivalent class is required for the first two years in which an apprentice permit is held, regardless of the age of the permittee. A sponsor may not have more than three apprentices at any one time.
3. The permittee may not possess more than one raptor and may not obtain more than one raptor for replacement during any twelve month period.
4. The permittee shall possess only an American kestrel *(Falco sparverius),* a red-tailed hawk *(Buteo jamaicensis),* a red-shouldered hawk *(Buteo lineatus),* or, in Alaska, a goshawk *(Accipter gentilis).*

General Class

1. A permittee must be at least 18 years old.
2. A permittee must have at least two years' experience in the practice of falconry at the apprentice level or its equivalent.
3. A permittee may not possess more than two raptors and may not obtain more than two raptors for replacement during any twelve month period.
4. A permittee may not take, transport, or possess any golden eagle or any species listed as Threatened or Endangered under the Endangered Species Act.

Master Class

1. An applicant must have at least five years' experience in the practice of falconry at the general class level or its equivalent.
2. A permittee may not possess more than three raptors, and may not obtain more than two raptors for replacement birds during any twelve month period.
3. A permittee may not take, transport, or possess any species listed as Endangered under the Endangered Species Act.
4. A permittee may not take, transport or possess any golden eagle for falconry purposes unless authorized in writing by the FWS.
5. A permittee may not take, as part of his three-bird limitation, more than one raptor listed as Threatened under the Endangered Species Act, and then only in accordance with the regulations promulgated under the Endangered Species Act.

Examination

State regulations shall require that the applicant answer at least 80 percent of the questions on a supervised examination correctly. The examination will cover basic biology, care and handling of raptors, literature, laws, regulations or other appropriate subject matter.

Facilities and Equipment

State regulations must also provide for inspection of the applicant's raptor housing facilities and falconry equipment before a permit will be issued. The following standards for **facilities** must be met and the facilities must be kept at or above these standards at all times. The primary consideration for raptor housing facilities, whether indoors (mews) or outdoors (weathering area) is protection from the environment, predators, or undue disturbance. The applicant shall have the following facilities, except that, depending upon climatic conditions, the issuing authority may require only one of the facilities described below.

1. Indoor facilities (mews) shall be large enough to allow easy access for caring for the raptors housed in the facility. If more than one raptor is to be kept in the mews, the raptors shall be tethered or separated by partitions, and the area for each bird shall be large enough to allow the bird to fully extend its wings. There shall be at least one window, protected on the inside by vertical bars, with spaces narrower than the width of the bird's body, and a secure door that can be easily closed. The floor of the mews shall permit easy cleaning and shall be well drained. Adequate perches shall be provided.

2. Outdoor facilities (weathering area) shall be fenced and covered with netting or wire, or roofed to protect the birds from disturbance and attack by predators except that perches more than 6 and 1/2 feet high need not be covered or roofed. The enclosed area shall be large enough to insure the birds cannot strike the fence when flying from the perch. Protection from excessive sun, wind, and inclement weather shall be provided for each bird. Adequate perches shall be provided.

The following **equipment** shall be in the possession of the applicant before he can obtain a permit or license:

1. Jesses — At least one pair of Alymeri jesses or similar type, constructed of pliable, high-quality leather or suitable synthetic material, to be used when a raptor is flown free. (Traditional one-piece jesses may be used on raptors when not being flown.)
2. Leashes and swivels — At least one flexible, weather-resistant leash and one strong swivel of acceptable falconry design.
3. Bath container — At least one suitable container two to six inches deep and wider than the length of the raptor, for drinking and bathing for each raptor.
4. Outdoor perches — At least one weathering area perch of an acceptable design shall be provided for each raptor.
5. Weighing device — A reliable scale or balance suitable for weighing the raptor(s), and graduated in increments of not more than 1/2 ounce (15 grams) shall be provided.

Taking Restrictions

State laws or regulations shall provide the following restrictions on the taking of raptors from the wild:

1. Young birds not yet capable of flight (eyasses) may only be taken by a General or Master Falconer during the period specified by the state, and no more than two eyasses may be taken by the same permittee during the specified period.
2. First-year (passage) birds may be taken only during the period specified by the state.

3. In no case shall the total of all periods of taking of eyasses or passage birds exceed 180 days during a calendar year, except that a marked raptor may be retrapped at any time.
4. Only American kestrels *(Falco sparverius)* and great-horned owls *(Bubo virginianus)* may be taken when over one year old, except that any raptor other than Endangered or Threatened species taken under a depredation (or special purpose) permit may be used for falconry by General and Master falconers.

Other Restrictions

State Laws or regulations must provide the following restrictions or conditions:

1. A person who possesses a lawfully acquired raptor before the enactment of these regulations and who fails to meet the permit requirements shall be allowed to retain the raptors. All such birds shall be identified with markers supplied by the FWS, and may not be replaced if death, loss, release, or escape occurs.
2. A person who possesses, before the enactment of these regulations, raptors in excess of the number allowed under his class permit, shall be allowed to retain the extra raptors. All such birds shall be identified with markers supplied by the FWS, and no replacement can occur, nor may an additional raptor be obtained, until the number in possession is at least one less than the total number authorized by the class of permit held by the permittee.
3. A falconry permit holder shall obtain written authorization from the appropriate state wildlife department before any species not indigenous to that state is intentionally released to the wild, at which time the marker from the released bird shall be removed and surrendered to the state wildlife department. The marker from an intentionally released bird which is indigenous to that state shall also be removed and surrendered to the state wildlife department. A standard federal bird band shall be attached to such bird by the state or FWS authorized federal bird bander whenever possible.
4. A person may care for the birds of a permittee only if the caretaker is authorized to possess raptors and only if the raptor is accompanied at all times by a properly completed Form 3-186A (Migratory Bird Acquisition/Disposition Report) designating the permittee as the possessor of record. The Report must be accompanied by a signed, dated Statement from the permittee authorizing the temporary possession.
5. Feathers that are molted or those feathers from birds held in captivity that die, may be retained and exchanged by permittees only for imping purposes.

NOTE: FWS also issues raptor propagation permits under 50 CFR 21.30.

TURN TO PAGE A-97, "APPLICATION INFORMATION: FALCONRY"

## APPLICATION INFORMATION: FALCONRY

A permit application for Falconry consists of three parts:

1. FORM 3-200
   Form 3-200 requests general information about you and your proposed activity. (A detailed explanation of each question may be found in Appendix B.)
2. SUPPLEMENTARY INFORMATION
   A series of questions (usually found on the back of Form 3-200) which requests specific information on your proposed activity.
3. APPLICATION FEE
   The application fee must be paid by certified check or money order, made payable to the U.S. Fish and Wildlife Service. The fee for this permit is $25.

**Be sure to answer all questions and provide all of the information required.** An incomplete application will be returned to you for completion, resulting in considerable delay.

### WHERE TO OBTAIN AND SUBMIT APPLICATION FORMS

The FWS Special Agent in Charge in your area or the Assistant Regional Director, Law Enforcement, for the FWS District in which you live. See 50 CFR 10.22.

### WHEN TO APPLY

Submit your completed application and accompanying documents to the address listed AT LEAST 30 days before you need the permit.

### WHERE TO MAIL THE COMPLETED APPLICATION

Mail your completed application to the FWS Special Agent in Charge in your area or the Assistant Regional Director, Law Enforcement, for the FWS District in which you live. See 50 CFR 10.22.

TURN TO PAGE A-104, "OTHER CONSIDERATIONS"

## APPLICATION INFORMATION: TAXIDERMY

A permit application for Taxidermy consists of three parts:

1. FORM 3-200
   Form 3-200 requests general information about you and your proposed activity. (A detailed explanation of each question may be found in Appendix B.)
2. SUPPLEMENTARY INFORMATION
   A series of questions (usually found on the back of Form 3-200) which requests specific information on your proposed activity.
3. APPLICATION FEE
   The charge for a permit is $25.

**Be sure to answer all questions and provide all of the information required.** An incomplete application will be returned to you for completion, resulting in considerable delay.

### WHERE TO OBTAIN AND SUBMIT APPLICATION FORMS

The FWS Special Agent in Charge in your area or the Assistant Regional Director, Law Enforcement, for the FWS District in which you live. See 50 CFR 10.22.

### WHEN TO APPLY

Submit your completed application and accompanying documents to the address listed AT LEAST 30 days before you need the permit.

### WHERE TO MAIL THE COMPLETED APPLICATION

Mail your completed application to the FWS Special Agent in Charge in your area or the Assistant Regional Director, Law Enforcement, for the FWS District in which you live. See 50 CFR 10.22.

TURN TO APPENDIX B, "APPLICATION REQUIREMENTS: TAXIDERMY"
**AND**
TURN TO PAGE A-104, "OTHER CONSIDERATIONS"

## APPLICATION INFORMATION: BANDING OR MARKING

A permit application for banding or marking consists of three parts:

1. FORM 3-200
   Form 3-200 requests general information about you and your proposed activity. (A detailed explanation of each question may be found in Appendix B.)
2. SUPPLEMENTARY INFORMATION
   A series of questions (usually found on the back of Form 3-200) which requests specific information on your proposed activity.
3. APPLICATION FEE
   There is no charge for this permit.

**Be sure to answer all questions and provide all of the information required.** An incomplete application will be returned to you for completion, resulting in considerable delay.

### WHERE TO OBTAIN APPLICATION FORMS

Bird Banding Laboratory
Office of Migratory Bird Management
U.S. Fish & Wildlife Service
Laurel, Maryland 20708

### WHEN TO APPLY

Submit your completed application and accompanying documents to the address listed below AT LEAST 30 days before you need the permit.

### WHERE TO MAIL THE COMPLETED APPLICATION

Bird Banding Laboratory
Office of Migratory Bird Management
U.S. Fish & Wildlife Service
Laurel, Maryland 20708

TURN TO APPENDIX B, "APPLICATION REQUIREMENTS: BANDING OR MARKING"
**AND**
TURN TO PAGE A-104, "OTHER CONSIDERATIONS"

## APPLICATION INFORMATION: SCIENTIFIC COLLECTING

A permit application for Scientific Collecting consists of three parts:

1. FORM 3-200
   Form 3-200 requests general information about you and your proposed activity. (A detailed explanation of each question may be found in Appendix B.)
2. SUPPLEMENTARY INFORMATION
   A series of questions (usually found on the back of Form 3-200) which requests specific information on your proposed activity.
3. APPLICATION FEE
   There is a $25 charge for this permit.

**Be sure to answer all questions and provide all of the information required.** An incomplete application will be returned to you for completion, resulting in considerable delay.

### WHERE TO OBTAIN APPLICATION FORMS

The FWS Special Agent in Charge in your area or the Assistant Regional Director, Law Enforcement, for the FWS District in which you live. See 50 CFR 10.22.

### WHEN TO APPLY

Submit your completed application and accompanying documents to the address listed AT LEAST 30 days before you need the permit.

### WHERE TO MAIL THE COMPLETED APPLICATION

Mail your completed application to the FWS Special Agent in Charge in your area or the Assistant Regional Director, Law Enforcement, for the FWS District in which you live. See 50 CFR 10.22.

TURN TO APPENDIX B, "APPLICATION REQUIREMENTS: SCIENTIFIC COLLECTING"
**AND**
TURN TO PAGE A-104, "OTHER CONSIDERATIONS"

## APPLICATION INFORMATION: WATERFOWL SALE AND DISPOSAL

An application for Waterfowl Sale and Disposal consists of three parts:

1. FORM 3-200
   Form 3-200 requests general information about you and your proposed activity. (A detailed explanation of each question may be found in Appendix B.)
2. SUPPLEMENTARY INFORMATION
   A series of questions (usually found on the back of Form 3-200) which requests specific information on your proposed activity.
3. APPLICATION FEE
   There is a $25 charge for this permit.

**Be sure to answer all questions and provide all of the information required.** An incomplete application will be returned to you for completion, resulting in considerable delay.

### WHERE TO OBTAIN APPLICATION FORMS

The FWS Special Agent in Charge in your area or the Assistant Regional Director, Law Enforcement, for the FWS District in which you live. See 50 CFR 10.22.

### WHEN TO APPLY

Submit your completed application and accompanying documents to the address listed AT LEAST 30 days before you need the permit.

### WHERE TO MAIL THE COMPLETED APPLICATION

Mail your completed application to the FWS Special Agent in Charge in your area or the Assistant Regional Director, Law Enforcement, for the FWS District in which you live. See 50 CFR 10.22.

TURN TO APPENDIX B, "APPLICATION REQUIREMENTS: WATERFOWL SALE AND DISPOSAL"
**AND**
TURN TO PAGE A-104, "OTHER CONSIDERATIONS"

## APPLICATION INFORMATION: DEPREDATION CONTROL

A permit application for Depredation Control consists of three parts:

1. FORM 3-200
   Form 3-200 requests general information about you and your proposed activity. (A detailed explanation of each question may be found in Appendix B.)
2. SUPPLEMENTARY INFORMATION
   A series of questions (usually found on the back of Form 3-200) which requests specific information on your proposed activity.
3. APPLICATION FEE
   There is a $25 charge for this permit.

**Be sure to answer all questions and provide all of the information required.** An incomplete application will be returned to you for completion, resulting in considerable delay.

### WHERE TO OBTAIN APPLICATION FORMS

The FWS Special Agent in Charge in your area or the Assistant Regional Director, Law Enforcement, for the FWS District in which you live. See 50 CFR 10.22.

### WHEN TO APPLY

Submit your completed application and accompanying documents to the address listed AT LEAST 30 days before you need the permit.

### WHERE TO MAIL THE COMPLETED APPLICATION

Mail your completed application to the FWS Special Agent in Charge in your area or the Assistant Regional Director, Law Enforcement, for the FWS District in which you live. See 50 CFR 10.22.

TURN TO APPENDIX B, "APPLICATION REQUIREMENTS: DEPREDATION CONTROL"
**AND**
TURN TO PAGE A-104, "OTHER CONSIDERATIONS"

## APPLICATION INFORMATION: SPECIAL PURPOSES

A permit application for Special Purposes consists of three parts:

1. FORM 3-200
   Form 3-200 requests general information about you and your proposed activity. (A detailed explanation of each question may be found in Appendix B.)
2. SUPPLEMENTARY INFORMATION
   A series of questions (usually found on the back of Form 3-200) which requests specific information on your proposed activity.
3. APPLICATION FEE
   There is a $25 charge for this permit.

**Be sure to answer all questions and provide all of the information required.** An incomplete application will be returned to you for completion, resulting in considerable delay.

### WHERE TO OBTAIN APPLICATION FORMS

The FWS Special Agent in Charge in your area or the Assistant Regional Director, Law Enforcement, for the FWS District in which you live. See 50 CFR 10.22.

### WHEN TO APPLY

Submit your completed application and accompanying documents to the address listed AT LEAST 30 days before you need the permit.

### WHERE TO MAIL THE COMPLETED APPLICATION

Mail your completed application to the FWS Special Agent in Charge in your area or the Assistant Regional Director, Law Enforcement, for the FWS District in which you live. See 50 CFR 10.22.

TURN TO APPENDIX B, "APPLICATION REQUIREMENTS: SPECIAL PURPOSES"
**AND**
TURN TO PAGE A-104, "OTHER CONSIDERATIONS"

## OTHER CONSIDERATIONS

If you have followed the steps outlined in this chapter, you have completed the permit process under the MBTA. However, you must also fulfill the requirements of **each** law that applies to your species. Be sure to check each applicable section of this volume.



IF YOU HAVE CONSULTED ALL OF THE SECTIONS THAT PERTAIN TO YOUR SPECIES, TURN TO PAGE A-149, "GENERAL REQUIREMENTS: ANIMALS"

## BALD EAGLE PROTECTION ACT
## U.S. Fish and Wildlife Service

## INTRODUCTION

The Bald Eagle Protection Act, enacted on June 8, 1940, prohibits the taking, possession, or transportation of bald eagles *(Haliaeetus leucocephalus)* AND golden eagles *(Aquila chrysaetos)*, or their parts, nests, or eggs, without a permit. It also prohibits the sale, exportation, or importation of bald and golden eagles, their parts, nests, or eggs; and the FWS cannot issue permits to authorize these activities. Permits are available from the FWS for scientific or exhibition purposes, Indian religious purposes, depredation control, falconry (with golden eagles only), and the removal of golden eagle nests for resource development or recovery operations. 50 CFR 22.21–22.25.

| | | |
|---|---|---|
| Was your bald eagle acquired before June 8, 1940, or your golden eagle acquired before October 24, 1962? | —YES— | TURN TO PAGE A-106, "SPECIAL SITUATION: PRE-ACT SPECIMENS" |

NO

TURN TO PAGE A-111, "OTHER CONSIDERATIONS" **AND** PAGE A-5, "MULTIPLE LAWS"

## SPECIAL SITUATION: PRE-ACT SPECIMENS

Possession or transportation of specimens acquired before the date the Bald Eagle Protection Act applied to them (June 8, 1940, for bald eagles and October 24, 1962, for golden eagles) is allowed; purchase, sale, import, or export of Pre-Act specimens is prohibited. No exemption from any statute or regulation applies to the offspring of Pre-Act birds.

Does your proposed activity meet the criteria described above?

—YES— If you can document the exempt status of your specimen, you are exempt from BEPA requirements. HOWEVER, you must either qualify for an exemption or meet the requirements under **each** of the laws that protects your species. TURN TO PAGE A-111, "OTHER CONSIDERATIONS"

NO

TURN TO PAGE A-111, "OTHER CONSIDERATIONS" **AND** PAGE A-5, "MULTIPLE LAWS"

## ACTIVITIES REQUIRING A PERMIT

Are you a public educational or scientific institution planning to exhibit bald or golden eagles, or to use them for scientific purposes?

—YES — TURN TO PAGE A-108, "APPLICATION INFORMATION: SCIENTIFIC RESEARCH OR EXHIBITION"

NO

Are you an American Indian planning to engage in religious activities involving the bald or golden eagle, or its parts or products?

—YES — TURN TO PAGE A-109, "APPLICATION INFORMATION: INDIAN RELIGIOUS PURPOSES"

NO

Do you plan to take bald or golden eagles for depredation control?

—YES — TURN TO PAGE A-110, "APPLICATION INFORMATION: DEPREDATION CONTROL"

NO

Do you plan to engage in falconry activities with golden eagles?

—YES — TURN TO PAGE A-110, "APPLICATION INFORMATION: FALCONRY"

NO

Your activity is not allowed. Contact the FWS Special Agent in Charge in your area.

## APPLICATION INFORMATION: SCIENTIFIC RESEARCH OR EXHIBITION

A permit application for Scientific Research or Exhibition consists of three parts:

1. FORM 3-200
   Form 3-200 requests general information about you and your proposed activity. (A detailed explanation of each question may be found in Appendix B.)
2. SUPPLEMENTARY INFORMATION
   A series of questions (usually found on the back of Form 3-200) which requests specific information on your proposed activity.
3. APPLICATION FEE
   There is no charge for a permit under the BEPA.

**Be sure to answer all questions, provide all of the information required, and include a check or money order for the application fee.** An incomplete application will be returned to you for completion, resulting in considerable delay.

### WHERE TO OBTAIN APPLICATION FORMS

The FWS Law Enforcement Special Agent in Charge in your area or the Assistant Regional Director, Law Enforcement, for the FWS District in which you live. See 50 CFR 10.22.

### WHEN TO APPLY

Submit your completed application and accompanying documents to the address listed AT LEAST 30 days before you need the permit.

### WHERE TO MAIL THE COMPLETED APPLICATION

Mail your completed application to the FWS Special Agent in Charge in your area or the Assistant Regional Director, Law Enforcement, for the FWS District in which you live. See 50 CFR 10.22.

TURN TO APPENDIX B, "APPLICATION REQUIREMENTS: SCIENTIFIC RESEARCH OR EXHIBITION"
**AND**
TURN TO PAGE A-111, "OTHER CONSIDERATIONS"

## APPLICATION INFORMATION: INDIAN RELIGIOUS PURPOSES

A permit application for Indian Religious Purposes consists of three parts.

1. FORM 3-200
   Form 3-200 requests general information about you and your proposed activity. (A detailed explanation of each question may be found in Appendix B.)
2. SUPPLEMENTARY INFORMATION
   A series of questions (usually found on the back of Form 3-200) which requests specific information on your proposed activity.
3. APPLICATION FEE
   There is no charge for a permit under the BEPA.

**Be sure to answer all questions and provide all of the information required.** An incomplete application will be returned to you for completion, resulting in considerable delay.

### WHERE TO OBTAIN APPLICATION FORMS

The FWS Law Enforcement Special Agent in Charge in your area or the Assistant Regional Director, Law Enforcement, for the FWS District in which you live. See 50 CFR 10.22.

### WHEN TO APPLY

Submit your completed application and accompanying documents to the address listed AT LEAST 30 days before you need the permit.

### WHERE TO MAIL THE COMPLETED APPLICATION

Mail your completed application to the FWS Special Agent in Charge in your area or the Assistant Regional Director, Law Enforcement, for the FWS District in which you live. See 50 CFR 10.22.

TURN TO APPENDIX B, "APPLICATION REQUIREMENTS: INDIAN RELIGIOUS PURPOSES"
**AND**
TURN TO PAGE A-111, "OTHER CONSIDERATIONS"

## APPLICATION INFORMATION: DEPREDATION CONTROL

A permit application for Depredation Control consists of three parts:

1. FORM 3-200
   Form 3-200 requests general information about you and your proposed activity. (A detailed explanation of each question may be found in Appendix B.)
2. SUPPLEMENTARY INFORMATION
   A series of questions (usually found on the back of Form 3-200) which requests specific information on your proposed activity.
3. APPLICATION FEE
   There is no charge for a permit under the BEPA.

**Be sure to answer all questions and provide all of the information required.** An incomplete application will be returned to you for completion, resulting in considerable delay.

### WHERE TO OBTAIN AND SUBMIT APPLICATION FORMS

The FWS Law Enforcement Special Agent in Charge in your area or the Assistant Regional Director, Law Enforcement, for the FWS District in which you live. See 50 CFR 10.22. Submit your completed application and accompanying documents to the address listed AT LEAST 30 days before you need the permit.

## APPLICATION INFORMATION: FALCONRY

A permit application for Falconry consists of three parts:

1. FORM 3-200
   Form 3-200 requests general information about you and your proposed activity. (A detailed explanation of each question may be found in Appendix B.)
2. SUPPLEMENTARY INFORMATION
   A series of questions (usually found on the back of Form 3-200) which requests specific information on your proposed activity.
3. APPLICATION FEE
   There is no charge for a permit under the BEPA.

**Be sure to answer all questions and provide all of the information required.** An incomplete application will be returned to you for completion, resulting in considerable delay.

### WHERE TO OBTAIN AND SUBMIT APPLICATION FORMS

The FWS Law Enforcement Special Agent in Charge in your area or the Assistant Regional Director, Law Enforcement, for the FWS District in which you live. See 50 CFR 10.22. Submit your completed application and accompanying documents to the address listed AT LEAST 30 days before you need the permit.

TURN TO APPENDIX B, "APPLICATION REQUIREMENTS: DEPREDATION CONTROL" AND "APPLICATION REQUIREMENTS: FALCONRY"
**AND**
TURN TO PAGE A-111, "OTHER CONSIDERATIONS"

## OTHER CONSIDERATIONS

If you have followed the steps outlined in this chapter, you have completed the permit process under the BEPA. However, you must also fulfill the requirements of any other laws that apply to your species. Be sure to check each applicable section of this volume.



IF YOU HAVE CONSULTED ALL OF THE SECTIONS THAT PERTAIN TO YOUR SPECIES, TURN TO PAGE A-149, "GENERAL REQUIREMENTS: ANIMALS"

This page intentionally left blank.

# FUR SEAL ACT
## National Marine Fisheries Service

## INTRODUCTION

The Fur Seal Act (FSA) is administered by the National Marine Fisheries Service (NMFS), a department of the National Oceanic and Atmospheric Administration. The FSA prohibits the taking of northern fur seals *(Callorhinus ursinus)* in the North Pacific Ocean or on lands or waters under the jurisdiction of the U.S. It also prohibits the sale, importation, transportation, or possession of northern fur seals or their parts. However, the prohibition against taking fur seals does not apply to Indians, Aleuts, and Eskimos who live on the coasts of the North Pacific Ocean, although certain restrictions and requirements must be observed. The northern fur seal is specifically exempted from the Marine Mammal Protection Act, but animals used for public display or to be maintained alive for research purposes are subject to the requirements of the Animal Welfare Act.

Does your activity involve the northern fur seal (*Callorhinus ursinus*)?

— NO — The Fur Seal Act does not apply to your species. Determine which laws control your species, **AND** TURN TO PAGE A-116 "OTHER CONSIDERATIONS"

YES

SEE BELOW, "SPECIAL SITUATIONS AND EXEMPTIONS"

## SPECIAL SITUATIONS AND EXEMPTIONS

In certain cases, exemptions may be claimed from the standard FSA permit requirements if specific criteria are met. These exemptions include the activities listed in the box below. Turn to the first section which seems to apply to your situation. The information provided there will help you determine whether or not you qualify for that exemption, and what documentation is required, if any.

CAUTION: Some form of documentation is nearly always required for any transaction involving wildlife, whether or not an exemption or special situation applies. If you cannot document the fact that your activity is exempt, and you have not obtained a permit, you are in violation of the law. In other words, you may not need an FSA permit, but you must be able to prove that you don't.

To determine if any exemptions apply to your proposed activity, or if a permit is required, refer to the sections listed below:

## SPECIAL SITUATION: SCIENTIFIC RESEARCH

Permission to conduct research involving northern fur seals must be obtained from:

National Marine Mammal Laboratory
National Marine Fisheries Service
7600 Sand Point Way, NE
Building 32
Seattle, WA 98115

or

NMFS Office of Protected Resources
1335 East-West Highway
Silver Spring, Maryland 20910

In addition, research conducted on fur seals held in captivity is subject to the requirements of the Animal Welfare Act.

TURN TO PAGE A-116, "OTHER CONSIDERATIONS"

## EXEMPTION: TAKING BY INDIANS, ALEUTS, ESKIMOS

The taking of northern fur seals by Indians, Aleuts, and Eskimos living on the coast of the North Pacific Ocean is permitted, provided that the following conditions are met:

1. The fur seals must be taken only from canoes not transported by or used in connection with other vessels, and propelled entirely by oars, paddles, or sails, and manned by not more than five persons.
2. The skins must be officially marked and certified by a person authorized by the Secretary of the Interior before they are disposed of.
3. The exemption does not apply to Indians, Aleuts, and Eskimos who are employed by any person for the purpose of taking fur seals, or who are under contract to deliver the skins to any person.
4. For activities on the Pribilof Islands, NMFS prescribes special limitations in 50 CFR 215.31–215.34.

Does your proposed activity meet the criteria described above?

—YES — There are no further requirements under the FSA. HOWEVER, you must either qualify for an exemption or meet the requirements of **each** of the laws that protects your species. TURN TO PAGE A-116, "OTHER CONSIDERATIONS"

NO

TURN TO PAGE A-115, "ACTIVITIES REQUIRING A PERMIT"

## OTHER ACTIVITIES REQUIRING A PERMIT

| | | |
|---|---|---|
| Do you plan to take, transport or possess northern fur seals for the purpose of public display? | —YES — | SEE BELOW, "APPLICATION INFORMATION: PUBLIC DISPLAY" |
| NO | | |
| Your activities are not allowed. Contact the NMFS for further information. | | |

## APPLICATION INFORMATION: PUBLIC DISPLAY

The NMFS issues permits which authorize the possession and transportation of northern fur seals for public display. The actual taking of the fur seals is done by NMFS personnel. The animal is then made available to a permit holder through that agency. A $600 fee is charged per animal for the services provided by the NMFS in capturing, caring for and holding fur seals taken for public display. (Note: the $600 fee does not include transportation of the animal from the Pribilof Islands to its final destination.) To obtain a northern fur seal for public display purposes, first contact the Pribilof program manager to arrange for the capture of the fur seal. Once you have the approval of the Pribilof program manager, you must then file a permit application on the same form used for a Marine Mammal Protection Act public display permit.

TURN TO PAGE A-85, "APPLICATION INFORMATION: MARINE MAMMAL PROTECTION ACT (NMFS)"

## OTHER CONSIDERATIONS

If you have followed the steps outlined in this chapter, you have completed the permit process under the FSA. However, you must also fulfill the requirements of **each** law that applies to your species.



TURN TO PAGE A-125, "ANIMAL WELFARE ACT"
**AND**
TURN TO PAGE A-149, "GENERAL REQUIREMENTS: ANIMALS"

# FEATHER IMPORT QUOTA—TARIFF CLASSIFICATION ACT
## U.S. Fish and Wildlife Service

## INTRODUCTION

The Tariff Classification Act generally prohibits the import of feathers into the U.S. However, the Feather Import Quota sets limits on the importation of skins and feathers of the six bird species listed below. (The quotas do not apply to live birds.)

Blue-eared pheasant *(Crossoptilon auritum)*
Golden pheasant *(Chrysolophus pictus)*
Lady Amherst pheasant *(Chrysolophus amherstiae)*
Mandarin duck *(Aix galericulata)*
Reeves pheasant *(Syrmaticus reevesii)*
Silver pheasant *(Lophura nycthemera)*

The annual quota currently stands at 1,000 mandarin duck skins, and a total aggregate of 45,000 pheasant skins of the species listed above. (Any part of a severed skin is considered a whole skin.) The annual quota is shared among all qualified applicants.

There are numerous exemptions from the Act's prohibitions and quota. These exemptions are listed in the diagram below.

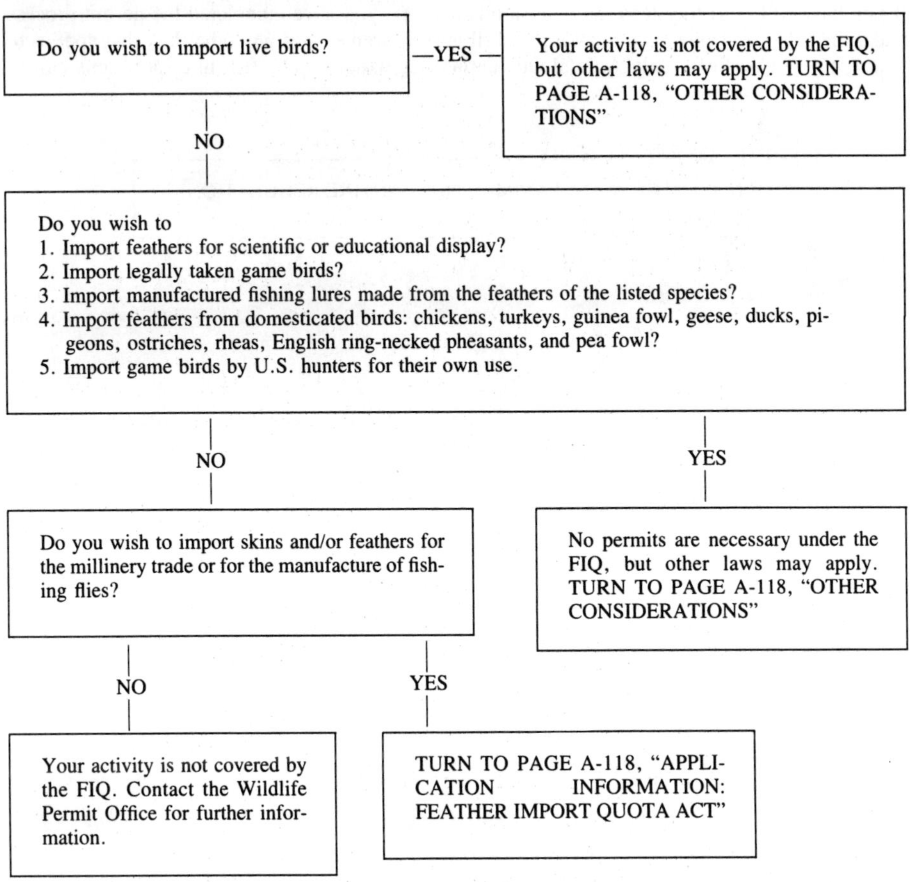

## APPLICATION INFORMATION: FEATHER IMPORT QUOTA

Feather quotas are divided among the qualified applicants twice each year. The first half of a calendar year is called the "allocation period." The second half is the "reallocation period." The reallocation period is designed to allow others to share in the quota for the portion of skins that were not imported during the allocation period. Applications to participate in the initial allocation of quotas must be postmarked during September of the year preceding the calendar year for which the import authorization is sought. Applications to participate in the reallocation of unused portions of quotas must be postmarked during July of the calendar year in which the unused portion of the quota becomes available.

TURN TO APPENDIX B, "SAMPLE APPLICATION: FEATHER IMPORT"
**AND**
SEE BELOW, "OTHER CONSIDERATIONS"

## OTHER CONSIDERATIONS

If you have followed the steps outlined in this chapter, you have completed the permit process under the FIQ. However, you must also fulfill the requirements of any other law that applies to your species. Currently, only Animal Quarantine Regulations apply (for live specimens only).

TURN TO PAGE A-137, "ANIMAL QUARANTINE REGULATIONS"

# LACEY ACT (INJURIOUS WILDLIFE PROVISIONS)
## U.S. Fish and Wildlife Service

## INTRODUCTION

The Injurious Wildlife provisions of the Lacey Act prohibit importation, transportation, or acquisition, without a permit, of certain animals (or their eggs) which have been determined to be injurious wildlife. The Wildlife Permit Office issues permits for importation of such injurious wildlife for zoological, education, medical, or scientific purposes.

## SPECIAL SITUATIONS AND EXEMPTIONS

In certain cases, exemptions may be claimed from the standard Injurious Wildlife permit requirements if specific criteria are met. These exemptions include the activities listed in the box below. Turn to the first section which seems to apply to your situation. The information provided there will help you determine whether or not you qualify for that exemption, and what documentation is required, if any.

CAUTION: Some form of documentation is nearly always required for any transaction involving a listed species, whether or not an exemption or special situation applies. If you cannot document the fact that your activity is exempt, and you have not obtained a permit, you cannot import or transport injurious wildlife. In other words, you may not need an Injurious Wildlife permit, but you must be able to prove that you don't.

To determine if any exemptions or special situations apply to your proposed activity, refer to the sections listed below:



THEN

IF NO EXEMPTIONS OR SPECIAL SITUATIONS APPLY, is your species covered by other laws?

YES

TURN TO PAGE A-123, "OTHER CONSIDERATIONS" **AND** PAGE A-5, MULTIPLE LAWS"

NO

TURN TO PAGE A-121, "ACTIVITIES REQUIRING A PERMIT"

## EXEMPTION: FAMILY SALMONIDAE

Injurious wildlife regulations restrict the importation of species of fish within the salmon family, including eggs. Import can be allowed, however, under certain conditions:

1. Processed salmon, or
2. Salmon landed in North America and brought into the U.S. for processing or sale, or
3. Salmon caught in the wild in North America under a sport or commercial fishing license, or
4. Salmon or salmon products originating outside North America and imported under fish pathology RAW certificates, as described below.

To qualify under this exemption, the shipment must have been processed by canning, pickling, smoking, or otherwise prepared in such a way as to kill all spores of the Protozoan *Myxosoma cerebralis,* the causative agent of "whirling disease," and the virus causing viral hemorrhagic septicema, also known as "Egtved disease." The shipment of raw fish or fish products must be accompanied by a certification to that effect, signed in the country of origin by a designated official qualified in fish pathology, approved by the Secretary of the Interior (50 CFR 16.13(b)), or in the U.S. by a qualified fish pathologist designated for this purpose by the Secretary of the Interior.

Does your proposed activity meet the criteria described above?

—YES— No further documentation is required under the Lacey Act Injurious Wildlife provisions. HOWEVER, you must either qualify for an exemption or meet the requirements of **each** of the laws that protect or control your species.

NO

In addition to the Lacey Act Injurious Wildlife provisions, is your species also protected by other laws?

—YES— TURN TO PAGE A-123, "OTHER CONSIDERATIONS" **AND** PAGE A-5, MULTIPLE LAWS"

NO

TURN TO PAGE A-121, "ACTIVITIES REQUIRING A PERMIT"

## EXEMPTION: REPTILES AND AMPHIBIANS

Almost all species of live reptiles, amphibians or their eggs may be imported, transported, and possessed in captivity, without a permit, for scientific, medical, educational, exhibition, or propagation purposes. (An exception is the brown tree snake, for which a permit is required. See 50 CFR 16.15(a).) However, no such live amphibians or reptiles, or any progeny or eggs thereof, may be released into the wild except when approved by the state wildlife conservation agency having jurisdiction over the area of release, or by persons having prior written permission for release from such agency.

Does your proposed activity meet the criteria described above?

—YES— No further documentation is required under the Injurious Wildlife provisions of the Lacey Act. HOWEVER, you must either qualify for an exemption or meet the requirements of each of the laws that protects or controls your species. TURN TO PAGE A-123, "OTHER CONSIDERATIONS"

NO

Is your species also controlled or protected by other laws?

—YES— TURN TO PAGE A-123, "OTHER CONSIDERATIONS" **AND** PAGE A-5, "MULTIPLE LAWS"

NO

SEE BELOW, "ACTIVITIES REQUIRING A PERMIT"

## ACTIVITIES REQUIRING A PERMIT

Do you wish to import, transport or acquire injurious wildlife for zoological, educational, medical or scientific purposes?

—YES— TURN TO PAGE A-122, "APPLICATION INFORMATION: INJURIOUS WILDLIFE"

NO

Your activity is not allowed. Contact the Wildlife Permit Office for further information.

## APPLICATION INFORMATION: INJURIOUS WILDLIFE

A permit application for Injurious Wildlife consists of three parts:

1. FORM 3-200
   Form 3-200 requests general information about you and your proposed activity. (A detailed explanation of each question may be found in Appendix B.)
2. SUPPLEMENTARY INFORMATION
   A series of questions (usually found on the back of Form 3-200) which requests specific information on your proposed activity.
3. APPLICATION FEE
   The application fee must be paid by certified check or money order, made payable to the U.S. Fish and Wildlife Service. The fee for this permit is $25.

**Be sure to answer all questions, provide all of the information required, and include a check or money order for the application fee.** An incomplete application will be returned to you for completion, resulting in considerable delay.

### WHERE TO OBTAIN APPLICATION FORMS

Federal Wildlife Permit Office
U.S. Fish and Wildlife Service
4401 N. Fairfax Drive, Room 432
Arlington, Virginia 22203

### WHEN TO APPLY

Submit your completed application, accompanying documents and a check or money order for $25 to the address listed below AT LEAST 30 days before you need the permit.

### WHERE TO MAIL THE COMPLETED APPLICATION

Federal Wildlife Permit Office
U.S. Fish and Wildlife Service
4401 N. Fairfax Drive, Room 432
Arlington, Virginia 22203

TURN TO APPENDIX B, "SAMPLE APPLICATION: INJURIOUS WILDLIFE"
**AND**
TURN TO PAGE A-123, "OTHER CONSIDERATIONS"

## OTHER CONSIDERATIONS

If you have followed the steps outlined in this chapter, you have completed the permit process under the Injurious Wildlife portion of the Lacey Act. However, you must also fulfill the requirements of **each** law that applies to your species. Be sure to check each applicable section of this volume.



IF YOU HAVE CONSULTED ALL OF THE SECTIONS THAT PERTAIN TO YOUR SPECIES, TURN TO PAGE A-149, "GENERAL REQUIREMENTS: ANIMALS"

This page intentionally left blank.

## ANIMAL WELFARE ACT
## Animal and Plant Health Inspection Service

## INTRODUCTION

The Animal Welfare Act (AWA) was intended to insure the humane treatment of warm-blooded animals intended for use in research or exhibition, or as pets. It is administered by the U.S. Department of Agriculture and authorizes regulations which provide for the licensing or registration of animal dealers, exhibitors, operators of animal auctions, research facilities, carriers and intermediate handlers. USDA regulations also include very specific animal care standards which must be met by any organization operating under the authority of the AWA. For information on animal care standards, and the name of the Veterinarian in Charge in your state, contact the Regional Director, Animal and Plant Health Inspection Service.

The AWA applies to:

> Any live dog, cat, nonhuman primate, guinea pig, hamster, rabbit, or other warm-blooded animal intended for use in research, testing, teaching, experimentation, or exhibition, or as a pet.

The AWA does NOT apply to:

> Horses not used for research purposes, other farm animals (such as livestock or poultry) intended for use as food or fiber, or for improving animal nutrition, breeding, management, or production efficiency, or for improving the quality of food or fiber.

The USDA issues dealer's licenses and exhibitor's licenses to applicants meeting specific requirements. It also registers certain types of research facilities which routinely use animals for research purposes, carriers which transport animals, and intermediate handlers which handle animals in connection with their transportation.

| Does your activity involve a warm-blooded animal, other than a farm animal intended for use as food or fiber, intended for research or exhibition use, or as a pet? | — NO — | Your activity is not covered by the Animal Welfare Act. TURN TO PAGE A-130, "OTHER CONSIDERATIONS" |
|---|---|---|

YES

| Check the following list to determine whether your business or activity requires licensing or registration, or is considered controlled or exempt. Then, TURN TO PAGE A-129, "ACTIVITIES REQUIRING A PERMIT" |
|---|

| ACTIVITY | STATUS | CONDITIONS |
|---|---|---|
| **ANIMAL DEALERS** | | |
| **Animal Sales (general)** | | |
| Auction operators— | | |
| Dogs or cats sold | Licensed | — |
| No dogs or cats sold | Exempt | (but must comply with standards) |
| Boarding Kennels— | | |
| Holding facilities for dealers | Controlled | — |
| Intermediate handlers transport | Registered | — |
| Other boarding kennels | Exempt | — |
| Brokers | Licensed | — |
| Hobby breeders— | | |
| Direct sales | Exempt | — |
| Sales under $500 | Exempt | (does not apply to dogs, cats or wild animals) |
| Wholesale transactions | Licensed | — |
| Nonregulated species | Exempt | — |
| Pounds, public | Exempt | — |
| Promoters (animal prizes) | Licensed | — |
| Shelters, private | Exempt | (unless they sell to licensed dealers, exhibitors or for research) |
| Trade-day sale sponsors | Exempt | (but must comply with standards) |
| **Laboratory animal trade** | | |
| Breeders | Licensed | — |
| Brokers | Licensed | — |
| Bunchers | Licensed | — |
| Dealers | Licensed | — |
| Holding facilities | Controlled | — |
| Importers | Licensed | — |
| Warm blooded animals (all sales) | Licensed | — |
| Specimens (all sales) | Licensed | — |
| **Pet animal trade** | | |
| Breeders— | | |
| Direct sales | Exempt | (except for wild or exotic species) |
| Sales via pet stores | Licensed | — |
| Sales of breeding stock | Licensed | — |
| Brokers | Licensed | — |
| Bunchers | Licensed | — |
| Chain stores— | | |
| No wild animals sold | Exempt | — |
| Wild animals sold | Licensed | — |
| Importers | Licensed | — |
| Rabbit breeders— | | |
| Direct sales | Exempt | — |
| Sales via pet stores | Licensed | — |
| Retailers— | | |
| No wild animals sold | Exempt | — |
| Wild animals sold | Licensed | — |

| | | |
|---|---|---|
| Trade-day sale sponsors | Exempt | — |
| Wholesalers | Licensed | — |
| **Working dog trade** | | |
| Hunting dogs | Licensed | — |
| Seeing-eye dogs | Exempt | — |
| Watchdogs | Licensed | — |
| **Exotic animal trade** | | |
| Chain stores— | | |
| No wild animals sold | Exempt | — |
| Wild animals sold | Licensed | — |
| Importers | Licensed | — |
| Retailers— | | |
| No wild animals sold | Exempt | — |
| Wild animals sold | Licensed | — |
| Wholesalers | Licensed | — |
| Wild animal dealers | Licensed | — |
| **ANIMAL EXHIBITORS** | | |
| **Zoological parks** | | |
| Aquariums— | | |
| Marine mammal exhibits | Licensed | — |
| All others | Exempt | — |
| Aviaries | Exempt | — |
| City zoos | Licensed | — |
| Farm exhibits | Exempt | — |
| Federal government zoos | Controlled | — |
| Marine mammal exhibits | Licensed | — |
| Pet stores | Exempt | — |
| Petting zoos | Licensed | — |
| Private zoos— | | |
| Closed to the public | Exempt | — |
| Open to the public | Licensed | — |
| Rabbits, exhibits of | Licensed | — |
| Registered exhibitors | Registered | — |
| Reptile houses | Exempt | — |
| Roadside zoos | Licensed | — |
| State zoos | Licensed | — |
| **Businesses with nonperforming animals** | | |
| Carnivals— | | |
| Animals used as prizes | Licensed | — |
| Animals on exhibit | Licensed | — |
| Game preserves | Exempt | — |
| Hunting preserves | Exempt | — |
| Nonregulated species | Exempt | — |
| Promotional exhibits | Licensed | — |
| **Businesses with performing animals** | | |
| Amusement parks— | | |
| Owning animals | Licensed | — |
| Not owning animals | Exempt | — |
| Animal acts | Licensed | — |

| | | |
|---|---|---|
| Aquatic shows | Licensed Registered | — |
| Circus acts | Licensed | — |
| Marine mammal acts | Licensed | — |
| Nonregulated species | Exempt | — |
| Booking agents | Exempt | — |
| TV and movie acts | Licensed | — |

**Competition involving animals**

| | | |
|---|---|---|
| Cockfighting ventures | Controlled | — |
| Dogfighting ventures | Prohibited | — |
| Fighting ventures (mammals) | Prohibited | — |
| Horse shows | Exempt | — |
| Hunts | Exempt | — |
| Pet shows | Exempt | — |
| Rodeos | Exempt | — |
| Sporting events | Exempt | — |

**ANIMAL TRANSPORTERS**

| | | |
|---|---|---|
| Carriers' terminals | Controlled | — |
| Dealer-owned transport | Licensed | — |
| Intermediate handlers | Registered | — |
| Nonregulated businesses | Exempt | — |
| Private carriers | Licensed | — |
| Public carriers | Registered | — |

**RESEARCH FACILITIES**

**Diagnostic laboratories**

| | | |
|---|---|---|
| Dogs and cats used | Registered | — |
| Large-scale | Registered | — |
| Small-scale | Controlled | — |

**Institutions selling or trading surplus animals**

| | | |
|---|---|---|
| State-owned facilities | Registered | — |
| Private and local facilities | Licensed Registered | — |

**Types of research facilities**

| | | |
|---|---|---|
| Agricultural research | Exempt | — |
| Animal studies, nonfarm | Registered | — |
| Behavioral studies | Registered | — |
| Biological specimens | Exempt | — |
| College laboratories | Registered | — |
| Drug firms | Registered | — |
| Federal facilities | Controlled | — |
| Laboratory tests | Registered | — |
| Marine mammal research | Registered | — |
| Nonregulated species | Exempt | — |
| Privately owned facilities | Registered | — |
| Quality-control studies | Registered | — |
| School laboratories | Exempt | (only at primary or secondary level) |
| State-owned facilities | Registered | — |
| Animals used for teaching | Registered | (if above secondary level) |

## ACTIVITIES REQUIRING A PERMIT

| | | |
|---|---|---|
| Is your business or activity listed as exempt? | —YES— | Your proposed activity is exempt from AWA registration and licensing requirements. TURN TO PAGE A-130, "OTHER CONSIDERATIONS" |
| NO | | |
| Is your business or activity listed as requiring licensing or registration? | —YES— | TURN TO PAGE A-130, "APPLICATION INFORMATION: AWA LICENSE AND REGISTRATION" **AND** TURN TO PAGE A-130, "OTHER CONSIDERATIONS" |
| NO | | |

To verify the status of your activity or business, contact:

Animal Care Staff<br>APHIS<br>Federal Building<br>6505 Belcrest Rd.<br>Room 565<br>Hyattsville, MD 20782

## APPLICATION INFORMATION: AWA LICENSE AND REGISTRATION

To obtain a dealer's or exhibitor's license, or to register as a research facility, carrier, or intermediate handler, you must contact the Veterinarian in Charge in the sector office in which you will be operating or the Animal Care Staff at the address listed on page A-129. If you will be operating in more than one state, contact the Veterinarian in Charge in the sector office in which you maintain your principal place of business. The five animal care sector offices are located in Annapolis (Northeast Region); Tampa (Southeast Region); Fort Worth (South Central Region); Minneapolis (North Central Region); and Sacramento (Western Region).

The Veterinarian in Charge will provide a description of the standards you must maintain in your facility and an application, which must be completed and returned to him. For license applications, a $10 fee must accompany the application; annual license fees are also levied, with the amount depending on the activity to be authorized. If you register under AWA as a research facility, you will be required to submit an annual report, the details of which accompany the license. USDA regulations also require detailed record-keeping by anyone obtaining a license or registration. Details on the information required accompany the license or registration.

TURN TO APPENDIX B, "SAMPLE APPLICATION: AWA LICENSE"
**OR**
"SAMPLE APPLICATION: AWA REGISTRATION"

## OTHER CONSIDERATIONS

If you have followed the steps outlined in this chapter, you have completed the licensing and registration process under the AWA. However, the AWA also prescribes very specific, detailed standards for the care of the animals affected; call APHIS for detailed information. In addition, you must also fulfill the requirements of **each** law that applies to your species. Be sure to check each applicable section of this volume.

Page



IF YOU HAVE CONSULTED ALL OF THE SECTIONS THAT PERTAIN TO YOUR SPECIES, TURN TO PAGE A-149, "GENERAL REQUIREMENTS: ANIMALS"

# PUBLIC HEALTH SERVICE ACT
## Department of Health and Human Services

## INTRODUCTION

The Public Health Service Act, PHSA, was enacted to prevent the spread of communicable diseases in connection with the importation of certain animals. Current PHSA regulations are printed in 42 CFR Part 71. Responsibility for enforcement of PHSA regulations lies with the Department of Health and Human Services, which is based at the Centers for Disease Control in Atlanta, Georgia. Unless noted otherwise, inquiries concerning the requirements of PHSA should be directed to:

Director
Center for Disease Control
Public Health Service
Department of Health and Human Services
Atlanta, GA 30333

Does your activity involve the importation of psittacine birds, turtles, non-human primates, or domestic cats or dogs?

— NO — Although additional species were covered at one time, current CDC regulations apply only to turtles, non-human primates and domestic cats and dogs. Special information on psittacine birds is included on page A-135. ALSO TURN TO PAGE A-136, "OTHER CONSIDERATIONS"

YES

TURN TO PAGE A-132, "ACTIVITIES REQUIRING A PERMIT OR OTHER SPECIAL INFORMATION"

## ACTIVITIES REQUIRING A PERMIT OR OTHER SPECIAL INFORMATION

Do you plan to import domestic cats or dogs?

—YES — TURN TO PAGE A-133, "APPLICATION INFORMATION: IMPORTATION OF DOMESTIC CATS AND DOGS

NO

Do you plan to import live nonhuman primates?

—YES — TURN TO PAGE A-134, "APPLICATION INFORMATION: IMPORTATION OF NONHUMAN PRIMATES"

NO

Do you plan to import live turtles?

—YES — TURN TO PAGE A-135, "APPLICATION INFORMATION: IMPORTATION OF TURTLES"

NO

TURN TO PAGE A-135, "SPECIAL INFORMATION: IMPORTATION OF PSITTACINE BIRDS"

## PUBLIC HEALTH SERVICE ACT
### Department of Health and Human Services

## APPLICATION INFORMATION: IMPORTATION OF DOMESTIC CATS AND DOGS

No advance authorization is required from the Department of Health and Human Services to import domestic cats or dogs. Inspection is required for all cats and dogs which arrive at a U.S. port. Admission into the United States is allowed only to those cats and dogs that show no signs of communicable disease. The person responsible for the care of the cats or dogs must maintain a record of sickness or death of the animals while they are enroute to the U.S. and must submit the record to the quarantine officer at the port of entry. Dog shipments must be accompanied by valid rabies vaccination certificates for each animal, unless evidence is presented that (42 CFR 71.51):

1. for the previous six months the animals have been only in a country declared rabies-free. Contact the Division of Quarantine for a current list of rabies-free countries.
2. the animals are to be taken to a research facility and vaccination would interfere with their use for research.

TURN TO PAGE A-136, "OTHER CONSIDERATIONS"

## APPLICATION INFORMATION: IMPORTATION OF NONHUMAN PRIMATES

Anyone who possesses non-human primates for research, teaching, or exhibition purposes or sells or transports them in commerce must be licensed or registered as a dealer, researcher, or exhibitor with the U.S. Department of Agriculture (USDA) in accordance with the Animal Welfare Act (AWA). For information you should contact: Veterinary Services, Animal and Plant Health Inspection Service (APHIS), Federal Center Building, Hyattsville, Maryland 20782.

Many non-human primates are listed as Endangered or Threatened under ESA. Interstate sale of listed species is allowed only under a permit from the U.S. Fish and Wildlife Service, Office of Management Authority (OMA). Permits are available for scientific purposes or for enhancement of propagation or survival if the animal is endangered and, in addition to those purposes, for zoological exhibition, educational purposes, or special purposes consistent with the ESA if the animal is threatened.

Import and export of many non-human primates is regulated under ESA and CITES. Import and export under ESA can be allowed by a permit from WPO for the purposes described above. All non-human primates are listed under CITES, and import and export of Appendix I species for commercial purposes are not permitted. In addition, import can be made only for *bona fide* scientific, educational, or exhibition purposes by an importer registered with the Public Health Service. Imports as a pet owner are not allowed. Application for registration should be made to: Director, Center for Disease Control, Public Health Service, Department of Health and Human Services, Atlanta, Georgia 30333.

There are no exceptions to the requirements explained above for the AWA, CITES, or general import regulations. However, 50 CFR 17.40(c) exempts some non-human primates from the ESA if specified conditions are met.

TURN TO PAGE A-136, "OTHER CONSIDERATIONS"

## PUBLIC HEALTH SERVICE ACT
## Department of Health and Human Services

## APPLICATION INFORMATION: IMPORTATION OF TURTLES

A permit is required from the Department of Health and Human Services to import viable turtle eggs or live turtles with shell lengths of four inches or less. The term "turtle" as used in this section refers to turtles, tortoises, terrapins and all other animals of the order Testudinata. It excludes marine species (the families *Dermochelidae* and *Chelontidae*). The Public Health Service issues permits for scientific, educational or exhibition purposes. Permits are issued only to those persons who can demonstrate that the turtles will be isolated or confined in appropriate holding facilities to prevent the infection of persons with bacteria of the *Salmonella* and *Arizona* genera. A permit is **not** required under the PHSA to:

1. import six or fewer turtles (counting eggs);
2. import turtles from the families *Dermochelidae* or *Chelontidae;* or
3. import turtles with shell lengths greater than four inches.

A permit request for turtle importation must be made in writing (may be in the form of a letter) to the Department of Health and Human Services in advance of the shipment, and contain your name and address, the number of specimens to be imported, the scientific and common names of the species, a description of the holding facilities and the intended use of the turtles. The letter must also include a description of the precautions to be taken to prevent infection of persons with the aforementioned bacteria genera.

***Warning***: Certain types of turtles are protected under ESA and CITES, with prohibitions or restrictions on importing or trafficking in live or dead specimens, their parts, or products.

TURN TO PAGE A-136, "OTHER CONSIDERATIONS"

## SPECIAL INFORMATION: IMPORTATION OF PSITTACINE BIRDS

In 1985 the Center for Disease Control deleted its pre-import treatment regulations for psittacine birds. USDA, however, has regulations requiring that all commercial birds, zoological birds, and research birds imported from any part of the world must be inspected at the Customs port of entry by an APHIS veterinary inspector. 9 CFR 92.105. The USDA regulations provide that psittacine birds must be given a chlortetracycline prophylactic treatment during quarantine. 9 CFR 92.106(b)(3)(ii)(C).

TURN TO PAGE A-136, "OTHER CONSIDERATIONS"

## OTHER CONSIDERATIONS

If you have followed the steps outlined in this chapter, you have completed the permit process under the PHSA. However, you must also fulfill the requirements of **each** law that applies to your species. Be sure to check each applicable section of this volume.



IF YOU HAVE CONSULTED ALL OF THE SECTIONS THAT PERTAIN TO YOUR SPECIES, TURN TO PAGE A-149, "GENERAL REQUIREMENTS: ANIMALS"

## ANIMAL QUARANTINE REGULATIONS
## Animal and Plant Health Inspection Service

The U.S. Department of Agriculture regulates the importation and exportation of certain animals and animal products to minimize the spread of disease. These regulations are extremely detailed, covering more than 100 pages in 9 CFR. Refer to the specific sections applicable to the species or products with which you are concerned.

For example, the rules for birds other than poultry are found in 9 CFR Part 92, Subpart A; for ruminants, Part 92, Subpart D. The rules for elephants, hippopotami, rhinoceroses, and tapirs are found in 9 CFR Part 93. The rules for animal byproducts (hides, skins, wool, hair, horns, bones, and trophies) are found in 9 CFR Part 95.

These rules are subject to frequent amendment. For information on the current rules, contact:

The Office of Import/Export
Animal and Plant Health Inspection Building
Federal Building
6505 Belcrest Road
Hyattsville, MD 20782

This page intentionally left blank.

## NOXIOUS WEED ACT
## Animal and Plant Health Inspection Service

### INTRODUCTION

The Federal Noxious Weed Act of 1974 is designed to prevent the spread of certain plant species which interfere with the growth of other plants, clog waterways, cause disease or adversely affect agriculture. These species, designated "Noxious Weeds" by the Department of Agriculture, are subject to particularly stringent controls. The movement of any Noxious Weed into or through the United States or interstate is prohibited. Purchase, barter, exchange, gift or receipt of noxious weeds is also prohibited. However, a written permit may be obtained to authorize movement of Noxious Weeds under conditions which would prevent the dissemination of the weed in the United States. The Canada-U.S. Free Trade Agreement also relaxes the restriction on importation of noxious weeds from Canada. The specific conditions under which the permit is granted will be stated in the permit.

TURN TO APPENDIX B, "SAMPLE APPLICATION: LIVE PLANT PESTS AND NOXIOUS WEEDS"
**AND**
SEE BELOW, "OTHER CONSIDERATIONS"

### OTHER CONSIDERATIONS

If you have followed the steps outlined in this chapter, you have completed the permit process under the Noxious Weed Act. However, you must also fulfill the requirements of each law that applies to your species. Be sure to check each applicable section of this appendix.



IF YOU HAVE CONSULTED ALL OF THE SECTIONS THAT PERTAIN TO YOUR SPECIES, TURN TO PAGE A-167, "GENERAL REQUIREMENTS: PLANTS"

This page intentionally left blank.

## CONTROLLED SUBSTANCES ACT
### Drug Enforcement Administration

The Controlled Substances Act (21 USC 801-971) regulates trafficking in controlled substances, including five plant species:

Coca leaves, *(Erythoxulum novagranatense)* and *(Erythoxulum coca)*
Marihuana, *(Cannabis sativa)*
Opium Poppy, *(Papaver somniferum)*
Peyote, *(Lophophora williamsii)*

Responsibility for the implementation and enforcement of the CSA rests with the Department of Justice's Drug Enforcement Administration (DEA). Only persons registered with the DEA may apply for permits. To determine which registration status is appropriate in your case, you must contact the local DEA office in your area. The local office will also be able to advise you of any state registration requirements as well as directing you to the appropriate state agency.

## OTHER CONSIDERATIONS

You must fulfill the requirements of **each** law that applies to your species. Be sure to check each applicable section of this volume.



IF YOU HAVE CONSULTED ALL OF THE SECTIONS THAT PERTAIN TO YOUR SPECIES, TURN TO PAGE A-167, "GENERAL REQUIREMENTS: PLANTS"

This page intentionally left blank.

# GENERAL REQUIREMENTS: ANIMALS
## U.S. Fish and Wildlife Service

## INTRODUCTION

In addition to the laws discussed earlier in this Appendix, there are a number of federal requirements which apply to certain transactions involving wildlife or plants, regardless of species. Answer the questions below to determine which general requirements apply to your proposed activity.

Do you wish to amend, modify or renew an existing FWS permit? —YES — TURN TO PAGE A-150, "GENERAL INFORMATION: PERMIT MODIFICATION"

NO

Does your activity involve **plants** or their parts or products? —YES — TURN TO PAGE A-167, "GENERAL REQUIREMENTS: PLANTS"

NO

Do you intend to do $25,000 or more of business in importing or exporting of wildlife (or wildlife products) during the calendar year? —YES — TURN TO PAGE A-153, "GENERAL INFORMATION: IMPORT/EXPORT LICENSES"

NO

TURN TO PAGE A-156, "SPECIAL SITUATIONS AND EXEMPTIONS: PORTS OF ENTRY"

## GENERAL INFORMATION: PERMIT MODIFICATION

### Permit Amendment

To amend the terms or conditions of your permit, you must request an amendment in writing and include the full justification and supporting information required in the general regulations and in the regulations dealing with your specific activity. An application for modification is subject to the same issuance criteria as the original application.

### Permit Renewal

To renew your permit, you must file a written request for renewal stating that the information in the original application is current and correct, or a statement of all changes to be incorporated into the original application, accompanied by any required fee at least 30 days prior to the expiration of your permit. If you hold a valid, renewable permit and have complied with the renewal process described in this paragraph, you may continue your activities until the renewal request is acted upon. Each permit bears a serial number which may be reassigned to you upon renewal of your permit, as long as the permit is not allowed to lapse.

### Other Modifications

Any change in a permit must be endorsed by the Director or issuing officer. Modifications other than those discussed below will be granted or denied at the discretion of the Director. If you have furnished your permit for modification to the Federal Wildlife Permit Office or the Special Agent in Charge of your Law Enforcement District for endorsement and have followed the procedures outlined below, you may continue your operations pending its return to you.

### Transferability of Permits

Permits are generally not transferable. However, in the following cases, limited transfer is allowed, provided that the successor submits the permit to the issuing officer for endorsement within 90 days from the date he begins to carry out the activity:

1. The surviving spouse, child, executor, administrator, or other legal representative of a deceased permit holder.
2. A receiver or trustee in bankruptcy, or a court-designated assignee for the benefit of creditors.

NOTE: Unless your permit states otherwise, any person under your direct control, or any person who is employed by you or under contract to you for the activities authorized by the permit, may carry out those activities.

### Change of Mailing Address

If you change your mailing address during the term of your permit, you must notify the issuing office within 10 days.

Change of Name

If your name or the name of your business is changed during the term of your permit, you must notify the issuing office within 10 days from the date you begin to conduct the activity under your new name.

Discontinuing Authorized Activities

If you discontinue your activities, you must mail your permit and a request for cancellation to the issuing officer within 30 days. The permit will be deemed void upon receipt. No refund of the permit fee, full or partial, will be granted.

TURN TO PAGE A-152, "APPLICATION INFORMATION: PERMIT RENEWAL OR MODIFICATION"

## APPLICATION INFORMATION: PERMIT RENEWAL OR MODIFICATION

An application for permit renewal or modification consists of:

1. FORM
A renewal form is available from WPO.

2. APPLICATION FEE
The application fee must be paid by certified check or money order, made payable to the U.S. Fish and Wildlife Service. The fee for this permit is $25.

**Be sure to answer all questions, provide all of the information required, and include a check or money order for the application fee.** An incomplete application will be returned to you for completion, resulting in considerable delay.

### WHERE TO OBTAIN APPLICATION FORMS

Federal Wildlife Permit Office
U.S. Fish and Wildlife Service
4401 N. Fairfax Drive, Room 432
Arlington, Virginia 22203

### WHEN TO APPLY

Submit your completed application, accompanying documents and a check or money order for $25 to the address listed below AT LEAST 30 to 60 days before you need the permit.

### WHERE TO MAIL THE COMPLETED APPLICATION

Federal Wildlife Permit Office
U.S. Fish and Wildlife Service
4401 N. Fairfax Drive, Room 432
Arlington, Virginia 22203

TURN TO APPENDIX B, "SAMPLE APPLICATION: PERMIT RENEWAL OR MODIFICATION"

## GENERAL INFORMATION: IMPORT/EXPORT LICENSES

An import/export license from the FWS is required before anyone may engage in business as an importer or exporter of wildlife, which are defined as follows:

"for a person to devote time, attention, labor or effort to any activity for gain or profit that involves the importation or exportation of wildlife, whether or not such person is an importer or exporter within the meaning of the customs laws of the United States."

However, you are exempt from this requirement if your business in importing or exporting of wildlife during a calendar year is less than $25,000. For example, the following persons are required to be licensed:

1. Persons importing or exporting wildlife for trade, sale, or resale, (such as animal dealers, animal brokers, pet dealers and pet suppliers, laboratory research suppliers).
2. Persons importing or exporting wildlife in the form of furs for tanning, manufacture, or sale, such as fur trappers, fur dealers, fur brokers, and fur manufacturers.
3. Persons importing or exporting wildlife in the form of hides and skins for tanning, manufacture or sale, such as hide and skin dealers, hide and skin brokers, leather dealers, and leather brokers.
4. Persons importing or exporting wildlife products (such as garments, bags, shoes, boots, jewelry, rugs or curios) for sale, such as wholesalers, retailers, distributors, and brokers.
5. Taxidermists importing or exporting wildlife in connection with the mounting, processing, or storage of trophies or specimens.
6. Freight forwarders.

Exceptions: Wildlife

An import/export license is not required to engage in business as an importer or exporter of the following wildlife:

1. Shellfish and fishery products imported or exported for purposes of human or animal consumption, or taken in waters under the jurisdiction of the U.S. or on the high seas for recreational purposes.
2. Fox, nutria, rabbit, mink, chinchilla, marten, fisher, muskrat, and karakul (or their products) if the animals were bred and born in captivity.

NOTE: The African Elephant Conservation Act of 1988 imposed special restrictions on the import, export, or reexport of ivory from African elephants. Turn to page A-28.

Exceptions: Persons

No import/export license is required for the following persons to engage in business as importers or exporters of wildlife, provided that complete records of each importation or exportation are maintained. FWS officers must be provided access, upon notice, to the place of business to examine the inventory of imported wildlife and the records required above.

1. Common carriers.
2. Customs house brokers.
3. Public museums or other public, scientific or educational institutions importing or exporting wildlife for research or educational purposes and not for resale.
4. Federal, state, or municipal agencies.
5. Circuses importing or exporting wildlife for exhibition purposes only.
6. Persons who import or export wildlife with a value of less than $25,000.

Do your proposed activities meet the criteria described above?

— NO — TURN TO PAGE A-155, "APPLICATION INFORMATION: IMPORT/EXPORT LICENSE"

YES

TURN TO PAGE A-156, "SPECIAL SITUATIONS AND EXEMPTIONS: PORTS OF ENTRY"

## APPLICATION INFORMATION: IMPORT/EXPORT LICENSE

An application for an Import/Export License consists of three parts:

1. FORM 3-200
   Form 3-200 requests general information about you and your proposed activity. (A detailed explanation of each question may be found in Appendix B.)
2. SUPPLEMENTARY INFORMATION
   A series of questions (usually found on the back of Form 3-200) which requests specific information on your proposed activity.
3. APPLICATION FEE
   The application fee must be paid by certified check or money order, made payable to the U.S. Fish and Wildlife Service. The fee for this permit is $125.

**Be sure to answer all questions, provide all of the information required, and include a check or money order for the application fee.** An incomplete application will be returned to you for completion, resulting in considerable delay.

### WHERE TO OBTAIN APPLICATION FORMS

Federal Wildlife Permit Office
U.S. Fish and Wildlife Service
4401 N. Fairfax Drive, Room 432
Arlington, Virginia 22203

### WHEN TO APPLY

Submit your completed application, accompanying documents and a check or money order for $125 to the address listed below AT LEAST 30 days before you need the permit.

### WHERE TO MAIL THE COMPLETED APPLICATION

Federal Wildlife Permit Office
U.S. Fish and Wildlife Service
4401 N. Fairfax Drive, Room 432
Arlington, Virginia 22203

TURN TO APPENDIX B, "SAMPLE APPLICATION: IMPORT/EXPORT DECLARATION"
**AND**
TURN TO PAGE A-156, "SPECIAL SITUATIONS AND EXEMPTIONS: PORTS OF ENTRY"

## SPECIAL SITUATIONS AND EXEMPTIONS: PORTS OF ENTRY

Shipments of wildlife and wildlife products may be lawfully imported, exported or reexported through a number of U.S. ports of entry, depending on the circumstances of your particular transactions. The questions below will help you determine which regulations or exceptions apply to your situation.

To determine if any exemptions or special situations apply to your proposed activity, refer to the sections listed below:



**THEN**

IF NO SPECIAL SITUATIONS OR EXEMPTIONS APPLY, TURN TO PAGE A-159, "GENERAL INFORMATION: PORTS OF ENTRY"

## EXEMPTION: IN-TRANSIT SHIPMENTS

Wildlife moving in transit through the United States from one foreign country to another may enter and exit the U.S. at any port, as long as the shipment proceeds under Customs bond.

| Does your activity meet the criteria described above? | —YES— | No further documentation is required. TURN TO PAGE A-166, "FINAL CONSIDERATIONS" |
|---|---|---|
| NO | | |
| To determine if any **other** exemptions or special situations apply to your proposed activity, TURN TO PAGE A-156, "SPECIAL SITUATIONS AND EXEMPTIONS: PORTS OF ENTRY" | | |

## EXEMPTION: PERSONAL BAGGAGE AND HOUSEHOLD EFFECTS

Persons moving their residence to or from the U.S. may import products or manufactured articles made from wildlife, including mounted game trophies and tanned hides, at any port, as long as those articles are part of their household effects and not intended for sale, and do not require a permit under another section of the federal wildlife regulations.

| Does your proposed activity meet the criteria described above? | —YES— | No special documentation is required. TURN TO PAGE A-166, "FINAL CONSIDERATIONS" |
|---|---|---|
| NO | | |
| To determine if any **other** exemptions or special situations apply to your proposed activity, TURN TO PAGE A-156, "SPECIAL SITUATIONS AND EXEMPTIONS: PORTS OF ENTRY" | | |

## EXEMPTION: SHELLFISH AND FISHERY PRODUCTS

Except for species which require a permit under the ESA, shellfish and fishery products imported or exported for purposes of human or animal consumption, or taken in waters under the jurisdiction of the U.S. or on the high seas for recreational purposes, may be imported or exported at any port.

Does your proposed activity meet the criteria described above?

—YES— No special documentation required. TURN TO PAGE A-166, "FINAL CONSIDERATIONS"

NO

To determine if any **other** exemptions or special situations apply to your proposed activity, TURN TO PAGE A-156, "SPECIAL SITUATIONS AND EXEMPTIONS: PORTS OF ENTRY"

## GENERAL INFORMATION: PORTS OF ENTRY

Three "classes" of ports of entry for the importation and exportation of wildlife and wildlife products are established in the regulations at:

| | |
|---|---|
| Designated Ports | 50 CFR 14.12 |
| Border Ports | 50 CFR 14.16 |
| Special Ports | 50 CFR 14.19 |

All wildlife or their products must be imported or exported through a designated port; however, except when a federal permit is required, wildlife imported from or exported to Canada and Mexico may be shipped through any border port. Special ports have been designated for wildlife shipments whose final destination is Alaska, Puerto Rico, the Virgin Islands or Guam, and for shipments which originate in Guam. In addition, permits are available for importation through other ports of entry for the following purposes:

Scientific purposes
To minimize deterioration or loss
To alleviate undue economic hardship

An "Exception to Designated Port" permit is available if the circumstances of your transaction make it impractical to use one of the designated ports of entry. This permit may be granted if the purpose of the requested exception is:

To minimize deterioration or loss,
To alleviate undue economic hardship,
For scientific purposes.

The permittee is liable for all costs incurred by the FWS in examining shipments, including per diem, salary and travel cost.

Do you plan to apply for an "Exception to Designated Port" permit?

—YES— TURN TO PAGE A-161, "APPLICATION INFORMATION: EXCEPTION TO DESIGNATED PORT"

NO

TURN TO PAGE A-162, "GENERAL INFORMATION: INSPECTION AND CLEARANCE OF WILDLIFE"

## APPLICATION INFORMATION: EXCEPTION TO DESIGNATED PORT

An application for an Exception to Designated Port permit consists of three parts:

1. FORM 3-200
   Form 3-200 requests general information about you and your proposed activity. (A detailed explanation of each question may be found in Appendix B.)
2. SUPPLEMENTARY INFORMATION
   A series of questions (usually found on the back of Form 3-200) which requests specific information to your proposed activity.
3. APPLICATION FEE
   The application fee must be paid by certified check or money order, made payable to the U.S. Fish and Wildlife Service. The fee for this permit is $25.

**Be sure to answer all questions, provide all of the information required, and include a check or money order for the application fee.** An incomplete application will be returned to you for completion, resulting in considerable delay.

**WHEN TO APPLY**

Submit your completed application, accompanying documents and a check or money order for $25 to the address listed below AT LEAST 30 days before you need the permit.

TURN TO APPENDIX B, "SAMPLE APPLICATION: EXCEPTION TO DESIGNATED PORT"
**AND**
TURN TO PAGE A-162, "GENERAL INFORMATION: INSPECTION AND CLEARANCE OF WILDLIFE"

## GENERAL INFORMATION: INSPECTION AND CLEARANCE OF WILDLIFE

Officers of the U.S. Fish and Wildlife Service may detain and inspect any container of wildlife or wildlife products and all accompanying documents before importation or exportation.

Clearance of Imported Wildlife

All wildlife imports into the U.S. must be cleared by an officer of the FWS before they can be released from detention by Customs. Clearance by the FWS may be obtained only at designated ports, border ports, special ports, or at any other port where importation has been authorized by permit. Any wildlife released without an FWS clearance or clearance by Customs (if an FWS officer is not available) must be returned immediately to a port where clearance may be obtained. The following must be made available to the FWS officer to obtain clearance for your shipment:

1. All shipping documents (including bills of lading, waybills and packing lists or invoices).
2. All permits or other documents required under U.S. law.
3. All permits or other documents required by the laws of any foreign country.
4. The wildlife being imported.
5. Completed Wildlife Declaration (Form 3-177).

FWS clearance does not constitute a certification that the import is legal.

Denial of Clearance

Clearance will be denied when there is reason to believe that:

1. You have violated a federal law.
2. You have violated a law in the country of origin in obtaining or exporting that specimen.
3. The identity of the wildlife has not been correctly established.
4. You have failed to provide the export and/or import permits and documentation (if required).
5. You have filed an incorrect or incomplete wildlife declaration, Form 3-177.
6. You have failed to pay inspection fees.

Unavailability of FWS Officers

Imported wildlife may be cleared by Customs officers if no FWS officer is available within a reasonable period of time. However, the wildlife is then subject to post-clearance inspection by the FWS.

Does your proposed activity involve import?

—YES— TURN TO PAGE A-163, "GENERAL INFORMATION: IMPORTATION DECLARATIONS"

NO

TURN TO PAGE A-164, "GENERAL INFORMATION: EXPORTATION DECLARATIONS"

## GENERAL INFORMATION: IMPORTATION DECLARATIONS

At the time and place where clearance for importation is requested, a Declaration for Importation or Exportation of Fish or Wildlife (Form 3-177) must be filed. If the wildlife or wildlife product is to be transshipped under Customs bond to a different port, a Customs declaration must be filed with the District Director of Customs at that port before release from Customs custody.

Exceptions

1. No Form 3-177 is required for shellfish and fishery products imported for the purpose of human or animal consumption or taken on the high seas for recreational purposes, unless the species are protected by the Endangered Species Act.

2. No Form 3-177 is required in the following cases (unless the wildlife in question requires a permit under the Endangered Species Act, the Convention on International Trade in Endangered Species of Wild Fauna and Flora, the Marine Mammal Protection Act, the Migratory Bird Treaty Act, or Lacey Act):
   a. Fish taken for recreational purposes in Canada or Mexico.
   b. Game mammals or birds from Canada or Mexico for which a Declaration for Free Entry of Game Mammals or Bird Killed by United States Residents (Customs Form 3315) has been filed with the U.S. Customs Service.
   c. Wildlife products which are not intended for sale and are worn as clothing or are contained in personal baggage. However, a Form 3-177 must be filed for raw or dressed furs; for raw, salted or crusted hides or skins; and for game or game trophies not covered in paragraph 2(b) above.
   d. Wildlife products which are not intended for sale and are part of the household effects of a person moving to the United States. However, a Wildlife Declaration (Form 3-177) must be filed for raw or dressed furs and for raw, salted, or crusted hides or skins.

3. Lawfully acquired specimens exported or imported between CITES-registered institutions for the purpose of taxonomic surveys may be described in general on the Form 3-177, provided that an amended form specifically describing the wildlife is filed within 180 days of the filing of the original Form 3-177. Extensions may be granted by the Director.

TURN TO APPENDIX B, "SAMPLE APPLICATION: IMPORT/EXPORT DECLARATION"
**AND**
TURN TO PAGE A-165, "GENERAL INFORMATION: MARKING REQUIREMENTS"

## GENERAL INFORMATION: EXPORTATION DECLARATIONS

A Declaration for Importation or Exportation of Fish or Wildlife (Form 3-177) must be filed with the U.S. Fish and Wildlife Service at the port of exportation prior to the exportation of any wildlife, unless one of the special situations described below applies to your proposed activities:

1. No Form 3-177 is required for the exportation of shellfish and fishery products exported for the purpose of human or animal consumption or taken on the high seas for recreational purposes, unless they are protected by the Endangered Species Act.
2. No Form 3-177 is required in the following cases (unless the wildlife in question requires a permit under the Endangered Species Act, the Convention on International Trade in Endangered Species of Wild Fauna and Flora, the Marine Mammal Protection Act, the Migratory Bird Treaty Act, or Lacey Act):

   a. Wildlife not intended for sale with a value of less than $250.
   b. Wildlife products, including game trophies, which are not intended for sale and are worn as clothing or are contained in the personal baggage, or are part of the household effects of persons moving their residence from the United States.
3. Specimens exchanged between CITES-registered scientific institutions for the purpose of taxonomic surveys may be described in general on the Form 3-177, provided that an amended form specifically describing the wildlife is filed within 180 days of the filing of the original Form 3-177. Extensions may be granted by the Director.

TURN TO APPENDIX B, "SAMPLE APPLICATION: IMPORT/EXPORT DECLARATION"
**AND**
TURN TO PAGE A-165, "GENERAL INFORMATION: MARKING REQUIREMENTS"

## GENERAL INFORMATION: MARKING REQUIREMENTS

Under the 1981 Lacey Act Amendments, no person may export, import, or transport in interstate commerce any container or package containing fish or wildlife (including shellfish) unless it is marked in compliance with law. The marking requirements are specified in 50 CFR 14.81 and 14.82. The primary requirement is that the container or package be conspicuously marked on the outside with both the shipper's and the consignee's names and addresses, as well as an accurate list of the contents by species and number of each species. The regulations, however, provide alternatives and exceptions to this primary marking requirement.

## GENERAL INFORMATION: HUMANE AND HEALTHFUL TRANSPORT OF WILD MAMMALS AND BIRDS TO THE U.S.

In the 1981 Lacey Act Amendments, the Fish and Wildlife Service was directed to promulgate regulations "to ensure that live wild mammals and birds shipped to the United States arrive alive, healthful, and un-injured, and that transportation of such animals occurs under humane and healthful conditions." 50 CFR 14.101.

The regulations for transporting wild mammals and birds include standards for veterinarian certificates, consignments to carriers, primary enclosures (cages), transport vehicles, care in transit, handling, and terminal facilities. Additionally, the regulations contain specific rules for non-human primates, marine mammals, elephants, ungulates, terrestrial mammals, sloths, bats, flying lemurs, and birds.

TURN TO PAGE A-166, "FINAL CONSIDERATIONS"

## FINAL CONSIDERATIONS

This Appendix has covered the federal permit process for your activity. However, you must also comply with state laws as well as local and municipal ordinances.

CAUTION: Statues and regulations change. To be certain that you are meeting **all requirements** for your proposed activity, you should consult with the appropriate federal and state agencies.

## GENERAL REQUIREMENTS: PLANTS

## PLANT PEST ACT AND PLANT QUARANTINE ACT

|  | |  |
|---|---|---|
| Does your proposed activity involve **importation** of plants or plant products? | —YES— | SEE BELOW AND TURN TO PAGE A-168, "APPLICATION INFORMATION." |
| NO | | |
| Does your proposed activity involve movement of Plant pests or noxious weeds. | ——— | SEE BELOW AND TURN TO PAGE A-168, "APPLICATION INFORMATION." |

The Plant Pest Act, 7 USC 150aa et seq., (PPA), the Plant Quarantine Act, 7 USC 151 et seq., (PPQ), and the Federal Noxious Weed Act, 7 USC 2801 et seq., are the basis of the regulations that affect importation of plant materials, including plant test organisms and products altered or produced through genetic engineering. Although this legislation was designed to protect domestic agriculture, the restrictions may apply to transactions that do not appear to be related to agriculture, such as importation of scientific specimens. Under these laws, permits are required for the arrival, unloading or landing, or the movement into or through the United States of any plants, plant products, plant pests and soil.

The regulations governing the import, interstate movement, and introduction of such materials are found in 7 CFR Parts 319, 321, 330, 340, 351, 352, and 360 and 50 CFR Part 24.

Two levels of regulation for plant species are established in the USDA regulations: prohibited species and restricted species. Prohibited species are those species whose listing indicates that they are prohibited if imported from the countries listed. Restricted species are all other plants, including those requiring post-entry quarantine or covered by special requirements. A species is often prohibited for import from certain countries, but may be imported from other countries if it is grown under post-entry quarantine. Documentation and permit requirements differ, depending on the degree of control exercised over a particular species.

Plants listed under the Endangered Species Act (ESA) or the Convention on International Trade in Endangered Species of Wild Fauna and Flora (CITES) may be imported, exported, or reexported only through ports designated on 50 CFR 24.12. The designated ports for other plant species are also published in 50 CFR Part 24.

Persons engaged in business as an importer, exporter, or reexporter of any terrestrial plants listed under ESA or CITES must obtain a permit for engaging in such a business from USDA's Plant Protection and Quarantine Office. Such permits are valid for 2 years. Persons engaging in importing, exporting, or reexporting other terrestrial plants may do so without obtaining a general permit.

## APPLICATION INFORMATION

If entry is allowed by USDA, the plant materials must meet specific conditions of treatment, processing, growing, shipment, marking, and disposal. The exact conditions, including types of permits required, vary with the material involved and the proposed use. The regulations are very detailed and complex. Contact USDA for information. Describe the plant material desired (including the parts of the plants and the genus and species), the nature of the work to be done, how potential pests will be contained or destroyed, and how the material will be disposed of when the work is complete. Write to:

Regulatory Services Staff

Plant Protection and Quarantine

Animal and Plant Health Inspection Service

U.S. Department of Agriculture

Federal Building

6505 Belcrest Road

Hyattsville, MD 20782

If the material is included in an ESA or CITES listing and you engaged in the business importing, exporting, or reexporting ESA or CITES listed species, turn to Appendix B, "Sample Application: Plant Import/Export Business."

If your article is classified as a plant or plant product, turn to Appendix B, "Sample Application: USDA Importation of Plant or Plant Products."

If your article is classified as a Live Plant Pest or Noxious Weed, turn to Appendix B, "Sample Application: Live Plant Pests and Noxious Weeds."

## FINAL CONSIDERATIONS

CAUTION: Statutes and regulations change. To be certain that you are meeting **all requirements** for your proposed activity, contact the appropriate federal and state agencies.

# APPENDIX B
# PERMIT APPLICATION FORMS AND INSTRUCTIONS FOR USE

# Permit Application Forms and Instructions for Use B-1

OMB NO. 42-R1670

**DEPARTMENT OF THE INTERIOR**
**U.S. FISH AND WILDLIFE SERVICE**

**FEDERAL FISH AND WILDLIFE LICENSE/PERMIT APPLICATION**

1. APPLICATION FOR *(Indicate only one)*

☐ IMPORT OR EXPORT LICENSE ☐ PERMIT

2. BRIEF DESCRIPTION OF ACTIVITY FOR WHICH REQUESTED LICENSE OR PERMIT IS NEEDED.

3. APPLICANT. *(Name, complete address and phone number of individual, business, agency, or institution for which permit is requested)*

4. IF "APPLICANT" IS AN INDIVIDUAL, COMPLETE THE FOLLOWING:

| | | |
|---|---|---|
| ☐ MR. ☐ MRS. ☐ MISS ☐ MS. | HEIGHT | WEIGHT |
| DATE OF BIRTH | COLOR HAIR | COLOR EYES |
| PHONE NUMBER WHERE EMPLOYED | SOCIAL SECURITY NUMBER | |
| OCCUPATION | | |
| ANY BUSINESS, AGENCY, OR INSTITUTIONAL AFFILIATION HAVING TO DO WITH THE WILDLIFE TO BE COVERED BY THIS LICENSE/PERMIT | | |

5. IF "APPLICANT" IS A BUSINESS, CORPORATION, PUBLIC AGENCY, OR INSTITUTION, COMPLETE THE FOLLOWING:

EXPLAIN TYPE OR KIND OF BUSINESS, AGENCY, OR INSTITUTION

NAME, TITLE, AND PHONE NUMBER OF PRESIDENT, PRINCIPAL OFFICER, DIRECTOR, ETC.

IF "APPLICANT" IS A CORPORATION, INDICATE STATE IN WHICH INCORPORATED

6. LOCATION WHERE PROPOSED ACTIVITY IS TO BE CONDUCTED

7. DO YOU HOLD ANY CURRENTLY VALID FEDERAL FISH AND WILDLIFE LICENSE OR PERMIT? ☐ YES ☐ NO
*(If yes, list license or permit numbers)*

8. IF REQUIRED BY ANY STATE OR FOREIGN GOVERNMENT, DO YOU HAVE THEIR APPROVAL TO CONDUCT THE ACTIVITY YOU PROPOSE? ☐ YES ☐ NO
*(If yes, list jurisdictions and type of documents)*

9. CERTIFIED CHECK OR MONEY ORDER *(if applicable)* PAYABLE TO THE U.S. FISH AND WILDLIFE SERVICE ENCLOSED IN AMOUNT OF
$

10. DESIRED EFFECTIVE DATE

11. DURATION NEEDED

12. ATTACHMENTS. THE SPECIFIC INFORMATION REQUIRED FOR THE TYPE OF LICENSE/PERMIT REQUESTED *(See 50 CFR 13.12(b))* MUST BE ATTACHED. IT CONSTITUTES AN INTEGRAL PART OF THIS APPLICATION. LIST SECTIONS OF 50 CFR UNDER WHICH ATTACHMENTS ARE PROVIDED.

**CERTIFICATION**

**I HEREBY CERTIFY THAT I HAVE READ AND AM FAMILIAR WITH THE REGULATIONS CONTAINED IN TITLE 50, PART 13, OF THE CODE OF FEDERAL REGULATIONS AND THE OTHER APPLICABLE PARTS IN SUBCHAPTER B OF CHAPTER I OF TITLE 50, AND I FURTHER CERTIFY THAT THE INFORMATION SUBMITTED IN THIS APPLICATION FOR A LICENSE/PERMIT IS COMPLETE AND ACCURATE TO THE BEST OF MY KNOWLEDGE AND BELIEF. I UNDERSTAND THAT ANY FALSE STATEMENT HEREIN MAY SUBJECT ME TO THE CRIMINAL PENALTIES OF 18 U.S.C. 1001.**

| SIGNATURE *(In ink)* | DATE |
|---|---|

3-200
(6/74)

Application for Federal Fish and Wildlife License/Permit

NOTICE

In accordance with the Privacy Act of 1974 (PL 93-579), please be advised that:

1. The gathering of information on fish and wildlife is authorized by: (a) Bald Eagle Protection Act (16 U.S.C. 663a), (b) Endangered Species Act of 1973 (16 U.S.C. 1539), (c) Migratory Bird Treaty Act (16 U.S.C. 703-711), (d) Marine Mammal Protection Act of 1972 (16 U.S.C. 1371-1383), (e) Lacey Act (18 U.S.C. 42 & 44), (f) Tariff Classification Act of 1962 (19 U.S.C. 1202), and (g) Title 50, Part 13, of the Code of Federal Regulations.

2. The disclosure of the requested information is required in order to process applications for licenses or permits authorized under the above acts. With the exception of your social security number, failure to disclose all of the requested information may be sufficient cause for the U.S. Fish and Wildlife Service to deny you a permit.

3. Applications for licenses or permits authorized under the Endangered Species Act of 1973 (16 U.S.C. 1539) and the Marine Mammal Protection Act of 1972 (16 U.S.C. 1371-1383) will be published in the Federal Register as required by the two acts.

4. In the event there is indicated a violation of a statute, regulation, rule, order, or license, whether civil, criminal, or regulatory in nature, the requested information may be transferred to the appropriate Federal, State, local, or foreign agency charged with investigating or prosecuting such violations.

5. In the event of litigation involving the records or the subject matter of the records, the requested information may be transferred to the U.S. Department of Justice.

United States Department of the Interior

FISH AND WILDLIFE SERVICE
Washington, D.C. 20240

ADDRESS ONLY THE DIRECTOR
FISH AND WILDLIFE SERVICE

OMA 5/89

## Permit application Form: instructions for use

A standard License/Permit Form 3-200 has been designed to assist persons applying for all U.S. Fish and Wildlife Service permits. In addition to the Form-3-200, attachments are necessary to provide the additional information required for each specific type of permit. A complete application prevents delays caused by the applicant having to supply more information at a later date.

Most of the application form is self explanatory, but the following provides some further assistance for completing each numbered block.

1. "Application for" - Check the appropriate box. At present, only permits are issued.

2. "Brief description of activity for which requested license or permit is needed" - In this space write a brief statement of the proposed activity and its purpose.

3. "Applicant" - The responsible party, who will also be the permittee if a permit issued, is identified here. Use complete names including middle name or initial. If applicant is a sole proprietor or a partnership doing business under a business name, include that business name in addition to the applicant's full name. Provide the complete address and phone number, including zip and area code.

4. "If applicant is an individual, complete the following" - This is used to identify the applicant fully. If the applicant is a corporation, institution, or other legal entity, block 5 should be filled out, and block 4 should be marked "not applicable."

5. "If applicant is a business corporation, public agency, or institution, complete the following" - Give a brief description of of the type of business the applicant is engaged in, the name and phone number of the person fully or partly in charge, and if the company is incorporated, the state in which it was incorporated. If block 4 is completed, mark "not applicable" in this space.

6. "Location where proposed activity is to be conducted" - The address or geographical location where the desired activity is to take place. This should include such information as the location where wildlife would be removed from the wild, where experiments would be conducted, the address where commercial products would be held, or the ports through which import or export would occur.

7. "Do you hold any currently valid Federal Fish and Wildlife license or permits?" - Check the appropriate box. If "yes" list the complete license or permit numbers.

8. "If required by any state or foreign government, do you have their approval to conduct the activity you propose?" - If the proposed activity is regulated, check the appropriate box. If "yes", list the state or foreign countries involved, and the type of document required. Include a copy of these documents with the application. If "no" indicate what steps you have taken to secure approval (use attachment if necessary). If the proposed activity is not regulated write "not required" in this block.

9. "Certified or personal check or money order (if applicable)" Permit fees are required for some permits. If required indicate the amount of the check or money enclosed with application. The check or money order should be attached to the application form. If no fee is required, write "none required" in this space.

10. "Desired effective date" - Insert the earliest date you want to conduct the activity. Depending on the type of permit, complete applications may take 20 - 90 days to process.

11. "Duration needed" - Most permits have a limited duration, but the applicant should insert the desired duration of the permit. Otherwise the permit will be limited to the shortest reasonable time needed, in the Service's best estimate, to complete the permitted activity.

12. "Attachments" - Here the applicant must consult the portion of the applicable regulation or the Fact Sheet that explains the activity to be permitted. Provide any required additional information on either the continuation (back) side of the appropriate application form or on attachment sheets (plain paper). When known, provide the relevant section numbers of the regulations. Be as complete and descriptive as possible. If there is any doubt as to the information's relevance, include it with the application. An incomplete or unclear application may be denied or will cause delays in processing.

    "Signature and date" - The individual applicant or the person named in block 5 must sign and date the application in the space provided. This signature binds that person to the statement of certification. Be sure to read the statement and re-read the application before signing.

If you have additional questions about the application or the regulations, please write the Director, U.S. Fish and Wildlife Service, Office of Management Authority, 4401 N. Fairfax Drive, Room 432, Arlington, VA 22203.

SEND TO: Office of Management Authority
4401 North Fairfax Drive, Rm. 432
Arlington, Virginia 22203
PHONE: (703) 358-2104

OMB NO. 42-R1670

**DEPARTMENT OF THE INTERIOR**
**U.S. FISH AND WILDLIFE SERVICE**

**FEDERAL FISH AND WILDLIFE LICENSE/PERMIT APPLICATION**

1. APPLICATION FOR *(Indicate only one)*

☐ IMPORT OR EXPORT LICENSE [XX] PERMIT

2. BRIEF DESCRIPTION OF ACTIVITY FOR WHICH REQUESTED LICENSE OR PERMIT IS NEEDED.

CAPTIVE-BRED WILDLIFE REGISTRATION

3. APPLICANT. *(Name, complete address and phone number of individual, business, agency, or institution for which permit is requested)*

4. IF "APPLICANT" IS AN <u>INDIVIDUAL</u>, COMPLETE THE FOLLOWING:

☐ MR. ☐ MRS. ☐ MISS ☐ MS. | HEIGHT | WEIGHT

DATE OF BIRTH | COLOR HAIR | COLOR EYES

PHONE NUMBER WHERE EMPLOYED | SOCIAL SECURITY NUMBER

OCCUPATION

ANY BUSINESS, AGENCY, OR INSTITUTIONAL AFFILIATION HAVING TO DO WITH THE WILDLIFE TO BE COVERED BY THIS LICENSE/PERMIT

5. IF "APPLICANT" IS A <u>BUSINESS</u>, <u>CORPORATION</u>, <u>PUBLIC AGENCY</u>, OR <u>INSTITUTION</u>, COMPLETE THE FOLLOWING

EXPLAIN TYPE OR KIND OF BUSINESS, AGENCY, OR INSTITUTION

NAME, TITLE, AND PHONE NUMBER OF PRESIDENT, PRINCIPAL OFFICER, DIRECTOR, ETC.

IF "APPLICANT" IS A CORPORATION, INDICATE STATE IN WHICH INCORPORATED

6. LOCATION WHERE PROPOSED ACTIVITY IS TO BE CONDUCTED

7. DO YOU HOLD ANY CURRENTLY VALID FEDERAL FISH AND WILDLIFE LICENSE OR PERMIT? ☐ YES ☐ NO
*(If yes, list license or permit numbers)*

8. IF REQUIRED BY ANY STATE OR FOREIGN GOVERNMENT, DO YOU HAVE THEIR APPROVAL TO CONDUCT THE ACTIVITY YOU PROPOSE? ☐ YES ☐ NO
*(If yes, list jurisdictions and type of documents)*

9. CERTIFIED CHECK OR MONEY ORDER *(if applicable)* PAYABLE TO THE U.S. FISH AND WILDLIFE SERVICE ENCLOSED IN AMOUNT OF
$ 25.00

10. DESIRED EFFECTIVE DATE

11. DURATION NEEDED

12. ATTACHMENTS. THE SPECIFIC INFORMATION REQUIRED FOR THE TYPE OF LICENSE/PERMIT REQUESTED *(See 50 CFR 13.12(b))* MUST BE ATTACHED. IT CONSTITUTES AN INTEGRAL PART OF THIS APPLICATION. LIST SECTIONS OF 50 CFR UNDER WHICH ATTACHMENTS ARE PROVIDED.

SEE REVERSE

**CERTIFICATION**

I HEREBY CERTIFY THAT I HAVE READ AND AM FAMILIAR WITH THE REGULATIONS CONTAINED IN TITLE 50, PART 13, OF THE CODE OF FEDERAL REGULATIONS AND THE OTHER APPLICABLE PARTS IN SUBCHAPTER B OF CHAPTER I OF TITLE 50, AND I FURTHER CERTIFY THAT THE INFORMATION SUBMITTED IN THIS APPLICATION FOR A LICENSE/PERMIT IS COMPLETE AND ACCURATE TO THE BEST OF MY KNOWLEDGE AND BELIEF. I UNDERSTAND THAT ANY FALSE STATEMENT HEREIN MAY SUBJECT ME TO THE CRIMINAL PENALTIES OF 18 U.S.C. 1001.

SIGNATURE *(In ink)* | DATE

3-200
(6/74)

*Applicant listed in 3 above or principal officer listed in 5 above <u>must</u> sign and date the application.

CAPTIVE-BRED WILDLIFE REGISTRATION
APPLICATION CONTINUATION

Please respond in full on a separate piece of paper to each of the items below. Your responses must be legibly printed with an ink pen or typed. Use as many attachment sheets as necessary.

1. Provide the complete scientific name (genus and species) and common name of each species you are seeking to have covered by the registration.

2. Provide the name(s) and address(es) of the person(s) or institution(s) from whom you propose to acquire the wildlife.

3. Discuss how your proposed activity will serve to enhance the propagation or survival of the species identified in your response to number 1, including your long-term goals and intended disposition of any progeny.

4. Provide a complete description of your experience in maintaining <u>and</u> propagating the species listed in answer to #1 (above) or similar species, or in conducting research directly related to maintaining and propagating such wildlife. Your description must include: a) the specific species you have successfully maintained and bred and how long you have been involved in such activities; b) an inventory of the endangered or threatened species you currently possess, including those in or out on loan; c) the number of successful births of each species that have occurred at your facility (or approximate number if too numerous to list) and how many survived beyond 30 days from birth; d) the number of mortalities of such species that have occurred at your facility in the past two years and the causes of the mortalities. (If you have changed procedures to reduce the probability of such mortalities, please describe the changes you have implemented.); and e) if you conducted research directly related to maintaining and propagating the types of wildlife sought to be covered, please provide a complete description of your past research, including any published papers, articles, etc., a description of your research protocol and methodologies, and any published or unpublished results of the research.

5. If you intend to exhibit the wildlife to the public, provide a complete description of the means by which your exhibit would serve to educate the public about the affected species' ecological role and conservation needs. Your description must include actual copies of the hand-outs you plan to distribute, and/or legible photographs of the signage you plan to use, and/or an exact copy of the script you plan to use to provide the information verbally to the public. You must also provide a resume of your qualifications for presenting such information to the public, a complete listing of similar exhibits you have performed in the past, including the dates and locations of such exhibits, and a statement as to the type of audience you plan to educate through your exhibits.

6. Provide a complete description <u>and</u> photographs or adequate diagrams (not blueprints) clearly depicting your <u>existing</u> facilities where the wildlife listed in response to #1 (above) will be maintained.

7. Provide a copy of your license or registration, if any, under the Animal Welfare Act regulations of the U.S. Department of Agriculture (9 CFR 2).

SEND TO:
U.S. Fish and Wildlife Service
Office of Management Authority
4401 N. Fairfax Drive, Room 432
Arlington, VA 22203
Call: 703/358-2104 for more information

OMB NO. 42-R1670

**DEPARTMENT OF THE INTERIOR**
**U.S. FISH AND WILDLIFE SERVICE**

**FEDERAL FISH AND WILDLIFE LICENSE/PERMIT APPLICATION**

1. APPLICATION FOR (*Indicate only one*)

☐ IMPORT OR EXPORT LICENSE ☒ PERMIT

2. BRIEF DESCRIPTION OF ACTIVITY FOR WHICH REQUESTED LICENSE OR PERMIT IS NEEDED.

IMPORT OF SPORT-HUNTED TROPHY

3. APPLICANT. (*Name, complete address and phone number of individual, business, agency, or institution for which permit is requested*)

4. IF "APPLICANT" IS AN INDIVIDUAL, COMPLETE THE FOLLOWING:

| ☐ MR. ☐ MRS. ☐ MISS ☐ MS. | HEIGHT | WEIGHT |
|---|---|---|
| DATE OF BIRTH | COLOR HAIR | COLOR EYES |
| PHONE NUMBER WHERE EMPLOYED | SOCIAL SECURITY NUMBER | |
| OCCUPATION | | |
| ANY BUSINESS, AGENCY, OR INSTITUTIONAL AFFILIATION HAVING TO DO WITH THE WILDLIFE TO BE COVERED BY THIS LICENSE/PERMIT<br>N/A | | |

5. IF "APPLICANT" IS A BUSINESS, CORPORATION, PUBLIC AGENCY, OR INSTITUTION, COMPLETE THE FOLLOWING:

EXPLAIN TYPE OR KIND OF BUSINESS, AGENCY, OR INSTITUTION

N/A

NAME, TITLE, AND PHONE NUMBER OF PRESIDENT, PRINCIPAL OFFICER, DIRECTOR, ETC.

IF "APPLICANT" IS A CORPORATION, INDICATE STATE IN WHICH INCORPORATED

6. LOCATION WHERE PROPOSED ACTIVITY IS TO BE CONDUCTED
(include port of entry into the U.S.)

7. DO YOU HOLD ANY CURRENTLY VALID FEDERAL FISH AND WILDLIFE LICENSE OR PERMIT? ☐ YES ☐ NO
(*If yes, list license or permit numbers*)

8. IF REQUIRED BY ANY STATE OR FOREIGN GOVERNMENT, DO YOU HAVE THEIR APPROVAL TO CONDUCT THE ACTIVITY YOU PROPOSE? ☐ YES ☐ NO
(*If yes, list jurisdictions and type of documents*)

| 9. CHECK OR MONEY ORDER (*if applicable*) PAYABLE TO THE U.S. FISH AND WILDLIFE SERVICE ENCLOSED IN AMOUNT OF | 10. DESIRED EFFECTIVE DATE | 11. DURATION NEEDED |
|---|---|---|
| $ $25.00 | | 1 year. |

12. ATTACHMENTS. THE SPECIFIC INFORMATION REQUIRED FOR THE TYPE OF LICENSE/PERMIT REQUESTED (*See 50 CFR 13.12(b)*) MUST BE ATTACHED. IT CONSTITUTES AN INTEGRAL PART OF THIS APPLICATION. LIST SECTIONS OF 50 CFR UNDER WHICH ATTACHMENTS ARE PROVIDED.

SEE REVERSE

**CERTIFICATION**

I HEREBY CERTIFY THAT I HAVE READ AND AM FAMILIAR WITH THE REGULATIONS CONTAINED IN TITLE 50, PART 13, OF THE CODE OF FEDERAL REGULATIONS AND THE OTHER APPLICABLE PARTS IN SUBCHAPTER B OF CHAPTER I OF TITLE 50, AND I FURTHER CERTIFY THAT THE INFORMATION SUBMITTED IN THIS APPLICATION FOR A LICENSE/PERMIT IS COMPLETE AND ACCURATE TO THE BEST OF MY KNOWLEDGE AND BELIEF. I UNDERSTAND THAT ANY FALSE STATEMENT HEREIN MAY SUBJECT ME TO THE CRIMINAL PENALTIES OF 18 U.S.C. 1001.

| SIGNATURE (*in ink*) | DATE |
|---|---|
| | |

3-200
(6/74)

Application continuation sheet

IMPORT PERMIT FOR SPORT-HUNTED TROPHIES

CONVENTION ON INTERNATIONAL TRADE IN ENDANGERED SPECIES (CITES)

I. COMPLETE THE FOLLOWING:

| a. Quantity | Scientific Name | Common Name | If trophy already taken: Age | Sex |
|---|---|---|---|---|
| ____ | ____________________ | ____________________ | ___ | ___ |
| ____ | ____________________ | ____________________ | ___ | ___ |

b. At the time of application, wildlife is: ____ living in wild ____ dead

c. Describe trophy (be specific, e.g. skin, skull, claws, horn, etc.). If trophy is already taken, give size of parts.

d. Person from whom trophy is to be imported. If you have not taken the trophy and do not know who is going to send it to you, just state such.

Name ____________________

Address ____________________

City/Country ____________________

e. Country and PLACE wildlife was (or is to be) taken from the wild:

f. Date was (or is to be) taken:

g. Purposes and details of activities for which wildlife is to be imported. (Note: This application is for import of sport-hunted trophies of animals that were personally taken by the applicant and are for personal use.)

---

II. IN ADDITION, FOR LEOPARD TROPHIES TAKEN PRIOR to March 1, 1982, attach a copy of the following that shows (a) that the leopard was legally taken by you and (b) date and place of take. (Note: A copy of an export permit or trophy list from a taxidermist or professional hunting guide is NOT sufficient.)

--Botswana: "Single Game License" issued under Fauna Conservation Act.
--South West Africa (Namibia): not allowed to sport-hunt leopard prior to February 1, 1983.
--Transvaal Province, South Africa: Statement from the landowner that you legally took the leopard on his land.
--Tanzania: game license.
--Zambia: "Supplementary Game License" under National Parks and Wildlife Act.
--Zimbabwe: hunting permit, game license or statement from landowner, whichever was required at time of take (Zimbabwe legislation changed between the period of December 28, 1973, and March 1, 1982, so the type of authorization needed to hunt leopard varied with both time and place).

# United States Department of the Interior

FISH AND WILDLIFE SERVICE
WASHINGTON, D.C. 20240

ADDRESS ONLY THE DIRECTOR FISH AND WILDLIFE SERVICE

## Import of Leopard (Panthera pardus) and Southern White Rhinoceros (Ceratotherium simum simum) Sport-Hunted Trophies

These steps must be followed to import a trophy of a legally taken leopard and/or southern white rhinoceros into the United States:

1. First, obtain a CITES import permit from the Office of Management Authority (OMA). An application is enclosed.

   a. Permits are available for sport-hunted trophies only. This means the trophy must be imported by the person who shot it and must be for personal use or display only. It does not include leopards or southern white rhinoceros shot by other hunters or people, nor does it include purchased skins.

   b. For the leopard, the U.S. Scientific Authority has given a non-detriment finding for Botswana, Namibia, (South West Africa), Transvaal Province of South Africa, Tanzania, Zaire, Zambia, and Zimbabwe.

   c. For the southern white rhinoceros, the U.S. Scientific Authority has given a non-detriment finding for Namibia (South West Africa) and South Africa.

   d. Import permits are valid for one year from the date of issuance. Applications are processed in the order received. Sport hunters should allow approximately 60 days for processing. A word of caution, if you request a permit months in advance of the planned hunting trip, you may have to request renewal of your permit as it may have expired before the trophy is ready to be imported. The renewal has a $25.00 processing fee and takes approximately 60 days to process.

2. Take the leopard and/or Southern white rhinoceros according to the foreign country's laws.

3. Obtain a CITES export permit from CITES management Authority of Party country or equivalent CITES documentation from competent authority in non-Party country (addresses on the reverse of this page). ("In lieu of documents" are not acceptable from Party countries.)

4. Import through a port designated for wildlife: Chicago, Illinois; Dallas/Ft. Worth, Texas; Honolulu, Hawaii; Los Angeles and San Francisco California; Miami, Florida; New Orleans, Louisiana; New York, New York; Portland, Oregon; and Seattle, Washington.

5. Present original of CITES import and export permits and a completed wildlife Declaration (form 3-177) to a U.S. Fish and Wildlife Service inspector at a designated port upon import.

NOTE: The BONTEBOK (Damaliscus dorcas dorcas) is listed as Endangered under the U.S. Endangered Species Act and may not be imported without an Endangered Species import permit. Contact OMA (703/358-2104) for more information.

Rev. 6/90

Issuing Offices for Permits Under the Convention on International Trade in Endangered Species of Wild Fauna and Flora (CITES)

*Botswana
Department of Wildlife National Parks
P.O. Box 131
GABRONE

Export permits can be granted in the following District Offices:

Francistown
Ghanzi
Kasane
Machaneng
Maun
Molepolole
Serowe
Tshabong

Namibia (South West Africa)
Department van Landbou
en Natuurbewaring
and Nature Conservation
P/Bag 13306
WINDHOEK 9000

Rhodesia (see Zimbabwe)

*South Africa
Department of Environment Affairs
Environmental Conservation Branch
P/Bag X 447
PRETORIA 0001

The Director of Nature Conservation
Transvaal
P/Bag X 209
PRETORIA 0001

The Director of Nature Conservation
Orange Free State
P.O. Box 517
BLOEMFONTEIN 9300

The Director of Nature and
Environmental Conservation
Provincial Building, Dorp Street
P/Bag 9086
CAPE TOWN 8000

The Director
Natal Parks
P.O. Box 662
Pietermaritzburg 3200

South West Africa (see Namibia)

*Tanzania, United Republic of
Director of Wildlife
Wildlife Division
Ministry of Land, Natural Resources
and Tourism
P.O. Box 1994
DAR ES SALAAM

Trophy Export Certificates from Following Tanzanian Stations

Arusha
Dar es Salaam (P.O. Box 1994)
Dar es Salaam (Ivory Room)
Mbeya
Mtwara
Mwanza
Tanga

*Zaire
Department de l'environnment,
Conservation de la natural
et tourisme
Cabinet du Commissaire d'Etat
15, Avenue des Cliniques
B.P. - 12348 Kin I
KINSHASA/GOMBE

*Zambia
The Conservation Division of the
Department of National Park
and Wildlife Service
P/Bag 1
CHILANGA

*Zimbabwe
Department of National Parks
and Wildlife Management
P.O. Box 8365
Causeway
HARARE

The Warden
Marongora
P/Bag 5926
KAROI

The Warden
Matetsi Safari Area
P/Bag 5926
VICTORIA FALLS

The Senior Ranger
Tuli
P/Bag 5726
BEIT BRIDGE

Provincial Warden
Mashonaland North
P.O. Box 193
CHINOYI

Provincial Warden
Matabeleland North
P/Bag 5925
VICTORIA FALLS

Provincial Warden
Matabeleland South
P.O. Box 2283
BULAWAYO

Provincial Warden
Masvingo
P/Bag 9136
MASVINGO

The Warden
Kariba
P/Bag 2002
KARIBA

*Denotes Party Country to CITES
November 1984

SEND TO:
U.S. Fish and Wildlife Service
Office of Management Authority
4401 N. Fairfax Drive, Room 432
Arlington, VA 22203
Call: 703/358-2104

OMB NO. 42-R1673

**DEPARTMENT OF THE INTERIOR**
**U.S. FISH AND WILDLIFE SERVICE**

**FEDERAL FISH AND WILDLIFE LICENSE/PERMIT APPLICATION**

1. APPLICATION FOR *(Indicate only one)*

☐ IMPORT OR EXPORT LICENSE ☐ PERMIT

2. BRIEF DESCRIPTION OF ACTIVITY FOR WHICH REQUESTED LICENSE OR PERMIT IS NEEDED.

IMPORT OF SPORT-HUNTED
BONTEBOK TROPHY
(Endangered Species)

3. APPLICANT. *(Name, complete address and phone number of individual, business, agency, or institution for which permit is requested)*

4. IF "APPLICANT" IS AN INDIVIDUAL, COMPLETE THE FOLLOWING:

☐ MR. ☐ MRS. ☐ MISS ☐ MS.

HEIGHT

WEIGHT

DATE OF BIRTH

COLOR HAIR

COLOR EYES

PHONE NUMBER WHERE EMPLOYED

SOCIAL SECURITY NUMBER

OCCUPATION

ANY BUSINESS, AGENCY, OR INSTITUTIONAL AFFILIATION HAVING TO DO WITH THE WILDLIFE TO BE COVERED BY THIS LICENSE/PERMIT

5. IF "APPLICANT" IS A BUSINESS, CORPORATION, PUBLIC AGENCY, OR INSTITUTION, COMPLETE THE FOLLOWING:

EXPLAIN TYPE OR KIND OF BUSINESS, AGENCY, OR INSTITUTION

NAME, TITLE, AND PHONE NUMBER OF PRESIDENT, PRINCIPAL OFFICER, DIRECTOR, ETC.

IF "APPLICANT" IS A CORPORATION, INDICATE STATE IN WHICH INCORPORATED

6. LOCATION WHERE PROPOSED ACTIVITY IS TO BE CONDUCTED

(U.S. Port of import)

7. DO YOU HOLD ANY CURRENTLY VALID FEDERAL FISH AND WILDLIFE LICENSE OR PERMIT? ☐ YES ☐ NO
*(If yes, list license or permit numbers)*

8. IF REQUIRED BY ANY STATE OR FOREIGN GOVERNMENT, DO YOU HAVE THEIR APPROVAL TO CONDUCT THE ACTIVITY YOU PROPOSE? ☐ YES ☐ NO
*(If yes, list jurisdictions and type of documents)*

9. CERTIFIED CHECK OR MONEY ORDER *(if applicable)* PAYABLE TO THE U.S. FISH AND WILDLIFE SERVICE ENCLOSED IN AMOUNT OF

$ $25.00

10. DESIRED EFFECTIVE DATE

11. DURATION NEEDED

1 year

12. ATTACHMENTS. THE SPECIFIC INFORMATION REQUIRED FOR THE TYPE OF LICENSE/PERMIT REQUESTED *(See 50 CFR 13.12(b))* MUST BE ATTACHED. IT CONSTITUTES AN INTEGRAL PART OF THIS APPLICATION. LIST SECTIONS OF 50 CFR UNDER WHICH ATTACHMENTS ARE PROVIDED.

(SEE REVERSE)

**CERTIFICATION**

I HEREBY CERTIFY THAT I HAVE READ AND AM FAMILIAR WITH THE REGULATIONS CONTAINED IN TITLE 50, PART 13, OF THE CODE OF FEDERAL REGULATIONS AND THE OTHER APPLICABLE PARTS IN SUBCHAPTER B OF CHAPTER I OF TITLE 50, AND I FURTHER CERTIFY THAT THE INFORMATION SUBMITTED IN THIS APPLICATION FOR A LICENSE/PERMIT IS COMPLETE AND ACCURATE TO THE BEST OF MY KNOWLEDGE AND BELIEF. I UNDERSTAND THAT ANY FALSE STATEMENT HEREIN MAY SUBJECT ME TO THE CRIMINAL PENALTIES OF 18 U.S.C. 1001.

| SIGNATURE *(In ink)* | DATE |
|---|---|
| | |

3-200
(5/74) *Applicant listed in block 3 above must sign application.

Continuation Sheet for Import of Bontebok Trophy

I. COMPLETE THE FOLLOWING:

A. Quantity Scientific Name Common Name

1 Damaliscus dorcas dorcas Bontebok

B. At time of application, wildlife is: ___living ___dead**

**If dead, give date which it was taken: ________
If alive, give approximate date of proposed take: ________

C. Describe trophy (e.g., skin, skull, etc.).

D. Name and address of landowner on whose property the bontebok was or will be taken: ________________

E. Name and address of institution /facility where wildlife trophy will by used, displayed, or otherwise maintained:

II. ATTACH THE FOLLOWING TO APPLICATION:

A. Original letter of authorization from the landowner giving you permission to cull a bontebok from his captive herd.

B. If bontebok has already been taken, provide a copy of the certificate issued by the Cape Provincial Administration's Department of Nature and Environmental Conservation certifying that the bontebok was taken on the landowner's ranch.

---

NOTE: The bontebok is listed as endangered under the Endangered Species Act. Applications for endangered species permits must be published in the Federal Register and allowed a 30-day comment period. The processing of such permits can take about 60 days.

Call: 703/358-2104 for more information

OMB NO. 42-R1670

**DEPARTMENT OF THE INTERIOR**
**U.S. FISH AND WILDLIFE SERVICE**

**FEDERAL FISH AND WILDLIFE LICENSE/PERMIT APPLICATION**

1. APPLICATION FOR *(Indicate only one)*

☐ IMPORT OR EXPORT LICENSE ☒ PERMIT

2. BRIEF DESCRIPTION OF ACTIVITY FOR WHICH REQUESTED LICENSE OR PERMIT IS NEEDED.

ENDANGERED/THREATENED SPECIES

_____ Take

_____ Import

_____ Export

_____ Interstate Commerce

3. APPLICANT. *(Name, complete address and phone number of individual, business, agency, or institution for which permit is requested)*

4. IF "APPLICANT" IS AN INDIVIDUAL, COMPLETE THE FOLLOWING:

| ☐ MR. ☐ MRS. ☐ MISS ☐ MS. | HEIGHT | WEIGHT |
|---|---|---|
| DATE OF BIRTH | COLOR HAIR | COLOR EYES |
| PHONE NUMBER WHERE EMPLOYED | SOCIAL SECURITY NUMBER | |
| OCCUPATION | | |

ANY BUSINESS, AGENCY, OR INSTITUTIONAL AFFILIATION HAVING TO DO WITH THE WILDLIFE TO BE COVERED BY THIS LICENSE/PERMIT

5. IF "APPLICANT" IS A BUSINESS, CORPORATION, PUBLIC AGENCY, OR INSTITUTION, COMPLETE THE FOLLOWING:

EXPLAIN TYPE OR KIND OF BUSINESS, AGENCY, OR INSTITUTION

NAME, TITLE, AND PHONE NUMBER OF PRESIDENT, PRINCIPAL OFFICER, DIRECTOR, ETC.

IF "APPLICANT" IS A CORPORATION, INDICATE STATE IN WHICH INCORPORATED

6. LOCATION WHERE PROPOSED ACTIVITY IS TO BE CONDUCTED

7. DO YOU HOLD ANY CURRENTLY VALID FEDERAL FISH AND WILDLIFE LICENSE OR PERMIT? ☐ YES ☐ NO
*(If yes, list license or permit numbers)*

8. IF REQUIRED BY ANY STATE OR FOREIGN GOVERNMENT, DO YOU HAVE THEIR APPROVAL TO CONDUCT THE ACTIVITY YOU PROPOSE? ☐ YES ☐ NO
*(If yes, list jurisdictions and type of documents)*

9. CHECK OR MONEY ORDER *(if applicable)* PAYABLE TO THE U.S. FISH AND WILDLIFE SERVICE ENCLOSED IN AMOUNT OF

$ 25.00

10. DESIRED EFFECTIVE DATE

11. DURATION NEEDED

12. ATTACHMENTS. THE SPECIFIC INFORMATION REQUIRED FOR THE TYPE OF LICENSE/PERMIT REQUESTED *(See 50 CFR 13.12(b))* MUST BE ATTACHED. IT CONSTITUTES AN INTEGRAL PART OF THIS APPLICATION. LIST SECTIONS OF 50 CFR UNDER WHICH ATTACHMENTS ARE PROVIDED.

SEE REVERSE

**CERTIFICATION**

I HEREBY CERTIFY THAT I HAVE READ AND AM FAMILIAR WITH THE REGULATIONS CONTAINED IN TITLE 50, PART 13, OF THE CODE OF FEDERAL REGULATIONS AND THE OTHER APPLICABLE PARTS IN SUBCHAPTER B OF CHAPTER I OF TITLE 50, AND I FURTHER CERTIFY THAT THE INFORMATION SUBMITTED IN THIS APPLICATION FOR A LICENSE/PERMIT IS COMPLETE AND ACCURATE TO THE BEST OF MY KNOWLEDGE AND BELIEF. I UNDERSTAND THAT ANY FALSE STATEMENT HEREIN MAY SUBJECT ME TO THE CRIMINAL PENALTIES OF 18 U.S.C. 1001.

| ** SIGNATURE *(In ink)* | DATE |
|---|---|
| | |

3-200
(5 '74)

**Applicant listed in 3 above or principal officer listed in 5 above must sign.

## ENDANGERED OR THREATENED WILDLIFE & PLANTS

COMPLETE THE FOLLOWING:

a. Species:______________________________________
(scientific and common name)

b. Quantity:________ c. Birth date and sex of wildlife:______________

d. Identifying features of wildlife (e.g., tattoo #, ISIS #, scars etc.):

e. Name and address of party from whom wildlife or plant will be obtained:

______________________________________

______________________________________

f. At time of application, wildlife or plant (i) is still in the wild____; (ii) has been removed from the wild____; or (iii) was born in captivity or artificially propagated___. Provide country and specific location of wild origin or captive propagation: ______________________

ATTACH THE FOLLOWING INFORMATION ON PLAIN WHITE PAPER:

g. A description of your attempts to obtain the wildlife or plant in a manner which would not cause death or removal from the wild (i.e., the use of specimens currently in captivity or produced in captivity, etc.).

h. Name and address of institution or facility where wildlife or plant will be used, displayed or maintained.

i. A statement justifying the permit including: 1) purpose, objectives, whether similar work has already been done, and methods (attach research proposals, if appropriate), 2) resume of the technical expertise of the persons conducting the activities, and 3) planned disposition of specimens upon termination of activities.

j. Copies of contracts and agreements that identify duration of activities and persons involved in the activities for which the permit is sought. Will funding be available for the completion of the proposed activity?

k. Copy of any foreign, state or other Federal permits required. (Note: If species is listed on Appendix I of CITES, and you plan to export a specimen, send a copy (or evidence of issuance) of the CITES import permit issued by the Management Authority of the country to which you plan to export it; this is not required for specimens that qualify under CITES criteria as Pre-Convention, Captive-bred or Artificially Propagated.

l. If live wildlife or plants to be covered by permit are to be held in captivity:

1. Give a complete description, including photographs and/or diagrams, of the area and facilities where wildlife or plant will be held and/or maintained in captivity and describe arrangements for care during transportation and maintenance, if applicable.

2. Resume of persons who will care for live specimens including any experience they have had in raising, caring for, and propagating similar wildlife or plants.

3. List mortalities resulting from your activities with these or similar species in the last 2 years.

4. Indicate your willingness to participate in a cooperative breeding or propagation program or to contribute data to a studbook, if applicable.

5. If born in captivity or artificially propagated outside your facility, provide certification of such from breeder or propagator.

6. If planned activity includes import or export and the species are listed under CITES, describe the type, size and construction of any shipping containers and the arrangements of watering and otherwise caring for the wildlife or plants during transportation.

OMB NO. 42-R1573

**DEPARTMENT OF THE INTERIOR**
**U.S. FISH AND WILDLIFE SERVICE**

**FEDERAL FISH AND WILDLIFE LICENSE/PERMIT APPLICATION**

1. APPLICATION FOR *(Indicate only one)*

☐ IMPORT OR EXPORT LICENSE ☒ XX PERMIT

2. BRIEF DESCRIPTION OF ACTIVITY FOR WHICH REQUESTED LICENSE OR PERMIT IS NEEDED.

Artificially propagated Endangered-Threatened plants

_____ Interstate Commerce

_____ Export

3. APPLICANT. *(Name, complete address and phone number of individual, business, agency, or institution for which permit is requested)*

4. IF "APPLICANT" IS AN INDIVIDUAL, COMPLETE THE FOLLOWING

☐ MR. ☐ MRS. ☐ MISS ☐ MS.

| | | |
|---|---|---|
| | HEIGHT | WEIGHT |
| DATE OF BIRTH | COLOR HAIR | COLOR EYES |
| PHONE NUMBER WHERE EMPLOYED | SOCIAL SECURITY NUMBER | |

OCCUPATION

ANY BUSINESS, AGENCY, OR INSTITUTIONAL AFFILIATION HAVING TO DO WITH THE WILDLIFE TO BE COVERED BY THIS LICENSE/PERMIT

5. IF "APPLICANT" IS A BUSINESS, CORPORATION, PUBLIC AGENCY, OR INSTITUTION, COMPLETE THE FOLLOWING

EXPLAIN TYPE OR KIND OF BUSINESS, AGENCY, OR INSTITUTION

NAME, TITLE, AND PHONE NUMBER OF PRESIDENT, PRINCIPAL OFFICER, DIRECTOR, ETC.

IF "APPLICANT" IS A CORPORATION, INDICATE STATE IN WHICH INCORPORATED

6. LOCATION WHERE PROPOSED ACTIVITY IS TO BE CONDUCTED

7. DO YOU HOLD ANY CURRENTLY VALID FEDERAL FISH AND WILDLIFE LICENSE OR PERMIT? ☐ YES ☐ NO
*(If yes, list license or permit numbers)*

8. IF REQUIRED BY ANY STATE OR FOREIGN GOVERNMENT, DO YOU HAVE THEIR APPROVAL TO CONDUCT THE ACTIVITY YOU PROPOSE? ☐ YES ☐ NO
*(If yes, list jurisdictions and type of documents)*

9. CHECK OR MONEY ORDER *(if applicable)* PAYABLE TO THE U.S. FISH AND WILDLIFE SERVICE ENCLOSED IN AMOUNT OF $ 25.00

10. DESIRED EFFECTIVE DATE

11. DURATION NEEDED

12. ATTACHMENTS. THE SPECIFIC INFORMATION REQUIRED FOR THE TYPE OF LICENSE/PERMIT REQUESTED *(See 50 CFR 13.12(b))* MUST BE ATTACHED. IT CONSTITUTES AN INTEGRAL PART OF THIS APPLICATION. LIST SECTIONS OF 50 CFR UNDER WHICH ATTACHMENTS ARE PROVIDED.

**SEE REVERSE**

**CERTIFICATION**

I HEREBY CERTIFY THAT I HAVE READ AND AM FAMILIAR WITH THE REGULATIONS CONTAINED IN TITLE 50, PART 13, OF THE CODE OF FEDERAL REGULATIONS AND THE OTHER APPLICABLE PARTS IN SUBCHAPTER B OF CHAPTER I OF TITLE 50, AND I FURTHER CERTIFY THAT THE INFORMATION SUBMITTED IN THIS APPLICATION FOR A LICENSE/PERMIT IS COMPLETE AND ACCURATE TO THE BEST OF MY KNOWLEDGE AND BELIEF. I UNDERSTAND THAT ANY FALSE STATEMENT HEREIN MAY SUBJECT ME TO THE CRIMINAL PENALTIES OF 18 U.S.C. 1001.

| SIGNATURE *(In ink)* * | DATE |
|---|---|
| | |

3-200
(5/74)

*Applicant listed in 3 above or principal officer listed in 5 above must sign.

Application Continuation Sheet

## SEEDS AND ARTIFICIALLY PROPAGATED
## ENDANGERED AND THREATENED PLANTS

For each species, please provide the following information on a separate sheet of paper:

1. Genus, species and common name. (If available, please submit a copy of your most recent catalog.)
2. Approximate number of specimens you currently maintain.
3. Description of your method of propagation (seed, cutting, mericlone, etc.).
4. Source of parental stock. (If taken from the wild, state when and where—be specific. If purchased, provide the name, address and telephone number of the person from whom purchased and approximate date of purchase.)
5. A brief description of your background and expertise in working with this or similar species.
6. Photographs of your facilities and a brief description of the conditions under which your plants are grown.
7. Are you willing to cooperate in a propagation program and maintain or contribute data regarding propagation success?

Return to:

U.S. Fish and Wildlife Service
Office of Management Authority
4401 N. Fairfax Drive, Room 432
Arlington, VA 22201
Call: 703/358-2104

SEND TO:
U.S. Fish and Wildlife Service
Office of Management Authority
4401 N. Fairfax Drive, Room 432
Arlington, VA 22201
Call: 703/358-2104 for more information

OMB NO. 42-R1670

DEPARTMENT OF THE INTERIOR
U.S. FISH AND WILDLIFE SERVICE

FEDERAL FISH AND WILDLIFE LICENSE/PERMIT APPLICATION

1. APPLICATION FOR (Indicate only one)

☐ IMPORT OR EXPORT LICENSE  [XX] PERMIT

2. BRIEF DESCRIPTION OF ACTIVITY FOR WHICH REQUESTED LICENSE OR PERMIT IS NEEDED.

3. APPLICANT. (Name complete address and phone number of individual, business, agency, or institution for which permit is requested)

4. IF "APPLICANT" IS AN INDIVIDUAL, COMPLETE THE FOLLOWING:

| ☐ MR. ☐ MRS. ☐ MISS ☐ MS. | HEIGHT | WEIGHT |
|---|---|---|
| DATE OF BIRTH | COLOR HAIR | COLOR EYES |
| PHONE NUMBER WHERE EMPLOYED | SOCIAL SECURITY NUMBER | |
| OCCUPATION | | |
| ANY BUSINESS, AGENCY, OR INSTITUTIONAL AFFILIATION HAVING TO DO WITH THE WILDLIFE TO BE COVERED BY THIS LICENSE/PERMIT | | |

5. IF "APPLICANT" IS A BUSINESS, CORPORATION, PUBLIC AGENCY, OR INSTITUTION, COMPLETE THE FOLLOWING:

EXPLAIN TYPE OR KIND OF BUSINESS, AGENCY, OR INSTITUTION

NAME, TITLE, AND PHONE NUMBER OF PRESIDENT, PRINCIPAL OFFICER, DIRECTOR, ETC.

IF "APPLICANT" IS A CORPORATION, INDICATE STATE IN WHICH INCORPORATED

6. LOCATION WHERE PROPOSED ACTIVITY IS TO BE CONDUCTED

(Proposed port of export)

7. DO YOU HOLD ANY CURRENTLY VALID FEDERAL FISH AND WILDLIFE LICENSE OR PERMIT? ☐ YES ☐ NO
(If yes, list license or permit numbers)

8. IF REQUIRED BY ANY STATE OR FOREIGN GOVERNMENT, DO YOU HAVE THEIR APPROVAL TO CONDUCT THE ACTIVITY YOU PROPOSE? ☐ YES ☐ NO
(If yes, list jurisdictions and type of documents)

9. ~~XXXXXXX~~ CHECK OR MONEY ORDER (If applicable) PAYABLE TO THE U.S. FISH AND WILDLIFE SERVICE ENCLOSED IN AMOUNT OF

$ 25.00

10. DESIRED EFFECTIVE DATE

11. DURATION NEEDED

Two years

12. ATTACHMENTS. THE SPECIFIC INFORMATION REQUIRED FOR THE TYPE OF LICENSE/PERMIT REQUESTED (See 50 CFR 13.12(b)) MUST BE ATTACHED. IT CONSTITUTES AN INTEGRAL PART OF THIS APPLICATION. LIST SECTIONS OF 50 CFR UNDER WHICH ATTACHMENTS ARE PROVIDED.

SEE REVERSE

CERTIFICATION

I HEREBY CERTIFY THAT I HAVE READ AND AM FAMILIAR WITH THE REGULATIONS CONTAINED IN TITLE 50, PART 13, OF THE CODE OF FEDERAL REGULATIONS AND THE OTHER APPLICABLE PARTS IN SUBCHAPTER B OF CHAPTER I OF TITLE 50, AND I FURTHER CERTIFY THAT THE INFORMATION SUBMITTED IN THIS APPLICATION FOR A LICENSE/PERMIT IS COMPLETE AND ACCURATE TO THE BEST OF MY KNOWLEDGE AND BELIEF. I UNDERSTAND THAT ANY FALSE STATEMENT HEREIN MAY SUBJECT ME TO THE CRIMINAL PENALTIES OF 18 U.S.C. 1001.

| SIGNATURE (In ink) * | DATE |
|---|---|
| | |

3-200
(6/74)

*Applicant listed in 3 above or principal officer listed in 5 above must sign.

(Application continuation sheet)

## CITES CERTIFICATE FOR ARTIFICIALLY PROPAGATED PLANTS

For your information, under CITES, "artificial propagation. . . refers only to plants grown from seeds, cuttings, callus tissue, spores, or other propagules under controlled conditions." (Conf. 2.12)

PLEASE COMPLETE THE FOLLOWING INFORMATION FOR EACH SPECIES YOU WISH TO EXPORT UNDER THIS CERTIFICATE:

1. Scientific (genus and species) and common name.

   (If available, provide a copy of your current catalog or species list. In addition, indicate any species you wish to export that are NOT propagated at your facility but are propagated elsewhere. Provide the name and address of the facilities where these specimens are propagated.)

2. General size of plants.

3. Method of propagation (seed, cutting, mericlone, etc.).

4. Provide photographs of your facilities and briefly describe the conditions under which your plants are grown.

5. Attach copies of state or USDA nursery licenses as appropriate.

6. When and from where did you obtain the parental stock for the specimens to be exported.

7. How often do you supplement your parental or other stock with specimens that are taken from the wild?

NOTE: (a) CITES Certificates for Artificially Propagated Plants are issued only for the species you request which are listed on the inventory sheet attached to your Certificate. Therefore, you may wish to request authorization for species you currently maintain that are not listed in your catalog.

(b) When an entire family is protected under CITES (e.g., Orchidaceae), all species, hybrids, etc., therein require CITES documentation. While Certificates for Artificially Propagated Plants are not issued for specific hybrids, you must still address the information requested in 1 through 7 above. Prior to shipping, the exporter is responsible for listing the hybrids on the inventory sheet provided with the Certificate.

Return to: U.S. Fish and Wildlife Service
Office of Management Authority
4401 N. Fairfax Drive, Room 432
Arlington, VA 22203
Call: 703-358-2104 for more information

OMB NO 42-R1570

**DEPARTMENT OF THE INTERIOR**
**U.S. FISH AND WILDLIFE SERVICE**

**FEDERAL FISH AND WILDLIFE LICENSE/PERMIT APPLICATION**

1. APPLICATION FOR *(Indicate only one)*

☐ IMPORT OR EXPORT LICENSE ☒ PERMIT

2. BRIEF DESCRIPTION OF ACTIVITY FOR WHICH REQUESTED LICENSE OR PERMIT IS NEEDED

CITES Scientific Exchange Certificate

3. APPLICANT. *(Name, complete address and phone number of individual, business, agency, or institution for which permit is requested)*

4. IF "APPLICANT" IS AN INDIVIDUAL, COMPLETE THE FOLLOWING

| ☐ MR. ☐ MRS. ☐ MISS ☐ MS. | HEIGHT | WEIGHT |
|---|---|---|
| DATE OF BIRTH | COLOR HAIR | COLOR EYES |
| PHONE NUMBER WHERE EMPLOYED | SOCIAL SECURITY NUMBER | |
| OCCUPATION | | |

ANY BUSINESS, AGENCY, OR INSTITUTIONAL AFFILIATION HAVING TO DO WITH THE WILDLIFE TO BE COVERED BY THIS LICENSE/PERMIT

5. IF "APPLICANT" IS A BUSINESS, CORPORATION, PUBLIC AGENCY, OR INSTITUTION, COMPLETE THE FOLLOWING

EXPLAIN TYPE OR KIND OF BUSINESS, AGENCY, OR INSTITUTION

NAME, TITLE, AND PHONE NUMBER OF PRESIDENT, PRINCIPAL OFFICER, DIRECTOR, ETC.

IF "APPLICANT" IS A CORPORATION, INDICATE STATE IN WHICH INCORPORATED

6. LOCATION WHERE PROPOSED ACTIVITY IS TO BE CONDUCTED

7. DO YOU HOLD ANY CURRENTLY VALID FEDERAL FISH AND WILDLIFE LICENSE OR PERMIT? ☐ YES ☐ NO
*(If yes, list license or permit numbers)*

8. IF REQUIRED BY ANY STATE OR FOREIGN GOVERNMENT, DO YOU HAVE THEIR APPROVAL TO CONDUCT THE ACTIVITY YOU PROPOSE? ☐ YES ☐ NO
*(If yes, list jurisdictions and type of documents)*

9. [illegible] CHECK OR MONEY ORDER *(if applicable)* PAYABLE TO THE U.S. FISH AND WILDLIFE SERVICE ENCLOSED IN AMOUNT OF
25.00

10. DESIRED EFFECTIVE DATE

11. DURATION NEEDED
2 years

12. ATTACHMENTS. THE SPECIFIC INFORMATION REQUIRED FOR THE TYPE OF LICENSE/PERMIT REQUESTED *(See 50 CFR 13.12(b))* MUST BE ATTACHED. IT CONSTITUTES AN INTEGRAL PART OF THIS APPLICATION. LIST SECTIONS OF 50 CFR UNDER WHICH ATTACHMENTS ARE PROVIDED

SEE REVERSE

**CERTIFICATION**

I HEREBY CERTIFY THAT I HAVE READ AND AM FAMILIAR WITH THE REGULATIONS CONTAINED IN TITLE 50, PART 13, OF THE CODE OF FEDERAL REGULATIONS AND THE OTHER APPLICABLE PARTS IN SUBCHAPTER B OF CHAPTER I OF TITLE 50, AND I FURTHER CERTIFY THAT THE INFORMATION SUBMITTED IN THIS APPLICATION FOR A LICENSE/PERMIT IS COMPLETE AND ACCURATE TO THE BEST OF MY KNOWLEDGE AND BELIEF. I UNDERSTAND THAT ANY FALSE STATEMENT HEREIN MAY SUBJECT ME TO THE CRIMINAL PENALTIES OF 18 U.S.C. 1001.

| SIGNATURE *(in ink)* * | DATE |
|---|---|
| | |

3-200
(8/74) *Applicant listed in 3 above or principal officer listed in 5 above must sign.

APPLICATION FOR REGISTRATION OF SCIENTIFIC INSTITUTIONS

**Please complete the following:**

___Yes ___No 1. Are your collections and associated data permanently housed and professionally curated?
As appropriate, indicate approximate number of specimens of:

| | |
|---|---|
| ________Mammals | ________Insects/Arachnids |
| ________Birds | ________Other Invertebrates |
| ________Reptiles/Amphibians | ________Vascular Plants |
| ________Fish | ________Other |

___Yes ___No 2. Are specimens accessible to qualified users from outside your Institution?
Indicate approximate number of:

| | In U.S. | Outside U.S. |
|---|---|---|
| Loans last year: | ________ | ________ |
| Exchanges last year: | ________ | ________ |
| Donations last year: | ________ | ________ |

___Yes ___No 3. Are all accessions properly recorded in a permanent catalogue?

___Yes ___No 4. Are permanent records maintained on loans and transfers of specimens?

___Yes ___No 5. Are specimens acquired primarily for the purpose of research, the results of which are to be reported in scientific publications?

___Yes ___No 6. Are specimens prepared and the collections arranged in a manner that insures their utility?

___Yes ___No 7. Are data on specimen labels, permanent catalogues and other records as accurate as possible?

___Yes ___No 8. To the best of your knowledge, were the specimens in your collection acquired legally under the relevant laws of the United States?

___Yes ___No 9. Are all specimens of species included on Appendix I of the Convention on International Trade in Endangered Species permanently and centrally housed under your direct control?

___Yes ___No 10. Are Appendix I specimens managed in such a manner to preclude their use as decorations or trophies, or for other purposes incompatible with the principles of the Convention on International Trade in Endangered Species?

FORM 3 201A (12/82)

**CONVENTION ON INTERNATIONAL TRADE IN ENDANGERED SPECIES OF WILD FAUNA AND FLORA**

☐ IMPORT PERMIT
☐ EXPORT PERMIT
☐ RE EXPORT CERTIFICATE
☐ OTHER CERTIFICATES (See block 3)

Page ______ of ______

1 Original Permit/Certificate No
US

2 Valid until

3. Permittee (name and address, country)

4. Consignee/Consignor (name and address, country)

5. Special conditions

6 U S Management Authority

OFFICE OF MANAGEMENT AUTHORITY
U.S. FISH AND WILDLIFE SERVICE
DEPARTMENT OF THE INTERIOR
WASHINGTON, D.C. 20240
UNITED STATES OF AMERICA

Issuing Date — United States Management Authority

AUTHORITY Endangered Species Act of 1973 (16 USC 1531 et seq.)

| 7/8 Common Name and Scientific Name (genus and species) of Animal or Plant | 9. Description of part or derivative. Including identifying marks or numbers (age/sex if live) | 10 Appendix No and source (W. C. A or O) | 11. Quantity, number of specimens, and/or net weight (kg or lbs.) |
|---|---|---|---|
| A. COMMON NAME / SCIENTIFIC NAME | | 10 | 11. |
| | | 12 Country of origin* | |
| | | Country of origin permit/certificate no. | |
| B. COMMON NAME / SCIENTIFIC NAME | | 10 | 11. |
| | | 12 Country of origin* | |
| | | Country of origin permit/certificate no. | |
| C. COMMON NAME / SCIENTIFIC NAME | | 10 | 11. |
| | | 12 Country of origin* | |
| | | Country of origin permit/certificate no. | |
| D. COMMON NAME / SCIENTIFIC NAME | | 10 | 11. |
| | | 12 Country of origin* | |
| | | Country of origin permit/certificate no | |

13. Export/Re export Endorsement

The official who inspects shipment upon exportation/re exportation must enter the actual quantities of specimens being exported/re exported in this block

| See block 7 | Quantity |
|---|---|
| A | |
| B | |
| C | |
| D | |

14. Bill of Lading/Air Way-Bill Number

Port of Exportation/Re exportation

Total No. of Shipping Containers

15. This document valid only with inspecting official's ORIGINAL stamp, signature and date in this block.

Inspecting Official's Stamp, Signature and Date

This page intentionally left blank.

Office of Management Authority
4401 N. Fairfax Drive, Room 432
Arlington, VA 22201
Call: 703/358-2104 for more information

OMB NO. 42-R1670

DEPARTMENT OF THE INTERIOR
U.S. FISH AND WILDLIFE SERVICE

FEDERAL FISH AND WILDLIFE
LICENSE/PERMIT APPLICATION

1. APPLICATION FOR (Indicate only one)

☐ IMPORT OR EXPORT LICENSE ☒ PERMIT

2. BRIEF DESCRIPTION OF ACTIVITY FOR WHICH REQUESTED LICENSE OR PERMIT IS NEEDED.

Export of American ginseng
(Panax quinquefolius)

Check one:

_____ cultivated

_____ wild, taken from the ______ harvest season

3. APPLICANT. (Name, complete address and phone number of individual, business, agency, or institution for which permit is requested)

4. IF "APPLICANT" IS AN INDIVIDUAL, COMPLETE THE FOLLOWING:

☐ MR. ☐ MRS. ☐ MISS ☐ MS. | HEIGHT | WEIGHT

DATE OF BIRTH | COLOR HAIR | COLOR EYES

PHONE NUMBER WHERE EMPLOYED | SOCIAL SECURITY NUMBER

OCCUPATION

ANY BUSINESS, AGENCY, OR INSTITUTIONAL AFFILIATION HAVING TO DO WITH THE WILDLIFE TO BE COVERED BY THIS LICENSE/PERMIT

5. IF "APPLICANT" IS A BUSINESS, CORPORATION, PUBLIC AGENCY, OR INSTITUTION, COMPLETE THE FOLLOWING

EXPLAIN TYPE OR KIND OF BUSINESS, AGENCY, OR INSTITUTION

NAME, TITLE, AND PHONE NUMBER OF PRESIDENT, PRINCIPAL OFFICER, DIRECTOR, ETC.

IF "APPLICANT" IS A CORPORATION, INDICATE STATE IN WHICH INCORPORATED

6. LOCATION WHERE PROPOSED ACTIVITY IS TO BE CONDUCTED

7. DO YOU HOLD ANY CURRENTLY VALID FEDERAL FISH AND WILDLIFE LICENSE OR PERMIT? ☐ YES ☐ NO
(If yes, list license or permit numbers)

8. IF REQUIRED BY ANY STATE OR FOREIGN GOVERNMENT, DO YOU HAVE THEIR APPROVAL TO CONDUCT THE ACTIVITY YOU PROPOSE? ☐ YES ☐ NO
(If yes, list jurisdictions and type of documents)

9. CHECK OR MONEY ORDER (If applicable) PAYABLE TO THE U.S. FISH AND WILDLIFE SERVICE ENCLOSED IN AMOUNT OF

$ 25.00 (U.S. currency)

10. DESIRED EFFECTIVE DATE

11. DURATION NEEDED

12. ATTACHMENTS. THE SPECIFIC INFORMATION REQUIRED FOR THE TYPE OF LICENSE/PERMIT REQUESTED (See 50 CFR 13.12(b)) MUST BE ATTACHED. IT CONSTITUTES AN INTEGRAL PART OF THIS APPLICATION. LIST SECTIONS OF 50 CFR UNDER WHICH ATTACHMENTS ARE PROVIDED.

SEE REVERSE

CERTIFICATION

I HEREBY CERTIFY THAT I HAVE READ AND AM FAMILIAR WITH THE REGULATIONS CONTAINED IN TITLE 50, PART 13, OF THE CODE OF FEDERAL REGULATIONS AND THE OTHER APPLICABLE PARTS IN SUBCHAPTER B OF CHAPTER I OF TITLE 50, AND I FURTHER CERTIFY THAT THE INFORMATION SUBMITTED IN THIS APPLICATION FOR A LICENSE/PERMIT IS COMPLETE AND ACCURATE TO THE BEST OF MY KNOWLEDGE AND BELIEF. I UNDERSTAND THAT ANY FALSE STATEMENT HEREIN MAY SUBJECT ME TO THE CRIMINAL PENALTIES OF 18 U.S.C. 1001.

SIGNATURE (In ink) * | DATE

3-200 *Applicant listed in 3 above or principal officer listed in 5 above must sign.

Application Continuation Sheet

CONVENTION ON INTERNATIONAL TRADE IN ENDANGERED
SPECIES OF WILD FAUNA AND FLORA

**Directions:** Complete Part 1 or 2. If both artificially propagated and wild ginseng are to be exported make a separate application for each.

PART 1. Wild American Ginseng (*Panax quinquefolius*)

a. Approximate number of pounds expected to be exported ____________

b. Harvest season during which ginseng was collected; or will be collected:______
(State the year harvest season began.)

c. Describe type of goods: ______________________________________.

d. Does the applicant understand that all American ginseng to be exported must be accompanied by valid documents which certify that it was legally harvested in a state for which the U.S. Scientific Authority has approved export and the Management Authority has approved the state's management program? ____________________.

PART 2. Artifically Propagated Ginseng (*Panax quinquefolius*)

a. Approximate number of pounds expected to be exported ____________.

b. At time of application, the ginseng is: harvested ____________.
not harvested ____________.

c. Describe the type of goods ______________________________________.

d. Does the applicant understand that all cultivated American ginseng to be exported must be accompanied by valid state documents which certify that it was artifically propagated or derived therefrom?
____________________.

Office of Management Authority
U.S. Fish and Wildlife Service
4401 N. Fairfax Drive, Room 432
Arlington, Virginia 22203
Call: 703/358-2104 for more information

OMB NO. 42-R1670

**DEPARTMENT OF THE INTERIOR**
**U.S. FISH AND WILDLIFE SERVICE**

**FEDERAL FISH AND WILDLIFE LICENSE/PERMIT APPLICATION**

1. APPLICATION FOR *(Indicate only one)*

☐ IMPORT OR EXPORT LICENSE ☐ PERMIT

2. BRIEF DESCRIPTION OF ACTIVITY FOR WHICH REQUESTED LICENSE OR PERMIT IS NEEDED.

LETTER OF AUTHORIZATION for export/reexport of species circled on reverse and/or reexport of species listed on reverse

3. APPLICANT. *(Name, complete address and phone number of individual, business, agency, or institution for which permit is requested)*

4. IF "APPLICANT" IS AN INDIVIDUAL, COMPLETE THE FOLLOWING:

☐ MR. ☐ MRS. ☐ MISS ☐ MS. | HEIGHT | WEIGHT

DATE OF BIRTH | COLOR HAIR | COLOR EYES

PHONE NUMBER WHERE EMPLOYED | SOCIAL SECURITY NUMBER

OCCUPATION

ANY BUSINESS, AGENCY, OR INSTITUTIONAL AFFILIATION HAVING TO DO WITH THE WILDLIFE TO BE COVERED BY THIS LICENSE/PERMIT

5. IF "APPLICANT" IS A BUSINESS, CORPORATION, PUBLIC AGENCY, OR INSTITUTION, COMPLETE THE FOLLOWING:

EXPLAIN TYPE OR KIND OF BUSINESS, AGENCY, OR INSTITUTION

NAME, TITLE, AND PHONE NUMBER OF PRESIDENT, PRINCIPAL OFFICER, DIRECTOR, ETC.

IF "APPLICANT" IS A CORPORATION, INDICATE STATE IN WHICH INCORPORATED

6. LOCATION WHERE PROPOSED ACTIVITY IS TO BE CONDUCTED

7. DO YOU HOLD ANY CURRENTLY VALID FEDERAL FISH AND WILDLIFE LICENSE OR PERMIT? ☐ YES ☐ NO
*(If yes, list license or permit numbers)*

8. IF REQUIRED BY ANY STATE OR FOREIGN GOVERNMENT, DO YOU HAVE THEIR APPROVAL TO CONDUCT THE ACTIVITY YOU PROPOSE? ☐ YES ☐ NO
*(If yes, list jurisdictions and type of documents)*

9. CERTIFIED CHECK OR MONEY ORDER *(if applicable)* PAYABLE TO THE U.S. FISH AND WILDLIFE SERVICE ENCLOSED IN AMOUNT OF

$ NONE

10. DESIRED EFFECTIVE DATE

11. DURATION NEEDED

2 years

12. ATTACHMENTS. THE SPECIFIC INFORMATION REQUIRED FOR THE TYPE OF LICENSE/PERMIT REQUESTED *(See 50 CFR 13.12(b))* MUST BE ATTACHED. IT CONSTITUTES AN INTEGRAL PART OF THIS APPLICATION. LIST SECTIONS OF 50 CFR UNDER WHICH ATTACHMENTS ARE PROVIDED.

Complete reverse of this form

**CERTIFICATION**

I HEREBY CERTIFY THAT I HAVE READ AND AM FAMILIAR WITH THE REGULATIONS CONTAINED IN TITLE 50, PART 13, OF THE CODE OF FEDERAL REGULATIONS AND THE OTHER APPLICABLE PARTS IN SUBCHAPTER B OF CHAPTER I OF TITLE 50, AND I FURTHER CERTIFY THAT THE INFORMATION SUBMITTED IN THIS APPLICATION FOR A LICENSE/PERMIT IS COMPLETE AND ACCURATE TO THE BEST OF MY KNOWLEDGE AND BELIEF. I UNDERSTAND THAT ANY FALSE STATEMENT HEREIN MAY SUBJECT ME TO THE CRIMINAL PENALTIES OF 18 U.S.C. 1001.

* SIGNATURE *(In ink)* | DATE

3-200
(6/74) *Applicant listed in 3 above or principal officer listed in 5 above must sign.

Application continuation sheet

EXPORT/REEXPORT - LETTER OF AUTHORIZATION

**CONVENTION ON INTERNATIONAL TRADE IN ENDANGERED SPECIES OF WILD FAUNA AND FLORA**

**1. For EXPORT/REEXPORT of fur pelts, hides or products of the following CITES Appendix II wildlife:**

| Species: | Scientific name | Common name |
|---|---|---|
| CIRCLE SPECIES IN WHICH YOU WISH TO TRADE | Lynx rufus | Bobcat |
| | Lynx canadensis | Lynx |
| | Lutra canadensis | River otter |
| | Ursus arctos | Alaskan brown bear |
| | Canis lupus | Alaskan gray wolf |
| | Alligator mississippiensis | American alligator |

2. For REEXPORT of the following Appendix II and III wildlife (no Endangered or Threatened species under U.S. Endangered Species Act):

Species:

| Scientific name | Common name | Type of shipment (live animals or description of parts or products) |
|---|---|---|
| ______ | ______ | ______ |
| ______ | ______ | ______ |
| ______ | ______ | ______ |
| ______ | ______ | ______ |
| ______ | ______ | ______ |
| ______ | ______ | ______ |

a. Note: You may request authorization for general groupings of wildlife (for example, Appendix II and III reptiles, etc.)

b. LIVING ANIMALS ONLY:

(1) Describe the type, size, and construction of any shipping container:

(2) Describe the arrangements for watering and otherwise caring for the animal during transportation:

U.S. Fish and Wildlife Service
Office of Management Authority
4401 N. Fairfax Drive, Room 432
Arlington, VA 22203
Call: 703/358-2104 for more information

OMB NO. 42-R1670

**DEPARTMENT OF THE INTERIOR**
**U.S. FISH AND WILDLIFE SERVICE**

**FEDERAL FISH AND WILDLIFE LICENSE/PERMIT APPLICATION**

1. APPLICATION FOR *(Indicate only one)*
☐ IMPORT OR EXPORT LICENSE ☐ PERMIT

2. BRIEF DESCRIPTION OF ACTIVITY FOR WHICH REQUESTED LICENSE OR PERMIT IS NEEDED.

Convention on International Trade in Endangered SPECIES (CITES)
☐ Export Permit
☐ Reexport Certificate
☐ Pre-Convention Certificate

3. APPLICANT. *(Name, complete address and phone number of individual, business, agency, or institution for which permit is requested)*

4. IF "APPLICANT" IS AN INDIVIDUAL, COMPLETE THE FOLLOWING:

| ☐ MR. ☐ MRS. ☐ MISS ☐ MS. | HEIGHT | WEIGHT |
|---|---|---|
| DATE OF BIRTH | COLOR HAIR | COLOR EYES |
| PHONE NUMBER WHERE EMPLOYED | SOCIAL SECURITY NUMBER | |
| OCCUPATION | | |
| ANY BUSINESS, AGENCY, OR INSTITUTIONAL AFFILIATION HAVING TO DO WITH THE WILDLIFE TO BE COVERED BY THIS LICENSE/PERMIT | | |

5. IF "APPLICANT" IS A BUSINESS, CORPORATION, PUBLIC AGENCY, OR INSTITUTION, COMPLETE THE FOLLOWING:

EXPLAIN TYPE OR KIND OF BUSINESS, AGENCY, OR INSTITUTION

NAME, TITLE, AND PHONE NUMBER OF PRESIDENT, PRINCIPAL OFFICER, DIRECTOR, ETC.

IF "APPLICANT" IS A CORPORATION, INDICATE STATE IN WHICH INCORPORATED

6. LOCATION WHERE PROPOSED ACTIVITY IS TO BE CONDUCTED

7. DO YOU HOLD ANY CURRENTLY VALID FEDERAL FISH AND WILDLIFE LICENSE OR PERMIT? ☐ YES ☐ NO
*(If yes, list license or permit numbers)*

8. IF REQUIRED BY ANY STATE OR FOREIGN GOVERNMENT, DO YOU HAVE THEIR APPROVAL TO CONDUCT THE ACTIVITY YOU PROPOSE? ☐ YES ☐ NO
*(If yes, list jurisdictions and type of documents)*

9. CERTIFIED CHECK OR MONEY ORDER *(if applicable)* PAYABLE TO THE U.S. FISH AND WILDLIFE SERVICE ENCLOSED IN AMOUNT OF
$ 25.00

10. DESIRED EFFECTIVE DATE

11. DURATION NEEDED

12. ATTACHMENTS. THE SPECIFIC INFORMATION REQUIRED FOR THE TYPE OF LICENSE/PERMIT REQUESTED *(See 50 CFR 13.12(b))* MUST BE ATTACHED. IT CONSTITUTES AN INTEGRAL PART OF THIS APPLICATION. LIST SECTIONS OF 50 CFR UNDER WHICH ATTACHMENTS ARE PROVIDED.

SEE REVERSE

**CERTIFICATION**

I HEREBY CERTIFY THAT I HAVE READ AND AM FAMILIAR WITH THE REGULATIONS CONTAINED IN TITLE 50, PART 13, OF THE CODE OF FEDERAL REGULATIONS AND THE OTHER APPLICABLE PARTS IN SUBCHAPTER B OF CHAPTER I OF TITLE 50, AND I FURTHER CERTIFY THAT THE INFORMATION SUBMITTED IN THIS APPLICATION FOR A LICENSE/PERMIT IS COMPLETE AND ACCURATE TO THE BEST OF MY KNOWLEDGE AND BELIEF. I UNDERSTAND THAT ANY FALSE STATEMENT HEREIN MAY SUBJECT ME TO THE CRIMINAL PENALTIES OF 18 U.S.C. 1001.

** SIGNATURE *(In ink)* | DATE

3-200
(8/74)

**Applicant listed in 3 above or principal officer listed in 5 above must sign.

CITES -- APPLICATION CONTINUATION SHEET -- WILDLIFE

I. COMPLETE THE FOLLOWING for each individual animal:

(NOTE: For export or reexport of several of the same non-living wildlife items, applicant may describe such items under "Description" and designate the exact quantity of such samples to be shipped.)

a.

| Species: Scientific name (genus and species) | Common name | Birth date/ age | Sex | Country of Origin (If U.S. - Specific location of birth) | *Source (W, C) | Description: ID, tattoo, tag or band #, scars, house name, etc. If type of goods, describe (such as purse, rug, raw skin, type of trophy, etc.). If biological sample, include description of type and size of sample. |
|---|---|---|---|---|---|---|
| | | | | | | |
| | | | | | | |
| | | | | | | |
| | | | | | | |

b. Name and address of recipient: ______________________

*Source:
W = living in wild or removed from the wild.
C = captive-born (for export see II. e. below).
NOTE: For non-living wildlife, such as biological samples, hides, products, etc., the "Source" refers to the source of wildlife from which the items were obtained.

II. ATTACH THE FOLLOWING:

a. For EXPORT or REEXPORT of living wildlife: (i) describe the type, size, and construction of any shipping containers and (ii) describe the arrangements for watering and otherwise caring for the wildlife during transportation.

b. For EXPORT or REEXPORT of Appendix I wildlife: copy of CITES import permit issued by the Management Authority of the country to which you plan to export/reexport specimen (that is the country of the recipient named in I. b. above. (Not required if the specimen qualifies as Pre-Convention)

c. For EXPORT of Appendix I or II wildlife if taken from the wild: (i) evidence that it was legally taken (such as State hunting license and tag#) and (ii) purpose specimen was removed from the wild.

d. For EXPORT of Appendix III wildlife: evidence specimen was BORN in the United States. See II. e. below for details on what constitutes evidence of captive-born.

e. For EXPORT of captive-born wildlife: documents, sworn affidavits, or other evidence that the individual animal was born in captivity. Such documents must include birth or hatch date, sex, and the complete name and address of the breeder's facility. If you are not the breeder of the wildlife, you need to submit breeder's records or sworn affidavit from the breeder specifying the above information and copies of the invoice or other documentation showing that you acquired the wildlife from the breeder or history of multiple transactions.

f. For EXPORT of migratory birds [50 CFR 10.13], their parts, nests, or eggs: (i) purpose of the export, (ii) estimated date of departure of the shipment(s), (iii) port of exit from the U.S., and (iv) Federal and State permit numbers and type of permits authorizing possession, acquisition, or disposition of such birds, their parts, nests, or eggs, where such a permit is required.

In addition, for EXPORT of raptors, provide written certification from the Management Authority of the importing country that the recipient is an experienced falconer or raptor propagator who is required to maintain any raptors in his/her possession under conditions that are comparable to the conditions under which a permittee must maintain raptors under 50 CFR 21.29 or 21.30.

g. For REEXPORT: evidence the specimen was legally imported (a copy of the cancelled CITES export or reexport document issued by the Management Authority or its equivalent in country from which the wildlife was imported or a copy of the cleared Declaration for Importation (Form 3-177). (If you did not make the original import, you need to show both the importer's cancelled CITES document or cleared 3-177 AND copies of the invoice or other documentation showing that you acquired the wildlife from the importer or the history of multiple transactions.)

h. For PRE-CONVENTION: documents, sworn affidavits or other evidence that the wildlife was obtained prior to the date the Convention applied to it (such as bill of sale, U.S. Customs import declarations, ISIS documents, etc.)

SEND TO:
Office of Management Authority
U.S. Fish and Wildlife Service
4401 N. Fairfax Drive, Rm. 432
Arlington, Virginia 22203 (Call: 703/358-2104 for more information)

**PLANTS**

OMB NO. 42-R1670

**DEPARTMENT OF THE INTERIOR**
**U.S. FISH AND WILDLIFE SERVICE**

**FEDERAL FISH AND WILDLIFE LICENSE/PERMIT APPLICATION**

1. APPLICATION FOR *(Indicate only one)*
☐ IMPORT OR EXPORT LICENSE  [XX] PERMIT

2. BRIEF DESCRIPTION OF ACTIVITY FOR WHICH REQUESTED LICENSE OR PERMIT IS NEEDED.

CONVENTION ON INTERNATIONAL TRADE IN ENDANGERED SPECIES (CITES)

_____ Import
_____ Export
_____ Reexport
_____ Pre-Convention Certificate

3. APPLICANT. *(Name complete address and phone number of individual, business, agency, or institution for which permit is requested)*

4. IF "APPLICANT" IS AN INDIVIDUAL, COMPLETE THE FOLLOWING.

| ☐ MR. ☐ MRS. ☐ MISS ☐ MS. | HEIGHT | WEIGHT |
|---|---|---|
| DATE OF BIRTH | COLOR HAIR | COLOR EYES |
| PHONE NUMBER WHERE EMPLOYED | SOCIAL SECURITY NUMBER | |
| OCCUPATION | | |
| ANY BUSINESS, AGENCY, OR INSTITUTIONAL AFFILIATION HAVING TO DO WITH THE WILDLIFE TO BE COVERED BY THIS LICENSE/PERMIT | | |

5. IF "APPLICANT" IS A BUSINESS, CORPORATION, PUBLIC AGENCY, OR INSTITUTION, COMPLETE THE FOLLOWING

EXPLAIN TYPE OR KIND OF BUSINESS, AGENCY, OR INSTITUTION

NAME, TITLE, AND PHONE NUMBER OF PRESIDENT, PRINCIPAL OFFICER, DIRECTOR, ETC.

IF "APPLICANT" IS A CORPORATION, INDICATE STATE IN WHICH INCORPORATED

6. LOCATION WHERE PROPOSED ACTIVITY IS TO BE CONDUCTED
(U.S. port)

7. DO YOU HOLD ANY CURRENTLY VALID FEDERAL FISH AND WILDLIFE LICENSE OR PERMIT? ☐ YES ☐ NO
*(If yes, list license or permit numbers)*

8. IF REQUIRED BY ANY STATE OR FOREIGN GOVERNMENT, DO YOU HAVE THEIR APPROVAL TO CONDUCT THE ACTIVITY YOU PROPOSE? ☐ YES ☐ NO
*(If yes, list jurisdictions and type of documents)*

9. XXXXXX CHECK OR MONEY ORDER *(if applicable)* PAYABLE TO THE U.S. FISH AND WILDLIFE SERVICE ENCLOSED IN AMOUNT OF
$ 25.00

10. DESIRED EFFECTIVE DATE

11. DURATION NEEDED

12. ATTACHMENTS. THE SPECIFIC INFORMATION REQUIRED FOR THE TYPE OF LICENSE/PERMIT REQUESTED *(See 50 CFR 13.12(b))* MUST BE ATTACHED. IT CONSTITUTES AN INTEGRAL PART OF THIS APPLICATION. LIST SECTIONS OF 50 CFR UNDER WHICH ATTACHMENTS ARE PROVIDED.

SEE REVERSE

**CERTIFICATION**

I HEREBY CERTIFY THAT I HAVE READ AND AM FAMILIAR WITH THE REGULATIONS CONTAINED IN TITLE 50, PART 13, OF THE CODE OF FEDERAL REGULATIONS AND THE OTHER APPLICABLE PARTS IN SUBCHAPTER B OF CHAPTER I OF TITLE 50, AND I FURTHER CERTIFY THAT THE INFORMATION SUBMITTED IN THIS APPLICATION FOR A LICENSE/PERMIT IS COMPLETE AND ACCURATE TO THE BEST OF MY KNOWLEDGE AND BELIEF. I UNDERSTAND THAT ANY FALSE STATEMENT HEREIN MAY SUBJECT ME TO THE CRIMINAL PENALTIES OF 18 U.S.C. 1001.

| SIGNATURE *(In ink)* * | DATE |
|---|---|

3-200 (6/74) *Applicant listed in 3 above or principal officer listed in 5 above must sign.

I. COMPLETE THE FOLLOWING for each species:

a. Species:

| Scientific name (genus & species) | Common name | Quantity | Country of origin | *Source (W,L,D,C) | Description of goods if part or derivitive |
|---|---|---|---|---|---|
| | | | | | |
| | | | | | |
| | | | | | |
| | | | | | |
| | | | | | |

b. For EXPORT or REEXPORT, name and address of recipient: ______________

For IMPORT, person from whom imported: ______________

*Source:
W = living in wild
L = living but not in wild
D = dead
A = artificially propagated

II. ATTACH THE FOLLOWING:

a. For IMPORT of Appendix I species: (1) provide purposes and details of activities for which plants are to be imported or a copy of a developed research proposal); (2) brief resume of technical expertise of applicant or other persons assuming responsibility for specimens; and, (3) name, address and description or photographs of facility where specimens will be maintained.

b. For EXPORT of Appendix I or II plants taken from the wild: (1) specific location where taken and (2) evidence that the plants were legally collected.

c. For EXPORT or REEXPORT of living plants: (1) describe type of shipping container and (2) arrangements for care during shipping.

d. For EXPORT or REEXPORT of Appendix I plants: copy of CITES import permit issued by the Management Authority of the importing country. (Not required if specimen qualifies as Pre-Convention or Artificially Propagated.)

e. For EXPORT of Appendix III plants: evidence specimen was artificially propagated in the United States.

f. For REEXPORT: evidence the specimen was legally imported (CITES export or reexport document issued by the Management Authority or its equivalent in the country from which the plant was imported. For plants imported prior to January 1978, supply a copy of dated invoice and correspondingly dated way bills or foreign phytosanitary certificates. If you did not make the original import, you need to show both the importer's CITES document (or alternate documentation described above) and the invoice or other documentation showing that you purchased the plant(s) from the original importer, or the history of multiple transactions.)

g. For PRE-CONVENTION: documents, sworn affidavits or other evidence that the plant was obtained prior to the date the Convention applied to it (such as bill of sale, USDA or foreign phytosanitary certificate, etc.)

h. ARTIFICIALLY PROPAGATED: (1) statement from propagator, sworn affidavits or other evidence that the specimen was artificially propagated in the United States and (2) source of parental stock.

## SAMPLE APPLICATION: PRE-ACT AFFIDAVIT, REQUIREMENTS ESA

### U.S. ENDANGERED SPECIES ACT
### PRE-ACT WILDLIFE
### 50 CFR 17.4

(a) The prohibitions defined in subparts C and D of this part 17 shall not apply to any activity involving endangered or threatened wildlife which was held in captivity or in a controlled environment on December 28, 1973: *Provided,*

(1) That the purposes of such holding were not contrary to the purposes of the Act; and

(2) That the wildlife was not held in the course of a commercial activity.

*Example 1*. On January 25, 1974, a tourist buys a stuffed hawksbill turtle (an endangered species listed since June 1970), in a foreign country. On December 28, 1973, the stuffed turtle had been on display for sale. The tourist imports the stuffed turtle into the United States on January 26, 1974. This is a violation of the Act since the stuffed turtle was held for commercial purposes on December 28, 1973.

*Example 2*. On December 27, 1973 (or earlier), a tourist buys a leopard skin coat (the leopard has been listed as endangered since March 1972) for his wife in a foreign country. On January 5, he imports it into the United States. He has not committed a violation since on December 28, 1973, he was the owner of the coat, for personal purposes, and the chain of commerce had ended with the sale on the 27th. Even if he did not finish paying for the coat for another year, as long as he had possession of it, and he was not going to resell it, but was using it for personal purposes, the Act does not apply to that coat.

*Example 3*. On or before December 28, 1973, a hunter kills a leopard legally in Africa. He has the leopard mounted and imports it into the United States in March 1974. The importation is not subject to the Act. The hunter has not engaged in a commercial activity, even though he bought the services of a guide, outfitters, and a taxidermist to help him take, preserve, and import the leopard. This applies even if the trophy was in the possession of the taxidermist on December 28, 1973.

*Example 4*. On January 15, 1974, a hunter kills a leopard legally in Africa. He has the leopard mounted and imports it into the United States in June 1974. This importation is a violation of the Act since the leopard was not in captivity or a controlled environment on December 28, 1973.

(b) Service officers or Customs officers may refuse to clear endangered or threatened wildlife for importation into or exportation from the United States, pursuant to § 14.53 of this subchapter, until the importer or exporter can demonstrate that the exemption referred to in this section applies. Exempt status may be established by any sufficient evidence, including an affidavit containing the following:

(1) The affiant's name and address;

(2) Identification of the affiant;

(3) Identification of the endangered or threatened wildlife which is the subject of the affidavit;

(4) A statement by the affiant that to the best of his knowledge and belief, the endangered or threatened wildlife which is the subject of the affidavit was in captivity or in a controlled environment on December 28, 1973, and was not being held for purposes contrary to the Act or in the course of a commercial activity;

(5) A statement by the affiant in the following language:

The foregoing is principally based on the attached exhibits which, to the best of my knowledge and belief, are complete, true and correct. I understand that this affidavit is being submitted for the purpose of inducing the Federal Government to recognize an exempt status regarding *(insert description of wildlife)*, under the Endangered Species Act of 1973 (16 U.S.C. 1531–1543), and regulations promulgated thereunder, and that any false statements may be subject to the criminal penalties of 18 U.S.C. 1001.

(6) As an attachment, records or other available evidence to show:

(i) That the wildlife in question was being held in captivity or in a controlled environment on December 28, 1973;

(ii) The purpose for which the wildlife was being held; and

(iii) The nature of such holding (to establish that no commercial activity was involved).

(c) This section applies only to wildlife born on or prior to December 28, 1973. It does not apply to the progeny of any such wildlife born after December 28, 1973.—OCT. 1990

## U.S. MARINE MAMMAL PROTECTION ACT
## PRE-ACT MARINE MAMMALS
## 50 CFR 18.14

**§ 18.14 Marine mammals taken before the Act.**

(a) Section 102(e) of the Act provides in effect that the Act shall not apply to any marine mammal taken prior to December 21, 1972, or to any marine mammal product consisting of, or composed in whole or in part of, any marine mammal taken before such date. Such status may be established by submitting to the Director prior to, or at the time of importation, an affidavit containing the following:

(1) The affiant's name and address;

(2) Identification of the affiant;

(3) A description of the marine mammals or marine mammal products which the affiant desires to import;

(4) A statement by the affiant that to the best of his knowledge and belief, the marine mammals involved in the application were taken prior to December 21, 1972;

(5) A statement by the affiant in the following language:

The foregoing is principally based on the attached exhibits which, to the best of my knowledge and belief, are complete, true and correct. I understand that this affidavit is being submitted for the purpose of inducing the Federal Government to permit the importation of ——— under the Marine Mammal Protection Act of 1972 (16 U.S.C. 1361–1407) and regulations promulgated thereunder, and that any false statements may subject me to the criminal penalties of 18 U.S.C. 1001.

(b) Either one of two exhibits shall be attached to such affidavit, and will contain either:

(1) Records or other available evidence showing that the product consists of or is composed in whole or in part of marine mammals taken prior to December 21, 1972. Such records or other evidentiary material must include information on how, when, where, and by whom the animals were taken, what processing has taken place since taking, and the date and location of such processing; or

(2) A statement from a government agency of the country of origin exercising jurisdiction over marine mammals that any and all such mammals from which the products sought to be imported were derived were taken prior to December 21, 1972.

(c) Service agents, or Customs officers, may refuse to clear marine mammals or marine mammal products for importation into the United States; pursuant to § 14.53 of this subchapter, until the importer can demonstrate, by production of the affidavit referred in above or otherwise, that section 102(e) of the Act applies to all affected items.

(d) This section has no application to any marine mammal or marine mammal product intended to be imported pursuant to § 18.21, § 18.31 or § 18.32 of this part.—OCT. 1990

Call: 703-358-2104 for more information

OMB NO. 42-R1670

**DEPARTMENT OF THE INTERIOR**
**U.S. FISH AND WILDLIFE SERVICE**

**FEDERAL FISH AND WILDLIFE LICENSE/PERMIT APPLICATION**

1. APPLICATION FOR *(Indicate only one)*

☐ IMPORT OR EXPORT LICENSE   ☒ PERMIT

2. BRIEF DESCRIPTION OF ACTIVITY FOR WHICH REQUESTED LICENSE OR PERMIT IS NEEDED.

(__) To become registered as an agent under the Marine Mammal Protection Act.

(__) To become registered as a tannery under the Marine Mammal Protection Act.

3. APPLICANT. *(Name, complete address and phone number of individual, business, agency, or institution for which permit is requested)*

4. IF "APPLICANT" IS AN INDIVIDUAL, COMPLETE THE FOLLOWING

☐ MR. ☐ MRS. ☐ MISS ☐ MS.

| | HEIGHT | WEIGHT |
|---|---|---|
| DATE OF BIRTH | COLOR HAIR | COLOR EYES |
| PHONE NUMBER WHERE EMPLOYED | SOCIAL SECURITY NUMBER | |

OCCUPATION

ANY BUSINESS, AGENCY, OR INSTITUTIONAL AFFILIATION HAVING TO DO WITH THE WILDLIFE TO BE COVERED BY THIS LICENSE/PERMIT

5. IF "APPLICANT" IS A BUSINESS, CORPORATION, PUBLIC AGENCY, OR INSTITUTION, COMPLETE THE FOLLOWING

EXPLAIN TYPE OR KIND OF BUSINESS, AGENCY, OR INSTITUTION

NAME, TITLE, AND PHONE NUMBER OF PRESIDENT, PRINCIPAL OFFICER, DIRECTOR, ETC.

IF "APPLICANT" IS A CORPORATION, INDICATE STATE IN WHICH INCORPORATED

6. LOCATION WHERE PROPOSED ACTIVITY IS TO BE CONDUCTED

7. DO YOU HOLD ANY CURRENTLY VALID FEDERAL FISH AND WILDLIFE LICENSE OR PERMIT? ☐ YES ☐ NO
*(If yes, list license or permit numbers)*

8. IF REQUIRED BY ANY STATE OR FOREIGN GOVERNMENT, DO YOU HAVE THEIR APPROVAL TO CONDUCT THE ACTIVITY YOU PROPOSE? ☐ YES ☐ NO
*(If yes, list jurisdictions and type of documents)*

9. CERTIFIED CHECK OR MONEY ORDER *(if applicable)* PAYABLE TO THE U.S. FISH AND WILDLIFE SERVICE ENCLOSED IN AMOUNT OF

$ 25.00

10. DESIRED EFFECTIVE DATE

11. DURATION NEEDED

12. ATTACHMENTS. THE SPECIFIC INFORMATION REQUIRED FOR THE TYPE OF LICENSE/PERMIT REQUESTED *(See 50 CFR 13.12(b))* MUST BE ATTACHED. IT CONSTITUTES AN INTEGRAL PART OF THIS APPLICATION. LIST SECTIONS OF 50 CFR UNDER WHICH ATTACHMENTS ARE PROVIDED.

Refer to reverse side -- fulfills 50 CFR 18.23(d)

**CERTIFICATION**

I HEREBY CERTIFY THAT I HAVE READ AND AM FAMILIAR WITH THE REGULATIONS CONTAINED IN TITLE 50, PART 13, OF THE CODE OF FEDERAL REGULATIONS AND THE OTHER APPLICABLE PARTS IN SUBCHAPTER B OF CHAPTER I OF TITLE 50, AND I FURTHER CERTIFY THAT THE INFORMATION SUBMITTED IN THIS APPLICATION FOR A LICENSE/PERMIT IS COMPLETE AND ACCURATE TO THE BEST OF MY KNOWLEDGE AND BELIEF. I UNDERSTAND THAT ANY FALSE STATEMENT HEREIN MAY SUBJECT ME TO THE CRIMINAL PENALTIES OF 18 U.S.C. 1001.

| SIGNATURE *(In ink)* | DATE |
|---|---|
| | |

Application Continuation Sheet

REGISTERED AGENT -- 50 CFR 18.23(d)

I am applying for registration under the Marine Mammal Protection Act regulations as a Tannery and/or Agent:

_____Tannery _____Agent

I would like to deal in parts and products of the following animals:

_____Polar bear (Ursus maritimus)

_____Walrus (Odobenus rosmarus)

_____Alaskan sea otter (Enhydra lutris)

I have enclosed the following information with my application:

Description of my procedures for receiving, storing, processing and shipping marine mammal parts and products.

Description of my present or proposed system of bookkeeping and inventory segregation (copy of bookkeeping ledger sheet and inventory record that shows for each transaction the number and, in the case of walrus ivory, weight of parts and products received, from whom received, for whom held, to whom transferred, returned or sold and the date of each transaction).

_____I will keep records of each transaction with marine mammal parts and keep them separate and apart from all other records maintained in the ordinary course of business.

_____I will maintain such records for not less than three years.

I hereby certify that the foregoing information is complete, true, and correct to the best of my knowledge and belief. I understand that this information is submitted for the purpose of obtaining the benefit of an exception under the Marine Mammal Protection Act of 1972 (16 USC 1361-1407) and regulations promulgated thereunder, and that any false statement may subject me to the criminal penalties of 18 USC 1001.

_______________________________
Applicant's signature

## APPLICATION REQUIREMENTS: FALCONRY PERMITS

**§ 21.28 Falconry permits.**

(a) *Permit requirements*. A falconry permit is required before any person may take, possess, transport, sell, purchase, barter, offer to sell, purchase, or barter raptors for falconry purposes.

(b) *Application procedures*. (1) An applicant who wishes to practice falconry in a State listed in § 21.29(k) of this part and which has been designated as a participant in a cooperative Federal/State permit application program may submit an application for a falconry permit to the appropriate agency of that State. Each such application must incorporate a completed official form approved by the Service and must include in addition to the general information required by part 13 of this subchapter all of the following:

(i) The number of raptors the applicant possesses at the time the application is submitted, including the species, age (if known), sex (if known), date of acquisition, and source of each;

(ii) A check or money order made payable to "U.S. Fish and Wildlife Service" in the amount of the application fee listed in § 13.11(d) of this subchapter.

(iii) An original, signed certification concerning the validity of the information provided in the application in the form set forth in § 13.12(a)(5).

(iv) Any additional information requested by the State to which the application is submitted.

(2) Upon receipt of a joint application by a State listed in § 21.29(k) as a participant in a cooperative Federal/State permit application program, the State will process the application for a State falconry permit in accordance with its own procedures. A copy of the application, the check or money order for Federal permit fees, and the original, signed certification required by paragraph (b)(1)(iii) of this section will be forwarded to the issuing office of the Service designated by § 13.11(b) of this subchapter. If the State decides to issue a falconry permit based upon the application, a copy of the permit will also be forwarded to the appropriate issuing office of the Service.

(3) An applicant who wishes to practice falconry in a State listed in § 21.29(k) of this subchapter, but which does not participate in a cooperative Federal/State permit application program must submit a written application for a falconry permit to the issuing office designated by § 13.11(b) of this subchapter. Each application must contain the general information and certification required by § 13.12(a) of this subchapter plus a copy of a valid State falconry permit issued to the applicant by a State listed in § 21.19(k) of this subchapter.

(c) *Issuance criteria*. Upon receiving an application completed in accordance with paragraph (b) of this section that meets all requirements of this part, the Director will issue a permit. In addition to meeting the general criteria in § 13.21(b), the applicant must have a valid State falconry permit issued by a State listed in § 21.29(k) of this subchapter.

(d) *Permit conditions*. In addition to the general conditions set forth in part 13 of this subchapter, every permit issued under this section shall be subject to the following special conditions:

(1) A permittee may not take, transport, or possess a golden eagle *(Aquila chrysaetos)* unless authorized in writing under § 22.24 of this subchapter.

(2) A permit issued under this section is not valid unless the permittee has a valid State falconry permit issued by a State listed in § 21.29(k) of this subchapter.

(3) A permittee may not take, possess, transport, sell, purchase, barter, or transfer any raptor for falconry purposes except under authority of a Federal falconry permit issued under this section and in compliance with the Federal falconry standards set forth in § 21.29 of this subchapter.

(4) No permittee may take, purchase, receive, or otherwise acquire, sell, barter, transfer, or otherwise dispose of any raptor unless such permittee submits a form 3-186A (Migratory Bird Acquisition/Disposition Report), completed in accordance with the instructions on the form, to the issuing office within five (5) calendar days of any such transaction.

(5) No raptor may be possessed under authority of a falconry permit unless the permittee has a properly completed form 3-186A (Migratory Bird Acquisition/Disposition Report) for each bird possessed, except as provided in paragraph (d)(4) of this section.

(6) A raptor possessed under authority of a falconry permit may be temporarily held by a person other than the permittee for maintenance and care for a period not to exceed thirty (30) days. The raptor must be accompanied at all times by a properly completed form 3-186A (Migratory Bird Acquisition/Disposi-

tion Report) designating the person caring for the raptor as the possessor of record and by a signed, dated statement from the permittee authorizing the temporary possession.

(7) A permittee may not take, possess, or transport any peregrine falcon *(Falco peregrinus)*, gyrfalcon *(Falco rusticolus)*, or Harris hawk *(Parabuteo unicinctus)* unless such bird is banded either by a seamless numbered band provided by the Service or by a permanent, non-reusable band provided by the Service.

(i) Any peregrine falcon *(Falco peregrinus)*, gyrfalcon *(Falco rusticolus)*, or Harris Hawk *(Parabuteo unicinctus)* taken from the wild must be reported to the issuing office within five (5) days of taking and must be banded with a permanent, non-reusable band provided by the Service. No raptor removed from the wild may be banded with a seamless numbered band.

(ii) The loss or removal of any band must be reported to the issuing office within five (5) working days of the loss. The lost band must be replaced by a permanent, non-reusable band supplied by the Service. A form 3-186A (Migratory Bird Acquisition/Disposition Report) must be filed in accordance with paragraph (d)(4) of this section reporting the loss of the band and rebanding.

(8) A permittee may not sell, purchase, barter, or offer to sell, purchase or barter any raptor unless the raptor is marked on the matatarsus by a seamless, numbered band supplied by the Service.

(9) A permittee may not propagate raptors without prior acquisition of a valid raptor propagation permit issued under section 21.30 of this subchapter.

(e) *Term of permit*. A falconry permit issued or renewed under this part expires on the date designated on the face of the permit unless amended or revoked, but the term of the permit shall not exceed three (3) years from the date of issuance or renewal.

[54 FR 38152, Sept. 14, 1989]

## APPLICATION REQUIREMENTS: TAXIDERMY PERMITS

**§ 21.24 Taxidermist permits.**

(a) *Permit requirement.* A taxidermist permit is required before any person may perform taxidermy services on migratory birds or their parts, nests, or eggs for any person other than himself.

(b) *Application procedures.* Application for taxidermist permits shall be submitted to the appropriate Special Agent in Charge (see: § 13.11(b) of this subchapter). Each such application must contain the general information and certification set forth by § 13.12(a) of this subchapter plus the following additional information:

(1) The address of the premises where taxidermist services will be provided;

(2) A statement of the applicant's qualifications and experience as a taxidermist; and

(3) If a State permit is required by State law, a statement as to whether or not the applicant possesses such State permit, giving its number and expiration date.

(c) *Permit authorizations.* A permit authorizes a taxidermist to:

(1) Receive, transport, hold in custody or possession, mount or otherwise prepare migratory birds, and their parts, nests, or eggs, and return them to another.

(2) Sell properly marked, captive reared migratory waterfowl which he has lawfully acquired and mounted. Such mounted birds may be placed on consignment for sale and may be possessed by such consignee for the purpose of sale.

(d) *Additional permit conditions.* In addition to the general conditions set forth in part 13 of this subchapter B, taxidermist permits shall be subject to the following conditions:

(1) Permittees must keep accurate records of operations, on a calendar year basis, showing the names and addresses of persons from and to whom migratory birds or their parts, nests, or eggs were received or delivered, the number and species of such, and the dates of receipt and delivery. In addition to the other records required by this paragraph, the permittee must maintain in his files the original of the completed Form 3-186, Notice of Waterfowl Sale or Transfer, confirming his acquisition of captive reared, properly marked migratory waterfowl from the holder of a current waterfowl sale and disposal permit.

(2) Notwithstanding the provisions of paragraph (c) of this section, the receipt, possession, and storage by a taxidermist of any migratory game birds taken by another by hunting is not authorized unless they are tagged as required by § 20.36 of this subchapter. The required tags may be removed during the taxidermy operations but must be retained by the taxidermist with the other records required to be kept and must be reattached to the mounted specimen after mounting. The tag must then remain attached until the mounted specimen is delivered to the owner.

(e) *Term of permit.* A taxidermist permit issued or renewed under this part expires on the date designated on the face of the permit unless amended or revoked, but the term of the permit shall not exceed three (3) years from the date of issuance or renewal.

[39 FR 1178, Jan. 4, 1974, as amended at 54 FR 38151, Sept. 14, 1989]

## APPLICATION REQUIREMENTS: BANDING PERMITS

**§ 21.22 Banding or marking permits.**

(a) *Permit requirement.* A banding or marking permit is required before any person may capture migratory birds for banding or marking purposes or use official bands issued by the Service for banding or marking any migratory bird.

(b) *Application procedures.* Applications for banding or marking permits shall be submitted by letter of application addressed to the Bird Banding Laboratory, Office of Migratory Bird Management, U.S. Fish and Wildlife Service, Laurel, Maryland 20708. Each such application shall contain the general information and certification set forth by § 13.12(a) of this subchapter plus the following additional information:

(1) Species and numbers proposed to be banded or marked;

(2) Purpose of banding or marking;

(3) State or States in which authorization is requested; and

(4) Name and address of the public, scientific, or educational institution to which any specimens will be donated that are salvaged pursuant to paragraphs (c) (3) and (4) of this section.

(c) *Additional permit conditions.* In addition to the general conditions set forth in part 13 of this subchapter B, banding or marking permits shall be subject to the following conditions:

(1) The banding of migratory birds shall only be by official numbered leg bands issued by the Service. The use of any other band, clip, dye, or other method of marking is prohibited unless specifically authorized in the permit.

(2) All traps or nets used to capture migratory birds for banding or marking purposes shall have attached thereto a tag or label clearly showing the name and address of the permittee and his permit number, or the area in which such traps or nets are located must be posted with notice of banding operations posters (Form 3-1155, available upon request from the Bird Banding Laboratory, Office of Migratory Bird Management, U.S. Fish and Wildlife Service, Laurel, Md. 20708) which shall bear the name and address of the permittee and the number of his permit.

(3) The holder of a banding or marking permit may salvage, for the purpose of donating to a public scientific or educational institution, birds killed or found dead as a result of the permittee's normal banding operations, and casualties from other causes. All dead birds salvaged under authority of a migratory bird banding or marking permit must be donated and transferred to a public scientific or educational institution at least every six months or within 60 days of the time such permit expires or is revoked, unless the permittee has been issued a special permit authorizing possession for a longer period of time.

(4) Permittees must keep accurate records of their operations and file reports as set forth in the North American Bird Banding Manual, or supplements thereto, in accordance with instructions contained therein.

(d) *Term of permit.* A banding or marking permit issued or renewed under this part expires on the date designated on the face of the permit unless amended or revoked, but the term of the permit shall not exceed three (3) years from the date of issuance or renewal.

[39 FR 1178, Jan. 4, 1974, as amended at 54 FR 38151, Sept. 14, 1989]

## APPLICATION REQUIREMENTS: SCIENTIFIC COLLECTING PERMITS

**§ 21.23 Scientific collecting permits.**

(a) *Permit requirement*. A scientific collecting permit is required before any person may take, transport, or possess migratory birds, their parts, nests, or eggs for scientific research or educational purposes.

(b) *Application procedures*. Applications for scientific collecting permits shall be submitted to the appropriate issuing officer (see: § 13.11(b) of this subchapter). Each such application must contain the general information and certification required by § 13.12(a) of this subchapter plus the following additional information:

(1) Species and numbers of migratory birds or their parts, nests, or eggs to be taken or acquired when it is possible to determine same in advance;

(2) Location or locations where such scientific collecting is proposed;

(3) Statement of the purpose and justification for granting such a permit, including an outline of any research project involved;

(4) Name and address of the public scientific, or educational institution to which all specimens ultimately will be donated; and

(5) If a State permit is required by State law, a statement as to whether or not the applicant possesses such State permit, giving its number and expiration date.

(c) *Additional permit conditions*. In addition to the general conditions set forth in Part 13 of this Subchapter B, scientific collecting permits shall be subject to the following conditions:

(1) All specimens taken and possessed under authority of a scientific collecting permit must be donated and transferred to the public scientific or educational institution designated in the permit application within 60 days following the date such permit expires or is revoked, unless the permittee has been issued a special purpose permit (See § 21.27) authorizing possession for a longer period of time.

(2) Unless otherwise provided on the permit, all migratory game birds taken pursuant to a scientific collecting permit during the open hunting season for such birds must be in conformance with Part 20 of this subchapter;

(3) Unless specifically stated on the permit, a scientific collecting permit does not authorize the taking of live migratory birds from the wild.

(4) In addition to any reporting requirement set forth in the permit, a report of the scientific collecting activities conducted under authority of such permit shall be submitted to the issuing officer on or before January 10 of each calendar year following the year of issue unless a different date is stated in the permit.

(d) *Term of permit*. A scientific collecting permit issued or renewed under this part expires on the date designated on the face of the permit unless amended or revoked, but the term of the permit shall not exceed three (3) years from the date of issuance or renewal.

[39 FR 1178, Jan. 4, 1974, as amended at 54 FR 38151, Sept. 14, 1989]

## APPLICATION REQUIREMENTS: WATERFOWL SALE AND DISPOSAL

**§ 21.25 Waterfowl sale and disposal permits.**

(a) *Permit requirement.* A waterfowl sale and disposal permit is required before any person may lawfully sell, trade, donate, or otherwise dispose of, to another person, any species of captive-reared and properly marked migratory waterfowl or their eggs, except that such a permit is not required for such sales or disposals of captive-reared and properly marked mallard ducks or their eggs.

(b) *Application procedures.* Applications for waterfowl sale and disposal permits shall be submitted to the appropriate Special Agent in Charge (see: § 13.11(b) of this subchapter). Each such application must contain the general information and certification required in § 13.12(a) of this subchapter, plus the following additional information:

(1) A description of the area where waterfowl are to be kept;

(2) Species and numbers of waterfowl now in possession and a statement showing from whom these were obtained;

(3) A statement indicating the method by which individual birds are marked as required by the provisions of this part 21; and

(4) If a State permit is required by State law, a statement as to whether or not the applicant possesses such State permit, giving its number and expiration date.

(c) *Additional permit conditions.* In addition to the general conditions set forth in part 13 of this subchapter B, waterfowl sale and disposal permits shall be subject to the following conditions:

(1) Permittees may not take migratory waterfowl or their eggs from the wild, and may not acquire such birds or their eggs from any person not authorized by a valid permit issued pursuant to this part to dispose of such birds or their eggs.

(2) All live migratory waterfowl possessed in captivity under authority of a valid waterfowl sale and disposal permit shall have been, prior to 6 weeks of age, physically marked as defined in § 21.13(b). All offspring of such birds hatched, reared, and retained in captivity shall be so marked prior to attaining 6 weeks of age. The preceding does not apply to captive adult geese, swans, and brant which were marked previous to March 1, 1967, by a "V" notch in the web of one foot, nor to such birds held in captivity at public zoological parks, and public scientific or educational institutions.

(3) Such properly marked birds may be killed, in any number, at any time or place, by any means except shooting. Such birds may be killed by shooting only in accordance with all the applicable hunting regulations governing the taking of like species from the wild.

(4) At all times during possession, transportation, and storage until the raw carcasses of such birds are finally processed immediately prior to cooking, smoking, or canning, the marked foot or wing must remain attached to each carcass: *Provided,* That permittees who are also authorized to sell game under a State license, permit, or authorization may remove the marked foot or wing from the raw carcasses if the number of his State license, permit, or authorization has first been legibly stamped in ink on the back of each carcass and on the wrapping or container in which each carcass is maintained, or each carcass is identified by a State band on leg or wing pursuant to requirements of his State license, permit, or authorization.

(5) Such properly marked birds, alive or dead, or their eggs may be disposed of in any number, at any time or place, to any person: *Provided,* That all such birds shall be physically marked prior to sale or disposal regardless of whether or not they have attained 6 weeks of age: *And provided further,* That on each date that any such birds or their eggs are transferred to another person, the permittee must complete a Form 3-186, Notice of Waterfowl Sale or Transfer, indicating all information required by the form and the method or methods by which individual birds are marked as required by § 21.25(c)(2). (Service will provide supplies of form.) The permittee will furnish the original of completed Form 3-186 to the person acquiring the birds or eggs; retain one copy in his files as a record of his operations; attach one copy to the shipping container for the birds or eggs, or include the copy in shipping documents which accompany the shipment; and, on or before the last day of each month, mail two copies of each form completed during that month to the office of the Fish and Wildlife Service which issued his permit.

(6) Permittees shall submit an annual report within 10 days following the 31st day of December of each calendar year to the office of the Fish and Wildlife Service which issued the permit. The information provided shall give

the total number of waterfowl by species in possession on that date and the method or methods by which individual birds are marked as required by the provisions of this part 21.

(d) *Term of permit*. A waterfowl sale and disposal permit issued or renewed under this part expires on the date designated on the face of the permit unless amended or revoked, but the term of the permit shall not exceed three (3) years from the date of issuance or renewal.

[40 FR 28460, July 7, 1975, as amended at 54 FR 38151, Sept. 14, 1989]

## APPLICATION REQUIREMENTS: DEPREDATION PERMITS

**§ 21.41 Depredation permits.**

(a) *Permit requirement*. Except as provided in §§ 21.42 through 21.46, a depredation permit is required before any person may take, possess, or transport migratory birds for depredation control purposes. No permit is required merely to scare or herd depredating migratory birds other than endangered or threatened species or bald or golden eagles.

(b) *Applicant procedures*. Applications for depredation permits shall be submitted to the appropriate Special Agent in Charge (see § 13.11(b) of this subchapter). Each such application must contain the general information and certification required by § 13.12(a) of this subchapter plus the following additional information:

(1) A description of the area where depredations are occurring;

(2) The nature of the crops or other interests being injured;

(3) The extent of such injury; and

(4) The particular species of migratory birds committing the injury.

(c) *Additional permit conditions*. In addition to the general conditions set forth in part 13 of this subchapter B, depredation permits shall be subject to requires, in this section:

(1) Permittees may not kill migratory birds unless specifically authorized on the permit.

(2) Unless otherwise specifically authorized, when permittees are authorized to kill migratory birds they may do so only with a shotgun not larger than No. 10 gauge fired from the shoulder, and only on or over the threatened area or area described on the permit.

(3) Permittees may not use blinds, pits, or other means of concealment, decoys, duck calls, or other devices to lure or entice birds within gun range.

(4) All migratory birds killed shall be retrieved by the permittee and turned over to a Bureau representative or his designee for disposition to charitable or other worthy institutions for use as food, or otherwise disposed of as provided by law.

(5) Only persons named on the permit are authorized to act as agents of the permittee under authority of the permit.

(d) *Tenure of permits*. The tenure of depredation permits shall be limited to the dates which appear on its face, but in no case shall be longer than one year.

[39 FR 1178, Jan. 4, 1974, as amended at 42 FR 17122, Mar. 31, 1977]

## APPLICATION REQUIREMENTS: SPECIAL PURPOSE PERMITS

**§ 21.27 Special purpose permits.**

Permits may be issued for special purpose activities related to migratory birds, their parts, nests, or eggs, which are otherwise outside the scope of the standard form permits of this part. A special purpose permit for migratory bird related activities not otherwise provided for in this part may be issued to an applicant who submits a written application containing the general information and certification required by part 13 and makes a sufficient showing of benefit to the migratory bird resource, important research reasons, reasons of human concern for individual birds, or other compelling justification.

(a) *Permit requirement*. A special purpose permit is required before any person may lawfully take, salvage, otherwise acquire, transport, or possess migratory birds, their parts, nests, or eggs for any purpose not covered by the standard form permits of this part. In addition, a special purpose permit is required before any person may sell, purchase, or barter captive-bred, migratory game birds, other than waterfowl, that are marked in compliance with § 21.13(b) of this part.

(b) *Application procedures*. Applications for special purpose permits shall be submitted to the appropriate issuing officer (see § 13.11(b) of this subchapter). Each such application must contain the general information and certification required by § 13.12(a) of this subchapter plus the following additional information:

(1) A detailed statement describing the project or activity which requires issuance of a permit, purpose of such project or activity, and a delineation of the area in which it will be conducted. (Copies of supporting documents, research proposals, and any necessary State permits should accompany the application);

(2) Numbers and species of migratory birds involved where same can reasonably be determined in advance; and

(3) Statement of disposition which will be made of migratory birds involved in the permit activity.

(c) *Additional permit conditions*. In addition to the general conditions set forth in part 13 of this subchapter B, special purpose permits shall be subject to the following conditions:

(1) Permittees shall maintain adequate records describing the conduct of the permitted activity, the numbers and species of migratory birds acquired and disposed of under the permit, and inventorying and identifying all migratory birds held on December 31 of each calendar year. Records shall be maintained at the address listed on the permit; shall be in, or reproducible in English; and shall be available for inspection by Service personnel during regular business hours. A permittee may be required by the conditions of the permit to file with the issuing office an annual report of operation. Annual reports, if required, shall be filed no later than January 31 of the calendar year following the year for which the report is required. Reports, if required, shall describe permitted activities, numbers and species of migratory birds acquired and disposed of, and shall inventory and describe all migratory birds possessed under the special purpose permit on December 31 of the reporting year.

(2) Permittees shall make such other reports as may be requested by the issuing officer.

(3) All live, captive-bred, migratory game birds possessed under authority of a valid special purpose permit shall be physically marked as defined in § 21.13(b) of this part.

(4) No captive-bred migratory game bird may be sold or bartered unless marked in accordance with § 21.13(b) of this part.

(5) No permittee may take, purchase, receive or otherwise acquire, sell, barter, transfer, or otherwise dispose of any captive-bred migratory game bird unless such permittee submits a Service form 3-186A (Migratory Bird Acquisition/Disposition Report), completed in accordance with the instructions on the form, to the issuing office within five (5) days of such transaction.

(6) No permittee, who is authorized to sell or barter migratory game birds pursuant to a permit issued under this section, may sell or

barter such birds to any person unless that person is authorized to purchase and possess such migratory game birds under a permit issued pursuant to this part and part 13, or as permitted by regulations in this part.

(d) *Term of permit*. A special purpose permit issued or renewed under this part expires on the date designated on the face of the permit unless amended or revoked, but the term of the permit shall not exceed three (3) years from the date of issuance or renewal.

[39 FR 1178, Jan. 4, 1974, as amended at 54 FR 38152, Sept. 14, 1989]

## APPLICATION REQUIREMENTS: SCIENTIFIC RESEARCH OR EXHIBITION

### Subpart C—Eagle Permits

**§ 22.21 Permits for scientific or exhibition purposes.**

The Director may, upon receipt of an application and in accordance with the issuance criteria of this section, issue a permit authorizing taking, possession, or transportation of bald eagles or golden eagles, or their parts, nests, or eggs for the scientific or exhibition purposes of public museums, public scientific societies, or public zoological parks.

(a) *Application procedure.* Applications for permits to take, possess, or transport bald or golden eagles, their parts, nests or eggs for scientific or exhibition purposes shall be submitted to the appropriate Special Agent in Charge (see: § 13.11(b) of this subchapter). Each such application must contain the general information and certification required by § 13.12(a) of this subchapter plus the following information:

(1) Species of eagle and number of such birds, nests, or eggs proposed to be taken, possessed, or transported;

(2) Specific locality in which taking is proposed, if any;

(3) Method taking proposed, if any;

(4) If not taken, the source of eagles and other circumstances surrounding the proposed acquisition or transportation;

(5) Name and address of the public museum, public scientific societies, or public zoological park for which they are intended;

(6) Complete explanation and justification of request, nature of project or study, number of specimens now at institution, reason these are inadequate, and other appropriate explanations.

(b) *Additional permit conditions.* In addition to the general conditions set forth in part 13 of this subchapter B, permits to take, possess, or transport bald or golden eagles for scientific or exhibition purposes shall be subject to the following condition: In addition to any reporting requirement set forth in the permit, the permittee shall submit a report of activities conducted under the permit to the Special Agent in Charge within 30 days after expiration of the permit.

(c) *Issuance criteria.* The Director shall conduct an investigation and not issue a permit to take, possess, or transport bald or golden eagles for scientific or exhibition purposes unless he has determined that such taking, possession, or transportation is compatible with the preservation of the bald or golden eagle. In making such determination, the Director shall consider, among other criteria, the following:

(1) The direct or indirect effect which issuing such permit would be likely to have upon the wild population of bald and golden eagles;

(2) Whether the expertise, facilities, or other resources available to the applicant appear adequate to successfully accomplish the objectives stated in the application;

(3) Whether the justification of the purpose for which the permit is being requested is adequate to justify the removal of the eagle from the wild or otherwise change its status; and

(4) Whether the applicant has demonstrated that the permit is being requested for *bona fide* scientific or exhibition purposes of public museums, public scientific societies, or public zoological parks.

(d) *Tenure of permits.* The tenure of permits to take bald or golden eagles for scientific or exhibition purposes shall be that shown on the face of the permit.

## APPLICATION REQUIREMENTS: INDIAN RELIGIOUS PURPOSES

**§ 22.22 Permits for Indian religious purposes.**

The Director may, upon receipt of an application and in accordance with the issuance criteria of this section, issue a permit authorizing the taking, possession, and transportation of bald or golden eagles, or their parts, nests, or eggs for the religious use of Indians.

(a) *Application procedure*. Applications for permits to take, possess, and transport bald or golden eagles, their parts, nests, or eggs for the religious use of Indians shall be submitted to the appropriate Special Agent in Charge (see: § 13.11(b) of this subchapter). Only applications from individual Indians will be accepted. Each such application must contain the general information and certification required by § 13.12(a) of this subchapter plus the following additional information:

(1) Species and number of eagles or feathers proposed to be taken, or acquired by gift or inheritance.

(2) State and local area where the taking is proposed to be done, or from whom acquired.

(3) Name of tribe with which applicant is associated.

(4) Name of tribal religious ceremony(ies) for which required.

(5) Applicant must attach a certification from the Bureau of Indian Affairs that the applicant is an Indian.

(6) Applicant must attach a certification from a duly authorized official of the religious group that the applicant is authorized to participate in such ceremonies.

(b) *Additional permit conditions*. In addition to the general conditions set forth in part 13 of this subchapter B, permits to take, possess, and transport bald or golden eagles, their parts, nests or eggs, for the religious use of Indians shall be subject to the following conditions:

(1) Bald or golden eagles or their parts possessed under permits issued pursuant to this section are not transferable, except such birds or their parts may be handed down from generation to generation or from one Indian to another in accordance with tribal or religious customs; and

(2) Permittees shall make such reports or submit inventories of eagle feathers or parts on hand as may be requested by the Special Agent in Charge.

(c) *Issuance criteria*. The Director shall conduct an investigation and not issue a permit to take, possess, and transport bald or golden eagles, their parts, nests or eggs, for the religious use of Indians unless he has determined that such taking, possession, and transportation is compatible with the preservation of the bald or golden eagle. In making such determination, the Director shall consider, among other criteria, the following:

(1) The direct or indirect effect which issuing such permit would be likely to have upon the wild population of bald or golden eagles; and

(2) Whether the applicant is an Indian who is authorized to participate in *bona fide* tribal religious ceremonies.

(d) *Tenure of permits*. Any permit issued pursuant to this section under which the applicant is authorized to take eagles shall be valid during the period specified on the face thereof which shall in no case be longer than one year from date of issue. Any permit issued pursuant to this part which authorized the permittee to transport and possess eagles or their parts shall be valid for the life of the permittee unless sooner revoked.

## APPLICATION REQUIREMENTS: EAGLE DEPREDATION CONTROL

**§ 22.23 Permits to take depredating eagles.**

The Director may, upon receipt of an application and in accordance with the issuance criteria of this section, issue a permit authorizing the taking of depredating bald or golden eagles.

(a) *Application procedure*. Applications for permits to take depredating bald or golden eagles shall be submitted to the appropriate Special Agent in Charge (see: § 13.11(b) of this subchapter). Each such application must contain the general information and certification required by § 13.12(a) of this subchapter plus the following additional information:

(1) Species and number of eagles proposed to be taken;

(2) Location and description of property where taking is proposed;

(3) Inclusive dates for which permit is requested;

(4) Method of taking proposed;

(5) Kind and number of livestock or domestic animals owned by applicant;

(6) Kind and amount of alleged damage; and

(7) Name, address, age, and business relationship with applicant of any person the applicant proposes to act for him as his agent in the taking of such eagles.

(b) *Additional permit conditions*. In addition to the general conditions set forth in part 13 of this subchapter B, permits to take depredating bald or golden eagles shall be subject to the following conditions:

(1) Bald or golden eagles may be taken under permit by firearms, traps, or other suitable means except by poison or from aircraft;

(2) The taking of eagles under permit may be done only by the permittee or his agents named in the permit;

(3) Any eagle taken under authority of such permit will be promptly turned over to a Service agent or other game law enforcement officer designated in the permit; and

(4) In addition to any reporting requirement set forth in the permit, the permittee shall submit a report of activities conducted under the permit to the Special Agent in Charge within 10 days following completion of the taking operations or the expiration of the permit, whichever occurs first.

(c) *Issuance criteria*. The Director shall conduct an investigation and not issue a permit to take depredating bald or golden eagles unless he has determined that such taking is compatible with the preservation of the bald or golden eagle. In making such determination the Director shall consider the following:

(1) The direct or indirect effect which issuing such permit would be likely to have upon the wild population of bald or golden eagles;

(2) Whether there is evidence to show that bald or golden eagles have in fact become seriously injurious to wildlife or to agriculture or other interests in the particular locality to be covered by the permit, and the injury complained of is substantial; and

(3) Whether the only way to abate the damage caused by the bald or golden eagle is to take some or all of the offending birds.

(d) *Tenure of permits*. The tenure of any permit to take bald or golden eagles for depredation control purposes shall be that shown on the face thereof, and shall in no case be longer than 90 days from date of issue.

This page intentionally left blank.

OMB NO 42-R1675

**DEPARTMENT OF THE INTERIOR**
**U.S. FISH AND WILDLIFE SERVICE**

**FEDERAL FISH AND WILDLIFE LICENSE/PERMIT APPLICATION**

1 APPLICATION FOR *(Indicate only one)*

☐ IMPORT OR EXPORT LICENSE ☐ PERMIT

2. BRIEF DESCRIPTION OF ACTIVITY FOR WHICH REQUESTED LICENSE OR PERMIT IS NEEDED.

(__) To import Mandarin duck skins for making artificial flies used for fishing only.

(__) To import pheasant skins listed on reverse side for millinery purposes or for making artificial flies used for fishing.

3 APPLICANT. *(Name complete address and phone number of individual, business, agency, or institution for which permit is requested)*

4 IF "APPLICANT" IS AN INDIVIDUAL, COMPLETE THE FOLLOWING

| ☐ MR. ☐ MRS. ☐ MISS ☐ MS. | HEIGHT | WEIGHT |
|---|---|---|
| DATE OF BIRTH | COLOR HAIR | COLOR EYES |
| PHONE NUMBER WHERE EMPLOYED | SOCIAL SECURITY NUMBER | |
| OCCUPATION | | |

ANY BUSINESS, AGENCY, OR INSTITUTIONAL AFFILIATION HAVING TO DO WITH THE WILDLIFE TO BE COVERED BY THIS LICENSE/PERMIT

5. IF "APPLICANT" IS A BUSINESS CORPORATION, PUBLIC AGENCY, OR INSTITUTION, COMPLETE THE FOLLOWING

EXPLAIN TYPE OR KIND OF BUSINESS, AGENCY, OR INSTITUTION

NAME, TITLE, AND PHONE NUMBER OF PRESIDENT, PRINCIPAL OFFICER, DIRECTOR, ETC.

IF "APPLICANT" IS A CORPORATION, INDICATE STATE IN WHICH INCORPORATED

6 LOCATION WHERE PROPOSED ACTIVITY IS TO BE CONDUCTED

7. DO YOU HOLD ANY CURRENTLY VALID FEDERAL FISH AND WILDLIFE LICENSE OR PERMIT? ☐ YES ☐ NO
*(If yes, list license or permit numbers)*

8 IF REQUIRED BY ANY STATE OR FOREIGN GOVERNMENT, DO YOU HAVE THEIR APPROVAL TO CONDUCT THE ACTIVITY YOU PROPOSE? ☐ YES ☐ NO
*(If yes, list jurisdictions and type of documents)*

9. CERTIFIED CHECK OR MONEY ORDER *(if applicable)* PAYABLE TO THE U.S. FISH AND WILDLIFE SERVICE ENCLOSED IN AMOUNT OF

$ 25.00

10. DESIRED EFFECTIVE DATE

11. DURATION NEEDED

12 ATTACHMENTS. THE SPECIFIC INFORMATION REQUIRED FOR THE TYPE OF LICENSE/PERMIT REQUESTED *(See 50 CFR 13.12(b))* MUST BE ATTACHED. IT CONSTITUTES AN INTEGRAL PART OF THIS APPLICATION. LIST SECTIONS OF 50 CFR UNDER WHICH ATTACHMENTS ARE PROVIDED.

**CERTIFICATION**

I HEREBY CERTIFY THAT I HAVE READ AND AM FAMILIAR WITH THE REGULATIONS CONTAINED IN TITLE 50, PART 13, OF THE CODE OF FEDERAL REGULATIONS AND THE OTHER APPLICABLE PARTS IN SUBCHAPTER B OF CHAPTER I OF TITLE 50, AND I FURTHER CERTIFY THAT THE INFORMATION SUBMITTED IN THIS APPLICATION FOR A LICENSE/PERMIT IS COMPLETE AND ACCURATE TO THE BEST OF MY KNOWLEDGE AND BELIEF. I UNDERSTAND THAT ANY FALSE STATEMENT HEREIN MAY SUBJECT ME TO THE CRIMINAL PENALTIES OF 18 U.S.C. 1001.

| SIGNATURE *(In ink)* | DATE |
|---|---|
| | |

3-200 (6/74)

Return complete application to:

Office of Management Authority
U.S. Fish and Wildlife Service
4401 N. Fairfax Drive, Rm. 432
Arlington, Virginia 22203

Application continuation sheet

Answer the following questions:

1. How many of each species of bird skins or parts thereof do you wish to import?

| | |
|---|---|
| Mandarin duck | ________ |
| Lady Amherst Pheasant | ________ |
| Golden Pheasant | ________ |
| Silver Pheasant | ________ |
| Reeves Pheasant | ________ |
| Blue-eared Pheasant | ________ |

2. Give the port at which the entry will be made, or in the case of warehouse storage under bond, port at which importation was made and location and amount of bird skins presently in storage.

3. Why do you wish to import these feathered skins?

4. Are you applying for initial allocation for the calendar year or for reallocation of an unused portion of a calendar year portion (Check appropriate box)?

☐ Allocation (January - June)

☐ Reallocation (July - December)

BE SURE TO ENCLOSE YOUR $25.00 FEE

SEND TO:
U.S. Fish and Wildlife Service
Office of Management Authority
4401 N. Fairfax Drive, Room 432
Arlington, VA 22201
Call: 703/358-2104 for more information

OMB NO 42-R1675

**DEPARTMENT OF THE INTERIOR**
**U.S. FISH AND WILDLIFE SERVICE**

**FEDERAL FISH AND WILDLIFE LICENSE/PERMIT APPLICATION**

1. APPLICATION FOR *(Indicate only one)*

☐ IMPORT OR EXPORT LICENSE [X] PERMIT

2. BRIEF DESCRIPTION OF ACTIVITY FOR WHICH REQUESTED LICENSE OR PERMIT IS NEEDED.

INJURIOUS WILDLIFE

______ ACQUIRE

______ IMPORT

______ TRANSPORT

3. APPLICANT. *(Name, complete address and phone number of individual, business, agency, or institution for which permit is requested)*

4. IF "APPLICANT" IS AN INDIVIDUAL, COMPLETE THE FOLLOWING

| ☐ MR ☐ MRS ☐ MISS ☐ MS | HEIGHT | WEIGHT |
|---|---|---|
| DATE OF BIRTH | COLOR HAIR | COLOR EYES |
| PHONE NUMBER WHERE EMPLOYED | SOCIAL SECURITY NUMBER | |
| OCCUPATION | | |

ANY BUSINESS, AGENCY, OR INSTITUTIONAL AFFILIATION HAVING TO DO WITH THE WILDLIFE TO BE COVERED BY THIS LICENSE/PERMIT

5. IF "APPLICANT" IS A BUSINESS, CORPORATION, PUBLIC AGENCY OR INSTITUTION, COMPLETE THE FOLLOWING

EXPLAIN TYPE OR KIND OF BUSINESS, AGENCY, OR INSTITUTION

NAME, TITLE, AND PHONE NUMBER OF PRESIDENT, PRINCIPAL OFFICER, DIRECTOR, ETC.

IF "APPLICANT" IS A CORPORATION, INDICATE STATE IN WHICH INCORPORATED

6. LOCATION WHERE PROPOSED ACTIVITY IS TO BE CONDUCTED

7. DO YOU HOLD ANY CURRENTLY VALID FEDERAL FISH AND WILDLIFE LICENSE OR PERMIT? ☐ YES ☐ NO
*(If yes, list license or permit numbers)*

8. IF REQUIRED BY ANY STATE OR FOREIGN GOVERNMENT, DO YOU HAVE THEIR APPROVAL TO CONDUCT THE ACTIVITY YOU PROPOSE? ☐ YES ☐ NO
*(If yes, list jurisdictions and type of documents)*

9. [illegible] CHECK OR MONEY ORDER *(if applicable)* PAYABLE TO THE U.S. FISH AND WILDLIFE SERVICE ENCLOSED IN AMOUNT OF

$ 25.00 (U.S. currency)

10. DESIRED EFFECTIVE DATE

11. DURATION NEEDED

12. ATTACHMENTS. THE SPECIFIC INFORMATION REQUIRED FOR THE TYPE OF LICENSE/PERMIT REQUESTED *(See 50 CFR 13.12(b))* MUST BE ATTACHED. IT CONSTITUTES AN INTEGRAL PART OF THIS APPLICATION. LIST SECTIONS OF 50 CFR UNDER WHICH ATTACHMENTS ARE PROVIDED

50 CFR 16.22 (SEE REVERSE)

**CERTIFICATION**

I HEREBY CERTIFY THAT I HAVE READ AND AM FAMILIAR WITH THE REGULATIONS CONTAINED IN TITLE 50, PART 13, OF THE CODE OF FEDERAL REGULATIONS AND THE OTHER APPLICABLE PARTS IN SUBCHAPTER B OF CHAPTER I OF TITLE 50, AND I FURTHER CERTIFY THAT THE INFORMATION SUBMITTED IN THIS APPLICATION FOR A LICENSE/PERMIT IS COMPLETE AND ACCURATE TO THE BEST OF MY KNOWLEDGE AND BELIEF. I UNDERSTAND THAT ANY FALSE STATEMENT HEREIN MAY SUBJECT ME TO THE CRIMINAL PENALTIES OF 18 U.S.C. 1001.

| SIGNATURE *(In ink)* * | DATE |
|---|---|
| | |

3-200
10/74

*Applicant listed in 3 above or principal officer listed in 5 above must sign.

Application Continuation Sheet

INJURIOUS WILDLIFE

IMPORTATION - TRANSPORTATION - ACQUISITION

1. Species ____________ ____________ ____________
(scientific name) (common name) (quantity)

____________
(parts - specific)

2. Activity sought: ☐ Import ☐ Transportation ☐ Acquisition

3. Premises where such wildlife is to be kept: ____________
(street)
   a. include photos of facilities to clearly show escape-proof cages

____________
(city, state, territory, zip code)

4. Purpose of import/transportation/acquisition (scientific/zoological/educational/medical) (submit project proposal if available):

5. Statement of applicant's qualifications and previous experience in caring for and handling captive wildlife:

6. Name and address of person/institution from whom you wish to obtain the animals:

This page intentionally left blank.

Public reporting burden for this collection of information is estimated to average 25 hours per response including the time for reviewing instructions, searching existing data sources, gathering and maintaining the data needed, and completing and reviewing the collection of information. Send comments regarding this burden estimate or any other aspect of this collection of information, including suggestions for reducing this burden, to Department of Agriculture Clearance Officer, OIRM, Room 404-W, Washington, D.C. 20250, and to the Office of Information and Regulatory Affairs, Office of Management and Budget, Washington, D.C. 20503

FORM APPROVED OMB NO. 0579-0036

No license may be issued unless a completed application has been received (7 U.S.C. 2133-2143), and the applicant is in compliance with the standards and regulations Section 2133

U.S. DEPARTMENT OF AGRICULTURE
ANIMAL AND PLANT HEALTH INSPECTION SERVICE

# APPLICATION FOR LICENSE

*(TYPE OR PRINT)*

☐ NEW LICENSE ☐ RENEWALS

| DO NOT USE THIS SPACE - OFFICIAL USE ONLY | | | |
|---|---|---|---|
| SEND THE COMPLETED FORM TO: | | | |
| LICENSE NO. | RENEWAL DATE | FEES | |
| | | AMOUNT | DATE RECEIVED |

**1. NAME(S) OF OWNER(S) AND MAILING ADDRESS**

COUNTY: TELEPHONE ( )

**2. ALL BUSINESS NAMES, LOCATIONS, AND ALL SITES HOUSING ANIMALS** *(P.O. Box not acceptable)*

COUNTY TELEPHONE ( )

**3. IF PREVIOUSLY LICENSED - NAME AND ADDRESS**

PREVIOUS LICENSE NO.

**4. NAME AND ADDRESS OF OTHER BUSINESS(S) HANDLING ANIMALS IN WHICH APPLICANT/LICENSEE HAS AN INTEREST**

**5. TYPE OF LICENSE**

☐ A - Dealer *(Breeder)* ☐ B - Dealer ☐ C - Exhibitor

**6. DATE OF LAST BUSINESS YEAR**

| FROM | | | TO | | |
|---|---|---|---|---|---|
| MO | DAY | YEAR | MO | DAY | YEAR |
| | | | | | |

**7. LIST OWNERS, PARTNERS, AND OFFICERS**

| NAME AND TITLE | ADDRESS |
|---|---|
| | |

**8. DEALER ONLY**

| | |
|---|---|
| TOTAL NO. OF ANIMALS PURCHASED IN THE LAST BUSINESS YEAR | |
| TOTAL NO. OF ANIMALS SOLD IN THE LAST BUSINESS YEAR | |
| TOTAL GROSS AMOUNT DERIVED FROM THE SALE OF ANIMALS | |
| DOLLAR AMOUNT ON WHICH FEE IS BASED *(Sections 2.6 and 2.7)* | |

**9. EXHIBITOR ONLY** *(No. of animals holding now or held during the last business year whichever is greater.)*

| | | | |
|---|---|---|---|
| DOGS | | RABBITS | |
| CATS | | NONHUMAN PRIMATES | |
| GUINEA PIGS | | MARINE MAMMALS | |
| HAMSTERS | | WILD OR EXOTIC MAMMALS | |
| OTHER *(List Species and No.)* | | | |

## CERTIFICATION

I hereby make application for a license under the Animal Welfare Act 7 U.S.C. 2131 et seq. I certify that the information provided herein is true and correct to the best of my knowledge. I hereby acknowledge receipt of and agree to comply with all the regulations and standards in 9 CFR, Subpart A, Parts 1, 2 and 3. I certify that I am over 18 years of age.

| 10. SIGNATURE | 11. NAME AND TITLE *(Type or Print.)* | 12. DATE |
|---|---|---|
| | | |

APHIS FORM 7003 (AUG 91) (Replaces APHIS FORM 7003 (MAY 90), which is obsolete.) PART 1 - SECTOR OFFICE

Every research facility, exhibitor, carrier, and intermediate handler not required to be licensed under Section 3 of the Animal Welfare Act, shall register with the USDA (7 USC 2136) This application provides information for such registration See reverse side for additional OMB information

See reverse for additional OMB information

FORM APPROVED
OMB NO 0579-0036

U.S. DEPARTMENT OF AGRICULTURE
ANIMAL AND PLANT HEALTH INSPECTION SERVICE

## APPLICATION FOR REGISTRATION

*(TYPE OR PRINT)*

- ☐ **Research Facility** *(Complete items 1, 2, and Sections A, B, and C)*
- ☐ **Exhibitor** *(Complete items 1, 2, and Sections B and C)*
- ☐ **Carrier** *(Complete items 1, 2, and Section C)*
- ☐ **Intermediate Handler** *(Complete items 1, 2, and Section C)*

**USDA USE ONLY**

**Applicant should send four (4) completed copies to this address:**

| REGISTRATION NO. | DATE REGISTERED |
|---|---|
| | |

| 1. REGISTRANT *(Name and permanent mailing address, including Zip Code)* | 2. LOCATION(S) OF BUSINESS, EXHIBITION SITE(S), OR RESEARCH FACILITIES *(Use additional sheets if necessary)* |
|---|---|
| | |

**SECTION A**

3. DO YOU USE OR INTEND TO USE DOGS OR CATS OR OTHER ANIMALS COVERED BY THE ANIMAL WELFARE ACT ☐ Yes ☐ No

4. DO YOU PURCHASE OR TRANSPORT DOGS OR CATS OR OTHER ANIMALS AS DEFINED IN THE ANIMAL WELFARE ACT ☐ Yes ☐ No

5. ARE YOU USING FEDERAL FUNDS TO CARRY OUT RESEARCH, TESTS, OR EXPERIMENTS ☐ Yes ☐ No

6. IF "YES" IN ITEM 5, "X" OR SPECIFY ☐ Grant ☐ Award ☐ Loan ☐ Contract — Other *(Specify)*

7. NAME OF FEDERAL AGENCY(S) SUPPLYING FUNDS

8. NAME AND LOCATION OF EACH RESEARCH REPORTING FACILITY *(see 9 CFR, Section 2.36)* WHERE TEACHING, RESEARCH, TESTS, OR EXPERIMENTS ARE CONDUCTED WITH ANIMALS WHICH ARE COVERED BY THIS REGISTRATION. *(Use reverse or attach additional sheeets.)*

**SECTION B**

9. NO. ANIMALS USED OR EXHIBITED ANNUALLY *(Attach additional sheets if needed)*

| A. Dogs | B. Cats | C. Guinea Pigs | D. Hamsters | H. Other *(Specify and give No.)* |
|---|---|---|---|---|
| E. Rabbits | F. Non-human Primates | G. Marine Mammals | | |

**SECTION C**

10. NATURE OR ORGANIZATION OR BUSINESS *("X" one)* ☐ Private ☐ Commercial ☐ State, County or Municipal ☐ Federal

11. TYPE OF OPERATION *("X" each applicable operation)* ☐ College or University ☐ Hospital ☐ Exhibitor ☐ Carrier ☐ Intermediate Handler ☐ Air ☐ Rail ☐ Marine ☐ Truck

| 12. TYPE OF ORGANIZATION ☐ Partnership ☐ Corporation ☐ Individual ☐ Association | Other *(Specify)* | 13. STATE WHERE INCORPORATED | 14. DATE INCORPORATED |
|---|---|---|---|

15. IF PARTNERSHIP, IDENTIFY EACH PARTNER OR OFFICER
IF CORPORATION OR ORGANIZATION, IDENTIFY PRINCIPAL OFFICERS *(Use reverse, if needed)*

| A. NAME | B. TITLE | C. ADDRESS *(full address, including zip code)* |
|---|---|---|
| | | |
| | | |
| | | |

**CERTIFICATION**

I hereby register as a Research Facility, Exhibitor, Carrier, or Intermediate Handler under the Animal Welfare Act, 7 U.S.C. 2131 et seq.; and I certify that the information provided herein is true and correct to the best of my knowledge and belief

| 16. SIGNATURE | 17. NAME AND TITLE *(Type or Print)* | 18. DATE SIGNED |
|---|---|---|
| | | |

**ACKNOWLEDGEMENT OF RECEIPT OF REGULATIONS AND STANDARDS**

I hereby acknowledge receipt of and agree to comply with all the regulations and standards contained in 9 CFR Chapter 1, Subchapter A

| 19. SIGNATURE | 20. NAME AND TITLE *(Type or Print)* | 21. DATE SIGNED |
|---|---|---|
| | | |

APHIS FORM 7011
(MAY 91)

(Replaces VS FORM 18-11 (SEP 77), which is obsolete.)

This page intentionally left blank.

This report is required by law (7 USC 2143). Failure to report according to the regulations can result in an order to cease and desist and to be subject to penalties as provided for in Section 2150

See reverse side for additional information

Interagency Report Control No. 0180-DOA-AN

UNITED STATES DEPARTMENT OF AGRICULTURE
ANIMAL AND PLANT HEALTH INSPECTION SERVICE

## ANNUAL REPORT OF RESEARCH FACILITY
*(TYPE OR PRINT)*

1. REGISTRATION NO.

FORM APPROVED
OMB NO. 0579-0036

2. HEADQUARTERS RESEARCH FACILITY *(Name and Address, as registered with USDA, include Zip Code)*

3. REPORTING FACILITY (List all locations where animals were housed or used in actual research, testing, teaching, or experimentation, or held for these purposes. Attach additional sheets if necessary.)

FACILITY LOCATIONS *(Sites)*

REPORT OF ANIMALS USED BY OR UNDER CONTROL OF RESEARCH FACILITY *(Attach additional sheets if necessary or use APHIS FORM 7023A.)*

| A. Animals Covered By The Animal Welfare Regulations | B. Number of animals being bred, conditioned, or held for use in teaching, testing, experiments, research, or surgery but not yet used for such purposes | C. Number of animals upon which teaching, research, experiments, or tests were conducted involving no pain, distress, or use of pain-relieving drugs | D. Number of animals upon which experiments, teaching, research, surgery, or tests were conducted involving accompanying pain or distress to the animals and for which appropriate anesthetic, analgesic, or tranquilizing drugs were used | E. Number of animals upon which teaching, experiments, research, surgery or tests were conducted involving accompanying pain or distress to the animals and for which the use of appropriate anesthetic, analgesic, or tranquilizing drugs would have adversely affected the procedures, results, or interpretation of the teaching, research, experiments, surgery, or tests. *(An explanation of the procedures producing pain or distress in these animals and the reasons such drugs were not used must be attached to this report)* | F. TOTAL NO. OF ANIMALS (Cols. C + D + E) |
|---|---|---|---|---|---|
| 4. Dogs | | | | | |
| 5. Cats | | | | | |
| 6. Guinea Pigs | | | | | |
| 7. Hamsters | | | | | |
| 8. Rabbits | | | | | |
| 9. Non-human Primates | | | | | |
| 10. Sheep | | | | | |
| 11. Pigs | | | | | |
| 12. Other Farm Animals | | | | | |
| | | | | | |
| 13. Other Animals | | | | | |
| | | | | | |
| | | | | | |
| | | | | | |

ASSURANCE STATEMENTS

1) Professionally acceptable standards governing the care, treatment, and use of animals, including appropriate use of anesthetic, analgesic, and tranquilizing drugs, prior to, during, and following actual research, teaching, testing, surgery, or experimentation were followed by this research facility.

2) Each principal investigator has considered alternatives to painful procedures.

3) This facility is adhering to the standards and regulations under the Act, and it has required that exceptions to the standards and regulations be specified and explained by the principal investigator and approved by the Institutional Animal Care and Use Committee (IACUC). **A summary of all such exceptions is attached to this annual report.** In addition to identifying the IACUC approved exceptions, this summary includes a brief explanation of the exceptions, as well as the species and number of animals affected.

4) The attending veterinarian for this research facility has appropriate authority to ensure the provision of adequate veterinary care and to oversee the adequacy of other aspects of animal care and use.

**CERTIFICATION BY HEADQUARTES RESEARCH FACILITY OFFICIAL**
**(Chief Executive Officer or Legally Responsible Institutional Official)**
I certify that the above is true, correct, and complete (7 U.S.C. Section 2143)

| SIGNATURE OF C.E.O. OR INSTITUTIONAL OFFICIAL | NAME & TITLE OF C.E.O. OR INSTITUTIONAL OFFICIAL *(Type or Print)* | DATE SIGNED |
|---|---|---|
| | | |

APHIS FORM 7023 (AUG 91) (Replaces VS FORM 18-23 (OCT 88), which is obsolete.)

PART 1 - HEADQUARTERS

## INSTRUCTIONS FOR COMPLETION OF APHIS FORM 7023

*(Refer to 9 CFR Part 2, Subpart C, Sections 2.33 and 2.36)*

**ITEM 1 -** Enter registration number as assigned to the Research Facility by United States Department of Agriculture (USDA).

**ITEM 2 -** Enter the complete name and address of the Headquarters Research Facility as registered with USDA.

**ITEM 3 -** List location of each Facility or Site where animals were housed or used in actual research, testing, teaching, or experimentation, or held for these purposes. *(Attached additional sheets if necessary.)*

**ITEM 4 - 13 - DO NOT** enter numbers in Column A. **DO NOT** add numbers entered in Column B into the total in Column F. **Column F** is to show total of numbers entered in Columns **C + D + E.** Entries in Column E must be explained on attached sheet(s).

**ITEM 12 -** List by common name all other farm animal species.

**ITEM 13 - Other:** List, by common name, all other warm-blooded animal species covered by the Regulations. *(This will include all wild or exotic species.)* Attach additional sheets if necessary or use APHIS Form 7023A.

**CERTIFICATION:** Must be signed by the Chief Executive Officer (C.E.O.) of the Registered Research Facility or other Institutional Official (I.O.) having authority to legally commit on behalf of the Registered Research Facility. Sign, Print or type Name and Title, and Date.

**RETURN COMPLETED FORM WITH AN ORIGINAL SIGNATURE OF C.E.O. OR I.O. TO APPROPRIATE SECTOR OFFICE.**

**APHIS FORM 7023 (Reverse)**

NO BIRDS MAY BE IMPORTED UNLESS ACCOMPANIED BY A VALIDATED IMPORT PERMIT (9 CFR 92)

FORM APPROVED: OMB NO. 40-R3859

UNITED STATES DEPARTMENT OF AGRICULTURE
ANIMAL AND PLANT HEALTH INSPECTION SERVICE
VETERINARY SERVICES
WASHINGTON, D.C. 20250

RCS# 34-VS-64

**UNITED STATES APPLICATION / PERMIT TO IMPORT BIRDS**

**INSTRUCTIONS TO IMPORTER:** Complete items 1 thru 13 in Section A. Illegibility, typographical errors or lack of information may delay the validation of permits. Mailing instructions are on the reverse of the last page. The application for an import permit becomes a valid permit when Section B is completed. See responsibilities below.

**This document not valid unless Section B completed by an employee of Veterinary Service.**

**SECTION A—TO BE COMPLETED BY APPLICANT** *(Please type)*

1. NAME AND ADDRESS OF QUARANTINE FACILITY *(Street, City, State and Zip Code)*

2. COUNTRY OF ORIGIN *(Specify)*

**Note: Name and address of shipper (Exporter) is to be verified (on reverse side of this page) at the time of arrival of birds.**

3. NAME AND MAILING ADDRESS OF PERSON IN U.S. TO WHOM PERMITS ARE TO BE MAILED

TELEPHONE NO. *(Include Area Code)*

4. BIRDS

| NO. A | COMMON OR SCIENTIFIC NAME *(Genus and Species)* *(Be specific)* B |
|---|---|
| | |
| | **Total Birds authorized for Importation** *(Limited to Facility Capacity)* |

5. PURPOSE OF IMPORTATION

6. PORT OF EMBARKATION & COUNTRY

7. PROPOSED SHIPPING DATE

8. ROUTE OF TRAVEL INCLUDING ALL CARRIER STOPS ENROUTE *(Detailed flight data may be requested)*

NO OTHER STOPS PERMITTED

CERTIFICATION OF OPERATOR OF QUARANTINE FACILITY *(If Operator same as Importer sign item 11 only) As the operator of the facility (in item 1) I agree to handle the shipment for the Importer (in item 11) and further agree to comply with the conditions for Importation as listed on the reverse of the Original copy of this form.*

9. SIGNATURE OF OPERATOR OF FACILITY *(In item 1)*

10. DATE SIGNED

*I have read the conditions for importation listed on the reverse and do agree to comply with these conditions and understand that non compliance jeopardizes the issuance of future permits.*

11. SIGNATURE OF IMPORTER

12. NAME AND ADDRESS OF IMPORTER *(If different from item 1)*

13. DATE SIGNED

**SECTION B—USDA OFFICIAL USE ONLY**

14. DATES VALIDATED

FROM | TO

15. PERMIT NO.

16. VALID ONLY AT THIS U.S. PORT OF ENTRY

QUARANTINE AT PORT OF ENTRY REQUIRED

17. MINIMUM NO. DAYS

18. NAME AND ADDRESS OF PORT VETERINARIAN

19. VALIDATING SEAL, OFFICIALS SIGNATURE AND REMARKS

20. NAME AND TITLE OF VALIDATING OFFICIAL

21. **THIS PERMIT VOID AFTER**

**NOTE: Conditions for Importation and Health Certification on reverse. Health Certification must be executed, failure to do so could necessitate rejection at the Port of Entry.**

**THE U.S. IMPORTER** must forward the "Original" and "Carrier's Copy" to the shipper in the country of origin; and must make arrangements at the U.S. Port of Entry for Customs brokers' service if desired, necessary quarantine space and transportation of the shipment to and from quarantine. The "Importer's Copy" to be retained.
**THE SHIPPER** in the country of origin must make certain the Health Certification *(On the reverse of Original)* is completed by a salaried veterinary officer of the National Government of the country from which the birds are shipped: and deliver "Original" and Carrier's Copy" to the initial transporting carrier.
**THE SALARIED VETERINARY OFFICER** of the National Government of the country of origin is being forwarded a copy of this permit and is responsible for insuring that the necessary inspections and Health Certification *(On reverse of Original)* are completed, provided circumstances are such that the certification be properly issued.
**THE INITIAL CARRIER** must make certain that the Health Certification *(On reverse of Original)* has been completed and signed by a salaried veterinary officer of the National Government of the country from which the birds are shipped; make sure that the "Original" *(With Health Certification on reverse)* accompany the birds to the U.S. Port of Entry; and make certain the "Carrier's Copy" is available for the final carrier who will transport the shipment to the U.S. Port of Entry.
**VS VETERINARIAN AT PORT OF ENTRY** will hold the "Customs Copy" until the shipment is received, then forward it to the U.S. Collector of Customs. The "Original" *(With the signed Health Certification on the reverse)* will be retained by the VS veterinarian at U.S. Port of Entry.

VS FORM 17-29 (DEC 79) *Previous editions are obsolete.*

**ORIGINAL-TO ACCOMPANY SHIPMENT**

## CONDITIONS FOR IMPORTATION

1. The importer agrees to import the birds authorized by this permit in accordance with the provisions of Part 92, Title 9, CFR, all agreements existing between Veterinary Services and the owner of the facility.
2. The birds will be shipped by the route indicated on the face of the permit.
3. The importer agrees upon arrival of the birds at the port of entry that they shall be accepted from the carrier in the presence of Veterinary Services personnel and transported in a sealed vehicle or accompanied by Veterinary Services personnel to the quarantine facility.
4. Lots refused entry shall be removed from the United States or disposed of by the importer after official notification by the U.S. Department of Agriculture, as provided in Section 92.8(a), Part 92, Title 9, Code of Federal Regulations.
5. If USDA approved quarantine space is not available to handle this shipment upon arrival, this permit is automatically cancelled and the shipment will be refused entry. The Deputy Administrator, Veterinary Services, for other reasons may cancel the permit.
6. Applicable U.S. Department of the Interior's regulations 50 CFR, Parts 14, 16, 17, and 21 must be met.

---

## HEALTH CERTIFICATION

***The following certification must be signed by a full-time salaried veterinary officer of the national government of the country of export:***

***I certify that I personally inspected all of the birds, immediately prior to exportation, described in item 4 of VS Form 17-20, and that no evidence of Newcastle disease, ornithosis, or other communicable disease of poultry was found, nor insofar as has been possible to determine, were the birds exposed to any such diseases during the 90 days immediately prior to the inspection date listed below. The birds were placed in new shipping containers at the premises of origin and insofar as is known, the birds have not been vaccinated with Newcastle disease vaccine, Newcastle disease has not occurred on the premises of origin, nor on adjoining premises during the 90-day period immediately prior to exportation and that these premises are not located in an area under quarantine for poultry diseases during the preceding 90 days.***

***I further certify that the name and address of the exporter below was furnished to me by the shipper of the birds which I inspected.***

(See Item 2 "NOTE" on front of this page.)

EXPORTER'S NAME AND ADDRESS *(Print or type in English. — Verify at time of arrival of birds.)*

NAME AND ADDRESS OF VETERINARY OFFICER *(Print or type.)*

SIGNATURE

| TITLE *(Print or type.)* | DATE SIGNED |
| --- | --- |
| | |

## CONDITIONS FOR IMPORTATION

1. The importer agrees to import the birds authorized by this permit in accordance with the provisions of Part 92, Title 9, CFR, all agreements existing between Veterinary Services and the owner of the facility.

2. The birds will be shipped by the route indicated on the face of the permit.

3. The importer agrees upon arrival of the birds at the port of entry that they shall be accepted from the carrier in the presence of Veterinary Services personnel and transported in a sealed vehicle or accompanied by Veterinary Services personnel to the quarantine facility.

4. Lots refused entry shall be removed from the United States or disposed of by the importer after official notification by the U.S. Department of Agriculture, as provided in Section 92.8(a), Part 92, Title 9, Code of Federal Regulations.

5. If USDA approved quarantine space is not available to handle this shipment upon arrival, this permit is automatically cancelled and the shipment will be refused entry. The Deputy Administrator, Veterinary Services, for other reasons may cancel the permit.

6. Applicable U.S. Department of the Interior's regulations 50 CFR Parts 14 16, 17, and 21 must be met.

---

MAIL APPLICATION AS INDICATED BELOW

| IF QUARANTINE FACILITY LOCATED IN: A | SEND FORM VS 17-20 TO B | IF QUARANTINE FACILITY LOCATED IN: A | SEND FORM VS 17-20 TO: B | IF QUARANTINE FACILITY LOCATED IN: A | SEND FORM VS 17-20 TO: B |
|---|---|---|---|---|---|
| New York | USDA, APHIS, VS<br>80 Wolf Road, Suite 503<br>Albany, NY 12205 | Florida | USDA, APHIS, VS<br>P.O. Box 660400<br>Miami Springs, FL 33166 | California | USDA, APHIS, VS<br>83 Scripps Drive<br>Sacramento, CA 95825 |
| Michigan | USDA, APHIS VS<br>300 South Walnut<br>Lewis Cass Building<br>Lansing, MI 48913 | Louisiana | USDA, APHIS, VS<br>P.O. Box 1391<br>Baton Rouge, LA 70821 | Washington | USDA, APHIS, VS<br>406 General Administration Bldg.<br>Olympia, WA 98504 |
| Illinois | USDA, APHIS, VS<br>P.O. Box 3126<br>Springfield, IL 62708 | Texas | USDA, APHIS, VS<br>702 Colorado Street<br>Room 301<br>Austin, TX 78701 | | |

VS FORM 17-20 (Reverse Part 7)

No animals, animal semen, animal embryos, birds, poultry, or hatching eggs may be imported unless a completed application has been received (9 CFR 92 and CFR 93.)

FORM APPROVED
OMB NO. 0579-0040

U.S. DEPARTMENT OF AGRICULTURE
ANIMAL AND PLANT HEALTH INSPECTION SERVICE
VETERINARY SERVICES

**APPLICATION FOR IMPORT OR IN TRANSIT PERMIT**
*(Animals, Animal Semen, Animal Embryos, Birds, Poultry, Or Hatching Eggs)*

**INSTRUCTIONS TO IMPORTER:** Complete and submit one copy to the Veterinary Services, APHIS, U. S. Department of Agriculture, Federal Center Building, Hyattsville, Maryland 20782. Prepare a separate application for each shipment.

1. NAME AND ADDRESS OF SHIPPER IN COUNTRY OF ORIGIN

2. NAME AND ADDRESS OF IMPORTER *(Include Zip Code)*

TELEPHONE NUMBER *(Include Area Code)*

3. PORT OF EMBARKATION *(From Canada show only for ocean vessel or airplane shipments)*

4. COUNTRY FROM WHICH SHIPPED

5. MODE OF TRANSPORTATION *(Name of Airline or Vessel, flight no.)*

6. ANIMALS, ANIMAL SEMEN, ANIMAL EMBRYOS, BIRDS, POULTRY, OR HATCHING EGGS

| A. NO. | B. BREED | C. SPECIES | D. DESCRIPTION *(Sex, Age, Registered Name and No., Tattoo, Tag No., other Markings)* |
|---|---|---|---|
| | | | |

6E. PURPOSE OF IMPORTATION

7. ROUTE OF TRAVEL INCLUDING ALL CARRIER STOPS ENROUTE *(From Canada show route of travel only for ocean vessel or airplane shipment)*

8. PROPOSED SHIPPING DATE *(From Canada show only for ocean vessel or airplane shipment)*

9. PROPOSED ARRIVAL DATE

10. UNITED STATES PORT OF ENTRY

11. NAME AND MAILING ADDRESS OF PERSON TO WHOM DELIVERY WILL BE MADE *(After quarantine, when required) (Include Zip Code)*

TELEPHONE NUMBER *(Include Area Code)*

12. WHERE DELIVERY WILL BE MADE IN U. S. *(After quarantine, when required) (Location of place)*

13. REMARKS

14. SIGNATURE OF IMPORTER

15. DATE SIGNED

VS FORM 17-129
(JAN 78)

No permit can be issued to move live plant pests or noxious weeds until an application is received (7 CFR 330 (live plant pests) or 7 CFR 360 (noxious weeds))

See reverse side for additional information

FORM APPROVED
OMB NO 0579-0054

U.S. DEPARTMENT OF AGRICULTURE
ANIMAL AND PLANT HEALTH INSPECTION SERVICE
PLANT PROTECTION AND QUARANTINE
BIOLOGICAL ASSESSMENT AND TAXONOMIC SUPPORT
HYATTSVILLE, MARYLAND 20782

**APPLICATION AND PERMIT TO MOVE LIVE PLANT PESTS AND NOXIOUS WEEDS**

**SECTION A - TO BE COMPLETED BY THE APPLICANT**

1. NAME, TITLE, AND ADDRESS *(Include Zip Code)*

2. TELEPHONE NO.

3. TYPE OF PEST TO BE MOVED

☐ Arthropods ☐ Noxious Weeds
☐ Pathogens ☐ Other *(Specify)*

| | A. SCIENTIFIC NAMES OF PESTS TO BE MOVED | B. CLASSIFICATION *(Orders, Families, Races, or Strains)* | C. LIFE STAGES IF APPLICABLE | D. NUMBER OF SPECIMENS OR UNITS | E. SHIPPED FROM *(Country or State)* | F. ARE PESTS ESTABLISHED IN U.S. | G. MAJOR HOST(S) OF THE PEST |
|---|---|---|---|---|---|---|---|
| 4. | | | | | | | |
| 5. | | | | | | | |
| 6. | | | | | | | |

7. WHAT HOST MATERIALS WILL ACCOMPANY WHICH PESTS *(Indicate by line number)*

8. DESTINATION

9. PORT OF ARRIVAL

10. APPROXIMATE DATE OF ARRIVAL OR INTERSTATE MOVEMENT

11. NO. OF SHIPMENTS

12. SUPPLIER

13. METHOD OF SHIPMENT ☐ Air Mail ☐ Air Freight ☐ Baggage ☐ Auto

14. INTENDED USE *(Be specific, attach outline of intended research)*

15. METHODS TO BE USED TO PREVENT PLANT PEST ESCAPE

16. METHOD OF FINAL DISPOSITION

17. *Applicant must be a resident of the U.S.A. I/We agree to comply with the safeguards printed on the reverse of this form, and understand that a permit may be subject to other conditions specified in Sections B and C.*

SIGNATURE OF APPLICANT *(Must be person named in Item 1)*

18. DATE

**SECTION B - TO BE COMPLETED BY STATE OFFICIAL**

19. RECOMMENDATION

☐ Approve ☐ Disapprove

☐ Accept USDA Decision

20. CONDITIONS RECOMMENDED

21. SIGNATURE

22. TITLE

STATE

23. DATE

**SECTION C - TO BE COMPLETED BY FEDERAL OFFICIAL**

**PERMIT**

24. PERMIT NO.

**(Permit not valid unless signed by an authorized official of the Animal and Plant Health Inspection Service)**

**Under authority of the Federal Plant Pest Act of May 23, 1957 or the Federal Noxious Weed Act of 1974, permission is hereby granted to the applicant named above to move the pests described, except as deleted, subject to the conditions stated on, or attached to this application. (See standard conditions on reverse side).**

This permit does not authorize the introduction, importation, interstate movement, or release into the environment of any genetically engineered organisms or products

25. SIGNATURE OF PLANT PROTECTION AND QUARANTINE OFFICIAL

26. DATE

27. LABELS ISSUED

28. VALID UNTIL

29. PEST CATEGORY

PPQ FORM 526 (OCT 88) *Previous edition may be used*

## STANDARD SAFEGUARDS OF PERMIT

1. All pests must be shipped in sturdy, escape-proof containers.

2. Upon receipt of pests, all packing material and shipping containers shall be sterilized or destroyed immediately after removing pests.

3. Pests shall be kept only within the laboratory or designated area at the permittee's address.

4. No living pests kept under this permit shall be removed from confined area except by prior approval from State and Federal regulatory officials.

5. Without prior notice and during reasonable hours, authorized PPQ and State regulatory officials shall be allowed to inspect the conditions under which the pests are kept.

6. All pests kept under this permit shall be destroyed at the completion of the intended use, and not later than the expiration date, unless an extension is granted by this issuing office.

7. All necessary precautions must be taken to prevent escape of pests. In the event of an escape, notify this office.

**Public reporting burden for this collection of information is estimated to average 0.17 hours per response, including the time for reviewing instructions, searching existing data sources, gathering and maintaining the data needed, and completing and reviewing the collection of information. Send comments regarding this burden estimate or any other aspect of this collection of information, including suggestions for reducing this burden, to Department of Agriculture, Clearance Officer, OIRM, Room 404-W, Washington, D.C. 20250; and to the Office of Information and Regulatory Affairs, Office of Management and Budget, Washington, D.C. 20503.**

SEND TO:
U.S. Fish and Wildlife Service
Office of Management Authority
4401 N. Fairfax Drive, Room 432
Arlington, VA 22201
Call: 703/358-2104 for more information

OMB NO. 42-R1670

**DEPARTMENT OF THE INTERIOR**
**U.S. FISH AND WILDLIFE SERVICE**

**FEDERAL FISH AND WILDLIFE LICENSE/PERMIT APPLICATION**

1. APPLICATION FOR *(Indicate only one)*
   ☐ IMPORT OR EXPORT LICENSE ☒ PERMIT

2. BRIEF DESCRIPTION OF ACTIVITY FOR WHICH REQUESTED LICENSE OR PERMIT IS NEEDED

3. APPLICANT *(Name, complete address and phone number of individual, business, agency, or institution for which permit is requested)*

4. IF "APPLICANT" IS AN INDIVIDUAL, COMPLETE THE FOLLOWING

| ☐ MR ☐ MRS ☐ MISS ☐ MS | HEIGHT | WEIGHT |
|---|---|---|
| DATE OF BIRTH | COLOR HAIR | COLOR EYES |
| PHONE NUMBER WHERE EMPLOYED | SOCIAL SECURITY NUMBER | |
| OCCUPATION | | |
| ANY BUSINESS, AGENCY, OR INSTITUTIONAL AFFILIATION HAVING TO DO WITH THE WILDLIFE TO BE COVERED BY THIS LICENSE/PERMIT | | |

5. IF "APPLICANT" IS A BUSINESS, CORPORATION, PUBLIC AGENCY, OR INSTITUTION, COMPLETE THE FOLLOWING
   EXPLAIN TYPE OR KIND OF BUSINESS, AGENCY, OR INSTITUTION
   NAME, TITLE, AND PHONE NUMBER OF PRESIDENT, PRINCIPAL OFFICER, DIRECTOR, ETC.
   IF "APPLICANT" IS A CORPORATION, INDICATE STATE IN WHICH INCORPORATED

6. LOCATION WHERE PROPOSED ACTIVITY IS TO BE CONDUCTED

7. DO YOU HOLD ANY CURRENTLY VALID FEDERAL FISH AND WILDLIFE LICENSE OR PERMIT? ☐ YES ☐ NO
   *(If yes, list license or permit numbers)*

8. IF REQUIRED BY ANY STATE OR FOREIGN GOVERNMENT, DO YOU HAVE THEIR APPROVAL TO CONDUCT THE ACTIVITY YOU PROPOSE? ☐ YES ☐ NO
   *(If yes, list jurisdictions and type of documents)*

9. CHECK OR MONEY ORDER *(if applicable)*, PAYABLE TO THE U.S. FISH AND WILDLIFE SERVICE ENCLOSED IN AMOUNT OF
   $ $25.00

10. DESIRED EFFECTIVE DATE

11. DURATION NEEDED

12. ATTACHMENTS. THE SPECIFIC INFORMATION REQUIRED FOR THE TYPE OF LICENSE/PERMIT REQUESTED *(See 50 CFR 13.12(b))* MUST BE ATTACHED. IT CONSTITUTES AN INTEGRAL PART OF THIS APPLICATION. LIST SECTIONS OF 50 CFR UNDER WHICH ATTACHMENTS ARE PROVIDED.

SEE REVERSE

**CERTIFICATION**

I HEREBY CERTIFY THAT I HAVE READ AND AM FAMILIAR WITH THE REGULATIONS CONTAINED IN TITLE 50, PART 13, OF THE CODE OF FEDERAL REGULATIONS AND THE OTHER APPLICABLE PARTS IN SUBCHAPTER B OF CHAPTER I OF TITLE 50, AND I FURTHER CERTIFY THAT THE INFORMATION SUBMITTED IN THIS APPLICATION FOR A LICENSE/PERMIT IS COMPLETE AND ACCURATE TO THE BEST OF MY KNOWLEDGE AND BELIEF. I UNDERSTAND THAT ANY FALSE STATEMENT HEREIN MAY SUBJECT ME TO THE CRIMINAL PENALTIES OF 18 U.S.C. 1001.

| SIGNATURE *(In ink)* * | DATE |
|---|---|
| | |

3-200 (6/74) *Applicant listed in 3 above or principal officer listed in 5 above must sign.

Please complete ONE of the statements below to renew your permit:

1. I certify that the information submitted in support of my original application for USFWS permit PRT ______ is still currently correct and hereby request renewal of that permit.

_______________________________
Permittee's signature

Date_______________________________

2. I certify that the information submitted in support of my original application for USFWS permit PRT ______ is still currently correct except for the changes listed below and hereby request renewal of that permit.

   Description of changes:

_______________________________
Permittee's signature

Date_______________________________

RETURN TO:
U.S. Fish and Wildlife Service
Office of Management Authority
4401 N. Fairfax Drive, Room 432
Arlington, VA 22201

OMB NO. 42-R1670

**DEPARTMENT OF THE INTERIOR**
**U.S. FISH AND WILDLIFE SERVICE**

**FEDERAL FISH AND WILDLIFE LICENSE/PERMIT APPLICATION**

1. APPLICATION FOR *(Indicate only one)*

☐ IMPORT OR EXPORT LICENSE  ☒ PERMIT

2. BRIEF DESCRIPTION OF ACTIVITY FOR WHICH REQUESTED LICENSE OR PERMIT IS NEEDED.

Use of a non-designated port.

3. APPLICANT. *(Name, complete address and phone number of individual, business, agency, or institution for which permit is requested)*

4. IF "APPLICANT" IS AN INDIVIDUAL, COMPLETE THE FOLLOWING:

☐ MR. ☐ MRS. ☐ MISS ☐ MS. | HEIGHT | WEIGHT

DATE OF BIRTH | COLOR HAIR | COLOR EYES

PHONE NUMBER WHERE EMPLOYED | SOCIAL SECURITY NUMBER

OCCUPATION

ANY BUSINESS, AGENCY, OR INSTITUTIONAL AFFILIATION HAVING TO DO WITH THE WILDLIFE TO BE COVERED BY THIS LICENSE/PERMIT

5. IF "APPLICANT" IS A BUSINESS, CORPORATION, PUBLIC AGENCY, OR INSTITUTION, COMPLETE THE FOLLOWING:

EXPLAIN TYPE OR KIND OF BUSINESS, AGENCY, OR INSTITUTION

NAME, TITLE, AND PHONE NUMBER OF PRESIDENT, PRINCIPAL OFFICER, DIRECTOR, ETC.

IF "APPLICANT" IS A CORPORATION, INDICATE STATE IN WHICH INCORPORATED

6. LOCATION WHERE PROPOSED ACTIVITY IS TO BE CONDUCTED

7. DO YOU HOLD ANY CURRENTLY VALID FEDERAL FISH AND WILDLIFE LICENSE OR PERMIT? ☐ YES ☐ NO
*(If yes, list license or permit numbers)*

8. IF REQUIRED BY ANY STATE OR FOREIGN GOVERNMENT, DO YOU HAVE THEIR APPROVAL TO CONDUCT THE ACTIVITY YOU PROPOSE? ☐ YES ☐ NO
*(If yes, list jurisdictions and type of documents)*

9. CERTIFIED CHECK OR MONEY ORDER *(if applicable)* PAYABLE TO THE U.S. FISH AND WILDLIFE SERVICE ENCLOSED IN AMOUNT OF

10. DESIRED EFFECTIVE DATE

11. DURATION NEEDED

12. ATTACHMENTS. THE SPECIFIC INFORMATION REQUIRED FOR THE TYPE OF LICENSE/PERMIT REQUESTED *(See 50 CFR 13.12(b))* MUST BE ATTACHED. IT CONSTITUTES AN INTEGRAL PART OF THIS APPLICATION. LIST SECTIONS OF 50 CFR UNDER WHICH ATTACHMENTS ARE PROVIDED.

See reverse, or 50 CFR 14.31, 14.32, 14.33

**CERTIFICATION**

**I HEREBY CERTIFY THAT I HAVE READ AND AM FAMILIAR WITH THE REGULATIONS CONTAINED IN TITLE 50, PART 13, OF THE CODE OF FEDERAL REGULATIONS AND THE OTHER APPLICABLE PARTS IN SUBCHAPTER B OF CHAPTER I OF TITLE 50, AND I FURTHER CERTIFY THAT THE INFORMATION SUBMITTED IN THIS APPLICATION FOR A LICENSE/PERMIT IS COMPLETE AND ACCURATE TO THE BEST OF MY KNOWLEDGE AND BELIEF. I UNDERSTAND THAT ANY FALSE STATEMENT HEREIN MAY SUBJECT ME TO THE CRIMINAL PENALTIES OF 18 U.S.C. 1001.**

SIGNATURE *(In ink)* | DATE

3-200
(6/74)

Application Continuation Sheet

NON-DESIGNATED PORT PERMIT

Directions: All applicants must complete section A. If for scientific purposes, only section A must be complete. For all other purposes, also complete either section B or section C, in addition to section A. Attach additional sheets as necessary.

A. ALL APPLICANTS (50 CFR 14.31)

1. Species: ____________________ ____________________ ________
(scientific name) (common name) (quantity)

2. Country or place of origin: ______________________________

3. Port(s) requested: ______________________________

4. Import or Export(choose one or both): ______________________________

5. ( ) Single shipment
( ) Series of shipments
Where possible, give date(s) of intended shipment(s).

6. Explain reasons shipment should be allowed at the requested port(s) rather than at a designated port.

7. What is the scientific purpose or uses of the wildlife to be imported or exported?

B. COMPLETE THIS PORTION FOR DETERIORATION OR LOSS (50 CFR 14.32)

1. Explain how substantial deterioration or loss of wildlife could be avoided by using a non-designated port. Be specific.

C. COMPLETE THIS PORTION FOR ECONOMIC HARDSHIP. (50 CFR 14.33)

1. Form of wildlife to be shipped (live, frozen, raw hides, etc.).

2. Name and address of supplier(s).

3. Attach cost data showing monetary difference between the cost of shipment at port(s) requested and the lowest cost of shipment at a designated port.

USFWS Form 3-177
(revised Sept. 1978)

Form Approved O.M.B. No. 42-R1476

U.S. FISH AND WILDLIFE SERVICE

**DECLARATION FOR IMPORTATION OR EXPORTATION OF FISH OR WILDLIFE**

Indicate One:
☐ import ☐ export

Port of:

Date:

For Imports Only

Customs Identification No.:

Name of Carrier:

Airway Bill or Bill of Lading No.:

Imported or Exported via:
☐ air cargo ☐ ocean cargo ☐ truck
☐ rail ☐ mail ☐ personal baggage
☐ automobile: license no. ______
state ______

Location where wildlife is available for inspection:

Package or Bale Marks and Nos.:

Please Type or Print Legibly

(indicate one)
☐ U.S. Importer of Record
☐ U.S. Exporter ______ (name) ______ (address - street, city, state, zip code)

Foreign Consignor or Consignee ______ (name) ______ (address - street, city, country)

Customs Broker or Agent ______

Shipping Agent or Freight Forwarder ______

Furnish All Information Below (invoices or lists providing required information may be attached)

| QUANTITY | SCIENTIFIC NAME Genus Species | COMMON NAME | DESCRIPTION If live, so state. If product, describe. | DECLARED VALUE | COUNTRY OF ORIGIN |
|---|---|---|---|---|---|
| | | | | | |
| | | | | | |
| | | | | | |
| | | | | | |
| | | | | | |
| | | | | | |

U.S. License and/or Permit Nos.:

Foreign License and/or Permits:
Country No.

I certify the information contained herein is true and complete to the best of my knowledge and belief.

______ signature ______ date

FOR OFFICIAL USE ONLY

Action Taken: Date:
☐ cleared
☐ clearance refused
☐ seized

______ % of Wildlife Inspected:

Officer Signature and Badge No.:

SEE REVERSE OF THIS FORM FOR INSTRUCTIONS AND PRIVACY ACT NOTICE

## FILING INSTRUCTIONS

File original declaration only. Copies may be retained by importer or broker if desired. Print or type legibly. Provide all relevant information. Declared value need not be shown for scientific specimens, game, or game trophies not imported or exported for a commercial purpose.

"Country of Origin" means the country where the animal was taken from the wild or the country of natal origin of the animal.

When And Where To File.

At Designated Ports: File with the U.S. Fish and Wildlife Service Office serving the designated port. For imports, file declarations when requesting wildlife clearance. For exports, file declaration in sufficient time in advance of actual departure of wildlife from U.S. to allow reasonable time for inspection.

At Nondesignated Ports: File with U.S. Customs. For imports, file declaration prior to removal of wildlife from Customs custody. For exports, file prior to departure of wildlife from U.S.

Note To Customs Officers. Mail all Forms 3-177 collected to Special Agent in Charge, U.S. Fish and Wildlife Service for your district at end of each month.

Regulations concerning the importation and exportation of wildlife may be found in 50 CFR Part 14. Specific regulations concerning the filing of declarations for the importation or exportation of wildlife may be found in 50 CFR 14.61-14.64.

Failure to file a declaration for importation or exportation of fish or wildlife when required by the regulations in 50 CFR 14.61-14.64 is a violation of the Endangered Species Act of 1973 (16 USC 1531-1543).

Knowingly making a false statement in a Declaration for Importation or Exportation of Fish or Wildlife may subject the declarant to the penalty provided by 18 USC 1001.

## NOTICE

In accordance with the Privacy Act of 1974 (P.L. 93-579), please be advised that:

1. The gathering of information on the importation or exportation of wildlife, including any wild mammal, bird, fish, amphibian, reptile, mollusk, or crustacean, is authorized by the Endangered Species Act of 1973 (16 USC 1531-1543) and Title 50, Parts 14 and 17, of the Code of Federal Regulations.

2. The disclosure of the requested information is required to provide information about wildlife imports or exports, including products and parts, to facilitate enforcement of the act and to carry out the provisions of the Convention on International Trade in Endangered Species of Wild Fauna and Flora.

3. Failure to provide all of the requested information is sufficient cause for the U.S. Fish and Wildlife Service to deny you permission to import or export wildlife.

4. In the event there is indicated a violation of a statute, regulation, rule, order, or license, whether civil, criminal, or regulatory in nature, the requested information may be transferred to the appropriate Federal, State, local, or foreign agency charged with investigating or prosecuting such violations.

5. In the event of litigation involving the records or the subject matter of the records, the requested information may be transferred to the U.S. Department of Justice.

6. The requested information may be subject to disclosure under provisions of the Freedom of Information Act, 5 USC 552.

GPO : 1980 O - 316-883

# United States Department of the Interior

**FISH AND WILDLIFE SERVICE**
**WASHINGTON, D.C. 20240**

ADDRESS ONLY THE DIRECTOR
FISH AND WILDLIFE SERVICE

Implemented May 1982

GENERAL PERMIT CONDITIONS

1. All sections of Title 50 Code of Federal Regulations Part 13 attached to this page are conditions of the permit.

2. All applicable foreign, state, local or other federal laws, including those requiring permits, must be observed.

3. Living specimens must be handled and shipped so as to minimize risk of injury, damage to health or cruel treatment.

4. Container in which authorized wildlife is shipped must be plainly marked with name and address of shipper consignee and an accurate description of the contents including common and scientific name and number of each within, OR with a symbol authorized by a Symbol Marking Permit.

5. Permittee must carry a copy of permit while conducting authorized activities.

6. Permit number must be legibly printed on all documents and advertisements involving activities conducted under permit.

For permits authorizing import, export or reexport:

7. The permit and a completed copy of the Wildlife Declaration (Form 3-177) must be presented to a USFWS officer at the port upon import, export or reexport of wildlife shipments.

8. Import, export or reexport of pre-Act wildlife under the U.S. Endangered Species Act must be accompanied by documentation required by 50 CFR 17.4.

9. Import of species listed in Appendix I, II or III of CITES must be accompanied by proper foreign documentation from the country of export.

10. Import, export or reexport of plants must be made through a U.S. Department of Agriculture (USDA) port (list attached if applicable). Permittee shall allow an authorized USDA agent to enter his premises at any reasonable hour to inspect any specimens held, or to inspect any records.

11. Import, export or reexport of wildlife must be made through one of the following designated ports or as authorized by an Exception to Designated Port permit: New York, NY; Miami, FL; New Orleans, LA; Los Angeles and San Francisco, CA; Dallas/Ft. Worth, TX; Honolulu, HI; Chicago, IL; Seattle, WA and Portland, OR.

    Exception to Designated Port Permittee:

    a. Permittee is liable for all costs incurred by USFWS in examining shipments including per diem, salary and travel costs. Payment shall be by certified check or money order, payable to U.S. Fish and Wildlife Service prior to Delivery of shipment to the consignee.

    b. The nearest USFWS Law Enforcement Office (list attached) must be notified at least 72 hours prior to import, export or reexport.

# SAMPLE APPLICATION: IMPORT/EXPORT: GENERAL PERMIT CONDITIONS CONTINUATION

**§ 13.22 Renewal of permits.**

(a) *Application for renewal.* Applicants for renewal of a permit must submit a written application at least 30 days prior to the expiration date of the permit. Applicants must certify in the form required by § 13.12(a)(5) that all statements and information in the original application remain current and correct, unless previously changed or corrected. If such information is no longer current or correct, the applicant must provide corrected information.

(b) *Renewal criteria.* The Service shall issue a renewal of a permit if the applicant meets the criteria for issuance in § 13.21(b) and is not disqualified under § 13.21(c).

(c) *Continuation of permitted activity.* Any person holding a valid, renewable permit, who has complied with this section, may continue the activities authorized by the expired permit until the Service has acted on such person's application for renewal.

(d) *Denial.* The issuing officer may deny renewal of a permit to any applicant who fails to meet the issuance criteria set forth in § 13.21 of this part, or in the part(s) or section(s) specifically governing the activity for which the renewal is requested.

[54 FR 38148, Sept. 14, 1989]

**§ 13.23 Amendment of permits.**

(a) *Permittee's request.* Where circumstances have changed so that a permittee desires to have any condition of his permit modified, such permittee must submit a full written justification and supporting information in conformity with this part and the part under which the permit was issued.

(b) *Service reservation.* The Service reserves the right to amend any permit for just cause at any time during its term, upon written finding of necessity.

(c) *Change of name or address.* A permittee is not required to obtain a new permit if there is a change in the legal individual or business name, or in the mailing address of the permittee. A permittee is required to notify the issuing office within 10 calendar days of such change. This provision does not authorize any change in location of the conduct of the permitted activity when approval of the location is a qualifying condition of the permit.

[54 FR 38148, Sept. 14, 1989]

**§ 13.24 Right of succession by certain persons.**

(a) Certain persons, other than the permittee are granted the right to carry on a permitted activity for the remainder of the term of a current permit provided they comply with the provisions of paragraph (b) of this section. Such persons are the following:

(1) The surviving spouse, child, executor, administrator, or other legal representative of a deceased permittee; and

(2) A receiver or trustee in bankruptcy or a court designated assignee for the benefit of creditors.

(b) In order to secure the right provided in this section the person or persons desiring to continue the activity shall furnish the permit to the issuing officer for endorsement within 90 days from the date the successor begins to carry on the activity.

[54 FR 38149, Sept. 14, 1989]

**§ 13.25 Permits not transferable; agents.**

(a) Permits issued under this part are not transferable or assignable. Some permits authorize certain activities in connection with a business or commercial enterprise and in the event of any lease, sale, or transfer of such business entity, the successor must obtain a permit prior to continuing the permitted activity. However, certain limited rights of succession are provided in § 13.24.

(b) Except as otherwise stated on the face of the permit, any person who is under the direct control of the permittee, or who is employed by or under contract to the permittee for purposes authorized by the permit, may carry out the activity authorized by the permit, as an agent for the permittee.

[54 FR 38149, Sept. 14, 1989]

**§ 13.26 Discontinuance of permit activity.**

When a permittee, or any successor to a permittee as provided for by § 13.24, discontinues activities authorized by a permit, the permittee shall within 30 calendar days of the discontinuance return the permit to the issuing officer together with a written statement surrendering the permit for cancellation. The permit shall be deemed void and cancelled upon its receipt by the issuing office. No refund of any fees paid for issuance of the permit or for any other fees or costs associated with a permitted activity shall be made when a permit is surrendered for cancellation for any reason prior to the expiration date stated on the face of the permit.

[54 FR 38149, Sept. 14, 1989]

**§ 13.27 Permit suspension.**

(a) *Criteria for suspension.* The privileges of exercising some or all of the permit authority may be suspended at any time if the permittee is not in compliance with the conditions of the permit, or with any applicable laws or regulations governing the conduct of the permitted activity. The issuing officer may also suspend all or part of the privileges authorized by a permit if the permittee fails to pay any fees, penalties, or costs owed to the Government. Such suspension shall remain in effect until the issuing officer determines that the permittee has corrected the deficiencies.

(b) *Procedure for suspension.* (1) When the issuing officer believes there are valid grounds for suspending a permit the permittee shall be notified in writing of the proposed suspension by certified or registered mail. This notice shall identify the permit to be suspended, the reason(s) for such suspension, the actions necessary to correct the deficiencies, and inform the permittee of the right to object to the proposed suspension. The issuing officer may amend any notice of suspension at any time.

(2) Upon receipt of a notice of proposed suspension the permittee may file a written objection to the proposed action. Such objection must be in writing, must be filed within 45 calendar days of the date of the notice of proposal, must state the reasons why the permittee objects to the proposed suspension, and may include supporting documentation.

(3) A decision on the suspension shall be made within 45 days after the end of the objection period. The issuing officer shall notify the permittee in writing of the Service's decision and the reasons therefore. The issuing officer shall also provide the applicant with the information concerning the right to request reconsideration of the decision under § 13.29 of this part and the procedures for requesting reconsideration.

[54 FR 38149, Sept. 14, 1989]

**§ 13.28 Permit revocation.**

(a) *Criteria for revocation.* A permit may be revoked for any of the following reasons:

(1) The permittee willfully violates any Federal or State statute or regulation, or any Indian tribal law or regulation, or any law or regulation of any foreign country, which involves a violation of the conditions of the permit or of the laws or regulations governing the permitted activity; or

(2) The permittee fails within 60 days to correct deficiencies that were the cause of a permit suspension; or

(3) The permittee becomes disqualified under § 13.21(c) of this part; or

(4) A change occurs in the statute or regulation authorizing the permit that prohibits the continuation of a permit issued by the Service; or

(5) The population(s) of the wildlife or plant that is subject of the permit declines to the extent that continuation of the permitted activity would be detrimental to maintenance or recovery of the affected population.

(b) *Procedure for revocation.* (1) When the issuing officer believes there are valid grounds for revoking a permit, the permittee shall be notified in writing of the proposed revocation by certified or registered mail. This notice shall identify the permit to be revoked, the reason(s) for such revocation, the proposed disposition of the wildlife, if any, and inform the permittee of the right to object to the proposed revocation. The issuing officer may amend any notice of revocation at any time.

(2) Upon receipt of a notice of proposed revocation the permittee may file a written objection to the proposed action. Such objection must be in writing, must be filed within 45 calendar days of the date of the notice of proposal, must state the reasons why the permittee objects to the proposed revocation, and may include supporting documentation.

(3) A decision on the revocation shall be made within 45 days after the end of the objection period. The issuing officer shall notify the permittee in writing of the Service's decision and the reasons therefore, together with the information concerning the right to request and the procedures for requesting reconsideration.

(4) Unless a permittee files a timely request for reconsideration, any wildlife held under authority of a permit that is revoked must be disposed of in accordance with instructions of the issuing officer. If a permittee files a timely request for reconsideration of a proposed revocation, such permittee may retain possession of any wildlife held under authority of the permit until final disposition of the appeal process.

[54 FR 38149, Sept. 14, 1989]

**§ 13.29 Review procedures.**

(a) *Request for reconsideration*. Any person may request reconsideration of an action under this part if that person is one of the following:

(1) An applicant for a permit who has received written notice of denial;

(2) An applicant for renewal who has received written notice that a renewal is denied;

(3) A permittee who has a permit amended, suspended, or revoked, except for those actions which are required by changes in statutes or regulations, or are emergency changes of limited applicability for which an expiration date is set within 90 days of the permit change; or

(4) A permittee who has a permit issued or renewed but has not been granted authority by the permit to perform all activities requested in the application, except when the activity requested is one for which there is no lawful authority to issue a permit.

(b) *Method of requesting reconsideration*. Any person requesting reconsideration of an action under this part must comply with the following criteria;

(1) Any request for reconsideration must be in writing, signed by the person requesting reconsideration or by the legal representative of that person, and must be submitted to the issuing officer.

(2) The request for reconsideration must be received by the issuing officer within 45 calendar days of the date of notification of the decision for which reconsideration is being requested.

(3) The request for reconsideration shall state the decision for which reconsideration is being requested and shall state the reason(s) for the reconsideration, including presenting any new information or facts pertinent to the issue(s) raised by the request for reconsideration.

(4) The request for reconsideration shall contain a certification in substantially the same form as that provided by § 13.12(a)(5). If a request for reconsideration does not contain such certification, but is otherwise timely and appropriate, it shall be held and the person submitting the request shall be given written notice of the need to submit the certification within 15 calendar days. Failure to submit certification shall result in the request being rejected as insufficient in form and content.

(c) *Inquiry by the Service*. The Service may institute a separate inquiry into the matter under consideration.

(d) *Determination of grant or denial of a request for reconsideration*. The issuing officer shall notify the permittee of the Service's decision within 45 days of the receipt of the request for reconsideration. This notification shall be in writing, shall state the reasons for the decision, and shall contain a description of the evidence which was relied upon by the issuing officer. The notification shall also provide information concerning the right to appeal, the official to whom an appeal may be addressed, and the procedures for making an appeal.

(e) *Appeal*. A person who has received an adverse decision following submission of a request for reconsideration may submit a written appeal to the Regional Director for the region in which the issuing office is located, or to the Director for offices which report directly to the Director. An appeal must be submitted within 45 days of the date of the notification of the decision on the request for reconsideration. The appeal shall state the reason(s) and issue(s) upon which the appeal is based and may contain any additional evidence or arguments to support the appeal.

(f) *Decision on appeal*. (1) Before a decision is made concerning the appeal the appellant may present oral arguments before the Regional Director or the Director, as appropriate, if such official judges oral arguments are necessary to clarify issues raised in the written record.

(2) The Service shall notify the appellant in writing of its decision within 45 calendar days of receipt of the appeal, unless extended for good cause and the appellant notified of the extension.

(3) The decision of the Regional Director or the Director shall constitute the final administrative decision of the Department of the Interior.

[54 FR 38149, Sept. 14, 1989]

**Subpart D—Conditions**

**§ 13.41 Humane conditions.**

Any live wildlife possessed under a permit must be maintained under humane and healthful conditions.

[54 FR 38150, Sept. 14, 1989]

**§ 13.42 Permits are specific.**

The authorizations on the face of a permit which set forth specific times, dates, places, methods of taking, numbers and kinds of wildlife or plants, location of activity, authorize certain circumscribed transactions, or otherwise permit a specifically limited matter, are to be strictly construed and shall not be interpreted to permit similar or related matters outside the scope of strict construction.

[39 FR 1161, Jan. 4, 1974, as amended at 42 FR 32377, June 24, 1977]

**§ 13.43 Alteration of permits.**

Permits shall not be altered, erased, or mutilated, and any permit which has been altered, erased, or mutilated shall immediately become invalid. Unless specifically permitted on the face thereof, no permit shall be copied, nor shall any copy of a permit issued pursuant to this subchapter B be displayed, offered for inspection, or otherwise used for any official purpose for which the permit was issued.

**§ 13.44 Display of permit.**

Any permit issued under this part shall be displayed for inspection upon request to the Director or his agent, or to any other person relying upon its existence.

**§ 13.45 Filing of reports.**

Permittees may be required to file reports of the activities conducted under the permit. Any such reports shall be filed not later than March 31 for the preceding calendar year ending December 31, or any portion thereof, during which a permit was in force, unless the regulations of this subchapter B or the provisions of the permit set forth other reporting requirements.

**§ 13.46 Maintenance of records.**

From the date of issuance of the permit, the permittee shall maintain complete and accurate records of any taking, possession, transportation, sale, purchase, barter, exportation, or importation of plants obtained from the wild (excluding seeds) or wildlife pursuant to such permit. Such records shall be kept current and shall include names and addresses of persons with whom any plant obtained from the wild (excluding seeds) or wildlife has been purchased, sold, bartered, or otherwise transferred, and the date of such transaction, and such other information as may be required or appropriate. Such records shall be legibly written or reproducible in English and shall be maintained for five years from the date of expiration of the permit.

[39 FR 1161, Jan. 4, 1974, as amended at 42 FR 32377, June 24, 1977; 54 FR 38150, Sept. 14, 1989]

**§ 13.47 Inspection requirement.**

Any person holding a permit under this subchapter B shall allow the Director's agent to enter his premises at any reasonable hour to inspect any wildlife or plant held or to inspect, audit, or copy any permits, books, or records required to be kept by regulations of this subchapter B.

[39 FR 1161, Jan. 4, 1974, as amended at 42 FR 32377, June 24, 1977]

**§ 13.48 Compliance with conditions of permit.**

Any person holding a permit under subchapter B and any person acting under authority of such permit must comply with all conditions of the permit and with all applicable laws and regulations governing the permitted activity.

[54 FR 38150, Sept. 14, 1989]

United States Department of the Interior
Fish and Wildlife Service

Rev. 1/91

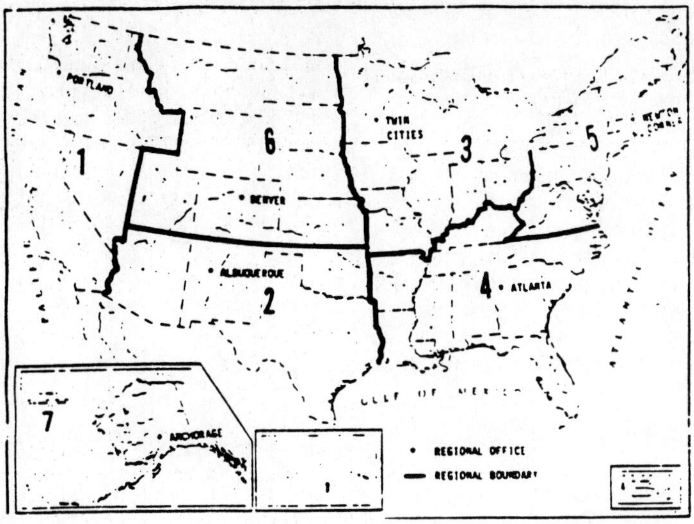


**Jurisdiction**

**Region 1:** California, Hawaii Idaho, Nevada, Oregon, Washington, American Samoa, Commonwealth of the Northern Mariana Islands, Guam, and the Pacific Trust Territories

**Region 2:** Arizona, New Mexico, Oklahoma, and Texas

**Region 3:** Illinois, Indiana, Iowa, Michigan, Minnesota, Missouri, Ohio, and Wisconsin

**Region 4:** Alabama, Arkansas, Florida, Georgia, Kentucky, Louisiana, Mississippi, North Carolina, South Carolina, Tennessee, Puerto Rico, and the U.S. Virgins Islands

**Region 5:** Connecticut, Delaware, District of Columbia, Maine, Maryland, Massachusetts, New Hampshire, New Jersey, New York, Pennsylvania, Rhode Island, Vermont, Virginia and West Virginia

**Region 6:** Colorado, Kansas, Montana, Nebraska, North Dakota, South Dakota, Utah, and Wyoming

**Region 7:** Alaska

**REGIONAL DIRECTORS**

1. Marvin Plenert
   Eastside Federal Complex
   911 N.E. 11th Avenue
   Portland, Oregon 97232-4181
   503-231-2234 FTS 429-2234
2. Michael J. Spear
   P.O. Box 1306
   Albuquerque, New Mexico 87103
   505-766-2321 FTS 474-2321
3. James C. Gritman
   P.O. Box 45
   Federal Building, Fort Snelling
   Twin Cities, Minnesota 55111
   612-725-3563 FTS 725-3563
4. James W. Pulliam, Jr.
   75 Spring Street, SW Rm. 1200
   Atlanta, Georgia 30303
   404-331-3588 FTS 841-3555
5. Ronald E. Lambertson
   One Gateway Center, Suite 700
   Newton Corner, Massachusetts 02158
   617-968-5100 FTS 829-9200
6. Galen L. Butterbaugh
   P.O. Box 25486
   Denver Federal Center
   Denver, Colorado 80225
   303-236-7920 FTS 776-7920
7. Walter O. Stieglitz
   1100 E. Tudor Road
   Anchorage, Alaska 99503
   907-786-3542 FTS 869-3542

Assistant Regional Directors
**LAW ENFORCEMENT**

1. David L. McMullen
   Eastside Federal Complex
   911 N.E. 11th Avenue
   Portland, Oregon 97232-4181
   503-231-6125 FTS: 429-6125
2. John E. Cross
   P.O. Box 329
   Albuquerque, New Mexico
   505-766-2091 FTS: 474-2091
3. Larry Hood
   Box 45
   Federal Building, Fort Snelling
   Twin Cities, Minnesota 55111
   612-725-3530 FTS: 725-3530
4. Richard Endress (Acting)
   P.O. Box 4839
   Atlanta, Georgia 30302
   404-331-5872 FTS: 841-5872
5. A. Eugene Hester
   P.O Box 129, New Town Branch
   Boston, Massachusetts 02258
   617-965-2298 FTS: 829-9254
6. Terry Grosz
   P.O. Box 25486
   Denver Federal Center
   Denver, Colorado 80225
   303-231-5270 FTS: 554-5270
7. R. David Puriton
   P.O. Box 92597
   Anchorage, Alaska 99509-2597
   907-786-3311 FTS: NONE

**U.S. Fish and Wildlife Service Designated Ports**
(50 CFR 14.12)

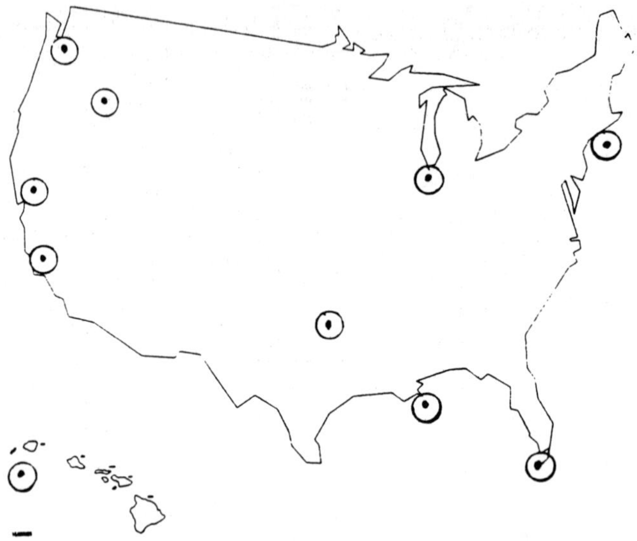

DESIGNATED PORTS (50 CFR 14.12)

CHICAGO
10600 Higgins Rd., Suite 707
Rosemont, Il 60018
312/298-3250

DALLAS/FT. WORTH
1205 Royal Lane
P.O. Box 610069
Ft. Worth, TX 75261
214/574-3254

HONOLULU
300 Ala Moana Blvd., Rm. 6307A
P.O. Box 50223
Honolulu, HI 96850
808/541-2681

LOS ANGELES
1149 W. 190th St., Suite 2024
Gardena, CA 90248802
213/297-0063

MIAMI
Monterey Bldg., Rm 118
8410 N.W. 53rd Terrace
Miami, FL 33166
305/536-4809 or 4788

NEW ORLEANS
1010 Gause Blvd., Bldg. 936
Slidell, LA 70458
504/837-2095

NEW YORK
Savings of Amer. Bank Bldg.
700 Rockaway Turnpike, 2nd fl.
Lawrence, NY 11559
718/917-1767

PORTLAND
847 NE 19th Ave., Room 225
Portland, OR 97232
503/231-6135 (Airport)
503/231-6186 (SRA Office)

SAN FRANCISCO
1290 Howard Ave., Suite 325
Burlingame, CA 94010
415/344-5900

SEATTLE
121 107th N.E. Suite 127
Bellevue, WA 98004
206/442-5543 or 764-3463

REV 11/90

**PLEASE PRINT**

U.S. DEPARTMENT OF AGRICULTURE
ANIMAL AND PLANT HEALTH INSPECTION SERVICE
PLANT PROTECTION AND QUARANTINE PROGRAMS

## APPLICATION FOR PERMIT TO IMPORT PLANTS OR PLANT PRODUCTS

1. DATE OF APPLICATION

2. PLANTS OR PLANT PRODUCTS TO BE IMPORTED

| COUNTRY OF ORIGIN (If Canada, give city and province. If Mexico, give State. **Make separate entry for each country.**) A | QUANTITY AND NAMES OF PLANTS OR PLANT PRODUCTS Scientific (Botanical) or English names must be included (Colloquial names are **not acceptable**). List whether seeds, bulbs, plants, cuttings, cut flowers, fruits, etc. Indicate whether for planting, consumption or other purposes. B | U.S. PORT OR PORTS OF ARRIVAL IF SHIPPED OTHER THAN BY MAIL C |
|---|---|---|
| | | |
| | | |
| | | |
| | | |
| | | |
| | | |
| | | |
| | | |
| | | |
| | | |
| | | |
| | | |
| | | |
| | | |
| | | |

*Use the reverse side if more space is needed, and check box* ☐

3. CHECK MEANS OF IMPORTATION: AIR MAIL OR AIR PARCEL POST ☐ AIR FREIGHT ☐ SURFACE MAIL OR PARCEL POST ☐ TRUCK, RAIL OR WATER FREIGHT ☐ BAGGAGE OR CAR ☐

4. APPROXIMATE DATE OF DEPARTURE FROM U.S.A. | ARRIVAL DATE

5. ARE OTHER IMPORTATIONS CONTEMPLATED WITHIN THE NEXT TWO YEARS YES ☐ NO ☐

**ANSWER 6, 7, 8, AND 9 ONLY IF IMPORTED MATERIAL WILL BE RESHIPPED TO ANOTHER COUNTRY**

6. RESHIPMENT WILL BE BY AIR ☐ WATER ☐ RAIL ☐ TRUCK ☐

7. UNDER THE FOLLOWING TYPE CUSTOMS ENTRY IE ☐ T & E ☐

8. PORT OF EXIT FROM UNITED STATES

9. COUNTRY OF FINAL DESTINATION

10. PRINT NAME AND UNITED STATES ADDRESS OF APPLICANT *(Including street address, P.O. Box, if any, and Zip Codes.)*

11. SIGNATURE OF APPLICANT

12. TELEPHONE NO. *(Include Area Code)*

13. FORWARD THIS APPLICATION TO

U.S. Department of Agriculture, APHIS
Plant Protection and Quarantine Programs
Permit Unit
Federal Building
Hyattsville, Maryland 20782

PPQ FORM 587 (MD) (6/77) PREVIOUS EDITION MAY BE USED UNTIL EXHAUSTED ☆U.S. G.P.O. 1977-729-353/3251

SEND TO:
U.S. Fish and Wildlife Service
Office of Management Authority
4401 N. Fairfax Drive, Room 432
Arlington, VA 22201
Call: 703/358-2104 for more information

OMB NO. 42-R1672

**DEPARTMENT OF THE INTERIOR**
**U.S. FISH AND WILDLIFE SERVICE**

**FEDERAL FISH AND WILDLIFE LICENSE/PERMIT APPLICATION**

1. APPLICATION FOR *(Indicate only one)*

☐ IMPORT OR EXPORT LICENSE  [X] PERMIT

2. BRIEF DESCRIPTION OF ACTIVITY FOR WHICH REQUESTED LICENSE OR PERMIT IS NEEDED.

MARINE MAMMAL PERMIT

Take _____ Import _____

Species: ____________________

For: Scientific Research _____
Public Display _____
Enhancement of Survival or Recovery _____

3. APPLICANT. *(Name, complete address and phone number of individual, business, agency, or institution for which permit is requested)*

4. IF "APPLICANT" IS AN <u>INDIVIDUAL</u>, COMPLETE THE FOLLOWING.

☐ MR. ☐ MRS. ☐ MISS ☐ MS.

| | HEIGHT | WEIGHT |
|---|---|---|
| DATE OF BIRTH | COLOR HAIR | COLOR EYES |
| PHONE NUMBER WHERE EMPLOYED | SOCIAL SECURITY NUMBER | |
| OCCUPATION | | |

ANY BUSINESS, AGENCY, OR INSTITUTIONAL AFFILIATION HAVING TO DO WITH THE WILDLIFE TO BE COVERED BY THIS LICENSE/PERMIT

5. IF "APPLICANT" IS A <u>BUSINESS</u>, <u>CORPORATION</u>, <u>PUBLIC AGENCY</u>, OR <u>INSTITUTION</u>, COMPLETE THE FOLLOWING

EXPLAIN TYPE OR KIND OF BUSINESS, AGENCY, OR INSTITUTION

NAME, TITLE, AND PHONE NUMBER OF PRESIDENT, PRINCIPAL OFFICER, DIRECTOR, ETC.

IF "APPLICANT" IS A CORPORATION, INDICATE STATE IN WHICH INCORPORATED

6. LOCATION WHERE PROPOSED ACTIVITY IS TO BE CONDUCTED

7. DO YOU HOLD ANY CURRENTLY VALID FEDERAL FISH AND WILDLIFE LICENSE OR PERMIT? ☐ YES ☐ NO
*(If yes, list license or permit numbers)*

8. IF REQUIRED BY ANY STATE OR FOREIGN GOVERNMENT, DO YOU HAVE THEIR APPROVAL TO CONDUCT THE ACTIVITY YOU PROPOSE? ☐ YES ☐ NO
*(If yes, list jurisdictions and type of documents)*

9. CERTIFIED CHECK OR MONEY ORDER *(if applicable)* PAYABLE TO THE U.S. FISH AND WILDLIFE SERVICE ENCLOSED IN AMOUNT OF

$ 100.00

10. DESIRED EFFECTIVE DATE

11. DURATION NEEDED

12. ATTACHMENTS. THE SPECIFIC INFORMATION REQUIRED FOR THE TYPE OF LICENSE/PERMIT REQUESTED *(See 50 CFR 13.12(b))* MUST BE ATTACHED. IT CONSTITUTES AN INTEGRAL PART OF THIS APPLICATION. LIST SECTIONS OF 50 CFR UNDER WHICH ATTACHMENTS ARE PROVIDED.

Attached is the information required by the Act & 50 CFR 18.31.

**CERTIFICATION**

I HEREBY CERTIFY THAT I HAVE READ AND AM FAMILIAR WITH THE REGULATIONS CONTAINED IN TITLE 50, PART 13, OF THE CODE OF FEDERAL REGULATIONS AND THE OTHER APPLICABLE PARTS IN SUBCHAPTER B OF CHAPTER I OF TITLE 50, AND I FURTHER CERTIFY THAT THE INFORMATION SUBMITTED IN THIS APPLICATION FOR A LICENSE/PERMIT IS COMPLETE AND ACCURATE TO THE BEST OF MY KNOWLEDGE AND BELIEF. I UNDERSTAND THAT ANY FALSE STATEMENT HEREIN MAY SUBJECT ME TO THE CRIMINAL PENALTIES OF 18 U.S.C. 1001.

| SIGNATURE *(In ink)* * | DATE |
|---|---|

3-200 (6/74)

* The applicant listed in 3 above, or principal officer listed in 5 above if applicant is a business, must sign the application.

MARINE MAMMAL APPLICATION CONTINUATION SHEET

Please respond to the questions below. Details may be given on attached sheets. If a particular section does not apply to your application, enter N/A (not applicable).

Synopsis of request: ____ New permit Species:____________

____ Permit renewal* ____________

____ Amendment of PRT-________*

Please provide a brief description of your permit or amendment request.

______________________________________________

______________________________________________

______________________________________________

*If you are requesting renewal or amendment of an existing permit between reporting dates, please include an update of any activity that has occurred under the permit since the last report.

* * * * * * * *

I. Type of activity requested

A. Take ____ B. Import ____

II. Type of permit requested

A. Scientific Research____ B. Public Display____

C. Enhancement of Survival or Recovery ____

III. Objective for Taking: ______________________________

______________________________________________

IV. Animals, parts, or products thereof requested. (If more space is needed use Table 1.)

A. Species: 1. Scientific name______________________

2. Common name______________________

B. Number_____ C. Size_____ D. Sex_____ E. Age_____

F. Reproductive Condition______________________

G. Description of Product______________________

V. Location and dates of taking as specifically as possible for each animal described in item IV above.______________________________

______________________________________________

VI. Status of affected population(s)

A. Population numbers______________________________

B. Legal status

1. Special designation (endangered, threatened, depleted)_____

______________________________________________

2. Need for taking animal with the designation indicated above

______________________________________________

3. Is requested taking consistent with restrictions placed upon the taking of animals with this designation?__________

______________________________________________

4. Is the species protected under the Convention on International Trade in Endangered Species (CITES)? ______

VII. Source of marine mammals: What efforts have been made to utilize captive animals (e.g., captive held, captive born or beached/stranded), or parts thereof, in lieu of taking animals from the wild? ______________________________

______________________________________________

VIII. Type of Take: Number of animals to be taken by age, sex, reproductive condition, etc., the specific activities (capture, tag, radio tag, kill etc.) to which each animal will be subjected, and the number of times that each animal will be taken. (If necessary use Table 1.)

______________________________________________
______________________________________________
______________________________________________
______________________________________________

IX. Importation

A. Exporting country: ______________________________

B. Country where animal was taken: ____________________

C. Was animal taken in a lawful manner? ____________

D. If the wildlife was born in captivity, provide a statement of such from the exporter.

E. Was the animal pregnant or nursing at the time of taking? ____________

F. What was the age of the animal at the time of taking? ________

G. Was the animal taken in a humane manner? ____________

X. Method of Take

A. Capture:

1. Specify the collector of record if applicable____________

2. If a collector of record will not collect the animals, how will animals be captured?

a. Describe the method of capture and gear: ________

b. Provide names and qualifications of personnel: ____________

c. Holding time required prior to transport or release___

B. Drugs

1. Purpose____________

2. Method of application and equipment____________

3. Kind and combinations of drugs and dosage rates (ml./kg.) ____________

4. Experience or other evidence that drugs will work without significant adverse impacts____________

5. Provisions to minimize the chance that drugged animals will not escape prior to immobilization________________

6. Provisions to insure animal is fully recovered prior to release________________

7. Holding time required prior to transport or release________

C. Marking

1. Tagging

   a. Description of tag including weight and size________

   b. Number and kinds of tags per animal________

   c. Number of animals to be tagged. (If necessary use Table 1.) ________

   d. Method and location of attachment________

   e. Duration of attachment________

   f. Method of release, if any________

2. Other types of marking (freeze, laser, tatoo, notch, etc.)

   a. Method________

   b. Type________

   c. Location on animal________

   d. Number of animals to be tagged________

3. Electronic devices

   a. Description of package________

   b. Number of animals to be tagged________

   c. Method and location of attachment________

d. Duration of attachment____________________

e. Method of release, if any____________________

4. Will recapture be necessary? If so, when, to do what, and how many times?____________________
____________________

5. Have the tagging or marking agents been used previously on the subject species?____________________

a. If so, what have been its effects on the animals?____
____________________

b. If not,

1) How will the animals be monitored in order to assess the impact of the tagging and/or marking activities? (Include information on the frequency of monitoring and the number of individuals that will be responsible for conducting the monitoring.)
____________________
____________________
____________________

2) What actions will the applicant take in the event that the tagging and/or marking activities have a significant adverse impact on the animal?_____
____________________
____________________

D. Harassment

1. Intentional

a. Activities causing harassment____________________
____________________
____________________

2. Unintentional

a. Activities that may cause unintentional harassment in the course of conducting the principal activities
____________________
____________________

b. Number of animals that may be harassed ___________
____________________

c. What precautions will be taken to minimize the likelihood that harassment will occur? ____________

d. What will you do if harassment occurs? ____________

E. Biological Sampling

1. Specimens to be taken ____________

2. Sampling methods ____________

3. Number of animals to be sampled ____________

4. Number of times each animal will be sampled ____________

5. Purpose for each type of sampling ____________

XI. Scientific Research

A. Please attach a copy of the formal research proposal or contract or else a detailed description of the proposed project, the objectives, anticipated results, and a statement of how the proposed project will enhance or benefit the wild population.

B. Will animals be sacrificed? If so, how and why? ____________

C. What is the proposed disposition of specimen materials or animals after completion of research?

____________

XII. Public Display

A. Describe the manner, location and times of display: ____________

B. Is the display open to the general public without limitations or restrictions (other than by the charging of an admission fee)? ____________

C. Is the display for profit? ____________________

D. Describe any pertinent educational or conservation programs provided: ____________________
____________________

XIII. Transportation

A. Modes of transportation ____________________

B. Dimensions and construction of container or cage ____________________
____________________

C. Qualifications of person accompanying animal
____________________

D. Duration of transit(s) ____________________

E. Attach certification by a licensed veterinarian that the transportation plans are adequate.

XIV. Maintenance

A. Dimensions of pools and haul-out areas ____________________
____________________

B. How many specimens of the requested species are currently maintained in the facility (include age, sex and source)? ____________________
____________________

C. Is there room for additional animals without exceeding USDA/APHIS standards? ________ If not, how do you intend to meet APHIS standards? ____________________
____________________

D. Has the facility been approved by APHIS? ____________________

1. Date of last inspection ____________________

2. Is an inspection needed ____________________

3. License or Registration Number ____________________

F. If the facility is not located in the United States, provide certification from a licensed veterinarian that the facilities intended to house the animals have been tested and are operating properly.

G. List any other marine mammals (species and quantity of each) maintained at the facility: ____________________
____________________
____________________
____________________

H. Describe the mortalities and provide necropsy reports for all marine mammal deaths which occurred to animals held under your care or in your facility during the past three years (five years for endangered or threatened species) giving for each loss the date, location, cause and steps taken to prevent or decrease similar mortalities. ______________________________
______________________________
______________________________

XV. Have any of the requirements for information been waived? If so,

A. What information requirements?______________________________
______________________________

B. What is the basis for these waivers?______________________________
______________________________

XVI. If applicant is a foreign entity, provide appropriate assurances for compliance with the MMPA, applicable regulations (including APHIS standards), and permit conditions and terms.

XVII. Have you submitted reports under previous permits? If so, please provide the permit number. ______________________________

(rev.12.89)

Table 1.

| Checklist Item No. | Species | Sex | Size, Age, Reproductive Condition | Number | No. of times each animal taken | Specific activities | Location of take | Population | Special legal status |
|---|---|---|---|---|---|---|---|---|---|
| | | | | | | | | | |
| | | | | | | | | | |
| | | | | | | | | | |
| | | | | | | | | | |
| | | | | | | | | | |
| | | | | | | | | | |
| | | | | | | | | | |
| | | | | | | | | | |
| | | | | | | | | | |
| | | | | | | | | | |

SEND APPLICATION TO: U.S. Fish and Wildlife Service
Office of Management Authority
4401 N. Fairfax Drive, Room 432 (703/358-2104)
Arlington, VA 22203

**INCIDENTAL TAKE**

OMB NO. 42-R1670

**DEPARTMENT OF THE INTERIOR**
**U.S. FISH AND WILDLIFE SERVICE**

**FEDERAL FISH AND WILDLIFE LICENSE/PERMIT APPLICATION**

1. APPLICATION FOR *(Indicate only one)*

[XX] IMPORT OR EXPORT LICENSE ☐ PERMIT

2. BRIEF DESCRIPTION OF ACTIVITY FOR WHICH REQUESTED LICENSE OR PERMIT IS NEEDED.

INCIDENTAL TAKE OF ENDANGERED OR THREATENED SPECIES

3. APPLICANT. *(Name, complete address and phone number of individual, business, agency, or institution for which permit is requested)*

4. IF "APPLICANT" IS AN INDIVIDUAL, COMPLETE THE FOLLOWING

☐ MR. ☐ MRS. ☐ MISS ☐ MS. | HEIGHT | WEIGHT

DATE OF BIRTH | COLOR HAIR | COLOR EYES

PHONE NUMBER WHERE EMPLOYED | SOCIAL SECURITY NUMBER

OCCUPATION

ANY BUSINESS, AGENCY, OR INSTITUTIONAL AFFILIATION HAVING TO DO WITH THE WILDLIFE TO BE COVERED BY THIS LICENSE/PERMIT

5. IF "APPLICANT" IS A BUSINESS, CORPORATION, PUBLIC AGENCY, OR INSTITUTION, COMPLETE THE FOLLOWING

EXPLAIN TYPE OR KIND OF BUSINESS, AGENCY, OR INSTITUTION

NAME, TITLE, AND PHONE NUMBER OF PRESIDENT, PRINCIPAL OFFICER, DIRECTOR, ETC.

IF "APPLICANT" IS A CORPORATION, INDICATE STATE IN WHICH INCORPORATED

6. LOCATION WHERE PROPOSED ACTIVITY IS TO BE CONDUCTED

7. DO YOU HOLD ANY CURRENTLY VALID FEDERAL FISH AND WILDLIFE LICENSE OR PERMIT? ☐ YES ☐ NO
*(If yes, list license or permit numbers)*

8. IF REQUIRED BY ANY STATE OR FOREIGN GOVERNMENT, DO YOU HAVE THEIR APPROVAL TO CONDUCT THE ACTIVITY YOU PROPOSE? ☐ YES ☐ NO
*(If yes, list jurisdictions and type of documents)*

9. ~~CERTIFIED~~ CHECK OR MONEY ORDER *(if applicable)* PAYABLE TO THE U.S. FISH AND WILDLIFE SERVICE ENCLOSED IN AMOUNT OF

$ $25.00

10. DESIRED EFFECTIVE DATE

11. DURATION NEEDED

12. ATTACHMENTS. THE SPECIFIC INFORMATION REQUIRED FOR THE TYPE OF LICENSE/PERMIT REQUESTED *(See 50 CFR 13.12(b))* MUST BE ATTACHED. IT CONSTITUTES AN INTEGRAL PART OF THIS APPLICATION. LIST SECTIONS OF 50 CFR UNDER WHICH ATTACHMENTS ARE PROVIDED.

SEE 50 CFR 17.22(b) & 17.32(b); Also 50 CFR 13

**CERTIFICATION**

I HEREBY CERTIFY THAT I HAVE READ AND AM FAMILIAR WITH THE REGULATIONS CONTAINED IN TITLE 50, PART 13, OF THE CODE OF FEDERAL REGULATIONS AND THE OTHER APPLICABLE PARTS IN SUBCHAPTER B OF CHAPTER I OF TITLE 50, AND I FURTHER CERTIFY THAT THE INFORMATION SUBMITTED IN THIS APPLICATION FOR A LICENSE/PERMIT IS COMPLETE AND ACCURATE TO THE BEST OF MY KNOWLEDGE AND BELIEF. I UNDERSTAND THAT ANY FALSE STATEMENT HEREIN MAY SUBJECT ME TO THE CRIMINAL PENALTIES OF 18 U.S.C. 1001.

SIGNATURE *(In ink)* | DATE

3-200
(6/74)

*****If applicant is a business, the principal officer listed in block 5 should sign the application.

Application for Federal Fish and Wildlife License/Permit

**NOTICE**

In accordance with the Privacy Act of 1974 (PL 93-579), please be advised that:

1. The gathering of information on fish and wildlife is authorized by: (a) Bald Eagle Protection Act (16 U.S.C. 663a), (b) Endangered Species Act of 1973 (16 U.S.C. 1539), (c) Migratory Bird Treaty Act (16 U.S.C. 703-711), (d) Marine Mammal Protection Act of 1972 (16 U.S.C. 1371-1383), (e) Lacey Act (18 U.S.C. 42 & 44), (f) Tariff Classification Act of 1962 (19 U.S.C. 1202), and (g) Title 50, Part 13, of the Code of Federal Regulations.

2. The disclosure of the requested information is required in order to process applications for licenses or permits authorized under the above acts. With the exception of your social security number, failure to disclose all of the requested information may be sufficient cause for the U.S. Fish and Wildlife Service to deny you a permit.

3. Applications for licenses or permits authorized under the Endangered Species Act of 1973 (16 U.S.C. 1539) and the Marine Mammal Protection Act of 1972 (16 U.S.C. 1371-1383) will be published in the Federal Register as required by the two acts.

4. In the event there is indicated a violation of a statute, regulation, rule, order, or license, whether civil, criminal, or regulatory in nature, the requested information may be transferred to the appropriate Federal, State, local, or foreign agency charged with investigating or prosecuting such violations.

5. In the event of litigation involving the records or the subject matter of the records, the requested information may be transferred to the U.S. Department of Justice.

No general permit may be issued until an application has been approved (7 CFR 355) *See reverse for additional information.*

FORM APPROVED
OMB NO 0579-0076

U.S. DEPARTMENT OF AGRICULTURE
ANIMAL AND PLANT HEALTH INSPECTION SERVICE
PLANT PROTECTION AND QUARANTINE

**APPLICATION FOR GENERAL PERMIT TO ENGAGE IN THE BUSINESS OF IMPORTING, EXPORTING, OR REEXPORTING TERRESTRIAL PLANTS**

MAIL COMPLETED APPLICATION WITH CHECK TO:
USDA-APHIS-PPQ-Permit Unit
Federal Building
Hyattsville, MD 20782

INSTRUCTIONS One copy of this application must be accompanied by a check or money order for $70 00 made payable to Plant Protection and Quarantine This fee shall not be refunded if the application is denied or abandoned If a General Permit is issued based on this application, it shall be valid for two years from date of issue

1. NAME AND ADDRESS OF APPLICANT *(include ZIP Code)*

TELEPHONE NUMBER: AC (

2. APPLICATION IS IN THE NAME OF *("X" one)*

☐ AN INDIVIDUAL

☐ A BUSINESS

3. DESCRIBE THE NATURE OF YOUR ACTIVITIES RELATING TO IMPORTING, EXPORTING, OR REEXPORTING PLANTS LISTED IN 50 CFR 17.12 AND 23.23 *(If more space is needed, continue on reverse side)*

4A. NAME OF BUSINESS AFFILIATION *(if any)* HAVING TO DO WITH IMPORTING, EXPORTING OR REEXPORTING PLANTS LISTED IN 50 CFR 17.12 AND 23.23 *(If none, so state)*

B. FORM OF BUSINESS *("X" one if applying as a business)*

☐ CORPORATION ☐ FIRM ☐ PARTNERSHIP ☐ OTHER *(specify)*

C. LIST THE NAME AND ADDDRESS OF EACH PARTNER, OFFICER, DIRECTOR, HOLDER, AND OWNER OF 10% OR MORE OF VOTING STOCK, AND EMPLOYEE IN A MANAGERIAL OR EXECUTIVE CAPACITY *(if more space is needed continue on reverse side)*

5. ADDRESS(ES) WHERE PLANTS LISTED IN 50 CFR 17.12 AND 23.23 WOULD BE GROWN OR STORED AND ANY OTHER LOCATION WHERE ACTIVITIES RELATED TO SUCH PLANTS WOULD BE CONDUCTED

6. STREET ADDRESSES WHERE BOOKS OR RECORDS CONCERNING THE IMPORTATION, EXPORTATION OR REEXPORTING OF PLANTS LISTED IN 50 CFR 17.12 AND 23.23 WILL BE KEPT

7. NAME AND ADDRESS OF THE PERSON AUTHORIZED TO MAKE RECORDS OR PLANT INVENTORIES AVAILABLE FOR EXAMINATION BY INSPECTORS

TELEPHONE NUMBER: AC ( )

**I hereby certify that the information is this application is complete and accurate to the best of my knowledge and belief.**
**False Statement:** Falsification of any item on this application may result in a fine of not more than $10,000 or imprisonment for not more than 5 years or both (18 USC 1001)

| 8. SIGNATURE *(partner or officer if a business)* | 9. DATE |
|---|---|
| | |

PPQ FORM 621
(APR 84)

**Public reporting burden for this collection of information is estimated to average 1 hour per response, including the time for reviewing instructions, searching existing data sources, gathering and maintaining the data needed, and completing and reviewing the collection of information. Send comments regarding this burden estimate or any other aspect of this collection of information, including suggestions for reducing this burden, to Department of Agriculture, Clearance Office, OIRM, Room 404-W, Washington, D.C. 20250; and to the Office of Management and Budget, Paperwork Reduction Project (OMB #0579-0076), Washington, D.C. 20503.**

PPQ FORM 621 Reverse

...blic reporting burden for this collection of information is estimated to average .083 hours per response, including the ...me for reviewing instructions, searching existing data sources, gathering and maintaining the data needed, and ...mpleting and reviewing the collection of information. Send comments regarding this burden estimate or any other ...spect of this collection of information including suggestions for reducing this burden, to Department of Agriculture, ...earance Officer OIRM, Room 404-W, Washington, D.C. 20250; and to the Office of Information and Regulatory Affairs, ...fice of Management and Budget, Washington, D.C. 20503

FORM APPROVED - OMB NO. 0579-00[illegible]

This permit is required by law (9 CFR 92). Failure to certify Health Certificate on reverse could necessitate rejection at the Port of Entry.

U.S. DEPARTMENT OF AGRICULTURE
ANIMAL AND PLANT HEALTH INSPECTION SERVICE
VETERINARY SERVICES

## APPLICATION/PERMIT FOR RATITE(S) OR RATITE HATCHING EGGS AND SPACE RESERVATION REQUEST

| | |
|---|---|
| NUMBER & TYPE OF RATITE(S) OR RATITE HATCHING EGGS | 2. LOCATION OF THE PREMISES WHERE THE FLOCK OF ORIGIN IS KEPT *(Complete Mailing Address)* |
| IMPORTER'S NAME AND ADDRESS *(Complete Mailing Address)*<br><br>Telephone No. | 4. BROKER'S NAME AND ADDRESS *(Complete Mailing Address)*<br><br>Telephone No. |

| | | |
|---|---|---|
| NAME AND ADDRESS OF SHIPPER IN COUNTRY OF ORIGIN | 6. PROPOSED ARRIVAL DATE | 7. ARRIVAL TIME |
| DATE OF THIS REQUEST | 9. PORT OF EMBARKATION | 10. COUNTRY OF ORIGIN |
| FARM OF ORIGIN *(Owner's Name & Telephone No.)* | 12. SIZE OF FLOCK OF ORIGIN | 13. TOTAL DEPOSIT ENCLOSED FOR LIVE RATITE(S) ONLY *(Make checks payable to USDA, APHIS, VS)* |

4. SUBMIT FORM TO

New York Animal Import Center
USDA, APHIS, Veterinary Services
200 Drury Lane
Rock Tavern, NY 12575
(914) 564-2950

OR

Hawaii Animal Import Center
USDA, APHIS, Veterinary Services
P.O. Box 50001
Honolulu, HI 96850
(808) 541-2603

OR

Port Veterinary in Charge of the Quarantine Facility

5. REMARKS

**AUTHORIZATION OF SITE INSPECTION**

*From the date of application through the date of export Animal and Plant Health Inspection Service representatives shall be granted access to the premises where the flock of origin is kept.*

| | |
|---|---|
| 6. SIGNATURE OF IMPORTER | 17. DATE SIGNED |

**FOR IMPORTATION OF RATITE(S) ONLY, NOT RATITE HATCHING EGGS**

**I/We understand and accept that the reservation fee is non-refundable if the ratite(s) do not arrive as per this confirmed reservation unless the Veterinarian in Charge at the Import Center is notified of cancellation, in writing, at least 15 working days prior to the scheduled time of arrival. All cancellations will have a $40.00 fee deducted from the refund.**

| | |
|---|---|
| 18. REQUESTER'S SIGNATURE | 19. REQUESTER'S ADDRESS *(Complete Mailing Address)* |
| 20. TELEPHONE NO. | |

**NOTE: Health Certificate on reverse must be executed. Failure to do so could necessitate rejection at the Port of Entry.**

**FOR USDA USE ONLY**

| | | |
|---|---|---|
| 21. DATE RESERVATION RECEIVED | 22. AMOUNT OF DEPOSIT RECEIVED | 23. RESERVATION NUMBER |
| 24. NUMBER & TYPE OF RATITE(S) RESERVED | 25. CONFIRMED ARRIVAL DATE | 26. DATE OF SITE INSPECTION |

| | |
|---|---|
| 27. NAME OF THE USDA REPRESENTATIVE APPROVING THE SITE INSPECTION | 28. SIGNATURE OF AUTHORIZING OFFICIAL |

VS FORM 17-128
(AUG 91)

## RESPONSIBILITIES

**THE U.S. IMPORTER** must forward the "Original" and "Carrier's Copy" to the shipper in the country of origin. The U.S. importer shall make arrangements at the U.S. port of entry for Customs broker's service if desired, and shall arrange for necessary quarantine space and transportation of the shipment to and from quarantine, when required. Retain "Importer's Copy."

**THE SHIPPER** in the country of origin must make certain that the Health Certificate below is completed by a veterinarian authorized for this purpose by the National Governement of the country from which the ratite(s) or ratite hatching eggs are shipped and the certificate endorsed (signed) by a salaried veterinary officer of the same government. Deliver the "Original" and "Carrier's Copy" to the initial transporting carrier.

**THE VETERINARY OFFICER** of the National Government in charge of the animal disease programs in the country of origin may have been forwarded a copy of this permit in order that they can determine whether the necessary inspections and certification on the "Original" can be completed.

**THE INITIAL CARRIER** must make certain that the Health Certificate below has been issued and endorsed (signed) by a salaried veterinary officer of the National Government of the country from which the ratite(s) or ratite hatching eggs are shipped; make sure that the Original Health Certificate accompanies the ratite(s) or ratite hatching eggs to the U.S. port of entry; and make certain that the "Carrier's Copy" is available for the final carrier who will transport the shipment to the U.S. port of entry.

**VS VETERINARIAN AT PORT OF ENTRY** will hold the "Customs Copy" until the shipment is received, then forward it to the U.S. Collector of Customs. The signed "Original" Health Certificate will be retained by the VS veterinarian at the U.S. port of entry.

## HEALTH CERTIFICATE

*(Must be completeded by a salaried veterinarian of the National Government of the country from which shipped.)*

### RATITE(S)

I certify that I personally inspected the ratite(s) and the flock of origin* immediately prior to exportation described in Item 1 and that no evidence of Newcastle disease, ornithosis, or other communicable diseases of poultry were found, nor insofar as has been possible to determine, were the ratites exposed to any such disease during the 90 days immediately prior to the exportation date. The ratites were placed in unused shipping containers free of hay, straw, grasses, wood chips, sawdust, or other materials likely to harbor ectoparasites at the premises of origin and insofar as is know, the ratite(s) to be shipped have not been vaccinated with Newcastle disease vaccine. Newcastle disease has not occurred on the premises of origin nor on adjacent premises during the 90-day period immediately prior to exportation and that these premises are not located in an area under quarantine for poultry diseases during the preceding 90 days.

I further certify that the ratite(s) in the shipment were produced by and maintained in a pen-raised flock* and were treated with a pesticide of a type and concentration sufficient to kill ectoparasites at least 3 days but not more than 14 days before shipment to the United States. The pesticide was applied under my supervision, to all body surfaces and after being treated they did not have physical contact with or share a pen or bedding materials with any ratite not in the same shipment to the United States.

*When ratites intended for importation are zoological birds, only the ratites to be imported must be inspected, and the birds do not have to be from a pen-raised flock.

| NAME OF PESTICIDE | CONCENTRATION | DATE OF TREATMENT |
|---|---|---|
| | | |

### RATITE HATCHING EGGS

I certify that I personnally inspected the flock of origin immediately prior to exportation described in item 1 and that no evidence of Newcastle disease, ornithosis, or other communicable diseases of poultry were found, nor insofar as has been possible to determine, were the ratites exposed to any such disease during the 90 days immediately prior to the exportation date. The ratite hatching eggs were placed in unused shipping containers at the premises from which the eggs were to be exported. The shipping containers were free of hay, straw, grasses, wood chips, sawdust, or other materials likely to harbor ectoparasites. Newcastle disease has not occurred on the premises of origin nor on adjacent premises during the 90-day period immediately prior to exportation and that these premises are not located in an area under quarantine for poultry disease during the preceding 90 days.

I further certify that the ratite hatching eggs were produced by a pen-raised flock.

*This hereby certifies compliance with the application certification above for the import shown in Item 1 on the face of this form.*

| TYPE OR PRINT NAME AND ADDRESS OF ISSUING VETERINARIAN | TITLE *(Show in detail to reflect official connection with National Government of the country from which shipped.)* |
|---|---|
| | |

| SIGNATURE | DATE |
|---|---|
| | |

VS FORM 17-128 (Reverse)

# APPENDIX C
# ENDANGERED SPECIES ACT OF 1973

As Amended through the

100th Congress

Prepared by

U.S. Fish and Wildlife Service

U.S. Department of the Interior

Washington, D.C. 20240

1988

## TABLE OF CONTENTS

# ENDANGERED SPECIES ACT OF 1973*

## FINDINGS, PURPOSES, AND POLICY

SEC. 2. (a) FINDINGS.—The Congress finds and declares that—

(1) various species of fish, wildlife, and plants in the United States have been rendered extinct as a consequence of economic growth and development untempered by adequate concern and conservation;

(2) other species of fish, wildlife, and plants have been so depleted in numbers that they are in danger of or threatened with extinction;

(3) these species of fish, wildlife, and plants are of esthetic, ecological, educational, historical, recreational, and scientific value to the Nation and its people;

(4) the United States has pledged itself as a sovereign state in the international community to conserve to the extent practicable the various species of fish or wildlife and plants facing extinction, pursuant to—

(A) migratory bird treaties with Canada and Mexico;

(B) the Migratory and Endangered Bird Treaty with Japan;

(C) the Convention on Nature Protection and Wildlife Preservation in the Western Hemisphere;

(D) the International Convention for the Northwest Atlantic Fisheries;

(E) the International Convention for the High Seas Fisheries of the North Pacific Ocean;

(F) the Convention on International Trade in Endangered Species of Wild Fauna and Flora; and

(G) other international agreements; and

(5) encouraging the States and other interested parties, through Federal financial assistance and a system of incentives, to develop and maintain conservation programs which meet national and international standards is a key to meeting the Nation's international commitments and to better safeguarding, for the benefit of all citizens, the Nation's heritage in fish, wildlife, and plants.

(b) PURPOSES.—The purposes of this Act are to provide a means whereby the ecosystems upon which endangered species and threatened species depend may be conserved, to provide a program for the conservation of such endangered species and threatened species, and to take such steps as may be appropriate to achieve

*As amended by P.L. 94-325, June 30, 1976; P.L. 94-359, July 12, 1976; P.L. 95-212, December 19, 1977; P.L. 95-632, November 10, 1978; P.L. 96-159, December 28, 1979; P.L. 97-304, October 13, 1982; P.L. 98-327, June 25, 1984; and P.L. 100-478, October 7, 1988.

the purposes of the treaties and conventions set forth in subsection (a) of this section.

(c) POLICY.—(1) It is further declared to be the policy of Congress that all Federal departments and agencies shall seek to conserve endangered species and threatened species and shall utilize their authorities in furtherance of the purposes of this Act.

(2) It is further declared to be the policy of Congress that Federal agencies shall cooperate with State and local agencies to resolve water resource issues in concert with conservation of endangered species.

DEFINITIONS

SEC. 3. For the purposes of this Act—

(1) The term "alternative courses of action" means all alternatives and thus is not limited to original project objectives and agency jurisdiction.

(2) The term "commercial activity" means all activities of industry and trade, including, but not limited to, the buying or selling of commodities and activities conducted for the purpose of facilitating such buying and selling: *Provided, however,* That it does not include exhibitions of commodities by museums or similar cultural or historical organizations.

(3) The terms "conserve," "conserving," and "conservation" mean to use and the use of all methods and procedures which are necessary to bring any endangered species or threatened species to the point at which the measures provided pursuant to this Act are no longer necessary. Such methods and procedures include, but are not limited to, all activities associated with scientific resources management such as research, census, law enforcement, habitat acquisition and maintenance, propagation, live trapping, and transplantation, and, in the extraordinary case where population pressures within a given ecosystem cannot be otherwise relieved, may include regulated taking.

(4) The term "Convention" means the Convention on International Trade in Endangered Species of Wild Fauna and Flora, signed on March 3, 1973, and the appendices thereto.

(5)(A) The term "critical habitat" for a threatened or endangered species means—

(i) the specific areas within the geographical area occupied by the species, at the time it is listed in accordance with the provisions of section 4 of this Act, on which are found those physical or biological features (I) essential to the conservation of the species and (II) which may require special management considerations or protection; and

(ii) specific areas outside the geographical area occupied by the species at the time it is listed in accordance with the provisions of section 4 of this Act, upon a determination by the Secretary that such areas are essential for the conservation of the species.

(B) Critical habitat may be established for those species now listed as threatened or endangered species for which no critical habitat has heretofore been established as set forth in subparagraph (A) of this paragraph.

(C) Except in those circumstances determined by the Secretary, critical habitat shall not include the entire geographical area which can be occupied by the threatened or endangered species.

(6) The term "endangered species" means any species which is in danger of extinction throughout all or a significant portion of its range other than a species of the Class Insecta determined by the Secretary to constitute a pest whose protection under the provisions of this Act would present an overwhelming and overriding risk to man.

(7) The term "Federal agency" means any department, agency, or instrumentality of the United States.

(8) The term "fish or wildlife" means any member of the animal kingdom, including without limitation any mammal, fish, bird (including any migratory, nonmigratory, or endangered bird for which protection is also afforded by treaty or other international agreement), amphibian, reptile, mollusk, crustacean, arthropod or other invertebrate, and includes any part, product, egg, or offspring thereof, or the dead body or parts thereof.

(9) The term "foreign commerce" includes, among other things, any transaction—

(A) between persons within one foreign country;

(B) between persons in two or more foreign countries;

(C) between a person within the United States and a person in a foreign country; or

(D) between persons within the United States, where the fish and wildlife in question are moving in any country or countries outside the United States.

(10) The term "import" means to land on, bring into, or introduce into, or attempt to land on, bring into, or introduce into, any place subject to the jurisdiction of the United States, whether or not such landing, bringing, or introduction constitutes an importation within the meaning of the customs laws of the United States.

(11) The term "permit or license applicant" means, when used with respect to an action of a Federal agency for which exemption is sought under section 7, any person whose application to such agency for a permit or license has been denied primarily because of the application of section 7(a) to such agency action.

(12) "The term person means an individual, corporation, partnership, trust, association, or any other private entity; or any officer, employee, agent, department, or instrumentality of the Federal Government, of any State, municipality, or political subdivision of a State, or of any foreign government; any State, muncipality, or political subdivision of a State; or any other entity subject to the jurisdiction of the United States."

(13) The term "plant" means any member of the plant kingdom, including seeds, roots and other parts thereof.

(14) The term "Secretary" means, except as otherwise herein provided, the Secretary of the Interior or the Secretary of Commerce as program responsibilities are vested pursuant to the provisions of Reorganization Plan Numbered 4 of 1970; except that with respect to the enforcement of the provisions of this Act and the Convention which pertain to the importation or exportation of terrestrial plants, the term also means the Secretary of Agriculture.

(15) The term "species" includes any subspecies of fish or wildlife or plants, and any distinct population segment of any species or vertebrate fish or wildlife which interbreeds when mature.

(16) The term "State" means any of the several States, the District of Columbia, the Commonwealth of Puerto Rico, American Samoa, the Virgin Islands, Guam, and the Trust Territory of the Pacific Islands.

(17) The term "State agency" means any State agency, department, board, commission, or other governmental entity which is responsible for the management and conservation of fish, plant, or wildlife resources within a State.

(18) The term "take" means to harass, harm, pursue, hunt, shoot, wound, kill, trap, capture, or collect, or to attempt to engage in any such conduct.

(19) The term "threatened species" means any species which is likely to become an endangered species within the foreseeable future throughout all or a significant portion of its range.

(20) The term "United States," when used in a geographical context, includes all States.

DETERMINATION OF ENDANGERED SPECIES AND THREATENED SPECIES

SEC. 4. (a) GENERAL.—(1) The Secretary shall by regulation promulgated in accordance with subsection (b) determine whether any species is an endangered species or a threatened species because of any of the following factors:

(A) the present or threatened destruction; modification, or curtailment of its habitat or range;

(B) overutilization for commercial, recreational, scientific, or educational purposes;

(C) disease or predation;

(D) the inadequacy of existing regulatory mechanisms;

(E) other natural or manmade factors affecting its continued existence.

(2) With respect to any species over which program responsibilities have been vested in the Secretary of Commerce pursuant to Reorganization Plan Numbered 4 of 1970—

(A) in any case in which the Secretary of Commerce determines that such species should—

(i) be listed as an endangered species or a threatened species, or

(ii) be changed in status from a threatened species to an endangered species, he shall so inform the Secretary of the Interior, who shall list such species in accordance with this section;

(B) in any case in which the Secretary of Commerce determines that such species should—

(i) be removed from any list published pursuant to subsection (c) of this section, or

(ii) be changed in status from an endangered species to a threatened species, he shall recommend such action to the Secretary of the Interior, and the Secretary of the Interior, if he concurs in the recommendation, shall implement such action; and

(C) the Secretary of the Interior may not list or remove from any list any such species, and may not change the status of any such species which are listed, without a prior favorable determination made pursuant to this section by the Secretary of Commerce.

(3) The Secretary, by regulation promulgated in accordance with subsection (b) and to the maximum extent prudent and determinable—

(A) shall, concurrently with making a determination under paragraph (1) that a species is an endangered species or a threatened species, designate any habitat of such species which is then considered to be critical habitat; and

(B) may, from time-to-time thereafter as appropriate, revise such designation.

(b) Basis for Determinations.—(1)(A) The Secretary shall make determinations required by subsection (a)(1) solely on the basis of the best scientific and commercial data available to him after conducting a review of the status of the species and after taking into account those efforts, if any, being made by any State or foreign nation, or any political subdivision of a State or foreign nation, to protect such species, whether by predator control, protection of habitat and food supply, or other conservation practices, within any area under its jurisdiction, or on the high seas.

(B) In carrying out this section, the Secretary shall give consideration to species which have been—

(i) designated as requiring protection from unrestricted commerce by any foreign nation, or pursuant to any international agreement; or

(ii) identified as in danger of extinction, or likely to become so within the foreseeable future, by any State agency or by any agency of a foreign nation that is responsible for the conservation of fish or wildlife or plants.

(2) The Secretary shall designate critical habitat, and make revisions thereto, under subsection (a)(3) on the basis of the best scientific data available and after taking into consideration the economic impact, and any other relevant impact, of specifying any particular area as critical habitat. The Secretary may exclude any area from critical habitat if he determines that the benefits of such exclusion outweigh the benefits of specifying such area as part of the critical habitat, unless he determines, based on the best scientific and commercial data available, that the failure to designate such area as critical habitat will result in the extinction of the species concerned.

(3)(A) To the maximum extent practicable, within 90 days after receiving the petition of an interested person under section 553(e) of title 5, United States Code, to add a species to, or to remove a species from, either of the lists published under subsection (c), the Secretary shall make a finding as to whether the petition presents substantial scientific or commercial information indicating that the petitioned action may be warranted. If such a petition is found to present such information, the Secretary shall promptly commence a review of the status of the species concerned. The Secretary shall promptly publish each finding made under this subparagraph in the Federal Register.

(B) Within 12 months after receiving a petition that is found under subparagraph (A) to present substantial information indicating that the petitioned action may be warranted, the Secretary shall make one of the following findings:

(i) The petitioned action is not warranted, in which case the Secretary shall promptly publish such finding in the Federal Register.

(ii) The petitioned action is warranted in which case the Secretary shall promptly publish in the Federal Register a general notice and the complete text of a proposed regulation to implement such action in accordance with paragraph (5).

(iii) The petitioned action is warranted but that—

(I) the immediate proposal and timely promulgation of a final regulation implementing the petitioned action in accordance with paragraphs (5) and (6) is precluded by pending proposals to determine whether any species is an endangered species or a threatened species, and

(II) expeditious progress is being made to add qualified species to either of the lists published under subsection (c) and to remove from such lists species for which the protections of the Act are no longer necessary.

in which case the Secretary shall promptly publish such finding in the Federal Register, together with a description and evaluaton of the reasons and data on which the finding is based.

(C)(i) A petition with respect to which a finding is made under subparagraph (B)(iii) shall be treated as a petition that is resubmitted to the Secretary under subparagraph (A) on the date of such finding and that presents substantial scientific or commerical information that the petitioned action may be warranted.

(ii) Any negative finding described in subparagraph (A) and any finding described in subparagraph (B) (i) or (iii) shall be subject to judicial review.

(iii) The Secretary shall implement a system to monitor effectively the status of all species with respect to which a finding is made under subparagraph (B)(iii) and shall make prompt use of the authority under paragraph 7 to prevent a significant risk to the well being of any such species.

(D)(i) To the maximum extent practicable, within 90 days after receiving the petition of an interested person under section 553(e) of title 5, United States Code, to revise a critical habitat designation, the Secretary shall make a finding as to whether the petition presents substantial scientific information indicating that the revision may be warranted. The Secretary shall promptly publish such finding in the Federal Register.

(ii) Within 12 months after receiving a petition that is found under clause (i) to present substantial information indicating that the requested revision may be warranted, the Secretary shall determine how he intends to proceed with the requested revision, and shall promptly publish notice of such intention in the Federal Register.

(4) Except as provided in paragraphs (5) and (6) of this subsection, the provisions of section 553 of title 5, United States Code (relating

to rulemaking procedures), shall apply to any regulation promulgated to carry out the purposes of this Act.

(5) With respect to any regulation proposed by the Secretary to implement a determination, designation, or revision referred to in subsection (a) (1) or (3), the Secretary shall—

(A) not less than 90 days before the effective date of the regulation—

(i) publish a general notice and the complete text of the proposed regulation in the Federal Register, and

(ii) give actual notice of the proposed regulation (including the complete text of the regulation) to the State agency in each State in which the species is believed to occur, and to each county or equivalent jurisdiction in which the species is believed to occur, and invite the comment of such agency, and each such jurisdiction, thereon;

(B) insofar as practical, and in cooperation with the Secretary of State, give notice of the proposed regulation to each foreign nation in which the species is believed to occur or whose citizens harvest the species on the high seas, and invite the comment of such nation thereon;

(C) give notice of the proposed regulation to such professional scientific organizations as he deems appropriate;

(D) publish a summary of the proposed regulation in a newspaper of general circulation in each area of the United States in which the species is believed to occur; and

(E) promptly hold one public hearing on the proposed regulation if any person files a request for such a hearing within 45 days after the date of publication of general notice.

(6)(A) Within the one-year period beginning on the date on which general notice is published in accordance with paragraph (5)(A)(i) regarding a proposed regulation, the Secretary shall publish in the Federal Register—

(i) if a determination as to whether a species is an endangered species or a threatened species, or a revision of critical habitat, is involved, either—

(I) a final regulation to implement such determination,

(II) a final regulation to implement such revision or a finding that such revision should not be made,

(III) notice that such one-year period is being extended under subparagraph (B)(i), or

(IV) notice that the proposed regulation is being withdrawn under subparagraph (B)(ii), together with the finding on which such withdrawal is based; or

(ii) subject to subparagraph (C), if a designation of critical habitat is involved, either—

(I) a final regulation to implement such designation, or

(II) notice that such one-year period is being extended under such subparagraph.

(B)(i) If the Secretary finds with respect to a proposed regulation referred to in subparagraph (A)(i) that there is substantial disagreement regarding the sufficiency or accuracy of the available data relevant to the determination or revision concerned the Secretary may extend the one-year period specified in subparagraph (A) for not more than six months for purposes of soliciting additional data.

(ii) If a proposed regulation referred to in subparagraph (a)(i) is not promulgated as a final regulation within such one-year period (or longer period if extension under clause (i) applies) because the Secretary finds that there is not sufficient evidence to justify the action proposed by the regulation the Secretary shall immediately withdraw the regulation. The finding on which a withdrawal is based shall be subject to judicial review. The Secretary may not propose a regulation that has previously been withdrawn under this clause unless he determines that sufficient new information is available to warrant such proposal.

(iii) If the one-year period specified in subparagraph (A) is extended under clause (i) with respect to a proposed regulation, then before the close of such extended period the Secretary shall publish in the Federal Register either a final regulation to implement the determination or revision concerned, a finding that the revision should not be made, or a notice of withdrawal of the regulation under clause (ii), together with the finding on which the withdrawal is based.

(C) A final regulation designating critical habitat of an endangered species or a threatened species shall be published concurrently with the final regulation implementing the determination that such species is endangered or threatened, unless the Secretary deems that—

(i) it is essential to the conservation of such species that the regulation implementing such determination be promptly published; or

(ii) critical habitat of such species is not then determinable, in which case the Secretary, with respect to the proposed regulation to designate such habitat, may extend the one-year period specified in subparagraph (A) by not more than one additional year, but not later than the close of such additional year the Secretary must publish a final regulation, based on such data as may be available at that time, designating, to the maximum extent prudent, such habitat.

(7) Neither paragraph (4), (5), or (6) of this subsection nor section 553 of title 5, United States Code, shall apply to any regulation issued by the Secretary in regard to any emergency posing a significant risk to the well-being of any species of fish and wildlife or plants, but only if—

(A) at the time of publication of the regulation in the Federal Register the Secretary publishes therein detailed reasons why such regulation is necessary; and

(B) in the case such regulation applies to resident species of fish or wildlife, or plants, the Secretary gives actual notice of such regulation to the State agency in each State in which such species is believed to occur.

Such regulation shall, at the discretion of the Secretary, take effect immediately upon the publication of the regulation in the Federal Register. Any regulation promulgated under the authority of this paragraph shall cease to have force and effect at the close of the 240-day period following the date of publication unless, during such 240-day period, the rulemaking procedures which would apply to such regulation without regard to this paragraph are complied with. If at any time after issuing an emergency regulation the Secretary determines, on the basis of the best appropriate data available to him, that substantial evidence does not exist to warrant such regulation, he shall withdraw it.

(8) The publication in the Federal Register of any proposed or final regulation which is necessary or appropriate to carry out the purposes of this Act shall include a summary by the Secretary of the data on which such regulation is based and shall show the relationship of such data to such regulation; and if such regulation designates or revises critical habitat, such summary shall, to the maximum extent practicable, also include a brief description and evaluation of those activities (whether public or private) which, in the opinion of the Secretary, if undertaken may adversely modify such habitat, or may be affected by such designation.

(c) LISTS.—(1) The Secretary of the Interior shall publish in the Federal Register a list of all species determined by him or the Secretary of Commerce to be endangered species and a list of all species determined by him or the Secretary of Commerce to be threatened species. Each list shall refer to the species contained therein by scientific and common name or names, if any, specify with respect to such species over what portion of its range it is endangered or threatened, and specify any critical habitat within such range. The Secretary shall from time to time revise each list published under the authority of this subsection to reflect recent determinations, designations, and revisions made in accordance with subsections (a) and (b).

(2) The Secretary shall—

(A) conduct, at least once every five years, a review of all species included in a list which is published pursuant to paragraph (1) and which is in effect at the time of such review; and

(B) determine on the basis of such review whether any such species should—

(i) be removed from such list;

(ii) be changed in status from an endangered species to a threatened species; or

(iii) be changed in status from a threatened species to an endangered species.

Each determination under subparagraph (B) shall be made in accordance with the provisions of subsection (a) and (b).

(d) PROTECTIVE REGULATIONS.—Whenever any species is listed as a threatened species pursuant to subsection (c) of this section, the Secretary shall issue such regulations as he deems necessary and advisable to provide for the conservation of such species. The Secretary may by regulation prohibit with respect to any threatened species any act prohibited under section 9(a)(1), in the case of fish or wildlife, or section 9(a)(2), in the case of plants, with respect to endangered species; except that with respect to the taking of resident species of fish or wildlife, such regulations shall apply in any State which has entered into a cooperative agreement pursuant to section 6(c) of this Act only to the extent that such regulations have also been adopted by such State.

(e) SIMILARITY OF APPEARANCE CASES.—The Secretary may, by regulation of commerce or taking, and to the extent he deems advisable, treat any species as an endangered species or threatened species even though it is not listed pursuant to section 4 of this Act if he finds that—

(A) such species so closely resembles in appearance, at the point in question, a species which has been listed pursuant to such section that enforcement personnel would have substantial difficulty in attempting to differentiate between the listed and unlisted species;

(B) the effect of this substantial difficulty is an additional threat to an endangered or threatened species; and

(C) such treatment of an unlisted species will substantially facilitate the enforcement and further the policy of this Act.

(f)(1) RECOVERY PLANS.—The Secretary shall develop and implement plans (hereinafter in this subsection referred to as 'recovery plans') for the conservation and survival of endangered species and threatened species listed pursuant to this section, unless he finds that such a plan will not promote the conservation of the species. The Secretary, in development and implementing recovery plans, shall, to the maximum extent practicable—

(A) give priority to those endangered species or threatened species, without regard to taxonomic classification, that are most likely to benefit from such plans, particularly those species that are, or may be, in conflict with construction or other development projects or other forms of economic activity;

(B) incorporate in each plan—

(i) a description of such site-specific management actions as may be necessary to achieve the plan's goal for the conservation and survival of the species;

(ii) objective, measurable criteria which, when met, would result in a determination, in accordance with the provisions of this section, that the species be removed from the list; and

(iii) estimates of the time required and the cost to carry out those measures needed to achieve the plan's goal and to achieve intermediate steps toward that goal.

(2) The Secretary, in developing and implementing recovery plans, may procure the services of appropriate public and private agencies and institutions, and other qualified persons. Recovery teams appointed pursuant to this subsection shall not be subject to the Federal Advisory Committee Act.

(3) The Secretary shall report every two years to the Committee on Environment and Public Works of the Senate and the Committee on Merchant Marine and Fisheries of the House of Representatives on the status of efforts to develop and implement recovery plans for all species listed pursuant to this section and on the status of all species for which such plans have been developed.

(4) The Secretary shall, prior to final approval of a new or revised recovery plan, provide public notice and an opportunity for public review and comment on such plan. The Secretary shall consider all information presented during the public comment period prior to approval of the plan.

(5) Each Federal agency shall, prior to implementation of a new or revised recovery plan, consider all information presented during the public comment period under paragraph (4).

(g) MONITORING.—(1) The Secretary shall implement a system in cooperation with the States to monitor effectively for not less than five years the status of all species which have recovered to the point at which the measures provided pursuant to this Act are no longer necessary and which, in accordance with the provisions of this section, have been removed from either of the lists published under subsection (c).

(2) The Secretary shall make prompt use of the authority under paragraph 7 of subsection (b) of this section to prevent a significant risk to the well being of any such recovered species.

(h) AGENCY GUIDELINES.—The Secretary shall establish, and publish in the Federal Register, agency guidelines to insure that the purposes of this section are achieved efficiently and effectively. Such guidelines shall include, but are not limited to—

(1) procedures for recording the receipt and the disposition of petitions submitted under subsection (b)(3) of this section;

(2) criteria for making the findings required under such subsection with respect to petitions;

(3) a ranking system to assist in the identification of species that should receive priority review under subsection (a)(1) of the section; and

(4) a system for developing and implementing, on a priority basis, recovery plans under subsection (f) of this section. The Secretary shall provide to the public notice of, and opportunity to submit written comments on, any guideline (including any amendment thereto) proposed to be established under this subsection.

(i) If, in the case of any regulation proposed by the Secretary under the authority of this section, a State agency to which notice thereof was given in accordance with subsection (b)(5)(A)(ii) files comments disagreeing with all or part of the proposed regulation, and the Secretary issues a final regulation which is in conflict with such comments, or if the Secretary fails to adopt a regulation pursuant to an action petitioned by a State agency under subsection (b)(3), the Secretary shall submit to the State agency a written justification for his failure to adopt regulations consistent with the agency's comments or petition.

## LAND ACQUISITION

SEC. 5. (a) PROGRAM.—The Secretary, and the Secretary of Agriculture with respect to the National Forest System, shall establish and implement a program to conserve fish, wildlife, and plants, including those which are listed as endangered species or threatened species pursuant to section 4 of this Act. To carry out such a program, the appropriate Secretary—

(1) shall utilize the land acquisition and other authority under the Fish and Wildlife Act of 1956, as amended, the Fish and Wildlife Coordination Act, as amended, and the Migratory Bird Conservation Act, as appropriate; and

(2) is authorized to acquire by purchase, donation, or otherwise, lands, waters, or interest therein, and such authority shall be in addition to any other land acquisition vested in him.

(b) ACQUISITIONS.—Funds made available pursuant to the Land and Water Conservation Fund Act of 1965, as amended, may be used for the purpose of acquiring lands, waters, or interests therein under subsection (a) of this section.

COOPERATION WITH THE STATES

SEC. 6. (a) GENERAL.—In carrying out the program authorized by this Act, the Secretary shall cooperate to the maximum extent practicable with the States. Such cooperation shall include consultation with the States concerned before acquiring any land or water, or interest therein, for the purpose of conserving any endangered species or threatened species.

(b) MANAGEMENT AGREEMENTS.—The Secretary may enter into agreements with any State for the administration and management of any area established for the conservation of endangered species or threatened species. Any revenues derived from the administration of such areas under these agreements shall be subject to the provisions of section 401 of the Act of June 15, 1935 (49 Stat. 383; 16 U.S.C. 715s).

(c)(1) COOPERATIVE AGREEMENTS.—In furtherance of the purposes of this Act, the Secretary is authorized to enter into a cooperative agreement in accordance with this section with any State which establishes and maintains an adequate and active program for the conservation of endangered species and threatened species. Within one hundred and twenty days after the Secretary receives a certified copy of such a proposed State program, he shall make a determination whether such program is in accordance with this Act. Unless he determines, pursuant to this paragraph, that the State program is not in accordance with this Act, he shall enter into a cooperative agreement with the State for the purpose of assisting in implementation of the State program. In order for a State program to be deemed an adequate and active program for the conservation of endangered species and threatened species, the Secretary must find, and annually thereafter reconfirm such finding, that under the State program—

(A) authority resides in the State agency of conserve resident species of fish or wildlife determined by the State agency or the Secretary to be endangered or threatened;

(B) the State agency has established acceptable conservation programs, consistent with the purposes and policies of this Act, for all resident species of fish or wildlife in the State which are deemed by the Secretary to be endangered or threatened, and has furnished a copy of such plan and program together with all pertinent details, information, and data requested to the Secretary;

(C) the State agency is authorized to conduct investigations to determine the status and requirements for survival of resident species of fish and wildlife;

(D) the State agency is authorized to establish programs, including the acquisition of land or aquatic habitat or interests therein, for the conservation of resident endangered or threatened species of fish or wildlife; and

(E) provision is made for public participation in designating resident species of fish or wildlife as endangered or threatened, or that under the State program—

(i) the requirements set forth in paragraphs (3), (4), and (5) of this subsection are complied with, and

(ii) plans are included under which immediate attention will be given to those resident species of fish and wildlife which are determined by the Secretary or the State agency to be endangered or threatened and which the Secretary and the State agency agree are most urgently in need of conservation programs; except that a cooperative agreement entered into with a State whose program is deemed adequate and active pursuant to clause (i) and this clause and this subparagraph shall not affect the applicability of prohibitions set forth in or authorized pursuant to section 4(d) or section 9(a)(1) with respect to the taking of any resident endangered or threatened species.

(2) In furtherance of the purposes of this Act, the Secretary is authorized to enter into a cooperative agreement in accordance with this section with any State which establishes and maintains an adequate and active program for the conservation of endangered species and threatened species of plants. Within one hundred and twenty days after the Secretary receives a certified copy of such a proposed State program, he shall make a determination whether such program is in accordance with this Act. Unless he determines, pursuant to this paragraph, that the State program is not in accordance with this Act, he shall enter into a cooperative agreement with the State for the purpose of assisting in implementation of the State program. In order for a State program to be deemed an adequate and active program for the conservation of endangered species of plants and threatened species of plants, the Secretary must find, and annually thereafter reconfirm such finding, that under the State program—

(A) authority resides in the State agency to conserve resident species of plants determined by the State agency or the Secretary to be endangered or threatened;

(B) the State agency has established acceptable conservation programs, consistent with the purposes and policies of this Act, for all resident species of plants in the State which are deemed by the Secretary to be endangered or threatened, and has furnished a copy of such plan and program together with all pertinent details, information, and data requested to the Secretary;

(C) the State agency is authorized to conduct investigations to determine the status and requirements for survival of resident species of plants; and

(D) provision is made for public participation in designating resident species of plants as endangered or threatened; or that under the State program—

(i) the requirements set forth in subparagraphs (C) and (D) of this paragraph are complied with, and

(ii) plans are included under which immediate attention will be given to those resident species of plants which are determined by the Secretary or the State agency to be endangered or threatened and which the Secretary and the State agency agree are most urgently in need of conservation programs; except that a cooperative agreement entered into with a State whose program is deemed adequate and active pursuant to clause (i) and this clause shall not affect the applicability of prohibitions set forth in or authorized pursuant to section 4(d) or section 9(a)(1) with respect to the taking of any resident endangered or threatened species.

(d) ALLOCATION OF FUNDS.—(1) The Secretary is authorized to provide financial assistance to any State, through its respective State agency, which has entered into a cooperative agreement pursuant to subsection (c) of this section to assist in development of programs for the conservation of endangered and threatened species or to assist in monitoring the status of candidate species pursuant to subparagraph (C) of section 4(b)(3) and recovered species pursuant to section 4(g). The Secretary shall allocate each annual appropriation made in accordance with the provisions of subsection (i) of this section to such States based on consideration of—

(A) the international commitments of the United States to protect endangered species or threatened species;

(B) the readiness of a State to proceed with a conservation program consistent with the objectives and purposes of this Act;

(C) the number of endangered species and threatened species within a State;

(D) the potential for restoring endangered species and threatened species within a State;

(E) the relative urgency to initiate a program to restore and protect an endangered species or threatened species in terms of survival of the species;

(F) the importance of monitoring the status of candidate species within a State to prevent a significant risk to the well being of any such species; and

(G) the importance of monitoring the status of recovered species within a State to assure that such species do not return to the point at which the measures provided pursuant to this Act are again necessary.

So much of the annual appropriation made in accordance with provisions of subsection (i) of this section allocated for obligation to any State for any fiscal year as remains unobligated at the close thereof is authorized to be made available to that State until the close of the succeeding fiscal year. Any amount allocated to any State which is unobligated at the end of the period during which it is available for expenditure is authorized to be made available for expenditure by the Secretary in conducting programs under this section.

(2) Such cooperative agreements shall provide for (A) the actions to be taken by the Secretary and the States; (B) the benefits that are expected to be derived in connection with the conservation of endangered or threatened species; (C) the estimated cost of these actions; and (D) the share of such costs to be borne by the Federal Government and by the States; except that—

(i) the Federal share of such program costs shall not exceed 75 percent of the estimated program cost stated in the agreement; and

(ii) the Federal share may be increased to 90 percent whenever two or more States having a common interest in one or more endangered or threatened species, the conservation of which may be enhanced by cooperation of such States, enter jointly into agreement with the Secretary.

The Secretary may, in his discretion, and under such rules and regulations as he may prescribe, advance funds to the State for financing the United States pro rata share agreed upon in the cooperative agreement. For the purposes of this section, the non-Federal share may, in the discretion of the Secretary, be in the form of money or real property, the value of which will be determined by the Secretary whose decision shall be final.

(e) Review of State Programs.—Any action taken by the Secretary under this section shall be subject to his periodic review at no greater than annual intervals.

(f) Conflicts Between Federal and State Laws.—Any State law or regulation which applies with respect to the importation or exportation of, or interstate or foreign commerce in, endangered species or threatened species is void to the extent that it may effectively (1) permit what is prohibited by this Act of by any regulation which implements this Act, or (2) prohibit what is authorized pursuant to an exemption or permit provided for in this Act or in any regulation which implements this Act. This Act shall not otherwise be construed to void any State law or regulation which is intended to conserve migratory, resident, or introduced fish or wildlife, or to permit or prohibit sale of such fish or wildlife. Any State law or regulation respecting the taking of an endangered species or threatened species may be more restrictive than the exemptions or permits provided for in this Act or in any regulation which implements this Act but not less restrictive than the prohibitions so defined.

(g) Transition.—(1) For purposes of this subsection, the term "establishment period" means, with respect to any State, the period beginning on the date of enactment of this Act and ending on whichever of the following dates first occurs: (A) the date of the close of the 120-day period following the adjournment of the first regular session of the legislature of such State which commences after such date of enactment, or (B) the date of the close of the 15-month period following such date of enactment.

(2) The prohibitions set forth in or authorized pursuant to sections 4(d) and 9(a)(1)(B) of this Act shall not apply with respect to the taking of any resident endangered species or threatened species (other than species listed in Appendix I to the Convention or otherwise specifically covered by any other treaty or Federal law) within any State—

(A) which is then a party to a cooperative agreement with the Secretary pursuant to section 6(c) of this Act (except to the extent that the taking of any such species is contrary to the law of such State); or

(B) except for any time within the establishment period when—

(i) the Secretary applies such prohibition to such species at the request of the State, or

(ii) the Secretary applies such prohibition after he finds, and publishes his finding, that an emergency exists posing a significant risk to the well-being of such species and that the prohibition must be applied to protect such species. The Secretary's finding and publication may be made without regard to the public hearing or comment provisions of section 553 of title 5, United States Code, or any other provision of this Act; but such prohibition shall expire 90 days after the date of its imposition unless the Secretary further extends such prohibition by publishing notice and a statement of justification of such extension.

(h) REGULATIONS.—The Secretary is authorized to promulgate such regulations as may be appropriate to carry out the provisions of this section relating to financial assistance to States.

(i) APPROPRIATIONS.—(1) To carry out the provisions of this section for fiscal years after September 30, 1988, there shall be deposited into a special fund known as the cooperative endangered species conservation fund, to be administered by the Secretary, an amount equal to five percent of the combined amounts covered each fiscal year into the Federal aid to wildlife restoration fund under section 3 of the Act of September 2, 1937, and paid, transferred, or otherwise credited each fiscal year to the Sport Fishing Restoration Account established under 1016 of the Act of July 18, 1984.

(2) Amounts deposited into the special fund are authorized to be appropriated annually and allocated in accordance with subsection (d) of this section.

INTERAGENCY COOPERATION

SEC. 7. (a) FEDERAL AGENCY ACTIONS AND CONSULTATIONS.—(1) The Secretary shall review other programs administered by him and utilize such programs in furtherance of the purposes of this Act. All other Federal agencies shall, in consultation with and with the assistance of the Secretary, utilize their authorities in furtherance of the purposes of this Act by carrying out programs for the conservation of endangered species and threatened species listed pursuant to section 4 of this Act.

(2) Each Federal agency shall, in consultation with and with the assistance of the Secretary, insure that any action authorized, funded, or carried out by such agency (hereinafter in this section referred to as an "agency action") is not likely to jeopardize the continued existence of any endangered species or threatened species or result in the destruction or adverse modification of habitat of such species which is determined by the Secretary, after consultation as appropriate with affected States, to be critical, unless such agency has been granted an exemption for such action by the Committee pursuant to subsection (h) of this section. In fulfilling the requirements of this paragraph each agency shall use the best scientific and commercial data available.

(3) Subject to such guidelines as the Secretary may establish, a Federal agency shall consult with the Secretary on any prospective

agency action at the request of, and in cooperation with, the prospective permit or license applicant if the applicant has reason to believe that an endangered species or a threatened species may be present in the area affected by his project and that implementation of such action will likely affect such species.

(4) Each Federal agency shall confer with the Secretary on any agency action which is likely to jeopardize the continued existence of any species proposed to be listed under section 4 or result in the destruction or adverse modification of critical habitat proposed to be designated for such species. This paragraph does not require a limitation on the commitment of resources as described in subsection (d).

(b) OPINION OF SECRETARY.—(1)(A) Consultation under subsection (a)(2) with respect to any agency action shall be concluded within the 90-day period beginning on the date on which initiated or, subject to subparagraph (B), within such other period of time as is mutually agreeable to the Secretary and the Federal agency;

(B) in the case of an agency action involving a permit or license applicant, the Secretary and the Federal agency may not mutually agree to conclude consultation within a period exceeding 90 days unless the Secretary, before the close of the 90th day referred to in subparagraph (A)—

(i) if the consultation period proposed to be agreed to will end before the 150th day after the date on which consultation was initiated, submits to the applicant a written statement setting forth—

(I) the reasons why a longer period is required;

(II) the information that is required to complete the consultation; and

(III) the estimated date on which consultation will be completed; or

(ii) if the consultation period proposed to be agreed to will end 150 or more days after the date on which consultation was initiated, obtains the consent of the applicant to such period.

The Secretary and the Federal agency may mutually agree to extend a consultation period established under the preceding sentence if the Secretary, before the close of such period, obtains the consent of the applicant to the extension.

(2) Consultation under subsection (a)(3) shall be concluded within such period as is agreeable to the Secretary, the Federal agency, and the applicant concerned.

(3)(A) Promptly after conclusion of consultation under paragraph (2) or (3) of subsection (a), the Secretary shall provide to the Federal agency and the applicant, if any, a written statement setting forth the Secretary's opinion, and a summary of the information on which the opinion is based, detailing how the agency action affects the species or its critical habitat. If jeopardy or adverse modification is found, the Secretary shall suggest those reasonable and prudent alternatives which he believes would not violate subsection (a)(2) and can be taken by the Federal agency or applicant in implementing the agency action.

(B) Consultation under subsection (a)(3), and an opinion based by the Secretary incident to such consultation, regarding an agency action shall be treated respectively as a consultation under subsection (a)(2), and as an opinion issued after consultation under such subsection, regarding that action if the Secretary reviews the action before it is commenced by the Federal agency and finds, and notifies such agency, that no significant changes have been made with respect to the action and that no significant change has occurred regarding the information used during the initial consultation.

(4) If after consultation under subsection (a)(2) of this section, the Secretary concludes that—

(A) the agency action will not violate such subsection, or offers reasonable and prudent alternatives which the Secretary believes would not violate such subsection;

(B) the taking of an endangered species or a threatened species incidental to the agency action will not violate such subsection; and

(C) if an endangered species or threatened species of a marine mammal is involved, the taking is authorized pursuant to section 1371(a)(5) of this title;

the Secretary shall provide the Federal agency and the applicant concerned, if any, with a written statement that—

(i) specifies the impact of such incidental taking on the species,

(ii) specifies those reasonable and prudent measures that the Secretary considers necessary or appropriate to minimize such impact,

(iii) in the case of marine mammals, specifies those measures that are necessary to comply with section 1371(a)(5) of this title with regard to such taking, and

(iv) sets forth the terms and conditions (including, but not limited to, reporting requirements) that must be complied with by the Federal agency or applicant (if any), or both, to implement the measures specified under clauses (ii) and (iii).

(c) BIOLOGICAL ASSESSMENT.—(1) To facilitate compliance with the requirements of subsection (a)(2) each Federal agency shall, with respect to any agency action of such agency for which no contract for construction has been entered into and for which no construction has begun on the date of enactment of the Endangered Species Act Amendments of 1978, request of the Secretary information whether any species which is listed or proposed to be listed may be present in the area of such proposed action. If the Secretary advises, based on the best scientific and commercial data available, that such species may be present, such agency shall conduct a biological assessment for the purpose of identifying any endangered species or threatened species which is likely to be affected by such action. Such assessment shall be completed within 180 days after the date on which initiated (or within such other period as is mutually agreed to by the Secretary and such agency, except that if a permit or license applicant is involved, the 180-day period may not be extended unless such agency provides the applicant, before the close of such period, with a written statement setting forth the estimated length of the proposed extension and the reasons therefor) and, before any contract for construction is entered into and before construction is begun with respect to such action. Such assessment may be undertaken as part of a Federal agency's compliance with the requirements of section 102 of the National Environmental Policy Act of 1969 (42 U.S.C. 4332).

(2) Any person who may wish to apply for an exemption under subsection (g) of this section for that action may conduct a biological assessment to identify any endangered species or threatened species which is likely to be affected by such action. Any such biological assessment must, however, be conducted in cooperation with the Secretary and under the supervision of the appropriate Federal agency.

(d) LIMITATION ON COMMITMENT OF RESOURCES.—After initiation of consultation required under subsection (a)(2), the Federal agency and the permit or license applicant shall not make any irreversible or irretrievable commitment of resources with respect to the agency action which has the effect of foreclosing the formulation or implementation of any reasonable and prudent alternative measures which would not violate subsection (a)(2).

(e)(1) ESTABLISHMENT OF COMMITTEE.—There is established a committee to be known as the Endangered Species Committee (hereinafter in this section referred to as the "Committee").

(2) The Committee shall review any application submitted to it pursuant to this section and determine in accordance with subsection (h) of this section whether or not to grant an exemption from the requirements of subsection (a)(2) of this action for the action set forth in such application.

(3) The Committee shall be composed of seven members as follows:

(A) The Secretary of Agriculture.

(B) The Secretary of the Army.

(C) The Chairman of the Council of Economic Advisors.

(D) The Administrator of the Environmental Protection Agency. Agency.

(E) The Secretary of the Interior.

(F) The Administrator of the National Oceanic and Atmospheric Administration.

(G) The President, after consideration of any recommendations received pursuant to subsection (g)(2)(B) shall appoint one individual from each affected State, as determined by the Secretary, to be a member of the Committee for the consideration of the application for exemption for an agency action with respect to which such recommendations are made, not later than 30 days after an application is submitted pursuant to this section.

(4)(A) Members of the Committee shall receive no additional pay on account of their service on the Committee.

(B) While away from their homes or regular places of business in the performance of services for the Committee, members of the Committee shall be allowed travel expenses, including per diem in lieu of subsistence, in the same manner as persons employed intermittently in the Government service are allowed expenses under section 5703 of title 5 of the United States Code

(5)(A) Five members of the Committee or their representatives shall constitute a quorum for the transaction of any function of the Committee, except that, in no case shall any representative be considered in determining the existence of a quorum for the transaction of any function of the Committee if that function involves a vote by the Committee on any matter before the Committee.

(B) The Secretary of the Interior shall be the Chairman of the Committee.

(C) The Committee shall meet at the call of the Chairman or five of its members.

(D) All meetings and records of the Committee shall be open to the public.

(6) Upon request of the Committee, the head of any Federal agency is authorized to detail, on a nonreimbursable basis, any of the personnel of such agency to the Committee to assist it in carrying out its duties under this section.

(7)(A) The Committee may for the purpose of carrying out its duties under this section hold such hearings, sit and act at such times and places, take such testimony, and receive such evidence, as the Committee deems advisable.

(B) When so authorized by the Committee, any member or agent of the Committee may take any action which the Committee is authorized to take by this paragraph.

(C) Subject to the Privacy Act, the Committee may secure directly from any Federal agency information necessary to enable it to carry out its duties under this section. Upon request of the Chairman of the Committee, the head of such Federal agency shall furnish such information to the Committee.

(D) The Committee may use the United States mails in the same manner and upon the same conditions as a Federal agency.

(E) The Administrator of General Services shall provide to the Committee on a reimbursable basis such administrative support services as the Committee may request.

(8) In carrying out its duties under this section, the Committee may promulgate and amend such rules, regulations, and procedures, and issue and amend such orders as it deems necessary.

(9) For the purpose of obtaining information necessary for the consideration of an application for an exemption under this section the Committee may issue subpoenas for the attendance and testimony of witnesses and the production of relevant papers, books, and documents.

(10) In no case shall any representative, including a representative of a member designated pursuant to paragraph (3)(G) of this subsection, be eligible to cast a vote on behalf of any member.

(f) REGULATIONS.—Not later than 90 days after the date of enactment of the Endangered Species Act Amendments of 1978, the Secretary shall promulgate regulations which set forth the form and manner in which applications for exemption shall be submitted to the Secretary and the information to be contained in such applications. Such regulations shall require that information submitted in an application by the head of any Federal agency with respect to any agency action include but not be limited to—

(1) a description of the consultation process carried out pursuant to subsection (a)(2) of this section between the head of the Federal agency and the Secretary; and

(2) a statement describing why such action cannot be altered or modified to conform with the requirements of subsection (a)(2) of this section.

(g) APPLICATION FOR EXEMPTION AND REPORT TO THE COMMITTEE.—(1) A Federal agency, the Governor of the State in which an agency action will occur, if any, or a permit or license applicant may apply to the Secretary for an exemption for an agency action of such agency if, after consultation under subsection (a)(2), the Secretary's opinion under subsection (b) indicates that the agency action would violate subsection (a)(2). An application for an exemption shall be considered initially by the Secretary in the manner provided for in this subsection, and shall be considered by the Committee for a final determination under subsection (h) after a report is made pursuant to paragraph (5). The applicant for an exemption shall be referred to as the "exemption applicant" in this section.

(2)(A) An exemption applicant shall submit a written application to the Secretary, in a form prescribed under subsection (f), not later than 90 days after the completion of the consultation process; except that, in the case of any agency action involving a permit or license applicant, such application shall be submitted not later than 90 days after the date on which the Federal agency concerned takes final agency action with respect to the issuance of the permit or license. For purposes of the preceding sentence, the term "final agency action" means (i) a disposition by an agency with respect to the issuance of a permit or license that is subject to administrative review, whether or not such disposition is subject to judicial review; or (ii) if administrative review is sought with respect to such disposition, the decision resulting after such review. Such application shall set forth the reasons why the exemption applicant considers that the agency action meets the requirements for an exemption under this subsection.

(B) Upon receipt of an application for exemption for an agency action under paragraph (1), the Secretary shall promptly (i) notify the Governor of each affected State, if any, as determined by the Secretary, and request the Governors so notified to recommend individuals to be appointed to the Endangered Species Committee for consideration of such application; and (ii) publish notice of receipt of the application in the Federal Register, including a summary of the information contained in the application and a description of the agency action with respect to which the application for exemption has been filed.

(3) The Secretary shall within 20 days after the receipt of an application for exemption, or within such other period of time as is mutually agreeable to the exemption applicant and the Secretary—

(A) determine that the Federal agency concerned and the exemption applicant have—

(i) carried out the consultation responsibilities described in subsection (a) in good faith and made a reasonable and responsible effort to develop and fairly consider modifications or reasonable and prudent alternatives to the proposed agency action which would not violate subsection (a)(2);

(ii) conducted any biological assessment required by subsection (c); and

(iii) to the extent determinable within the time provided herein, refrained from making any irreversible or irretrievable commitment of resources prohibited by subsection (d); or

(B) deny the application for exemption because the Federal agency concerned or the exemption applicant have not met the requirements set forth in subparagraph (A) (i), (ii), and (iii).

The denial of an application under subparagraph (B) shall be considered final agency action for purposes of chapter 7 of title 5, United States Code.

(4) If the Secretary determines that the Federal agency concerned and the exemption applicant have met the requirements set forth in paragraph (3)(A) (i), (ii) and (iii) he shall, in consultation with the Members of the Committee, hold a hearing on the application for exemption in accordance with sections 554, 555, and 556 (other than subsection (b) (1) and (2) thereof) of title 5, United States Code, and prepare the report to be submitted pursuant to paragraph (5).

(5) Within 140 days after making the determinations under paragraph (3) or within such other period of time as is mutually agreeable to the exemption applicant and the Secretary, the Secretary shall submit to the Committee a report discussing—

(A) the availability of reasonable and prudent alternatives to the agency action, and the nature and extent of the benefits of the agency action and of alternative courses of action consistent with conserving the species of the critical habitat;

(B) a summary of the evidence concerning whether or not the agency action is in the public interest and is of national or regional significance;

(C) appropriate reasonable mitigation and enhancement measures which should be considered by the Committee; and

(D) whether the Federal agency concerned and the exemption applicant refrained from making any irreversible or irretrievable commitment of resources prohibited by subsection (d).

(6) To the extent practicable within the time required for action under subsection (g) of this section, and except to the extent inconsistent with the requirements of this section, the consideration of any application for an exemption under this section and the conduct of any hearing under this subsection shall be in accordance with sections 554, 555, and 556 (other than subsection (b)(3) of section 556) of title 5, United States Code.

(7) Upon request of the Secretary, the head of any Federal agency is authorized to detail, on a nonreimbursable basis, any of the personnel of such agency to the Secretary to assist him in carrying out his duties under this section.

(8) All meetings and records resulting from activities pursuant to this subsection shall be open to the public.

(h) EXEMPTION.—(1) The Committee shall make a final determination whether or not to grant an exemption within 30 days after receiving the report of the Secretary pursuant to subsection (g)(5). The Committee shall grant an exemption from the requirements of subsection (a)(2) for an agency action if, by a vote of not less than five of its members voting in person—

(A) it determines on the record, based on the report of the Secretary, the record of the hearing held under subsection (g)(4), and on such other testimony or evidence as it may receive, that—

(i) there are no reasonable and prudent alternatives to the agency action;

(ii) the benefits of such action clearly outweigh the benefits of alternative courses of action consistent with conserving the species or its critical habitat, and such action is in the public interest;

(iii) the action is of regional or national significance; and

(iv) neither the Federal agency concerned nor the exemption applicant made any irreversible or irretrievable commitment of resources prohibited by subsection (d); and

(B) it establishes such reasonable mitigation and enhancement measures, including, but not limited to, live propagation, transplantation, and habitat acquisition and improvement, as are necessary and appropriate to minimize the adverse effects of the agency action upon the endangered species, threatened species, or critical habitat concerned.

Any final determination by Committee under this subsection shall be considered final agency action for purposes of chapter 7 of title 5 of the United States Code.

(2)(A) Except as provided in subparagraph (B), an exemption for an agency action granted under paragraph (1) shall constitute a permanent exemption with respect to all endangered or threatened species for the purposes of completing such agency action—

(i) regardless whether the species was identified in the biological assessment; and

(ii) only if a biological assessment has been conducted under subsection (c) with respect to such agency action.

(B) An exemption shall be permanent under subparagraph (A) unless—

(i) the Secretary finds, based on the best scientific and commercial data available, that such exemption would result in the extinction of a species that was not the subject of consultation under subsection (a)(2) or was not identified in any biological assessment conducted under subsection (c), and

(ii) the Committee determines within 60 days after the date of the Secretary's finding that the exemption should not be permanent.

If the Secretary makes a finding described in clause (i), the Committee shall meet with respect to the matter within 30 days after the date of the finding.

(i) Review by Secretary of State.—Notwithstanding any other provision of this Act, the Committee shall be prohibited from considering for exemption any application made to it, if the Secretary of State, after a review of the proposed agency action and its potential implications, and after hearing, certifies, in writing, to the Committee within 60 days of any application made under this section that the granting of any such exemption and the carrying out of such action would be in violation of an international treaty obligation or other international obligation of the United States. The Secretary of State shall, at the time of such certification, publish a copy thereof in the Federal Register.

(j) Notwithstanding any other provision of this Act, the Committee shall grant an exemption for any agency action if the Secretary of Defense finds that such exemption is necessary for reasons of national security.

(k) SPECIAL PROVISIONS.—An exemption decision by the Committee under this section shall not be a major Federal action for purposes of the National Environmental Policy Act of 1969 (42 U.S.C. 4321 et seq.): *Provided,* That an environmental impact statement which discusses the impacts upon endangered species or threatened species or their critical habitats shall have been previously prepared with respect to any agency action exempted by such order.

(l) COMMITTEE ORDERS.—(1) If the Committee determines under subsection (h) that an exemption should be granted with respect to any agency action, the Committee shall issue an order granting the exemption and specifying the mitigation and enhancement measures established pursuant to subsection (h) which shall be carried out and paid for by the exemption applicant in implementing the agency action. All necessary mitigation and enhancement measures shall be authorized prior to the implementing of the agency action and funded concurrently with all other project features.

(2) The applicart receiving such exemption shall include the costs of such mitigation and enhancement measures within the overall costs of continuing the proposed action. Notwithstanding the preceding sentence the costs of such measures shall not be treated as project costs for the purpose of computing benefit-cost or other ratios for the proposed action. Any applicant may request the Secretary to carry out such mitigation and enhancement measures. The costs incurred by the Secretary in carrying out any such measures shall be paid by the applicant receiving the exemption. No later than one year after the granting of an exemption, the exemption applicant shall submit to the Council on Environmental Quality a report describing its compliance with the mitigation and enhancement measures prescribed by this section. Such report shall be submitted annually until all such mitigation and enhancement measures have been completed. Notice of the public availability of such reports shall be published in the Federal Register by the Council on Environmental Quality.

(m) NOTICE.—The 60-day notice requirement of section 11(g) of this Act shall not apply with respect to review of any final determination of the Committee under subsection (h) of this section granting an exemption from the requirements of subsection (a)(2) of this section.

(n) JUDICIAL REVIEW.—Any person, as defined by section 3(13) of this Act, may obtain judicial review, under chapter 7 of title 5 of the United States Code, of any decision of the Endangered Species Committee under subsection (h) in the United States Court of Appeals for (1) any circuit wherein the agency action concerned will be, or is being, carried out, or (2) in any case in which the agency action will be, or is being, carried out outside of any circuit, the District of Columbia, by filing in such court within 90 days after the date of issuance of the decision, a written petition for review. A copy of such petition shall be transmitted by the clerk of the court to the Committee and the Committee shall file in the court the record in the proceeding, as provided in section 2112, of title 28,

United States Code. Attorneys designated by the Endangered Species Committee may appear for, and represent the Committee in any action for review under this subsection.

(o) EXEMPTION AS PROVIDING EXCEPTION ON TAKING OF ENDANGERED SPECIES.—Notwithstanding sections 1533(d) and 1538(a)(1)(B) and (C) of this title, sections 1371 and 1372 of this title, or any regulation promulgated to implement any such section—

(1) any action for which an exemption is granted under subsection (h) of this section shall not be considered to be a taking of any endangered species or threatened species with respect to any activity which is necessary to carry out such action; and

(2) any taking that is in compliance with the terms and conditions specified in a written statement provided under subsection (b)(4)(iv) of this section shall not be considered to be a prohibited taking of the species concerned.

(p) EXEMPTIONS IN PRESIDENTIALLY DECLARED DISASTER AREAS.—In any area which has been declared by the President to be a major disaster area under the Disaster Relief Act of 1974, the President is authorized to make the determinations required by subsections (g) and (h) of this section for any project for the repair or replacement of a public facility substantially as it existed prior to the disaster under section 401 or 402 of the Disaster Relief Act of 1974, and which the President determines (1) is necessary to prevent the recurrence of such a natural disaster and to reduce the potential loss of human life, and (2) to involve an emergency situation which does not allow the ordinary procedures of this section to be followed. Notwithstanding any other provision of this section, the Committee shall accept the determinations of the President under this subsection.

## INTERNATIONAL COOPERATION

SEC. 8. (a) FINANCIAL ASSISTANCE.—As a demonstration of the commitment of the United States to the worldwide protection of endangered species and threatened species, the President may, subject to the provisions of section 1415 of the Supplemental Appropriation Act, 1953 (31 U.S.C. 724), use foreign currencies accruing to the United States Government under the Agricultural Trade Development and Assistance Act of 1954 or any other law to provide to any foreign country (with its consent) assistance in the development and management of programs in that country which the Secretary determines to be necessary or useful for the conservation of any endangered species or threatened species listed by the Secretary pursuant to section 4 of this Act. The President shall provide assistance (which includes, but is not limited to, the acquisition, by lease or otherwise, of lands, waters, or interests therein) to foreign countries under this section under such terms and conditions as he deems appropriate. Whenever foreign currencies are available for the provision of assistance under this section, such currencies shall be used in preference to funds appropriated under the authority of section 15 of this Act.

(b) ENCOURAGEMENT OF FOREIGN PROGRAMS.—In order to carry out further the provisions of this Act, the Secretary, through the Secretary of State shall encourage—

(1) foreign countries to provide for the conservation of fish or wildlife and plants including endangered species and threatened species listed pursuant to section 4 of this Act;

(2) the entering into of bilateral or multilateral agreements with foreign countries to provide for such conservation; and

(3) foreign persons who directly or indirectly take fish or wildlife or plants in foreign countries or on the high seas for importation into the United States for commercial or other purposes to develop and carry out with such assistance as he may provide, conservation practices designed to enhance such fish or wildlife or plants and their habitat.

(c) PERSONNEL.—After consultation with the Secretary of State, the Secretary may—

(1) assign or otherwise make available any officer or employee of his department for the purpose of cooperating with foreign countries and international organizations in developing personnel resources and programs which promote the conservation of fish or wildlife or plants, and

(2) conduct or provide financial assistance for the educational training of foreign personnel, in this country or abroad, in fish, wildlife, or plant management, research and law enforcement and to render professional assistance abroad in such matters.

(d) INVESTIGATIONS.—After consultation with the Secretary of State and the Secretary of the Treasury, as appropriate, the Secretary may conduct or cause to be conducted such law enforcement investigations and research abroad as he deems necessary to carry out the purposes of this Act.

CONVENTION IMPLEMENTATION

SEC. 8A. (a) MANAGEMENT AUTHORITY AND SCIENTIFIC AUTHORITY.—The Secretary of the Interior (hereinafter in this section referred to as the "Secretary") is designated as the Management Authority and the Scientific Authority for purposes of the Convention and the respective functions of each such Authority shall be carried out through the United States Fish and Wildlife Service.

(b) MANAGEMENT AUTHORITY FUNCTIONS.—The Secretary shall do all things necessary and appropriate to carry out the functions of the Management Authority under the Convention.

(c) SCIENTIFIC AUTHORITY FUNCTIONS.—(1) The Secretary shall do all things necessary and appropriate to carry out the functions of the Scientific Authority under the Convention.

(2) The Secretary shall base the determinations and advice given by him under Article IV of the Convention with respect to wildlife upon the best available biological information derived from professionally accepted wildlife management practices; but is not required to make, or require any State to make, estimates of population size in making such determinations or giving such advice.

(d) RESERVATIONS BY THE UNITED STATES UNDER CONVENTION.—If the United States votes against including any species in Appendix I or II of the Convention and does not enter a reservation pursuant to paragraph (3) of Article XV of the Convention with respect to that species, the Secretary of State, before the 90th day after the last day on which such a reservation could be entered, shall submit to the Committee on Merchant Marine and Fisheries of the House of Representatives, and to the Committee on the Environment and Public Works of the Senate, a written report setting forth the reasons why such a reservation was not entered.

(e) Wildlife Preservation in Western Hemisphere.—(1) The Secretary of the Interior (hereinafter in this subsection referred to as the "Secretary"), in cooperation with the Secretary of State, shall act on behalf of, and represent, the United States in all regards as required by the Convention on Nature Protection and Wildlife Preservation in the Western Hemisphere (56 Stat. 1354, T.S. 982, hereinafter in this subsection referred to as the "Western Convention"). In the discharge of these responsibilities, the Secretary and the Secretary of State shall consult with the Secretary of Agriculture, the Secretary of Commerce, and the heads of other agencies with respect to matters relating to or affecting their areas of responsibility.

(2) The Secretary and the Secretary of State shall, in cooperation with the contracting parties to the Western Convention and, to the extent feasible and appropriate, with the participation of State agencies, take such steps as are necessary to implement the Western Convention. Such steps shall include, but not be limited to—

(A) cooperation with contracting parties and international organizations for the purpose of developing personnel resources and programs that will facilitate implementation of the Western Convention;

(B) identification of those species of birds that migrate between the United States and other contracting parties, and the habitats upon which those species depend, and the implementation of cooperative measures to ensure that such species will not become endangered or threatened; and

(C) identification of measures that are necessary and appropriate to implement those provisions of the Western Convention which address the protection of wild plants.

(3) No later than September 30, 1985, the Secretary and the Secretary of State shall submit a report to Congress describing those steps taken in accordance with the requirements of this subsection and identifying the principal remaining actions yet necessary for comprehensive and effective implementation of the Western Convention.

(4) The provisions of this subsection shall not be construed as affecting the authority, jurisdiction, or responsibility of the several States to manage, control, or regulate resident fish or wildlife under State law or regulations.

PROHIBITED ACTS

Sec. 9. (a) General.—(1) Except as provided in sections 6(g)(2) and 10 of this Act, with respect to any endangered species of fish or wildlife listed pursuant to section 4 of this Act it is unlawful for any person subject to the jurisdiction of the United States to—

(A) import any such species into, or export any such species from the United States;

(B) take any such species within the United States or the territorial sea of the United States;

(C) take any such species upon the high seas;

(D) possess, sell, deliver, carry, transport, or ship, by any means whatsoever, any such species taken in violation of subparagraphs (B) and (C);

(E) deliver, receive, carry, transport, or ship in interstate or foreign commerce, by any means whatsoever and in the course of a commercial activity, any such species;

(F) sell or offer for sale in interstate or foreign commerce any such species; or

(G) violate any regulation pertaining to such species or to any threatened species of fish or wildlife listed pursuant to section 4 of this Act and promulgated by the Secretary pursuant to authority provided by this Act.

(2) Except as provided in sections 6(g)(2) and 10 of this Act, with respect to any endangered species of plants listed pursuant to section 4 of this Act, it is unlawful for any person subject to the jurisdiction of the United States to—

(A) import any such species into, or export any such species from, the United States;

(B) remove and reduce to possession any such species from areas under Federal jurisdiction; maliciously damage or destroy any such species on any such area; or remove, cut, dig up, or damage or destroy any such species on any other area in knowing violation of any law or regulation of any state or in the course of any violation of a state criminal trespass law;".

(C) deliver, receive, carry, transport, or ship in interstate or foreign commerce, by any means whatsoever and in the course of a commercial activity, any such species;

(D) sell or offer for sale in interstate or foreign commerce any such species; or

(E) violate any regulation pertaining to such species or to any threatened species of plants listed pursuant to section 4 of this Act and promulgated by the Secretary pursuant to authority provided by this Act.

(b)(1) Species Held in Captivity or Controlled Environment.—The provisions of subsections (a)(1)(A) and (a)(1)(G) of this section shall not apply to any fish or wildlife which was held in captivity or in a controlled environment on (A) December 28, 1973, or (B) the date of the publication in the Federal Register of a final regulation adding such fish or wildlife species to any list published pursuant to subsection (c) of section 4 of this Act: *Provided,* That such holding and any subsequent holding or use of the fish or wildlife was not in the course of a commercial activity. With respect to any act prohibited by subsections (a)(1)(A) and (a)(1)(G) of this section which occurs after a period of 180 days from (i) December 28, 1973, or (ii) the date of publication in the Federal Register of a final regulation adding such fish or wildlife species to any list published pursuant to subsection (c) of section 4 of this Act, there shall be a rebuttable presumption that the fish or wildlife involved in such act is not entitled to the exemption contained in this subsection.

(2)(A) The provisions of subsections (a)(1) shall not apply to—

(i) any raptor legally held in captivity or in a controlled environment on the effective date of the Endangered Species Act Amendments of 1978; or

(ii) any progeny of any raptor described in clause (i); until such time as any such raptor or progeny is intentionally returned to a wild state.

(B) Any person holding any raptor or progeny described in subparagraph (A) must be able to demonstrate that the raptor or progeny does, in fact, qualify under the provisions of this paragraph, and shall maintain and submit to the Secretary, on request, such inventories, documentation, and records as the Secretary may by regulation require as being reasonably appropriate to carry out the purposes of this paragraph. Such requirements shall not unnecessarily duplicate the requirements of other rules and regulations promulgated by the Secretary.

(c) Violation of Convention.—(1) It is unlawful for any person subject to the jurisdiction of the United States to engage in any trade in any specimens contrary to the provisions of the Convention, or to possess any specimens traded contrary to the provisions of the Convention, including the definitions of terms in article I thereof.

(2) Any importation into the United States of fish or wildlife shall, if—

(A) such fish or wildlife is not an endangered species listed pursuant to section 4 of this Act but is listed in Appendix II of the Convention;

(B) the taking and exportation of such fish or wildlife is not contrary to the provisions of the Convention and all other applicable requirements of the Convention have been satisfied;

(C) the applicable requirements of subsections (d), (e), and (f) of this section have been satisfied; and

(D) such importation is not made in the course of a commercial activity;

be presumed to be an importation not in violation of any provision of this Act or any regulation issued pursuant to this Act.

(d) Imports and Exports.—

(1) In general.—It is unlawful for any person, without first having obtained permission from the Secretary, to engage in business—

(A) as an importer or exporter of fish or wildlife (other than shellfish and fishery products which (i) are not listed pursuant to section 4 of this Act as endangered species or threatened species, and (ii) are imported for purposes of human or animal consumption or taken in waters under the jurisdiction of the United States or on the high seas for recreational purposes) or plants; or

(B) as an importer or exporter of any amount of raw or worked African elephant ivory.

(2) Requirements.—Any person required to obtain permission under paragraph (1) of this subsection shall—

(A) keep such records as will fully and correctly disclose each importation or exportation of fish, wildlife, plants, or African elephant ivory made by him and the subsequent disposition made by him with respect to such fish, wildlife, plants, or ivory;

(B) at all reasonable times upon notice by a duly authorized representative of the Secretary, afford such representative access to his place of business, an opportunity to examine his inventory of imported fish, wildlife, plants, or African elephant ivory and the records required to be kept under subparagraph (A) of this paragraph, and to copy such records; and

(C) file such reports as the Secretary may require.

(3) REGULATIONS.—The Secretary shall prescribe such regulations as are necessary and appropriate to carry out the purposes of this subsection.

(4) RESTRICTION ON CONSIDERATION OF VALUE OR AMOUNT OF AFRICAN ELEPHANT IVORY IMPORTED OR EXPORTED.—In granting permission under this subsection for importation or exportation of African elephant ivory, the Secretary shall not vary the requirements for obtaining such permission on the basis of the value or amount of ivory imported or exported under such permission.

(e) REPORTS.—It is unlawful for any person importing or exporting fish or wildlife (other than shellfish and fishery products which (1) are not listed pursuant to section 4 of this Act as endangered or threatened species, and (2) are imported for purposes of human or animal consumption or taken in waters under the jurisdiction of the United States or on the high seas for recreational purposes) or plants to fail to file any declaration or report as the Secretary deems necessary to facilitate enforcement of this Act or to meet the obligations of the Convention.

(f) DESIGNATION OF PORTS.—(1) It is unlawful for any person subject to the jurisdiction of the United States to import into or export from the United States any fish or wildlife (other than shellfish and fishery products which (A) are not listed pursuant to section 4 of this Act as endangered species or threatened species, and (B) are imported for purposes of human or animal consumption or taken in waters under the jurisdiction of the United States or on the high seas for recreational purposes) or plants, except at a port or ports designated by the Secretary of the Interior. For the purposes of facilitating enforcement of this Act and reducing the costs thereof, the Secretary of the Interior, with approval of the Secretary of the Treasury and after notice and opportunity for public hearing, may, by regulation, designate ports and change such designations. The Secretary of the Interior, under such terms and conditions as he may prescribe, may permit the importation or exportation at nondesignated ports in the interest of the health or safety of the fish or wildlife or plants, or for other reasons if, in his discretion, he deems it appropriate and consistent with the purpose of this subsection.

(2) Any port designated by the Secretary of the Interior under the authority of section 4(d) of the Act of December 5, 1969 (16 U.S.C. 666cc-4(d), shall, if such designation is in effect on the day before the date of the enactment of this Act, be deemed to be a port designated by the Secretary under paragraph (1) of this subsection until such time as the Secretary otherwise provides.

(g) VIOLATIONS.—It is unlawful for any person subject to the jurisdiction of the United States to attempt to commit, solicit another to commit, or cause to be committed, any offense defined in this section.

EXCEPTIONS

SEC. 10. (a) PERMITS.—(1) The Secretary may permit, under such terms and conditions as he shall prescribe—

(A) any act otherwise prohibited by section 9 for scientific purposes or to enhance the propagation or survival of the affected species, including, but not limited to, acts necessary for the establishment and maintenance of experimental populations pursuant subsection (j); or

(B) any taking otherwise prohibited by section 9(a)(1)(B) if such taking is incidental to, and not the purpose of, the carrying out of an otherwise lawful activity.

(2)(A) No permit may be issued by the Secretary authorizing any taking referred to in paragraph (1)(B) unless the applicant therefor submits to the Secretary a conservation plan that specifies—

(i) the impact which will likely result from such taking;

(ii) what steps the applicant will take to minimize and mitigate such impacts, and the funding that will be available to implement such steps;

(iii) what alternative actions to such taking the applicant considered and the reasons why such alternatives are not being utilized; and

(iv) such other measures that the Secretary may require as being necessary or appropriate for purposes of the plan.

(B) If the Secretary finds, after opportunity for public comment, with respect to a permit application and the related conservation plan that—

(i) the taking will be incidental;

(ii) the applicant will, to the maximum extent practicable, minimize and mitigate the impacts of such taking;

(iii) the applicant will ensure that adequate funding for the plan will be provided;

(iv) the taking will not appreciably reduce the likelihood of the survival and recovery of the species in the wild; and

(v) the measures, if any, required under subparagraph (A)(iv) will be met;

and he has received such other assurances as he may require that the plan will be implemented, the Secretary shall issue the permit. The permit shall contain such terms and conditions as the Secretary deems necessary or appropriate to carry out the purposes of this paragraph, including, but not limited to, such reporting requirements as the Secretary deems necessary for determining whether such terms and conditions are being complied with.

(C) The Secretary shall revoke a permit issued under this paragraph if he finds that the permittee is not complying with the terms and conditions of the permit.

(b) HARDSHIP EXEMPTIONS.—(1) If any person enters into a contract with respect to a species of fish or wildlife or plant before the date of the publication in the Federal Register of notice of consideration of that species as an endangered species and the subsequent listing of that species as an endangered species pursuant to section 4 of this Act will cause undue hardship to such person under the contract, the Secretary, in order to minimize such hardship, may exempt such person from the application of section 9(a) of this Act to the extent the Secretary deems appropriate if such person applies to him for such exemption and includes with such application such information as the Secretary may require to prove such hardship; except that (A) no such exemption shall be for a duration of more than one year from the date of publication in the Federal Register of notice of consideration of the species concerned, or shall apply to a quantity of fish or wildlife or plants in excess of that specified by the Secretary; (B) the one-year period for those species of fish or wildlife listed by the Secretary as endangered prior to the effective date of this Act shall expire in accordance with the terms of section 3 of the Act of December 5, 1969 (83 Stat. 275); and (C) no such exemption may be granted for the importation or exportation of a specimen listed in Appendix I of the Convention which is to be used in a commercial activity.

(2) As used in this subsection, the term "undue economic hardship" shall include, but not be limited to:

(A) substantial economic loss resulting from inability caused by this Act to perform contracts with respect to species of fish and wildlife entered into prior to the date of publication in the Federal Register of a notice of consideration of such species as an endangered species;

(B) substantial economic loss to persons who, for the year prior to the notice of consideration of such species as an endangered species, derived a substantial portion of their income from the lawful taking of any listed species, which taking would be made unlawful under this Act; or

(C) curtailment of subsistence taking made unlawful under this Act by persons (i) not reasonably able to secure other sources of subsistence; and (ii) dependent to a substantial extent upon hunting and fishing for subsistence; and (iii) who must engage in such curtailed taking for subsistence purposes.

(3) The Secretary may make further requirements for a showing of undue economic hardship as he deems fit. Exceptions granted under this section may be limited by the Secretary in his discretion as to time, area, or other factor of applicability.

(c) Notice and Review.—The Secretary shall publish notice in the Federal Register of each application for an exemption or permit which is made under this section. Each notice shall invite the submission from interested parties, within thirty days after the date of the notice, of written data, views, or arguments with respect to the application; except that such thirty-day period may be waived by the Secretary in an emergency situation where the health or life of an endangered animal is threatened and no reasonable alternative is available to the applicant, but notice of any such waiver shall be published by the Secretary in the Federal Register within ten days following the issuance of the exemption or permit. Information received by the Secretary as part of any application shall be available to the public as a matter of public record at every stage of the proceeding.

(d) PERMIT AND EXEMPTION POLICY.—The Secretary may grant exceptions under subsections (a)(1)(A) and (b) of this section only if he finds and publishes his finding in the Federal Register that (1) such exceptions were applied for in good faith, (2) if granted and exercised will not operate to the disadvantage of such endangered species, and (3) will be consistent with the purposes and policy set forth in section 2 of this Act.

(e) ALASKA NATIVES.—(1) Except as provided in paragraph (4) of this subsection the provisions of this Act shall not apply with respect to the taking of any endangered species or threatened species, or the importation of any such species taken pursuant to this section, by—

(A) any Indian, Aleut, or Eskimo who is an Alaskan Native who resides in Alaska; or

(B) any non-native permanent resident of an Alaskan native village;

if such taking is primarily for subsistence purposes. Non-edible byproducts of species taken pursuant to this section may be sold in interstate commerce when made into authentic native articles of handicrafts and clothing; except that the provisions of this subsection shall not apply to any non-native resident of an Alaskan native village found by the Secretary to be not primarily dependent upon the taking of fish and wildlife for consumption or for the creation and sale of authentic native articles of handicrafts and clothing.

(2) Any taking under this subsection may not be accomplished in a wasteful manner.

(3) As used in this subsection—

(i) The term "subsistence" includes selling any edible portion of fish or wildlife in native villages and towns in Alaska for native consumption within native villages or towns; and

(ii) The term "authentic native articles of handicrafts and clothing" means items composed wholly or in some significant respect to natural materials, and which are produced, decorated or fashioned in the exercise of traditional native handicrafts without the use of pantographs, multiple carvers, or other mass copying devices. Traditional native handicrafts include, but are not limited to, weaving, carving, stitching, sewing, lacing, beading, drawing, and painting.

(4) Notwithstanding the provisions of paragraph (1) of this subsection, whenever the Secretary determines that any species of fish or wildlife which is subject to taking under the provisions of this subsection is an endangered species or threatened species, and that such taking materially and negatively affects the threatened or endangered species, he may prescribe regulations upon the taking of such species by any such Indian, Aleut, Eskimo, or non-native Alaskan resident of an Alaskan native village. Such regulations may be established with reference to species, geographical description of the area included, the season for taking, or any other factors related to the reason for establishing such regulations and consistent with the policy of this Act. Such regulations shall be prescribed after a notice and hearings in the affected judicial districts of Alaska and as otherwise required by section 103 of the Marine Mammal Protection Act of 1972, and shall be removed as soon as

the Secretary determines that the need for their impositions has disappeared.

(f)(1) As used in this subsection—

(A) The term "pre-Act endangered species part" means—

(i) any sperm whale oil, including derivatives thereof, which was lawfully held within the United States on December 28, 1973, in the course of a commercial activity; or

(ii) any finished scrimshaw product, if such product or the raw material for such product was lawfully held within the United States on December 28, 1973, in the course of a commercial activity.

(B) The term "scrimshaw product" means any art form which involves the substantial etching or engraving of designs upon, or the substantial carving of figures, patterns, or designs from, any bone or tooth of any marine mammal of the order Cetacea. For purposes of this subsection, polishing or the adding of minor superficial markings does not constitute substantial etching, engraving, or carving.

(2) The Secretary, pursuant to the provisions of this subsection, may exempt, if such exemption is not in violation of the Convention, any pre-Act endangered species part from one or more of the following prohibitions:

(A) The prohibition on exportation from the United States set forth in section 9(a)(1)(A) of this Act.

(B) Any prohibition set forth in section 9(a)(1) (E) or (F) of this Act.

(3) Any person seeking an exemption described in paragraph (2) of this subsection shall make application therefor to the Secretary in such form and manner as he shall prescribe, but no such application may be considered by the Secretary unless the application—

(A) is received by the Secretary before the close of the one-year period beginning on the date on which regulations promulgated by the Secretary to carry out this subsection first take effect;

(B) contains a complete and detailed inventory of all pre-Act endangered species parts for which the applicant seeks exemption;

(C) is accompanied by such documentation as the Secretary may require to prove that any endangered species part or product claimed by the applicant to be a pre-Act endangered species part is in fact such a part; and

(D) contains such other information as the Secretary deems necessary and appropriate to carry out the purposes of this subsection.

(4) If the Secretary approves any application for exemption made under this subsection, he shall issue to the applicant a certificate of exemption which shall specify—

(A) any prohibition in section 9(a) of this Act which is exempted;

(B) the pre-Act endangered species parts to which the exemption applies;

(C) the period of time during which the exemption is in effect, but no exemption made under this subsection shall have force and effect after the close of the three-year period beginning on the date of issuance of the certificate unless such exemption is renewed under paragraph (8); and

(D) any term or condition prescribed pursuant to paragraph (5) (A) or (B), or both, which the Secretary deems necessary or appropriate.

(5) The Secretary shall prescribe such regulations as he deems necessary and appropriate to carry out the purposes of this subsection. Such regulations may set forth—

(A) terms and conditions which may be imposed on applicants for exemptions under this subsection (including, but not limited to, requirements that applicants register inventories, keep complete sales records, permit duly authorized agents of the Secretary to inspect such inventories and records, and periodically file appropriate reports with the Secretary); and

(B) terms and conditions which may be imposed on any subsequent purchaser of any pre-Act endangered species part covered by an exemption granted under this subsection;

to insure that any such part so exempted is adequately accounted for and not disposed of contrary to the provisions of this Act. No regulation prescribed by the Secretary to carry out the purposes of this subsection shall be subject to section 4(f)(2)(A)(i) of this Act.

(6)(A) Any contract for the sale of pre-Act endangered species parts which is entered into by the Administrator of General Services prior to the effective date of this subsection and pursuant to the notice published in the Federal Register on January 9, 1973, shall not be rendered invalid by virtue of the fact that fulfillment of such contract may be prohibited under section 9(a)(1)(F).

(B) In the event that this paragraph is held invalid, the validity of the remainder of the Act, including the remainder of this subsection, shall not be affected.

(7) Nothing in this subsection shall be construed to—

(A) exonerate any person from any act committed in violation of paragraphs (1)(A), (1)(E), or (1)(F) of section 9(a) prior to the date of enactment of this subsection; or

(B) immunize any person from prosecution for any such act.

(8)(A)(i) Any valid certificate of exemption which was renewed after October 13, 1982, and was in effect on March 31, 1988, shall be deemed to be renewed for a 6-month period beginning on the date of enactment of the Endangered Species Act Amendments of 1988. Any person holding such a certificate may apply to the Secretary for one additional renewal of such certificate for a period not to exceed 5 years beginning on the date of such enactment.

(B) If the Secretary approves any application for renewal of an exemption under this paragraph, he shall issue to the applicant a certificate of renewal of such exemption which shall provide that all terms, conditions, prohibitions, and other regulations made applicable by the previous certificate shall remain in effect during the period of the renewal.

(C) No exemption or renewal of such exemption made under this subsection shall have force and effect after the expiration date of the certificate of renewal of such exemption issued under this paragraph.

(D) No person may, after January 31, 1984, sell or offer for sale in interstate or foreign commerce, any pre-Act finished scrimshaw product unless such person holds a valid certificate of exemption issued by the Secretary under this subsection, and unless such product or the raw material for such product was held by such person on October 13, 1982.

(g) In connection with any action alleging a violation of section 9, any person claiming the benefit of any exemption or permit under this Act shall have the burden of proving that the exemption or permit is applicable, has been granted, and was valid and in force at the time of the alleged violation.

(h) CERTAIN ANTIQUE ARTICLES.—(1) Sections 4(d), 9(a), and 9(c) do not apply to any article which—

(A) is not less than 100 years of age;

(B) is composed in whole or in part of any endangered species or threatened species listed under section 4;

(C) has not been repaired or modified with any part of any such species on or after the date of the enactment of this Act; and

(D) is entered at a port designated under paragraph (3).

(2) Any person who wishes to import an article under the exception provided by this subsection shall submit to the customs officer concerned at the time of entry of the article such documentation as the Secretary of the Treasury, after consultation with the Secretary of the Interior, shall by regulation require as being necessary to establish that the article meets the requirements set forth in paragraph (1) (A), (B), and (C).

(3) The Secretary of the Treasury, after consultation with the Secretary of the Interior, shall designate one port within each customs region at which articles described in paragraph (1) (A), (B), and (C) must be entered into the customs territory of the United States.

(4) Any person who imported, after December 27, 1973, and on or before the date of the enactment of the Endangered Species Act Amendments of 1978, any article described in paragraph (1) which—

(A) was not repaired or modified after the date of importation with any part of any endangered species or threatened species listed under section 4;

(B) was forfeited to the United States before such date of the enactment, or is subject to forfeiture to the United States on such date of enactment, pursuant to the assessment of a civil penalty under section 11; and

(C) is in the custody of the United States on such date of enactment;

may, before the close of the one-year period beginning on such date of enactment make application to the Secretary for return of the article. Application shall be made in such form and manner, and contain such documentation, as the Secretary prescribes. If on the basis of any such application which is timely filed, the Secretary is satisfied that the requirements of this paragraph are met with respect to the article concerned, the Secretary shall return the article to the applicant and the importation of such article shall, on and after the date of return, be deemed to be a lawful importation under this Act.

(i) NONCOMMERCIAL TRANSSHIPMENTS.—Any importation into the United States of fish or wildlife shall, if—

(1) such fish or wildlife was lawfully taken and exported from the country of origin and country of reexport, if any;

(2) such fish or wildlife is in transit or transshipment through any place subject to the jurisdiction of the United States en route to a country where such fish or wildlife may be lawfully imported and received;

(3) the exporter or owner of such fish or wildlife gave explicit instructions not to ship such fish or wildlife through any place subject to the jurisdiction of the United States, or did all that could have reasonably been done to prevent transshipment, and the circumstances leading to the transshipment were beyond the exporter's or owner's control;

(4) the applicable requirements of the Convention have been satisfied; and

(5) such importation is not made in the course of a commercial activity,

be an importation not in violation of any provision of this Act or any regulation issued pursuant to this Act while such fish or wildlife remains in the control of the United States Customs Service.

(j) EXPERIMENTAL POPULATIONS.—(1) For purposes of this subsection, the term "experimental population" means any population (including any offspring arising solely therefrom) authorized by the Secretary for release under paragraph (2), but only when, and at such times as, the population is wholly separate geographically from nonexperimental populations of the same species.

(2)(A) The Secretary may authorize the release (and the related transportation) of any population (including eggs, propagules, or individuals) of an endangered species or a threatened species outside the current range of such species if the Secretary determines that such release will further the conservation of such species.

(B) Before authorizing the release of any population under subparagraph (A), the Secretary shall by regulation identify the population and determine, on the basis of the best available information, whether or not such population is essential to the continued existence of an endangered species or a threatened species.

(C) For the purposes of this Act, each member of an experimental population shall be treated as a threatened species; except that—

(i) solely for purposes of section 7 (other than subsection (a)(1) thereof), an experimental population determined under subparagraph (B) to be not essential to the continued existence of a species shall be treated, except when it occurs in an area within the National Wildlife Refuge System or the National Park System, as a species proposed to be listed under section 4; and

(ii) critical habitat shall not be designated under this Act for any experimental population determined under subparagraph (B) to be not essential to the continued existence of a species.

(3) The Secretary, with respect to populations of endangered species or threatened species that the Secretary authorized, before the date of the enactment of this subsection, for release in geographical areas separate from the other populations of such species, shall determine by regulation which of such populations are an experimen-

tal population for the purposes of this subsection and whether or not each is essential to the continued existence of an endangered species or a threatened species.

PENALTIES AND ENFORCEMENT

SEC. 11. (a) CIVIL PENALTIES.—(1) Any person who knowingly violates, and any person engaged in business as an importer or exporter of fish, wildlife, or plants who violates, any provision of this Act, or any provision of any permit or certificate issued hereunder, or of any regulation issued in order to implement subsection (a)(1)(A), (B), (C), (D), (E), or (F), (a)(2)(A), (B), (C), or (D), (c), (d) (other than regulation relating to recordkeeping or filing of reports), (f), or (g) of section 9 of this Act, may be assessed a civil penalty by the Secretary of not more than $25,000 for each violation. Any person who knowingly violates, and any person engaged in business as an importer or exporter of fish, wildlife, or plants who violates, any provision of any other regulation issued under this Act may be assessed a civil penalty by the Secretary of not more than $12,000 for each such violation. Any person who otherwise violates any provision of this Act, or any regulation, permit, or certificate issued hereunder, may be assessed a civil penalty by the Secretary of not more than $500 for each such violation. No penalty may be assessed under this subsection unless such person is given notice and opportunity for a hearing with respect to such violation. Each violation shall be a separate offense. Any such civil penalty may be remitted or mitigated by the Secretary. Upon any failure to pay a penalty assessed under this subsection, the Secretary may request the Attorney General to institute a civil action in a district court of the United States for any district in which such person is found, resides, or transacts business to collect the penalty and such court shall have jurisdiction to hear and decide any such action. The court shall hear such action on the record made before the Secretary and shall sustain his action if it is supported by substantial evidence on the record considered as a whole.

(2) Hearings held during proceedings for the assessment of civil penalties by paragraph (1) of this subsection shall be conducted in accordance with section 554 of title 5, United States Code. The Secretary may issue subpoenas for the attendance and testimony of witnesses and the production of relevant papers, books, and documents, and administer oaths. Witnesses summoned shall be paid the same fees and mileage that are paid to witnesses in the courts of the United States. In case of contumacy or refusal to obey a subpoena served upon any person pursuant to this paragraph, the district court of the United States for any district in which such person is found or resides or transacts business, upon application by the United States and after notice to such person, shall have jurisdiction to issue an order requiring such person to appear and give testimony before the Secretary or to appear and produce documents before the Secretary, or both, and any failure to obey such order of the court may be punished by such court as a contempt thereof.

(3) Notwithstanding any other provision of this Act, no civil penalty shall be imposed if it can be shown by a preponderance of the

evidence that the defendant committed an act based on a good faith belief that he was acting to protect himself or herself, a member of his or her family, or any other individual from bodily harm, from any endangered or threatened species.

(b) CRIMINAL VIOLATIONS.—(1) Any person who knowingly violates any provision of this Act, of any permit or certificate issued hereunder, or of any regulation issued in order to implement subsection (a)(1)(A), (B), (C), (D), (E), or (F); (a)(2)(A), (B), (C), or (D), (c), (d) (other than a regulation relating to recordkeeping, or filing of reports), (f), or (g) of section 9 of this Act shall, upon conviction, be fined not more than $50,000 or imprisoned for not more than one year, or both. Any person who knowingly violates any provision of any other regulation issued under this Act shall, upon conviction, be fined not more than $25,000 or imprisoned for not more than six months, or both.

(2) The head of any Federal agency which has issued a lease, license, permit, or other agreement authorizing a person to import or export fish, wildlife, or plants, or to operate a quarantine station for imported wildlife, or authorizing the use of Federal lands, including grazing of domestic livestock, to any person who is convicted of a criminal violation of this Act or any regulation, permit, or certificate issued hereunder may immediately modify, suspend, or revoke each lease, license, permit, or other agreement. The Secretary shall also suspend for a period of up to one year, or cancel, any Federal hunting or fishing permits or stamps issued to any person who is convicted of a criminal violation of any provision of this Act or any regulation, permit, or certificate issued hereunder. The United States shall not be liable for the payments of any compensation, reimbursement, or damages in connection with the modification, suspension, or revocation of any leases, licenses permits stamps, or other agreements pursuant to this section.

(3) Notwithstanding any other provision of this Act, it shall be a defense to prosecution under this subsection if the defendant committed the offense based on a good faith belief that he was acting to protect himself or herself, a member of his or her family, or any other individual, from bodily harm from any endangered or threatened species.

(c) DISTRICT COURT JURISDICTION.—The several district courts of the United States; including the courts enumerated in section 460 of title 28, United States Code, shall have jurisdiction over any actions arising under this Act. For the purpose of this Act, American Samoa shall be included within the judicial district of the District Court of the United States for the District of Hawaii.

(d) REWARDS AND CERTAIN INCIDENTAL EXPENSES.—The Secretary or the Secretary of the Treasury shall pay, from sums received as penalties, fines, or forfeitures of property for any violation of this chapter or any regulation issued hereunder (1) a reward to any person who furnishes information which leads to an arrest, a criminal conviction, civil penalty assessment, or forfeiture of property for any violation of this chapter or any regulation issued hereunder, and (2) the reasonable and necessary costs incurred by any person in providing temporary care for any fish, wildlife, or plant pending the disposition of any civil or criminal proceeding alleging a violation of this chapter with respect to that fish, wildlife, or plant. The amount of the reward, if any, is to be designated by the Secretary or the Secretary of the Treasury, as appropriate. Any officer or employee of the United States or any State or local government who furnishes information or renders service in the performance of his official duties is ineligible for payment under this subsection. Whenever the balance of sums received under this section and section 6(d) of the Act of November 16, 1981 (16 U.S.C. 3375(d)) as penalties or fines, or from forfeitures of property, exceed $500,000, the Secretary of the Treasury shall deposit an amount equal to such excess balance in the cooperative endangered species conservation fund established under section 6(i) of this Act.

(e) ENFORCEMENT.—(1) The provisions of this Act and any regulations or permits issued pursuant thereto shall be enforced by the Secretary, the Secretary of the Treasury, or the Secretary of the Department in which the Coast Guard is operating, or all such Secretaries. Each such Secretary may utilize by agreement, with or without reimbursement, the personnel, services, and facilities of any other Federal agency or any State agency for purposes of enforcing this Act.

(2) The judges of the district courts of the United States and the United States magistrates may within their respective jurisdictions, upon proper oath or affirmation showing probable cause, issue such warrants or other process as may be required for enforcement of this Act and any regulation issued thereunder.

(3) Any person authorized by the Secretary, the Secretary of the Treasury, or the Secretary of the Department in which the Coast Guard is operating, to enforce this Act may detain for inspection and inspect any package, crate, or other container, including its contents, and all accompanying documents, upon importation or exportation. Such persons may make arrests without a warrant for any violation of this Act if he has reasonable grounds to believe that the person to be arrested is committing the violation in his presence or view and may execute and serve any arrest warrant, search warrant, or other warrant or civil or criminal process issued by any officer or court of competent jurisdiction for enforcement of this Act. Such person so authorized may search and seize, with or without a warrant, as authorized by law. Any fish, wildlife, property, or item so seized shall be held by any person authorized by the Secretary, the Secretary of the Treasury, or the Secretary of the Department in which the Coast Guard is operating pending disposition of civil or criminal proceedings, or the institution of an action in rem for forfeiture of such fish, wildlife, property, or item pursuant to paragraph (4) of the subsection; except that the Secretary may, in lieu of holding such fish, wildlife, property, or item, permit the owner or consignee to post a bond or other surety satisfactory to the Secretary, but upon forfeiture of any such property to the United States, or the abandonment or waiver of any claim to any such property, it shall be disposed of (other than by sale to the general public) by the Secretary in such a manner, consistent with the purposes of this Act, as the Secretary shall by regulation prescribe.

(4)(A) All fish or wildlife or plants taken, possessed, sold, purchased, offered for sale or purchase, transported, delivered, received, carried, shipped, exported, or imported contrary to the provisions of this Act, any regulation made pursuant thereto, or any permit or certificate issued hereunder shall be subject to forfeiture to the United States.

(B) All guns, traps, nets, and other equipment, vessels, vehicles, aircraft, and other means of transportation used to aid the taking, possessing, selling, purchasing, offering for sale or purchase, transporting, delivering, receiving, carrying, shipping, exporting, or importing of any fish or wildlife or plants in violation of this Act, any regulation made pursuant thereto, or any permit or certificate issued thereunder shall be subject to forfeiture to the United States upon conviction of a criminal violation pursuant to section 11(b)(1) of this Act.

(5) All provisions of law relating to the seizure, forfeiture, and condemnation of a vessel for violation of the customs laws, the disposition of such vessel or the proceeds from the sale thereof, and the remission or mitigation of such forfeiture, shall apply to the seizures and forfeitures incurred, or alleged to have been incurred, under the provisions of this Act, insofar as such provisions of law are applicable and not inconsistent with the provisions of this Act; except that all powers, rights, and duties conferred or imposed by the customs laws upon any officer or employee of the Treasury Department shall, for the purposes of this Act, be exercised or performed by the Secretary or by such persons as he may designate.

(6) The Attorney General of the United States may seek to enjoin any person who is alleged to be in violation of any provision of this Act or regulation issued under authority thereof.

(f) Regulations.—The Secretary, the Secretary of the Treasury, and the Secretary of the Department in which the Coast Guard is operating, are authorized to promulgate such regulations as may be appropriate to enforce this Act, and charge reasonable fees for expenses to the Government connected with permits or certificates authorized by this Act including processing applications and reasonable inspections, and with the transfer, board, handling, or storage of fish or wildlife or plants and evidentiary items seized and forfeited under this Act. All such fees collected pursuant to this subsection shall be deposited in the Treasury to the credit of the appropriation which is current and chargeable for the cost of furnishing the services. Appropriated funds may be expended pending reimbursement from parties in interest.

(g) Citizen Suits.—(1) Except as provided in paragraph (2) of this subsection any person may commence a civil suit on his own behalf—

(A) to enjoin any person, including the United States and any other governmental instrumentality or agency (to the extent permitted by the eleventh amendment to the Constitution), who is alleged to be in violation of any provision of this Act or regulation issued under the authority thereof; or

(B) to compel the Secretary to apply, pursuant to section 6(g)(2)(B)(ii) of this Act, the prohibitions set forth in or authorized pursuant to section 4(d) or section 9(a)(1)(B) of this Act with respect to the taking of any resident endangered species or threatened species within any State; or

(C) against the Secretary where there is alleged a failure of the Secretary to perform any act or duty under section 4 which is not discretionary with the Secretary.

The district courts shall have jurisdiction, without regard to the amount in controversy or the citizenship of the parties, to enforce any such provision or regulation or to order the Secretary to perform such act or duty, as the case may be. In any civil suit commenced under subparagraph (B) the district court shall compel the Secretary to apply the prohibition sought if the court finds that the allegation that an emergency exists is supported by substantial evidence.

(2)(A) No action may be commenced under subparagraph (1)(A) of this section—

(i) prior to sixty days after written notice of the violation has been given to the Secretary, and to any alleged violator of any such provision or regulation;

(ii) if the Secretary has commenced action to impose a penalty pursuant to subsection (a) of this section; or

(iii) if the United States has commenced and is diligently prosecuting a criminal action in a court of the United States or a State to redress a violation of any such provision or regulation.

(B) No action may be commenced under subparagraph (1)(B) of this section—

(i) prior to sixty days after written notice has been given to the Secretary setting forth the reasons why an emergency is thought to exist with respect to an endangered species or a threatened species in the State concerned; or

(ii) if the Secretary has commenced and is diligently prosecuting action under section 6(g)(2)(B)(ii) of this Act to determine whether any such emergency exists.

(C) No action may be commenced under subparagraph (1)(C) of this section prior to sixty days after written notice has been given to the Secretary; except that such action may be brought immediately after such notification in the case of an action under this section respecting an emergency posing a significant risk to the well-being of any species of fish or wildlife or plants.

(3)(A) Any suit under this subsection may be brought in the judicial district in which the violation occurs.

(B) In any such suit under this subsection in which the United States is not a party, the Attorney General, at the request of the Secretary, may intervene on behalf of the United States as a matter of right.

(4) The court, in issuing any final order in any suit brought pursuant to paragraph (1) of this subsection, may award costs of litigation (including reasonable attorney and expert witness fees) to any party, whenever the court determines such award is appropriate.

(5) The injunctive relief provided by this subsection shall not restrict any right which any person (or class of persons) may have under any statute or common law to seek enforcement of any standard or limitation or to seek any other relief (including relief against the Secretary or a State agency).

(h) Coordination With Other Laws.—The Secretary of Agriculture and the Secretary shall provide for appropriate coordination of the administration of this Act with the administration of the animal quarantine laws (21 U.S.C. 101–105, 111–135b, and 612–614) and section 306 of the Tariff Act of 1930 (19 U.S.C. 1306). Nothing in this Act or any amendment made by this Act shall be construed as superseding or limiting in any manner the functions of the Secretary of Agriculture under any other law relating to prohibited or restricted importations or possession of animals and other articles and no proceeding or determination under this Act shall preclude any proceeding or be considered determinative of any issue of fact or law in any proceeding under any Act administered by the Secretary of Agriculture. Nothing in this Act shall be construed as superseding or limiting in any manner the functions and responsibilities of the Secretary of the Treasury under the Tariff Act of 1930, including, without limitation, section 527 of that Act (19 U.S.C. 1527), relating to the importation of wildlife taken, killed, possessed, or exported to the United States in violation of the laws or regulations of a foreign country.

### ENDANGERED PLANTS

SEC. 12. The Secretary of the Smithsonian Institution, in conjunction with other affected agencies, is authorized and directed to review (1) species of plants which are now or may become endangered, or threatened and (2) methods of adequately conserving such species, and to report to Congress, within one year after the date of the enactment of this Act, the results of such review including recommendations for new legislation or the amendment of existing legislation.

### CONFORMING AMENDMENTS

SEC. 13. (a) Subsection 4(c) of the Act of October 15, 1966 (80 Stat. 928, 16 U.S.C. 668dd(c)), is further amended by revising the second sentence thereof to read as follows: "With the exception of endangered species and threatened species listed by the Secretary pursuant to section 4 of the Endangered Species Act of 1973 in States wherein a cooperative agreement does not exist pursuant to section 6(c) of that Act, nothing in this Act shall be construed to authorize the Secretary to control or regulate hunting or fishing of resident fish and wildlife on lands not within the system."

(b) Subsection 10(a) of the Migratory Bird Conservation Act (45 Stat. 1224, 16 U.S.C. 715i(a)) and subsection 401(a) of the Act of June 15, 1935 (49 Stat. 383, 16 U.S.C. 715s(a)) are each amended by striking out "threatened with extinction," and inserting in lieu thereof the following: "listed pursuant to section 4 of the Endangered Species Act of 1973 as endangered species or threatened species."

(c) Section 7(a)(1) of the Land and Water Conservation Fund Act of 1965 (16 U.S.C. 4601-9(a)(1)) is amended by striking out:

> "THREATENED SPECIES.—For any national area which may be authorized for the preservation of species of fish or wildlife that are threatened with extinction." and inserting in lieu thereof the following:
>
> "ENDANGERED SPECIES AND THREATENED SPECIES.—For lands, waters, or interests therein, the acquisition of which is authorized under section 5(a) of the Endangered Species Act of 1973, needed for the purpose of conserving endangered or threatened species of fish or wildlife or plants."

(d) The first sentence of section 2 of the Act of September 28, 1962, as amended (76 Stat. 653, 16 U.S.C. 460k-1), is amended to read as follows:

"The Secretary is authorized to acquire areas of land, or interests therein, which are suitable for—

"(1) incidental fish and wildlife-oriented recreational development;

"(2) the protection of natural resources;

"(3) the conservation of endangered species or threatened species listed by the Secretary pursuant to section 4 of the Endangered Species Act of 1973; or

"(4) carrying out two or more of the purposes set forth in paragraphs (1) through (3) of this section, and are adjacent to, or within, the said conservation areas, except that the acquisition of any land or interest therein pursuant to this section shall be accomplished only with such funds as may be appropriated therefor by the Congress or donated for such purposes, but such property shall not be acquired with funds obtained from the sale of Federal migratory bird hunting stamps."

(e) The Marine Mammal Protection Act of 1972 (16 U.S.C. 1361–1407) is amended—

(1) by striking out "Endangered Species Conservation Act of 1969" in section 3(l)(B) thereof and inserting in lieu thereof the following: "Endangered Species Act of 1973";

(2) by striking out "pursuant to the Endangered Species Conservation Act of 1969" in section 101(a)(3)(B) thereof and inserting in lieu thereof the following: "or threatened species pursuant to the Endangered Species Act of 1973";

(3) by striking out "endangered under the Endangered Species Conservation Act of 1969" in section 102(b)(3) thereof and inserting in lieu thereof the following: "an endangered species or threatened species pursuant to the Endangered Species Act of 1973"; and

(4) by striking out "of the Interior and revisions of the Endangered Species List, authorized by the Endangered Species Conservation Act of 1969," in section 202(a)(6) thereof and inserting in lieu thereof the following: "such revisions of the endangered species list and threatened species list published pursuant to section 4(c)(1) of the Endangered Species Act of 1973".

(f) Section 2(l) of the Federal Environmental Pesticide Control Act of 1972 (Public Law 92–516) is amended by striking out the words "by the Secretary of the Interior under Public Law 91–135" and inserting in lieu thereof the words "or threatened by the Secretary pursuant to the Endangered Species Act of 1973".

REPEALER

SEC. 14. The Endangered Species Conservation Act of 1969 (sections 1 through 3 of the Act of October 15, 1966, and sections 1 through 6 of the Act of December 5, 1969; 16 U.S.C. 668aa—668cc–6), is repealed.

AUTHORIZATION OF APPROPRIATIONS

SEC. 15. (a) IN GENERAL.—Except as provided in subsections (b), (c), and (d), there are authorized to be appropriated—

(1) not to exceed $35,000,000 for fiscal year 1988, $36,500,000 for fiscal year 1989, $38,000,000 for fiscal year 1990, $39,500,000 for fiscal year 1991, and $41,500,000 for fiscal year 1992 to enable the Department of the Interior to carry out such functions and responsibilities as it may have been given under this Act;

(2) not to exceed $5,750,000 for fiscal year 1988, $6,250,000 for each of fiscal years 1989 and 1990, and $6,750,000 for each of fiscal years 1991 and 1992 to enable the Department of Commerce to carry out such functions and responsibilities as it may have been given under this Act; and

(3) not to exceed $2,200,000 for fiscal year 1988, $2,400,000 for each of fiscal years 1989 and 1990, and $2,600,000 for each of fiscal years 1991 and 1992, to enable the Department of Agriculture to carry out its functions and responsibilities with respect to the enforcement of this Act and the Convention which pertain to the importation or exportation of plants.

(b) EXEMPTIONS FROM ACT.—There are authorized to be appropriated to the Secretary to assist him and the Endangered Species Committee in carrying out their functions under section 7 (e), (g) and (h) not to exceed $600,000 for each for fiscal years 1988, 1989, 1990, 1991, and 1992.

(c) CONVENTION IMPLEMENTATION.—There are authorized to be appropriated to the Department of the Interior for purposes of carrying out section 8A(e) not to exceed $400,000 for each of fiscal years 1988, 1989, and 1990, and $500,000 for each of fiscal years 1991 and 1992, and such sums shall remain available until expended.

EFFECTIVE DATE

SEC. 16. This Act shall take effect on the date of its enactment.

MARINE MAMMAL PROTECTION ACT OF 1972

SEC. 17. Except as otherwise provided in this Act, no provision of this Act shall take precedence over any more restrictive conflicting provision of the Marine Mammal Protection Act of 1972.

ANNUAL COST ANALYSIS BY THE FISH AND WILDLIFE SERVICE

SEC. 18. On or before January 15, 1990, and each January 15 thereafter, the Secretary of the Interior, acting through the Fish and Wildlife Service, shall submit to the Congress an annual report covering the preceding fiscal year which shall contain—

(1) an accounting on a species by species basis of all reasonably unidentifiable Federal expenditures made primarily for the conservation of endangered or threatened species pursuant to this Act; and

(2) an accounting on a species by species basis for all reasonably identifiable expenditures made primarily for the conservation of endangered or threatened species pursuant to this Act by states receiving grants under section 6.

☆ U. S. Government Printing Office: 1990 - 258-990 (20159)

# APPENDIX D

# ENDANGERED AND THREATENED WILDLIFE AND PLANTS

50 CFR 17.11 and 17.12

July 15, 1991

**Title 50—Wildlife and Fisheries**

## PART 17—ENDANGERED AND THREATENED WILDLIFE AND PLANTS

* * * * *

### Subpart B—Lists

**Source:** 48 FR 34182, July 27, 1983, unless otherwise noted.

**§ 17.11 Endangered and threatened wildlife.**

(a) The list in this section contains the names of all species of wildlife which have been determined by the Services to be Endangered or Threatened. It also contains the names of species of wildlife treated as Endangered or Threatened because they are sufficiently similar in appearance to Endangered or Threatened species (see § 17.50 *et seq.*).

(b) The columns entitled "Common Name," "Scientific Name," and "Vertebrate Population Where Endangered or Threatened" define the species of wildlife within the meaning of the Act. Thus, differently classified geographic populations of the same vertebrate subspecies or species shall be identified by their differing geographic boundaries, even though the other two columns are identical. The term "Entire" means that all populations throughout the present range of a vertebrate species are listed. Although common names are included, they cannot be relied upon for identification of any specimen, since they may vary greatly in local usage. The Services shall use the most recently accepted scientific name. In cases in which confusion might arise, a synonym(s) will be provided in parentheses. The Services shall rely to the extent practicable on the *International Code of Zoological Nomenclature.*

(c) In the "Status" column the following symbols are used: "E" for Endangered, "T" for Threatened, and "E [or T] (S/A)" for similarity of appearance species.

(d) The other data in the list are nonregulatory in nature and are provided for the information of the reader. In the annual revision and compilation of this title, the following information may be amended without public notice: the spelling of species' names, historical range, footnotes, references to certain other applicable portions of this title, synonyms, and more current names. In any of these revised entries, neither the species, as defined in paragraph (b) of this section, nor its status may be changed without following the procedures of Part 424 of this title.

(e) The "historic range" indicates the known general distribution of the species or subspecies as reported in the current scientific literature. The present distribution may be greatly reduced from this historic range. This column does not imply any limitation on the application of the prohibitions in the Act or implementing rules. Such prohibitions apply to all individuals of the species, wherever found.

(f)(1) A footnote to the **Federal Register** publication(s) listing or reclassifying a species is indicated under the column "When listed." Footnote numbers to §§ 17.11 and 17.12 are in the same numerical sequence, since plants and animals may be listed in the same **Federal Register** document. That document, at least since 1973, includes a statement indicating the basis for the listing, as well as the effective date(s) of said listing.

(2) The "Special rules" and "Critical habitat" columns provide a cross reference to other sections in Parts 17, 222, 226, or 227. The "Special rules" column will also be used to cite the special rules that describe experimental populations and determine if they are essential or nonessential. Separate listing will be made for experimental populations, and the status column will include the following symbols: "XE" for an essential experimental population and "XN" for a nonessential experimental population. The term "NA" (not applicable) appearing in either of these two columns indicates that there are no special rules and/or critical habitat for that particular species. However, all other appropriate rules in Parts 17, 217 through 227, and 402 still apply to that species. In addition, there may be other rules in this title that relate to such wildlife, e.g., port-of-entry requirements. It is not intended that the references in the "Special rules" column list all the regulations of the two Services which might apply to the species or to the regulations of other Federal agencies or State or local governments.

(g) The listing of a particular taxon includes all lower taxonomic units. For example, the genus *Hylobates* (gibbons) is listed as Endangered throughout its entire range (China, India, and SE Asia); consequently, all species, subspecies, and populations of that genus are considered listed as Endangered for the purposes of the Act. In 1978 (43 FR 6230–6233) the species *Haliaeetus leucocephalus* (bald eagle) was listed as Threatened in "USA (WA, OR, MN, WI, MI)" rather than its entire population; thus, all individuals of the bald eagle found in those five States are considered listed as Threatened for the purposes of the Act.

(h) The "List of Endangered and Threatened Wildlife" is provided below:

**Editorial Note:** This is a compilation and special reprint of 50 CFR 17.11 and 17.12 and is current as of the date shown on the cover. Minor changes and corrections to the October 1, 1990, compilation of 50 CFR have been incorporated in this printing, as well as all published final rules that have subsequently appeared in the **Federal Register.** Otherwise no entry in these lists has been significantly affected. This list has been prepared by the staff of the Division of Endangered Species, U.S. Fish and Wildlife Service, Washington, D.C. 20240. Readers are requested to advise the Service of any errors in this list. Copies are available from the Publication Unit, U.S. Fish and Wildlife Service, 130-ARLSQ, Washington, D.C. 20240.

**2**

| Species: Common name | Species: Scientific name | Historic range | Vertebrate population where endangered or threatened | Status | When listed | Critical habitat | Special rules |
|---|---|---|---|---|---|---|---|
| **MAMMALS** | | | | | | | |
| Anoa, lowland | *Bubalus depressicornis* (=*B. anoa depressicornis*). | Indonesia | Entire | E | 3 | NA | NA |
| Anoa, mountain | *Bubalus quarlesi* (=*B. anoa quarlesi*) | ......do | ......do | E | 15 | NA | NA |
| Antelope, giant sable | *Hippotragus niger variani* | Angola | ......do | E | 15 | NA | NA |
| Argali | *Ovis ammon hodgsoni* | China (Tibet, Himalayas) | ......do | E | 15 | NA | NA |
| Armadillo, giant | *Priodontes maximus* (=*giganteus*) | Venezuela and Guyana to Argentina | ......do | E | 15 | NA | NA |
| Armadillo, pink fairy | *Chlamyphorus truncatus* | Argentina | ......do | E | 3 | NA | NA |
| Ass, African wild | *Equus asinus* (=*africanus*) | Somalia, Sudan, Ethiopia | Somalia, Sudan, Ethiopia. | E | 3, 22 | NA | NA |
| Ass, Asian wild (=kulan, onager) | *Equus hemionus* | Southwestern and Central Asia | Entire | E | 3 | NA | NA |
| Avahi | *Avahi* (=*Lichanotus*) *laniger* (=entire genus). | Malagasy Republic (=Madagascar) | ......do | E | 3 | NA | NA |
| Aye-Aye | *Daubentonia madagascariensis* | Malagasy Republic (=Madagascar) | ......do | E | 3 | NA | NA |
| Babirusa | *Babyrousa babyrussa* | Indonesia | ......do | E | 15 | NA | NA |
| Baboon, gelada | *Theropithecus gelada* | Ethiopia | ......do | T | 16 | NA | 17.40(c) |
| Bandicoot, barred | *Perameles bougainville* | Australia | ......do | E | 4 | NA | NA |
| Bandicoot, desert | *Perameles eremiana* | ......do | ......do | E | 6 | NA | NA |
| Bandicoot, lesser rabbit | *Macrotis leucura* | ......do | ......do | E | 4 | NA | NA |
| Bandicoot, pig-footed | *Chaeropus ecaudatus* | ......do | ......do | E | 4 | NA | NA |
| Bandicoot, rabbit | *Macrotis lagotis* | ......do | ......do | E | 4 | NA | NA |
| Banteng | *Bos javanicus* (=*banteng*) | Southeast Asia | ......do | E | 3 | NA | NA |
| Bat, Bulmer's fruit (flying fox) | *Aproteles bulmerae* | Papua New Guinea | ......do | E | 139 | NA | NA |
| Bat, bumblebee | *Craseonycteris thonglongyai* | Thailand | ......do | E | 139 | NA | NA |
| Bat, gray | *Myotis grisescens* | Central and Southeastern U.S.A | ......do | E | 13 | NA | NA |
| Bat, Hawaiian hoary | *Lasiurus cinereus semotus* | U.S.A. (HI) | ......do | E | 2 | NA | NA |
| Bat, Indiana | *Myotis sodalis* | Eastern and Midwestern U.S.A. | ......do | E | 1 | 17.95(a) | NA |
| Bat, little Mariana fruit | *Pteropus tokudae* | Western Pacific Ocean: U.S.A. (Guam) | ......do | E | 156 | NA | NA |
| Bat, Mariana fruit | *Pteropus mariannus mariannus* | Western Pacific Ocean: U.S.A. (Guam, Rota, Tinian, Saipan, Agiguan). | Guam | E | 156 | NA | NA |
| Bat, Mexican long-nosed | *Leptonycteris nivalis* | U.S.A. (NM, TX), Mexico, Central America. | Entire | E | 336 | NA | NA |
| Bat, Ozark big-eared | *Plecotus townsendii ingens* | U.S.A. (MO, OK, AR) | ......do | E | 85 | NA | NA |
| Bat, Rodrigues fruit (flying fox) | *Pteropus rodricensis* | Indian Ocean: Rodrigues Island | ......do | E | 139 | NA | NA |
| Bat, Sanborn's long-nosed | *Leptonycteris sanborni* (=*yerbabuenae*). | U.S.A. (AZ, NM), Mexico, Central America. | ......do | E | 336 | NA | NA |
| Bat, Singapore roundleaf horseshoe | *Hipposideros ridleyi* | Malaysia | ......do | E | 139 | NA | NA |
| Bat, Virginia big-eared | *Plecotus townsendii virginianus* | U.S.A. (KY, NC, WV, VA) | ......do | E | 85 | 17.95(a) | NA |
| Bear, Baluchistan | *Ursus thibetanus gedrosianus* | Iran, Pakistan | ......do | E | 233 | NA | NA |
| Bear, brown | *Ursus arctos pruinosus* | China (Tibet) | ......do | E | 15 | NA | NA |
| Do | *Ursus arctos arctos* | Palearctic | Italy | E | 15, 15A | NA | NA |
| Bear, brown or grizzly | *Ursus arctos* (=*U.a. horribilis*) | Holarctic | U.S.A.—48 conterminous States. | T | 1, 2D, 9 | NA | 17.40(b) |
| Do | *Ursus arctos* (=*U.a. nelsoni*) | ......do | Mexico | E | 3 | NA | NA |
| Beaver | *Castor fiber birulai* | Mongolia | Entire | E | 15 | NA | NA |
| Bison, wood | *Bison bison athabascae* | Canada, Northwestern U.S.A | Canada | E | 3 | NA | NA |
| Bobcat | *Felis rufus escuinapae* | Central Mexico | Entire | E | 15 | NA | NA |
| Bontebok (antelope) | *Damaliscus dorcas dorcas* | South Africa | ......do | E | 15 | NA | NA |
| Camel, Bactrian | *Camelus bactrianus* (=*ferus*) | Mongolia, China | ......do | E | 15 | NA | NA |

| | | | | | | | |
|---|---|---|---|---|---|---|---|
| Caribou, woodland | *Rangifer tarandus caribou* | Canada, U.S.A. (AK, ID, ME, MI, MN, MT, NH, VT, WA, WI). | Canada (that part of S.E. Brit. Col. bounded by the Can.-USA border, Columbia R., Kootenay R., Kootenay L., and Kootenai R.), U.S.A. (ID, WA). | E | 128E, 136E, 143 | NA | NA |
| Cat, Andean | *Felis jacobita* | Chile, Peru, Bolivia, Argentina | Entire | E | 15 | NA | NA |
| Cat, black-footed | *Felis nigripes* | Southern Africa | do | E | 15 | NA | NA |
| Cat, flat-headed | *Felis planiceps* | Malaysia, Indonesia | do | E | 15 | NA | NA |
| Cat, Iriomote | *Felis (Mayailurus) iriomotensis* | Japan (Iriomote Island, Ryukyu Islands) | do | E | 50 | NA | NA |
| Cat, leopard | *Felis bengalensis bengalensis* | India, Southeast Asia | do | E | 15 | NA | NA |
| Cat, marbled | *Felis marmorata* | Nepal, Southeast Asia, Indonesia | do | E | 15 | NA | NA |
| Cat, Pakistan sand | *Felis margarita scheffeli* | Pakistan | do | E | 139 | NA | NA |
| Cat, Temminck's (=golden cat) | *Felis temmincki* | Nepal, China, Southeast Asia, Indonesia (Sumatra). | do | E | 15 | NA | NA |
| Cat, tiger | *Felis tigrinus* | Costa Rica to northern Argentina | do | E | 5 | NA | NA |
| Chamois, Apennine | *Rupicapra rupicapra ornata* | Italy | do | E | 15 | NA | NA |
| Cheetah | *Acinonyx jubatus* | Africa to India | do | E | 3, 5 | NA | NA |
| Chimpanzee | *Pan troglodytes* | Africa-see 17.40(c)(3) | Wherever found in the wild. | E | 16, 376 | NA | NA |
| Do | do | do | Wherever found in captivity. | T | 16, 376 | NA | 17.40(c) |
| Chimpanzee, pygmy | *Pan paniscus* | Zaire | Entire | E | 16, 376 | NA | NA |
| Chinchilla | *Chinchilla brevicaudata boliviana* | Bolivia | do | E | 15 | NA | NA |
| Civet, Malabar large-spotted | *Viverra megaspila civettina* | India | do | E | 50 | NA | NA |
| Cochito (=Gulf of California harbor porpoise). | *Phocoena sinus* | Mexico (Gulf of California) | do | E | 169 | NA | NA |
| Cougar, eastern | *Felis concolor couguar* | Eastern North America | do | E | 6 | NA | NA |
| Deer, Bactrian | *Cervus elaphus bactrianus* | U.S.S.R., Afghanistan | do | E | 50 | NA | NA |
| Deer, Barbary | *Cervus elaphus barbarus* | Morocco, Tunisia, Algeria | do | E | 50 | NA | NA |
| Deer, Bawean | *Axis (=Cervus) porcinus kuhli* | Indonesia | do | E | 3 | NA | NA |
| Deer, Cedros Island mule | *Odocoileus hemionus cedrosensis* | Mexico (Cedros Island) | do | E | 10 | NA | NA |
| Deer, Columbian white-tailed | *Odocoileus virginianus leucurus* | U.S.A. (WA, OR) | do | E | 1 | NA | NA |
| Deer, Corsican red | *Cervus elaphus corsicanus* | Corsica, Sardinia | do | E | 50 | NA | NA |
| Deer, Eld's brow-antlered | *Cervus eldi* | India to Southeast Asia | do | E | 3 | NA | NA |
| Deer, Formosan sika | *Cervus nippon taiouanus* | Taiwan | do | E | 50 | NA | NA |
| Deer, hog | *Axis (=Cervus) porcinus annamiticus* | Thailand, Indochina | do | E | 15 | NA | NA |
| Deer, key | *Odocoileus virginianus clavium* | U.S.A. (FL) | do | E | 1 | NA | NA |
| Deer, marsh | *Blastocerus dichotomus* | Argentina, Uruguay, Paraguay, Bolivia, Brazil. | do | E | 3 | NA | NA |
| Deer, McNeill's | *Cervus elaphus macneilli* | China (Sinkiang, Tibet) | do | E | 3 | NA | NA |
| Deer, musk | *Moschus* spp. (all species) | Central and East Asia | Afghanistan, Bhutan, Burma, China (Tibet, Yunnan), India, Nepal, Pakistan, Sikkim. | E | 15 | NA | NA |
| Deer, North China sika | *Cervus nippon mandarinus* | China (Shantung and Chihli Provinces) | Entire | E | 50 | NA | NA |
| Deer, pampas | *Ozotoceros bezoarticus* | Brazil, Argentina, Uruguay, Bolivia, Paraguay. | do | E | 15 | NA | NA |
| Deer, Persian fallow | *Dama dama mesopotamica* | Iraq, Iran | do | E | 3 | NA | NA |
| Deer, Philippine | *Axis (=Cervus) porcinus calamianensis.* | Philippines (Calamian Islands) | do | E | 15 | NA | NA |
| Deer, Ryukyu sika | *Cervus nippon keramae* | Japan (Ryukyu Islands) | do | E | 50 | NA | NA |
| Deer, Shansi sika | *Cervus nippon grassianus* | China (Shansi Province) | do | E | 50 | NA | NA |
| Deer, South China sika | *Cervus nippon kopschi* | Southern China | do | E | 50 | NA | NA |

4

| Species | | Historic range | Vertebrate population where endangered or threatened | Status | When listed | Critical habitat | Special rules |
|---|---|---|---|---|---|---|---|
| Common name | Scientific name | | | | | | |
| Deer, swamp (=barasingha) | *Cervus duvauceli* | India, Nepal | ......do | E | 3 | NA | NA |
| Deer, Visayan | *Cervus alfredi* | Philippines | ......do | E | 320 | NA | NA |
| Deer, Yarkand | *Cervus elaphus yarkandensis* | China (Sinkiang) | ......do | E | 50 | NA | NA |
| Dhole (=Asiatic wild dog) | *Cuon alpinus* | U.S.S.R., Korea, China, India, Southeast Asia. | ......do | E | 3 | NA | NA |
| Dibbler | *Antechinus apicalis* | Australia | ......do | E | 4 | NA | NA |
| Dog, African wild | *Lycaon pictus* | Sub-Saharan Africa | ......do | E | 139 | NA | NA |
| Dolphin, Chinese river (=whitefin) | *Lipotes vexillifer* | China | ......do | E | 350 | NA | NA |
| Dolphin, Indus River | *Platanista minor* | Pakistan (Indus R. and tributaries) | ......do | E | 417 | NA | NA |
| Drill | *Papio leucophaeus* | Equatorial West Africa | ......do | E | 16 | NA | NA |
| Dugong | *Dugong dugon* | East Africa to southern Japan, including U.S.A. (Trust Territories). | Entire, except U.S.A.. | E | 4 | NA | NA |
| Duiker, Jentink's | *Cephalophus jentinki* | Sierra Leone, Liberia, Ivory Coast | Entire | E | 50 | NA | NA |
| Eland, Western giant | *Taurotragus derbianus derbianus* | Senegal to Ivory Coast | ......do | E | 50 | NA | NA |
| Elephant, African | *Loxodonta africana* | Africa | ......do | T | 40 | NA | 17.40(e) |
| Elephant, Asian | *Elephas maximus* | South-central and Southeast Asia | ......do | E | 15 | NA | NA |
| Ferret, black-footed | *Mustela nigripes* | Western U.S.A., Western Canada | ......do | E | 1, 3 | NA | NA |
| Fox, Northern swift | *Vulpes velox hebes* | U.S.A. (northern plains), Canada | Canada | E | 3 | NA | NA |
| Fox, San Joaquin kit | *Vulpes macrotis mutica* | U.S.A. (CA) | Entire | E | 1 | NA | NA |
| Fox, Simien | *Canis (Simenia) simensis* | Ethiopia | ......do | E | 50 | NA | NA |
| Gazelle, Arabian | *Gazella gazella* | Arabian Peninsula, Palestine, Sinai | ......do | E | 50 | NA | NA |
| Gazelle, Clark's (=Dibatag) | *Ammodorcas clarkei* | Somalia, Ethiopia | ......do | E | 3 | NA | NA |
| Gazelle, Cuvier's | *Gazella cuvieri* | Morocco, Algeria, Tunisia | ......do | E | 3 | NA | NA |
| Gazelle, Mhorr | *Gazella dama mhorr* | Morocco | ......do | E | 3 | NA | NA |
| Gazelle, Moroccan (=Dorcas) | *Gazella dorcas massaesyla* | Morocco, Algeria, Tunisia | ......do | E | 3 | NA | NA |
| Gazelle, Pelzeln's | *Gazella dorcas pelzelni* | Somalia | ......do | E | 50 | NA | NA |
| Gazelle, Rio de Oro Dama | *Gazella dama lozanoi* | Western Sahara | ......do | E | 3 | NA | NA |
| Gazelle, sand | *Gazella subgutturosa marica* | Jordan, Arabian Peninsula | ......do | E | 50 | NA | NA |
| Gazelle, Saudi Arabian | *Gazella dorcas saudiya* | Israel, Iraq, Jordan, Syria, Arabian Peninsula. | ......do | E | 50 | NA | NA |
| Gazelle, slender-horned (=Rhim) | *Gazella leptoceros* | Sudan, Egypt, Algeria, Libya | ......do | E | 3 | NA | NA |
| Gibbons | *Hylobates* spp. (including *Nomascus*) | China, India, Southeast Asia | ......do | E | 3, 15 | NA | NA |
| Goat, wild (=Chiltan markhor) | *Capra aegagrus (=falconeri chiltanensis).* | Southwestern Asia | Chiltan Range of west-central Pakistan. | E | 15 | NA | NA |
| Goral | *Nemorhaedus goral* | East Asia | Entire | E | 15 | NA | NA |
| Gorilla | *Gorilla gorilla* | Central and Western Africa | ......do | E | 3 | NA | NA |
| Hare, hispid | *Caprolagus hispidus* | India, Nepal, Bhutan | ......do | E | 15 | NA | NA |
| Hartebeest, Swayne's | *Alcelaphus buselaphus swaynei* | Ethiopia, Somalia | ......do | E | 3, 50 | NA | NA |
| Hartebeest, Tora | *Alcelaphus buselaphus tora* | Ethiopia, Sudan, Egypt | ......do | E | 50 | NA | NA |
| Hog, pygmy | *Sus salvanius* | India, Nepal, Bhutan, Sikkim | ......do | E | 3 | NA | NA |
| Horse, Przewalski's | *Equus przewalskii* | Mongolia, China | ......do | E | 15 | NA | NA |
| Huemul, North Andean | *Hippocamelus antisensis* | Ecuador, Peru, Chile, Bolivia, Argentina | ......do | E | 15 | NA | NA |
| Huemul, South Andean | *Hippocamelus bisulcus* | Chile, Argentina | ......do | E | 15 | NA | NA |
| Hutia, Cabrera's | *Capromys angelcabrerai* | Cuba | ......do | E | 233 | NA | NA |
| Hutia, dwarf | *Capromys nana* | ......do | ......do | E | 233 | NA | NA |
| Hutia, large-eared | *Capromys auritus* | ......do | ......do | E | 233 | NA | NA |
| Hutia, little earth | *Capromys sanfelipensis* | ......do | ......do | E | 233 | NA | NA |
| Hyena, Barbary | *Hyaena hyaena barbara* | Morocco, Algeria, Tunisia | ......do | E | 3 | NA | NA |
| Hyena, brown | *Hyaena brunnea* | Southern Africa | ......do | E | 3 | NA | NA |
| Ibex, Pyrenean | *Capra pyrenaica pyrenaica* | Spain | ......do | E | 3 | NA | NA |
| Ibex, Walia | *Capra walie* | Ethiopia | ......do | E | 3 | NA | NA |
| Impala, black-faced | *Aepyceros melampus petersi* | Namibia, Angola | ......do | E | 3 | NA | NA |

| | | | | | | | |
|---|---|---|---|---|---|---|---|
| Indri | *Indri indri* (=entire genus) | Malagasy Republic (=Madagascar) | do | E | 3 | NA | NA |
| Jaguar | *Panthera onca* | U.S.A. (TX, NM, AZ), C. and S. America. | Mexico southward | E | 5 | NA | NA |
| Jaguarundi | *Felis yagouaroundi cacomitli* | U.S.A. (TX), Mexico | Entire | E | 15 | NA | NA |
| Do | *Felis yagouaroundi fossata* | Mexico, Nicaragua | do | E | 15 | NA | NA |
| Do | *Felis yagouaroundi panamensis* | Nicaragua, Costa Rica, Panama | do | E | 15 | NA | NA |
| Do | *Felis yagouaroundi tolteca* | U.S.A. (AZ), Mexico | do | E | 15 | NA | NA |
| Kangaroo, eastern gray | *Macropus giganteus* (all subspecies except *tasmaniensis*). | Australia | do | T | 7 | NA | 17.40(a) |
| Kangaroo, red | *Macropus* (*Megaleia*) *rufus* | do | do | T | 7 | NA | 17.40(a) |
| Kangaroo, Tasmanian forester | *Macropus giganteus tasmaniensis* | Australia (Tasmania) | do | E | 6 | NA | NA |
| Kangaroo, western gray | *Macropus fuliginosus* | Australia | do | T | 7 | NA | 17.40(a) |
| Kouprey | *Bos sauveli* | Vietnam, Laos, Cambodia, Thailand | do | E | 3 | NA | NA |
| Langur, capped | *Presbytis pileata* | India, Burma, Bangladesh | do | E | 15 | NA | NA |
| Langur, Douc | *Pygathrix nemaeus* | Cambodia, Laos, Vietnam | do | E | 3 | NA | NA |
| Langur, entellus | *Presbytis entellus* | China (Tibet), India, Pakistan, Kashmir, Sri Lanka, Sikkim, Bangladesh. | do | E | 15 | NA | NA |
| Langur, Francois' | *Presbytis francoisi* | China (Kwangsi), Indochina | do | E | 16 | NA | NA |
| Langur, golden | *Presbytis geei* | India (Assam), Bhutan | do | E | 15 | NA | NA |
| Langur, long-tailed | *Presbytis potenziani* | Indonesia | do | T | 16 | NA | 17.40(c) |
| Langur, Pagi Island | *Nasalis* (*Simias*) *concolor* | do | do | E | 3 | NA | NA |
| Langur, purple-faced | *Presbytis senex* | Sri Lanka (=Ceylon) | do | T | 16 | NA | 17.40(c) |
| Lechwe, red | *Kobus leche* | Southern Africa | do | T | 3, 15, 106 | NA | NA |
| Lemurs | Lemuridae (incl. Cheirogaleidae, Lepilemuridae); all members of genera *Lemur, Phaner, Hapalemur, Lepilemur, Microcebus, Allocebus, Cheirogaleus, Varecia*. | Malagasy Republic (=Madagascar) | do | E | 3, 15, 15A | NA | NA |
| Leopard | *Panthera pardus* | Africa, Asia | Wherever found, except where it is listed as Threatened as set forth below. | E | 3, 5, 114 | NA | NA |
| Do | do | do | In Africa, in the wild, south of, and including, the following countries: Gabon, Congo, Zaire, Uganda, Kenya. | T | 3, 5, 114 | NA | 17.40(f) |
| Leopard, clouded | *Neofelis nebulosa* | Southeast and south-central Asia, Taiwan. | Entire | E | 3, 15 | NA | NA |
| Leopard, snow | *Panthera uncia* | Central Asia | do | E | 5 | NA | NA |
| Linsang, spotted | *Prionodon pardicolor* | Nepal, Assam, Vietnam, Cambodia, Laos, Burma. | do | E | 15 | NA | NA |
| Lion, Asiatic | *Panthera leo persica* | Turkey to India | do | E | 3 | NA | NA |
| Loris, lesser slow | *Nycticebus pygmaeus* | Indochina | do | T | 16 | NA | 17.40(c) |
| Lynx, Spanish | *Felis* (=*Lynx*) *pardina* | Spain, Portugal | do | E | 3 | NA | NA |
| Macaque, Formosan rock | *Macaca cyclopis* | Taiwan | do | T | 16 | NA | 17.40(c) |
| Macaque, Japanese | *Macaca fuscata* | Japan (Shikoku, Kyushu and Honshu Islands). | do | T | 16 | NA | 17.40(c) |
| Macaque, lion-tailed | *Macaca silenus* | India | do | E | 3 | NA | NA |
| Macaque, stump-tailed | *Macaca arctoides* | India (Assam) to southern China | do | T | 16 | NA | 17.40(c) |
| Macaque, Toque | *Macaca sinica* | Sri Lanka (=Ceylon) | do | T | 16 | NA | 17.40(c) |
| Manatee, Amazonian | *Trichechus inunguis* | South America (Amazon River Basin) | do | E | 3 | NA | NA |
| Manatee, West African | *Trichechus senegalensis* | West Coast of Africa from Senegal River to Cuanza River. | do | T | 52 | NA | NA |

| Species | | Historic range | Vertebrate population where endangered or threatened | Status | When listed | Critical habitat | Special rules |
|---|---|---|---|---|---|---|---|
| Common name | Scientific name | | | | | | |
| Manatee, West Indian (Florida) | *Trichechus manatus* | U.S.A. (southeastern), Caribbean Sea, South America. | do | E | 1, 3 | 17.95(a) | NA |
| Mandrill | *Papio sphinx* | Equatorial West Africa | do | E | 16 | NA | NA |
| Mangabey, Tana River | *Cercocebus galeritus* | Kenya | do | E | 3 | NA | NA |
| Mangabey, white-collared | *Cercocebus torquatus* | Senegal to Ghana; Nigeria to Gabon | do | E | 16 | NA | NA |
| Margay | *Felis wiedii* | U.S.A. (TX), C. and S. America | Mexico southward | E | 5 | NA | NA |
| Markhor, Kabal | *Capra falconeri megaceros* | Afghanistan, Pakistan | Entire | E | 15 | NA | NA |
| Markhor, straight-horned | *Capra falconeri jerdoni* | do | do | E | 15 | NA | NA |
| Marmoset, buff-headed | *Callithrix flaviceps* | Brazil | do | E | 139 | NA | NA |
| Marmoset, buffy tufted-ear | *Callithrix jacchus aurita* | do | do | E | 233 | NA | NA |
| Marmoset, cotton-top | *Saguinus oedipus* | Costa Rica to Colombia | do | E | 16 | NA | NA |
| Marmoset, Goeldi's | *Callimico goeldii* | Brazil, Colombia, Ecuador, Peru, Bolivia. | do | E | 3 | NA | NA |
| Marmot, Vancouver Island | *Marmota vancouverensis* | Canada (Vancouver Island) | do | E | 139 | NA | NA |
| Marsupial, eastern jerboa | *Antechinomys laniger* | Australia | do | E | 4 | NA | NA |
| Marsupial-mouse, large desert | *Sminthopsis psammophila* | do | do | E | 4 | NA | NA |
| Marsupial-mouse, long-tailed | *Sminthopsis longicaudata* | do | do | E | 4 | NA | NA |
| Marten, Formosan yellow-throated | *Martes flavigula chrysospila* | Taiwan | do | E | 3 | NA | NA |
| Monkey, black colobus | *Colobus satanas* | Equatorial Guinea, People's Republic of Congo, Cameroon, Gabon. | do | E | 16 | NA | NA |
| Monkey, black howler | *Alouatta pigra* | Mexico, Guatemala, Belize | do | T | 16 | NA | 17.40(c) |
| Monkey, Diana | *Cercopithecus diana* | Coastal West Africa | do | E | 16 | NA | NA |
| Monkey, howler | *Alouatta palliata* (=*villosa*) | Mexico to South America | do | E | 15 | NA | NA |
| Monkey (=langur), Guizhou snub-nosed. | *Rhinopithecus* (=*Pygathrix*) *brelichi* | China | do | E | 400 | NA | NA |
| Monkey (=langur), Sichuan snub-nosed. | *Rhinopithecus* (=*Pygathrix*) *roxellana* | do | do | E | 400 | NA | NA |
| Monkey (=langur), Tonkin snub-nosed | *Rhinopithecus* (=*Pygathrix*) *avunculus* | Viet Nam | do | E | 16,400 | NA | NA |
| Monkey (=langur), Yunnan snub-nosed. | *Rhinopithecus* (=*Pygathrix*) *bieti* | China | do | E | 400 | NA | NA |
| Monkey, L'hoest's | *Cercopithecus lhoesti* | Upper Eastern Congo Basin, Cameroon. | do | E | 16 | NA | NA |
| Monkey, Preuss' red colobus | *Colobus badius preussi* | Cameroon | do | E | 139 | NA | NA |
| Monkey, proboscis | *Nasalis larvatus* | Borneo | do | E | 15 | NA | NA |
| Monkey, red-backed squirrel | *Saimiri oerstedii* | Costa Rica, Panama | do | E | 3 | NA | NA |
| Monkey, red-bellied | *Cercopithecus erythrogaster* | Western Nigeria | do | E | 16 | NA | NA |
| Monkey, red-eared nose-spotted | *Cercopithecus erythrotis* | Nigeria, Cameroon, Fernando Po | do | E | 16 | NA | NA |
| Monkey, spider | *Ateles geoffroyi frontatus* | Costa Rica, Nicaragua | do | E | 3 | NA | NA |
| Monkey, spider | *Ateles geoffroyi panamensis* | Costa Rica, Panama | do | E | 3 | NA | NA |
| Monkey, Tana River red colobus | *Colobus rufomitratus* (=*badius*) *rufomitratus*. | Kenya | do | E | 3, 16 | NA | NA |
| Monkey, woolly spider | *Brachyteles arachnoides* | Brazil | do | E | 3 | NA | NA |
| Monkey, yellow-tailed woolly | *Lagothrix flavicauda* | Andes of northern Peru | do | E | 16 | NA | NA |
| Monkey, Zanzibar red colobus | *Colobus kirki* | Tanzania | do | E | 3 | NA | NA |
| Mouse, Alabama beach | *Peromyscus polionotus ammobates* | U.S.A. (AL) | do | E | 183 | 17.95(a) | NA |
| Mouse, Anastasia Island beach | *Peromyscus polionotus phasma* | U.S.A. (FL) | do | E | 349 | NA | NA |
| Mouse, Australian native | *Zyzomys* (=*Notomys*) *pedunculatus* | Australia | do | E | 15 | NA | NA |
| Mouse, Australian native | *Notomys aquilo* | do | do | E | 15 | NA | NA |
| Mouse, Choctawhatchee beach | *Peromyscus polionotus allophrys* | U.S.A. (FL) | do | E | 183 | 17.95(a) | NA |
| Mouse, Field's | *Pseudomys fieldi* | Australia | do | E | 4 | NA | NA |
| Mouse, Gould's | *Pseudomys gouldii* | do | do | E | 6 | NA | NA |
| Mouse, Key Largo cotton | *Peromyscus gossypinus allapaticola* | U.S.A. (FL) | do | E | 131E, 160 | NA | NA |

| | | | | | | | |
|---|---|---|---|---|---|---|---|
| Mouse, New Holland | *Pseudomys novaehollandiae* | Australia | do | E | 4 | NA | NA |
| Mouse, Perdido Key beach | *Peromyscus polionotus trissyllepsis* | U.S.A. (AL, FL) | do | E | 183 | 17.95(a) | NA |
| Mouse, salt marsh harvest | *Reithrodontomys raviventris* | U.S.A. (CA) | do | E | 2 | NA | NA |
| Mouse, Shark Bay | *Pseudomys praeconis* | Australia | do | E | 4 | NA | NA |
| Mouse, Shortridge's | *Pseudomys shortridgei* | do | do | E | 4 | NA | NA |
| Mouse, Smoky | *Pseudomys fumeus* | do | do | E | 4 | NA | NA |
| Mouse, southeastern beach | *Peromyscus polionotus niveiventris* | U.S.A. (FL) | do | T | 349 | NA | NA |
| Mouse, western | *Pseudomys occidentalis* | Australia | do | E | 4 | NA | NA |
| Muntjac, Fea's | *Muntiacus feae* | Northern Thailand, Burma | do | E | 50 | NA | NA |
| Native-cat, eastern | *Dasyurus viverrinus* | Australia | do | E | 6 | NA | NA |
| Numbat | *Myrmecobius fasciatus* | do | do | E | 4, 6 | NA | NA |
| Ocelot | *Felis pardalis* | U.S.A. (AZ, TX) to C. and S. America | do | E | 5, 119 | NA | NA |
| Orangutan | *Pongo pygmaeus* | Borneo, Sumatra | do | E | 3 | NA | NA |
| Oryx, Arabian | *Oryx leucoryx* | Arabian Peninsula | do | E | 3 | NA | NA |
| Otter, Cameroon clawless | *Aonyx (Paraonyx) congica microdon* | Cameroon, Nigeria | do | E | 3 | NA | NA |
| Otter, giant | *Pteronura brasiliensis* | South America | do | E | 3 | NA | NA |
| Otter, long-tailed | *Lutra longicaudis* (incl. *platensis*) | do | do | E | 3, 15 | NA | NA |
| Otter, marine | *Lutra felina* | Peru south to Straits of Magellan | do | E | 15 | NA | NA |
| Otter, southern river | *Lutra provocax* | Chile, Argentina | do | E | 15 | NA | NA |
| Otter, southern sea | *Enhydra lutris nereis* | West Coast, USA (WA, OR, CA) south to Mexico (Baja California). | Entire, except where listed below. | T | 21, 284 | NA | NA |
| Do | do | do | All areas subject to U.S. jurisdiction south of Pt. Conception, CA (34°26.9′ N. Lat.) [Note: status governed by Pub. L. 99–625, 100 Stat. 3500.]. | [See 17.84 (d)] | 21, 284 | NA | 17.84(d) |
| Panda, giant | *Ailuropoda melanoleuca* | People's Republic of China | Entire | E | 139 | NA | NA |
| Pangolin (=scaly anteater) | *Manis temmincki* | Africa | do | E | 15 | NA | NA |
| Panther, Florida | *Felis concolor coryi* | U.S.A. (LA and AR east to SC and FL) | do | E | 1 | NA | NA |
| Planigale, little | *Planigale ingrami subtilissima* (formerly *P. subtilissima*). | Australia | do | E | 4 | NA | NA |
| Planigale, southern | *Planigale tenuirostris* | do | do | E | 4 | NA | NA |
| Porcupine, thin-spined | *Chaetomys subspinosus* | Brazil | do | E | 3 | NA | NA |
| Possum, Leadbeater's | *Gymnobelideus leadbeateri* | do | do | E | 233 | NA | NA |
| Possum, mountain pygmy | *Burramys parvus* | Australia | do | E | 4 | NA | NA |
| Possum, scaly-tailed | *Wyulda squamicaudata* | do | do | E | 4 | NA | NA |
| Prairie dog, Mexican | *Cynomys mexicanus* | Mexico | do | E | 3 | NA | NA |
| Prairie dog, Utah | *Cynomys parvidens* | U.S.A. (UT) | do | T | 6, 149 | NA | 17.40(g) |
| Pronghorn, peninsular | *Antilocapra americana peninsularis* | Mexico (Baja California) | do | E | 10 | NA | NA |
| Pronghorn, Sonoran | *Antilocapra americana sonoriensis* | U.S.A. (AZ), Mexico | do | E | 1, 3 | NA | NA |
| Pudu | *Pudu pudu* | Southern South America | do | E | 15 | NA | NA |
| Puma, Costa Rican | *Felis concolor costaricensis* | Nicaragua, Panama, Costa Rica | do | E | 15 | NA | NA |
| Quokka | *Setonix brachyurus* | Australia | do | E | 6 | NA | NA |
| Rabbit, Lower Keys | *Sylvilagus palustris hefneri* | U.S.A. (FL) | do | E | 390 | NA | NA |
| Rabbit, Ryukyu | *Pentalagus furnessi* | Japan (Ryukyu Islands) | do | E | 50 | NA | NA |
| Rabbit, volcano | *Romerolagus diazi* | Mexico | do | E | 3 | NA | NA |
| Rat, false water | *Xeromys myoides* | Australia | do | E | 4 | NA | NA |
| Rat, Fresno kangaroo | *Dipodomys nitratoides exilis* | U.S.A. (CA) | do | E | 170 | 17.95(a) | NA |
| Rat, giant kangaroo | *Dipodomys ingens* | do | do | E | 251 | NA | NA |
| Rat, Morro Bay kangaroo | *Dipodomys heermanni morroensis* | do | do | E | 2 | 17.95(a) | NA |
| Rat, rice (=silver rice) | *Oryzomys palustris natator* (=*O. argentatus*). | U.S.A. (FL) | Lower FL Keys (west of the Seven Mile Bridge). | E | 421 | NA | NA |

8

| Species: Common name | Species: Scientific name | Historic range | Vertebrate population where endangered or threatened | Status | When listed | Critical habitat | Special rules |
|---|---|---|---|---|---|---|---|
| Rat, Stephens' kangaroo | *Dipodomys stephensi* (incl. *D. cascus*) | U.S.A. (CA) | Entire | E | 338 | NA | NA |
| Rat, stick-nest | *Leporillus conditor* | Australia | do | E | 6 | NA | NA |
| Rat, Tipton kangaroo | *Dipodomys nitratoides nitratoides* | U.S.A. (CA) | do | E | 312 | NA | NA |
| Rat-kangaroo, brush-tailed | *Bettongia penicillata* | Australia | do | E | 4 | NA | NA |
| Rat-kangaroo, Gaimard's | *Bettongia gaimardi* | do | do | E | 6 | NA | NA |
| Rat-kangaroo, Lesuer's | *Bettongia lesueur* | do | do | E | 4 | NA | NA |
| Rat-kangaroo, plain | *Caloprymnus campestris* | do | do | E | 4 | NA | NA |
| Rat-kangaroo, Queensland | *Bettongia tropica* | do | do | E | 4 | NA | NA |
| Rhinoceros, black | *Diceros bicornis* | Sub-Saharan Africa | do | E | 97 | NA | NA |
| Rhinoceros, great Indian | *Rhinoceros unicornis* | India, Nepal | do | E | 4 | NA | NA |
| Rhinoceros, Javan | *Rhinoceros sondaicus* | Indonesia, Indochina, Burma, Thailand, Sikkim, Bangladesh, Malaysia. | do | E | 3 | NA | NA |
| Rhinoceros, northern white | *Ceratotherium simum cottoni* | Zaire, Sudan, Uganda, Central African Republic. | do | E | 3 | NA | NA |
| Rhinoceros, Sumatran | *Dicerorhinus* (=*Didermoceros*) *sumatrensis.* | Bangladesh to Vietnam to Indonesia (Borneo). | do | E | 3 | NA | NA |
| Saiga, Mongolian (antelope) | *Saiga tatarica mongolica* | Mongolia | do | E | 15 | NA | NA |
| Saki, southern beared | *Chiropotes satanas satanas* | Brazil | do | E | 233 | NA | NA |
| Saki, white-nosed | *Chiropotes albinasus* | do | do | E | 3 | NA | NA |
| Sea-lion, Steller (=northern) | *Eumetopias jubatus* | U.S.A. (AK, CA, OR, WA), Canada, Soviet Union; North Pacific Ocean. | do | T | 384E, 408 | NA | 227.12 |
| Seal, Caribbean monk | *Monachus tropicalis* | Caribbean Sea, Gulf of Mexico | do | E | 1, 2D, 45 | NA | NA |
| Seal, guadalupe fur | *Arctocephalus townsendi* | U.S.A. (Farallon Islands of CA) south to Mexico (Islas Revillagigedo). | do | T | 1, 2D, 212 | NA | 227.11 |
| Seal, Hawaiian monk | *Monachus schauinslandi* | U.S.A. (HI) | do | E | 18 | 226.11 | NA |
| Seal, Mediterranean monk | *Monachus monachus* | Mediterranean, Northwest African Coast and Black Sea. | do | E | 3 | NA | NA |
| Seledang (=Gaur) | *Bos gaurus* | Bangladesh, Southeast Asia, India | do | E | 3 | NA | NA |
| Serow | *Capricornis sumatraensis* | East Asia, Sumatra | do | E | 15 | NA | NA |
| Serval, Barbary | *Felis serval constantina* | Algeria | do | E | 3 | NA | NA |
| Shapo | *Ovis vignei vignei* | Kashmir | do | E | 15 | NA | NA |
| Shou | *Cervus elaphus wallichi* | Tibet, Bhutan | do | E | 3 | NA | NA |
| Shrew, Dismal Swamp southeastern | *Sorex longirostris fisheri* | U.S.A. (VA, NC) | do | T | 246 | NA | NA |
| Siamang | *Symphalangus syndactylus* | Malaysia, Indonesia | do | E | 15 | NA | NA |
| Sifakas | *Propithecus* spp. (all species) | Malagasy Republic (=Madagascar) | do | E | 4 | NA | NA |
| Sloth, Brazilian three-toed | *Bradypus torquatus* | Brazil | do | E | 3, 4 | NA | NA |
| Solenodon, Cuban | *Solenodon (Atopogale) cubanus* | Cuba | do | E | 3 | NA | NA |
| Solenodon, Haitian | *Solenodon paradoxus* | Dominican Republic, Haiti | do | E | 3 | NA | NA |
| Squirrel, Carolina northern flying | *Glaucomys sabrinus coloratus* | U.S.A. (NC, TN) | do | E | 189 | NA | NA |
| Squirrel, Delmarva Peninsula fox | *Sciurus niger cinereus* | U.S.A. (Delmarva Peninsula to southeast PA). | Entire, except Sussex Co., DE. | E | 1, 161, 168 | NA | NA |
| Do | do | do | U.S.A. (DE—Sussex County). | XN | 161 | NA | 17.84(a) |
| Squirrel, Mount Graham red | *Tamiasciurus hudsonicus grahamensis* | U.S.A. (AZ) | Entire | E | 268 | 17.95(a) | NA |
| Squirrel, Virginia northern flying | *Glaucomys sabrinus fuscus* | U.S.A. (VA, WV) | do | E | 189 | NA | NA |
| Stag, Barbary | *Cervus elaphus barbarus* | Tunisia, Algeria | do | E | 3 | NA | NA |
| Stag, Kashmir | *Cervus elaphus hanglu* | Kashmir | do | E | 3 | NA | NA |
| Suni, Zanzibar | *Neotragus (Nesotragus) moschatus moschatus.* | Zanzibar (and nearby islands) | do | E | 50 | NA | NA |
| Tahr, Arabian | *Hemitragus jayakari* | Oman | do | E | 50 | NA | NA |
| Tamaraw | *Bubalus mindorensis* | Philippines | do | E | 4 | NA | NA |

| | | | | | | | |
|---|---|---|---|---|---|---|---|
| Tamarin, golden-rumped (=golden-headed Tamarin; =golden-lion Marmoset). | *Leontopithecus* (=*Leontideus*) spp. (all species). | Brazil | ...do | E | 3 | NA | NA |
| Tamarin, pied | *Saguinus bicolor* | ...do | ...do | E | 16 | NA | NA |
| Tamarin, white-footed | *Saguinus leucopus* | Colombia | ...do | T | 16 | NA | 17.40(c) |
| Tapir, Asian | *Tapirus indicus* | Burma, Laos, Cambodia, Vietnam, Malaysia, Indonesia, Thailand. | ...do | E | 15 | NA | NA |
| Tapir, Brazilian | *Tapirus terrestris* | Colombia and Venezuela south to Paraguay and Argentina. | ...do | E | 3 | NA | NA |
| Tapir, Central American | *Tapirus bairdii* | Southern Mexico to Colombia and Ecuador. | ...do | E | 3 | NA | NA |
| Tapir, mountain | *Tapirus pinchaque* | Colombia, Ecuador and possibly Peru and Venezuela. | ...do | E | 3 | NA | NA |
| Tarsier, Philippine | *Tarsius syrichta* | Philippines | ...do | T | 16 | NA | 17.40(c) |
| Tiger | *Panthera tigris* | Temperate and Tropical Asia | ...do | E | 3, 5 | NA | NA |
| Tiger, Tasmanian (=Thylacine) | *Thylacinus cynocephalus* | Australia | ...do | E | 3 | NA | NA |
| Uakari (all species) | *Cacajao* spp. (all species) | Peru, Brazil, Ecuador, Colombia, Venezuela. | ...do | E | 3 | NA | NA |
| Urial | *Ovis musimon* (=*orientalis*) *ophion* | Cyprus | ...do | E | 15 | NA | NA |
| Vicuna | *Vicugna vicugna* | South America (Andes) | ...do | E | 3 | NA | NA |
| Vole, Amargosa | *Microtus californicus scirpensis* | U.S.A. (CA) | ...do | E | 166 | 17.95(a) | NA |
| Vole, Florida salt marsh | *Microtus pennsylvanicus dukecampbelli* | U.S.A. (FL) | ...do | E | 415 | NA | NA |
| Vole, Hualapai Mexican | *Microtus mexicanus hualpaiensis* | U.S.A. (AZ) | ...do | E | 292 | NA | NA |
| Wallaby, banded hare | *Lagostrophus fasciatus* | Australia | ...do | E | 4 | NA | NA |
| Wallaby, brindled nail-tailed | *Onychogalea fraenata* | ...do | ...do | E | 4 | NA | NA |
| Wallaby, crescent nail-tailed | *Onychogalea lunata* | ...do | ...do | E | 4 | NA | NA |
| Wallaby, Parma | *Macropus parma* | ...do | ...do | E | 4 | NA | NA |
| Wallaby, Western hare | *Lagorchestes hirsutus* | ...do | ...do | E | 4 | NA | NA |
| Wallaby, yellow-footed rock | *Petrogale xanthopus* | ...do | ...do | E | 6 | NA | NA |
| Whale, blue | *Balaenoptera musculus* | Oceanic | ...do | E | 3 | NA | NA |
| Whale, bowhead | *Balaena mysticetus* | Oceanic (north latitudes only) | ...do | E | 3 | NA | NA |
| Whale, finback | *Balaenoptera physalus* | Oceanic | ...do | E | 3 | NA | NA |
| Whale, gray | *Eschrichtius robustus* | North Pacific Ocean: coastal and Bering Sea, formerly North Atlantic Ocean. | ...do | E | 3 | NA | NA |
| Whale, humpback | *Megaptera novaeangliae* | Oceanic | ...do | E | 3 | NA | 222.31 |
| Whale, right | *Balaena glacialis* | ...do | ...do | E | 3 | NA | NA |
| Whale, Sei | *Balaenoptera borealis* | ...do | ...do | E | 3 | NA | NA |
| Whale, sperm | *Physeter catodon* | ...do | ...do | E | 3 | NA | NA |
| Wolf, gray | *Canis lupus* | Holarctic | U.S.A. (48 conterminous States, except MN), Mexico. | E | 1, 6, 13, 15, 35 | 17.95(a) | NA |
| Do | ...do | ...do | U.S.A. (MN) | T | 35 | 17.95(a) | 17.40(d) |
| Wolf, maned | *Chrysocyon brachyurus* | Argentina, Bolivia, Brazil, Paraguay, Uruguay. | Entire | E | 4 | NA | NA |
| Wolf, red | *Canis rufus* | U.S.A. (SE U.S.A., west to central TX) | Entire, except Dare, Tyrrell, Hyde, and Washington Counties, NC. | E | 1, 248 | NA | NA |
| Do | ...do | ...do | U.S.A.: NC-Dare, Tyrrell, Hyde, & Washington Cos. | XN | 248 | NA | 17.84(c) |
| Wombat, hairy-nosed (=Barnard's and Queensland hairy-nosed). | *Lasiorhinus krefftii* (formerly *L. barnardi* and *L. gillespiei*). | Australia | Entire | E | 4, 6 | NA | NA |
| Woodrat, Key Largo | *Neotoma floridana smalli* | U.S.A. (FL) | ...do | E | 131E, 160 | NA | NA |
| Yak, wild | *Bos grunniens mutus* | China (Tibet), India | ...do | E | 3 | NA | NA |
| Zebra, Grevy's | *Equus grevyi* | Kenya, Ethiopia, Somalia | ...do | T | 54 | NA | NA |

| Species: Common name | Species: Scientific name | Historic range | Vertebrate population where endangered or threatened | Status | When listed | Critical habitat | Special rules |
|---|---|---|---|---|---|---|---|
| Zebra, Hartmann's mountain | *Equus zebra hartmannae* | Namibia, Angola | do | T | 54, 111 | NA | NA |
| Zebra, mountain | *Equus zebra zebra* | South Africa | do | E | 15, 111 | NA | NA |
| BIRDS | | | | | | | |
| Akepa, Hawaii (honeycreeper) | *Loxops coccineus coccineus* | U.S.A. (HI) | do | E | 2 | NA | NA |
| Akepa, Maui (honeycreeper) | *Loxops coccineus ochraceus* | do | do | E | 2 | NA | NA |
| Akialoa, Kauai (honeycreeper) | *Hemignathus procerus* | do | do | E | 1 | NA | NA |
| Akiapolaau (honeycreeper) | *Hemignathus munroi* (=*wilsoni*) | do | do | E | 1 | NA | NA |
| Albatross, short-tailed | *Diomedea albatrus* | North Pacific Ocean: Japan, U.S.S.R., U.S.A. (AK, CA, HI, OR, WA). | Entire, except U.S.A. | E | 3 | NA | NA |
| Blackbird, yellow-shouldered | *Agelaius xanthomus* | U.S.A. (PR) | Entire | E | 17 | 17.95(b) | NA |
| Bobwhite, masked (quail) | *Colinus virginianus ridgwayi* | U.S.A. (AZ), Mexico (Sonora) | do | E | 1, 3 | NA | NA |
| Booby, Abbott's | *Sula abbotti* | Indian Ocean: Christmas Island | do | E | 15 | NA | NA |
| Bristlebird, western | *Dasyornis brachypterus longirostris* | Australia | do | E | 3 | NA | NA |
| Bristlebird, western rufous | *Dasyornis broadbenti littoralis* | do | do | E | 15 | NA | NA |
| Broadbill, Guam | *Myiagra freycineti* | Western Pacific Ocean: U.S.A. (Guam) | do | E | 156 | NA | NA |
| Bulbul, Mauritius olivaceous | *Hypsipetes borbonicus olivaceus* | Indian Ocean: Mauritius | do | E | 3 | NA | NA |
| Bullfinch, Sao Miguel (finch) | *Pyrrhula pyrrhula murina* | Eastern Atlantic Ocean: Azores | do | E | 3 | NA | NA |
| Bushwren, New Zealand | *Xenicus longipes* | New Zealand | do | E | 3 | NA | NA |
| Bustard, great Indian | *Choriotis nigriceps* | India, Pakistan | do | E | 3 | NA | NA |
| Cahow (=Bermuda Petrel) | *Pterodroma cahow* | North Atlantic Ocean: Bermuda | do | E | 3 | NA | NA |
| Caracara, Audubon's crested | *Polyborus plancus audubonii* | U.S.A. (AZ, FL, LA, NM, TX) south to Panama; Cuba. | U.S.A. (FL) | T | 280 | NA | NA |
| Condor, Andean | *Vultur gryphus* | Colombia to Chile and Argentina | Entire | E | 4 | NA | NA |
| Condor, California | *Gymnogyps californianus* | U.S.A. (OR, CA), Mexico (Baja California). | U.S.A. only | E | 1 | 17.95(b) | NA |
| Coot, Hawaiian (=alae keo keo) | *Fulica americana alai* | U.S.A. (HI) | Entire | E | 2 | NA | NA |
| Cotinga, banded | *Cotinga maculata* | Brazil | do | E | 15 | NA | NA |
| Cotinga, white-winged | *Xipholena atropurpurea* | do | do | E | 15 | NA | NA |
| Crane, black-necked | *Grus nigricollis* | China (Tibet) | do | E | 15 | NA | NA |
| Crane, Cuba sandhill | *Grus canadensis nesiotes* | West Indies: Cuba | do | E | 15 | NA | NA |
| Crane, hooded | *Grus monacha* | Japan, U.S.S.R | do | E | 4 | NA | NA |
| Crane, Japanese | *Grus japonensis* | China, Japan, Korea, U.S.S.R | do | E | 3 | NA | NA |
| Crane, Mississippi sandhill | *Grus canadensis pulla* | U.S.A. (MS) | do | E | 6 | 17.95(b) | NA |
| Crane, Siberian white | *Grus leucogeranus* | U.S.S.R. (Siberia) to India, including Iran and China. | do | E | 4 | NA | NA |
| Crane, white-naped | *Grus vipio* | Mongolia | do | E | 15 | NA | NA |
| Crane, whooping | *Grus americana* | Canada, U.S.A. (Rocky Mountains east to Carolinas), Mexico. | do | E | 1, 3 | 17.95(b) | NA |
| Creeper, Hawaii | *Oreomystis* (=*Loxops*) *mana* | U.S.A. (HI) | do | E | 10 | NA | NA |
| Creeper, Molokai (=kakawahie) | *Paroreomyza* (=*Oreomystis*, =*Loxops*) *flammea*. | do | do | E | 2 | NA | NA |
| Creeper, Oahu (=alauwahio) | *Paroreomyza* (=*Oreomystis*, =*Loxops*) *maculata*. | do | do | E | 2 | NA | NA |
| Crow, Hawaiian (='alala) | *Corvus hawaiiensis* (=*tropicus*) | do | do | E | 1 | NA | NA |
| Crow, Mariana | *Corvus kubaryi* | Western Pacific Ocean: U.S.A. (Guam, Rota). | do | E | 156 | NA | NA |
| Crow, white-necked | *Corvus leucognaphalus* | U.S.A. (PR), Dominican Republic, Haiti | do | E | 419 | NA | NA |
| Cuckoo-shrike, Mauritius | *Coquus* (=*Coracina*) *typicus* | Indian Ocean: Mauritius | do | E | 3 | NA | NA |
| Cuckoo-shrike, Reunion | *Coquus* (=*Coracina*) *newtoni* | Indian Ocean: Reunion | do | E | 3 | NA | NA |
| Curassow, razor-billed | *Mitu* (=*Crax*) *mitu mitu* | Brazil (Eastern) | do | E | 15 | NA | NA |
| Curassow, red-billed | *Crax blumenbachii* | Brazil | do | E | 4 | NA | NA |
| Curassow, Trinidad white-headed | *Pipile pipile pipile* | West Indies: Trinidad | do | E | 3 | NA | NA |

| | | | | | | | |
|---|---|---|---|---|---|---|---|
| Curlew, Eskimo | *Numenius borealis* | Alaska and northern Canada to Argentina. | do | E | 1, 3 | NA | NA |
| Dove, cloven-feathered | *Drepanoptila holosericea* | Southwest Pacific Ocean: New Caledonia. | do | E | 3 | NA | NA |
| Dove, Grenada gray-fronted | *Leptotila rufaxilla wellsi* | West Indies: Grenada | do | E | 3 | NA | NA |
| Duck, Hawaiian (=koloa) | *Anas wyvilliana* | U.S.A. (HI) | do | E | 1 | NA | NA |
| Duck, Laysan | *Anas laysanensis* | do | do | E | 1 | NA | NA |
| Duck, pink-headed | *Rhodonessa caryophyllacea* | India | do | E | 15 | NA | NA |
| Duck, white-winged wood | *Cairina scutulata* | India, Malaysia, Indonesia, Thailand | do | E | 3 | NA | NA |
| Eagle, bald | *Haliaeetus leucocephalus* | North America south to northern Mexico. | U.S.A. (conterminous U.S., except WA, OR, MN, WI, MI). | E | 1, 34 | NA | NA |
| Do | do | do | U.S.A. (WA, OR, MN, WI, MI). | T | 34 | NA | 17.41(a) |
| Eagle, Greenland white-tailed | *Haliaeetus albicilla groenlandicus* | Greenland and adjacent Atlantic islands. | Entire | E | 15 | NA | NA |
| Eagle, harpy | *Harpia harpyja* | Mexico south to Argentina | do | E | 15 | NA | NA |
| Eagle, Philippine (=monkey-eating) | *Pithecophaga jefferyi* | Philippines | do | E | 3 | NA | NA |
| Eagle, Spanish imperial | *Aquila heliaca adalberti* | Spain, Morocco, Algeria | do | E | 3 | NA | NA |
| Egret, Chinese | *Egretta eulophotes* | China, Korea | do | E | 3 | NA | NA |
| Falcon, American peregrine | *Falco peregrinus anatum* | Nests from central Alaska across north-central Canada to central Mexico, winters south to South America. | do | E | 2, 3, 145 | 17.95(b) | NA |
| Falcon, Arctic peregrine | *Falco peregrinus tundrius* | Nests from northern Alaska to Greenland; winters south to Central and South America. | do | T | 2, 3, 145 | NA | NA |
| Falcon, Eurasian peregrine | *Falco peregrinus peregrinus* | Europe, Eurasia south to Africa and Mideast. | do | E | 15 | NA | NA |
| Falcon, northern aplomado | *Falco femoralis septentrionalis* | U.S.A. (AZ, NM, TX), Mexico, Guatemala. | do | E | 216 | NA | NA |
| Falcon, peregrine | *Falco peregrinus* | Worldwide, except Antarctica and most Pacific Islands. | Wherever found in wild in the conterminous 48 States. | E(S/A) | 145 | NA | NA |
| Finch, Laysan (honeycreeper) | *Telespyza* (=*Psittirostra*) *cantans* | U.S.A. (HI) | Entire | E | 1 | NA | NA |
| Finch, Nihoa (honeycreeper) | *Telespyza* (=*Psittirostra*) *ultima* | do | do | E | 1 | NA | NA |
| Flycatcher, Euler's | *Empidonax euleri johnstonei* | West Indies: Grenada | do | E | 3 | NA | NA |
| Flycatcher, Seychelles paradise | *Terpsiphone corvina* | Indian Ocean: Seychelles | do | E | 3 | NA | NA |
| Flycatcher, Tahiti | *Pomarea nigra* | South Pacific Ocean: Tahiti | do | E | 3 | NA | NA |
| Fody, Seychelles (weaver-finch) | *Foudia sechellarum* | Indian Ocean: Seychelles | do | E | 3 | NA | NA |
| Frigatebird, Andrew's | *Fregata andrewsi* | East Indian Ocean | do | E | 15 | NA | NA |
| Goose, Aleutian Canada | *Branta canadensis leucopareia* | U.S.A. (AK, CA, OR, WA), Japan | do | T | 1, 3, 410 | NA | NA |
| Goose, Hawaiian (=nene) | *Nesochen* (=*Branta*) *sandvicensis* | U.S.A. (HI) | do | E | 1 | NA | NA |
| Goshawk, Christmas Island | *Accipiter fasciatus natalis* | Indian Ocean: Christmas Island | do | E | 3 | NA | NA |
| Grackle, slender-billed | *Quisicalus* (=*Cassidix*) *palustris* | Mexico | do | E | 3 | NA | NA |
| Grasswren, Eyrean (flycatcher) | *Amytornis goyderi* | Australia | do | E | 3 | NA | NA |
| Grebe, Atitlan | *Podilymbus gigas* | Guatemala | do | E | 3 | NA | NA |
| Greenshank, Nordmann's | *Tringa guttifer* | U.S.S.R., Japan, south to Malaya, Borneo. | do | E | 15 | NA | NA |
| Guan, horned | *Oreophasis derbianus* | Guatemala, Mexico | do | E | 3 | NA | NA |
| Guan, white-winged | *Penelope albipennis* | Peru | do | E | 401 | NA | NA |
| Gull, Audouin's | *Larus audouinii* | Mediterranean Sea | do | E | 3 | NA | NA |
| Gull, relict | *Larus relictus* | India, China | do | E | 15 | NA | NA |
| Hawk, Anjouan Island sparrow | *Accipiter francesii pusillus* | Indian Ocean: Comoro Islands | do | E | 3 | NA | NA |
| Hawk, Galapagos | *Buteo galapagoensis* | Ecuador (Galapagos Islands) | do | E | 3 | NA | NA |
| Hawk, Hawaiian (=Io) | *Buteo solitarius* | U.S.A. (HI) | do | E | 1 | NA | NA |
| Hermit, hook-billed (hummingbird) | *Glaucis* (=*Ramphodon*) *dohrnii* | Brazil | do | E | 15 | NA | NA |

12

| Species | | Historic range | Vertebrate population where endangered or threatened | Status | When listed | Critical habitat | Special rules |
|---|---|---|---|---|---|---|---|
| Common name | Scientific name | | | | | | |
| Honeycreeper, crested (='akohekohe) | *Palmeria dolei* | U.S.A. (HI) | do | E | 1 | NA | NA |
| Honeyeater, helmeted | *Meliphaga cassidix* | Australia | do | E | 4 | NA | NA |
| Hornbill, helmeted | *Rhinoplax vigil* | Thailand, Malaysia | do | E | 15 | NA | NA |
| Ibis, Japanese crested | *Nipponia nippon* | China, Japan, U.S.S.R., Korea | do | E | 3 | NA | NA |
| Ibis, northern bald | *Geronticus eremita* | Southern Europe, southwestern Asia, northern Africa. | do | E | 401 | NA | NA |
| Jay, Florida scrub | *Aphelocoma coerulescens coerulescens.* | U.S.A. (FL) | do | T | 267 | NA | NA |
| Kagu | *Rhynochetos jubatus* | South Pacific Ocean: New Caledonia | do | E | 3 | NA | NA |
| Kakapo (=owl-parrot) | *Strigops habroptilus* | New Zealand | do | E | 3 | NA | NA |
| Kestrel, Mauritius | *Falco punctatus* | Indian Ocean: Mauritius | do | E | 3 | NA | NA |
| Kestrel, Seychelles | *Falco araea* | Indian Ocean: Seychelles Islands | do | E | 3 | NA | NA |
| Kingfisher, Guam Micronesian | *Halcyon cinnamomina cinnamomina* | West Pacific Ocean: U.S.A. (Guam) | do | E | 156 | NA | NA |
| Kite, Cuba hook-billed | *Chondrohierax uncinatus wilsonii* | West Indies: Cuba | do | E | 3 | NA | NA |
| Kite, Everglade snail | *Rostrhamus sociabilis plumbeus* | U.S.A. (FL), Cuba | Florida | E | 1 | 17.95(b) | NA |
| Kite, Grenada hook-billed | *Chondrohierax uncinatus mirus* | West Indies: Grenada | Entire | E | 3 | NA | NA |
| Kokako (wattlebird) | *Callaeas cinerea* | New Zealand | do | E | 3 | NA | NA |
| Macaw, glaucous | *Anodorhynchus glaucus* | Paraguay, Uruguay, Brazil | do | E | 15 | NA | NA |
| Macaw, indigo | *Anodorhynchus leari* | Brazil | do | E | 15 | NA | NA |
| Macaw, little blue | *Cyanopsitta spixii* | do | do | E | 15 | NA | NA |
| Magpie-robin, Seychelles (thrush) | *Copsychus sechellarum* | Indian Ocean: Seychelles Islands | do | E | 3 | NA | NA |
| Malkoha, red-faced (cuckoo) | *Phaenicophaeus pyrrhocephalus* | Sri Lanka (=Ceylon) | do | E | 3 | NA | NA |
| Mallard, Mariana | *Anas oustaleti* | West Pacific Ocean: U.S.A. (Guam, Mariana Islands). | do | E | 23 | NA | NA |
| Megapode, Maleo | *Macrocephalon maleo* | Indonesia (Celebes) | do | E | 3 | NA | NA |
| Megapode, Micronesian (=La Perouse's). | *Megapodius laperouse* | West Pacific Ocean: U.S.A. (Palau Island, Mariana Islands). | do | E | 3 | NA | NA |
| Millerbird, Nihoa (old world warbler) | *Acrocephalus familiaris kingi* | U.S.A. (HI) | do | E | 1 | NA | NA |
| Monarch, Tinian (old world flycatcher) | *Monarcha takatsukasae* | West Pacific Ocean: U.S.A. (Mariana Islands). | do | T | 3, 261 | NA | NA |
| Moorhen (=gallinule), Hawaiian common. | *Gallinula chloropus sandvicensis* | U.S.A. (HI) | do | E | 1 | NA | NA |
| Moorhen (=gallinule), Mariana common. | *Gallinula chloropus guami* | West Pacific Ocean: U.S.A. (Guam, Tinian, Saipan, Pagan). | do | E | 156 | NA | NA |
| Nightjar (=whip-poor-will), Puerto Rican. | *Caprimulgus noctitherus* | U.S.A. (PR) | do | E | 6 | NA | NA |
| Nukupu'u (honeycreeper) | *Hemignathus lucidus* | U.S.A. (HI) | do | E | 1, 2 | NA | NA |
| 'O'o, Kauai (='O'o 'A'a) (honeyeater) | *Moho braccatus* | do | do | E | 1 | NA | NA |
| Ostrich, Arabian | *Struthio camelus syriacus* | Jordan, Saudi Arabia | do | E | 3 | NA | NA |
| Ostrich, West African | *Struthio camelus spatzi* | Spanish Sahara | do | E | 3 | NA | NA |
| 'O'u (honeycreeper) | *Psittirostra psittacea* | U.S.A. (HI) | do | E | 1 | NA | NA |
| Owl, Anjouan scops | *Otus rutilus capnodes* | Indian Ocean: Comoro Island | do | E | 3 | NA | NA |
| Owl, giant scops | *Otus gurneyi* | Philippines: Marinduque and Mindanao Island. | do | E | 15 | NA | NA |
| Owl, Madagascar red | *Tyto soumagnei* | Madagascar | do | E | 401 | NA | NA |
| Owl, northern spotted | *Strix occidentalis caurina* | U.S.A. (CA, OR, WA), British Columbia | do | T | 393 | NA | NA |
| Owl, Seychelles | *Otus insularis* | Indian Ocean: Seychelles Islands | do | E | 3 | NA | NA |
| Owlet, Morden's (=Sokoke) | *Otus ireneae* | Kenya | do | E | 3 | NA | NA |
| Palila (honeycreeper) | *Loxioides (=Psittirostra) bailleui* | U.S.A. (HI) | do | E | 1 | 17.95(b) | NA |
| Parakeet, Forbes' | *Cyanoramphus auriceps forbesi* | New Zealand | do | E | 3, 15 | NA | NA |
| Parakeet, golden | *Aratinga guarouba* | Brazil | do | E | 4 | NA | NA |
| Parakeet, golden-shouldered (=hooded). | *Psephotus chrysopterygius* | Australia | do | E | 3 | NA | NA |

| | | | | | | | |
|---|---|---|---|---|---|---|---|
| Parakeet, Mauritius | *Psittacula echo* | Indian Ocean: Mauritius | ......do | E | 3 | NA | NA |
| Parakeet, Norfolk Island | *Cyanoramphus novaezelandiae cookii* | Australia (Norfolk Island) | ......do | E | 401 | NA | NA |
| Parakeet, ochre-marked | *Pyrrhura cruentata* | Brazil | ......do | E | 3 | NA | NA |
| Parakeet, orange-bellied | *Neophema chrysogaster* | Australia | ......do | E | 4 | NA | NA |
| Parakeet, paradise (=beautiful) | *Psephotus pulcherrimus* | ......do | ......do | E | 4 | NA | NA |
| Parakeet, scarlet-chested (=splendid) | *Neophema splendida* | ......do | ......do | E | 4 | NA | NA |
| Parakeet, turquoise | *Neophema pulchella* | ......do | ......do | E | 3 | NA | NA |
| Parrot, Australian | *Geopsittacus occidentalis* | ......do | ......do | E | 3 | NA | NA |
| Parrot, Bahaman or Cuban | *Amazona leucocephala* | West Indies: Cuba, Bahamas, Caymans. | ......do | E | 3, 15 | NA | NA |
| Parrot, ground | *Pezoporus wallicus* | Australia | ......do | E | 6 | NA | NA |
| Parrot, imperial | *Amazona imperialis* | West Indies: Dominica | ......do | E | 3 | NA | NA |
| Parrot, Puerto Rican | *Amazona vittata* | U.S.A. (PR) | ......do | E | 1 | NA | NA |
| Parrot, red-browed | *Amazona rhodocorytha* | Brazil | ......do | E | 3 | NA | NA |
| Parrot, red-capped | *Pionopsitta pileata* | ......do | ......do | E | 15 | NA | NA |
| Parrot, red-necked | *Amazona arausiaca* | West Indies: Dominica | ......do | E | 50 | NA | NA |
| Parrot, red-spectacled | *Amazona pretrei pretrei* | Brazil, Argentina | ......do | E | 15 | NA | NA |
| Parrot, red-tailed | *Amazona brasiliensis* | Brazil | ......do | E | 401 | NA | NA |
| Parrot, St. Lucia | *Amazona versicolor* | West Indies: St. Lucia | ......do | E | 3 | NA | NA |
| Parrot, St. Vincent | *Amazona guildingii* | West Indies: St. Vincent | ......do | E | 3 | NA | NA |
| Parrot, thick-billed | *Rhynchopsitta pachyrhyncha* | Mexico, U.S.A. (AZ, NM) | Mexico | E | 3 | NA | NA |
| Parrot, vinaceous-breasted | *Amazona vinacea* | Brazil | Entire | E | 15 | NA | NA |
| Parrotbill, Maui (honeycreeper) | *Pseudonestor xanthophrys* | U.S.A. (HI) | ......do | E | 1 | NA | NA |
| Pelican, brown | *Pelecanus occidentalis* | U.S.A (Carolinas to TX, CA), West Indies, C. and S. America: Coastal. | Entire, except U.S. Atlantic coast, FL, AL. | E | 2, 3, 171 | NA | NA |
| Penguin, Galapagos | *Spheniscus mendiculus* | Ecuador (Galapagos Islands) | Entire | E | 3 | NA | NA |
| Petrel, Hawaiian dark-rumped | *Pterodroma phaeopygia sandwichensis* | U.S.A. (HI) | ......do | E | 2, 4, 1 | NA | NA |
| Pheasant, bar-tailed | *Syrmaticus humaie* | Burma, China | ......do | E | 3 | NA | NA |
| Pheasant, Blyth's tragopan | *Tragopan blythii* | Burma, China, India | ......do | E | 3 | NA | NA |
| Pheasant, brown eared | *Crossoptilon mantchuricum* | China | ......do | E | 3 | NA | NA |
| Pheasant, Cabot's tragopan | *Tragopan caboti* | ......do | ......do | E | 3 | NA | NA |
| Pheasant, cheer | *Catreus wallichii* | India, Nepal, Pakistan | ......do | E | 401 | NA | NA |
| Pheasant, Chinese monal | *Lophophorus lhuysii* | China | ......do | E | 3 | NA | NA |
| Pheasant, Edward's | *Lophura edwardsi* | Vietnam | ......do | E | 3 | NA | NA |
| Pheasant, Elliot's | *Syrmaticus ellioti* | China | ......do | E | 15 | NA | NA |
| Pheasant, imperial | *Lophura imperialis* | Vietnam | ......do | E | 3 | NA | NA |
| Pheasant, Mikado | *Syrmaticus mikado* | Taiwan | ......do | E | 3 | NA | NA |
| Pheasant, Palawan peacock | *Polyplectron emphanum* | Philippines | ......do | E | 3 | NA | NA |
| Pheasant, Sclater's monal | *Lophophorus sclateri* | Burma, China, India | ......do | E | 3 | NA | NA |
| Pheasant, Swinhoe's | *Lophura swinhoii* | Taiwan | ......do | E | 3 | NA | NA |
| Pheasant, western tragopan | *Tragopan melanocephalus* | India, Pakistan | ......do | E | 3 | NA | NA |
| Pheasant, white eared | *Crossoptilon crossoptilon* | China (Tibet), India | ......do | E | 4 | NA | NA |
| Pigeon, Azores wood | *Columba palumbus azorica* | East Atlantic Ocean: Azores | ......do | E | 3 | NA | NA |
| Pigeon, Chatham Island | *Hemiphaga novaeseelandiae chathamensis.* | New Zealand | ......do | E | 3 | NA | NA |
| Pigeon, Mindoro zone-tailed | *Ducula mindorensis* | Philippines | ......do | E | 15 | NA | NA |
| Pigeon, Puerto Rican plain | *Columba inornata wetmorei* | U.S.A. (PR) | ......do | E | 2 | NA | NA |
| Piping-guan, black-fronted | *Pipile jacutinga* | Argentina | ......do | E | 15 | NA | NA |
| Pitta, Koch's | *Pitta kochi* | Philippines | ......do | E | 15 | NA | NA |
| Plover, New Zealand shore | *Thinornis novaeseelandiae* | New Zealand | ......do | E | 3 | NA | NA |
| Plover, piping | *Charadrius melodus* | U.S.A. (Great Lakes, northern Great Plains, Atlantic and Gulf coasts, PR VI), Canada, Mexico, Bahamas, West Indies. | Great Lakes watershed in States of IL, IN, MI, MN, NY, OH, PA, and WI and Province of Ontario. | E | 211 | NA | NA |

**14**

| Species: Common name | Species: Scientific name | Historic range | Vertebrate population where endangered or threatened | Status | When listed | Critical habitat | Special rules |
|---|---|---|---|---|---|---|---|
| Do | do | do | Entire, except those areas where listed as endangered above. | T | 211 | NA | NA |
| Po'ouli (honeycreeper) | *Melamprosops phaeosoma* | U.S.A. (HI) | Entire | E | 10 | NA | NA |
| Prairie-chicken, Attwater's greater | *Tympanuchus cupido attwateri* | U.S.A. (TX) | do | E | 1 | NA | NA |
| Quail, Merriam's Montezuma | *Cyrtonyx montezumae merriami* | Mexico (Vera Cruz) | do | E | 15 | NA | NA |
| Quetzel, resplendent | *Pharomachrus mocinno* | Mexico to Panama | do | E | 15 | NA | NA |
| Rail, Aukland Island | *Rallus pectoralis muelleri* | New Zealand | do | E | 3 | NA | NA |
| Rail, California clapper | *Rallus longirostris obsoletus* | U.S.A. (CA) | do | E | 2 | NA | NA |
| Rail, Guam | *Rallus owstoni* | Western Pacific Ocean: U.S.A. (Guam) | Entire, except Rota | E | 146E, 156 | NA | NA |
| Do | do | do | Rota | XN | 371 | NA | 17.84(f) |
| Rail, light-footed clapper | *Rallus longirostris levipes* | U.S.A. (CA), Mexico (Baja California) | U.S.A. only | E | 2 | NA | NA |
| Rail, Lord Howe wood | *Tricholimnas sylvestris* | Australia (Lord Howe Island) | Entire | E | 15 | NA | NA |
| Rail, Yuma clapper | *Rallus longirostris yumanensis* | Mexico, U.S.A. (AZ, CA) | U.S.A. only | E | 1 | NA | NA |
| Rhea, Darwin's | *Pterocnemia pennata* | Argentina, Bolivia, Peru, Uruguay | Entire | E | 3 | NA | NA |
| Robin, Chatham Island | *Petroica traversi* | New Zealand | do | E | 3 | NA | NA |
| Robin, scarlet-breasted (flycatcher) | *Petroica multicolor multicolor* | Australia (Norfolk Island) | do | E | 3 | NA | NA |
| Rockfowl, grey-necked | *Picathartes oreas* | Cameroon, Gabon | do | E | 3 | NA | NA |
| Rockfowl, white-necked | *Picathartes gymnocephalus* | Africa: Togo to Sierra Leone | do | E | 3 | NA | NA |
| Roller, long-tailed ground | *Uratelornis chimaera* | Malagasy Republic (=Madagascar) | do | E | 3 | NA | NA |
| Scrub-bird, noisy | *Atrichornis clamosus* | Australia | do | E | 3 | NA | NA |
| Shama, Cebu black (thrush) | *Copsychus niger cebuensis* | Philippines | do | E | 3 | NA | NA |
| Shearwater, Newell's Townsend's (formerly Manx) (='A'o). | *Puffinus auricularis* (formerly *P. newelli*). | U.S.A. (HI) | do | T | 10 | NA | NA |
| Shrike, San Clemente loggerhead | *Lanius ludovicianus mearnsi* | U.S.A. (CA) | do | E | 26 | NA | NA |
| Siskin, red | *Carduelis* (=*Spinus*) *cucullata* | South America | do | E | 15 | NA | NA |
| Sparrow, Cape Sable seaside | *Ammodramus* (=*Ammospiza*) *maritimus mirabilis*. | U.S.A. (FL) | do | E | 1 | 17.95(b) | NA |
| Sparrow, dusky seaside | *Ammodramus* (=*Ammospiza*) *maritimus nigrescens*. | do | do | E | 1 | 17.95(b) | NA |
| Sparrow, Florida grasshopper | *Ammodramus savannarum floridanus* | do | do | E | 239 | NA | NA |
| Sparrow, San Clemente sage | *Amphispiza belli clementeae* | U.S.A. (CA) | do | T | 26 | NA | NA |
| Starling, Ponape mountain | *Aplonis pelzelni* | West Pacific Ocean: Federated States of Micronesia. | do | E | 3 | NA | NA |
| Starling, Rothschild's (myna) | *Leucopsar rothschildi* | Indonesia (Bali) | do | E | 3 | NA | NA |
| Stilt, Hawaiian (=Ae'o) | *Himantopus mexicanus* (=*himantopus*) *knudseni*. | U.S.A. (Hawaii) | do | E | 2 | NA | NA |
| Stork, oriental white | *Ciconia ciconia boyciana* | China, Japan, Korea, U.S.S.R. | do | E | 3 | NA | NA |
| Stork, wood | *Mycteria americana* | U.S.A., (CA, AZ, TX, to Carolinas), Mexico, Central and South America. | U.S.A. (AL, FL, GA, NC, SC). | E | 142 | NA | NA |
| Swiftlet, Mariana gray (=Vanikoro) | *Aerodramus* (=*Collocalia*) *vanikorensis bartschi*. | Western Pacific Ocean: U.S.A. (Guam, Rota, Tinian, Saipan, Agiguan). | Entire | E | 156 | NA | NA |
| Teal, Campbell Island flightless | *Anas aucklandica nesiotis* | New Zealand (Campbell Island) | do | E | 15 | NA | NA |
| Tern, California least | *Sterna antillarum* (=*albifrons*) *browni* | Mexico, U.S.A. (CA) | do | E | 2, 3 | NA | NA |

| | | | | | | | |
|---|---|---|---|---|---|---|---|
| Tern, least | *Sterna antillarum* | U.S.A. (Atlantic and Gulf coasts, Miss. R. Basin, CA), Gr. and Lesser Antilles, Bahamas, Mexico; winters C. America, northern S. America. | U.S.A. [AR, CO, IA, IL, IN, KS, KY, LA (Miss. R. and tribs. N of Baton Rouge), MS (Miss. R.), MO, MT, NE, NM, ND, OK, SD, TN, TX (Except within 50 miles of coast)]. | E | 182 | NA | NA |
| Tern, roseate | *Sterna dougallii dougallii* | Tropical and temperate coasts of Atlantic Basin and East Africa.. | U.S.A. (Atlantic Coast south to NC), Canada (NF, NS, QU), Bermuda.. | E | 296 | NA | NA |
| Do | do | do | Western Hemisphere and adjacent oceans, incl. U.S.A. (FL, PR, VI), where not listed as endangered.. | T | 296 | NA | NA |
| Thrasher, white-breasted | *Ramphocinclus brachyurus* | West Indies: St. Lucia, Martinique | Entire | E | 3 | NA | NA |
| Thrush, large Kauai | *Myadestes (=Phaeornis) myadestinus* | U.S.A. (HI) | do | E | 2 | NA | NA |
| Thrush, Molokai (=oloma'o) | *Myadestes (=Phaeornis) lanaiensis (=obscurus) rutha.* | do | do | E | 2 | NA | NA |
| Thrush, New Zealand (wattlebird) | *Turnagra capensis* | New Zealand | do | E | 3 | NA | NA |
| Thrush, small Kauai (=puaiohi) | *Myadestes (=Phaeornis) palmeri* | U.S.A. (HI) | do | E | 1 | NA | NA |
| Tinamou, solitary | *Tinamus solitarius* | Brazil, Paraguay, Argentina | do | E | 15 | NA | NA |
| Towhee, Inyo California (=brown) | *Pipilo crissalis (=fuscus) eremophilus* | U.S.A. (CA) | do | T | 282 | 17.95(b) | NA |
| Trembler, Martinique (thrasher) | *Cinclocerthia ruficauda gutturalis* | West Indies: Martinique | do | E | 3 | NA | NA |
| Vireo, black-capped | *Vireo atricapillus* | U.S.A. (KS, LA, NE, OK, TX), Mexico. | do | E | 294 | NA | NA |
| Vireo, least Bell's | *Vireo bellii pusillus* | U.S.A. (CA), Mexico | do | E | 228 | NA | NA |
| Wanderer, plain (collared-hemipode) | *Pedionomous torquatus* | Australia | do | E | 6 | NA | NA |
| Warbler (wood), Bachman's | *Vermivora bachmanii* | U.S.A.(Southeastern), Cuba | do | E | 1, 3 | NA | NA |
| Warbler (wood), golden-cheeked | *Dendroica chrysoparia* | U.S.A. (TX), Mexico, Guatemala, Honduras, Nicaragua, Belize. | do | E | 387E, 411 | NA | NA |
| Warbler (wood), Barbados yellow | *Dendroica petechia petechia* | West Indies: Barbados | do | E | 3 | NA | NA |
| Warbler (wood), Kirtland's | *Dendroica kirtlandii* | U.S.A. (principally MI), Canada, West Indies: Bahama Islands. | do | E | 1, 3 | NA | NA |
| Warbler (old world), nightingale reed | *Acrocephalus luscinia* | Western Pacific Ocean | U.S.A. (Mariana Islands). | E | 3, 4 | NA | NA |
| Warbler (old world), Rodriques | *Bebrornis rodericanus* | Mauritius (Rodrigues Islands) | Entire | E | 3 | NA | NA |
| Warbler (wood), Semper's | *Leucopeza semperi* | West Indies: St. Lucia | do | E | 3 | NA | NA |
| Warbler (old world), Seychelles | *Bebrornis sechellensis* | Indian Ocean: Seychelles Island | do | E | 3 | NA | NA |
| Whipbird, Western | *Psophodes nigrogularis* | Australia | do | E | 3 | NA | NA |
| White-eye, bridled | *Zosterops conspicillatus conspicillatus* | Western Pacific Ocean: U.S.A. (Guam) | do | E | 156 | NA | NA |
| White-eye, Norfolk Island | *Zosterops albogularis* | Indian Ocean: Norfolk Islands | do | E | 15 | NA | NA |
| White-eye, Ponape greater | *Rukia longirostra (=sanfordi)* | West Pacific Ocean: Federated States of Micronesia. | do | E | 3 | NA | NA |
| White-eye, Seychelles | *Zosterops modesta* | Indian Ocean: Seychelles | do | E | 3 | NA | NA |
| Woodpecker, imperial | *Campephilus imperialis* | Mexico | do | E | 3 | NA | NA |
| Woodpecker, ivory-billed | *Campephilus principalis* | U.S.A. (southcentral and southeastern), Cuba. | do | E | 1, 3 | NA | NA |
| Woodpecker, red-cockaded | *Picoides (=Dendrocopos) borealis* | U.S.A. (southcentral and southeastern) | do | E | 2 | NA | NA |
| Woodpecker, Tristam's | *Dryocopus javensis richardsi* | Korea | do | E | 3 | NA | NA |
| Wren, Guadeloupe house | *Troglodytes aedon guadeloupensis* | West Indies: Guadeloupe | do | E | 3 | NA | NA |
| Wren, St. Lucia house | *Troglodytes aedon mesoleucus* | West Indies: St. Lucia | do | E | 3 | NA | NA |

| Species: Common name | Species: Scientific name | Historic range | Vertebrate population where endangered or threatened | Status | When listed | Critical habitat | Special rules |
|---|---|---|---|---|---|---|---|
| **REPTILES** | | | | | | | |
| Alligator, American | *Alligator mississippiensis* | Southeastern U.S.A. | do | T(S/A) | 1, 11, 20, 47, 51, 60, 113, 134, 186, 269 | NA | 17.42(a) |
| Alligator, Chinese | *Alligator sinensis* | China | do | E | 15 | NA | NA |
| Anole, Culebra Island giant | *Anolis roosevelti* | U.S.A. (PR: Culebra Island) | do | E | 25 | 17.95(c) | NA |
| Boa, Jamaican | *Epicrates subflavus* | Jamaica | do | E | 3 | NA | NA |
| Boa, Mona | *Epicrates monensis monensis* | U.S.A. (PR) | do | T | 33 | 17.95(c) | NA |
| Boa, Puerto Rican | *Epicrates inornatus* | do | do | E | 2 | NA | NA |
| Boa, Round Island [no common name]. | *Casarea dussumieri* | Indian Ocean: Mauritius | do | E | 88 | NA | NA |
| Boa, Round Island [no common name]. | *Bolyeria multocarinata* | do | do | E | 88 | NA | NA |
| Boa, Virgin Islands tree | *Epicrates monensis granti* | U.S. and British Virgin Islands | do | E | 2, 86 | NA | NA |
| Caiman, Apaporis River | *Caiman crocodilus apaporiensis* | Colombia | do | E | 15 | NA | NA |
| Caiman, black | *Melanosuchus niger* | Amazon basin | do | E | 15 | NA | NA |
| Caiman, broad-snouted | *Caiman latirostris* | Brazil, Argentina, Paraguay, Uruguay | do | E | 15 | NA | NA |
| Caiman, Yacare | *Caiman crocodilus yacare* | Bolivia, Argentina, Peru, Brazil | do | E | 3 | NA | NA |
| Chuckwalla, San Esteban Island | *Sauromalus varius* | Mexico | do | E | 88 | NA | NA |
| Crocodile, African dwarf | *Osteolaemus tetraspis tetraspis* | West Africa | do | E | 15 | NA | NA |
| Crocodile, African slender-snouted | *Crocodylus cataphractus* | Western and central Africa | do | E | 5 | NA | NA |
| Crocodile, American | *Crocodylus acutus* | U.S.A. (FL), Mexico, South America, Central America, Caribbean. | do | E | 10, 87 | 17.95(c) | NA |
| Crocodile, Ceylon mugger | *Crocodylus palustris kimbula* | Sri Lanka | do | E | 15 | NA | NA |
| Crocodile, Congo dwarf | *Osteolaemus tetraspis osborni* | Congo River drainage | do | E | 15 | NA | NA |
| Crocodile, Cuban | *Crocodylus rhombifer* | Cuba | do | E | 3 | NA | NA |
| Crocodile, Morelet's | *Crocodylus moreletii* | Mexico, Belize, Guatemala | do | E | 3 | NA | NA |
| Crocodile, mugger | *Crocodylus palustris palustris* | India, Pakistan, Iran, Bangladesh | do | E | 15 | NA | NA |
| Crocodile, Nile | *Crocodylus niloticus* | Africa, Middle East | Entire, except populations in Zimbabwe. | E | 3, 334 | NA | NA |
| Do | do | do | Zimbabwe | T | 3, 334 | NA | 17.42(c) |
| Crocodile, Orinoco | *Crocodylus intermedius* | South America: Orinoco River Basin | Entire | E | 3 | NA | NA |
| Crocodile, Philippine | *Crocodylus novaeguineae mindorensis* | Philippine Islands | do | E | 15 | NA | NA |
| Crocodile, saltwater (=estuarine) | *Crocodylus porosus* | Southeast Asia, Australia, Papua-New Guinea, Pacific Islands. | Entire, except Papua-New Guinea. | E | 87 | NA | NA |
| Crocodile, Siamese | *Crocodylus siamensis* | Southeast Asia, Malay Peninsula | Entire | E | 15 | NA | NA |
| Gavial (=gharial) | *Gavialis gangeticus* | Pakistan, Burma, Bangladesh, India, Nepal. | do | E | 3, 15 | NA | NA |
| Gecko, day | *Phelsuma edwardnewtoni* | Indian Ocean: Mauritius | do | E | 3 | NA | NA |
| Gecko, Monito | *Sphaerodactylus micropithecus* | U.S.A. (PR) | do | E | 125 | 17.95(c) | NA |
| Gecko, Round Island day | *Phelsuma guentheri* | Indian Ocean: Mauritius | do | E | 3 | NA | NA |
| Gecko, Serpent Island | *Cyrtodactylus serpensinsula* | do | do | T | 129 | NA | NA |
| Iguana, Acklins ground | *Cyclura rileyi nuchalis* | West Indies: Bahamas | do | T | 129 | NA | NA |
| Iguana, Allen's Cay | *Cyclura cychlura inornata* | do | do | T | 129 | NA | NA |
| Iguana, Andros Island ground | *Cyclura cychlura cychlura* | do | do | T | 129 | NA | NA |
| Iguana, Anegada ground | *Cyclura pinguis* | West Indies: British Virgin Islands (Anegada Island). | do | E | 3 | NA | NA |
| Iguana, Barrington land | *Conolophus pallidus* | Ecuador (Galapagos Islands) | do | E | 3 | NA | NA |

| | | | | | | | |
|---|---|---|---|---|---|---|---|
| Iguana, Cayman Brac ground | *Cyclura nubila caymanensis* | West Indies: Cayman Islands | ......do | T | 129 | NA | NA |
| Iguana, Cuban ground | *Cyclura nubila nubila* | Cuba | Entire (excluding population introduced in Puerto Rico). | T | 129 | NA | NA |
| Iguana, Exuma Island | *Cyclura cychlura figginsi* | West Indies: Bahamas | Entire | T | 129 | NA | NA |
| Iguana, Fiji banded | *Brachylophus fasciatus* | Pacific: Fiji, Tonga | ......do | E | 88 | NA | NA |
| Iguana, Fiji crested | *Brachylophus vitiensis* | Pacific: Fiji | ......do | E | 88 | NA | NA |
| Iguana, Grand Cayman ground | *Cyclura nubila lewisi* | West Indies: Cayman Islands | ......do | E | 129 | NA | NA |
| Iguana, Jamaican | *Cyclura collei* | West Indies: Jamaica | ......do | E | 129 | NA | NA |
| Iguana, Mayaguana | *Cyclura carinata bartschi* | West Indies: Bahamas | ......do | T | 129 | NA | NA |
| Iguana, Mona ground | *Cyclura stejnegeri* | U.S.A. (PR: Mona Island) | ......do | T | 33 | 17.95(c) | NA |
| Iguana, Turks and Caicos | *Cyclura carinata carinata* | West Indies: Turks and Caicos Islands | ......do | T | 129 | NA | NA |
| Iguana, Watling Island ground | *Cyclura rileyi rileyi* | West Indies: Bahamas | ......do | E | 129 | NA | NA |
| Iguana, White Cay ground | *Cyclura rileyi cristata* | ......do | ......do | T | 129 | NA | NA |
| Lizard, blunt-nosed leopard | *Gambelia* (=*Crotaphytus*) *silus* | U.S.A. (CA) | ......do | E | 1 | NA | NA |
| Lizard, Coachella Valley fringe-toed | *Uma inornata* | ......do | ......do | T | 105 | 17.95(c) | NA |
| Lizard, Hierro giant | *Gallotia simonyi simonyi* | Spain (Canary Islands) | ......do | E | 144 | NA | NA |
| Lizard, Ibiza wall | *Podarcis pityusensis* | Spain (Balearic Islands) | ......do | T | 144 | NA | NA |
| Lizard, Island night | *Xantusia* (=*Klauberina*) *riversiana* | U.S.A. (CA) | ......do | T | 26 | NA | NA |
| Lizard, St. Croix ground | *Ameiva polops* | U.S.A. (VI) | ......do | E | 24 | 17.95(c) | NA |
| Monitor, Bengal | *Varanus bengalensis* | Iran, Iraq, India, Sri Lanka, Malaysia, Afghanistan, Burma, Vietnam, Thailand. | ......do | E | 15 | NA | NA |
| Monitor, desert | *Varanus griseus* | North Africa to Neareast, Caspian Sea through U.S.S.R. to Pakistan, Northwest India. | ......do | E | 15 | NA | NA |
| Monitor, Komodo Island | *Varanus komodoensis* | Indonesia (Komodo, Rintja, Padar, and western Flores Island). | ......do | E | 15 | NA | NA |
| Monitor, yellow | *Varanus flavescens* | West Pakistan through India to Bangladesh. | ......do | E | 15 | NA | NA |
| Python, Indian | *Python molurus molurus* | Sri Lanka and India | ......do | E | 15 | NA | NA |
| Rattlesnake, Aruba Island | *Crotalus unicolor* | Aruba Island (Netherland Antilles) | ......do | T | 129 | NA | NA |
| Rattlesnake, New Mexican ridge-nosed | *Crotalus willardi obscurus* | U.S.A. (NM), Mexico | ......do | T | 43 | 17.95(c) | NA |
| Skink, blue-tailed mole | *Eumeces egregius lividus* | U.S.A. (FL) | ......do | T | 299 | NA | 17.42(d) |
| Skink, Round Island | *Leiolopisma telfairi* | Indian Ocean: Mauritius | ......do | T | 129 | NA | NA |
| Skink, sand | *Neoseps reynoldsi* | U.S.A. (FL) | ......do | T | 299 | NA | 17.42(d) |
| Snake, Atlantic salt marsh | *Nerodia fasciata taeniata* | ......do | ......do | T | 30 | NA | NA |
| Snake, Concho water | *Nerodia harteri paucimaculata* | U.S.A. (TX) | ......do | T | 241 | NA | NA |
| Snake, eastern indigo | *Drymarchon corais couperi* | U.S.A. (AL, FL, GA, MS, SC) | ......do | T | 32 | NA | NA |
| Snake, San Francisco garter | *Thamnophis sirtalis tetrataenia* | U.S.A. (CA) | ......do | E | 1 | NA | NA |
| Tartaruga | *Podocnemis expansa* | South America: Orinoco and Amazon River basins. | ......do | E | 3 | NA | NA |
| Terrapin, river (=Tuntong) | *Batagur baska* | Malaysia, Bangladesh, Burma, India, Indonesia. | ......do | E | 3 | NA | NA |
| Tomistoma | *Tomistoma schlegelii* | Malaysia, Indonesia | ......do | E | 15 | NA | NA |
| Tortoise, angulated | *Geochelone yniphora* | Malagasy Republic (=Madagascar) | ......do | E | 15 | NA | NA |
| Tortoise, Bolson | *Gopherus flavomarginatus* | Mexico | ......do | E | 46 | NA | NA |
| Tortoise, desert | *Gopherus* (=*Xerobates*, =*Scaptochelys*) *agassizii*. | U.S.A. (AZ, CA, NV, UT), Mexico | Entire, except AZ south and east of the Colorado River, and Mexico.. | T | 103, 357E, 378 | 17.95(c) | NA |

18

| Species: Common name | Species: Scientific name | Historic range | Vertebrate population where endangered or threatened | Status | When listed | Critical habitat | Special rules |
|---|---|---|---|---|---|---|---|
| Do | ......do | ......do | U.S.A. (AZ, south and east of Colorado River) and Mexico when found outside of AZ, south and east of Colorado River, and Mexico.. | T(S/A) | 357E, 378 | NA | 17.42(e) |
| Tortoise, Galapagos | *Geochelone elephantopus* | Ecuador (Galapagos Islands) | Entire | E | 3 | NA | NA |
| Tortoise, gopher | *Gopherus polyphemus* | U.S.A. (AL, FL, GA, LA, MS, SC) | Wherever found west of Mobile and Tombigbee Rivers in AL, MS, and LA. | T | 281 | NA | NA |
| Tortoise, radiated | *Geochelone* (=*Testudo*) *radiata* | Malagasy Republic (=Madagascar) | Entire | E | 3 | NA | NA |
| Tracaja | *Podocnemis unifilis* | South America: Orinoco and Amazon River basins. | ......do | E | 3 | NA | NA |
| Tuatara | *Sphenodon punctatus* | New Zealand | ......do | E | 3 | NA | NA |
| Turtle, Alabama red-bellied | *Pseudemys alabamensis* | U.S.A. (AL) | ......do | E | 278 | NA | NA |
| Turtle, aquatic box | *Terrapene coahuila* | Mexico | ......do | E | 6 | NA | NA |
| Turtle, black softshell | *Trionyx nigricans* | Bangladesh | ......do | E | 15 | NA | NA |
| Turtle, Burmese peacock | *Morenia ocellata* | Burma | ......do | E | 15 | NA | NA |
| Turtle, Central American river | *Dermatemys mawii* | Mexico, Belize, Guatemala | ......do | E | 129 | NA | NA |
| Turtle, Cuatro Cienegas softshell | *Trionyx ater* | Mexico | ......do | E | 15 | NA | NA |
| Turtle, flattened musk | *Sternotherus depressus* | U.S.A. (AL) | Black Warrior River system upstream from Bankhead Dam. | T | 272 | NA | NA |
| Turtle, geometric | *Psammobates geometricus* (=*Geochelone geometrica*). | South Africa | Entire | E | 15 | NA | NA |
| Turtle, green sea | *Chelonia mydas* (incl. *agassizi*) | Circumglobal in tropical and temperate seas and oceans. | Wherever found except where listed as endangered below. | T | 2, 42 | NA | 17.42(b) and Parts 220 and 227. |
| Do | ......do | ......do | Breeding colony populations in FL and on Pacific coast of Mexico. | E | 2, 42 | NA | 222.41 |
| Turtle, hawksbill sea (=carey) | *Eretmochelys imbricata* | Tropical seas | Entire | E | 3 | 17.95(c) | 222.41 |
| Turtle, Indian sawback | *Kachuga tecta tecta* | India | ......do | E | 15 | NA | NA |
| Turtle, Indian softshell | *Trionyx gangeticus* | Pakistan, India | ......do | E | 15 | NA | NA |
| Turtle, Kemp's (=Atlantic) ridley sea | *Lepidochelys kempii* | Tropical and temperate seas in Atlantic Basin, incl. Gulf of Mexico. | ......do | E | 4 | NA | 222.41 |
| Turtle, leatherback sea | *Dermochelys coriacea* | Tropical, temperate, and subpolar seas | ......do | E | 3 | 17.95(c), 226.71 | 222.41 |
| Turtle, loggerhead sea | *Caretta caretta* | Circumglobal in tropical and temperate seas and oceans. | ......do | T | 42 | NA | 17.42(b) and Parts 220 and 227. |

| | | | | | | | |
|---|---|---|---|---|---|---|---|
| Turtle, olive (Pacific) ridley sea | *Lepidochelys olivacea* | Tropical and temperate seas in Pacific Basin. | Wherever found except where listed as endangered below. | T | 42 | NA | 17.42(b) and Parts 220 and 227. |
| Do | ......do | ......do | Breeding colony populations on Pacific coast of Mexico. | E | 42 | NA | 222.41 |
| Turtle, peacock softshell | *Trionyx hurum* | India, Bangladesh | Entire | E | 15 | NA | NA |
| Turtle, Plymouth red-bellied | *Pseudemys* (=*Chrysemys*) *rubriventris bangsi*. | U.S.A. (MA) | ......do | E | 90 | 17.95(c) | NA |
| Turtle, ringed sawback | *Graptemys oculifera* | U.S.A. (LA, MS) | ......do | T | 250 | NA | NA |
| Turtle, short-necked or western swamp | *Pseudemydura umbrina* | Australia | ......do | E | 3 | NA | NA |
| Turtle, spotted pond | *Geoclemys* (=*Damonia*) *hamiltonii* | North India, Pakistan | ......do | E | 15 | NA | NA |
| Turtle, three-keeled Asian | *Melanochelys* (=*Geoemyda*, =*Nicoria*) *tricarinata*. | Central India to Bangladesh and Burma. | ......do | E | 15 | NA | NA |
| Turtle, yellow-blotched map (=sawback). | *Graptemys flavimaculata* | U.S.A. (MS) | ......do | T | 416 | NA | NA |
| Viper, Lar Valley | *Vipera latifii* | Iran | ......do | E | 129 | NA | NA |
| AMPHIBIANS | | | | | | | |
| Coqui, golden | *Eleutherodactylus jasperi* | U.S.A. (PR) | ......do | T | 29 | 17.95(d) | NA |
| Frog, Israel painted | *Discoglossus nigriventer* | Israel | ......do | E | 3 | NA | NA |
| Frog, Panamanian golden | *Atelopus varius zeteki* | Panama | ......do | E | 15 | NA | NA |
| Frog, Stephen Island | *Leiopelma hamiltoni* | New Zealand | ......do | E | 3 | NA | NA |
| Salamander, Cheat Mountain | *Plethodon nettingi* | U.S.A. (WV) | ......do | T | 358 | NA | NA |
| Salamander, Chinese giant | *Andrias davidianus davidianus* | Western China | ......do | E | 15 | NA | NA |
| Salamander, desert slender | *Batrachoseps aridus* | U.S.A. (CA) | ......do | E | 6 | NA | NA |
| Salamander, Japanese giant | *Andrias davidianus japonicus* | Japan | ......do | E | 15 | NA | NA |
| Salamander, Red Hills | *Phaeognathus hubrichti* | U.S.A. (AL) | ......do | T | 19 | NA | NA |
| Salamander, San Marcos | *Eurycea nana* | U.S.A. (TX) | ......do | T | 98 | 17.95(d) | 17.43(a) |
| Salamander, Santa Cruz long-toed | *Ambystoma macrodactylum croceum* | U.S.A. (CA) | ......do | E | 1 | NA | NA |
| Salamander, Shenandoah | *Plethodon shenandoah* | U.S.A. (VA) | ......do | E | 358 | NA | NA |
| Salamander, Texas blind | *Typhlomolge rathbuni* | U.S.A. (TX) | ......do | E | 1 | NA | NA |
| Toad, African viviparous | *Nectophrynoides* spp | Tanzania, Guinea, Ivory Coast, Cameroon, Liberia, Ethiopia. | ......do | E | 15 | NA | NA |
| Toad, Cameroon | *Bufo superciliaris* | Equatorial Africa | ......do | E | 15 | NA | NA |
| Toad, Houston | *Bufo houstonensis* | U.S.A. (TX) | ......do | E | 2 | 17.95(d) | NA |
| Toad, Monte Verde | *Bufo periglenes* | Costa Rica | ......do | E | 15 | NA | NA |
| Toad, Puerto Rican crested | *Peltophryne lemur* | U.S.A. (PR), British Virgin Islands | ......do | T | 283 | NA | NA |
| Toad, Wyoming | *Bufo hemiophrys baxteri* | U.S.A. (WY) | ......do | E | 138 | NA | NA |
| FISHES | | | | | | | |
| Ala Balik (trout) | *Salmo platycephalus* | Turkey | ......do | E | 3 | NA | NA |
| Ayumodoki (loach) | *Hymenophysa* (=*Botia*) *curta* | Japan | ......do | E | 3 | NA | NA |
| Blindcat, Mexican (catfish) | *Prietella phreatophila* | Mexico | ......do | E | 3 | NA | NA |
| Bonytoungue, Asian | *Scleropages formosus* | Thailand, Indonesia, Malaysia | ......do | E | 15 | NA | NA |
| Catfish [no common name] | *Pangasius sanitwongsei* | Thailand | ......do | E | 3 | NA | NA |
| Catfish, giant | *Pangasianodon gigas* | ......do | ......do | E | 3 | NA | NA |
| Catfish, Yaqui | *Ictalurus pricei* | U.S.A. (AZ), Mexico | ......do | T | 157 | 17.95(e) | 17.44(g) |
| Cavefish, Alabama | *Speoplatyrhinus poulsoni* | U.S.A. (AL) | ......do | E | 28, 328 | 17.95(e) | NA |
| Cavefish, Ozark | *Amblyopsis rosae* | U.S.A. (AR, MO, OK) | ......do | T | 164 | NA | NA |
| Chub, bonytail | *Gila elegans* | U.S.A. (AZ, CA, CO, NV, UT, WY) | ......do | E | 92 | NA | NA |
| Chub, Borax Lake | *Gila boraxobius* | U.S.A. (OR) | ......do | E | 124 | 17.95(e) | NA |
| Chub, Chihuahua | *Gila nigrescens* | U.S.A. (NM), Mexico (Chihuahua) | ......do | T | 132 | NA | 17.44(g) |
| Chub, humpback | *Gila cypha* | U.S.A. (AZ, CO, UT, WY) | ......do | E | 1 | NA | NA |
| Chub, Hutton tui | *Gila bicolor* ssp | U.S.A. (OR) | ......do | T | 174 | NA | 17.44(j) |
| Chub, Mohave tui | *Gila bicolor mohavensis* | U.S.A. (CA) | ......do | E | 2 | NA | NA |

| Species | | Historic range | Vertebrate population where endangered or threatened | Status | When listed | Critical habitat | Special rules |
|---|---|---|---|---|---|---|---|
| Common name | Scientific name | | | | | | |
| Chub, Owens tui | *Gila bicolor snyderi* | do | do | E | 195 | 17.95(e) | NA |
| Chub, Pahranagat roundtail (=bonytail) | *Gila robusta jordani* | U.S.A. (NV) | do | E | 2 | NA | NA |
| Chub, slender | *Erimystax (=Hybopsis) cahni* | U.S.A. (TN, VA) | do | T | 28 | 17.95(e) | 17.44(c) |
| Chub, Sonora | *Gila ditaenia* | U.S.A., (AZ), Mexico | do | T | 227 | 17.95(e) | 17.44(o) |
| Chub, spotfin | *Cyprinella (=Hybopsis) monacha* | U.S.A. (AL, GA, NC, TN, VA) | do | T | 28 | 17.95(e) | 17.44(c) |
| Chub, Virgin River | *Gila robusta semidnuda* | U.S.A. (AZ, NV, UT) | do | E | 361 | NA | NA |
| Chub, Yaqui | *Gila purpurea* | U.S.A. (AZ), Mexico | do | E | 157 | 17.95(e) | NA |
| Cicek (minnow) | *Acanthorutilus handlirschi* | Turkey | do | E | 3 | NA | NA |
| Cui-ui | *Chasmistes cujus* | U.S.A. (NV) | do | E | 1 | NA | NA |
| Dace, Ash Meadows speckled | *Rhinichthys osculus nevadensis* | do | do | E | 117E, 127E, 130 | 17.95(e) | NA |
| Dace, blackside | *Phoxinus cumberlandensis* | U.S.A. (TN, KY) | do | T | 273 | NA | NA |
| Dace, Clover Valley speckled | *Rhinichthys osculus oligoporus* | U.S.A. (NV) | do | E | 370 | NA | NA |
| Dace, desert | *Eremichthys acros* | U.S.A. (NV) | do | T | 1, 2D, 210 | 17.95(e) | 17.44(m) |
| Dace, Foskett speckled | *Rhinichthys osculus* ssp | U.S.A. (OR) | do | T | 174 | NA | 17.44(j) |
| Dace, Independence Valley speckled | *Rhinichthys osculus lethoporus* | U.S.A. (NV) | do | E | 370, 372 | NA | NA |
| Dace, Kendall Warm Springs | *Rhinichthys osculus thermalis* | U.S.A. (WY) | do | E | 2 | NA | NA |
| Dace, Moapa | *Moapa coriacea* | U.S.A. (NV) | do | E | 1 | NA | NA |
| Darter, amber | *Percina antesella* | U.S.A. (GA, TN) | do | E | 196 | 17.95(e) | NA |
| Darter, bayou | *Etheostoma rubrum* | U.S.A. (MS) | do | T | 10 | NA | 17.44(b) |
| Darter, boulder (=Elk River) | *Etheostoma wapiti* | U.S.A. (TN, AL) | do | E | 322 | NA | NA |
| Darter, fountain | *Etheostoma fonticola* | U.S.A. (TX) | do | E | 2 | 17.95(e) | NA |
| Darter, leopard | *Percina pantherina* | U.S.A. (AR, OK) | do | T | 31 | 17.95(e) | 17.44(d) |
| Darter, Maryland | *Etheostoma sellare* | U.S.A. (MD) | do | E | 1 | 17.95(e) | NA |
| Darter, Niangua | *Etheostoma nianguae* | U.S.A. (MO) | do | T | 185 | 17.95(e) | 17.44(k) |
| Darter, Okaloosa | *Etheostoma okaloosae* | U.S.A. (FL) | do | E | 6 | NA | NA |
| Darter, slackwater | *Etheostoma boschungi* | U.S.A. (AL, TN) | do | T | 28 | 17.95(e) | 17.44(c) |
| Darter, snail | *Percina tanasi* | U.S.A. (AL, GA, TN) | do | T | 12, 150 | NA | NA |
| Darter, watercress | *Etheostoma nuchale* | U.S.A. (AL) | do | E | 2 | NA | NA |
| Gambusia, Big Bend | *Gambusia gaigei* | U.S.A. (TX) | do | E | 1 | NA | NA |
| Gambusia, Clear Creek | *Gambusia heterochir* | do | do | E | 1 | NA | NA |
| Gambusia, Pecos | *Gambusia nobilis* | U.S.A. (NM, TX) | do | E | 2 | NA | NA |
| Gambusia, San Marcos | *Gambusia georgei* | U.S.A. (TX) | do | E | 98 | 17.95(e) | NA |
| Killifish, Pahrump | *Empetrichthys latos* | U.S.A. (NV) | do | E | 1 | NA | NA |
| Logperch, Conasauga | *Percina jenkinsi* | U.S.A. (GA, TN) | do | E | 196 | 17.95(e) | NA |
| Logperch, Roanoke | *Percina rex* | U.S.A. (VA) | do | E | 359 | NA | NA |
| Madtom, Neosho | *Notorus placidus* | U.S.A. (KS, MO, OK) | do | T | 388 | NA | NA |
| Madtom, Scioto | *Noturus trautmani* | U.S.A. (OH) | do | E | 10 | NA | NA |
| Madtom, Smoky | *Noturus baileyi* | U.S.A. (TN) | do | E | 163 | 17.95(e) | NA |
| Madtom, yellowfin | *Noturus flavipinnis* | U.S.A. (TN, VA) | Entire, except where listed as an experimental population below. | T | 28, 317 | 17.95(e) | 17.44(c) |

| | | | | | | | |
|---|---|---|---|---|---|---|---|
| Do | ......do | ......do | N. Fork Holston R., VA, TN; S. Fork Holston R., upstream to Ft. Patrick Henry Dam, TN; Holston R., downstream to John Sevier Detention Lake Dam, TN; and all tributaries thereto. | XN | 317 | NA | 17.84(e) |
| Minnow, loach | *Tiaroga cobitis* | U.S.A. (AZ, NM), Mexico | Entire | T | 247 | NA | 17.44(q) |
| Nekogigi (catfish) | *Coreobagrus ichikawai* | Japan | ......do | E | 3 | NA | NA |
| Pupfish, Ash Meadows Amargosa | *Cyprinodon nevadensis mionectes* | U.S.A. (NV) | ......do | E | 117E, 127E, 130 | 17.95(e) | NA |
| Pupfish, Comanche Springs | *Cyprinodon elegans* | U.S.A. (TX) | ......do | E | 1 | NA | NA |
| Pupfish, desert | *Cyprinodon macularius* | U.S.A. (AZ, CA) Mexico | ......do | E | 222 | 17.95(e) | NA |
| Pupfish, Devils Hole | *Cyprinodon diabolis* | U.S.A. (NV) | ......do | E | 1 | NA | NA |
| Pupfish, Leon Springs | *Cyprinodon bovinus* | U.S.A. (TX) | ......do | E | 102 | 17.95(e) | NA |
| Pupfish, Owens | *Cyprinodon radiosus* | U.S.A. (CA) | ......do | E | 1 | NA | NA |
| Pupfish, Warm Springs | *Cyprinodon nevadensis pectoralis* | U.S.A. (NV) | ......do | E | 2 | NA | NA |
| Salmon, chinook | *Oncorhynchus tshawytscha* | Pacific Ocean | U.S.A. (CA: Sacramento R. winter run). | T | 383E, 407 | 226.21 | 227.21 |
| Sculpin, pygmy | *Cottus pygmaeus* | U.S.A. (AL) | Entire | T | 365 | NA | 17.44(u) |
| Shiner, beautiful | *Cyprinella* (=*Notropis*) *formosa* (=*formosus*). | U.S.A. (AZ, NM), Mexico | ......do | T | 157 | 17.95(e) | 17.44(g) |
| Shiner, Cahaba | *Notropis cahabae* | U.S.A. (AL) | ......do | E | 405 | NA | NA |
| Shiner, Cape Fear | *Notropis mekistocholas* | U.S.A. (NC) | ......do | E | 290 | 17.95(e) | NA |
| Shiner, Pecos bluntnose | *Notropis simus pecosensis* | U.S.A. (NM) | ......do | T | 258 | 17.95(e) | 17.44(r) |
| Silverside, Waccamaw | *Menidia extensa* | U.S.A. (NC) | ......do | T | 265 | 17.95(e) | 17.44(s) |
| Spikedace | *Meda fulgida* | U.S.A. (NM) | ......do | T | 236 | NA | 17.44(p) |
| Spinedace, Big Spring | *Lepidomeda mollispinis pratensis* | U.S.A. (NV) | ......do | T | 173 | 17.95(e) | 17.44(i) |
| Spinedace, Little Colorado | *Lepidomeda vittata* | U.S.A. (AZ) | ......do | T | 287 | 17.95(e) | 17.44(t) |
| Spinedace, White River | *Lepidomeda albivallis* | U.S.A. (NV) | ......do | E | 203 | 17.95(e) | NA |
| Springfish, Hiko White River | *Crenichthys baileyi grandis* | ......do | ......do | E | 206 | 17.95(e) | NA |
| Springfish, Railroad Valley | *Crenichthys nevadae* | ......do | ......do | T | 224 | 17.95(e) | 17.44(n) |
| Springfish, White River | *Crenichthys baileyi baileyi* | ......do | ......do | E | 206 | 17.95(e) | NA |
| Squawfish, Colorado | *Ptychocheilus lucius* | U.S.A. (AZ, CA, CO, NM, NV, UT, WY), Mexico. | Entire, except Salt and Verde R. drainages, AZ. | E | 1, 193 | NA | NA |
| Do | ......do | ......do | Salt and Verde R. drainages, AZ. | XN | 193 | NA | 17.84(b) |
| Stickleback, unarmored threespine | *Gasterosteus aculeatus williamsoni* | U.S.A. (CA) | Entire | E | 2 | NA | NA |
| Sturgeon, pallid | *Scaphirhynchus albus* | U.S.A. (AR, IA, IL, KS, KY, LA, MO, MS, MT, ND, NE, SD, TN). | ......do | E | 399 | NA | NA |
| Sturgeon, shortnose | *Acipenser brevirostrum* | U.S.A. and Canada (Atlantic Coast) | ......do | E | 1 | NA | NA |
| Sucker, June | *Chasmistes liorus* | U.S.A. (UT) | ......do | E | 223 | 17.95(e) | NA |
| Sucker, Lost River | *Deltistes luxatus* | U.S.A. (OR, CA) | ......do | E | 313 | NA | NA |
| Sucker, Modoc | *Catostomus microps* | U.S.A. (CA) | ......do | E | 184 | 17.95(e) | NA |
| Sucker, short-nose | *Chasmistes brevirostris* | U.S.A. (OR, CA) | ......do | E | 313 | NA | NA |
| Sucker, Warner | *Catostomus warnerensis* | U.S.A. (OR) | ......do | T | 205 | 17.95(e) | 17.44(l) |
| Tango, Miyako (Tokyo bitterling) | *Tanakia tanago* | Japan | ......do | E | 3 | NA | NA |
| Temolek, Ikan (minnow) | *Probarbus jullieni* | Thailand, Cambodia, Vietnam, Malaysia, Laos. | ......do | E | 15 | NA | NA |
| Topminnow, Gila (incl. Yaqui) | *Poeciliopsis occidentalis* | U.S.A. (AZ, NM), Mexico | U.S.A. only | E | 1 | NA | NA |
| Totoaba (seatrout or weakfish) | *Cynoscion macdonaldi* | Mexico (Gulf of California) | Entire | E | 45 | NA | NA |

| Species | | Historic range | Vertebrate population where endangered or threatened | Status | When listed | Critical habitat | Special rules |
|---|---|---|---|---|---|---|---|
| Common name | Scientific name | | | | | | |
| Trout, Apache (=Arizona) | *Oncorhynchus* (=*Salmo*) *apache* | U.S.A. (AZ) | do | T | 1, 8 | NA | 17.44(a) |
| Trout, Gila | *Oncorhynchus* (=*Salmo*) *gilae* | U.S.A. (AZ, NM) | do | E | 1 | NA | NA |
| Trout, greenback cutthroat | *Oncorhynchus* (=*Salmo*) *clarki stomias.* | U.S.A. (CO) | do | T | 1, 38 | NA | 17.44(f) |
| Trout, Lahontan cutthroat | *Oncorhynchus* (=*Salmo*) *clarki henshawi.* | U.S.A. (CA, NV, OR) | do | T | 2, 8 | NA | 17.44(a) |
| Trout, Little Kern golden | *Oncorhynchus* (=*Salmo*) *aguabonita whitei.* | U.S.A. (CA) | do | T | 37 | 17.95(e) | 17.44(e) |
| Trout, Paiute cutthroat | *Oncorhynchus* (=*Salmo*) *clarki seleniris.* | do | do | T | 1, 8 | NA | 17.44(a) |
| Woundfin | *Plagopterus argentissimus* | U.S.A. (AZ, NV, UT) | Entire, except Gila R. drainage, AZ, NM. | E | 2, 193 | NA | NA |
| Do | do | do | Gila R. drainage AZ, NM. | XN | 193 | NA | 17.84(b) |
| SNAILS | | | | | | | |
| Shagreen, Magazine Mountain | *Mesodon magazinensis* | U.S.A. (AR) | NA | T | 348 | NA | NA |
| Snail, Chittenango ovate amber | *Succinea chittenangoensis* | U.S.A. (NY) | NA | T | 41 | NA | NA |
| Snail, flat-spired three-toothed | *Triodopsis platysayoides* | U.S.A. (WV) | NA | T | 41 | NA | NA |
| Snail, Iowa Pleistocene | *Discus macclintocki* | U.S.A. (IA) | NA | E | 41 | NA | NA |
| Snail, Manus Island tree | *Papustyla pulcherrima* | Pacific Ocean: Admiralty Is. (Manus Is.) | NA | E | 3 | NA | NA |
| Snail, noonday | *Mesodon clarki nantahala* | U.S.A. (NC) | NA | T | 41 | NA | NA |
| Snail, Oahu tree | *Achatinella* spp. (all species) | U.S.A. (HI) | NA | E | 108, 112 | NA | NA |
| Snail, painted snake coiled forest | *Anguispira picta* | U.S.A. (TN) | NA | T | 41 | NA | NA |
| Snail, Stock Island tree | *Orthalicus reses* (not incl. *nesodryas*) | U.S.A. (FL) | NA | T | 41 | NA | NA |
| Snail, tulotoma (=Alabama live-bearing). | *Tulotoma magnifica* | U.S.A. (AL) | NA | E | 412 | NA | NA |
| Snail, Virginia fringed mountain | *Polygyriscus virginianus* | U.S.A. (VA) | NA | E | 41 | NA | NA |
| CLAMS | | | | | | | |
| Fanshell | *Cyprogenia stegaria* (=*irrorata*) | U.S.A. (AL, IL, IN, KY, OH, PA, TN, VA, WV). | NA | E | 391 | NA | NA |
| Fatmucket, Arkansas | *Lampsilis powelli* | U.S.A. (AR) | NA | T | 382 | NA | NA |
| Heelsplitter, inflated | *Potamilus inflatus* | U.S.A. (AL, LA, MS) | NA | T | 404 | NA | NA |
| Mussel, Cumberland pigtoe | *Pleurobema gibberum* | U.S.A. (TN) | NA | E | 423 | NA | NA |
| Mussel, Curtus' | *Pleurobema curtum* | U.S.A. (AL, MS) | NA | E | 262 | NA | NA |
| Mussel, dwarf wedge | *Alasmidonta heterodon* | U.S.A. (CT, DC, DE, MA, MD, NC, NH, NJ, PA, VA, VT), Canada (NB). | NA | E | 377 | NA | NA |
| Mussel, Judge Tait's | *Pleurobema taitianum* | U.S.A. (AL, MS) | NA | E | 262 | NA | NA |
| Mussel, Marshall's | *Pleurobema marshalli* | do | NA | E | 262 | NA | NA |
| Mussel, penitent | *Epioblasma* (=*Dysnomia*) *penita* | do | NA | E | 262 | NA | NA |
| Mussel, ring pink (=golf stick pearly) | *Obovaria retusa* | U.S.A. (AL, IL, IN, KY, OH, PA, TN, WV). | NA | E | 369 | NA | NA |
| Mussel, winged mapleleaf | *Quandrula fragosa* | U.S.A. (WI, IL, MN, MO, OH, NE, TN, KY, IN, IA, OK). | NA | E | 426 | NA | NA |
| Pearlshell, Louisiana | *Margaritifera hembeli* | U.S.A. (LA) | NA | E | 304 | NA | NA |
| Pearly mussel, Alabama lamp | *Lampsilis virescens* | U.S.A. (AL, TN) | NA | E | 15 | NA | NA |
| Pearly mussel, Appalachian monkeyface. | *Quadrula sparsa* | U.S.A. (TN, VA) | NA | E | 15 | NA | NA |
| Pearly mussel, birdwing | *Conradilla caelata* | do | NA | E | 15 | NA | NA |
| Pearly mussel, cracking | *Hemistena* (=*Lastena*) *lata* | U.S.A. (AL, IL, IN, KY, OH, TN, and VA). | NA | E | 366 | NA | NA |

| | | | | | | | | |
|---|---|---|---|---|---|---|---|---|
| Pearly mussel, Cumberland bean | *Villosa* (=*Micromya*) *trabalis* | U.S.A. (KY, TN) | NA | E | 15 | NA | NA |
| Pearly mussel, Cumberland monkey-face. | *Quadrula intermedia* | U.S.A. (AL, TN, VA) | NA | E | 15 | NA | NA |
| Pearly mussel, Curtis' | *Epioblasma* (=*Dysnomia*) *florentina curtisi.* | U.S.A. (MO) | NA | E | 15 | NA | NA |
| Pearly mussel, dromedary | *Dromus dromas* | U.S.A. (TN, VA) | NA | E | 15 | NA | NA |
| Pearly mussel, green-blossom | *Epioblasma* (=*Dysnomia*) *torulosa gubernaculum.* | ......do | NA | E | 15 | NA | NA |
| Pearly mussel, Higgins' eye | *Lampsilis higginsi* | U.S.A. (IL, IA, MN, MO, NE, WI) | NA | E | 15 | NA | NA |
| Pearly mussel, little-wing | *Pegias fabula* | U.S.A. (AL, KY, NC, TN, VA) | NA | E | 342 | NA | NA |
| Pearly mussel, Nicklin's | *Megalonaias nicklineana* | Mexico | NA | E | 15 | NA | NA |
| Pearly mussel (=pimple back), orange-footed. | *Plethobasus cooperianus* | U.S.A. (AL, IN, IA, KY, OH, PA, TN) | NA | E | 15 | NA | NA |
| Pearly mussel, pale lilliput | *Toxolasma* (=*Carunculina*) *cylindrellus* | U.S.A. (AL, TN) | NA | E | 15 | NA | NA |
| Pearly mussel, pink mucket | *Lampsilis orbiculata* | U.S.A. (AL, IL, IN, KY, MO, OH, PA, TN, WV). | NA | E | 15 | NA | NA |
| Pearly mussel, purple cat's paw | *Epioblasma* (=*Dysnomia*) *obliquata obliquata* (=*E. sulcata sulcata*). | U.S.A. (AL, IL, IN, KY, OH, TN) | NA | E | 394 | NA | NA |
| Pearly mussel, Tampico | *Cyrtonaias ampicoensis tecomatensis* | Mexico | NA | E | 15 | NA | NA |
| Pearly mussel, tubercled-blossom | *Epioblasma* (=*Dysnomia*) *torulosa torulosa.* | U.S.A. (IL, IN, KY, TN, WV) | NA | E | 15 | NA | NA |
| Pearly mussel, turgid-blossom | *Epioblasma* (=*Dysnomia*) *turgidula* | U.S.A. (AL, TN) | NA | E | 15 | NA | NA |
| Pearly mussel, white cat's paw | *Epioblasma* (=*Dysnomia*) *sulcata delicata.* | U.S.A. (IN, MI, OH) | NA | E | 15 | NA | NA |
| Pearly mussel, white wartyback | *Plethobasus cicatricosus* | U.S.A. (AL, IN, TN) | NA | E | 15 | NA | NA |
| Pearly mussel, yellow-blossom | *Epioblasma* (=*Dysnomia*) *florentina florentina.* | U.S.A. (AL, TN) | NA | E | 15 | NA | NA |
| Pigtoe, fine-rayed | *Fusconaia cuneolus* | U.S.A. (AL, TN, VA) | NA | E | 15 | NA | NA |
| Pigtoe, rough | *Pleurobema plenum* | U.S.A. (IN, KY, TN, VA) | NA | E | 15 | NA | NA |
| Pigtoe, shiny | *Fusconaia edgariana* | U.S.A. (AL, TN, VA) | NA | E | 15 | NA | NA |
| Pocketbook, fat | *Potamilus* (=*Proptera*) *capax* | U.S.A. (AR, IN, MO, OH) | NA | E | 15 | NA | NA |
| Pocketbook, speckled | *Lampsilis streckeri* | U.S.A. (AR) | NA | E | 345 | NA | NA |
| Riffle shell, tan | *Epioblasma walkeri* | U.S.A. (KY, TN, VA) | NA | E | 27 | NA | NA |
| Spinymussel, James River (=Virginia) | *Pleurobema* (=*Fusconaia*, =*Elliptio*, =*Canthyria*) *collina.* | U.S.A. (VA, WV) | NA | E | 316 | NA | NA |
| Spinymussel, Tar River | *Elliptio* (*Canthyria*) *steinstansana* | U.S.A. (NC) | NA | E | 188 | NA | NA |
| Stirrup shell | *Quadrula stapes* | U.S.A. (AL, MS) | NA | E | 262 | NA | NA |
| CRUSTACEANS | | | | | | | |
| Amphipod, Hay's Spring | *Stygobromus hayi* | U.S.A. (DC) | NA | E | 115 | NA | NA |
| Crayfish (no common name) | *Cambarus zophonastes* | U.S.A. (AR) | NA | E | 263 | NA | NA |
| Crayfish, Nashville | *Orconectes shoupi* | U.S.A. (TN) | NA | E | 242 | NA | NA |
| Crayfish, Shasta (=placid) | *Pacifastacus fortis* | U.S.A. (CA) | NA | E | 337 | NA | NA |
| Isopod, Madison Cave | *Antrolana lira* | U.S.A. (VA) | NA | T | 123 | NA | 17.46(a) |
| Isopod, Socorro | *Thermosphaeroma* (=*Exosphaeroma*) *thermophilus.* | U.S.A. (NM) | NA | E | 36 | NA | NA |
| Shrimp, Alabama cave | *Palaemonias alabamae* | U.S.A. (AL) | NA | E | 323 | NA | NA |
| Shrimp, California freshwater | *Syncaris pacifica* | U.S.A. (CA) | NA | E | 340 | NA | NA |
| Shrimp, Kentucky cave | *Palaemonias ganteri* | U.S.A. (KY) | NA | E | 135 | 17.95(h) | NA |
| Shrimp, Squirrel Chimney (=Florida) Cave. | *Palaemonetes cummingi* | U.S.A. (FL) | NA | T | 390 | NA | NA |
| INSECTS | | | | | | | |
| Beetle, American burying (=Giant carrion beetle). | *Nicrophorus americanus* | U.S.A. (eastern States south to FL, west to SD and TX), eastern Canada. | NA | E | 351 | NA | NA |
| Beetle, delta green ground | *Elaphrus viridis* | U.S.A. (CA) | NA | T | 100 | 17.95(i) | NA |
| Beetle, Kretschmarr Cave mold | *Texamaurops reddelli* | U.S.A. (TX) | NA | E | 327 | NA | NA |
| Beetle, northeastern beach tiger | *Cicindela dorsalis dorsalis* | U.S.A. (CT, MA, MD, NJ, NY, PA, RI, VA). | NA | T | 396 | NA | NA |

| Species | | Historic range | Vertebrate population where endangered or threatened | Sta-tus | When listed | Critical habitat | Special rules |
|---|---|---|---|---|---|---|---|
| Common name | Scientific name | | | | | | |
| Beetle, Puritan tiger | *Cicindela puritana* | U.S.A. (CT, MA, MD, NH, VT) | NA | T | 396 | NA | NA |
| Beetle, Tooth Cave ground | *Rhadine persephone* | U.S.A. (TX) | NA | E | 327 | NA | NA |
| Beetle, valley elderberry longhorn | *Desmocerus californicus dimorphus* | U.S.A. (CA) | NA | T | 99 | 17.95(i) | NA |
| Butterfly, bay checkerspot | *Euphydryas editha bayensis* | ......do | NA | T | 288 | NA | NA |
| Butterfly, El Segundo blue | *Euphilotes* (=*Shijimiaeoides*) *battoides allyni.* | ......do | NA | E | 14 | NA | NA |
| Butterfly, Lange's metalmark | *Apodemia mormo langei* | ......do | NA | E | 14 | NA | NA |
| Butterfly, lotis blue | *Lycaeides argyrognomon lotis* | ......do | NA | E | 14 | NA | NA |
| Butterfly, mission blue | *Icaricia icarioides missionensis* | ......do | NA | E | 14 | NA | NA |
| Butterfly, Mitchell's satyr | *Neonympha mitchellii mitchellii* | U.S.A. (IN, MI, NJ, OH) | NA | E | NA | NA | |
| Butterfly, Oregon silverspot | *Speyeria zerene hippolyta* | U.S.A. (OR, WA) | NA | T | 95 | 17.95(i) | NA |
| Butterfly, Palos Verdes blue | *Glaucopsyche lygdamus palosverdesensis.* | U.S.A. (CA) | NA | E | 96 | 17.95(i) | NA |
| Butterfly, Queen Alexandra's birdwing | *Troides* (=*Ornithoptera*) *alexandrae* | Papua New Guinea | NA | E | 364 | NA | NA |
| Butterfly, San Bruno elfin | *Callophrys mossii bayensis* | U.S.A. (CA) | NA | E | 14 | NA | NA |
| Butterfly, Schaus swallowtail | *Heraclides* (=*Papilio*) *aristodemus ponceanus.* | U.S.A. (FL) | NA | E | 13,159 | NA | NA |
| Butterfly, Smith's blue | *Euphilotes* (=*Shijimiaeoides*) *enoptes smithi.* | U.S.A. (CA) | NA | E | 14 | NA | NA |
| Butterfly, Uncompahgre fritillary | *Boloria acrocnema* | U.S.A. (C0) | NA | E | 427 | NA | NA |
| Moth, Kern primrose sphinx | *Euproserpinus euterpe* | U.S.A. (CA) | NA | T | 91 | NA | NA |
| Naucorid, Ash Meadows | *Ambrysus amargosus* | U.S.A. (NV) | NA | T | 181 | 17.95(i) | NA |
| Skipper, Pawnee montane | *Hesperia leonardus* (=*pawnee*) *montana.* | U.S.A. (CO) | NA | T | 289 | NA | NA |
| ARACHNIDS | | | | | | | |
| Harvestman, Bee Creek Cave | *Texella reddelli* | U.S.A. (TX) | NA | E | 327 | NA | NA |
| Pseudoscorpion, Tooth Cave | *Microcreagris texana* | ......do | NA | E | 327 | NA | NA |
| Spider, Tooth Cave | *Leptoneta myopica* | ......do | NA | E | 327 | NA | NA |

Symbols used in the "when listed" column:

D—Indicates FR where species was Delisted; relisting of the species is indicated by subsequent number(s).
E—Indicates Emergency rule publication (see FR document for effective dates); subsequent number(s) indicate FR final rule, if applicable, under "When listed".

EDITORIAL NOTE: See the following list for the "when listed" citations.

1—32 FR 4001; March 11, 1967.
2—35 FR 16047; October 13, 1970.
3—35 FR 8495; June 2, 1970.
4—35 FR 18320; December 2, 1970.
5—37 FR 6176; March 30, 1972.
6—38 FR 14678; June 4, 1973.
7—39 FR 44991; December 30, 1974.
8—40 FR 29864; July 16, 1975.
9—40 FR 31736; July 28, 1975.
10—40 FR 44151; September 25, 1975.
11—40 FR 44418; September 26, 1975.
12—40 FR 47506; October 9, 1975.
13—41 FR 17740; April 28, 1976.
14—41 FR 22044; June 1, 1976.
15—41 FR 24064; June 14, 1976.
15A—41 FR 26019, June 24, 1976.
16—41 FR 45993; October 19, 1976.
17—41 FR 51021; November 19, 1976.
18—41 FR 51612; November 23, 1976.
19—41 FR 53034; December 3, 1976.
20—42 FR 2076; January 10, 1977.
21—42 FR 2968; January 14, 1977.
22—42 FR 15971, March 24, 1977.
23—42 FR 28137; June 2, 1977.
24—42 FR 28545; June 3, 1977.
25—42 FR 37373; July 21, 1977.
26—42 FR 40685; August 11, 1977.
27—42 FR 42353; August 23, 1977.
28—42 FR 45528; September 9, 1977.
29—42 FR 58755; November 11, 1977.
30—42 FR 60745; November 29, 1977.
31—43 FR 3715; January 27, 1978.
32—43 FR 4028; January 31, 1978.
33—43 FR 4621; February 3, 1978.
34—43 FR 6233; February 14, 1978.
35—43 FR 9612; March 9, 1978.
36—43 FR 12691; March 27, 1978.
37—43 FR 15429; April 13, 1978.
38—43 FR 16345; April 18, 1978.
40—43 FR 20504; May 12, 1978.
41—43 FR 28932; July 3, 1978.
42—43 FR 32808; July 28, 1978.
43—43 FR 34479; August 4, 1978.
45—44 FR 21289; April 10, 1979.
46—44 FR 23064; April 17, 1979.
48—44 FR 29480; May 21, 1979.
50—44 FR 37126; June 25, 1979.
51—44 FR 37132; June 25, 1979.
52—44 FR 42911; July 20, 1979.
54—44 FR 49220; August 21, 1979.
55—44 FR 54007; September 17, 1979.
60—44 FR 59084; October 12, 1979.
85—44 FR 69208; November 30, 1979.
86—44 FR 70677; December 7, 1979.
87—44 FR 75076; December 18, 1979.
88—45 FR 18010; March 20, 1980.
90—45 FR 21833; April 2, 1980.
91—45 FR 24090; April 8, 1980.
92—45 FR 27713; April 23, 1980.
93—45 FR 28722; April 30, 1980.
94—45 FR 35821; May 28, 1980.
95—45 FR 44935; July 2, 1980.
96—45 FR 44939; July 2, 1980.
97—45 FR 47352; July 14, 1980.
98—45 FR 47355; July 14, 1980.
99—45 FR 52803; August 8, 1980.
100—45 FR 52807; August 8, 1980.
102—45 FR 54678; August 15, 1980.
103—45 FR 55654; August 20, 1980.
105—45 FR 63812; September 25, 1980.
106—45 FR 65132; October 1, 1980.
108—46 FR 3178; January 13, 1981.
111—46 FR 11665; February 10, 1981.
112—46 FR 40025; August 6, 1981.
113—46 FR 40664; August 10, 1981.
114—47 FR 4204; January 28, 1982.
115—47 FR 5425; February 5, 1982.
117—47 FR 19995; May 10, 1982.
119—47 FR 31670; July 21, 1982.
123—47 FR 43701; October 4, 1982.
124—47 FR 43962; October 5, 1982.
125—47 FR 46093; October 15, 1982.
127—48 FR 612; January 5, 1983.
128—48 FR 1726; January 14, 1983.
129—48 FR 28464; June 22, 1983.
130—48 FR 40184; September 2, 1983.
131—48 FR 43043; September 21, 1983.
132—48 FR 46057; October 11, 1983.
134—48 FR 46336; October 12, 1983.
135—48 FR 46341; October 12, 1983.
136—48 FR 49249; October 25, 1983.
138—49 FR 1994; January 17, 1984.
139—49 FR 2783; January 23, 1984.
142—49 FR 7335; February 28, 1984.
143—49 FR 7394; February 29, 1984.
144—49 FR 7398; February 29, 1984.
145—49 FR 10526; March 20, 1984.
146—49 FR 14356; April 11, 1984.
149—49 FR 22334; May 29, 1984.
150—49 FR 27514; July 5, 1984.
156—49 FR 33885; August 27, 1984.
157—49 FR 34494; August 31, 1984.
159—49 FR 34504; August 31, 1984.
160—49 FR 34510; August 31, 1984.
161—49 FR 35954; September 13, 1984.
163—49 FR 43069; October 26, 1984.
164—49 FR 43969; November 1, 1984.
166—49 FR 45163; November 15, 1984.
168—49 FR 49639; December 21, 1984.
169—50 FR 1056; January 9, 1985.
170—50 FR 4226; January 30, 1985.
171—50 FR 4945; February 4, 1985.
173—50 FR 12302; March 28, 1985.
174—50 FR 12305; March 28, 1985.
181—50 FR 20786; May 20, 1985.
182—50 FR 21792; May 28, 1985.
183—50 FR 23884; June 6, 1985.
184—50 FR 24530; June 11, 1985.
185—50 FR 24653; June 12, 1985.
186—50 FR 25678; June 20, 1985.
188—50 FR 26575; June 27, 1985.
189—50 FR 27002; July 1, 1985.
193—50 FR 30194; July 24, 1985.
195—50 FR 31596; August 5, 1985.
196—50 FR 31603; August 5, 1985.
203—50 FR 37198; September 12, 1985.
205—50 FR 39117; September 27, 1985.
206—50 FR 39123; September 27, 1985.
210—50 FR 50308; December 10, 1985.
211—50 FR 50733; December 11, 1985.
212—50 FR 51252; December 16, 1985.
216—51 FR 6690; February 25, 1986.
222—51 FR 10850; March 31, 1986.
223—51 FR 10857; March 31, 1986.
224—51 FR 10864; March 31, 1986.
227—51 FR 16047; April 30, 1986.
228—51 FR 16482; May 2, 1986.
233—51 FR 17980; May 16, 1986.
236—51 FR 23781; July 1, 1986.
239—51 FR 27495; July 31, 1986.
241—51 FR 31422; September 3, 1986.
242—51 FR 34412; September 26, 1986.
246—51 FR 34425; September 26, 1986.
247—51 FR 39478; October 28, 1986.
248—51 FR 41796; November 19, 1986.
250—51 FR 45910; December 23, 1986.
251—52 FR 288; January 5, 1987.
258—52 FR 5302; February 20, 1987.
261—52 FR 10892; April 6, 1987.
262—52 FR 11169; April 7, 1987.
263—52 FR 11172; April 7, 1987.
265—52 FR 11286; April 8, 1987.
267—52 FR 20719; June 3, 1987.
268—52 FR 20999; June 3, 1987.
269—52 FR 21063; June 4, 1987.
272—52 FR 22430; June 11, 1987.
273—52 FR 22585; June 12, 1987.
278—52 FR 22943; June 16, 1987.
279—52 FR 23151; June 17, 1987.
280—52 FR 25232; July 6, 1987.
281—52 FR 25380; July 7, 1987.
282—52 FR 28785; August 3, 1987.
283—52 FR 28831; August 4, 1987.
284—52 FR 29780; August 11, 1987.
287—52 FR 35040; September 16, 1987.
288—52 FR 35378; September 18, 1987.
289—52 FR 36180; September 25, 1987.
290—52 FR 36038; September 25, 1987.
292—52 FR 36779; October 1, 1987.
294—52 FR 37423; October 6, 1987.
296—52 FR 42068; November 2, 1987.
299—52 FR 42662; November 6, 1987.
304—53 FR 3570; February 5, 1988.
312—53 FR 25611; July 8, 1988.
313—53 FR 27134; July 18, 1988.
316—53 FR 27693; July 22 1988.
317—53 FR 29337; August 4, 1988.
320—53 FR 33992; September 1, 1988.
322—53 FR 33998; September 1, 1988.
323—53 FR 34698; September 7, 1988.
327—53 FR 36033; September 16, 1988.
328—53 FR 37970; September 28, 1988.
334—53 FR 38453; September 30, 1988.
336—53 FR 38460; September 30, 1988.
337—53 FR 38465; September 30, 1988.
338—53 FR 38469; September 30, 1988.
340—53 FR 43889; October 30, 1988.
342—53 FR 45865; November 14, 1988.
345—54 FR 8341; February 28, 1989.
348—54 FR 15208; April 17, 1989.
349—54 FR 20602; May 12, 1989.
350—54 FR 22906; May 30, 1989.
351—54 FR 29655; July 13, 1989.
357—54 FR 32331; August 4, 1989.
358—54 FR 34468; August 18, 1989.
359—54 FR 34472; August 18, 1989.
361—54 FR 35311; August 24, 1989.
364—54 FR 38951; September 21, 1989.
365—54 FR 39849; September 28, 1989.
366—54 FR 39853; September 28, 1989.
369—54 FR 40112; September 29, 1989.
370—54 FR 41453; October 10, 1989.
371—54 FR 43969; October 30, 1989.
372—54 FR 47861; November 17, 1989.
376—55 FR 9135; March 12, 1990.
377—55 FR 9451; March 14, 1990.
378—55 FR 12191; April 2, 1990.
382—55 FR 12801; April 5, 1990.
383—55 FR 12832; April 6, 1990.
384—55 FR 13488; April 10, 1990.
387—55 FR 18845; May 4, 1990.
388—55 FR 21153; May 22, 1990.
390—55 FR 25591; June 21, 1990.
391—55 FR 25595; June 21, 1990.
393—55 FR 26194; June 26, 1990.
394—55 FR 28213; July 10, 1990.
396—55 FR 32094; August 7, 1990.
399—55 FR 36647; September 6, 1990.
400—55 FR 39416; September 27, 1990.
401—55 FR 39860; September 28, 1990.
404—55 FR 39872; September 28, 1990.
405—55 FR 42966; October 25, 1990.
407—55 FR 49623; November 30, 1990.
408—55 FR 50006; December 4, 1990.
410—55 FR 51112; December 12, 1990.
411—55 FR 53160; December 27, 1990.
412—56 FR 800; January 9, 1991.

415—56 FR 1459; January 14, 1991.
416—56 FR 1463; January 14, 1991.
417—56 FR 1463; January 14, 1991.
419—56 FR 13600; April 3, 1991.
421—56 FR 19814; April 30, 1991.
423—56 FR 21087; May 7, 1991.
426—56 FR 28349; June 20, 1991.
427—56 FR 28717; June 24, 1991.
428—56 FR 28828; June 25, 1991.

[48 FR 34182, July 27, 1983]

**Editorial Note:** For **Federal Register** citations affecting § 17.11, see the List of CFR Sections Affected appearing in the Finding Aids section of this volume.

**Editorial Note:** For **Federal Register** citations affecting the table in § 17.11(h), see the listing above.

**§ 17.12 Endangered and threatened plants.**

(a) The list in this section contains the names of all species of plants which have been determined by the Services to be Endangered or Threatened. It also contains the names of species of plants treated as Endangered or Threatened because they are sufficiently similar in appearance to Endangered or Threatened species (see § 17.50 *et seq.*).

(b) The columns entitled "Scientific name" and "Common name" define the species of plant within the meaning of the Act. Although common names are included, they cannot be relied upon for identification of any specimen, since they may vary greatly in local usage. The Services shall use the most recently accepted scientific name. In cases in which confusion might arise, a synonym(s) will be provided in parentheses. The Services shall rely to the extent practicable on the *International Code of Botanical Nomenclature*.

(c) In the "Status" column the following symbols are used: "E" for Endangered, "T" for Threatened, and "E [or T] (S/A)" for similarity of appearance species.

(d) The other data in the list are nonregulatory in nature and are provided for the information of the reader. In the annual revision and compilation of this title, the following information may be amended without public notice: the spelling of species' names, historical range, footnotes, references to certain other applicable portions of this title, synonyms, and more current names. In any of these revised entries, neither the species, as defined in paragraph (b) of this section, nor its status may be changed without following the procedures of Part 424 of this title.

(e) The "Historic range" indicates the known general distribution of the species or subspecies as reported in the current scientific literature. The present distribution may be greatly reduced from this historic range. This column does not imply any limitation on the application of the prohibitions in the Act or implementing rules. Such prohibitions apply to all individuals of the plant species, wherever found.

(f)(1) A footnote to the **Federal Register** publication(s) listing or reclassifying a species is indicated under the column "When listed." Footnote numbers to §§ 17.11 and 17.12 are in the same numerical sequence, since plants and animals may be listed in the same **Federal Register** document. That document, at least since 1973, includes a statement indicating the basis for the listing, as well as the effective date(s) of said listing.

(2) The "Special rules" and "Critical habitat" columns provide a cross reference to other sections in Parts 17, 222, 226, or 227. The "Special rules" column will also be used to cite the special rules which describe experimental populations and determine if they are essential or nonessential. Separate listings will be made for experimental populations, and the status column will include the following symbols: "XE" for an essential experimental population and "XN" for a nonessential experimental population. The term "NA" (not applicable) appearing in either of these two columns indicates that there are no special rules and/or critical habitat for that particular species. However, all other appropriate rules in Parts 17, 217 through 227, and 402 still apply to that species. In addition, there may be other rules in this title that relate to such plants, e.g., port-of-entry requirements. It is not intended that the references in the "Special rules" column list all the regulations of the two Services which might apply to the species or to the regulations of other Federal agencies or State or local governments.

(g) The listing of a particular taxon includes all lower taxonomic units (see § 17.11(g) for examples).

(h) The "List of Endangered and Threatened Plants" is provided below:

| Species: Scientific name | Species: Common name | Historic range | Status | When listed | Critical habitat | Special rules |
|---|---|---|---|---|---|---|
| Acanthaceae—Acanthus family: | | | | | | |
| *Justicia cooleyi* | Cooley's water-willow | U.S.A. (FL) | E | 356 | NA | NA |
| Agavaceae—Agave family: | | | | | | |
| *Agave arizonica* | Arizona agave | U.S.A. (AZ) | E | 147 | NA | NA |
| Alismataceae—Water-plantain family: | | | | | | |
| *Sagittaria fasciculata* | Bunched arrowhead | U.S.A. (NC, SC) | E | 53 | NA | NA |
| *Sagittaria secundifolia* | Kral's water-plantain | U.S.A. (AL, GA) | T | 386 | NA | NA |
| Amaranthaceae—Amaranth family: | | | | | | |
| *Achyranthes splendens* var. *rotundata* | None | U.S.A. (HI) | E | 220 | NA | NA |
| Anacardiaceae—Cashew family: | | | | | | |
| *Rhus michauxii* | Michaux's sumac | U.S.A. (NC, SC, GA) | E | 367 | NA | NA |
| Annonaceae—Custard-apple family: | | | | | | |
| *Asimina tetramera* | Four-petal pawpaw | U.S.A. (FL) | E | 244 | NA | NA |
| *Deeringothamnus pulchellus* | Beautiful pawpaw | do | E | 244 | NA | NA |
| *Deeringothamnus rugelii* | Rugel's pawpaw | do | E | 244 | NA | NA |
| Apiaceae—Parsley family: | | | | | | |
| *Eryngium constancei* | Loch Lomond coyote-thistle | U.S.A. (CA) | E | 194E, 249 | NA | NA |
| *Eryngium cuneifolium* | Snakeroot | U.S.A. (FL) | E | 256 | NA | NA |
| *Lomatium bradshawii* | Bradshaw's desert-parsley | U.S.A. (OR) | E | 333 | NA | NA |
| *Oxypolis canbyi* | Canby's dropwort | U.S.A. (DE, GA, MD, NC, SC). | E | 217 | NA | NA |
| *Ptilimnium nodosum* (= *P. fluviatile*) | Harperella | U.S.A. (AL, GA, MD, NC, SC, WV). | E | 332 | NA | NA |
| Apocynaceae—Dogbane family: | | | | | | |
| *Amsonia kearneyana* | Kearney's blue-star | U.S.A. (AZ) | E | 343 | NA | NA |
| *Cycladenia humilis* var. *jonesii* | Jones cycladenia | U.S.A. (AZ, UT) | T | 229 | NA | NA |
| Aquifoliaceae—Holly family: | | | | | | |
| *Ilex cookii* | Cook's holly | U.S.A. (PR) | E | 277 | NA | NA |
| Arecaceae—Palm family: | | | | | | |
| *Calyptronoma rivalis* | Palma de manaca | do | T | 375 | NA | NA |
| Aristolochiaceae—Heartleaf family: | | | | | | |
| *Hexastylis naniflora* | Dwarf-flowered heartleaf | U.S.A. (NC, SC) | T | 347 | NA | NA |
| Asclepiadaceae—Milkweed family: | | | | | | |
| *Asclepias meadii* | Mead's milkweed | U.S.A. (IL, IN, IA, KS, MO, WI). | T | 321 | NA | NA |
| *Asclepias welshii* | Welsh's milkweed | U.S.A. (AZ, UT) | T | 295 | 17.96(a) | NA |
| Aspleniaceae—Spleenwort family: | | | | | | |
| *Phyllitis scolopendrium* var. *americana* (=*P. japonica* ssp. *americana.*). | American hart's-tongue fern | U.S.A. (AL, MI, NY, TN), Canada (ON). | T | 354 | NA | NA |
| *Polystichum aleuticum* | Aleutian shield-fern (=Aleutian holly-fern) | U.S.A. (AK) | E | 305 | NA | NA |
| Asteraceae—Aster family: | | | | | | |
| *Argyroxiphium sandwicense* ssp. *sandwicense* | 'Ahinahina (=Mauna Kea silversword) | U.S.A. (HI) | E | 219 | NA | NA |
| *Bidens cuneata* | Cuneate bidens | do | E | 141 | NA | NA |
| *Boltonia decurrens* | Decurrent false aster | U.S.A. (IL, MO) | T | 341 | NA | NA |

| Species | | Historic range | Status | When listed | Critical habitat | Special rules |
|---|---|---|---|---|---|---|
| Scientific name | Common name | | | | | |
| *Chrysopsis floridana* (=*Heterotheca f.*) | Florida golden aster | U.S.A. (FL) | E | 232 | NA | NA |
| *Cirsium pitcheri* | Pitcher's thistle | U.S.A. (IL, IN, MI, WI), Canada (ON). | T | 315 | NA | NA |
| *Cirsium vinaceum* | Sacramento Mountains thistle | U.S.A. (NM) | T | 276 | NA | NA |
| *Echinacea tennesseensis* | Tennessee purple coneflower | U.S.A. (TN) | E | 49 | NA | NA |
| *Enceliopsis nudicaulis* var. *corrugata* | Ash Meadows sunray | U.S.A. (NV) | T | 181 | 17.96(a) | NA |
| *Erigeron maguirei* var. *maguirei* | Maguire daisy | U.S.A. (UT) | E | 202 | NA | NA |
| *Erigeron rhizomatus* | Zuni (=Rhizome) fleabane | U.S.A. (NM) | T | 177 | NA | NA |
| *Grindelia fraxinopratensis* | Ash Meadows gumplant | U.S.A. (CA, NV) | T | 181 | 17.96(a) | NA |
| *Helianthus schweinitzii* | Schweinitz's sunflower | U.S.A. (NS, SC) | E | 424 | NA | NA |
| *Hymenoxys acaulis var. glabra* | Lakeside daisy | U.S.A. (OH, IL) Canada (ON). | T | 310 | NA | NA |
| *Hymenoxys texana* | Texas prairie dawn-flower (=Texas bitterweed) | U.S.A. (TX) | E | 218 | NA | NA |
| *Lembertia congdonii* | San Joaquin wooly-threads | U.S.A. (CA) | E | 395 | NA | NA |
| *Liatris helleri* | Heller's blazingstar | U.S.A. (NC) | T | 300 | NA | NA |
| *Liatris ohlingerae* | Scrub blazingstar | U.S.A. (FL) | E | 356 | NA | NA |
| *Lipochaeta venosa* | None | U.S.A. (HI) | E | 73 | NA | NA |
| *Marshallia mohrii* | Mohr's Barbara's buttons | U.S.A. (AL, GA) | T | 324 | NA | NA |
| *Pityopsis ruthii* (=*Heterotheca r., Chrysopsis r.*) | Ruth's golden aster | U.S.A. (TN) | E | 191 | NA | NA |
| *Remya kauaiensis* | None | U.S.A. (HI) | E | 413 | NA | NA |
| *Remya mauiensis* | Maui remya | ......do | E | 413 | NA | NA |
| *Remya montgomeryi* | None | ......do | E | 413 | NA | NA |
| *Senecio franciscanus* | San Francisco Peaks groundsel | U.S.A. (AZ) | T | 137 | 17.96(a) | NA |
| *Solidago albopilosa* | White-haired goldenrod | U.S.A. (KY) | T | 308 | NA | NA |
| *Solidago houghtonii* | Houghton's goldenrod | U.S.A. (MI), Canada (Ont.). | T | 314 | NA | NA |
| *Solidago shortii* | Short's goldenrod | U.S.A. (KY) | E | 201 | NA | NA |
| *Solidago spithamaea* | Blue Ridge goldenrod | U.S.A. (NC, TN) | T | 175 | NA | NA |
| *Stephanomeria malheurensis* | Malheur wire-lettuce | U.S.A. (OR) | E | 126 | 17.96(a) | NA |
| *Thymophylla tephroleuca* (=*Dyssodia t.*) | Ashy dogweed | U.S.A. (TX) | E | 152 | NA | NA |
| *Townsendia aprica* | Last Chance townsendia | U.S.A. (UT) | T | 200 | NA | NA |
| Berberidaceae—Barberry family: | | | | | | |
| *Berberis sonnei* (=*Mahonia s.*) | Truckee barberry | U.S.A. (CA) | E | 76 | NA | NA |
| Betulaceae—Birch family: | | | | | | |
| *Betula uber* | Virginia round-leaf birch | U.S.A. (VA) | E | 39 | NA | NA |
| Bignoniaceae—Bignonia family: | | | | | | |
| *Crescentia portoricensis* | Higuero de Sierra | U.S.A. (PR) | E | 301 | NA | NA |
| Boraginaceae—Borage family: | | | | | | |
| *Amsinckia grandiflora* | Large-flowered fiddleneck | U.S.A. (CA) | E | 179 | 17.96(a) | NA |
| Brassicaceae—Mustard family: | | | | | | |
| *Arabis mcdonaldiana* | McDonald's rock-cress | ......do | E | 44 | NA | NA |
| *Arabis serotina* | Shale barren rock-cress | U.S.A. (VA, WV) | E | 352 | NA | NA |
| *Cardamine micranthera* | Small-anthered bittercress | U.S.A. (NC) | E | 363 | NA | NA |
| *Caulanthus californicus* | California jewelflower | U.S.A. (CA) | E | 395 | NA | NA |
| *Erysimum capitatum* var. *angustatum* | Contra Costa wallflower | ......do | E | 39 | 17.96(a) | NA |
| *Glaucocarpum suffrutescens* | Toad-flax cress | U.S.A. (UT) | E | 293 | NA | NA |
| *Lepidium barnebyanum* | Barneby ridge-cress (=peppercress) | ......do | E | 402 | NA | NA |
| *Lesquerella congesta* | Dudley Bluffs bladderpod | U.S.A. (CO) | T | 374 | NA | NA |
| *Lesquerella filiformis* | Missouri bladderpod | U.S.A. (MO) | E | 253 | NA | NA |
| *Lesquerella lyrata* | Lyrate bladderpod | U.S.A. (AL) | T | 403 | NA | NA |
| *Lesquerella pallida* | White bladderpod | U.S.A. (TX) | E | 260 | NA | NA |

| | | | | | | |
|---|---|---|---|---|---|---|
| *Physaria obcordata* | Dudley Bluffs twinpod | U.S.A. (CO) | T | 374 | NA | NA |
| *Thelypodium stenopetalum* | Slender-petaled mustard | U.S.A. (CA) | E | 158 | NA | NA |
| *Warea amplexifolia* | Wide-leaf warea | U.S.A. (FL) | E | 266 | NA | NA |
| *Warea carteri* | Carter's mustard | do | E | 256 | NA | NA |
| Buxaceae—Boxwood family: | | | | | | |
| *Buxus vahlii* | Vahl's boxwood | U.S.A. (PR) | E | 197 | NA | NA |
| Cactaceae—Cactus family: | | | | | | |
| *Ancistrocactus tobuschii* (=*Echinocactus t., Mammillaria t.*) | Tobusch fishhook cactus | U.S.A. (TX) | E | 80 | NA | NA |
| *Cereus eriophorus* var. *fragrans* | Fragrant prickly-apple | U.S.A. (FL) | E | 208 | NA | NA |
| *Cereus robinii* | Key tree-cactus | U.S.A. (FL), Cuba | E | 153 | NA | NA |
| *Coryphantha minima* (=*C. nellieae, Escobaria n., Mammillaria n.*). | Nellie cory cactus | U.S.A. (TX) | E | 81 | NA | NA |
| *Coryphantha ramillosa* | Bunched cory cactus | U.S.A. (TX), Mexico (Coahuila). | T | 77 | NA | NA |
| *Coryphantha robbinsorum* (=*Cochiseia r., Escobaria r.*) | Cochise pincushion cactus | U.S.A. (AZ), Mexico (Sonora). | T | 214 | NA | NA |
| *Coryphantha sneedii* var. *leei* (=*Escobaria l., Mammillaria l.*) | Lee pincushion cactus | U.S.A. (NM) | T | 61 | NA | NA |
| *Coryphantha sneedii* var. *sneedii* (=*Escobaria s., Mammillaria s.*). | Sneed pincushion cactus | U.S.A. (TX, NM) | E | 82 | NA | NA |
| *Echinocactus horizonthalonius* var. *nicholii* | Nichol's Turk's head cactus | U.S.A. (AZ) | E | 71 | NA | NA |
| *Echinocereus chisosensis* var. *chisosensis* (=*E. reichenbachii* var. *c.*). | Chisos Mountain hedgehog cactus | U.S.A. (TX) | T | 335 | NA | NA |
| *Echinocereus fendleri* var. *kuenzleri* (=*E. kuenzleri, E. hempelii* of authors, not Fobe). | Kuenzler hedgehog cactus | U.S.A. (NM) | E | 70 | NA | NA |
| *Echinocereus lloydii* (=*E. roetteri* var. *l.*) | Lloyd's hedgehog cactus | U.S.A. (TX) | E | 67 | NA | NA |
| *Echinocereus reichenbachii* var. *albertii* (=*E. melanocentrus*) | Black lace cactus | do | E | 68 | NA | NA |
| *Echinocereus triglochidiatus* var. *arizonicus* (=*E. arizonicus*) | Arizona hedgehog cactus | U.S.A. (AZ) | E | 62 | NA | NA |
| *Echinocereus triglochidiatus* var. *inermis* (=*E. coccineus* var. *i., E. phoeniceus* var. *i.*). | Spineless hedgehog cactus | U.S.A. (CO, UT) | E | 83 | NA | NA |
| *Echinocereus viridiflorus* var. *davisii* (=*E. davisii*) | Davis' green pitaya | U.S.A. (TX) | E | 81 | NA | NA |
| *Harrisia* (=*Cereus*) *portoricensis* | Higo chumbo | U.S.A. (PR) | T | 397 | NA | NA |
| *Neolloydia mariposensis* (=*Echinocactus m., Echinomastus m.*). | Lloyd's Mariposa cactus | U.S.A. (TX), Mexico (Coahuila). | T | 77 | NA | NA |
| *Opuntia treleasei* | Bakersfield cactus | U.S.A. (CA) | E | 395 | NA | NA |
| *Pediocactus bradyi* (=*Toumeya b.*) | Brady pincushion cactus | U.S.A. (AZ) | E | 63 | NA | NA |
| *Pediocactus despainii* | San Rafael cactus | U.S.A. (UT) | E | 286 | NA | NA |
| *Pediocactus knowltonii* (=*P. bradyi* var. *k. Toumeya k.*) | Knowlton cactus | U.S.A. (NM, CO) | E | 72 | NA | NA |
| *Pediocactus peeblesianus* var. *peeblesianus* (=*Echinocactus p., Navajoa p., Toumeya p., Utahia p.*). | Peebles Navajo cactus | U.S.A. (AZ) | E | 69 | NA | NA |
| *Pediocactus sileri* (=*Echinocactus s., Utahia s.*) | Siler pincushion cactus | U.S.A. (AZ, UT) | E | 64 | NA | NA |
| *Sclerocactus glaucus* (=*Echinocactus g., E. subglaucus, E. whipplei* var. *g., Pediocactus g., S. franklinii, S. whipplei* var. *g.*). | Uinta Basin hookless cactus | U.S.A. (CO, UT) | T | 59 | NA | NA |
| *Sclerocactus mesae-verdae* (=*Coloradoa m., Echinocactus m., Pediocactus m.*). | Mesa Verde cactus | U.S.A. (CO, NM) | T | 75 | NA | NA |
| *Sclerocactus wrightiae* (=*Pediocactus w.*) | Wright fishhook cactus | U.S.A. (UT) | E | 58 | NA | NA |
| Caesalpiniaceae-Cassia family: | | | | | | |
| *Cassia mirabilis* | None | U.S.A. (PR) | E | 379 | NA | NA |
| Campanulaceae—Bellflower family: | | | | | | |
| *Campanula robinsiae* | Brooksville (=Robins') bellflower | U.S.A. (FL) | E | 356 | NA | NA |
| Caryophyllaceae—Pink family: | | | | | | |
| *Arenaria cumberlandensis* | Cumberland sandwort | U.S.A. (KY, TN) | E | 311 | NA | NA |
| *Geocarpon minimum* | None | U.S.A. (AR, MO) | T | 275 | NA | NA |
| *Paronychia chartacea* (=*Nyachia pulvinata*) | Papery whitlow-wort | U.S.A. (FL) | T | 256 | NA | NA |
| *Schiedea adamantis* | Diamond Head schiedea | U.S.A. (HI) | E | 141 | NA | NA |
| *Silene polypetala* | Fringed campion | U.S.A. (FL, GA) | E | 418 | NA | NA |

| Species | | Historic range | Status | When listed | Critical habitat | Special rules |
|---|---|---|---|---|---|---|
| Scientific name | Common name | | | | | |
| Chenopodiaceae—Goosefoot family: | | | | | | |
| *Nitrophila mohavensis* | Amargosa niterwort | U.S.A. (CA) | E | 181 | 17.96(a) | NA |
| Cistaceae—Rockrose family: | | | | | | |
| *Hudsonia montana* | Mountain golden heather | U.S.A. (NC) | T | 107 | 17.96(a) | NA |
| Convolvulaceae—Morning-glory family: | | | | | | |
| *Bonamia grandiflora* | Florida bonamia | U.S.A. (FL) | T | 297 | NA | NA |
| Crassulaceae—Stonecrop family: | | | | | | |
| *Dudleya traskiae* | Santa Barbara Island liveforever | U.S.A. (CA) | E | 39 | NA | NA |
| Cucurbitaceae—Gourd family: | | | | | | |
| *Tumamoca macdougalii* | Tumamoc globe-berry | U.S.A. (AZ), Mexico (Sonora). | E | 226 | NA | NA |
| Cupressaceae—Cypress family: | | | | | | |
| *Cupressus abramsiana* | Santa Cruz Cypress | U.S.A. (CA) | E | 252 | NA | NA |
| *Fitzroya cupressoides* | Chilean false larch (=alerce) | Chile, Argentina | T | 79 | NA | NA |
| Cyatheaceae—Tree-fern family: | | | | | | |
| *Cyathea dryopteroides* | Elfin tree fern | U.S.A. (PR) | E | 277 | NA | NA |
| Cyperaceae—Sedge family: | | | | | | |
| *Carex specuicola* | Navajo sedge | U.S.A. (AZ) | T | 178 | 17.96(a) | NA |
| *Scirpus ancistrochaetus* | Northeastern bulrush (=Barbed bristle bulrush) | U.S.A. (VA, MD, WV, PA, NY, MA, VT). | E | 425 | NA | NA |
| Ericaceae—Heath family: | | | | | | |
| *Arctostaphylos pungens* var. *ravenii* (=*A. hookeri* ssp. *r.*) | Presidio (=Raven's) manzanita | U.S.A. (CA) | E | 65 | NA | NA |
| *Rhododendron chapmanii* | Chapman rhododendron | U.S.A. (FL) | E | 47 | NA | NA |
| Euphorbiaceae—Spurge family: | | | | | | |
| *Chamaesyce deltoidea* ssp. *deltoidea* (=*Euphorbia d.* spp. *d.*). | Deltoid spurge | ......do | E | 192 | NA | NA |
| *Chamaesyce garberi* (=*Euphorbia g.*) | Garber's spurgeNone | ......do | T | 192 | NA | NA |
| *Chamaesyce skottsbergii* var. *kalaeloana* (=*Euphorbia s.* var. *k.*). | Ewa Plains 'akoko | U.S.A. (HI) | E | 120 | NA | NA |
| *Jatropha costaricensis* | Costa Rican jatropha | Costa Rica | E | 154 | NA | NA |
| Fabaceae—Pea family: | | | | | | |
| *Amorpha crenulata* | Crenulate lead-plant | U.S.A. (FL) | E | 192 | NA | NA |
| *Apios priceana* | Price's Potato-bean | U.S.A. (AL, IL, KY, MS, TN). | T | 373 | NA | NA |
| *Astragalus cremnophylax* var. *cremnophylax* | Sentry milk-vetch | U.S.A. (AZ) | E | 409 | NA | NA |
| *Astragalus humillimus* | Mancos milk-vetch | U.S.A. (CO, NM) | E | 187 | NA | NA |
| *Astragalus montii* (=*A. limnocharis* var. *m.*) | Heliotrope milk-vetch | U.S.A. (UT) | T | 298 | 17.96(a) | NA |
| *Astragalus osterhoutii* | Osterhout milk-vetch | U.S.A. (CO) | E | 353 | NA | NA |
| *Astragalus phoenix* | Ash Meadows milk-vetch | U.S.A. (NV) | T | 181 | 17.96(a) | NA |
| *Astragalus robbinsii* var. *jesupi* | Jesup's milk-vetch | U.S.A. (NH, VT) | E | 271 | NA | NA |
| *Baptisia arachnifera* | Hairy rattleweed | U.S.A. (GA) | E | 39 | NA | NA |
| *Caesalpinia kavaiense* (=*Mezoneuron k.*) | Uhiuhi | U.S.A. (HI) | E | 238 | NA | NA |
| *Cassia mirabilis* | None | U.S.A. (PR) | E | 379 | NA | NA |
| *Dalea foliosa* (=*Petalostemum foliosum*) | Leafy prairie-clover | U.S.A. (AL, IL, TN) | E | 422 | NA | NA |
| *Galactia smallii* | Small's milkpea | U.S.A. (FL) | E | 192 | NA | NA |
| *Hoffmannseggia tenella* | Slender rush-pea | U.S.A. (TX) | E | 209 | NA | NA |

| | | | | | | |
|---|---|---|---|---|---|---|
| *Lespedeza leptostachya* | Prairie bush-clover | U.S.A. (IA, IL, MN, WI). | T | 254 | NA | NA |
| *Lotus dendroideus* ssp. *traskiae* (=*L. scoparius* ssp. *t.*) | San Clemente Island broom | U.S.A. (CA) | E | 26 | NA | NA |
| *Lupinus aridorum* | Scrub lupine | U.S.A. (FL) | E | 264 | NA | NA |
| *Oxytropis campestris* var. *chartacea* | Fassett's locoweed | U.S.A. (WI) | T | 329 | NA | NA |
| *Serianthes nelsonii* | Hayun lagu (Guam), Tronkon guafi (Rota) | Western Pacific Ocean: U.S.A. (Guam, Rota). | E | 257, 259 | NA | NA |
| *Stahlia monosperma* | Cobana negra | U.S.A. (PR), Dominican Republic. | T | 380 | NA | NA |
| *Trifolium stoloniferum* | Running buffalo clover | U.S.A. (AR, IL, IN, KS, KY, MO, OH, WV). | E | 270 | NA | NA |
| *Vicia menziesii* | Hawaiian vetch | U.S.A. (HI) | E | 39 | NA | NA |
| Fagaceae—Oak family: | | | | | | |
| *Quercus hinckleyi* | Hinckley's oak | U.S.A. (TX) | T | 318 | NA | NA |
| Flacourtiaceae—Flacourtia family: | | | | | | |
| *Banara vanderbiltii* | Palo de Ramon | U.S.A. (PR) | E | 255 | NA | NA |
| Frankeniaceae—Frankenia family: | | | | | | |
| *Frankenia johnstonii* | Johnston's frankenia | U.S.A. (TX), Mexico (Nuevo Leon). | E | 155 | NA | NA |
| Gentianaceae—Gentian family: | | | | | | |
| *Centaurium namophilum* | Spring-loving centaury | U.S.A. (CA, NV) | T | 181 | 17.96(a) | NA |
| Goodeniaceae—Goodenia family: | | | | | | |
| *Scaevola coriacea* | Dwarf naupaka | U.S.A. (HI) | E | 231 | NA | NA |
| Hydrophyllaceae—Waterleaf family: | | | | | | |
| *Phacelia argillacea* | Clay phacelia | U.S.A. (UT) | E | 44 | NA | NA |
| *Phacelia formosula* | North Park phacelia | U.S.A. (CO) | E | 121 | NA | NA |
| Hypericaceae—St. Johns-Wort family: | | | | | | |
| *Hypericum cumulicola* | Highlands scrub hypericum | U.S.A. (FL) | E | 256 | NA | NA |
| Icacinacea—Icacina family: | | | | | | |
| *Ottoschulzia rhodoxylon* | Palo de rosa | U.S.A. (PR), Dominican Republic. | E | 385 | NA | NA |
| Iridaceae—Iris family: | | | | | | |
| *Iris lacustris* | Dwarf lake iris | U.S.A. (MI, WI), Canada (ON). | T | 330 | NA | NA |
| Isoetaceae—Quillwort family: | | | | | | |
| *Isoetes melanospora* | Black-spored quillwort | U.S.A. (GA,SC) | E | 302 | NA | NA |
| *Isoetes tegetiformans* | Mat-forming quillwort | U.S.A. (GA) | E | 302 | NA | NA |
| Lamiaceae—Mint family: | | | | | | |
| *Acanthomintha obovata* ssp. *duttonii* | San Mateo thornmint | U.S.A. (CA) | E | 204 | NA | NA |
| *Dicerandra christmanii* | Garrett's mint | U.S.A. (FL) | E | 207, 362 | NA | NA |
| *Dicerandra cornutissima* | Longspurred mint | ...do | E | 207 | NA | NA |
| *Dicerandra frutescens* | Scrub mint | ...do | E | 207, 362 | NA | NA |
| *Dicerandra immaculata* | Lakela's mint | ...do | E | 180 | NA | NA |
| *Haplostachys haplostachya* var. *angustifolia* | None | U.S.A. (HI) | E | 73 | NA | NA |
| *Hedeoma apiculatum* | McKittrick pennyroyal | U.S.A. (TX, NM) | T | 118 | 17.96(a) | NA |
| *Hedeoma todsenii* | Todsen's pennyroyal | U.S.A. (NM) | E | 110, 112 | 17.96(a) | NA |
| *Pogogyne abramsii* | San Diego mesa mint | U.S.A. (CA) | E | 44 | NA | NA |

| Species | | Historic range | Status | When listed | Critical habitat | Special rules |
|---|---|---|---|---|---|---|
| Scientific name | Common name | | | | | |
| *Scutellaria montana* | Large-flowered skullcap | U.S.A. (GA,TN) | E | 234 | NA | NA |
| *Stenogyne angustifolia* var. *angustifolia* | None | U.S.A. (HI) | E | 73 | NA | NA |
| Lauraceae—Laurel family: | | | | | | |
| *Lindera melissifolia* | Pondberry | U.S.A. (AL, AR, FL, GA, LA, MO, MS, NC, SC). | E | 240 | NA | NA |
| Liliaceae—Lily family: | | | | | | |
| *Erythronium propullans* | Minnesota trout lily | U.S.A. (MN) | E | 221 | NA | NA |
| *Harperocallis flava* | Harper's beauty | U.S.A. (FL) | E | 57 | NA | NA |
| *Helonias bullata* | Swamp pink | U.S.A. (DE, GA, MD, NC, NJ, NY, SC, VA). | T | 326 | NA | NA |
| *Trillium persistens* | Persistent trillium | U.S.A. (GA, SC) | E | 39 | NA | NA |
| *Trillium reliquum* | Relict trillium | U.S.A. (AL, GA, SC) | E | 306 | NA | NA |
| Loasaceae—Loasa family: | | | | | | |
| *Mentzelia leucophylla* | Ash Meadows blazing-star | U.S.A. (NV) | T | 181 | 17.96(a) | NA |
| Loganiaceae—Logania family: | | | | | | |
| *Spigelia gentianoides* | Gentian pinkroot | U.S.A. (FL) | E | 406 | NA | NA |
| Malvaceae—Mallow family: | | | | | | |
| *Abutilon menziesii* | Ko'oloa'ula | U.S.A. (HI) | E | 243 | NA | NA |
| *Callirhoe scabriuscula* | Texas poppy-mallow | U.S.A. (TX) | E | 109, 112 | NA | NA |
| *Eremalche kernensis* | Kern mallow | U.S.A. (CA) | E | 395 | NA | NA |
| *Hibiscadelphus distans* | Kauai hau kuahiwi | U.S.A. (HI) | E | 225 | NA | NA |
| *Iliamna corei* | Peter's Mountain mallow | U.S.A. (VA) | E | 230 | NA | NA |
| *Kokia cookei* | Cooke's kokio | U.S.A. (HI) | E | 74 | NA | NA |
| *Kokia drynarioides* | Koki'o (=hau-hele'ula or Hawaii tree cotton) | ......do | E | 167 | 17.96(a) | NA |
| *Malacothamnus clementinus* | San Clemente Island bush-mallow | U.S.A. (CA) | E | 26 | NA | NA |
| *Sidalcea pedata* | Pedate checker-mallow | ......do | E | 158 | NA | NA |
| Meliaceae—Mahogany family: | | | | | | |
| *Trichilia triacantha* | Bariaco | U.S.A. (PR) | E | 303 | NA | NA |
| Nyctaginaceae—Four-o'clock family: | | | | | | |
| *Abronia macrocarpa* | Large-fruited sand-verbena | U.S.A. (TX) | E | 331 | NA | NA |
| *Mirabilis macfarlanei* | MacFarlane's four-o'clock | U.S.A. (ID, OR) | E | 66 | NA | NA |
| Olacaceae—Olax family: | | | | | | |
| *Schoepfia arenaria* | None | U.S.A. (PR) | T | 420 | NA | NA |
| Oleaceae—Olive family: | | | | | | |
| *Chionanthus pygmaeus* | Pygmy fringe-tree | U.S.A. (FL) | E | 256 | NA | NA |
| Onagraceae—Evening-primrose family: | | | | | | |
| *Camissonia benitensis* | San Benito evening-primrose | U.S.A. (CA) | T | 172 | NA | NA |
| *Oenothera avita* ssp. *eurekensis* | Eureka Valley evening-primrose | ......do | E | 39 | NA | NA |
| *Oenothera deltoides* ssp. *howellii* | Antioch Dunes evening-primrose | ......do | E | 39 | 17.96(a) | NA |

| | | | | | | |
|---|---|---|---|---|---|---|
| Orchidaceae—Orchid family: | | | | | | |
| *Isotria medeoloides* | Small whorled pogonia | U.S.A. (CT, DC, DE, GA, IL, MA, MD, ME, MI, MO, NC, NH, NJ, NY, PA, RI, SC, TN, VA, VT), Canada (ON). | E | 122 | NA | NA |
| *Platanthera leucophaea* | Eastern prairie fringed orchid | U.S.A (AR, IA, IL, IN, ME, MI, MO, NE, NJ, NY, OH, OK, PA, VA, WI), Canada (ON, NB). | T | 368 | NA | NA |
| *Platanthera praeclara* | Western prairie fringed orchid | U.S.A (IA, MN, MO, NE, ND, OK, KS, SD), Canada (MB). | T | 368 | NA | NA |
| *Spiranthes parksii* | Navasota ladies'-tresses | U.S.A. (TX) | E | 116 | NA | NA |
| Papaveraceae—Poppy family: | | | | | | |
| *Arctomecon humilis* | Dwarf bear-poppy | U.S.A. (UT) | E | 78 | NA | NA |
| *Argemone pleiacantha* ssp. *pinnatisecta* | Sacramento prickly-poppy | U.S.A. (NM) | E | 360 | NA | NA |
| Pinaceae—Pine family: | | | | | | |
| *Abies guatemalensis* | Guatemalan fir (=pinabete) | Mexico, Guatemala, Honduras, El Salvador. | T | 84 | NA | NA |
| Piperaceae—Pepper family: | | | | | | |
| *Peperomia wheeleri* | Wheeler's peperomia | U.S.A. (PR) | E | 255 | NA | NA |
| Poaceae—Grass family: | | | | | | |
| *Aristida portoricensis* | Pelos del diablo | ......do | E | 398 | NA | NA |
| *Panicum fauriei* var. *carteri* | Carter's panicgrass | U.S.A. (HI) | E | 133 | 17.96(a) | NA |
| *Swallenia alexandrae* | Eureka Dune grass | U.S.A. (CA) | E | 39 | NA | NA |
| *Tuctoria mucronata* (=*Orcuttia m.*) | Solano grass | ......do | E | 44 | NA | NA |
| *Zizania texana* | Texas wild-rice | U.S.A. (TX) | E | 39 | 17.96(a) | NA |
| Polemoniaceae—Phlox family: | | | | | | |
| *Eriastrum densifolium* ssp. *sanctorum* | Santa Ana River woolly-star | U.S.A. (CA) | E | 291 | NA | NA |
| *Eriastrum hooveri* | Hoover's woolly-star | ......do | T | 395 | NA | NA |
| Polygalaceae—Milkwort family: | | | | | | |
| *Polygala smallii* | Tiny polygala | U.S.A. (FL) | E | 192 | NA | NA |
| Polygonaceae—Buckwheat family: | | | | | | |
| *Dodecahema* (=*Centrostegia l.*) *leptoceras* | Slender-horned spineflower | U.S.A. (CA) | E | 291 | NA | NA |
| *Eriogonum gypsophilum* | Gypsum wild-buckwheat | U.S.A. (NM) | T | 110, 112 | 17.96(a) | NA |
| *Eriogonum ovalifolium* var. *williamsiae* | Steamboat buckwheat | U.S.A. (NV) | E | 237 | NA | NA |
| *Eriogonum pelinophilum* | Clay-loving wild-buckwheat | U.S.A. (CO) | E | 151 | 17.96(a) | NA |
| *Polygonella basiramia* (=*P. ciliata* var. *b.*) | Wireweed | U.S.A. (FL) | E | 256 | NA | NA |
| Primulaceae—Primrose family: | | | | | | |
| *Lysimachia asperulaefolia* | Rough-leaved loosestrife | U.S.A. (NC, SC) | E | 274 | NA | NA |
| *Primula maguirei* | Maguire primrose | U.S.A. (UT) | T | 199 | NA | NA |
| Ranunculaceae—Buttercup family: | | | | | | |
| *Aconitum noveboracense* | Northern wild monkshood | U.S.A. (IA, NY, OH, WI). | T | 39 | NA | NA |
| *Clematis socialis* | Alabama leather flower | U.S.A. (AL) | E | 245 | NA | NA |
| *Delphinium kinkiense* | San Clemente Island larkspur | U.S.A. (CA) | E | 26 | NA | NA |
| *Ranunculus acriformis* var. *aestivalis* (=*R. acris* var. *aestivalis*). | Autumn buttercup | U.S.A. (UT) | E | 355 | NA | NA |
| *Thalictrum cooleyi* | Cooley's meadowrue | U.S.A. (NC, FL) | E | 344 | NA | NA |

| Species: Scientific name | Species: Common name | Historic range | Status | When listed | Critical habitat | Special rules |
|---|---|---|---|---|---|---|
| Rhamnaceae—Buckthorn family: | | | | | | |
| *Gouania hillebrandii* | None | U.S.A. (HI) | E | 165 | 17.96(a) | NA |
| *Ziziphus celata* | Florida ziziphus | U.S.A. (FL) | E | 356 | NA | NA |
| Rosaceae—Rose family: | | | | | | |
| *Geum radiatum* | Spreading avens | U.S.A. (NC, TN) | E | 381 | NA | NA |
| *Ivesia kingii* var. *eremica* | Ash Meadows ivesia | U.S.A. (NV) | T | 181 | 17.96(a) | NA |
| *Potentilla robbinsiana* | Robbins' cinquefoil | U.S.A. (NH, VT) | E | 104 | 17.96(a) | NA |
| *Prunus geniculata* | Scrub plum | U.S.A. (FL) | E | 256 | NA | NA |
| *Purchia subintegra* (=*Cowania s.*) | Arizona cliffrose | U.S.A. (AZ) | E | 148 | NA | NA |
| *Spiraea virginiana* | Virginia spiraea | U.S.A. (GA, KY, NC, PA, TN, VA, WV). | T | 389 | NA | NA |
| Rubiaceae—Coffee family: | | | | | | |
| *Gardenia brighamii* | Na'u (Hawaiian gardenia) | U.S.A. (HI) | E | 198 | NA | NA |
| *Hedyotis purpurea* var. *montana* | Roan Mountain bluet | U.S.A. (NC, TN) | E | 381 | NA | NA |
| Rutaceae—Citrus family: | | | | | | |
| *Zanthoxylum thomasianum* | St. Thomas prickly-ash | U.S.A. (PR, VI) | E | 213 | NA | NA |
| Santalaceae—Sandalwood family: | | | | | | |
| *Santalum freycinetianum* var. *lanaiense* | Lanai sandalwood or 'iliahi | U.S.A. (HI) | E | 215 | NA | NA |
| Sarraceniaceae—Pitcher-plant family: | | | | | | |
| *Sarracenia oreophila* | Green pitcher-plant | U.S.A. (AL, GA, TN) | E | 56, 89 | NA | NA |
| *Sarracenia rubra* ssp. *alabamensis* (=*S. alabamensis* ssp. *a.*). | Alabama canebrake pitcher-plant | U.S.A. (AL) | E | 346 | NA | NA |
| *Sarracenia rubra* ssp. *jonesii* (=*S. jonesii*) | Mountain sweet pitcher-plant | U.S.A. (NC, SC) | E | 339 | NA | NA |
| Saxifragaceae—Saxifrage family: | | | | | | |
| *Ribes echinellum* | Miccosukee gooseberry | U.S.A. (FL, SC) | T | 190 | NA | NA |
| Scrophulariaceae—Snapdragon family: | | | | | | |
| *Agalinis acuta* | Sandplain gerardia | U.S.A. (CT, MA, MD, NY, RI). | E | 325 | NA | NA |
| *Amphianthus pusillus* | Little amphianthus | U.S.A. (AL, GA, SC) | T | 302 | NA | NA |
| *Castilleja grisea* | San Clemente Island Indian paintbrush | U.S.A. (CA) | E | 26 | NA | NA |
| *Cordylanthus maritimus* ssp. *maritimus* | Salt marsh bird's-beak | U.S.A. (CA), Mexico (Baja California). | E | 44 | NA | NA |
| *Cordylanthus palmatus* | Palmate-bracted bird's-beak | U.S.A. (CA) | E | 235 | NA | NA |
| *Mimulus glabratus* var. *michiganensis* | Michigan monkey-flower | U.S.A. (MI) | E | 392 | NA | NA |
| *Pedicularis furbishiae* | Furbish lousewort | U.S.A. (ME), Canada (NB). | E | 39 | NA | NA |
| *Penstemon haydenii* | Blowout penstemon | U.S.A. (NE) | E | 285 | NA | NA |
| *Penstemon penlandii* | Penland beardtongue | U.S.A. (CO) | E | 353 | NA | NA |
| Solanaceae—Nightshade family: | | | | | | |
| *Goetzea elegans* | Beautiful goetzea, matabuey | U.S.A. (PR) | E | 176 | NA | NA |
| *Solanum drymophilum* | Erubia | ......do | E | 319 | NA | NA |
| Styracaceae—Styrax family: | | | | | | |
| *Styrax texana* | Texas snowbells | U.S.A. (TX) | E | 162 | NA | NA |
| Taxaceae—Yew family: | | | | | | |
| *Torreya taxifolia* | Florida torreya | U.S.A. (FL, GA) | E | 140 | NA | NA |
| Thymelaeaceae—Mezereum family: | | | | | | |
| *Daphnopsis hellerana* | None | U.S.A. (PR) | E | 309 | NA | NA |

| | | | | | | |
|---|---|---|---|---|---|---|
| Verbenaceae—Verbena family: | | | | | | |
| *Cornutia obovata* | Palo de Nigua | U.S.A. (PR) | E | 307 | NA | NA |
| Violaceae—Violet family: | | | | | | |
| *Isodendrion hosakae* | Aupaka | U.S.A. (HI) | E | 414 | NA | NA |

Symbol used in the "when listed" columm:
E—Indicates Emergency rule publication (see FR document for effective dates); subsequent number(s) indicate FR final rule, if applicable, under "When listed".

EDITORIAL NOTE: See the following list for the "when listed" citations.

26—42 FR 40685; August 11, 1977.
39—43 FR 17916; April 26, 1978.
44—43 FR 44812; September 28, 1978.
47—44 FR 24250; April 24, 1979.
49—44 FR 32605; June 6, 1979.
53—44 FR 43701; July 25, 1979.
56—44 FR 54923; September 21, 1979.
57—44 FR 58863; October 2, 1979.
58—44 FR 58868; October 11, 1979.
59—44 FR 58870; October 11, 1979.
61—44 FR 61556; October 25, 1979.
62—44 FR 61558; October 25, 1979.
63—44 FR 61786; October 26, 1979.
64—44 FR 61788; October 26, 1979
65—44 FR 61911; October 26, 1979.
66—44 FR 61913; October 26, 1979.
67—44 FR 61916; October 26, 1979.
68—44 FR 61920; October 26, 1979.
69—44 FR 61924; October 26, 1979.
70—44 FR 61927; October 26, 1979.
71—44 FR 61929; October 26, 1979.
72—44 FR 62246; October 29, 1979.
73—44 FR 62469; October 30, 1979.
74—44 FR 62471; October 30, 1979.
75—44 FR 62474; October 30, 1979.
76—44 FR 64247; November 6, 1979.
77—44 FR 64250; November 6, 1979.
78—44 FR 64252; November 6, 1979.
79—44 FR 64733; November 7, 1979.
80—44 FR 64738; November 7, 1979.
81—44 FR 64740; November 7, 1979.
82—44 FR 64743; November 7, 1979.
83—44 FR 64746; Nobember 7, 1979.
84—44 FR 65005; November 8, 1979.
89—45 FR 18929; March 24, 1980.
104—45 FR 61944; September 17, 1980.
107—45 FR 69360; October 20, 1980.
109—46 FR 3184; January 13, 1981.
110—46 FR 5730; January 19, 1981.
112—46 FR 40025; August 6, 1981.
116—47 FR 19539; May 6, 1982.
118—47 FR 30440; July 13, 1982.
120—47 FR 36846; August 24, 1982.
121—47 FR 38540; September 1, 1982.
122—47 FR 38927; September 10, 1982.
126—47 FR 50885; November 10, 1982.
133—48 FR 46331; October 12, 1983.
137—48 FR 52747; November 22, 1983.
140—49 FR 2786; January 23, 1984.
141—49 FR 6102; February 17, 1984.
147—49 FR 21058; May 18, 1984.
148—49 FR 22329; May 29, 1984.
151—49 FR 28565; July 13, 1984.
152—49 FR 29234; July 19, 1984.
153—49 FR 29237; July 19, 1984.
154—49 FR 30201; July 27, 1984.
155—49 FR 31421; Aug. 7, 1984.
158—49 FR 34500; Aug. 31, 1984.
162—49 FR 40038; October 12, 1984.
165—49 FR 44756; November 9, 1984.
167—49 FR 47400; December 4, 1984.
168—49 FR 49639; December 21, 1984.
172—50 FR 5758; February 12, 1985.
175—50 FR 12309; March 28, 1985.
176—50 FR 15567; April 19, 1985.
177—50 FR 16682; April 26, 1985.
178—50 FR 19373; May 8, 1985.
179—50 FR 19377; May 8, 1985.
180—50 FR 20214; May 15, 1985.
181—50 FR 20786; May 20, 1985.
187—50 FR 26572; June 27, 1985.
190—50 FR 29341; July 18, 1985.
191—50 FR 29344; July 18, 1985.
192—50 FR 29349; July 18, 1985.
194—50 FR 31190; August 1, 1985.
197—50 FR 32575; August 13, 1985.
198—50 FR 33731; August 21, 1985.
199—50 FR 33734; August 21, 1985.
200—50 FR 33737; August 21, 1985.
201—50 FR 36089; September 5, 1985.
202—50 FR 36091; September 5, 1985.
204—50 FR 37863; September 18, 1985.
207—50 FR 45618; November 1, 1985.
208—50 FR 45621; November 1, 1985.
209—50 FR 45624; November 1, 1985.
213—50 FR 51870; December 21, 1985.
214—51 FR 956; January 9, 1986.
215—51 FR 3185; January 24, 1986.
217—51 FR 6693; February 25, 1986.
218—51 FR 8683; March 13, 1986.
219—51 FR 9820; March 21, 1986.
220—51 FR 10521; March 26, 1986.
221—51 FR 10523; March 26, 1986.
225—51 FR 15906; April 29, 1986.
226—51 FR 15911; April 29, 1986.
229—51 FR 16530; May 5, 1986.
230—51 FR 17346; May 12, 1986.
231—51 FR 17974; May 16, 1986.
232—51 FR 17977; May 16, 1986.
234—51 FR 22524; June 20, 1986.
235—51 FR 23769; July 1, 1986.
237—51 FR 24672; July 8, 1986.
238—51 FR 24675; July 8, 1986.
240—51 FR 27500; July 31, 1986.
243—51 FR 34415; September 26, 1986.
244—51 FR 34419; September 26, 1986.
245—51 FR 34422; September 26, 1986.
249—51 FR 45907; December 23, 1986.
252—52 FR 679; January 8, 1987.
253—52 FR 682; January 8, 1987.
254—52 FR 784; January 9, 1987.
255—52 FR 1462; January 14, 1987.
256—52 FR 2234; January 21, 1987.
257—52 FR 4910; February 18, 1987.
259—52 FR 6651; March 4, 1987.
260—52 FR 7426; March 11, 1987.
264—52 FR 11175; April 7, 1987.
266—52 FR 15505; April 29, 1987.
270—52 FR 21480; June 5, 1987.
271—52 FR 21484; June 5, 1987.
274—52 FR 22589; June 12, 1987.
275—52 FR 22933; June 16, 1987.
276—52 FR 22936; June 16, 1987.
277—52 FR 22939; June 16, 1987.
285—52 FR 32929; September 1, 1987.
286—52 FR 34917; September 16, 1987.
291—52 FR 36270; September 28, 1987.
293—52 FR 37420; October 6, 1987.
295—52 FR 41440; October 28, 1987.
297—52 FR 42071; November 2, 1987.
298—52 FR 42657; November 6, 1987.
300—52 FR 44401; November 19, 1987.
301—52 FR 46087; December 4, 1987.
302—53 FR 3565; February 5, 1988.
303—53 FR 3567; February 5, 1988.
305—53 FR 4629; February 17, 1988.
306—53 FR 10884; April 4, 1988.
307—53 FR 11612; April 7, 1988.
308—53 FR 11615; April 7, 1988.
309—53 FR 23742; June 23, 1988.
310—53 FR 23745; June 23, 1988.
311—53 FR 23748; June 23, 1988.
314—53 FR 27137; July 18, 1988.
315—53 FR 27141; July 18, 1988.
318—53 FR 32827; August 26, 1988.
319—53 FR 32830; August 26, 1988.
321—53 FR 33996; September 1, 1988.
324—53 FR 34701; September 7, 1988.
325—53 FR 34705; September 7, 1988.
326—53 FR 35080; September 9, 1988.
329—53 FR 37972; September 28, 1988.
330—53 FR 37975; September 28, 1988.
331—53 FR 37978; September 28, 1988.
332—53 FR 37982; September 28, 1988.
333—53 FR 38451; September 30, 1988.
335—53 FR 38456; September 30, 1988.
339—53 FR 38474; September 30, 1988.
341—53 FR 45861; November 14, 1988.
343—54 FR 2134; January 19, 1989.
344—54 FR 5938; February 7, 1989.
346—54 FR 10154; March 10, 1989.
347—54 FR 14967; April 14, 1989.
352—54 FR 29658; July 13, 1989.
353—54 FR 29663; July 13, 1989.
354—54 FR 29730; July 14, 1989.
355—54 FR 30554; July 21, 1989.
356—54 FR 31196; July 27, 1989.
360—54 FR 35305; August 24, 1989.
362—54 FR 38947; September 21, 1989.
363—54 FR 38950; September 21, 1989.
367—54 FR 39857; September 28, 1989.
368—54 FR 39863; September 28, 1989.
373—55 FR 433; January 5, 1990.
374—55 FR 4157; February 6, 1990.
375—55 FR 4159; February 6, 1990.
379—55 FR 12790; April 5, 1990.
380—55 FR 12793; April 5, 1990.
381—55 FR 12797; April 5, 1990.
385—55 FR 13491; April 10, 1990.
386—55 FR 13911; April 13, 1990.
389—55 FR 24246; June 15, 1990.
392—55 FR 25599; June 21, 1990.
395—55 FR 29370; July 19, 1990.
397—55 FR 32255; August 8, 1990.
398—55 FR 32257; August 8, 1990.
402—55 FR 39864; September 28, 1990.
403—55 FR 39867; September 28, 1990.
406—55 FR 49050; November 26, 1990.
409—55 FR 50187; December 5, 1990.
413—56 FR 1453; January, 14, 1991.
414—56 FR 1457; January, 14, 1991.
418—56 FR 1936; January, 18, 1991.
420—56 FR 16024; April 19, 1991.
422—56 FR 19959; May 1, 1991.
424—56 FR 21091; May 7, 1991.
425—56 FR 21096; May 7, 1991.

[48 FR 34182, July 27, 1983]

**Editorial Note:** For **Federal Register** citations affecting § 17.12, see the List of CFR Sections Affected appearing in the Finding Aids section of this volume.

### SPECIES REMOVED FROM THE ENDANGERED AND THREATENED LISTS

The following list of wildlife removed from the list at § 17.11 is provided for informational purposes only and is not codified in the Code of Federal Regulations. Only species completely removed from the list are included below. In cases where only a portion of the vertebrate species is delisted, the entry remains in § 17.11 in the modified form with the citation to the **Federal Register** indicated under "When listed."

The Service's listing regulations at 50 CFR 424.11(c) and (d) are as follows:

(c) A species shall be listed or reclassified if the Secretary determines, on the basis of the best scientific and commercial data available after conducting a review of the species' status, that the species is endangered or threatened because of any one or a combination of the following factors:

(1) The present or threatened destruction, modification, or curtailment of its habitat or range;

(2) Overutilization for commercial, recreational, scientific, or educational purposes;

(3) Disease or predation;

(4) The inadequacy of existing regulatory mechanisms; or

(5) Other natural or manmade factors affecting its continued existence.

(d) The factors considered in delisting a species are those in paragraph (c) of this section as they relate to the definitions of endangered or threatened species. Such removal must be supported by the best scientific and commercial data available to the Secretary after conducting a review of the status of the species. A species may be delisted only if such data substantiate that it is neither endangered nor threatened for one or more of the following reasons:

(1) *Extinction.* Unless all individuals of the listed species had been previously identified and located, and were later found to be extirpated from their previous range, a sufficient period of time must be allowed before delisting to indicate clearly that the species is extinct.

(2) *Recovery.* The principal goal of the U.S. Fish and Wildlife Service and the National Marine Fisheries Services is to return listed species to a point at which protection under the Act is no longer required. A species may be delisted on the basis of recovery only if the best scientific and commercial data available indicate that it is no longer endangered or threatened.

(3) *Original data for classification in error.* Subsequent investigations may show that the best scientific or commercial data available when the species was listed, or the interpretation of such data, were in error.

| Species | | Historic range | Former vertebrate population where endangered or threatened | Former status | Delisted | |
|---|---|---|---|---|---|---|
| Common name | Scientific name | | | | Citation | Reason |
| Duck, Mexican | *Anas "diazi"* | U.S.A. (AZ, NM, TX) to central Mexico. | U.S. only | E | 43 FR 32258-61; July 25, 1978. | Original data in error. |
| Pupfish, Tecopa | *Cyprinodon nevadensis calidae.* | U.S.A. (CA) | Entire | E | 47 FR 2317-19; January 15, 1982. | Extinct. |
| Cisco, longjaw | *Coregonus alpenae* | U.S.A. and Canada (Lakes Michigan, Huron, Erie). | ......do | E | 48 FR 39941-43; September 2, 1983. | Do. |
| Pike, blue | *Stizostedion vitreum glaucum.* | U.S.A. and Canada (Lakes Erie, Ontario). | ......do | E | ......do | Do. |
| Sparrow, Santa Barbara song. | *Melospiza melodia graminea.* | U.S.A. (CA) | ......do | E | 48 FR 46336-37; October 12, 1983. | Do. |
| Treefrog, Pine Barrens | *Hyla andersonii* | U.S.A. (FL, AL, NC, SC, NJ) | Florida | E | 48 FR 52740-43; November 22, 1983. | Original data in error. |
| Pearly mussel, Sampson's | *Epioblasma (=Dysnomia) sampsoni.* | U.S.A. (IL, IN) | NA | E | 49 FR 1057-58; January 9, 1984. | Extinct. |
| Turtle, Indian flap-shelled | *Lissemys punctata punctata* | India, Pakistan, Bangladesh | Entire | E | 49 FR 7394-98; February 29, 1984. | Original data in error. |
| Butterfly, Bahama swallowtail. | *Heraclides (=Papilio) andraemon bonhotei.* | U.S.A. (FL), Bahamas | NA | T | 49 FR 34501-04; August 31, 1984. | Do. |
| Dove, Palau | *Gallicolumba canifrons* | W. Pacific: U.S.A. (Palau Islands). | Entire | E | 50 FR 37192-94; September 12, 1985. | Recovered. |
| Fantail, Palau (Old World flycatcher). | *Rhipidura lepida* | ......do | ......do | E | ......do | Do. |
| Owl, Palau | *Pyroglaux (=Otus) podargina.* | ......do | ......do | E | ......do | Do. |
| Gambusia, Amistad | *Gambusia amistadensis* | U.S.A. (TX) | ......do | E | 52 FR 86083-85; December 4, 1987. | Extinct. |
| Milk-vetch, Rydberg | *Astragalus perianus* | U.S.A. (UT) | NA | T | 54 FR 37941-43; September 14, 1989. | Recovered. |
| Cactus, purple-spined hedgehog. | *Echinocereus engelmannii* var. *purpureus.* | ......do | NA | E | 54 FR 48749-51; November 27, 1989. | Original data in error. |
| Sparrow, dusky seaside | *Ammodramus (=Ammospiza) maritimus mirabilis.* | U.S.A. (FL) | Entire | E | 55 FR 51112-14; December 12, 1990. | Extinct. |

* U.S. G.P.O.:1991-296-520:50024

# APPENDIX E

# TEXT OF THE

# CONVENTION ON INTERNATIONAL TRADE IN ENDANGERED SPECIES OF WILD FAUNA AND FLORA

# Convention on International Trade in Endangered Species of Wild Fauna and Flora

Signed at Washington, D.C., on March 3, 1973

The Contracting States,

*Recognizing* that wild fauna and flora in their many beautiful and varied forms are an irreplaceable part of the natural systems of the earth which must be protected for this and the generations to come;

*Conscious* of the ever-growing value of wild fauna and flora from aesthetic, scientific, cultural, recreational and economic points of view;

*Recognizing* that peoples and States are and should be the best protectors of their own wild fauna and flora;

*Recognizing*, in addition, that international cooperation is essential for the protection of certain species of wild fauna and flora against over-exploitation through international trade;

*Convinced* of the urgency of taking appropriate measures to this end;

*Have agreed* as follows:

### *Article I*
### Definitions

For the purpose of the present Convention, unless the context otherwise requires:

(a) "Species" means any species, subspecies, or geographically separate population thereof;

(b) "Specimen" means:

- (i) any animal or plant, whether alive or dead;
- (ii) in the case of an animal: for species included in Appendices I and II, any readily recognizable part or derivative thereof; and for species included in Appendix III, any readily recognizable part or derivative thereof specified in Appendix III in relation to the species; and
- (iii) in the case of a plant: for species included in Appendix I, any readily recognizable part or derivative thereof; and for species included in Appendices II and III, any readily recognizable part or derivative thereof specified in Appendices II and III in relation to the species;

(c) "Trade" means export, re-export, import and introduction from the sea;

(d) "Re-export" means export of any specimen that has previously been imported;

(e) "Introduction from the sea" means transportation into a State of specimens of any species which were taken in the marine environment not under the jurisdiction of any State;

(f) "Scientific Authority" means a national scientific authority designated in accordance with Article IX;

(g) "Management Authority" means a national management authority designated in accordance with Article IX;

(h) "Party" means a State for which the present Convention has entered into force.

### *Article II*
### Fundamental Principles

1. Appendix I shall include all species threatened with extinction which are or may be affected by trade. Trade in specimens of these species must be subject to particularly strict regulation in order not to endanger further their survival and must only be authorized in exceptional circumstances.

2. Appendix II shall include:

(a) all species which although not necessarily now threatened with extinction may become so unless trade in specimens of such species is subject to strict regulation in order to avoid utilization incompatible with their survival; and

(b) other species which must be subject to regulation in order that trade in specimens of certain species referred to in sub-paragraph (a) of this paragraph may be brought under effective control.

3. Appendix III shall include all species which any Party identified as being subject to regulation within its jurisdiction for the purpose of preventing or restricting exploitation, and as needing the cooperation of other parties in the control of trade.

4. The Parties shall not allow trade in specimens of species included in Appendices I, II and III except in accordance with the provisions of the present Convention.

### *Article III*
### Regulation of Trade in Specimens of Species Included in Appendix I

1. All trade in specimens of species included in Appendix I shall be in accordance with the provisions of this Article.

2. The export of any specimen of a species included in Appendix I shall require the prior grant and presentation of an export permit. An export permit shall only be granted when the following conditions have been met:

(a) a Scientific Authority of the State of export has advised that such export will not be detrimental to the survival of that species;

(b) a Management Authority of the State of export is satisfied that the specimen was not obtained in contravention of the laws of that State for the protection of fauna and flora;

(c) a Management Authority of the State of export is satisfied that any living specimen will be so prepared and shipped as to minimize the risk of injury, damage to health or cruel treatment; and

(d) a Management Authority of the State of export is satisfied that an import permit has been granted for the specimen.

3. The import of any specimen of a species included in Appendix I shall require the prior grant and presentation of an import permit and either an export permit or a re-export certi-

Special Supplement to IUCN Bulletin 4 (3) March 1973

*Reprinted April 1983*

ficate. An import permit shall only be granted when the following conditions have been met:

(a) a Scientific Authority of the State of import has advised that the import will be for purposes which are not detrimental to the survival of the species involved;

(b) a Scientific Authority of the State of import is satisfied that the proposed recipient of a living specimen is suitably equipped to house and care for it; and

(c) a Management Authority of the State of import is satisfied that the specimen is not to be used for primarily commercial purposes.

4. The re-export of any specimen of a species included in Appendix I shall require the prior grant and presentation of a re-export certificate. A re-export certificate shall only be granted when the following conditions have been met:

(a) a Management Authority of the State of re-export is satisfied that the specimen was imported into that State in accordance with the provisions of the present Convention;

(b) a Management Authority of the State of re-export is satisfied that any living specimen will be so prepared and shipped as to minimize the risk of injury, damage to health or cruel treatment; and

(c) a Management Authority of the State of re-export is satisfied that an import permit has been granted for any living specimen.

5. The introduction from the sea of any specimen of a species included in Appendix I shall require the prior grant of a certificate from a Management Authority of the State of introduction. A certificate shall only be granted when the following conditions have been met:

(a) a Scientific Authority of the State of introduction advises that the introduction will not be detrimental to the survival of the species involved;

(b) a Management Authority of the State of introduction is satisfied that the proposed recipient of a living specimen is suitably equipped to house and care for it; and

(c) a Management Authority of the State of introduction is satisfied that the specimen is not to be used for primarily commercial purposes.

*Article IV*

**Regulation of Trade in Specimens of Species included in Appendix II**

1. All trade in specimens of species included in Appendix II shall be in accordance with the provisions of this Article.

2. The export of any specimen of a species included in Appendix II shall require the prior grant and presentation of an export permit. An export permit shall only be granted when the following conditions have been met:

(a) a Scientific Authority of the State of export has advised that such export will not be detrimental to the survival of that species;

(b) a Management Authority of the State of export is satisfied that the specimen was not obtained in contravention of the laws of that State for the protection of fauna and flora; and

(c) a Management Authority of the State of export is satisfied that any living specimen will be so prepared and shipped as to minimize the risk of injury, damage to health or cruel treatment.

3. A Scientific Authority in each Party shall monitor both the export permits granted by that State for specimens of species included in Appendix II and the actual exports of such specimens. Whenever a Scientific Authority determines that the export of specimens of any such species should be limited in order to maintain that species throughout its range at a level consistent with its role in the ecosystems in which it occurs and well above the level at which that species might become eligible for inclusion in Appendix I, the Scientific Authority shall advise the appropriate Management Authority of suitable measures to be taken to limit the grant of export permits for specimens of that species.

4. The import of any specimen of a species included in Appendix II shall require the prior presentation of either an export permit or a re-export certificate.

5. The re-export of any specimen of a species included in Appendix II shall require the prior grant and presentation of a re-export certificate. A re-export certificate shall only be granted when the following conditions have been met:

(a) a Management Authority of the State of re-export is satisfied that the specimen was imported into that State in accordance with the provisions of the present Convention; and

(b) a Management Authority of the State of re-export is satisfied that any living specimen will be so prepared and shipped as to minimize the risk of injury, damage to health or cruel treatment.

6. The introduction from the sea of any specimen of a species included in Appendix II shall require the prior grant of a certificate from a Management Authority of the State of introduction. A certificate shall only be granted when the following conditions have been met:

(a) a Scientific Authority of the State of introduction advises that the introduction will not be detrimental to the survival of the species involved; and

(b) a Management Authority of the State of introduction is satisfied that any living specimen will be so handled as to minimize the risk of injury, damage to health or cruel treatment.

7. Certificates referred to in paragraph 6 of this Article may be granted on the advice of a Scientific Authority, in consultation with other national scientific authorities or, when appropriate, international scientific authorities, in respect of periods not exceeding one year for total numbers of specimens to be introduced in such periods.

*Article V*

**Regulation of Trade in Specimens of Species included in Appendix III**

1. All trade in specimens of species included in Appendix III shall be in accordance with the provisions of this Article.

2. The export of any specimen of a species included in Appendix III from any State which has included that species in Appendix III shall require the prior grant and presentation of an export permit. An export permit shall only be granted when the following conditions have been met:

(a) a Management Authority of the State of export is satisfied that the specimen was not obtained in contravention of the laws of that State for the protection of fauna and flora; and

(b) a Management Authority of the State of export is satisfied that any living specimen will be so prepared and shipped as to minimize the risk of injury, damage to health or cruel treatment.

3. The import of any specimen of a species included in Appendix III shall require, except in circumstances to which paragraph 4 of this Article applies, the prior presentation of a certificate of origin and, where the import is from a State which has included that species in Appendix III, an export permit.

4. In the case of re-export, a certificate granted by the Management Authority of the State of re-export that the specimen was processed in that State or is being re-exported shall be accepted by the State of import as evidence that the provisions of the present Convention have been complied with in respect of the specimen concerned.

*Article VI*

**Permits and Certificates**

1. Permits and certificates granted under the provisions of Articles III, IV, and V shall be in accordance with the provisions of this Article.

2. An export permit shall contain the information specified in the model set forth in Appendix IV, and may only be used for export within a period of six months from the date on which it was granted.

3. Each permit or certificate shall contain the title of the present Convention, the name and any identifying stamp of the Management Authority granting it and a control number assigned by the Management Authority.

4. Any copies of a permit or certificate issued by a Management Authority shall be clearly marked as copies only and no such copy may be used in place of the original, except to the extent endorsed thereon.

5. A separate permit or certificate shall be required for each consignment of specimens.

6. A Management Authority of the State of import of any specimen shall cancel and retain the export permit or re-export certificate and any corresponding import permit presented in respect of the import of that specimen.

7. Where appropriate and feasible a Management Authority may affix a mark upon any specimen to assist in identifying the specimen. For these purposes "mark" means any indelible imprint, lead seal or other suitable means of identifying a specimen, designed in such a way as to render its imitation by unauthorized persons as difficult as possible.

*Article VII*

**Exemptions and Other Special Provisions Relating to Trade**

1. The provisions of Articles III, IV and V shall not apply to the transit or trans-shipment of specimens through or in the territory of a Party while the specimens remain in Customs control.

2. Where a Management Authority of the State of export or re-export is satisfied that a specimen was acquired before the provisions of the present Convention applied to that specimen, the provisions of Articles III, IV and V shall not apply to that specimen where the Management Authority issues a certificate to that effect.

3. The provisions of Articles III, IV and V shall not apply to specimens that are personal or household effects. This exemption shall not apply where:

(a) in the case of specimens of a species included in Appendix I, they were acquired by the owner outside his State of usual residence, and are being imported into that State; or

(b) in the case of specimens of species included in Appendix II:

(i) they were acquired by the owner outside his State of usual residence and in a State where removal from the wild occurred;

(ii) they are being imported into the owner's State of usual residence; and

(iii) the State where removal from the wild occurred requires the prior grant of export permits before any export of such specimens;

unless a Management Authority is satisfied that the specimens were acquired before the provisions of the present Convention applied to such specimens.

4. Specimens of an animal species included in Appendix I bred in captivity for commercial purpose, or of a plant species included in Appendix I artificially propagated for commercial purposes, shall be deemed to be specimens of species included in Appendix II

5. Where a Management Authority of the State of export is satisfied that any specimen of an animal species was bred in captivity or any specimen of a plant species was artificially propagated, or is a part of such an animal or plant or was derived therefrom, a certificate by that Management Authority to that effect shall be accepted in lieu of any of the permits or certificates required under the provisions of Articles III, IV or V.

6. The provisions of Articles III, IV and V shall not apply to the non-commercial loan, donation or exchange between scientists or scientific institutions registered by a Management Authority of their State, of herbarium specimens, other preserved, dried or embedded museum specimens, and live plant material which carry a label issued or approved by a Management Authority.

7. A Management Authority of any State may waive the requirements of Articles III, IV and V and alow the movement without permits or certificates of specimens which form part of a travelling zoo, circus, menagerie, plant exhibition or other travelling exhibition provided that:

(a) the exporter or importer registers full details of such specimens with that Management Authority;

(b) the specimens are in either of the categories specified in paragraphs 2 or 5 of this Article; and

(c) the Management Authority is satisfied that any living specimen will be so transported and cared for as to minimize the risk of injury, damage to health or cruel treatment.

*Article VIII*

**Measures to be Taken by the Parties**

1. The Parties shall take appropriate measures to enforce the provisions of the present Convention and to prohibit trade in specimens in violation thereof. These shall include measures:

(a) to penalize trade in, or possession of, such specimens, or both; and

(b) to provide for the confiscation or return to the State of export of such specimens.

2. In addition to the measures taken under paragraph 1 of this Article, a Party may, when it deems it necessary, provide for any method of internal reimbursement for expenses incurred as a result of the confiscation of a specimen traded in violation of the measures taken in the application of the provisions of the present Convention.

3. As far as possible, the Parties shall ensure that specimens shall pass through any formalities required for trade with a minimum of delay. To facilitate such passage, a Party may designate ports of exit and ports of entry at which specimens must be presented for clearance. The Parties shall ensure further that all living specimens, during any period of transit, holding or shipment, are properly cared for so as to minimize the risk of injury, damage to health or cruel treatment.

4. Where a living specimen is confiscated as a result of measures referred to in paragraph 1 of this Article:

(a) the specimen shall be entrusted to a Management Authority of the State of confiscation;

(b) the Management Authority shall, after consultation with the State of export, return the specimen to that State at the expense of that State, or to a rescue centre or such other place as the Management Authority deems appropriate and consistent with the purposes of the present Convention; and

(c) the Management Authority may obtain the advice of a Scientific Authority, or may, whenever it considers it desirable, consult the Secretariat in order to facilitate the decision under subparagraph (b) of this paragraph, including the choice of a rescue centre or other place.

5. A rescue centre as referred to in paragraph 4 of this Article means an institution designated by a Management Authority to look after the welfare of living specimens, particularly those that have been confiscated.

6. Each Party shall maintain records of trade in specimens of species included in Appendices I, II and III which shall cover:

(a) the names and addresses of exporters and importers; and

(b) the number and type of permits and certificates granted; the States with which such trade occurred; the numbers or quantities and types of specimens, names of species as included in Appendices I, II and III and, where applicable, the size and sex of the specimens in question.

7. Each Party shall prepare periodic reports on its implementation of the present Convention and shall transmit to the Secretariat:

(a) an annual report containing a summary of the information specified in sub-paragraph (b) of paragraph 6 of this Article; and

(b) a biennial report on legislative, regulatory and administrative measures taken to enforce the provisions of the present Convention.

8. The information referred to in paragraph 7 of this Article shall be available to the public where this is not inconsistent with the law of the Party concerned.

*Article IX*

**Management and Scientific Authorities**

1. Each Party shall designate for the purpose of the present Convention:

(a) one or more Management Authorities competent to grant permits or certificates on behalf of that Party; and

(b) one or more Scientific Authorities.

2. A State depositing an instrument of ratification, acceptance, approval or accession shall at that time inform the Depositary Government of the name and address of the Management Authority authorized to communicate with other Parties and with the Secretariat.

3. Any changes in the designations or authorizations under the provisions of this Article shall be communicated by the Party concerned to the Secretariat for transmission to all other Parties.

4. Any Management Authority referred to in paragraph 2 of this Article shall if so requested by the Secretariat or the Management Authority of another Party, communicate to it impression of stamps, seals or other devices used to authenticate permits or certificates.

*Article X*

**Trade with States not Party to the Convention**

Where export or re-export is to, or import is from, a State not a party to the present Convention, comparable documentation issued by the competent authorities in that State which substantially conforms with the requirements of the present Convention for permits and certificates may by accepted in lieu thereof by any Party.

*Article XI*

**Conference of the Parties**

1. The Secretariat shall call a meeting of the Conference of the Parties not later than two years after the entry into force of the present Convention.

2. Thereafter the Secretariat shall convene regular meetings at least once every two years, unless the Conference decides otherwise, and extraordinary meetings at any time on the written request of at least one-third of the Parties.

3. At meetings, whether regular or extraordinary, the Parties shall review the implementation of the present Convention and may:

(a) make such provision as may be necessary to enable the Secretariat to carry out its duties;

(b) consider and adopt amendements to Appendices I and II in accordance with Article XV;

(c) review the progress made towards the restoration and conservation of the species included in Appendices I, II and III;

(d) receive and consider any reports presented by the Secretariat or by any Party; and

(e) where appropriate, make recommendations for improving the effectiveness of the present Convention.

4. At each regular meeting, the Parties may determine the time and venue of the next regular meeting to be held in accordance with the provisions of paragraph 2 of this Article.

5. At any meeting, the Parties may determine and adopt rules of procedure for the meeting.

6. The United Nations, its Specialized Agencies and the International Atomic Energy Agency, as well as any State not a Party to the present Convention, may be represented at meetings of the Conference by observers, who shall have the right to participate but not to vote.

7. Any body or agency technically qualified in protection, conservation or management of wild fauna and flora, in the following categories, which has informed the Secretariat of its desire to be represented at meetings of the Conference by observers, shall be admitted unless at least one-third of the Parties present object:

(a) international agencies or bodies, either governmental or non-governmental, and national governmental agencies and bodies; and

(b) national non-governmental agencies or bodies which have been approved for this purpose by the State in which they are located.

Once admitted, these observers shall have the right to participate but not to vote.

*Article XII*

**The Secretariat**

1. Upon entry into force of the present Convention, a Secretariat shall be provided by the Executive Director of the United Nations Environment Programme. To the extent and in the manner he considers appropriate, he may be assisted by suitable inter-governmental or non-governmental, international or national agencies and bodies technically qualified in protection, conservation and management of wild fauna and flora.

2. The functions of the Secretariat shall be:

(a) to arrange for and service meetings of the Parties;

(b) to perform the functions entrusted to it under the provisions of Articles XV and XVI of the present Convention;

(c) to undertake scientific and technical studies in accordance with programmes authorized by the Conference of the Parties as will contribute to the implementation of the present Convention, including studies concerning standards for appropriate preparation and shipment of living specimens and the means of identifying specimens;

(d) to study the reports of Parties and to request from Parties such further information with respect thereto as it deems necessary to ensure implementation of the present Convention;

(e) to invite the attention of the Parties to any matter pertaining to the aims of the present Convention;

(f) to publish periodically and distribute to the Parties current editions of Appendices I, II and III together with any information which will facilitate identification of specimens of species included in those Appendices.

(g) to prepare annual reports to the Parties on its work and on the implementation of the present Convention and such other reports as meetings of the Parties may request;

(h) to make recommendations for the implementation of the aims and provisions of the present Convention, including the exchange of information of a scientific or technical nature,

(i) to perform any other function as may be entrusted to it by the Parties.

*Article XIII*

**International Measures**

1. When the Secretariat in the light of information received is satisfied that any species included in Appendices I or II is being affected adversely by trade in specimens of that species or that the provisions of the present Convention are not being effectively implemented, it shall communicate such information to the authorized Management Authority of the Party or Parties concerned.

2. When any Party receives a communication as indicated in paragraph 1 of this Article, it shall, as soon as possible, inform the Secretariat of any relevant facts insofar as its laws permit and, where appropriate, propose remedial action. Where the Party considers that an inquiry is desirable, such inquiry may be carried out by one or more persons expressly authorized by the Party.

3. The information provided by the Party or resulting from any inquiry as specified in paragraph 2 of this Article shall be reviewed by the next Conference of the Parties which may make whatever recommendations it deems appropriate.

*Article XIV*

**Effect on Domestic Legislation and International Conventions**

1. The provisions of the present Convention shall in no way affect the right of Parties to adopt:

(a) stricter domestic measures regarding the conditions for trade, taking, possession or transport of specimens of species included in Appendices I, II and III, or the complete prohibition thereof; or

(b) domestic measures restricting or prohibiting trade, taking, possession, or transport of species not included in Appendices I, II or III.

2. The provisions of the present Convention shall in no way affect the provisions of any domestic measures or the obligations of Parties deriving from any treaty, convention, or international agreement relating to other aspects of trade, taking, possession, or transport of specimens which is in force or subsequently may enter into force for any Party including any measure pertaining to the Customs, public health, veterinary or plant quarantine fields.

3. The provisions of the present Convention shall in no way affect the provisions of, or the obligations deriving from, any treaty, convention or international agreement concluded or which may be concluded between States creating a union or regional trade agreement establishing or maintaining a common external customs control and removing customs control between the parties thereto insofar as they relate to trade among the States members of that union agreement.

4. A State Party to the present Convention, which is also a party to any other treaty, convention or international agreement which is in force at the time of the coming into force of the present Convention and under the provisions of which protection is afforded to marine species included in Appendix II, shall be relieved of the obligation imposed on it under the provisions of the present Convention with respect to trade in specimens of species included in Appendix II that are taken by ships registered in that State and in accordance with the provisions of such other treaty, convention or international agreement.

5. Notwithstanding the provisions of Articles III, IV and V, any export of a specimen taken in accordance with paragraph 4 of this Article shall only require a certificate from a Management Authority of the State of introduction to the effect that the specimen was taken in accordance with the provisions of the other treaty, convention or international agreement in question.

6. Nothing in the present Convention shall prejudice the codification and development of the law of the sea by the United Nations Conference on the Law of the Sea convened pursuant to Resolution 2750 C (XXV) of the General Assembly of the United Nations nor the present or future claims and legal views of any State concerning the law of the sea and the nature and extent of coastal and flag State jurisdiction.

*Article XV*

**Amendments to Appendices I and II**

1. The following provisions shall apply in relation to amendments to Appendices I and II at meetings of the Conference of the Parties:

(a) Any Party may propose an amendment to Appendix I or II for consideration at the next meeting. The text of the proposed amendment shall be communicated to the Secretariat at least 150 days before the meeting. The Secretariat shall consult the other Parties and interested bodies on the amendment in accordance with the provisions of sub-paragraph (b) and (c) of paragraph 2 of this Article and shall communicate the response to all Parties not later than 30 days before the meeting.

(b) Amendments shall be adopted by a two-thirds majority of Parties present and voting. For these purposes "Parties present and voting" means Parties present and casting an affirmative or negative vote. Parties abstaining from voting shall not be counted among the two-thirds required for adopting an amendment.

(c) Amendments adopted at a meeting shall enter into force 90 days after that meeting for all Parties except those which make a reservation in accordance with paragraph 3 of this Article.

2. The following provisions shall apply in relation to amendments to Appendices I and II between meetings of the Conference of the Parties:

(a) Any Party may propose an amendment to Appendix I or II for consideration between meetings by the postal procedures set forth in this paragraph.

(b) For marine species, the Secretariat shall, upon receiving the text of the proposed amendment, immediately communicate it to the Parties. It shall also consult inter-governmental bodies having a function in relation to those species especially with a view to obtaining scientific data these bodies may be able to provide and to ensuring coordination with any conservation measures enforced by such bodies. The Secretariat shall communicate the views expressed and data provided by these bodies and its own findings and recommendations to the Parties as soon as possible.

(c) For species other than marine species, the Secretariat shall, upon receiving the text of the proposed amendment, immediately communicate it to the Parties, and, as soon as possible thereafter, its own recommendations.

(d) Any Party may, within 60 days of the date on which the Secretariat communicated its recommendations to the Parties under sub-paragraphs (b) or (c) of this paragraph, transmit to the Secretariat any comments on the proposed amendment together with any relevant scientific data and information.

(e) The Secretariat shall communicate the replies received together with its own recommendations to the Parties as soon as possible.

(f) If no objection to the proposed amendment is received by the Secretariat within 30 days of the date the replies and recommendations were communicated under the provisions of sub-paragraph (e) of this paragraph, the amendment shall enter into force 90 days later for all Parties except those which make a reservation in accordance with paragraph 3 of this Article.

(g) If an objection by any Party is received by the Secretariat, the proposed amendment shall be submitted to a postal vote in accordance with the provisions of sub-paragraphs (h), (i) and (j) of this paragraph.

(h) The Secretariat shall notify the Parties that notification of objection has been received.

(i) Unless the Secretariat receives the votes for, against or in abstention from at least one-half of the Parties within 60 days of the date of notification under sub-paragraph (h) of this paragraph, the proposed amendment shall be referred to the next meeting of the Conference for further consideration.

(j) Provided that votes are received from one-half of the Parties, the amendment shall be adopted by a two-thirds majority of Parties casting an affirmative or negative vote.

(k) The Secretariat shall notify all Parties of the result of the vote.

(l) If the proposed amendment is adopted it shall enter into force 90 days after the date of the notification by the Secretariat of its acceptance for all Parties except those which make a reservation in accordance with paragraph 3 of this Article.

3. During the period of 90 days provided for by sub-paragraph (c) of paragraph 1 or sub-paragraph (l) of paragraph 2 of this Article any Party may by notification in writing to the Depositary Government make a reservation with respect to the amendment. Until such reservation is withdrawn the Party shall be treated as a State not a Party to the present Convention with respect to trade in the species concerned.

*Article XVI*

**Appendix III and Amendments thereto**

1. Any party may at any time submit to the Secretariat a list of species which it identifies as being subject to regulation within its jurisdiction for the purpose mentioned in paragraph 3 of Article II. Appendix III shall include the names of the Parties submitting the species for inclusion therein, the scientific names of the species so submitted, and any parts or derivatives of the animals or plants concerned that are specified in relation to the species for the purposes of sub-paragraph (b) of Article I.

2. Each list submitted under the provisions of paragraph 1 of this Article shall be communicated to the Parties by the Secretariat as soon as possible after receiving it. The list shall take effect as part of Appendix III 90 days after the date of such communication. At any time after the communication of such list, any Party may by notification in writing to the Depositary Government enter a reservation with respect to any species or any parts or derivatives, and until such reservation is withdrawn, the State shall be treated as a State not a Party to the present Convention with respect to trade in the species or part or derivative concerned.

3. A Party which has submitted a species for inclusion in Appendix III may withdraw it at any time by notification to the Secretariat which shall communicate the withdrawal to all Parties. The withdrawal shall take effect 30 days after the date of such communication.

4. Any Party submitting a list under the provisions of paragraph 1 of this Article shall submit to the Secretariat a copy of all domestic laws and regulations applicable to the protection of such species, together with any interpretations which the Party may deem appropriate or the Secretariat may request. The Party shall, for as long as the species in questions is included in Appendix III, submit any amendment of such laws and regulations or any new interpretations as they are adopted.

*Article XVII*

**Amendment of the Convention**

1. An extraordinary meeting of the Conference of the Parties shall be convened by the Secretariat on the written request of at least one-third of the Parties to consider and adopt amendments to the present Convention. Such amendments shall be adopted by a two-thirds majority of Parties present and voting. For these purposes "Parties present and voting" means Parties present and casting an affirmative or negative vote. Parties abstaining from voting shall not be counted among the two-thirds required for adopting an amendment.

2. The text of any proposed amendment shall be communicated by the Secretariat to all Parties at least 90 days before the meeting.

3. An amendment shall enter into force for the Parties which have accepted it 60 days after two-thirds of the Parties have deposited an instrument of acceptance of the amendment with the Depositary Government. Thereafter, the amendment shall enter into force for any other Party 60 days after that Party deposits its instrument of acceptance of the amendment.

*Article XVIII*

**Resolution of Disputes**

1. Any dispute which may arise between two or more Parties with respect to the interpretation or application of the provisions of the present Convention shall be subject to negotiation between the Parties involved in the dispute.

2. If the dispute cannot be resolved in accordance with paragraph 1 of this Article, the Parties may, by mutual consent, submit the dispute to arbitration, in particular that of the Permanent Court of Arbitration at The Hague and the Parties submitting the dispute shall be bound by the arbitral decision.

*Article XIX*

**Signature**

The present Convention shall be open for signature at Washington until 30th April 1973 and thereafter at Berne until 31st December 1974.

*Article XX*

**Ratification, Acceptance, Approval**

The present Convention shall be subject to ratification, acceptance or approval. Instruments of ratification, acceptance or approval shall be deposited with the Government of the Swiss Confederation which shall be the Depositary Government.

*Article XXI*

**Accession**

The present Convention shall be open indefinitely for accession. Instruments of accession shall be deposited with the Depositary Government.

*Article XXII*

**Entry into Force**

1. The present Convention shall enter into force 90 days after the date of deposit of the tenth instrument of ratification, acceptance, approval or accession, with the Depositary Government.

2. For each State which ratifies, accepts or approves the present Convention or accedes thereto after the deposit of the tenth instrument of ratification, acceptance, approval or accession, the present Convention shall enter into force 90 days after the deposit by such State of its instrument of ratification, acceptance, approval or accession.

*Article XXIII*

**Reservations**

1. The provisions of the present Convention shall not be subject to general reservations. Specific reservations may be entered in accordance with the provisions of this Article and Articles XV and XVI.

2. Any State may, on depositing its instrument of ratification, acceptance, approval or accession, enter a specific reservation with regard to:

(a) any species included in Appendix I, II or III; or

(b) any parts or derivatives specified in relation to a species concluded in Appendix III.

3. Until a Party withdraws its reservation entered under the provisions of this Article, it shall be treated as a State not a party to the present Convention with respect to trade in the particular species or parts or derivatives specified in such reservation.

*Article XXIV*

**Denunciation**

Any Party may denounce the present Convention by written notification to the Depositary Government at any time. The denunciation shall take effect twelve months after the Depositary Government has received the notification.

*Article XXV*

**Depositary**

1. The original of the present Convention, in the Chinese, English, French, Russian and Spanish languages, each version being equally authentic, shall be deposited with the Depositary Government, which shall transmit certified copies thereof to all States that have signed it or deposited instruments of accession to it.

2. The Depositary Government shall inform all signatory and acceding States and the Secretariat of signatures, deposit of instruments of ratification, acceptance, approval or accession, entry into force of the present Convention, amendments thereto, entry and withdrawal of reservations and notifications of denunciation.

3. As soon as the present Convention enters into force, a certified copy thereof shall be transmitted by the Depositary Government to the Secretariat of the United Nations for registration and publication in accordance with Article 102 of the Charter of the United Nations.

*In witness whereof* the undersigned Plenipotentiaries, being duly authorized to that effect, have signed the present Convention.

*Done* at Washington this third day of March, One Thousand Nine Hundred and Seventy-three.

---

*Editor's note: The Appendices I, II and III, subject to periodical changes, as well as Appendix IV are not reproduced in this document. (January 1980)*

# APPENDIX F

# CITES: APPENDICES I, II, AND III TO THE CONVENTION ON INTERNATIONAL TRADE IN ENDANGERED SPECIES OF WILD FAUNA AND FLORA

September 30, 1991

**Title 50—Wildlife and Fisheries**

**PART 23—ENDANGERED SPECIES CONVENTION**

* * * * *

**Subpart C—Appendices I, II and III to the Convention on International Trade in Endangered Species of Wild Fauna and Flora**

* * * * *

**§ 23.23 Species listed in Appendices I, II, and III.**

(a) The list in this section includes species of wildlife and plants placed in Appendix I, II or III in accordance with the provisions of Articles XV and XVI of the Convention.

The list of species is organized as follows:

| Major group | Subgroups |
|---|---|
| Mammals | Orders, in taxonomic sequence. |
| Birds | Orders, in taxonomic sequence. |
| Reptiles | Orders, in taxonomic sequence. |
| Amphibians | Orders, in taxonomic sequence. |
| Fishes | Orders, in taxonomic sequence. |
| Molluscs | Classes. |
| Arthropods | Classes. |
| Plants | Families, in alphabetical sequence. |

In each group, species are listed in alphabetical sequence. The scientific name takes precedence over the common name in determining if a species is listed.

(b) The appendix column of the list includes the annotation "pe" (=possibly extinct) for certain species. It also contains the names of Parties including species in Appendix III.

(c) For purposes of issuing United States certificates of exemption under Article VII(3), the date when the Convention applies to a species is the date when the inclusion of that species in the appendices enters into force under the terms of Article XV or XVI of the Convention. The date of first listing is retained if a species is transferred from one appendix to another or if a listed species is subsequently included with other species in the listing of a taxon above the species level. Such species are shown separately in this publication of the appendices. The date of a subsequent listing is used only if a species is entirely deleted from the appendices and is subsequently reincluded after an intervening period of time.

(d) All living or dead animals and plants in Appendix I or II and all readily recognizable parts and derivatives thereof are subject to the regulations of this part, except for the following for plants in Appendix II:

(1) Seeds, spores, and pollen (including pollinia);

(2) Tissue cultures and flasked seedling cultures;

(3) Parts and derivatives, other than roots and readily recognizable parts thereof, of *Panax quinquefolius*;

(4) Fruits and parts and derivatives thereof of naturalized or artificially propagated Cactaceae spp., and separate stem joints (pads) and parts and derivatives thereof of naturalized or artificially propagated species of *Opuntia* subgenus *Opuntia*;

(5) Separate leaves and parts and derivatives thereof of naturalized or artificially propagated *Aloe vera*; and

(6) Cut flowers of artificially propagated Orchidaceae spp., and fruits and parts and derivatives thereof of artificially propagated *Vanilla* spp.

All living or dead animals and plants included in Appendix III, and readily recognizable parts or derivatives thereof (unless specified otherwise for particular species in the list) are subject to the regulations of this part.

(e) [Reserved]

(f) The list of species in the Appendices to the Convention on International Trade in Endangered Species of Wild Fauna and Flora is provided below:

| Species | Common name | Appendix | Date listed (month/day/year) |
|---|---|---|---|
| CLASS MAMMALIA: | MAMMALS: | | |
| Order Monotremata: | Monotremes: | | |
| *Zaglossus* spp. | Spiny anteaters | II | 2/4/77 |
| Order Marsupialia: | Marsupials: | | |
| *Bettongia* spp. (except species listed below) | Rat-kangaroo | I | 6/28/79 |
| *B. lesueuri* | Lesueur's rat-kangaroo, Boodie | I | 7/1/75 |
| *B. penicillata* | Brush-tailed rat-kangaroo, Woylie | I | 7/1/75 |
| *B. tropica* | Queensland rat-kangaroo, Northern rat-kangaroo | I | 7/1/75 |
| *Burramys parvus* | Mountain pigmy possum | II | 7/1/75 |
| *Caloprymnus campestris* | Desert rat-kangaroo | I pe | 7/1/75 |
| *Chaeropus ecaudatus* | Pig-footed bandicoot | I pe | 7/1/75 |
| *Dendrolagus bennettianus* | Bennett's tree kangaroo, Dusky tree kangaroo | II | 6/28/79 |
| *D. inustus* | Grizzled tree kangaroo | II | 7/1/75 |
| *D. lumholtzi* | Lumholtz's tree kangaroo | II | 6/28/79 |
| *D. ursinus* | Vogelkop tree kangaroo | II | 7/1/75 |
| *Lagorchestes hirsutus* | Western hare wallaby, Wurrup | I | 7/1/75 |
| *Lagostrophus fasciatus* | Banded hare wallaby, Munning | I | 7/1/75 |
| *Lasiorhinus krefftii* | Queensland hairy-nosed wombat | I | 7/1/75 |
| *Macrotis lagotis* | Rabbit bandicoot, Bilby | I | 7/1/75 |
| *M. leucura* | Lesser rabbit bandicoot, Yallara | I | 7/1/75 |
| *Onychogalea fraenata* | Bridled nail-tailed wallaby | I | 7/1/75 |
| *O. lunata* | Crescent nail-tailed wallaby | I | 7/1/75 |
| *Perameles bougainville* | Barred bandicoot, Long-nosed bandicoot, Mari | I | 7/1/75 |
| *Phalanger maculatus* | Spotted cuscus | II | 6/28/79 |
| *P. orientalis* | Gray cuscus | II | 6/28/79 |
| *Sminthopsis longicaudata* | Long-tailed marsupial-mouse, Long-tailed dunnart | I | 7/1/75 |
| *S. psammophila* | Large desert marsupial-mouse, Sandhill dunnart | I | 7/1/75 |
| *Thylacinus cynocephalus* | Tasmanian wolf, Thylacine | I pe | 7/1/75 |
| Order Chiroptera: | Bats: | | |
| *Acerodon* spp. | Flying foxes | II | 1/18/90 |
| *Pteropus* spp. (all species except those in App. I or with earlier date in App. II). | Flying foxes | II | 1/18/90 |

**2**

| Species | Common name | Appendix | Date listed (month/day/year) |
|---|---|---|---|
| *P. insularis* | Truk flying fox | I | 10/22/87 |
| *P. macrotis* | Big-eared flying fox | II | 10/22/87 |
| *P. mariannus* | Mariana flying fox, Mariana fruit bat | I | 10/22/87 |
| *P. molossinus* | Ponape flying fox | I | 10/22/87 |
| *P. phaeocephalus* | Mortlock flying fox | I | 10/22/87 |
| *P. pilosus* | Palau flying fox | I | 10/22/87 |
| *P. samoensis* | Samoa flying fox | I | 10/22/87 |
| *P. tokudae* | Little Mariana fruit bat, Tokuda's flying fox | II | 10/22/87 |
| *P. tonganus* | Insular flying fox, Tonga fruit bat | I | 10/22/87 |
| *Vampyrops lineatus* | White-lined bat | III (Uruguay) | 7/14/76 |
| Order Primates: | Primates: Monkeys, Apes, etc: | | |
| All species except those in App. I or with earlier date in App. II. | | II | 2/4/77 |
| *Allocebus* spp. | Hairy-eared dwarf lemur | I | 7/1/75 |
| *Alouatta palliata* (=*villosa*) | Mantled howler monkey | I | 7/1/75 |
| *Ateles geoffroyi frontatus* | Black-handed spider monkey | I | 7/1/75 |
| *A. geoffroyi panamensis* | Black-handed spider monkey | I | 7/1/75 |
| *Avahi* spp. | Avahis, Woolly lemurs | I | 7/1/75 |
| *Brachyteles arachnoides* | Woolly spider monkey | I | 7/1/75 |
| *Cacajao* spp. | Uakaris | I | 7/1/75 |
| *Callimico goeldii* | Goeldi's monkey, Callimico | I | 7/1/75 |
| *Callithrix jacchus aurita* (=*C. aurita*) | White-eared marmoset | I | 2/4/77 |
| *C. jacchus flaviceps* (=*C. flaviceps*) | Buff-headed marmoset | I | 2/4/77 |
| *Cebus capucinus* | White-throated capuchin | II | 7/1/75 |
| *Cercocebus galeritus galeritus* | Tana River mangabey, Agile mangabey | I | 7/1/75 |
| *Cercopithecus diana* | Diana monkey | I | 2/4/77 |
| *Cheirogaleus* spp. | Dwarf lemurs | I | 7/1/75 |
| *Chiropotes albinasus* | White-nosed saki | I | 7/1/75 |
| *Colobus badius gordonorum* | Uhehe red colobus | II | 7/1/75 |
| *C. pennantii kirki* (=*C. badius kirki*) | Zanzibar red colobus | I | 7/1/75 |
| *C. rufomitratus* (=*C. badius rufomitratus*) | Tana River red colobus | I | 7/1/75 |
| *C. verus* | Olive colobus | II | 7/1/75 |
| *Daubentonia madagascariensis* | Aye-aye | I | 7/1/75 |
| *Gorilla gorilla* | Gorilla | I | 7/1/75 |
| *Hapalemur* spp. | Gentle lemurs | I | 7/1/75 |
| *Hylobates* spp. | Gibbons | I | 7/1/75 |
| *H.* (=*Symphalangus*) *syndactylus* | Siamang | I | 7/1/75 |
| *Indri* spp. | Indri | I | 7/1/75 |
| *Lagothrix flavicauda* | Yellow-tailed woolly monkey | I | 2/4/77 |
| *Lemur* spp. | Lemurs | I | 7/1/75 |
| *Leontopithecus* (=*Leontideus*) spp. | Golden lion tamarin | I | 7/1/75 |
| *Lepilemur* spp. | Sportive lemur, Weasel lemur | I | 7/1/75 |
| *Loris tardigradus* | Slender loris | II | 7/1/75 |
| *Macaca silenus* | Lion-tailed macaque | I | 7/1/75 |
| *M. sylvanus* | Barbary ape | II | 7/1/75 |
| *Microcebus* spp. | Mouse lemurs | I | 7/1/75 |
| *Nasalis* (=*Simias*) *concolor* | Pagai Island langur | I | 7/1/75 |
| *N. larvatus* | Proboscis monkey | I | 7/1/75 |
| *Nycticebus coucang* | Slow loris | II | 7/1/75 |
| *Pan paniscus* | Pygmy chimpanzee, Bonobo | I | 7/1/75 |
| *P. troglodytes* | Chimpanzee | I | 7/1/75 |
| *Papio* (=*Mandrillus*) *leucophaeus* | Drill | I | 2/4/77 |
| *P.* (=*Mandrillus*) *sphinx* | Mandrill | I | 2/4/77 |
| *Phaner* sp. | Fork mouse lemur, Fork-marked mouse lemur | I | 7/1/75 |
| Pongidae spp. (all species in family except those with earlier date). | Chimpanzees, Gorillas, Orangutans | I | 2/4/77 |
| *Pongo pygmaeus abelli* | Orangutan | I | 7/1/75 |
| *P. pygmaeus pygmaeus* | Orangutan | I | 7/1/75 |
| *Presbytis entellus* | Gray langur, Common Indian langur | I | 7/1/75 |
| *P. geei* | Golden langur | I | 7/1/75 |
| *P. johnii* | Nilgiri langur | II | 7/1/75 |
| *P. pileata* | Capped langur | I | 7/1/75 |
| *P. potenziani* | Long-tailed langur, Mentawai leaf monkey | I | 2/4/77 |
| *Propithecus* spp. | Sifakas | I | 7/1/75 |
| *Pygathrix* (=*Rhinopithecus*) spp. (except those species with earlier date). | Snub-nosed langurs | I | 2/4/77 |
| *P. nemaeus* | Douc langur | I | 7/1/75 |
| *P.* (=*Rhinopithecus*) *roxellanae* | Sichuan snub-nosed langur | I | 7/1/75 |
| *Saguinus bicolor* | Pied tamarin | I | 2/4/77 |
| *S. leucopus* | White-footed tamarin, Silvery-brown bare-face tamarin. | I | 2/4/77 |
| *S. oedipus* (including *S.o. geoffroyi*) | Cotton-top tamarin | I | 2/4/77 |
| *Saimiri oerstedii* | Red-backed squirrel monkey | I | 7/1/75 |
| Order Edentata: | Anteaters, Sloths, Armadillos: | | |
| *Bradypus variegatus* (=*boliviensis* or *griseus*) | Three-toed sloth | II | 7/1/75 |
| *Cabassous centralis* | Five-toed armadillo | III (Costa Rica) | 10/28/76 |
| *C. tatouay* (=*gymnurus*) | Naked-tailed armadillo | III (Uruguay) | 7/14/76 |
| *Choloepus hoffmanni* | Two-toed sloth | III (Costa Rica) | 10/28/76 |
| *Myrmecophaga tridactyla* | Giant anteater | II | 7/1/75 |
| *Priodontes maximus* (=*giganteus*) | Giant armadillo | I | 7/1/75 |

| Species | Common name | Appendix | Date listed (month/day/year) |
|---|---|---|---|
| *Tamandua tetradactyla* | Tamandua, Collared anteater | III (Guatemala) | 4/23/81 |
| *T. tetradactyla chapadensis* | Tamandua, Collared anteater | II | 7/1/75 |
| Order Pholidota: | Pangolins, Scaly Anteaters: | | |
| *Manis crassicaudata* | Thick-tailed pangolin, Indian pangolin | II | 7/1/75 |
| *M. gigantea* | Giant pangolin | III (Ghana) | 2/26/76 |
| *M. javanica* | Malayan pangolin | II | 7/1/75 |
| *M. pentadactyla* | Chinese pangolin | II | 7/1/75 |
| *M. temminckii* | Common African ground pangolin | I | 7/1/75 |
| *M. tetradactyla* (=*longicaudata*) | Long-tailed pangolin | III (Ghana) | 2/26/76 |
| *M. tricuspis* | African tree pangolin | III (Ghana) | 2/26/76 |
| Order Lagomorpha: | Rabbits, Hares: | | |
| *Caprolagus hispidus* | Hispid hare, Assam rabbit | I | 7/1/75 |
| *Romerolagus diazi* | Mexican volcano rabbit | I | 7/1/75 |
| Order Rodentia: | Rodents: | | |
| *Agouti* (=*Cuniculus*) *paca* | Greater paca, Spotted cavy | III (Honduras) | 4/13/87 |
| *Anomalurus beecrofti* | Beecroft's scaly-tailed flying squirrel | III (Ghana) | 2/26/76 |
| *A. derbianus* | Lord Derby's scaly-tailed flying squirrel | III (Ghana) | 2/26/76 |
| *A. peli* | Pel's scaly-tailed flying squirrel | III (Ghana) | 2/26/76 |
| *Chinchilla* spp. (except those chinchillas bred in countries outside of South America). | Chinchilla | I | 2/4/77 |
| *C. brevicaudata boliviana* (except those chinchillas bred in countries outside of South America). | Chinchilla | I | 7/1/75 |
| *Cynomys mexicanus* | Mexican prairie dog | I | 7/1/75 |
| *Dasyprocta punctata* | Common agouti | III (Honduras) | 4/13/87 |
| *Epixerus ebii* | African palm squirrel | III (Ghana) | 2/26/76 |
| *Hystrix cristata* | Crested porcupine | III (Ghana) | 2/26/76 |
| *Idiurus macrotis* | Long-eared pygmy flying squirrel | III (Ghana) | 2/26/76 |
| *Leporillus conditor* | Australian stick-nest rat | I | 7/1/75 |
| *Marmota caudata* | Long-tailed marmot | III (India) | 3/16/89 |
| *M. himalayana* | Himalayan marmot | III (India) | 3/16/89 |
| *Pseudomys praeconis* | Shark Bay mouse | I | 7/1/75 |
| *Ratufa* spp. | Giant squirrels | II | 7/1/75 |
| *Sciurus deppei* | Deppe's squirrel | III (Costa Rica) | 10/28/76 |
| *Sphiggurus* (=*Coendou*) *mexicanus* | Middle American prehensile-tailed porcupine, Coendou. | III (Honduras) | 4/13/87 |
| *S.* (=*Coendou*) *spinosus* | Prehensile-tailed porcupine | III (Uruguay) | 7/14/76 |
| *Xeromys myoides* | False water rat | I | 7/1/75 |
| *Zyzomys pedunculatus* | Australian native mouse, McDonnell Range rock rat | I | 7/1/75 |
| Order Cetacea: | Whales, Porpoises, Dolphins: | | |
| All species except those in App. I or with earlier date in App. II. | | II | 6/28/79 |
| *Balaena* (=*Eubalaena*) spp. | Right whale | I | 7/1/75 |
| *B. mysticetus* | Bowhead whale | I | 7/1/75 |
| *Balaenoptera acutorostrata* (all populations except that of West Greenland: entry into force as App. I on 1/1/86). | Minke Whale | I | 6/28/79 |
| *B. borealis* | Sei whale | I | 2/4/77 |
| *B. edeni* | Bryde's whale | I | 6/28/79 |
| *B. musculus* | Blue whale | I | 7/1/75 |
| *B. physalus* | Fin whale | I | 2/4/77 |
| *Berardius* spp. | Beaked whales | I | 6/28/79 |
| *Caperea marginata* (entry into force as App. I on 1/1/86). | Pygmy right whale | I | 6/28/79 |
| *Eschrichtius robustus* (=*glaucus*) | Gray whale | I | 7/1/75 |
| *Hyperoodon* spp. | Bottle-nosed whales | I | 6/28/79 |
| *Lipotes vexillifer* | White flag dolphin, Chinese river dolphin | I | 6/28/79 |
| *Megaptera novaeangliae* | Humpback whale | I | 7/1/75 |
| *Monodon monoceros* | Narwhal | II | 11/16/75 |
| *Neophocaena phocaenoides* | Finless porpoise | I | 6/28/79 |
| *Phocoena sinus* | Gulf of California harbor porpoise, Cochita | I | 6/28/79 |
| *Physeter macrocephalus* (=*catodon*) | Sperm whale | I | 2/4/77 |
| *Platanista* spp. | Ganges and Indus River dolphins | I | 7/1/75 |
| *Pontoporia* (=*Stenodelphis*) *blainvillei* | La Plata River dolphin | II | 7/14/76 |
| *Sotalia* spp. | Humpbacked dolphins | I | 6/28/79 |
| *Sousa* spp. | Humpbacked dolphins | I | 6/28/79 |
| Order Carnivora: | Carnivores: Cats, Bears, etc.: | | |
| *Acinonyx jubatus* | Cheetah | I | 7/1/75 |
| *Ailuropoda melanoleuca* | Giant panda | I | 3/14/84 |
| *Ailurus fulgens* | Lesser panda | II | 7/1/75 |
| *Aonyx congica* (=*microdon*) | West African "clawless" otter | I | 7/1/75 |
| *Arctictis binturong* | Binturong | III (India) | 3/16/89 |
| *Bassaricyon gabbii* | Bushy-tailed olingo | III (Costa Rica) | 10/28/76 |
| *Bassariscus sumichrasti* | Cacomistle | III (Costa Rica) | 10/28/76 |
| *Canis aureus* | Golden jackal | III (India) | 3/16/89 |
| *C. lupus* (all subspecies and populations except those listed below). | Gray wolf | II | 2/4/77 |
| *C. lupus* (India, Pakistan, Bhutan and Nepal populations). | Gray wolf | I | 2/4/77 |
| *C. lupus crassodon* | Gray wolf, Vancouver Island gray wolf | II | 7/1/75 |
| *C. lupus irremotus* | Gray wolf, Rocky Mountain gray wolf | II | 7/1/75 |

**4**

| Species | Common name | Appendix | Date listed (month/ day/year) |
|---|---|---|---|
| *C. lupus monstrabilis* | Gray wolf | II | 7/1/75 |
| *C. lupus pallipes* | Gray wolf, Middle East gray wolf | II | 7/1/75 |
| *Chrysocyon brachyurus* | Maned wolf | II | 7/1/75 |
| *Civettictis* (=*Viverra*) *civetta* | African civet | III (Botswana) | 4/24/78 |
| *Conepatus humboldtii* | Humboldt's hognose skunk | II | 6/28/79 |
| *Cryptoprocta ferox* | Fossa | II | 2/4/77 |
| *Cuon alpinus* | Dhole | II | 7/1/75 |
| *Cynogale bennettii* | Otter civet | II | 7/1/75 |
| *Dusicyon culpaeus* | Culpeo fox | II | 6/28/79 |
| *D. griseus* (=*fulvipes*) | Argentine gray fox | II | 6/28/79 |
| *D. gymnocercus* | Pampas fox | II | 10/22/87 |
| *Eira barbara* | Tayra | III (Honduras) | 4/13/87 |
| *Enhydra lutris nereis* | Southern sea otter | I | 7/1/75 |
| *Eupleres goudotii* (=*major*) | Malagasy mongoose | II | 2/4/77 |
| Felidae spp. (all species in family except those in App. I or *Felis catus*). | Cats (not including house cats) | II | 2/4/77 |
| *Felis bengalensis bengalensis* (execpt for Chinese population). | Leopard cat | I | 7/1/75 |
| *F. bengalensis bengalensis* (Chinese population) | Leopard cat | II | 7/1/75 |
| *F. caracal* (Asian population) | Caracal | I | 7/1/75 |
| *F. concolor coryi* | Florida panther, Florida puma | I | 7/1/75 |
| *F. concolor costaricensis* | Costa Rican puma | I | 7/1/75 |
| *F. concolor couguar* | Eastern puma, Adirondack cougar | I | 7/1/75 |
| *F. jacobita* | Andean cat | I | 7/1/75 |
| *F. marmorata* | Marbled cat | I | 7/1/75 |
| *F. nigripes* | Black-footed cat | I | 7/1/75 |
| *F. pardalis* (except subspecies with earlier date) | Ocelot | I | 2/4/77 |
| *F. pardalis mearnsi* | Ocelot | I | 7/1/75 |
| *F. pardalis mitis* | Brazilian ocelot | I | 7/1/75 |
| *F.* (=*Lynx*) *pardina* | Spanish lynx, Iberian lynx | I | 2/4/77 |
| *F. planiceps* | Flat-headed cat | I | 7/1/75 |
| *F. rubiginosa* (Indian population) | Rusty-spotted cat | I | 2/4/77 |
| *F.* (=*Lynx*) *rufa escuinapae* | Mexican bobcat | I | 7/1/75 |
| *F. temmincki* | Asian golden cat | I | 7/1/75 |
| *F. tigrina* (except subspecies with earlier date) | Tiger cat, Little spotted cat | I | 2/4/77 |
| *F. tigrina oncilla* | Tiger cat | I | 7/1/75 |
| *F. wiedii* (except subspecies with earlier date) | Margay | I | 2/4/77 |
| *F. wiedii nicaraguae* | Central American margay | I | 7/1/75 |
| *F. wiedii salvinia* | Guatemalan margay | I | 7/1/75 |
| *F. yagouaroundi* (North and Central American populations). | Jaguarundi | I | 7/1/75 |
| *F. yagouaroundi* (South American populations) | Jaguarundi | II | 7/1/75 |
| *Fossa fossa* | Fanaloka | II | 2/4/77 |
| *Galictis vittata* (=*allamandi*) | Grison | III (Costa Rica) | 10/28/76 |
| *Helarctos malayanus* | Sun bear | I | 7/1/75 |
| *Hemigalus derbyanus* | Banded palm civet | II | 2/4/77 |
| *Herpestes auropunctatus* | Small Indian mongoose | III (India) | 3/16/89 |
| *H. edwardsi* | Indian gray mongoose | III (India) | 3/16/89 |
| *H. fuscus* | Indian brown mongoose | III (India) | 3/16/89 |
| *H. smithii* | Ruddy mongoose | III (India) | 3/16/89 |
| *H. urva* | Crab-eating mongoose | III (India) | 3/16/89 |
| *H. vitticollis* | Stripe-necked mongoose | III (India) | 3/16/89 |
| *Hyaena brunnea* | Brown hyaena | I | 7/1/75 |
| Lutrinae spp. (all species in subfamily except those in App. I). | Otters | II | 2/4/77 |
| *Lutra felina* | Marine otter | I | 7/1/75 |
| *L. longicaudis* | Long-tailed otter, Neotropical otter | I | 7/1/75 |
| *L. lutra* | European otter | I | 2/4/77 |
| *L. provocax* | Southern river otter, South American river otter | I | 7/1/75 |
| *Martes flavigula* (including *M. gwatkinsi*) | Yellow-throated marten | III (India) | 3/16/89 |
| *M. foina intermedia* | Beech marten | III (India) | 3/16/89 |
| *Mellivora capensis* | Honey badger, Ratel | III (Ghana and Botswana) | 2/26/76 |
| *Melursus* (=*Ursus*) *ursinus* | Sloth bear | I | 9/21/88 |
| *Mustela altaica* | Mountain weasel | III (India) | 3/16/89 |
| *M. erminea* | Ermine | III (India) | 3/16/89 |
| *M. kathiah* | Yellow-bellied weasel | III (India) | 3/16/89 |
| *M. nigripes* | Black-footed ferret | I | 7/1/75 |
| *M. sibirica* | Siberian weasel | III (India) | 3/16/89 |
| *Nasua nasua* (=*narica*) | Common coati, Coatimundi | III (Honduras) | 4/13/87 |
| *N. nasua solitaria* | Coatimundi | III (Uruguay) | 7/14/76 |
| *Neofelis nebulosa* | Clouded leopard | I | 7/1/75 |
| *Paguma larvata* | Masked palm civet | III (India) | 3/16/89 |
| *Panthera leo persica* | Asiatic lion, Indian lion | I | 7/1/75 |
| *P. onca* | Jaguar | I | 7/1/75 |
| *P. pardus* | Leopard | I | 7/1/75 |
| *P. tigris* | Tiger | I | 7/1/75 |
| *P. uncia* | Snow leopard | I | 7/1/75 |
| *Paradoxurus hermaphroditus* | Common palm civet | III (India) | 3/16/89 |
| *P. jerdoni* | Jerdon's palm civet | III (India) | 3/16/89 |
| *Potos flavus* | Kinkajou | III (Honduras) | 4/13/87 |

| Species | Common name | Appendix | Date listed (month/day/year) |
|---|---|---|---|
| *Prionodon linsang* | Banded linsang | II | 7/1/75 |
| *P. pardicolor* | Spotted linsang | I | 7/1/75 |
| *Proteles cristatus* | Aardwolf | III (Botswana) | 4/24/78 |
| *Pteronura brasiliensis* | Giant otter | I | 7/1/75 |
| *Selenarctos* (=*Ursus*) *thibetanus* (except subspecies listed below). | Asiatic black bear | I | 6/28/79 |
| *S.* (=*Ursus*) *thibetanus gedrosianus* | Baluchistan black bear | I | 2/4/77 |
| *Speothos venaticus* | Bush dog | I | 2/4/77 |
| *Tremarctos ornatus* | Spectacled bear | I | 2/4/77 |
| *Ursus americanus* (except skull and/or skin with claws attached). | American black bear | III (Canada) | 9/18/91 |
| *U. arctos* (all North American populations except that listed below). | Brown bear, Grizzly | II | 7/1/75 |
| *U. arctos* (Asian populations, including populations in Iran, Iraq, Syria, and Turkey, but not populations in USSR except for subspecies listed in App. I). | Brown bear | II | 1/18/90 |
| *U. arctos* (European population, except USSR population). | Brown Bear | II | 7/29/83 |
| *U. arctos* (Italian population) (=*U.a. nelsoni*) | European brown bear | II | 7/1/75 |
| *U. arctos* (Mexican population) | Mexican grizzly bear | I | 7/1/75 |
| *U. arctos isabellinus* | Red bear | I | 6/28/79 |
| *U. arctos pruinosus* | Tibetan blue bear | I | 7/1/75 |
| *U.* (=*Thalarctos*) *maritimus* | Polar bear | II | 7/1/75 |
| *Viverra megaspila* | Large-spotted civet | III (India) | 3/16/89 |
| *V. zibetha* | Large Indian civet | III (India) | 3/16/89 |
| *Viverricula indica* | Lesser oriental civet, Small Indian civet | III (India) | 3/16/89 |
| *Vulpes bengalensis* | Bengal fox | III (India) | 3/16/89 |
| *V. cana* | Blanford's fox | II | 2/4/77 |
| *V. vulpes griffithi* | Griffith's red fox | III (India) | 3/16/89 |
| *V. vulpes montana* | Montane red fox | III (India) | 3/16/89 |
| *V. vulpes pusilla* (= *leucopus*) | Little red fox | III (India) | 3/16/89 |
| *V.* (=*Fennecus*) *zerda* | Fennec fox | II | 4/22/76 |
| Order Pinnipedia: | Seals, Sea lions: | | |
| *Arctocephalus* spp. (except species listed below) | Southern fur seals | II | 2/4/77 |
| *A. australis* | Southern fur seal | II | 7/1/75 |
| *A. galapagoensis* | Galapagos fur seal | II | 7/1/75 |
| *A. philippii* | Juan Fernandez fur seal | II | 7/1/75 |
| *A. townsendi* | Guadalupe fur seal | I | 7/1/75 |
| *Mirounga angustirostris* | Northern elephant seal | II | 7/1/75 |
| *M. leonina* | Southern elephant seal | II | 7/1/75 |
| *Monachus* spp. | Monk seals | I | 7/1/75 |
| *Odobenus rosmarus* | Walrus | III (Canada) | 11/16/75 |
| Order Tubulidentata: | Aardvarks: | | |
| *Orycteropus afer* | Aardvark | II | 7/1/75 |
| Order Proboscidea: | Elephants: | | |
| *Elephas maximus* | Asian elephant | I | 7/1/75 |
| *Loxodonta africana* | African elephant | I | 2/4/77 |
| Order Sirenia: | Dugongs, Manatees: | | |
| *Dugong dugon* (except for Australian population) | Dugong | I | 7/1/75 |
| *D. dugon* (Australian population) | Dugong | II | 7/1/75 |
| *Trichechus inunguis* | South American manatee, Amazonian manatee | I | 7/1/75 |
| *T. manatus* | West Indian manatee | I | 7/1/75 |
| *T. senegalensis* | West African manatee | II | 7/1/75 |
| Order Perissodactyla: | Odd-toed ungulates: | | |
| *Equus africanus* | African wild ass | I | 7/29/83 |
| *E. grevyi* | Grevy's zebra | I | 6/28/79 |
| *E. hemionus* (except subspecies listed below) | Asian wild ass | II | 7/1/75 |
| *E. hemionus hemionus* | Asian wild ass | I | 7/1/75 |
| *E. hemionus* (=*kiang* or *onager*) *khur* | Asian wild ass | I | 7/1/75 |
| *E. przewalskii* | Przewalski's horse | I | 7/1/75 |
| *E. zebra hartmannae* | Hartmann's mountain zebra | II | 6/28/79 |
| *E. zebra zebra* | Cape mountain zebra | I | 7/1/75 |
| *Tapirus bairdii* | Central American tapir | I | 7/1/75 |
| *T. indicus* | Asian tapir | I | 7/1/75 |
| *T. pinchaque* | Mountain tapir | I | 7/1/75 |
| *T. terrestris* | South American tapir | II | 7/1/75 |
| Rhinocerotidae spp. (all species in the family except those with earlier date in App. I). | Rhinoceroses | I | 2/4/77 |
| *Ceratotherium simum cottoni* | Northern white rhinoceros | I | 7/1/75 |
| *Dicerorhinus* (=*Didermocerus*) *sumatrensis* | Sumatran rhinoceros | I | 7/1/75 |
| *Diceros bicornis* | Black rhinoceros | I | 7/1/75 |
| *Rhinoceros sondaicus* | Javan rhinoceros | I | 7/1/75 |
| *R. unicornis* | Great Indian one-horned rhinoceros | I | 7/1/75 |
| Order Artiodactyla: | Even-toed ungulates: | | |
| *Addax nasomaculatus* | Addax | I | 7/1/75 |
| *Ammotragus lervia* | Barbary sheep, Aoudad | II | 4/22/76 |
| *Antilocapra americana mexicana* | Mexican pronghorn | II | 7/1/75 |
| *A. americana peninsularis* | Baja pronghorn | I | 7/1/75 |
| *A. americana sonoriensis* | Sonoran pronghorn | I | 7/1/75 |
| *Antilope cervicapra* | Blackbuck antelope | III (Nepal) | 11/16/75 |

6

| Species | Common name | Appendix | Date listed (month/day/year) |
|---|---|---|---|
| *Babyrousa babyrussa* | Babirusa | I | 7/1/75 |
| *Blastocerus dichotomus* | Marsh deer | I | 7/1/75 |
| *Bison bison athabascae* | Woods bison | I | 7/1/75 |
| *Boocercus* (=*Taurotragus*) *eurycerus* | Bongo antelope | III (Ghana) | 2/26/76 |
| *Bos gaurus* | Seladang, Gaur | I | 7/1/75 |
| *B.* (=*grunniens*) *mutus* | Wild yak | I | 7/1/75 |
| *B.* (=*Novibos*) *sauveli* | Kouprey | I | 7/1/75 |
| *Bubalus arnee* (formerly listed as *B. bubalis*, a non-protected, domesticated form). | Water buffalo | III (Nepal) | 11/16/75 |
| *B.* (=*Anoa*) *depressicornis* | Lowland anoa | I | 7/1/75 |
| *B.* (=*Anoa*) *mindorensis* | Tamaraw | I | 7/1/75 |
| *B.* (=*Anoa*) *quarlesi* | Mountain anoa | I | 7/1/75 |
| *Budorcas taxicolor* | Takin | II | 8/1/85 |
| *Capra falconeri* (except subspecies listed below) | Markhor | II | 7/1/75 |
| *C. falconeri chialtanensis* | Chialtan markhor | I | 7/1/75 |
| *C. falconeri jerdoni* | Straight-horned markhor | I | 7/1/75 |
| *C. falconeri megaceros* | Kabul markhor, Straight-horned markhor | I | 7/1/75 |
| *Capricornis sumatraensis* | Serow | I | 7/1/75 |
| *Catagonus wagneri* | Chacoan peccary, Giant peccary | I | 10/22/87 |
| *Cephalophus dorsalis* | Bay duiker | II | 7/29/83 |
| *C. jentinki* | Jentink's duiker | I | 7/29/83 |
| *C. monticola* | Blue duiker | II | 7/1/75 |
| *C. ogilbyi* | Ogilby's duiker | II | 7/29/83 |
| *C. sylvicultor* | Yellow-backed duiker | II | 7/29/83 |
| *C. zebra* | Zebra-banded duiker | II | 7/29/83 |
| *Cervus duvauceli* | Swamp deer | I | 7/1/75 |
| *C. elaphus bactrianus* | Bactrian deer | II | 7/1/75 |
| *C. elaphus barbarus* | Barbary deer | III (Tunisia) | 4/22/76 |
| *C. elaphus hanglu* | Kashmir stag | I | 7/1/75 |
| *C. eldi* | Eld's brow-antlered deer | I | 7/1/75 |
| *C. dama mesopotamicus* (=*Dama mesopotamica*) | Persian fallow deer | I | 2/4/77 |
| *C.* (=*Axis*) *porcinus annamiticus* | Indochina hog deer | I | 7/1/75 |
| *C.* (=*Axis*) *porcinus calamianensis* | Calamianes deer | I | 7/1/75 |
| *C.* (=*Axis*) *porcinus kuhli* | Kuhl's deer, Bawean hog deer | I | 7/1/75 |
| *Choeropsis liberiensis* | Pygmy hippopotamus | II | 7/1/75 |
| *Damaliscus dorcas dorcas* | Bontebok | II | 7/1/75 |
| *D. lunatus* | Sassaby antelope, Korrigum | III (Ghana) | 2/26/76 |
| *Gazella cuvieri* (=*G. gazella cuvieri*) | Mountain gazelle | III (Tunisia) | 4/22/76 |
| *G. dama* | Dama gazelle | I | 7/29/83 |
| *G. dorcas* | Dorcas gazelle | III (Tunisia) | 4/22/76 |
| *G. leptoceros* | Slender-horned gazelle | III (Tunisia) | 4/22/76 |
| *Hippocamelus antisensis* | North Andean huemal | I | 7/1/75 |
| *H. bisulcus* | South Andean huemal | I | 7/1/75 |
| *Hippopotamus amphibius* | Hippopotamus | III (Ghana) | 2/26/76 |
| *Hippotragus equinus* | Roan antelope | II | 2/26/76 |
| *H. niger variani* | Giant sable antelope | I | 7/1/75 |
| *Hyemoschus aquaticus* | Water chevrotain | III (Ghana) | 2/26/76 |
| *Kobus leche* | Lechwe | II | 7/1/75 |
| *Lama guanicoe* | Guanaco | II | 8/12/78 |
| *Mazama americana cerasina* | Red brocket deer | III (Guatemala) | 4/23/81 |
| *Moschus* spp. (all except populations in App. I) | Musk deer | II | 2/16/79 |
| *Moschus* spp. (populations of Afghanistan, Bhutan, Burma, India, Nepal and Pakistan). | Musk deer | I | 7/1/75 |
| *Muntiacus crinifrons* | Black muntjac | I | 8/1/85 |
| *Nemorhaedus goral* | Goral | I | 7/1/75 |
| *Odocoileus virginianus mayensis* | Whitetail deer | III (Guatemala) | 4/23/81 |
| *Oryx dammah* | Scimitar-horned oryx | I | 7/1/75 |
| *O. leucoryx* | Arabian oryx | I | 7/1/75 |
| *Ovis ammon* (except subspecies listed below) | Argali | II | 7/1/75 |
| *O. ammon hodgsoni* | Tibetan argali | I | 7/1/75 |
| *O. canadensis* (Mexican population) | Mexican bighorn sheep | II | 7/1/75 |
| *O. orientalis ophion* (=*O. musimon ophion*) | Urial, Cyprian red sheep | I | 7/1/75 |
| *O. vignei* | Shapo | I | 7/1/75 |
| *Ozotoceros bezoarticus* | Pampas deer | I | 7/1/75 |
| *Pantholops hodgsoni* | Tibetan antelope | I | 7/1/75 |
| *Pudu mephistophiles* | Northern pudu | II | 7/1/75 |
| *P. pudu* | Pudu | I | 7/1/75 |
| *Rupicapra rupicapra ornata* | Apennian chamois | I | 7/1/75 |
| *Sus salvanius* | Pygmy hog | I | 7/1/75 |
| *Tayassu* spp. (except populations in the United States) | Collared peccaries, White-lipped peccaries | II | 10/22/87 |
| *Tetracerus quadricornis* | Four-horned antelope | III (Nepal) | 11/16/75 |
| *Tragelaphus spekei* | Sitatunga antelope | III (Ghana) | 2/26/76 |
| *Vicugna vicugna* (except populations listed below) | Vicuna | I | 7/1/75 |

| Species | Common name | Appendix | Date listed (month/ day/year) |
|---|---|---|---|
| *V. vicugna* (populations in Paranicota Province, Ia. Region of Tarapaca in Chile, and populations of Pampa Galeras Natl. Reserve and Nuclear Zone, Pedregal, Oscconta and Sawacocha (Province of Lucanas), Sais Pictoani (Province of Azangaro), Sais Tupac Amaru (Province of Junin), and of Salinas Aguada Blance Natl. Reserve (Provinces of Arequipa and Cailloma) in Peru (under specific conditions including export of cloth only). | Vicuna | II | 10/22/87 |
| CLASS AVES: | BIRDS: | | |
| Order Struthioniformes: | Ostriches: | | |
| *Struthio camelus* (populations of Algeria, Central African Republic, Chad, Mali, Mauritania, Morocco, Niger, Nigeria, Senegal, Sudan, Cameroon and Upper Volta). | Ostrich | I | 7/29/83 |
| Order Rheiformes | Rheas: | | |
| *Pterocnemia pennata* (except subspecies listed below) | Lesser rhea | I | 6/28/79 |
| *P. pennata garleppi* | Lesser rhea | I | 7/1/75 |
| *P. pennata pennata* | Darwin's rhea | I | 7/1/75 |
| *Rhea americana* (except subspecies listed below) | Greater rhea, Common rhea | III (Uruguay) | 7/14/76 |
| *R. americana albescens* | Greater rhea | II | 7/1/75 |
| Order Sphenisciformes: | Penguins: | | |
| *Spheniscus demersus* | Jackass penguin, Blackfooted Cape penguin | II | 7/1/75 |
| *S. humboldti* | Humboldt penguin | I | 6/6/81 |
| Order Tinaminiformes: | Tinamous: | | |
| *Rhynchotus rufescens maculicollis* | Red-winged tinamou | II | 7/1/75 |
| *R. rufescens pallescens* | Southern red-winged tinamou | II | 7/1/75 |
| *R. rufescens rufescens* | Western red-winged tinamou | II | 7/1/75 |
| *Tinamus solitarius* | Solitary tinamou | I | 7/1/75 |
| Order Podicipediformes: | Grebes: | | |
| *Podilymbus gigas* | Atitlan grebe | I | 7/1/75 |
| Order Procellariformes: | Albatrosses, Shearwaters, Petrels: | | |
| *Diomedea albatrus* | Short-tailed albatross | I | 7/1/75 |
| Order Pelecaniformes: | Tropicbirds, Pelicans, Frigatebirds: | | |
| *Fregata andrewsi* | Andrew's frigatebird | I | 7/1/75 |
| *Pelecanus crispus* | Dalmatian pelican | I | 7/1/75 |
| *Sula abbotti* | Abbott's booby | I | 7/1/75 |
| Order Ciconiiformes: | Herons, Storks, Ibises, Flamingos: | | |
| *Ardea goliath* | Goliath heron | III (Ghana) | 2/26/76 |
| *Balaeniceps rex* | Whale-headed stork | II | 10/22/87 |
| *Bubulcus (=Ardeola) ibis* | Cattle egret | III (Ghana) | 2/26/76 |
| *Casmerodius (=Egretta) albus* | Great white egret | III (Ghana) | 2/26/76 |
| *Ciconia ciconia boyciana* | Oriental white stork | I | 7/1/75 |
| *C. nigra* | Black stork | II | 7/1/75 |
| *Egretta garzetta* | Little egret | III (Ghana) | 2/26/76 |
| *Ephippiorhynchus senegalensis* | Saddlebill stork | III (Ghana) | 2/26/76 |
| *Eudocimus ruber* | Scarlet ibis | II | 10/22/87 |
| *Geronticus calvus* | Southern bald ibis | II | 7/1/75 |
| *G. eremita* | Northern bald ibis, Hermit ibis | I | 6/28/79 |
| *Hagedashia hagedash* | Hadada ibis | III (Ghana) | 2/26/76 |
| *Jabiru mycteria* | Jabiru | I | 8/1/85 |
| *Lampribis rara* | Spotted-breasted ibis | III (Ghana) | 2/26/76 |
| *Leptoptilos crumeniferus* | Marabou stork | III (Ghana) | 2/26/76 |
| *Mycteria cinerea* | Milky wood stork | I | 10/22/87 |
| *Nipponia nippon* | Japanese crested ibis | I | 7/1/75 |
| *Phoenicoparrus andinus* | Andean flamingo | II | 7/1/75 |
| *P. jamesi* | James flamingo | II | 7/1/75 |
| Phoenicopteridae spp. (all species except those with earlier date in App. II). | Flamingos | II | 7/29/83 |
| *Phoenicopterus chilensis* | Chilean flamingo | II | 7/1/75 |
| *P. ruber ruber* | American flamingo | II | 6/28/79 |
| *Platalea leucorodia* | White spoonbill | II | 7/1/75 |
| *Threskiornis aethiopicus* | Sacred ibis | III (Ghana) | 2/26/76 |
| Order Anseriformes: | Ducks, Geese, Swans, Screamers: | | |
| *Alopochen aegyptiacus* | Egyptian goose | III (Ghana) | 2/26/76 |
| *Anas acuta* | Northern pintail | III (Ghana) | 2/26/76 |
| *A. aucklandica aucklandica* | Auckland Island flightless teal | II | 7/1/75 |
| *A. aucklandica chlorotis* | New Zealand brown teal | II | 7/1/75 |
| *A. aucklandica nesiotis* | Campbell Island flightless teal | I | 7/1/75 |
| *A. bernieri* | Madagascar teal | II | 7/1/75 |
| *A. capensis* | Cape wigeon | III (Ghana) | 2/26/76 |
| *A. clypeata* | Northern shoveler | III (Ghana) | 2/26/76 |
| *A. crecca* | Green-winged teal | III (Ghana) | 2/26/76 |
| *A. (=Platyrhynchos) laysanensis* | Laysan duck | I | 7/1/75 |
| *A. (=Platyrhynchos) oustaleti* | Marianas mallard | I | 7/1/75 |
| *A. penelope* | Europeon wigeon | III (Ghana) | 2/26/76 |
| *A. querquedula* | Garganey | III (Ghana) | 2/26/76 |
| *Aythya nyroca* | White-eyed pochard | III (Ghana) | 2/26/76 |
| *Branta canadensis leucopareia* | Aleutian goose | I | 7/1/75 |
| *B. ruficollis* | Red-breasted goose | II | 7/1/75 |
| *B. (=Nesochen) sandvicensis* | Hawaiian goose, Nene | I | 7/1/75 |

| Species | Common name | Appendix | Date listed (month/day/year) |
|---|---|---|---|
| Cairina moschata | Muscovy duck | III (Honduras) | 4/13/87 |
| C. scutulata | White-winged duck | I | 7/1/75 |
| Coscoroba coscoroba | Coscoroba | II | 7/1/75 |
| Cygnus columbianus (=bewickii) jankowskii | Jankowski's swan | II | 7/1/75 |
| C. melanocoryphus | Black-necked swan | II | 7/1/75 |
| Dendrocygna arborea | Cuban tree duck, West Indian whistling duck | II | 7/1/75 |
| D. autumnalis | Black-bellied whistling duck | III (Honduras) | 4/13/87 |
| D. bicolor (=fulva) | Fulvous whistling duck | III (Ghana and Honduras) | 2/26/76 |
| D. viduata | White-faced whistling duck | III (Ghana) | 2/26/76 |
| Nettapus auritus | African pygmy goose | III (Ghana) | 2/26/76 |
| Oxyura leucocephala | White-headed duck | II | 7/29/83 |
| Plectropterus gambensis | Spur-winged goose | III (Ghana) | 2/26/76 |
| Pteronetta hartlaubii | Hartlaub's duck | III (Ghana) | 2/26/76 |
| Rhodonessa caryophyllacea | Pink-headed duck | I pe | 7/1/75 |
| Sarkidiornis melanotos | Comb duck | II | 7/1/75 |
| Order Falconiformes: | Hawks, Falcons, Vultures, Eagles: | | |
| All species except Cathartidae and those species in App. I or with earlier date in App. II. | All species except New World vultures | II | 6/28/79 |
| Accipitridae spp. (all South American populations) | Hawks, Harriers | II | 10/28/76 |
| Accipiter gentilis | Northern goshawk | II | 2/4/77 |
| A. gundlachii | Gundlach's hawk | II | 2/4/77 |
| A. nisus | European sparrow hawk | II | 2/4/77 |
| Aegypius monachus | European black vulture, Cinerous vulture | II | 2/4/77 |
| Aquila spp. (all species except those in App. I or with earlier date in App. II). | Eagles | II | 2/4/77 |
| A. chrysaetos | Golden eagle | II | 7/1/75 |
| A. heliaca | Imperial eagle | I | 2/4/77 |
| Chondrohierax uncinatus wilsonii | Cuban hook-billed kite | I | 2/4/77 |
| Circaetus spp. | Snake eagles | II | 2/4/77 |
| Circus spp. | Harriers | II | 2/4/77 |
| Falconidae spp. (all species in family except those in App. I). | Falcons, Caracaras | II | 7/1/75 |
| Falco araea | Seychelles kestrel | I | 7/1/75 |
| F. jugger | Lagger falcon | I | 7/1/75 |
| F. newtoni aldabranus | Aldabra kestrel | I | 7/1/75 |
| F. peregrinus | Peregrine falcon | I | 7/1/75 |
| F. punctatus | Mauritius kestrel | I | 7/1/75 |
| F. rusticolus | Gyrfalcon | I | 7/1/75 |
| Gymnogyps californianus | California condor | I | 7/1/75 |
| Gypaetus barbatus | Lammergeier | II | 2/4/77 |
| Gyps fulvus | Griffon vulture | II | 2/4/77 |
| Haliaeetus spp. (except species in App.I) | Sea eagles, Fish eagles | II | 2/4/77 |
| H. albicilla (except subspecies listed below) | White-tailed eagle | I | 2/4/77 |
| H. albicilla greenlandicus | Greenland white-tailed sea eagle | I | 7/1/75 |
| H. leucocephalus (except subspecies listed below) | Bald eagle | I | 2/4/77 |
| H. leucocephalus leucocephalus | Southern bald eagle | I | 7/1/75 |
| Harpia harpyja | Harpy eagle | I | 7/1/75 |
| Harpyopsis novaeguineae | New Guinea harpy eagle | II | 2/4/77 |
| Milvus milvus | Red kite | II | 2/4/77 |
| Pandion haliaetus | Osprey | II | 2/4/77 |
| Pithecophaga jefferyi | Monkey-eating eagle | I | 7/1/75 |
| Sagittarius serpentarius | Secretary bird | II | 2/26/76 |
| Sarcoramphus papa | King vulture | III (Honduras) | 4/13/87 |
| Vultur gryphus | Andean condor | I | 7/1/75 |
| Order Galliformes: | Pheasants, Curassows, Megapodes, Hoatzins: | | |
| Aburria (=Pipile) jacutinga | Black-fronted piping-guan | I | 7/1/75 |
| A. (=Pipile) pipile pipile | Trinidad white-headed curassow | I | 7/1/75 |
| Agelastes meleagrides | White-breasted guineafowl | III (Ghana) | 2/26/76 |
| Agriocharis ocellata | Ocellated turkey | III (Guatemala | 4/23/81 |
| Arborophila brunneopectus | Bar-backed partridge, Bare-throated tree partridge | III (Malaysia) | 11/13/86 |
| A. (=Tropicoperdix) charltonii | Scaly-breasted partridge, Chestnut-breasted tree partridge. | III (Malaysia) | 11/13/86 |
| Argusianus argus | Great argus pheasant | II | 7/1/75 |
| Caloperdix oculea | Ferruginous wood partridge | III (Malaysia) | 11/13/86 |
| Catreus wallichii | Cheer pheasant | I | 7/1/75 |
| Colinus virginianus ridgwayi | Masked bobwhite | I | 7/1/75 |
| Crax alberti | Blue-bellied curassow | III (Colombia) | 9/21/88 |
| C. blumenbachi | Red-billed curassow | I | 7/1/75 |
| C. daubentoni | Yellow-knobbed curassow | III (Colombia) | 9/21/88 |
| C. globulosa | Wattled curassow | III (Colombia) | 9/21/88 |
| C. (=Mitu) mitu mitu | Mitu, Razor-billed curassow | I | 7/1/75 |
| C. pauxi (=Pauxi pauxi) | Northern helmeted curassow | III (Colombia) | 9/21/88 |
| C. rubra | Great curassow | III (Colombia, Costa Rica, Guatemala, and Honduras). | 10/28/76 |
| Crossoptilon crossoptilon | White-eared pheasant | I | 7/1/75 |
| C. mantchuricum | Brown-eared pheasant | I | 7/1/75 |
| Cyrtonyx montezumae mearnsi (Mexican population) | Mearn's harlequin quail | II | 7/1/75 |
| C. montezumae montezumae | Harlequin quail | II | 7/1/75 |
| Gallus sonneratii | Gray jungle fowl | II | 7/1/75 |
| Ithaginis cruentus | Blood pheasant | II | 7/1/75 |

| Species | Common name | Appendix | Date listed (month/day/year) |
|---|---|---|---|
| *Lophophorus impeyanus* | Himalayan monal | I | 7/1/75 |
| *L. lhuysii* | Chinese monal | I | 7/1/75 |
| *L. sclateri* | Sclater's monal | I | 7/1/75 |
| *Lophura edwardsi* | Edward's pheasant | I | 7/1/75 |
| *L. erythrophthalma* | Crestless fireback | III (Malaysia) | 11/13/86 |
| *L. ignita* | Crested fireback | III (Malaysia) | 11/13/86 |
| *L. imperialis* | Imperial pheasant | I | 7/1/75 |
| *L. swinhoii* | Swinhoe's pheasant | I | 7/1/75 |
| *Macrocephalon maleo* | Maleo | I | 7/1/75 |
| *Melanoperdix nigra* | Black wood partridge | III (Malaysia) | 11/13/86 |
| *Oreophasis derbianus* | Horned guan | I | 7/1/75 |
| *Ortalis vetula* | Plain chachalaca | III (Guatemala and Honduras) | 4/23/81 |
| *Pavo muticus* | Green peafowl | II | 2/4/77 |
| *Penelope albipennis* | White-winged guan | I | 6/6/81 |
| *P. purpurascens* | Northern crested guan | III (Honduras) | 4/13/87 |
| *Penelopina nigra* | Black chachalaca | III (Guatemala) | 4/23/81 |
| *Polyplectron bicalcaratum* | Gray peacock pheasant | II | 7/1/75 |
| *P. emphanum* | Palawan peacock pheasant | I | 7/1/75 |
| *P. germaini* | Germain's peacock pheasant | II | 7/1/75 |
| *P. inopinatum* | Rothschild's peacock pheasant, Mountain peacock pheasant. | III (Malaysia) | 11/13/86 |
| *P. malacense* | Malaysian peacock pheasant | II | 7/1/75 |
| *Rheinartia ocellata* | Rheinard's crested argus, Crested argus pheasant | I | 11/13/86 |
| *Rhizothera longirostris* | Long-billed wood partridge | III (Malaysia) | 11/13/86 |
| *Rollulus rouloul* | Crested wood partridge, Rouloul, Green-winged wood partridge. | III (Malaysia) | 11/13/86 |
| *Syrmaticus ellioti* | Elliot's pheasant | I | 7/1/75 |
| *S. humiae* | Bar-tailed pheasant | I | 7/1/75 |
| *S. mikado* | Mikado pheasant | I | 7/1/75 |
| *Tetraogallus caspius* | Caspian snowcock | I | 7/1/75 |
| *T. tibetanus* | Tibetan snowcock | I | 7/1/75 |
| *Tragopan blythii* | Blyth's tragopan | I | 7/1/75 |
| *T. caboti* | Cabot's tragopan | I | 7/1/75 |
| *T. melanocephalus* | Western tragopan | I | 7/1/75 |
| *T. satyra* | Satyr tragopan | III (Nepal) | 11/16/75 |
| *Tympanuchus cupido attwateri* | Attwater's greater prairie chicken | I | 7/1/75 |
| Order Gruiformes: | Cranes, Rails, Bustards: | | |
| *Anthropoides virgo* | Demoiselle crane | II | 7/29/83 |
| *Balearica rugulorum* | Crowned crane | II | 7/1/75 |
| *Chlamydotis undulata* | Houbara bustard | I | 7/1/75 |
| *Choriotis nigriceps* | Great Indian bustard | I | 7/1/75 |
| *Gallirallus australis hectori* | Eastern weka rail | II | 7/1/75 |
| Gruidae spp. (all species and subspecies except those in App. I and those with earlier date in App. II). | Cranes | II | 8/1/85 |
| *Grus americana* | Whooping Crane | I | 7/1/75 |
| *G. canadensis nesiotes* | Cuba sandhill crane | I | 7/1/75 |
| *G. canadensis pratensis* | Florida sandhill crane | II | 7/1/75 |
| *G. canadensis pulla* | Mississippi sandhill crane | I | 7/1/75 |
| *G. japonensis* | Manchurian crane | I | 7/1/75 |
| *G. leucogeranus* | Siberian white crane | I | 7/1/75 |
| *G. monacha* | Hooded crane | I | 7/1/75 |
| *G. nigricollis* | Black necked crane | I | 7/1/75 |
| *G. vipio* | White-naped crane | I | 7/1/75 |
| *Houbaropsis (=Eupodotis) bengalensis* | Bengal florican | I | 7/1/75 |
| Otididae spp. (all species except those in App. I or with earlier date in App. II). | Bustards | II | 10/22/87 |
| *Otis tarda* | Great bustard | II | 7/1/75 |
| *Pedionomus torquatus* | Collared hemipode | II | 6/28/79 |
| *Rhynochetos jubatus* | Kagu | I | 7/1/75 |
| *Tricholimnas sylvestris* | Lord Howe wood rail | I | 7/1/75 |
| *Turnix melanogaster* | Black-breasted button quail | II | 6/28/79 |
| Order Charadriiformes: | Shorebirds, Gulls, Auks: | | |
| *Burhinus bistriatus* | Double-striped thick-knee, Mexican stone curlew | III (Guatemala) | 4/23/81 |
| *Larus relictus* | Relict gull | I | 7/1/75 |
| *Numenius borealis* | Eskimo curlew | I | 7/1/75 |
| *N. tenuirostris* | Slender-billed curlew | I | 7/1/75 |
| *Tringa guttifer* | Nordmann's greenshank | I | 7/1/75 |
| Order Columbifomes: | Pigeons, Doves, Sand-grouse: | | |
| *Caloenas nicobarica* | Nicobar pigeon | I | 6/28/79 |
| *C. nicobarica pelewensis* | Nicobar pigeon | I | 7/1/75 |
| *Columba guinea* | Speckled pigeon | III (Ghana) | 2/26/76 |
| *C. iriditorques* | Bronze-necked pigeon, Bronze-naped pigeon | III (Ghana) | 2/26/76 |
| *C. livia* | Rock dove | III (Ghana) | 2/26/76 |
| *C. unicincta* | African wood pigeon | III (Ghana) | 2/26/76 |
| *Ducula mindorensis* | Mindoro imperial pigeon | I | 7/1/75 |
| *Gallicolumba luzonica* | Bleeding heart pigeon | II | 7/1/75 |
| *Goura cristata* | Common crowned pigeon | II | 7/1/75 |
| *G. scheepmakeri* | Maroon-breasted crowned pigeon | II | 7/1/75 |
| *G. victoria* | Victoria crowned pigeon | II | 7/1/75 |
| *Nesoenas (=Columba) mayeri* | Pink pigeon | III (Mauritius) | 12/4/75 |

**10**

| Species | Common name | Appendix | Date listed (month/ day/year) |
|---|---|---|---|
| *Oena capensis* | Namaqua dove, Masked dove | III (Ghana) | 2/26/76 |
| *Streptopelia decipiens* | African mourning dove, Mourning collared dove | III (Ghana) | 2/26/76 |
| *S. roseogrisea* | African turtle dove, African collared dove | III (Ghana) | 2/26/76 |
| *S. semitorquata* | Red-eyed dove | III (Ghana) | 2/26/76 |
| *S. senegalensis* | Laughing dove | III (Ghana) | 2/26/76 |
| *S. turtur* | Turtle dove | III (Ghana) | 2/26/76 |
| *S. vinacea* | Vinaceous dove | III (Ghana) | 2/26/76 |
| *Treron calva* | African green pigeon | III (Ghana) | 2/26/76 |
| *T. waalia* | Yellow-bellied green pigeon | III (Ghana) | 2/26/76 |
| *Turtur abyssinicus* | Black-billed wood dove | III (Ghana) | 2/26/76 |
| *T. afer* | Blue-spotted wood dove | III (Ghana) | 2/26/76 |
| *T. brehmeri* | Blue-headed wood dove | III (Ghana) | 2/26/76 |
| *T. tympanistria* | Tambourine dove | III (Ghana) | 2/26/76 |
| Order Psittaciformes: | Parrots, Parakeets, Macaws, Lories: | | |
| All species in order except those in App. I or with earlier date in App. II and except *Melopsittacus undulatus* and *Nymphicus hollandicus*. | All Parrots, Parakeets, Macaws and Lories (not including the Budgerigar and Cockatiel). | II | 6/6/81 |
| *Amazona arausiaca* | Red-necked parrot | I | 6/6/81 |
| *A. barbadensis* | Yellow-shouldered parrot | I | 6/6/81 |
| *A. brasiliensis* | Red-tailed parrot | I | 6/6/81 |
| *A. dufresniana rhodocorytha* | Red-browed parrot | I | 7/1/75 |
| *A. guildingii* | St. Vincent parrot | I | 7/1/75 |
| *A. imperialis* | Imperial parrot | I | 7/1/75 |
| *A. leucocephala* | Cuban parrot | I | 7/1/75 |
| *A. pretrei* | Red-spectacled parrot | I | 7/1/75 |
| *A. tucumana* | Tucuman amazon | I | 6/6/81 |
| *A. versicolor* | St. Lucia parrot | I | 7/1/75 |
| *A. vinacea* | Vinaceous parrot | I | 7/1/75 |
| *A. vittata* | Puerto Rican parrot | I | 7/1/75 |
| *Anodorhynchus glaucus* | Glaucous macaw | I | 7/1/75 |
| *A. hyacinthinus* | Hyacinth macaw | I | 6/6/81 |
| *A. leari* | Lear's macaw, Indigo macaw | I | 7/1/75 |
| *Ara ambigua* | Buffon's macaw, Great green macaw | I | 10/28/76 |
| *A. glaucogularis* | Caninde macaw | I | 6/6/81 |
| *A. macao* | Scarlet macaw | I | 10/28/76 |
| *A. maracana* | Illiger's macaw | I | 6/6/81 |
| *A. militaris* | Military macaw | I | 6/6/81 |
| *A. rubrogenys* | Red-fronted macaw | I | 6/6/81 |
| *Aratinga guarouba* | Golden conure | I | 7/1/75 |
| *Cacatua moluccensis* | Moluccan cockatoo | I | 6/6/81 |
| *C.* (=*Kakatoe*) *tenuirostris* | Long-billed corella, Slender-billed cockatoo | II | 2/4/77 |
| *Calyptorhynchus lathami* | Glossy cockatoo | II | 2/4/77 |
| *Coracopsis nigra barklyi* | Seychelles vasa parrot | II | 7/1/75 |
| *Cyanoliseus patagonus byroni* | Patagonian conure | II | 6/28/79 |
| *Cyanopsitta spixii* | Spix's macaw | I | 7/1/75 |
| *Cyanoramphus auriceps forbesi* | Forbe's parakeet, Yellow-fronted parakeet | I | 7/1/75 |
| *C. malherbi* | Orange-fronted parakeet | II | 7/1/75 |
| *C. novaezelandiae* | New Zealand parakeet, Red-fronted parakeet | I | 7/1/75 |
| *C. unicolor* | Antipodes green parakeet | II | 7/1/75 |
| *Eunymphicus cornutus* | Horned parakeet | II | 7/1/75 |
| *Geopsittacus occidentalis* | Blue-collared parrot, Australian night parrot | I pe. | 7/1/75 |
| *Neophema chrysogaster* | Orange-bellied parakeet | I | 7/1/75 |
| *N. splendida* | Scarlet-chested parakeet | II | 7/1/75 |
| *Ognorhynchus icterotis* | Yellow-cheeked conure | I | 6/6/81 |
| *Opopsitta* (=*Cyclopsitta*) *diophthalma coxeni* | Coxen's fig parrot | I | 2/4/77 |
| *Pezoporus wallicus* | Ground parrot | I | 2/4/77 |
| *Pionopsitta pileata* | Red-capped parrot, Pileated parrot | I | 7/1/75 |
| *Poicephalus robustus* | Cape parrot | II | 7/1/75 |
| *Polytelis alexandrae* | Princess parrot | II | 2/4/77 |
| *Probosciger aterrimus* | Great black cockatoo, Palm cockatoo | I | 7/1/75 |
| *Prosopoeia personata* | Masked shining parrot, Yellow-breasted musk parrot. | II | 7/1/75 |
| *Psephotus chrysopterygius* | Golden-shouldered parakeet | I | 7/1/75 |
| *P. pulcherrimus* | Paradise parakeet | I pe. | 7/1/75 |
| *P.* (=*Northiella*) *haematogaster narethae* | Blue-bonnet parakeet | II | 2/4/77 |
| *Psittacula echo* (=*P. krameri echo*) | Mauritius ring-neck parakeet | I | 7/1/75 |
| *P. krameri* | Ring-neck parakeet | III (Ghana) | 2/26/76 |
| *Psittacus erithacus princeps* | Principe parrot | I | 7/1/75 |
| *Pyrrhura cruentata* | Blue-throated parakeet, Ochre-marked parakeet | I | 7/1/75 |
| *Rhynchopsitta pachyrhyncha* | Thick-billed parrot | I | 7/1/75 |
| *R. pachyrhyncha terrisi* (=*R. terrisi*) | Maroon-fronted parrot | I | 6/6/81 |
| *Strigops habroptilus* | Kakapo, Owl parrot | I | 7/1/75 |
| *Tanygnathus lucionensis* | Blue-naped parrot | II | 2/4/77 |
| Order Cuculiformes: | Cuckoos, Plantain-eaters: | | |
| *Corythaeola cristata* | Great blue turaco | III (Ghana) | 2/4/77 |
| *Crinifer piscator* | Gray plantain eater | III (Ghana) | 2/4/77 |
| *Musophaga violacea* | Violet turaco | III (Ghana) | 2/4/77 |
| *Tauraco corythaix* | Knysna loury | II | 2/4/77 |
| *T. macrorhynchus* | Black-tip crested turaco | III (Ghana) | 2/4/77 |

| Species | Common name | Appendix | Date listed (month/day/year) |
|---|---|---|---|
| *T.* (=*Gallirex*) *porphyreolophus* | Violet-crested turaco | II | 7/1/75 |
| Order Strigiformes: | Owls: | | |
| All species except those in App. I or with earlier date in App. II. | | II | 6/28/79 |
| *Athene blewitti* | Forest little owl, Forest spotted owlet | I | 6/28/79 |
| *Bubo bubo* | Eurasian eagle owl | II | 2/4/77 |
| *Ninox novaeseelandiae royana* | Great hawk owl | I | 2/4/77 |
| *N. squamipila natalis* | Great hawk owl, Moluccan hawk owl | I | 2/4/77 |
| *Nyctea scandiaca* | Snowy owl | II | 2/4/77 |
| *Otus* (=*mimizyku*) *gurneyi* | Giant scops owl | I | 7/1/75 |
| *O. nudipes newtoni* | Virgin Island screech owl | II | 7/1/75 |
| Strigidae spp. (all species in family native to Ghana) | Owls | II | 2/26/76 |
| *Strix butleri* | Hume's wood owl | II | 2/4/77 |
| *S. nebulosa* | Great gray owl | II | 11/16/75 |
| Tytonidae spp. (all species in family native to Ghana) | Owls | II | 2/26/76 |
| *Tyto soumagnei* | Madagascar owl | I | 2/4/77 |
| Order Apodiformes: | Swifts, Hummingbirds: | | |
| *Glaucis* (=*Ramphodon*) *dohrnii* | Hook-billed hermit | I | 7/1/75 |
| Trochilidae spp. | Hummingbirds | II | 10/22/87 |
| Order Trogoniformes: | Trogons: | | |
| *Pharomachrus mocinno costaricensis* | Central resplendent quetzal | I | 7/1/75 |
| *P. mocinno mocinno* | Northern resplendent quetzal | I | 7/1/75 |
| Order Coraciiformes: | Hornbills, Kingfishers, Rollers, Bee-eaters, Motmots: | | |
| *Aceros narcondami* | Narcondam hornbill | II | 7/1/75 |
| *Buceros bicornis* | Great hornbill | II | 7/1/75 |
| *B. bicornis homrai* | Great Indian hornbill, Great pied hornbill | I | 7/1/75 |
| *B. hydrocorax hydrocorax* | Luzon-Marinduque rufous hornbill | II | 7/1/75 |
| *B. rhinoceros* (except subspecies with earlier date) | Rhinoceros hornbill | II | 1/18/90 |
| *B. rhinoceros rhinoceros* | Malay rhinoceros hornbill | II | 7/1/75 |
| *Rhinoplax vigil* | Helmeted hornbill | I | 7/1/75 |
| Order Piciformes: | Woodpeckers, Toucans, Jacamars, Barbets: | | |
| *Campephilus imperialis* | Imperial woodpecker | I | 7/1/75 |
| *Dryocopus javensis richardsi* | Tristam's white-bellied woodpecker | I | 7/1/75 |
| *Ramphastos sulphuratus* | Keel-billed toucan | III (Guatemala) | 4/23/81 |
| *Semnornis ramphastinus* | Toucan barbet | III (Colombia) | 5/28/89 |
| Order Passeriformes: | Perching birds: | | |
| *Amadina fasciata* | Cut-throat | III (Ghana) | 2/26/76 |
| *Amandava subflava* | Zebra waxbill | III (Ghana) | 2/26/76 |
| *Amblyospiza albifrons* | Grosbeak weaver | III (Ghana) | 2/26/76 |
| *Anomalospiza imberbis* | Parasitic weaver | III (Ghana) | 2/26/76 |
| *Atrichornis clamosus* | Noisy scrub-bird | I | 7/1/75 |
| *Bebrornis rodericanus* | Rodriquez Island warbler | III (Mauritius) | 12/4/75 |
| *Bubalornis albirostris* | Buffalo weaver | III (Ghana) | 2/26/76 |
| *Carduelis* (=*Spinus*) *cucullata* | Red siskin | I | 7/1/75 |
| *C.* (=*Spinus*) *yarrellii* | Yellow-faced siskin | II | 7/1/75 |
| *Cephalopterus ornatus* | Amazonian umbrellabird | III (Colombia) | 9/21/88 |
| *C. penduliger* | Long-wattled umbrellabird | III (Colombia) | 9/21/88 |
| *Cotinga maculata* | Banded cotinga | I | 7/1/75 |
| *Dasyornis broadbenti litoralis* | Western rufous bristlebird | I pe | 7/1/75 |
| *D. longirostris* (=*D. brachypterus longirostris*) | Western bristlebird | I | 7/1/75 |
| *Estrilda astrild* | Common waxbill | III (Ghana) | 2/26/76 |
| *E. caerulescens* | Lavender fire-finch | III (Ghana) | 2/26/76 |
| *E. melpoda* | Orange-cheeked waxbill | III (Ghana) | 2/26/76 |
| *E. troglodytes* | Black-rumped waxbill | III (Ghana) | 2/26/76 |
| *Euplectes afer* | Yellow-crowned bishop | III (Ghana) | 2/26/76 |
| *E. ardens* | Red-collared whydah | III (Ghana) | 2/26/76 |
| *E. hordeaceus* | Black-winged red bishop | III (Ghana) | 2/26/76 |
| *E. macrourus* | Yellow-mantled whydah | III (Ghana) | 2/26/76 |
| *E. orix* | Red bishop | III (Ghana) | 2/26/76 |
| *Gubernatrix cristata* | Yellow cardinal | II | 7/14/76 |
| *Lagonosticta larvata* | Vinaceous waxbill | III (Ghana) | 2/26/76 |
| *L. rara* | Black-bellied waxbill | III (Ghana) | 2/26/76 |
| *L. rubricata* | African waxbill | III (Ghana) | 2/26/76 |
| *L. rufopicta* | Bar-breasted waxbill | III (Ghana) | 2/26/76 |
| *L. senegala* | Red-billed fire finch, Red-billed waxbill | III (Ghana) | 2/26/76 |
| *Leucopsar rothschildi* | Rothschild's starling, Myna | I | 7/1/75 |
| *Lonchura bicolor* | Black-and white mannikin | III (Ghana) | 2/26/76 |
| *L. cucullata* | Bronze mannikin | III (Ghana) | 2/26/76 |
| *L. fringilloides* | Magpie mannikin, Pied mannikin | III (Ghana) | 2/26/76 |
| *L. malabarica* | White-throated munia | III (Ghana) | 2/26/76 |
| *Malimbus cassini* | Cassin's malimbe | III (Ghana) | 2/26/76 |
| *M. malimbicus* | Crested malimbe | III (Ghana) | 2/26/76 |
| *M. nitens* | Gray's malimbe | III (Ghana) | 2/26/76 |
| *M. rubriceps* | Red-headed malimbe | III (Ghana) | 2/26/76 |
| *M. rubricollis* | Red-headed weaver | III (Ghana) | 2/26/76 |
| *M. scutatus* | Red-vented malimbe | III (Ghana) | 2/26/76 |
| *Mandingoa nitidula* | Green-backed twin-spot | III (Ghana) | 2/26/76 |
| *Meliphaga cassidix* | Helmeted honey eater | I | 7/1/75 |
| *Nesocharis capistrata* | Gray-headed olive-back | III (Ghana) | 2/26/76 |
| *Nigrita bicolor* | Chestnut-breasted negro-finch | III (Ghana) | 2/26/76 |

| Species | Common name | Appendix | Date listed (month/day/year) |
|---|---|---|---|
| *N. canicapilla* | Gray-headed negro-finch | III (Ghana) | 2/26/76 |
| *N. fusconota* | White-breasted negro-finch | III (Ghana) | 2/26/76 |
| *N. luteifrons* | Pale-fronted negro-finch | III (Ghana) | 2/26/76 |
| *Niltava* (=*Muscicapa*) *ruecki* | Rueck's blue flycatcher, Niltava | II | 7/1/75 |
| *Ortygospiza atricollis* | Common quail-finch | III (Ghana) | 2/26/76 |
| Paradiseidae spp. (all species in family) | Birds of paradise | II | 7/1/75 |
| *Parmoptila woodhousei* | Flowerpecker weaver-finch | III (Ghana) | 2/26/76 |
| *Paroaria capitata* | Yellow-billed cardinal | II | 10/22/87 |
| *P. coronata* | Red-crested cardinal | II | 10/22/87 |
| *Passer griseus* | Gray-headed sparrow | III (Ghana) | 2/26/76 |
| *Petronia dentata* | Bush petronia | III (Ghana) | 2/26/76 |
| *Pholidornis rushiae* | Tit-hylia | III (Ghana) | 2/26/76 |
| *Picathartes gymnocephalus* | Bare-headed rock fowl, Yellow-headed rock fowl | I | 7/1/75 |
| *P. oreas* | Gray-necked rock fowl, Red-headed rock fowl | I | 7/1/75 |
| *Pitta brachyura nympha* | Fairy pitta, Blue-winged pitta | II | 7/1/75 |
| *P. guajana* | Blue-tailed pitta, Banded pitta | II | 12/7/87 |
| *P. gurneyi* | Gurney's pitta | I | 12/7/87 |
| *P. kochi* | Koch's pitta | I | 7/1/75 |
| *Plocepasser superciliosus* | Chestnut-crowned sparrow-weaver | III (Ghana) | 2/26/76 |
| *Ploceus albinucha* | White-naped black weaver | III (Ghana) | 2/26/76 |
| *P. aurantius* | Orange weaver | III (Ghana) | 2/26/76 |
| *P. cucullatus* | Black-headed weaver | III (Ghana) | 2/26/76 |
| *P. heuglini* | Heuglin's masked weaver | III (Ghana) | 2/26/76 |
| *P. luteolus* | Little weaver | III (Ghana) | 2/26/76 |
| *P. melanocephalus* | Yellow-backed weaver | III (Ghana) | 2/26/76 |
| *P. nigerrimus* | Viellot's weaver | III (Ghana) | 2/26/76 |
| *P. nigricollis* | Black-necked weaver | III (Ghana) | 2/26/76 |
| *P. pelzelni* | Slender-billed weaver | III (Ghana) | 2/26/76 |
| *P. preussi* | Golden-backed weaver | III (Ghana) | 2/26/76 |
| *P. superciliosus* | Compact weaver | III (Ghana) | 2/26/76 |
| *P. tricolor* | Yellow-mantled weaver | III (Ghana) | 2/26/76 |
| *P. velatus* | Vitelline masked weaver | III (Ghana) | 2/26/76 |
| *Poephila cincta cincta* | Black-throated finch, Parson finch | II | 10/17/80 |
| *Pseudochelidon sirintarae* | White-eyed river martin | I | 7/1/75 |
| *Pyrenestes ostrinus* | Black-bellied seedcracker | III (Ghana) | 2/26/76 |
| *Pytilia hypogrammica* | Yellow-winged pytilia | III (Ghana) | 2/26/76 |
| *P. phoenicoptera* | Red-winged pytilia | III (Ghana) | 2/26/76 |
| *Quelea erythrops* | Red-headed quelea | III (Ghana) | 2/26/76 |
| *Rupicola peruviana* | Andean cock-of-the-rock | II | 7/1/75 |
| *R. rupicola* | Guianan cock-of-the-rock | II | 7/1/75 |
| *Serinus gularis* | Streaky-headed seedeater | III (Ghana) | 2/26/76 |
| *S. leucopygius* | White-rumped seedeater | III (Ghana) | 2/26/76 |
| *S. mozambicus* | Yellow-fronted canary | III (Ghana) | 2/26/76 |
| *Spermophaga haematina* | Blue-bill | III (Ghana) | 2/26/76 |
| *Sporopipes frontalis* | Speckled fronted weaver | III (Ghana) | 2/26/76 |
| *Tchitrea* (=*Terpsiphone*) *bourbonnensis* | Coq de Boise, Mascarene paradise flycatcher | III (Mauritius) | 12/4/75 |
| *Uraeginthus bengalus* | Red-cheeked cordon-bleu | III (Ghana) | 2/26/76 |
| *Vidua* (=*Hypochera*) *chalybeata* | Village indigobird | III (Ghana) | 2/26/76 |
| *V. interjecta* | Uelle paradise whydah | III (Ghana) | 2/26/76 |
| *V. larvaticola* | Bako indigobird | III (Ghana) | 2/26/76 |
| *V. macroura* | Pin-tailed whydah | III (Ghana) | 2/26/76 |
| *V. paradisaea* | Paradise whydah | III (Ghana) | 2/26/76 |
| *V. raricola* | Jambandu indigobird | III (Ghana) | 2/26/76 |
| *V. togoensis* | Togo paradise whydah | III (Ghana) | 2/26/76 |
| *V. wilsoni* | Wilson's indigobird | III (Ghana) | 2/26/76 |
| *Xanthopsar flavus* | Saffron-cowled blackbird | III (Uruguay) | 7/14/76 |
| *Xipholena atropurpurea* | White-winged cotinga | I | 7/1/75 |
| *Zosterops albogularis* | White-breasted silver-eye, Norfolk Island silver-eye | I | 7/1/75 |
| CLASS REPTILIA: | REPTILES: | | |
| Order Crocodylia: | Crocodiles, Alligators, Caimans, Gavials: | | |
| Alligatoridae spp. (all species in family except those in App. I or with earlier date in App. II). | Alligators, Caimans | II | 2/4/77 |
| *Alligator mississippiensis* | American alligator | II | 7/1/75 |
| *A. sinensis* | Chinese alligator | I | 7/1/75 |
| *Caiman crocodilus apaporiensis* | Apaporis River caiman | I | 7/1/75 |
| *C. crocodilus crocodilus* | Common caiman | II | 7/1/75 |
| *C. crocodilus fuscus* (including *C. crocodilus chiapasius*) | Brown caiman | II | 7/1/75 |
| *C. crocodilus yacare* (=*C. yacare*) | Yacare | II | 7/1/75 |
| *C. latirostris* | Broad-snouted caiman | I | 7/1/75 |
| Crocodylidae spp. (all species in family except those in App. I or with earlier date in App. II). | Crocodiles | II | 2/4/77 |
| *Crocodylus acutus* | American crocodile | I | 7/1/75 |
| *C. cataphractus* (except Congo population) | African slender-snouted crocodile | I | 7/1/75 |
| *C. cataphractus* (Congo population) | African slender-snouted crocodile | II | 7/1/75 |
| *C. intermedius* | Orinoco crocodile | I | 7/1/75 |
| *C. johnsoni* | Johnson's crocodile | II | 7/1/75 |
| *C. moreletii* | Morelet's crocodile | I | 7/1/75 |
| *C. niloticus* (except those populations on App. II) | Nile crocodile | I | 7/1/75 |

| Species | Common name | Appendix | Date listed (month/ day/year) |
|---|---|---|---|
| *C. niloticus* (populations in Cameroon, Congo, Ethiopia, Kenya, Madagascar, Somalia, Sudan and Tanzania subject to export quotas described by the Secretariat). | Nile crocodile | II | 7/1/75 |
| *C. niloticus* (populations in Botswana, Malawi, Mozambique, Zambia and Zimbabwe pursuant to ranching). | Nile Crocodile | II | 7/1/75 |
| *C. novaeguineae* (except subspecies listed below) | New Guinea crocodile, Freshwater crocodile | II | 7/1/75 |
| *C. novaeguineae mindorensis* | Philippine crocodile | I | 7/1/75 |
| *C. palustris kimbula* | Ceylon mugger crocodile | I | 7/1/75 |
| *C. palustris palustris* | Mugger crocodile | I | 7/1/75 |
| *C. porosus* (except the population of Papua New Guinea, the Australia population subject to ranching, and Indonesian population subject to export quotas). | Saltwater Crocodile | I | 7/1/75 |
| *C. porosus* (Papua New Guinea population, the Australian population subject to ranching, and the Indonesian population subject to export quotas described by the Secretariat). | Saltwater Crocodile | II | 7/1/75 |
| *C. rhombifer* | Cuban crocodile | I | 7/1/75 |
| *C. siamensis* | Siamese crocodile | I | 7/1/75 |
| *Gavialis gangeticus* | Gavial, Gharial | I | 7/1/75 |
| *Melanosuchus niger* | Black caiman | I | 7/1/75 |
| *Osteolaemus tetraspis* (except subspecies and populations listed below). | Dwarf crocodile | I | 2/4/77 |
| *O. tetraspis* (Congo population) | Dwarf crocodile | II | 2/4/77 |
| *O. tetraspis osborni* | Dwarf crocodile | I | 7/1/75 |
| *O. tetraspis tetraspis* | Dwarf crocodile | I | 7/1/75 |
| *Paleosuchus trigonatus* | Smooth-fronted caiman | II | 7/1/75 |
| *Tomistoma schlegelii* | Tomistoma, False gavial | I | 7/1/75 |
| Order Testudinata: | Turtles, Tortoises: | | |
| *Batagur baska* | River terrapin, Tuntong | I | 7/1/75 |
| Cheloniidae spp. (all species in family) | Sea turtles | I | 7/1/75 |
| *Chersina* (=*Testudo*) spp. | Bow-sprit tortoises | II | 7/1/75 |
| *Clemmys muhlenbergi* | Bog turtle | II | 7/1/75 |
| *Dermatemys mawii* | Central American river turtle | II | 6/6/81 |
| *Dermochelys coriacea* | Leatherback sea turtle | I | 7/1/75 |
| *Erymnochelys madagascariensis* | Madagascar turtle | II | 7/1/75 |
| *Geochelone* spp. (except species listed below) | Land tortoises | II | 7/1/75 |
| *G.* (=*Testudo*) *elephantopus* | Galapagos tortoises | I | 7/1/75 |
| *G.* (=*Testudo*) *radiata* | Madagascar radiated tortoises | I | 7/1/75 |
| *G.* (=*Testudo*) *yniphora* | Angulated tortoises | I | 7/1/75 |
| *Geoclemys* (=*Damonia*) *hamiltonii* | Spotted pond turtle | I | 7/1/75 |
| *Gopherus* spp. (except species listed below) | Gopher tortoises | II | 7/1/75 |
| *G. flavomarginatus* | Bolson tortoise | I | 7/1/75 |
| *Homopus* spp. | African parrot-beaked tortoises | II | 7/1/75 |
| *Kachuga tecta tecta* | Indian sawback turtle | I | 7/1/75 |
| *Kinixys* spp. | Hinged-back tortoise | II | 7/1/75 |
| *Lissemys punctata punctata* | Indian flap-shell tortoise | I | 7/1/75 |
| *Malacochersus* spp. | Pancake tortoises | II | 7/1/75 |
| *Melanochelys* (=*Geoemyda*) *tricarinata* | Three-keeled Asian turtle | I | 7/1/75 |
| *Morenia ocellata* | Burmese peacock turtle | I | 7/1/75 |
| *Pelomedusa subrufa* | Helmeted terrapin | III (Ghana) | 2/26/76 |
| *Peltocephalus dumeriliana* | Big-headed Amazon River turtle | II | 7/1/75 |
| *Pelusios adansonii* | Adanson's hinged terrapin | III (Ghana) | 2/26/76 |
| *P. castaneus* | Brown hinged terrapin, Swamp hinged terrapin | III (Ghana) | 2/26/76 |
| *P. gabonensis* | Gabon hinged terrapin | III (Ghana) | 2/26/76 |
| *P. niger* | Black hinged terrapin | III (Ghana) | 2/26/76 |
| *Podocnemis* spp. | South American turtles | II | 7/1/75 |
| *Psammobates* (=*Testudo*) *geometricus* | Geometric turtle | I | 2/4/77 |
| *Pseudemydura umbrina* | Short-necked swamp turtle | I | 7/1/75 |
| *Pyxis* spp. | Madagascar spider tortoises | II | 7/1/75 |
| *Terrapene coahuila* | Aquatic box turtle | I | 7/1/75 |
| Testudinidae spp. (all species except those in App. I or with earlier date in App. II). | Land tortoises | II | 2/4/77 |
| *Testudo* spp. | Land tortoises | II | 7/1/75 |
| *Trionyx ater* | Cuatro Cienegas softshell turtle | I | 7/1/75 |
| *T. gangeticus* | Indian softshell turtle | I | 7/1/75 |
| *T. hurum* | Peacock softshell turtle | I | 7/1/75 |
| *T. nigricans* | Black softshell turtle | I | 7/1/75 |
| *T. triunguis* | Three-clawed turtle | III (Ghana) | 2/26/76 |
| Order Rhynchocephalia: | Tuatara: | | |
| *Sphenodon punctatus* | Tuatara | I | 7/1/75 |
| Order Squamata: | Lizards, Snakes: | | |
| *Acrantophis* spp. | Madagascar boas | I | 2/4/77 |
| *Agkistrodon bilineatus* | Cantil | III (Honduras) | 4/13/87 |
| *Amblyrhynchus cristatus* | Galapagos marine iguana | II | 7/1/75 |
| *Atretium schistosum* | Olive keelback water snake | III (India) | 2/12/84 |
| *Boa* (=*Constrictor*) *constrictor* | Boa constrictor | II | 7/1/75 |
| *Boa constrictor occidentalis* | Argentine boa constrictor | I | 2/4/77 |
| Boidae spp. (all species except those in App. I or with earlier date in App. II). | Boa constrictors, Pythons | II | 2/4/77 |

| Species | Common name | Appendix | Date listed (month/ day/year) |
|---|---|---|---|
| *Bolyeria multocarinata* | Round Island boa | I | 2/4/77 |
| *Bothrops asper* | Terciopelo | III (Honduras) | 4/13/87 |
| *B. nasutus* | Rainforest hognosed pit-viper | III (Honduras) | 4/13/87 |
| *B. nummifer* | Jumping pit-viper | III (Honduras) | 4/13/87 |
| *B. ophryomegas* | Slender hognosed pit-viper | III (Honduras) | 4/13/87 |
| *B. schlegelii* | Eyelash palm pit-viper | III (Honduras) | 4/13/87 |
| *Brachylophus* spp. | Fiji iguanas | I | 6/6/81 |
| *Bradypodion* spp. | Chameleons | II | 2/4/77 |
| *Casarea dussumieri* | Round Island boa | I | 2/4/77 |
| *Cerberus rhynchops* | Dog-faced water snake | III (India) | 2/12/84 |
| *Chamaeleo* spp. | Chamaeleons | II | 2/4/77 |
| *Clelia* (=*Pseudoboa*) *clelia* | Mussurana snake | II | 7/1/75 |
| *Cnemidophorus hyperythrus* | Orange-throated whiptail lizard | II | 7/1/75 |
| *Conolophus* spp. (except species listed below) | Land lizards | II | 2/4/77 |
| *C. pallidus* | Barrington Island land lizard | II | 7/1/75 |
| *C. subcristatus* | Galapagos land iguana | II | 7/1/75 |
| *Cordylus* spp. | Girdled lizards | II | 6/6/81 |
| *Crocodilurus lacertinus* | Dragon lizardet | II | 2/4/77 |
| *Crotalus durissus* | Tropical rattlesnake, Cascabel | III (Honduras) | 4/13/87 |
| *Cyclagras* (=*Hydrodynastes*) *gigas* | South American false water cobra | II | 7/1/75 |
| *Cyclura* spp. | Ground iguanas | I | 2/4/77 |
| *Cyrtodactylus serpensinsula* | Serpent Island gecko | II | 2/4/77 |
| *Dracaena guianensis* | Caiman lizard | II | 2/4/77 |
| *D. paraquayensis* | Caiman lizard | II | 1/18/90 |
| *Elachistodon westermanni* | Indian egg-eating snake | II | 7/1/75 |
| *Epicrates cenchris cenchris* | Rainbow boa | II | 7/1/75 |
| *E. inornatus* | Puerto Rican boa | I | 2/4/77 |
| *E. monensis* | Mona boa | I | 2/4/77 |
| *E. subflavus* | Jamaican boa | I | 7/1/75 |
| *Eunectes notaeus* | Yellow anaconda | II | 7/1/75 |
| *Gallotia simonyi* | Hierro giant lizard | I | 10/22/87 |
| *Heloderma* spp. | Beaded lizards, Gila monster | II | 7/1/75 |
| *Hoplocephalus bungaroides* | Broad-headed snake | II | 8/1/85 |
| *Iguana* spp. | Iguanas | II | 2/4/77 |
| *Micrurus diastema* | Atlanta coral snake | III (Honduras) | 4/13/87 |
| *M. nigrocinctus* | Black-banded coral snake | III (Honduras) | 4/13/87 |
| *Naja naja* | Indian cobra | II | 2/12/84 |
| *Ophiophagus hannah* | King cobra | II | 2/12/84 |
| *Phelsuma* spp. | Day geckos | II | 2/4/77 |
| *Phrynosoma coronatum blainvillei* | San Diego horned lizard | II | 7/1/75 |
| *Podarcis lilfordi* | Lilford's wall lizard | II | 10/22/87 |
| *P. pityusensis* | Ibiza wall lizard | II | 10/22/87 |
| *Pseudocordylus* spp. | Crag lizards | II | 6/6/81 |
| *Ptyas mucosus* | Oriental rat snake, Whipsnake | II | 2/12/84 |
| *Python* spp. (except subspecies listed below) | Pythons | II | 7/1/75 |
| *P. molurus molurus* | Indian python | I | 7/1/75 |
| *Sanzinia madagascariensis* | Tree boa | I | 2/4/77 |
| *Sauromalus varius* | San Esteban Island chuckwalla | I | 6/6/81 |
| *Shinisaurus crocodilurus* | Chinese crocodile lizard | II | 1/18/90 |
| *Tupinambis* spp. | Tegu lizards | II | 2/4/77 |
| *Uromastyx* spp. | Spiny-tailed lizards | II | 2/4/77 |
| *Varanus* spp. (all species except those in App. I) | Monitor lizards | II | 7/1/75 |
| *V. bengalensis* | Indian monitor, Bengal monitor | I | 7/1/75 |
| *V. flavescens* | Yellow monitor | I | 7/1/75 |
| *V. griseus* | Desert monitor | I | 7/1/75 |
| *V. komodoensis* | Komodo Island monitor, Komodo dragon | I | 7/1/75 |
| *Vipera russellii* | Russell's viper | III (India) | 2/12/84 |
| *V. ursinii* (except USSR populations) | Orsini's viper | I | 10/22/87 |
| *Xenochrophis* (=*Natrix*) *piscator* | Checkered keelback water snake | III (India) | 2/12/84 |
| CLASS AMPHIBIA: | AMPHIBIANS: | | |
| Order Caudata: | Salamanders: | | |
| *Ambystoma dumerilii* | Lake Patzcuaro salamander | II | 7/1/75 |
| *A. mexicanum* | Axolotl | II | 7/1/75 |
| *Andrias* (=*Megalobatrachus*) *davidianus* | Chinese giant salamander | I | 7/1/75 |
| *A.* (=*Megalobatrachus*) *japonicus* | Japanese giant salamander | I | 7/1/75 |
| Order Anura: | Frogs, Toads: | | |
| *Atelopus varius zeteki* | Panamanian golden frog | I | 7/1/75 |
| *Bufo periglenes* | Monte Verde toad | III (Costa Rica) | 7/1/75 |
| *B. retiformis* | Sonoran green toad | II | 7/1/75 |
| *B. superciliaris* | Cameroon toad | I | 7/1/75 |
| *Dendrobates* spp. | Poison dart frogs, Poison arrow frogs | II | 10/22/87 |
| *Dyscophus antongilii* | Tomato frog | I | 10/22/87 |
| *Nectophrynoides* spp. | African viviparous toads | I | 7/1/75 |
| *Phyllobates* spp. | Poison arrow frogs | II | 10/22/87 |
| *Rana hexadactyla* | Asian bullfrog | II | 8/1/85 |
| *Rana tigerina* | Indian bullfrog | II | 8/1/85 |
| *Rheobatrachus* spp. | Platypus frog | II | 8/1/85 |
| CLASS OSTEICHTHYES: | BONY FISHES: | | |
| Order Acipenseriformes: | Sturgeons: | | |
| *Acipenser brevirostrum* | Short-nosed sturgeon | I | 7/1/75 |

| Species | Common name | Appendix | Date listed (month/ day/year) |
|---|---|---|---|
| *A. oxyrhynchus* | Atlantic sturgeon | II | 7/1/75 |
| *A. sturio* | Baltic sturgeon | I | 7/1/75 |
| Order Osteoglossiformes: | Bonytongues: | | |
| *Arapaima gigas* | Arapaima | II | 7/1/75 |
| *Scleropages formosus* | Asian bonytongue | I | 7/1/75 |
| *S. formosus* (population in Indonesia subject to export quota described by the Secretariat). | Asian bonytongue | II | 7/1/75 |
| Order Cypriniformes: | | | |
| *Caecobarbus geertsi* | African blind barb, Congo blind barb | II | 6/6/81 |
| *Chasmistes cujus* | Cui-ui | I | 7/1/75 |
| *Probarbus jullieni* | Ikan temolek, Pla eesok | I | 7/1/75 |
| Order Atheriniformes: | Livebearers: | | |
| *Cynolebias constanciae* | Annual tropical killifish | II | 7/1/75 |
| *C. marmoratus* | Annual tropical killifish | II pe | 7/1/75 |
| *C. minimus* | Annual tropical killifish | II | 7/1/75 |
| *C. opalescens* | Annual tropical killifish | II pe | 7/1/75 |
| *C. splendens* | Annual tropical killifish | II | 7/1/75 |
| Order Coelacanthiformes: | Coelacanth: | | |
| *Latimeria chalumnae* | Coelacanth, Gombessa | I | 7/1/75 |
| Order Ceratodiformes: | Lungfishes: | | |
| *Neoceratodus forsteri* | Australian lungfish | II | 7/1/75 |
| Order Siluriformes: | Catfishes: | | |
| *Pangasianodon gigas* | Thailand giant catfish | I | 7/1/75 |
| Order Perciformes: | Perch-like fishes: | | |
| *Cynoscion macdonaldi* | Totoaba | I | 2/4/77 |
| PHYLUM MOLLUSCA: | MOLLUSCS: | | |
| CLASS Pelecypoda (=*Bivalvia*): | Clams, Mussels: | | |
| *Conradilla caelata* | Birdwing pearly mussel | I | 7/1/75 |
| *Cyprogenia aberti* | Edible pearly mussel | II | 7/1/75 |
| *Dromus dromas* | Dromedary pearly mussel | I | 7/1/75 |
| *Epioblasma* (=*Dysnomia*) *curtisi* (=*E. florentina curtisi*) | Curtis' pearly mussel | I | 7/1/75 |
| *E. florentina* (=*E. florentina florentina*) | Yellow-blossom pearly mussel | I | 7/1/75 |
| *E. sampsoni* | Sampson's pearly mussel | I | 7/1/75 |
| *E. sulcata perobliqua* | White cat's paw mussel | I | 7/1/75 |
| *E. torulosa gubernaculum* | Green-blossom pearly mussel | I | 7/1/75 |
| *E. torulosa rangiana* | Tan-blossom pearly mussel | II | 7/1/75 |
| *E. torulosa torulosa* | Tuberculed-blossom pearly mussel | I | 7/1/75 |
| *E. turgidula* | Turgid-blossom pearly mussel | I | 7/1/75 |
| *E. walkeri* | Brown-blossom pearly mussel | I | 7/1/75 |
| *Fusconaia cuneolus* | Fine-rayed pigtoe mussel | I | 7/1/75 |
| *F. edgariana* | Shiny pigtoe mussel | I | 7/1/75 |
| *F. subrotunda* | Long solid mussel | II | 7/1/75 |
| *Lampsilis brevicula* | Ozark lamp pearly mussel | II | 7/1/75 |
| *L. higginsi* | Higgin's eye mussel | I | 7/1/75 |
| *L. orbiculata orbiculata* | Pink mucket mussel | I | 7/1/75 |
| *L. satura* | Plain pocketbook mussel | I | 7/1/75 |
| *L. virescens* | Alabama lamp pearly mussel | I | 7/1/75 |
| *Lexingtonia dolabelloides* | Slab-side pearly mussel | II | 7/1/75 |
| *Plethobasus cicatricosus* | White wartyback mussel | I | 7/1/75 |
| *P. cooperianus* | Orange-footed pimpleback mussel | I | 7/1/75 |
| *Pleurobema clava* | Club pearly mussel | II | 7/1/75 |
| *P. plenum* | Rough pigtoe mussel | I | 7/1/75 |
| *Potamilus* (=*Proptera*) *capax* | Fat pocketbook mussel | I | 7/1/75 |
| *Quadrula intermedia* | Cumberland monkey-face mussel | I | 7/1/75 |
| *Q. sparsa* | Appalachian monkey-face mussel | I | 7/1/75 |
| *Toxolasma* (=*Carunculina*) *cylindrella* | Pale lilliput pearly mussel | I | 7/1/75 |
| *Tridacna deras* | Giant clam | II | 5/29/83 |
| *T. gigas* | Giant clam | II | 5/29/83 |
| Tridacnidae spp. (includes all species in genera *Hippopus* and *Tridacna* except those with earlier date in App. II). | Giant clams | II | 8/1/85 |
| *Unio* (=*Megalonaias*) *nickliniana* | Nicklin's pearly mussel | I | 7/1/75 |
| *U.* (=*Lampsilis* or *Cyrtonaias*) *tampicoensis tecomatensis*. | Tampico pearly mussel | I | 7/1/75 |
| *Villosa* (=*Micromya*) *trabalis* | Cumberland bean mussel | I | 7/1/75 |
| CLASS Gastropoda: | Snails: | | |
| *Achatinella* spp. | Oahu tree snails | I | 10/22/87 |
| *Papustyla* (=*Papuina*) *pulcherrima* | Manus Island tree snail | II | 7/1/75 |
| *Paryphanta* spp. (New Zealand species only) | New Zealand amber snails | II | 7/1/75 |
| PHYLUM ANNELIDA: | ANNELID WORMS: | | |
| CLASS Hirudinea: | Leeches: | | |
| Order Arhynchobdelliformes: | Rhynchobedellids: | | |
| *Hirudo medicinalis* | Medicinal leech | II | 10/22/87 |
| PHYLUM ARTHROPODA: | ARTHROPODS: | | |
| CLASS Arachnida: | Arachnids: | | |
| *Brachypelma smithi* | Red-kneed tarantula | II | 8/1/85 |
| CLASS Insecta: | Insects: | | |
| *Bhutanitis* spp. | Bhutan glory swallowtails | II | 10/22/87 |
| *Ornithoptera* spp. (all species except those in App. I or with earlier date in App. II). | Birdwing butterflies | II | 2/16/79 |

16

| Species | Common name | Appendix | Date listed (month/day/year) |
|---|---|---|---|
| *O. alexandrae* | Queen Alexandra's birdwing butterfly | I | 2/4/77 |
| *O. allotei* | Birdwing butterfly | II | 2/4/77 |
| *O. chimaera* | Birdwing butterfly | II | 2/4/77 |
| *O. goliath* | Birdwing butterfly | II | 2/4/77 |
| *O. meridionalis* | Birdwing butterfly | II | 2/4/77 |
| *O. paradisea* | Paradise birdwing butterfly | II | 2/4/77 |
| *O. victoriae* | Queen Victoria's birdwing butterfly | II | 2/4/77 |
| *Papilio chikae* | Luzon peacock swallowtail | I | 10/22/87 |
| *P. homerus* | Homerus swallowtail | I | 10/22/87 |
| *P. hospiton* | Corsican swallowtail | I | 10/22/87 |
| *Parnassius apollo* | Mountain apollo butterfly | II | 2/4/77 |
| *P. apollo apollo* | Mountain apollo butterfly | II | 7/1/75 |
| *Teinopalpus* spp. | Kaiser-I-Hind butterflies | II | 10/22/87 |
| *Trogonoptera* spp. | Birdwing butterflies | II | 2/16/79 |
| *Troides* spp. | Birdwing butterflies | II | 2/16/79 |
| PHYLUM CNIDARIA (=COELENTERATA): | CORAL-LIKE ANIMALS: | | |
| CLASS Anthozoa: | Corals, Sea anemones: | | |
| Order Antipatharia: | Black corals: | | |
| All species in the Order | | II | 6/6/81 |
| Order Scleractinia: | Stony corals: | | |
| All species in the Order (except the genera with earlier date). | | II | 1/18/90 |
| *Acropora* spp. | Staghorn corals | II | 8/1/85 |
| *Euphyllia* spp. | Trumpet corals | II | 8/1/85 |
| *Favia* spp. | Brain corals | II | 8/1/85 |
| *Fungia* spp. | Mushroom corals | II | 8/1/85 |
| *Halomitra* spp. | Bowl corals | II | 8/1/85 |
| *Lobophyllia* spp. | Brain corals | II | 8/1/85 |
| *Merulina* spp. | Merulinas | II | 8/1/85 |
| *Pavona* spp. | Cactus corals | II | 8/1/85 |
| *Pectinia* spp. | Lettuce corals | II | 8/1/85 |
| *Platygyra* spp. | Brain corals | II | 8/1/85 |
| *Pocillopora* spp. | Brush corals | II | 8/1/85 |
| *Polyphyllia* spp. | Feather corals | II | 8/1/85 |
| *Seriatopora* spp. | Bird nest corals | II | 8/1/85 |
| *Stylophora* spp. | Cauliflower corals | II | 8/1/85 |
| CLASS Hydrozoa: | Sea ferns, Fire corals, Stinging medusae: | | |
| Order Athecata: | | | |
| Milleporidae spp. (all species in family except genus with earlier date). | | II | 1/18/90 |
| *Millepora* spp. | Fire corals | II | 8/1/85 |
| Stylasteridae spp. (all species in family). | | II | 1/18/90 |
| CLASS Alcyonaria: | | | |
| Order Coenothecalia: | | | |
| All species in the Order (except those in genus with earlier date).. | | II | 1/18/90 |
| *Heliopora* spp. | Blue corals | II | 8/1/85 |
| Order Stolonifera: | | | |
| Tubiporidae spp. (all species in family except genus with earlier date).. | | II | 1/18/90 |
| *Tubipora* spp. | Organ-pipe corals | II | 8/1/85 |
| PLANT KINGDOM: | PLANTS: | | |
| Family Agavaceae: | Agave family: | | |
| *Agave arizonica* | New River agave | I | 7/29/83 |
| *A. parviflora* | Santa Cruz striped agave | I | 7/29/83 |
| *A. victoriae-reginae* | Queen Victoria agave | II | 7/29/83 |
| *Nolina interrata* | Dehesa bear-grass | I | 7/29/83 |
| Family Amaryllidaceae: | Amaryllis family: | | |
| *Galanthus* spp. (and their natural hybrids) | Snowdrops | II | 1/18/90 |
| *Sternbergia* spp. | Sternbergias | II | 1/18/90 |
| Family Apocynaceae: | Dogbane family: | | |
| *Pachypodium* spp. (except species listed in App. I) | Pachypodiums | II | 7/1/75 |
| *P. baronii* (and its natural hybrids) | | I | 7/1/75 |
| *P. brevicaule* (and its natural hybrids) | | I | 7/1/75 |
| *P. decaryi* (and its natural hybrids) | | I | 7/1/75 |
| *P. namaquanum* | Half-men, Ghost-men | I | 7/1/75 |
| *Rauvolfia serpentina* (except chemical derivatives) | Snake-root devil-pepper | II | 1/18/90 |
| Family Araceae: | Arum family: | | |
| *Alocasia sanderiana* | | I | 7/1/75 |
| Family Araliaceae: | Ginseng family: | | |
| *Panax quinquefolius* | American ginseng | II | 7/1/75 |
| Family Araucariaceae: | Monkey-puzzle tree family: | | |
| *Araucaria araucana* (all populations except that of Chile). | Monkey-puzzle tree | II | 7/1/75 |
| *A. araucana* (population of Chile) | Monkey-puzzle tree | I | 7/1/75 |
| Family Asclepiadaceae: | Milkweed family: | | |
| *Ceropegia* spp. | Ceropegias | II | 6/28/79 |
| *Frerea indica* | | II | 6/28/79 |

| Species | Common name | Appendix | Date listed (month/day/year) |
|---|---|---|---|
| Family Berberidaceae: | Barberry family: | | |
| *Podophyllum hexandrum* (=*P. emodi*) (except chemical derivatives). | Himalayan may-apple | II | 1/18/90 |
| Family Byblidaceae: | Byblis family: | | |
| *Byblis* spp. | Byblis, Rainbow plants | II | 6/28/79 |
| Family Cactaceae: | Cactus family: | | |
| All species except those in App. I | Cacti | II | 7/1/75 |
| *Ancistrocactus tobuschii* | Tobusch's fishhook cactus | I | 7/1/75 |
| *Ariocarpus agavoides* | Agave living-rock cactus | I | 7/1/75 |
| *A. scapharostrus* | Living-rock cactus | I | 7/1/75 |
| *A. trigonus* | Chaute | I | 7/1/75 |
| *Astrophytum* (=*Echinocactus*) *asterias* | Sea urchin cactus, Star cactus | I | 7/1/75 |
| *Aztekium ritteri* | Aztec cactus | I | 7/1/75 |
| *Backebergia militaris* | Teddy-bear cactus, Military cap | I | 7/1/75 |
| *Coryphantha minima* | Nellie's corycactus | I | 7/1/75 |
| *C. sneedii* (=*C. sneedii* var. *sneedii* and var. *leei*) | Sneed pincushion cactus, Lee pincushion cactus | I | 7/1/75 |
| *C. werdermannii* | Jabali pincushion cactus | I | 7/1/75 |
| *Echinocereus ferreirianus* var. *lindsayi* (=*E. lindsayi*) | Lindsay's hedgehog cactus | I | 7/1/75 |
| *E.* (=*Wilcoxia*) *schmollii* | Lamb's-tail cactus | I | 7/1/75 |
| *Echinomastus* (=*Neolloydia*) *erectocentrus* | | I | 7/1/75 |
| *E.* (=*Neolloydia*) *mariposensis* | Mariposa cactus | I | 7/1/75 |
| *Leuchtenbergia principis* | Agave cactus | I | 7/1/75 |
| *Mammillaria pectinifera* (=*Solisia pectinata*) | Conchilinque | I | 7/1/75 |
| *M. plumosa* | Feather cactus | I | 7/1/75 |
| *M. solisioides* | Pitayita | I | 7/1/75 |
| *Nopalxochia* (=*Lobeira*) *macdougallii* | MacDougall's cactus | I | 7/1/75 |
| *Obregonia denegrii* | Artichoke cactus | I | 7/1/75 |
| *Pediocactus bradyi* | Brady's pincushion cactus | I | 7/1/75 |
| *P. despainii* | San Rafael cactus | I | 7/1/75 |
| *P. knowltonii* | Knowlton's cactus | I | 7/1/75 |
| *P. papyracanthus* | Grama-grass cactus | I | 7/1/75 |
| *P. paradinei* | Houserock Valley cactus | I | 7/1/75 |
| *P. peeblesianus* | Peebles' Navajo cactus | I | 7/1/75 |
| *P. sileri* | Siler's pincushion cactus | I | 7/1/75 |
| *P. winkleri* | Winkler's cactus | I | 7/1/75 |
| *Pelecyphora aselliformis* | Hatchet cactus, Peyotillo | I | 7/1/75 |
| *P.* (=*Encephalocarpus*) *strobiliformis* | Pinecone cactus | I | 7/1/75 |
| *Sclerocactus glaucus* | Uinta Basin hookless cactus | I | 7/1/75 |
| *S. mesae-verdae* | Mesa Verde cactus | I | 7/1/75 |
| *S. pubispinus* | Great Basin fishhook cactus | I | 7/1/75 |
| *S. wrightiae* | Wright's fishhook cactus | I | 7/1/75 |
| *Strombocactus disciformis* | Disc cactus, Top cactus | I | 7/1/75 |
| *Turbinicarpus* (=*Neolloydia*) *laui* | Turbinicarpus | I | 7/1/75 |
| *T.* (=*Neolloydia*) *lophophoroides* | Turbinicarpus | I | 7/1/75 |
| *T.* (=*Neolloydia*) *pseudomacrochele* | Turbinicarpus | I | 7/1/75 |
| *T.* (=*Neolloydia*) *pseudopectinatus* | Turbinicarpus | I | 7/1/75 |
| *T.* (=*Neolloydia*) *schmiedickeanus* | Turbinicarpus | I | 7/1/75 |
| *T.* (=*Neolloydia*) *valdezianus* | Turbinicarpus | I | 7/1/75 |
| Family Caryocaraceae: | Souari family: | | |
| *Caryocar costaricense* | Ajo | II | 7/1/75 |
| Family Cephalotaceae: | Australian pitcher-plant family: | | |
| *Cephalotus follicularis* | West Australian pitcher plant | II | 6/28/79 |
| Family Compositae (=Asteraceae): | Aster family: | | |
| *Saussurea costus* (=*S. lappa*) | Costus, Kuth root | I | 7/1/75 |
| Family Crassulaceae: | Stonecrop family: | | |
| *Dudleya stolonifera* | Laguna Beach dudleya | I | 7/29/83 |
| *D. traskiae* | Santa Barbara Island dudleya | I | 7/29/83 |
| Family Cupressaceae: | Cypress family: | | |
| *Fitz-Roya cupressoides* | Fitzroya, Alerce | I | 7/1/75 |
| *Pilgerodendron uviferum* | Pilgerodendron | I | 7/1/75 |
| Family Cyatheaceae: | Tree-fern family: | | |
| All species in the family except those with earlier date | | II | 2/4/77 |
| *Cyathea* (=*Hemitelia*) *capensis* | | II | 7/1/75 |
| *C. dredgei* | | II | 7/1/75 |
| *C. mexicana* | | II | 7/1/75 |
| *C.* (=*Alsophila*) *salvinii* | | II | 7/1/75 |
| Family Cycadaceae: | Cycas family: | | |
| All species in the family except species in App. I | | II | 2/4/77 |
| *Cycas beddomei* | Beddome cycad | I | 2/4/77 |
| Family Diapensiaceae: | Diapensia family: | | |
| *Shortia galacifolia* | Oconee bells | II | 7/29/83 |
| Family Dicksoniaceae: | Tree fern family: | | |
| All species in the family | | II | 2/4/77 |
| Family Didiereaceae: | Alluaudia family: | | |
| All species in the family | | II | 2/4/77 |
| Family Dioscoreaceae: | Yam family: | | |
| *Dioscorea deltoidea* | Kniss, Kurta | II | 7/1/75 |
| Family Ericaceae: | Heath family: | | |
| *Kalmia cuneata* | White wicky | II | 7/29/83 |

**18**

| Species | Common name | Appendix | Date listed (month/day/year) |
|---|---|---|---|
| Family Euphorbiaceae: | Spurge family: | | |
| *Euphorbia* spp. (excluding non-succulent species) (all species except those in App. I). | Euphorbias | II | 7/1/75 |
| *E.* subgenus *Lacanthis* dwarf species in Madagascar (and their natural hybrids) as given below: | Malagasy dwarf euphorbias as shown: | | |
| *E. ambovombensis* (and its natural hybrids) | | I | 7/1/75 |
| *E. cylindrifolia* (and its natural hybrids) | | I | 7/1/75 |
| *E. decaryi* (and its natural hybrids) | | I | 7/1/75 |
| *E. francoisii* (and its natural hybrids) | | I | 7/1/75 |
| *E. moratii* (and its natural hybrids) | | I | 7/1/75 |
| *E. parvicyathophora* (and its natural hybrids) | | I | 7/1/75 |
| *E. primulifolia* (and its natural hybrids) | | I | 7/1/75 |
| *E. quartziticola* (and its natural hybrids) | | I | 7/1/75 |
| *E. tulearensis* (and its natural hybrids) | | I | 7/1/75 |
| Family Fagaceae: | Beech family: | | |
| *Quercus copeyensis* | Roble, Copey oak | II | 7/1/75 |
| Family Fouquieriaceae: | Ocotillo family: | | |
| *Fouquieria columnaris* | Boojum tree | II | 7/29/83 |
| *F. fasciculata* | Arbol del barril | I | 7/29/83 |
| *F. purpusii* | | I | 7/29/83 |
| Family Gnetaceae: | Gnetum family: | | |
| *Gnetum montanum* | | III (Nepal) | 11/16/75 |
| Family Humiriaceae: | Humiria family: | | |
| *Vantanea barbourii* | Ira chiricana | II | 7/1/75 |
| Family Juglandaceae: | Walnut family: | | |
| *Oreomunnea* (=*Engelhardia*) *pterocarpa* | Gavilan | I | 7/1/75 |
| Family Leguminosae (=Fabaceae): | Pea family: | | |
| *Cynometra hemitomophylla* | Guapinol negro | II | 7/1/75 |
| *Platymiscium pleiostachyum* | Cristobal, Granadillo | II | 7/1/75 |
| *Tachigali versicolor* | Cana fistula | II | 7/1/75 |
| Family Liliaceae: | Lily family: | | |
| *Aloe* spp. (all species except those in App. I) | Aloes | II | 7/1/75 |
| *A. albida* | | I | 7/1/75 |
| *A. pillansii* | Boomaalwyn | I | 7/1/75 |
| *A. polyphylla* | Spiral aloe | I | 7/1/75 |
| *A. thorncroftii* | | I | 7/1/75 |
| *A. vossii* | | I | 7/1/75 |
| Family Magnoliaceae: | Magnolia family: | | |
| *Talauma hodgsonii* | | III (Nepal) | 11/16/75 |
| Family Meliaceae: | Mahogany family: | | |
| *Swietenia humilis* | Pacific Coast mahogany | II | 7/1/75 |
| Family Moraceae: | Mulberry family: | | |
| *Batocarpus costaricensis* | Ojoche macho, Nispero colorado | II | 7/1/75 |
| Family Nepenthaceae: | Old World pitcher-plant family: | | |
| *Nepenthes* spp. (all species except those in App. I) | Tropical pitcher plants | II | 10/22/87 |
| *N. khasiana* | Indian tropical pitcher plant | I | 10/22/87 |
| *N. rajah* | Giant tropical pitcher plant | I | 6/6/81 |
| Family Orchidaceae: | Orchid family: | | |
| All species except those in App. I | Orchids | II | 7/1/75 |
| *Cattleya skinneri* | Guaria morada | I | 7/1/75 |
| *C. trianae* | Christmas orchid | I | 7/1/75 |
| *Didiciea cunninghamii* | | I | 7/1/75 |
| *Laelia jongheana* | | I | 7/1/75 |
| *L. lobata* | | I | 7/1/75 |
| *Lycaste skinneri* (=*virginalis*) var. *alba* | White nun, Monja blanca | I | 7/1/75 |
| *Paphiopedilum* spp. | Asian tropical lady's slippers | I | 7/1/75 |
| *P. druryi* | Drury tropical lady's slipper | I | 7/1/75 |
| *Peristeria elata* | Holy Ghost, Dove orchid | I | 7/1/75 |
| *Phragmipedium* spp. | New World tropical lady's slippers | I | 7/1/75 |
| *Renanthera imschootiana* | | I | 7/1/75 |
| *Vanda coerulea* | Blue vanda | I | 7/1/75 |
| Family Palmae (=Arecaceae): | Palm family: | | |
| *Areca ipot* | | II | 7/1/75 |
| *Chrysalidocarpus decipiens* | | II | 2/4/77 |
| *Neodypsis decaryi* | Triangle palm | II | 7/1/75 |
| Family Papaveraceae: | Poppy family: | | |
| *Meconopsis regia* | | III (Nepal) | 11/16/75 |
| Family Pinaceae: | Pine family: | | |
| *Abies guatemalensis* | Guatemalan fir | I | 7/1/75 |
| Family Podocarpaceae: | Podocarp family: | | |
| *Podocarpus neriifolius* | | III (Nepal) | 11/16/75 |
| *P. parlatorei* | Parlatore's podocarp, Monteromero | I | 7/1/75 |
| Family Podophyllaceae (see Berberidacae) | | | |
| Family Portulacaceae: | Portulaca family: | | |
| *Anacampseros* spp. | | II | 7/1/75 |
| *Lewisia cotyledon* | Siskiyou lewisia | II | 7/29/83 |
| *L. maguirei* | Maguire's lewisia | II | 7/29/83 |
| *L. serrata* | Saw-toothed lewisia | II | 7/29/83 |
| *L. tweedyi* | Tweedy's lewisia | II | 7/29/83 |

| Species | Common name | Appendix | Date listed (month/day/year) |
|---|---|---|---|
| Family Primulaceae: | Primrose family: | | |
| *Cyclamen* spp. | Cyclamens | II | 7/1/75 |
| Family Proteaceae: | Protea family: | | |
| *Orothamnus zeyheri* | Marsh-rose | I | 7/1/75 |
| *Protea odorata* | Ground-rose | I | 7/1/75 |
| Family Rubiaceae: | Coffee family: | | |
| *Balmea stormiae* | Ayuque | I | 7/1/75 |
| Family Sarraceniaceae: | New World pitcher-plant family: | | |
| *Darlingtonia californica* | Western pitcher plant, Cobra lily | II | 6/6/81 |
| *Sarracenia* spp. (all species and natural hybrids except species in App. I). | Trumpet pitcher plants | II | 10/22/87 |
| *S. alabamensis* subsp. *alabamensis* (=*S. rubra* subsp. *alabamensis* ). | Alabama canebrake pitcher plant | I | 6/6/81 |
| *S. jonesii* (=*S. rubra* subsp. *jonesii*) | Mountain sweet pitcher plant | I | 6/6/81 |
| *S. oreophila* | Green pitcher plant | I | 6/6/81 |
| Family Stangeriaceae: | Stangeria family: | | |
| *Stangeria eriopus* (=*S. paradoxa*) | Stangeria, Fern-leafed cycad | I | 7/1/75 |
| Family Tetracentraceae: | Tetracentron family: | | |
| *Tetracentron sinense* | Tetracentron | III (Nepal) | 11/16/75 |
| Family Theaceae: | Tea family: | | |
| *Camellia chrysantha* | Yellow-flowered camellia, Jinhuacha | II | 8/1/85 |
| Family Welwitschiaceae: | Welwitschia family: | | |
| *Welwitschia mirabilis* (=*W. bainesii*) | Welwitschia | II | 7/1/75 |
| Family Zamiaceae: | Cycad family: | | |
| All species except those in App. I | | II | 2/4/77 |
| *Ceratozamia* spp. | Ceratozamia, Horncone | I | 2/4/77 |
| *Chigua* spp. | | I | 2/4/77 |
| *Encephalartos* spp. | Bread palms, African cycads | I | 7/1/75 |
| *Microcycas calocoma* | Palma corcho, Microcycas | I | 7/1/75 |
| Family Zingiberaceae: | Ginger family: | | |
| *Hedychium philippinense* | Philippine garland flower | I | 7/1/75 |
| Family Zygophyllaceae: | Caltrop family: | | |
| *Guaiacum sanctum* | Holywood lignum vitae | II | 7/1/75 |

EDITORIAL NOTE: This is a reprint of the species list for the Convention on International Trade in Endangered Species (CITES) as given in the October 1, 1991, 50 CFR 23.23. The list incorporates the scientific names as adopted by the CITES Parties and published by the CITES Secretariat (January 18, 1990). Readers are requested to advise the Service of any errors in this list. Copies are available from the Publication Unit, U.S. Fish and Wildlife Service, 725-ARLSQ, Washington, D.C. 20240.

☆ U.S. GOVERNMENT PRINTING OFFICE : 1991 O - 301-316

# Table of Cases

Cases are referenced to chapter and footnote number(s) (e.g., ***7:*** 119 indicates the case is cited in chapter 7, footnote 119); alphabetization is letter-by-letter.

## C

## D



## E

## I



## J



## K



## L

## M



## N

## S



## T



## U

## V



## W



## Y

# Index

This index is alphabetized letter-by-letter (i.e., Seals precedes Sea mammals). References are to page numbers and Appendixes.

## D



## E

**F**

## G



## H



## I

## M

## N



## O



## P

## Q

## U



## V



## W



## Y



## Z

## About the Author

Richard Littell is a former general counsel of two federal regulatory agencies. Now in private law practice in Washington, D.C., Littell represents regulated businesses and also has done legal work for the World Conservation Union. Littell is a member of the international advisory board of the Fundacion Pro Iguana Verde, a Costa Rican foundation that promotes conservation by means of sustainable development. A graduate of the Harvard Law School, Littell is a member of the bar of the U.S. Supreme Court and is licensed as a lawyer in California, New York, and the District of Columbia. Littell attended the Ottawa (1987) and Kyoto (1992) meetings of the Convention on International Trade in Endangered Species.